Frommer's®

Madrid

4th Edition

by Peter Stone

Wiley Publishing, Inc

ABOUT THE AUTHOR

A contributor to a variety of European magazines, guidebooks, and travel brochures, **Peter Stone** has lived in Madrid since 1998. Born in London, he started his working life in the Foreign Office in Downing Street before moving on to translating and journalism. He previously resided in Greece, North Africa, and in various other Spanish cities, including Málaga, Barcelona, Alicante, Palma de Mallorca, and Las Palmas de Gran Canaria. A lifelong lover of Hispanic culture, history, and language, his publications include a book on Madrid province called *Madrid Escapes.* He has contributed to *Time Out* and *Insight* and is the author of *Frommer's Barcelona* and co-author of *Pauline Frommer's Spain.*

Published by:
WILEY PUBLISHING, INC.
111 River St.
Hoboken, NJ 07030-5774

ISBN 978-0-470-88144-6 (paper); 978-1-118-01304-5 (ebk); 978-1-118-01305-2 (ebk); 978-1-118-01306-9 (ebk)

Editor: Jamie Ehrlich
Production Editor: Jonathan Scott
Cartographer: Elizabeth Puhl
Photo Editor: Richard Fox
Production by Wiley Indianapolis Composition Services

Front cover photo: Equestrian statue of King Philip III in Plaza Mayo. ©Mark Thomas / Axiom Photographic Limited / SuperStock, Inc.
Back cover photo: People enjoying dinner and drinks at Bar La Recoba.©Santi Burgos / Fototeca9x12

For information on our other products and services or to obtain technical support, please contact our Customer Care Department within the U.S. at 877/762-2974, outside the U.S. at 317/572-3993 or fax 317/572-4002.

Wiley also publishes its books in a variety of electronic formats. Some content that appears in print may not be available in electronic formats.

Manufactured in the United States of America

5 4 3 2 1

CONTENTS

4 SUGGESTED MADRID ITINERARIES 65

5 WHERE TO STAY 81

6 WHERE TO DINE 115

7 EXPLORING MADRID 171

LIST OF MAPS

ACKNOWLEDGMENTS

I'd like to give special thanks to fellow writers and photojournalists Vicky Hayward, Ken Welsh, and Jean Dominique Dallet for their invaluable help and encouragement over the years and to Ken and Arlene Brown for publishing my very first book on Madrid. Thanks also to Laurie Saum, Kate White, and Jerry Rogers for their enthusiastic support in personally investigating the labyrinthine ins and outs of the Spanish capital.

HOW TO CONTACT US

In researching this book, we discovered many wonderful places—hotels, restaurants, shops, and more. We're sure you'll find others. Please tell us about them, so we can share the information with your fellow travelers in upcoming editions. If you were disappointed with a recommendation, we'd love to know that, too. Please write to:

Frommer's Madrid, 4th Edition
Wiley Publishing, Inc. • 111 River St. • Hoboken, NJ 07030-5774
frommersfeedback@wiley.com

AN ADDITIONAL NOTE

Please be advised that travel information is subject to change at any time—and this is especially true of prices. We therefore suggest that you write or call ahead for confirmation when making your travel plans. The authors, editors, and publisher cannot be held responsible for the experiences of readers while traveling. Your safety is important to us, however, so we encourage you to stay alert and be aware of your surroundings. Keep a close eye on cameras, purses, and wallets, all favorite targets of thieves and pickpockets.

FROMMER'S STAR RATINGS, ICONS & ABBREVIATIONS

Every hotel, restaurant, and attraction listing in this guide has been ranked for quality, value, service, amenities, and special features using a **star-rating system.** In country, state, and regional guides, we also rate towns and regions to help you narrow down your choices and budget your time accordingly. Hotels and restaurants are rated on a scale of zero (recommended) to three stars (exceptional). Attractions, shopping, nightlife, towns, and regions are rated according to the following scale: zero stars (recommended), one star (highly recommended), two stars (very highly recommended), and three stars (must-see).

In addition to the star-rating system, we also use **seven feature icons** that point you to the great deals, in-the-know advice, and unique experiences that separate travelers from tourists. Throughout the book, look for:

special finds—those places only insiders know about

fun facts—details that make travelers more informed and their trips more fun

kids—best bets for kids and advice for the whole family

special moments—those experiences that memories are made of

overrated—places or experiences not worth your time or money

insider tips—great ways to save time and money

great values—where to get the best deals

The following **abbreviations** are used for credit cards:

AE American Express **DISC** Discover **V** Visa

DC Diners Club **MC** MasterCard

TRAVEL RESOURCES AT FROMMERS.COM

Frommer's travel resources don't end with this guide. Frommer's website, **www.frommers.com**, has travel information on more than 4,000 destinations. We update features regularly, giving you access to the most current trip-planning information and the best airfare, lodging, and car-rental bargains. You can also listen to podcasts, connect with other Frommers.com members through our active-reader forums, share your travel photos, read blogs from guidebook editors and fellow travelers, and much more.

THE BEST OF MADRID

1

It's the vintage heart of this city that provides by far the richest concentration of fascinating sights. Here, narrow-laned old quarters and handsome plazas filled with regal statues are bordered by wide avenues and modern skyscrapers. World-class art galleries and museums vie for attention with secretive convents and tiny 17th-century churches. The Plaza Mayor, the city's photogenic main plaza, was once the stage for the Inquisition's horrific autos de fe; today it is filled with strolling families, tourists, lively cafes, and souvenir shops.

Yet hedonism has always played a vital part in the city's lifestyle, and in a spontaneous nonstop way that leaves you breathless. It is said that Madrid has more bars and cafes than Belgium or Holland. And the bars here not only open early but also close late (or never shut at all if you include the after-hours bars), and weekend dawn traffic jams of cars and night buses block the city thoroughfares as revelers weave their way to, from, or between their favorite spots. Madrileños also love to eat well—be it at a favorite neighborhood *tasca* or a fabled culinary mecca. Restaurants and chefs serving cuisine from recipes that haven't changed for generations compete for the citizens' affections with innovative newcomers experimenting with fusion and molecular gastronomy. The city's shoppers have their pick from ultrachic stores and boutiques selling the latest in international fashion to street markets where an elusive antique is bargained for a song.

You name it, Madrid has it.

THE most unforgettable MADRID EXPERIENCES

- **Sitting in Sol or Sombra at the Bullfights:** With origins as old as pagan Spain, the art of bullfighting is the expression of Iberian temperament and passions. Detractors object to the sport as cruel, bloody, violent, hot, and savage. Aficionados, however, understand bullfighting as a microcosm of death, catharsis, and rebirth. These philosophical underpinnings may not be immediately apparent, but if you strive to understand the bullfight, it can be one of the most evocative and memorable events in Spain. Head for the country's biggest ***plaza de toros*** (bullring), at Ventas (on the eastern border of Madrid's Salamanca district, close to the M-30 highway). Tickets are either *sol* (sunny side) or *sombra* (in the shade); you'll pay more to get out of the sun. Observe how the feverish crowds appreciate the ballet of the *banderilleros,* the thundering fury of the bull, the arrogance of the matador—all leading to "death in the afternoon." Peak time for attending bullfights is during the capital's San Isidro fiestas in May, when 4 consecutive weeks of daily *corridas* feature some of the biggest names in the bullfighting world. See p. 181.

- **Seeing the Masterpieces at the Prado:** It's one of the world's premier art museums, ranking with the Louvre. The Prado—which saw a bright and innovative expansion in 2007—is home to over 4,000 masterpieces, many of them acquired by kings through the ages. The wealth of Spanish art is staggering—everything from Goya's *Naked Maja* to the celebrated *Las Meninas (The Maids of Honor)* by Velázquez (my favorite). Masterpiece after masterpiece unfolds before your eyes: You can imagine your fate in Hieronymus Bosch's *Garden of Earthly Delights* or recoil from the horror of Goya's *Disasters of War* etchings. When the Spanish artistic soul gets too dark, escape to the Italian salons and view canvases by Caravaggio, Fra Angelico, and Botticelli. Be warned, though, that a quick run-through won't suffice: It would take a lifetime to savor the Prado's wonders. See p. 174.
- **Feasting on Tapas in the Tascas:** Tapas, those bite-size portions washed down with wine, beer, or sherry, are reason enough to go to Madrid! Spanish tapas are so good their once-secret recipes have been broadcast around the world, but they always taste better at home. A *tapeo* is akin to a London pub-crawl—you travel from one tapas bar to another. Each has a different specialty. Tapas bars, called *tascas,* are a quintessential Spanish experience, be it in Galicia, Andalusia, Catalonia, or Castile. Originally, tapas were cured ham or chorizo (spicy sausage). Today they are likely to include everything—*gambas* (deep-fried shrimp); anchovies marinated in vinegar; stuffed peppers; a cool, spicy gazpacho; or hake salad. To go really native, try *mollejas* (lamb sweetbreads) or *criadillas* (bull testicles). These dazzling spreads will hold you over until the fashionable 10pm dining hour. The best streets for your *tasca* crawl include Ventura de la Vega, the area around Plaza de Santa Ana or Plaza de Santa Bárbara, Cava Baja, or Calle de Cuchilleros. Calle Hartzenbusch, in the Chamberí district, also has some tempting places. See chapter 6.
- **Lounging in an Outdoor Cafe:** In sultry summertime, Madrileños come alive on their *terrazas.* The drinking and good times can go on until dawn. In glamorous hangouts or on lowly street corners, the cafe scene takes place mainly along an axis shaped by the Paseo de la Castellana, Paseo del Prado, and Paseo de Recoletos. The Paseo del Pintor Rosales, on the western edge of the Argüelles district, near the *teleférico* and overlooking the Casa de Campo, also has an attractive tree-fringed collection of open-air cafes; and down at the southern end of Lavapiés, the colorful Calle Argumasa offers a fashionable spill of lively alfresco bars. Wander up and down the boulevards and select a spot that appeals to you. For traditional atmosphere in a historic setting, the touristy but fun *terrazas* at Plaza Mayor win out. See chapter 6.
- **Shopping the Rastro:** Madrid's main flea market has been a local tradition for 500 years. Savvy shoppers arrive before 7am every Sunday to beat the rush and claim the best merchandise. It doesn't really get going until about 9am, and then it's

shoulder-to-shoulder all the way down Calle Ribera de Curtidores. Real or fake antiques, secondhand clothing, porno films, Franco-era furniture, paintings (endless copies of Velázquez), bullfight posters, old books, religious relics, and plenty of just plain junk, including motorcycles from World War II, are for sale. These streets also contain some of the finest permanent antiques shops in Madrid. But beware: Pickpockets are out in full force. More than a few mugging victims have later found their purses here for resale—thoroughly emptied, of course. (Shoppers will be pleased to know that earlier plans to move the Rastro from its handy central location to Mercamadrid, the city's outlying wholesale market, have been indefinitely shelved.)

- **Sunday Strolling in the Retiro:** Spread across 140 cool hectares (350 acres) in sweltering Madrid, Parque del Retiro was originally designed as the gardens of Buen Retiro palace, occupied by Philip IV in the 1630s. In 1767, Charles III opened part of the gardens to the general public. Only after the collapse of Isabella II's monarchy in 1868 did the park become available to all Madrileños. Statues dot the grounds (a towering 1902 monument to Alfonso XII presides over the lake), which also contain some 15,000 trees, a rose garden, and a few art galleries. The best time for a stroll is Sunday morning before lunch, when vendors hawk their wares, magicians perform their acts, fortunetellers read their tarot cards, and large Disney-style moving models of Tweety Bird and Bugs Bunny delight the kids. You can rent a rowboat and laze away the morning on its glittering waters, or take a short trip around it on a solar-energized pleasure boat. Don't be tempted to try and catch any of the silvery carp that dart below you, though. It could earn you a fine. See p. 192.
- **Picnicking in the Casa de Campo:** On a hot summer day, enjoy an alfresco repast in the shade of a fragrant pine in the heart of Madrid's largest park and look back at the shimmering city skyline. Afterward go boating on the lake or take the kids to the zoo or Parque de Atracciones. You can get here by *teleférico* chairlift, travel via the metro to Lago, or enter the park through its easterly gate after crossing the River Manzanares from Príncipe Pío. See p. 191.
- **Nursing a Drink at Museo Chicote (© 91-532-67-37):** The 1930s interior at Madrid's most famous bar looks the same as it did during the Spanish Civil War. Shells might have been flying along the Gran Vía, but the international press corps covering the war drank on—a tunnel is rumored to have connected it with the vintage Bar Cock on a parallel street, handy if they felt like a change of scene and didn't want to risk stepping into the street. After the war, the crowd of regulars included major writers, artists, and actors, including the likes of Frank Sinatra and Ava Gardner. By the late 1960s, it had degenerated into a pickup bar frequented by prostitutes. Today it has regained the *joie de vivre* of yore and is one of the smart, sophisticated spots to rendezvous in Madrid. See p. 247.
- **Experiencing the Madrid Night Scene:** The 1980s expression *movida,* roughly translated as the "shift" or the "movement," referred to the world of arts and entertainment released from practically all restrictions and censorship after the death of repressive dictator Franco. Then it covered all aspects of local life, encompassing a wide range of social projects and progressive causes. Today's *movida* is simply a lively, nonpolitical fun scene that doesn't really get going till after midnight, and even later on weekends. Madrileños hop from club to club as if they're afraid they'll miss out on something if they stay in one place too long. To truly catch a whiff of

the Madrileño action, head for the lively nightlife areas of Chueca, Huertas, and Malasaña, and the big clubs around Calle Arenal. See chapter 10, "Madrid After Dark."

- **Wandering around the Monasterio de las Descalzas Reales:** A haven of unexpected peace in the bustling heart of Madrid, barely a stone's throw from the Gran Vía, this charming, medieval former palace was converted into a monastery in the 16th century by Philip II's sister Juana. Ornate frescoes, Flemish tapestries, and paintings by the likes of Titian and Zurbarán fill its chapel-lined interior. Only 20 visitors are allowed in at a time, so be prepared to wait. See p. 183.
- **Exploring the Real Monasterio de San Lorenzo de El Escorial** (49km/30 miles north of Madrid): Philip II, who commissioned this monastery in the 1530s, envisioned it as a monastic fortress against the distractions of the secular world. More awesome than beautiful, it's the world's best example of the religious devotion of Renaissance Spain. This huge granite fortress, the burial place for Spanish kings, houses a wealth of paintings and tapestries—works by everyone from Titian to Velázquez. See p. 266.
- **Strolling through the Palacio Real at Aranjuez** (48km/30 miles south of Madrid.): In sharp contrast to the Castilian austerity of El Escorial, this sumptuous baroque-classical Bourbon palace, located in a richly fertile valley surrounded by a sun-soaked limestone plateau, boasts a hedonistically warm ambience. So do the magnificent French-designed 16th-century gardens whose tall trees extend for miles alongside the deep flowing Tagus River and shelter the tiny neighboring Casa del Labrador summer *palacete*. See p. 255.

THE best SPLURGE HOTELS

- **Hesperia Madrid (© 91-210-88-00)** doesn't show up on the "Leading Hotels of the World" list for nothing, as you'll see if you splash out on this Catalan-owned gem with its ultrasmart fittings, sophisticated amenities, and pared down Far Eastern decor. Add to this the Michelin-rated Santceloni dining room (see "The Most Unforgettable Dining Experiences," later) and you have as fine a combination of catering facilities as you'll find in Madrid. See p. 104.
- A recognized "in" place with top people, from movie stars to high ranking politicians, the **Park Hyatt Villa Magna** (**© 800/223-1234** in the U.S. and Canada, or 91-587-12-34) enjoys a prestigious reputation almost unique in the city. Behind its elegant garden setting is a classically styled hotel boasting the highest standards of service and facilities. See p. 105.
- In spite of an increasing number of worthy rivals, the grandiose Belle Epoque **Hotel Ritz Madrid** (**© 800/225-5843** in the U.S. and Canada, or 91-701-67-67) remains a world apart, a legend in its own lifetime. The granddaddy of all luxury hotels in the city—now approaching its hundredth anniversary—it's seen monarchs and dictators come and go and democracy suffer its ups and downs. Backed by gardens in the loveliest part of the Paseo del Prado, its incomparable setting and decor are matched by the inimitable service and attention. See p. 104.
- With more than a touch of luxury and the best views ever of the city and its surroundings, the huge emblematic **Eurostars Madrid Tower © 93-295-99-08** (24-hr. service) is Madrid's hottest new hotel. Immaculately planned and designed by two of Spain's top architects, it offers an almost unparalleled quality of service and room comforts. See p. 111.

THE best MODERATELY PRICED HOTELS

- Built in 1966 and still going strong, the reasonably priced **Ayre Gran Hotel Colón** (© **91-573-59-00**) is west of Retiro Park in a relatively safe area of Madrid that's easily connected to the center by subway. It's well maintained and kept up-to-date, offering well-designed bedrooms with comfortably traditional furnishings. See p. 108.
- Ideally located in a popular tiny square close to the Plaza Mayor, the 19th century **Hostal Persal** (© **91-369-46-43**) offers particularly good value, family-size rooms, and fine on-the-spot meals. See p. 90.
- If the prospect of a peaceful setting within easy reach of the center tickles your fancy, then the **Residencia El Viso** (© **91-564-03-70**) is the place for you. Comfortable rooms, a friendly atmosphere, and a leafy patio where you can enjoy home-cooked meals are all part of the deal. See p. 113.

THE most unforgettable DINING EXPERIENCES

- The **Sobrino de Botín** (© **91-366-30-26** or 91-366-42-17) may be touristy these days, but the setting and atmosphere of the city's oldest restaurant (it claims to be the oldest in the world) more than compensate. Rafters, beams, and nooks abound, and the effective service is accompanied by some first-rate Castilian specialties, such as *lechona.* See p. 128.
- Okay, so it's money-is-no-object time. With supreme Basque cuisine at **Zalacaín** (© **91-561-48-40**), you can let yourself go for once. Long rated as the best eating spot in Madrid, it's still holding out well against the Catalan tsunami of fashionable nouvelle cuisine. See p. 162.
- A stylish repository of fine Mediterranean cuisine located in the immaculate Hotel Hesperia (p. 106), **Santceloni** (© **91-210-88-40**) is, for many, the tops in town. Chef Santi Santamaría conjures up further-inspired Catalan dishes such as fennel-based John Dory. See p. 152.
- For those who do favor tradition-shattering gourmet delights, then **La Broche** (© **91-399-34-37**), the dining room of the Hotel Miguel Angel (p. 110), still provides some of the most imaginative offerings you'll encounter in the city, with Angel Palacio now ably replacing original star chef Sergi Arola to produce more Michelin-awarded cuisine. See p. 160.
- Sergi hasn't moved far: Just a five-minute stroll from La Broche is the acclaimed chef's new gourmet paradise **Sergi Arola Gastro** (© **91-310-21-69**). Its

The Best Train Ride

An old narrow-gauge railway takes you up 1,500m (5,000 ft.) through giant pinewoods from Cercedilla to the hamlet of Cotos, which enjoys winter skiing and summer walks up to the 2,300m (7,500 ft.) Peñalara, the highest point of the Guadarramas. See p. 258.

secluded location and low-key exterior cannily hide one of the city's genuine new gourmet treats. His tasting menus (be warned that they aren't cheap!) are in a class of their own.

THE best THINGS TO DO FOR FREE

- **Enjoy the Weekend Cultural Treats:** Saturday and Sunday are free at the **Nacional Centro de Arte Reina Sofía** (p. 174). The tiny **Casa Museo de Lope de Vega** (p. 181) is free on Saturday only. Sunday-morning-only treats include the **Museos de América** (p. 186), **Sorolla** (p. 186), and **Nacional de Artes Decorativas** (p. 182).
- **Don't Forget the Weekday Freebies, too: El Prado** (p. 174) is free in the evenings all week long (though it's closed on Mon). Some of the more individual private museums such as **Lazaro Galdiano** (p. 185) and **Cerralbo** (p. 183) are free on Wednesdays (also Sun for Cerralbo), while the **Museo San Isidro** in Plaza San Andrés gives you a daily rundown on the city's history for free (p. 177). Also permanently free are the **Bolsa** (Stock Exchange; p. 180 **Museo de Historia** (p. 182, **Museo Naval** (p. 182), and the **Conde Duque** cultural center (p. 182).
- **Take an Ecclesiastical Trip Back in Time:** I'm particularly fond of Madrid's two oldest churches, hidden in the heart of the Austrias district. They're both tiny, giving you an idea of what Madrid must have been like when it had a population of just around 10,000. **San Nicolás de los Servitas** (full title San Nicolás de Bari de los Servitas) was named after an Italian saint, and its 12th-century Arabic *torre* rises above a narrow lane just behind the Calle Mayor (p. 180). Nearby **San Pedro el Leal,** also known as San Pedro el Viejo, has the best-preserved 14th-century *Mudéjar* brick tower in the capital (p. 180). No entry fee for either, of course, though you may care to leave something in the collection box to help toward the preservation of these two gems.
- **Stroll in the Parks:** Madrid's best central *parques* are particularly rewarding to explore, especially the **Retiro** (p. 192), with its rose garden, fountains, statues (including the Angel Caído, or Fallen Angel, depicting Lucifer), and central lake; Casa de Vacas; and the 19th-century Palacios de Cristal and Velázquez cultural showrooms. Below the Palacio Real, the **Campo del Moro** has a verdant neatness more associated with Northern Europe, while on the edge of Argüelles the **Parque del Oeste**'s marked nature trails wend their way down past an international selection of trees and plants to the River Manzanares (where you can view the Ermita de San Antonio de la Florida's Goyan frescoes; p. 192). Most relaxing of all and only open weekends is **El Capricho** (p. 191), first laid out in the 19th century and complete with the original fountains, gazebos, and waterways. It's on the eastern edge of the city just a 5-minute walk from the El Capricho metro station.
- **See Madrid's "Little Egypt":** On the ridge overlooking the Casa de Campo, you can visit the **Templo de Debod,** a unique slice of Egypt in Spain. It's the real McCoy: shipped stone by stone from the banks of the Nile. See p. 184.
- **Be a Politician for a Day (or Morning, anyway):** Visit the **Congreso de Diputados** on Saturday mornings, and imagine yourself changing the state of the Spanish nation. No need to book. Just turn up at 10am (except during the summer recess). See p. 212.

THE best STUFF TO BRING HOME

- **Leather:** Leather has long been one of Spain's highest valued products, and best buys range from stylish belts and handbags to handmade shoes and fine jackets. Check out such top shops as **Loewe** in the Gran Vía and **Farrutx** in Calle Serrano (p. 230). Or rummage through Sunday's **Rastro** flea market for a secondhand bargain (p. 227).
- **Ceramics:** Though this is not a Madrid specialty, you'll find a wide selection of ceramic vases, dishes, and jugs, from nearby towns such as Toledo and Talavera de la Reina, some of whose wares have the style and finesse of fine art. There's also plenty of choice from areas farther afield, such as Seville, Granada, and Manises in Valencia province. Visit the **Antigua Casa Talavera** (p. 224) for some of the best.
- **Porcelain:** Most popular and widely available ornaments in this field are made by the Valencian company Lladró, similar in style to the Italian Capodimonte; and, though considered rather twee by some, they are extremely popular with the majority of visitors. Check out **Lasarte** (p. 231) in the Gran Vía.
- **Capes:** If your taste runs to the slightly eccentric, now's your chance to buy a genuine Spanish cape (or *capa*) and surprise your friends as you arrive at the theater in style! The place to find them is **Capas Seseña** (p. 224).

THE best UNIQUE TABERNAS

- You can't get more traditional than the much-copied, 200-year-old original **La Taberna de Antonio Sánchez** (© **91-539-78-26**). It's a vintage example of Old Madrid, complete with zinc counter, carved wooden bar top, barrels, honest wines, and a genial bartender. Formerly patronized by painters and playwrights, this small cavelike locale has also had long associations with the bullfight world. (The bull's head on the wall is not there just for decoration.) See p. 167.
- Perhaps because of its location up in the northern suburbs, few people realize the former coaching inn **Casa Pedro** (© **91-734-02-01**), with its secluded array of dining alcoves, is the second-oldest eating spot in Madrid (after Sobrino de Botín). Don't be put off. It's barely half an hour by metro, and the unique dining experience makes it more than worthwhile. See p. 170.
- Another genuine oldie, charismatic tavern **Casa Alberto** (© **91-429-93-56**) has been around since 1827. The dark maroon exterior and tunnel-like interior, with its zinc bar top, bullfight pictures, and engravings on the walls, create the ideal ambience to enjoy a tasty *tapa* or three. The restaurant at the rear provides more substantial versions of the traditional seafood and Castilian meat dishes available. See p. 166.

THE best BARS & CAFES

- **Best Cocktail Bar:** Try the daiquiris at **Del Diego** (© **91-523-31-06**), and you'll have to agree they're the best in town. Cool decor, low-key atmosphere, and smooth attentive service add to the charm of this discreet spot, tucked away in a quiet street just below the Gran Vía. See p. 247.

The Best Castle

The fairy tale *castillo* Manzanares el Real, set above a clear-water reservoir and backed by some of the most dramatic mountain scenery in central Spain, lies just 48km (30 miles) north of the capital beside a small, attractive town. Built in the 15th century by the powerful Mendoza family in a heady blend of Gothic and *Mudéjar,* its towers, ramparts, and crenulated walls form everyone's dream of what a castle in Spain should look like. See p. 261.

- **Best Literary Cafe:** Once several distinguished old-world cafes served the intellectuals, artists, and lesser mortals who would gather to enjoy a leisurely chat or stimulating *tertulia* (social gathering). Today, practically the sole survivor of these legendary watering holes is the 117-year-old **Gran Café de Gijón** (✆ **91-521-54-25**), with its wrought-iron columns and checkered tabletops. Get a window seat if you want to enjoy the ever-changing scene on the Paseo outside. See p. 141.
- **Best Place for Sherry:** The cavernous **La Venencia** (✆ **91-429-62-61**) sells sherry and nothing else, from ultradry *manzanillas* to hearty *olorosos.* The space *is* uncompromisingly preserved, with a run-down and untampered look. This means flaking tobacco-brown walls with tattered sherry posters, old barrels, and a basic wooden bar top. Olives, manchego cheese, and mountain ham are on the concise, no-nonsense tapas list. Check out the sitting area with tables and chairs at the back, too. See p. 247.
- **Best Wine Bar:** No less than 200 *vinos* are on offer at **Aloque** (✆ **91-528-36-62**), an understated modern bodega/*taberna* hidden away in a narrow lane in medieval multiethnic Lavapiés. In addition to the inevitable Riojas and Penedes, you'll find some exciting new wines from hitherto undervalued areas such as Yecla and Toro. Sit at the bar or at tables in a small alcove. There are a la carte *raciones* if you feel peckish. See p. 246.
- **Best Tapas:** Cited as a favorite snack 'n' wine locale by Oscar-winning cineaste Pedro Almodóvar, the stylish little **El Bocaíto** (✆ **91-532-12-19**) is set in the heart of bohemian Chueca. They will usually serve a free miniportion of *cecina* (smoked beef) or something similar with your vino before offering a wealth of marine delights that ranges from *salmonetes* (red mullet) to *pescaítos* (small fried fish). See p. 148.
- **Best "Celebrity" Bar:** At **La Bardemcilla** (✆ **91-521-42-56**), the "Bardem" bit comes from the name of Spain's number-one movie family—the equivalent of the Baldwins to the States and the Redgraves to the U.K. Actress mother Pilar's son Javier—an Academy Award winner for best supporting actor in *No Country for Old Men* in 2007—is co-owner with his sister Mónica. Tapas and *raciones* are accordingly named after other movies he's made: croquetas "Jamón, Jamón" and *tortilla* "Perdita Durango," for example. It's a warm, stylish bar with an ever-so-slightly pretentious ambience. See p. 149.

THE best MUSEUMS

The spectacular **Prado** in Madrid is no mere museum, but a travel experience. It's worth a journey to Spain by itself (see "The Most Unforgettable Madrid Experiences," earlier in this chapter).

- **Museo Lázaro Galdiano:** This rare collection demonstrates the evolution of enamel and ivory crafts from the Byzantine era to 19th-century Limoges. Of almost equal importance are displays of superb medieval gold and silver work along with Italian Renaissance jewelry. Galleries with rare paintings, include everything from Flemish primitives to works by Spanish masters of the golden age, including El Greco, Murillo, and Zurbarán. You will also encounter paintings from Goya's "Black Period," and from the English and Italian masters Constable and Tiepolo. See p. 185.
- **Thyssen-Bornemisza Museum:** Madrid's acquisition of this treasure-trove of art in the 1980s was one of the greatest coups in European art history. Amassed by a central European collector beginning around 1920, and formerly displayed in Lugano, Switzerland, its 700 canvasses, with works by artists ranging from El Greco to Picasso, are arranged in chronological order. The collection rivals the legendary holdings of the queen of England herself. See p. 175.
- **Museo Cerralbo:** This 19th-century mansion evokes the genuine aura of a sumptuous restored residence. Formerly owned by the 17th marquis of Argüelles, it houses one of the most personal collections in Madrid. Works by Zurburán and El Greco, especially the latter's *Ecstasy of St. Francis of Assisi,* are among its highlights; and the upper floor contains a unique collection of Western and Oriental armor and weapons. ***Note:*** The museum was closed at the time of writing but should be reopened by 2011. See p. 183.
- **Museo Sorolla:** Visit the great Valencian artist's own house in the residential heart of the Spanish capital. Built in 1910 and bequeathed as a museum by his wife after his death, its trademark works are luminous Levante coast beach scenes, with women in white dresses backed by the azure Mediterranean Sea. You can also see his eccentrically furnished studio, complete with a Turkish sofa on which he took his siesta. See p. 186.
- **Reina Sofía:** Spain's number one modern art exhibition features works by Dalí, Tapies, and Klein, plus an ever-interesting series of temporary exhibits ranging from anarchic to mainstream. The outside glass-walled elevator is popular with kids. See p. 174.
- **Caixa Forum:** A brave new rival to the Paseo del Prado's "Big Three," this imaginatively converted former office-cum-warehouse features an exciting range of traditional and innovative exhibitions, plus a unique vertical wall climbing garden. See p. 171.

MADRID IN DEPTH

2

So many aspects of Madrid have changed in the last decade, from the striking new riverside gardens and green areas created by landscape experts to the gleaming high-rise buildings designed by top modern architects, that visitors tend first to be surprised and exhilarated. Given some time to explore, though, they'll be comfortingly reassured by traditional sights such as the atmospheric old Austrias center and elegant Salamanca district, still the most stylish corner of town.

This creative, lively, and restless metropolis has never been one to let the grass grow under its feet. Today a vital need to move into the 21st century blends seamlessly with a need to preserve a glorious past. Even in the decades of a supposedly restrained and conservative past, when the city and its people were subjected to a ruling dictatorship and crushed by post–Civil War deprivation, when the Spanish capital assumed the cliché of a gray, gray place, Madrid never really was a quiet, depressive, early-to-bed city—whatever people may tell you. The spirit and energy were always there, latently during the hardest times, at full throttle when life was anything like normal.

This chapter seeks to unravel a bit of this fascinating city's history, art, and culture by raising the question: Is there still such a person as a real Madrileño (born and bred Madrid inhabitant), given the cultural changes that have transformed a once purely Spanish city into a multinational metropolis? Read on to learn about the forces that created today's Madrid and to get a good idea of what the future holds for this intriguing and dynamic city.

MADRID TODAY

Undeterred by such nagging issues as the economy and unemployment—both in a highly precarious state at the time of writing—Madrid's communication and ecological improvements continue to expand under the relentless guiding hand of Mayor Alberto Ruiz-Gallardón. His dream is to see the still-in-progress 14km/9 mile-long **Madrid Rio** development transform the Manzanares River in its section from the Puente de Toledo to the Parque del Oeste into a whole new airy green zone, light years away in mood from the claustrophobically narrow-laned old center. Most of its 811 hectares (just over 2,000 acres) have already been laid out with trees,

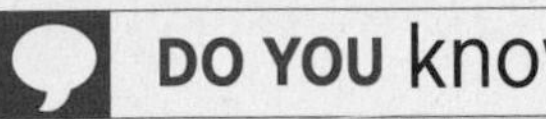

DO YOU know . . .

Why the bear and the madroño tree are the symbols of Madrid?

You see them everywhere—from the small bronze statue in the Puerta del Sol (moved in 2009 back to the eastern side of the square where Calle Alcalá ends)—to the insignia on the side of city taxis: A squat bear on its hind legs attempting to eat the berries on an equally squat *madroño,* or so-called strawberry tree. They are the official symbols of Madrid. But why? Opinions vary. The practical theory is that the bear, standing on its hind legs with its front paws on the tree trunk, represents possession and ownership of wood, necessary for constructing buildings. The sentimental theory is based on the fact that bears love sweet things and constantly try to extract honey from beehives. According to legend, because they suffer from sore eyes, they get stung and bleed from their wounds to such an extent that it relieves them of some of the pain. Next, they grope around desperately for a *madroño* tree and start gobbling the fruit, whose bitterness belies its rich red exterior (it only *looks* like a strawberry) and shocks the palate into further reducing the pain by the virtue of sheer distraction. So, masochistically, they rid themselves of their discomfort. The first theory makes sense as a metaphor for how Madrid has grown. The second is rather cute but doesn't seem to have any particular relevance. Take your pick.

flower-filled gardens, and lawns, though full completion is not expected until 2012. Additional small sandy "beaches," complete with adjoining solariums and sports centers, are also planned. (For more information on this, including a 5-min. video with English-language narration, check out www.munimadrid.es/madridrio).

The latest stage in metro travel, the *tren ligero* (a smaller streamlined TALGO-shaped tram, similar to those also facilitating commuters in Bilbao, Valencia, and Barcelona) has for the past few years been providing services to classy northerly suburbs such as Boadilla del Monte, Pozuelo de Alarcón, and Aravaca, while *cercanías* (suburban rail services) speed residents of other outlying satellite towns, such as San Sebastian de los Reyes and Colmenar Viejo, to Madrid's center in less than half an hour.

Expanded and renovated rail and bus stations, from the large main Atocha and Chamartín termini to the smaller Príncipe Pío and Moncloa stops, all function in ecologically friendly, well-ventilated underground locations. Public transport throughout the city is economical and efficient, with metro services extending as far as the airport; and the ubiquitous tunnels of pedestrian and subway underpasses, together with a widening of countless streets and avenues, have all improved road access into and around the city. The expanded Barajas airport—undaunted by the ETA terrorist bombings of its terminal 4 car park in December 2006—continues to develop its facilities and number of international flights and is now the third busiest in Europe.

The most visible symbol of all this progress is a brand new quartet of Spain's highest buildings, known in Spanglish as the Cuatro Torres Business Area (CTBA). The buildings stand on the site of the former Real Madrid sports grounds, just north of the twin sloping KIO glass and concrete office towers, which previously dominated Plaza Castilla and formed a kind of jet-age gateway to Madrid. Three of these soaring new concrete and glass icons, named Cristal, Espacio, and Sacyr Vallehermoso, were

DO YOU know . . .

Why the Manzanares River has had such bad press?
The insults and quips came thick and fast in the old days when the Manzanares River was a malodorous trickle that dried up in summer. "An apprentice river," the Golden Age poet Quevedo called it, "in which the water barely comes up to the sole of my foot." Another writer claimed that "the elms that decorate its banks die of thirst, and the river itself begs for an umbrella if it rains," adding that "the Manzanares barely dampens the ground, as if a finger moistened with saliva was stroking the soil." It is said that King Fernando VII, passing one day in summer, requested his consorts to water it so that the dust wouldn't rise so much. Visiting French writer Alexandre Dumas once pleaded with a friend not to throw away the glass of water he'd half finished but to throw it into the parched and needy Manzanares. And so on.

Today, if not quite comparable with the Seine or Thames, the Manzanares looks more like a real river, thanks to diverted water channels that have helped to replenish it (although that coyly secluded location in the dip btw. the Royal Palace and the Casa de Campo still prevents many visitors from realizing it's even there). Today a whole stretch from Príncipe Pío, close to the Campo del Moro, to Puente de Toledo, just below the street where the Sunday Rastro is held, has now been immaculately laid out with gardens, trees, walkways, cycle trails, and occasional pebbled piazzas. Quevedo wouldn't believe his eyes.

completed in 2008; the fourth, Caja Madrid—designed by the ubiquitous British architect Norman Foster and the highest of the four at 250m (750 ft.)—was finished in 2009. Collectively, they're an emphatic in-your-face reflection of capitalist wealth. Not so impressive is the news that (at the time of writing) two of them are still empty, having so far priced themselves out of the current market.

The city's increasingly mixed population is starting to rival those of London, Paris, and Berlin to an extent unthinkable just a couple of decades ago. For decades, Madrid was the most purely national and homogenous of European capitals, and foreign residents were a relative rarity—high-paid executives working in international businesses along the Castellana aside—who totaled barely 1%. Today's resident immigrants come mainly from Africa, South America, the Hispanic Caribbean islands, and Eastern Europe. Ecuadorians and Romanians tend to predominate. Latin Americans, for whom the language obviously presents no problems (Portuguese-speaking Brazilians aside), have opened large numbers of cafes, shops—especially bakeries—and *locutorios* (long-distance phone call centers). Meanwhile, the Russians, Poles, and Czechs who work on many of the eternally busy building sites and in practical fields such as plumbing and carpentry have shown great versatility in their work and in picking up Spanish.

The most rapid change in recent years, though, has been the growth of the Chinese population, which has now created a small world of its own in the southwesterly former working class suburb of Usera. Though this Lilliputian Chinatown pales in comparison with those of New York and San Francisco, it's burgeoning so fast in this ever-changing metropolis that it could soon approach them in stature.

Madrid is now officially one of the "greenest" cities in Europe, with verdant areas springing up every year thanks to its environmentally aware town hall. Traditionally the Retiro, where Madrileños over the past decades have relaxed amid the endless array of trees, flowers, and fountains, and the huge Casa de Campo moorland, with its copses and bird life, are the city's twin lungs, aided by the regular flow of pure mountain air from the Guadarramas, 97km (60 miles) away. Additionally, in the past few years, hundreds of thousands of trees have been planted in green zones in and around the city, intersected by walking and cycling lanes that now total nearly 100km (62 miles) and completely encompass the outer city. The above-mentioned Manzanares River development—with the adjoining M-30 highway running underground—now has newly pedestrianized and flower-filled parkland adjoining Casa de Campo. And several buses are in service using environmentally friendly fuel.

In spite of all these dramatic social, technological, and ecological changes, at the city's heart remain the old traditional Los Austrias, Plaza Mayor, and Royal Palace, still exuding their timeless atmosphere, and ringed in turn by regenerated Castizo (traditional) districts such as Chueca, Malasaña, and Lavapiés. These districts have remained unchanged architecturally for centuries, but offer a vibrant, stimulating blend of the bohemian and ethnically diverse, thanks to a resident bevy of artists and fresh influx of arrivals from other countries.

A BRIEF GUIDE TO ETIQUETTE IN SPAIN

Appropriate Attire

Though dress is becoming increasingly informal among Spaniards themselves in the workplace, even in banks and insurance offices and the like, when it comes to formal international meetings, elegance, style, and conservative quality clothing are still much appreciated. Shorts and Hawaiian shirts are not a good idea, and even in the hottest weather it's more acceptable for jackets to be kept on. Men usually wear dark colors during the winter and lighter shades during the summer.

For sightseeing, however, it's okay for visitors to dress down, especially in hot weather when even Madrileños often wear shorts and short-sleeved shirts. You'll still want something a little dressier for dining in nice restaurants and stepping out to the clubs.

In churches, the recommended attire is less prone to restrictions than in the past, though it would be a sign of respect for men not to wear shorts and women to cover bare shoulders in summer.

Avoiding Offense

In Madrid, it's tactful to avoid discussing Gibraltar, the late General Franco's regime, and politics in general until you're totally sure of your ground. Also avoid criticizing national activities that may be controversial elsewhere but not in Madrid, such as bullfights. (In more radical areas like the Basque Country and Cataluña, where Madrid tends to be regarded as the unacceptable face of authority, you may have more leeway on all these matters.) Sports, such as *fútbol* (soccer), and attractions of different regions of the country are good topics to discuss. Many resident Madrileños originated from another part of Spain and still retain a strong link with their home province, so if you know something about it, they will be appreciative.

Gestures

A firm handshake and eye contact are standard formal greetings for men and women alike, though on relaxed social occasions it's perfectly acceptable for two members of the opposite sex to kiss on both cheeks, even if they've never met before. When in doubt, the male can always follow the lead of the female. First names are generally okay after an introduction, unless you are addressing an older man or woman. It's acceptable to indulge in politely restrained conversational touching. With friends or close contacts, hugging and back-patting are common additional greeting gestures. Heterosexual men don't usually kiss each other on both cheeks—as in France—but it can be customary between close friends and members of the same family.

The "thumbs up" is not usually recognized as a sign for signaling okay; making a circle with thumb and first finger (the American symbol for "okay") is considered vulgar. To attract someone's attention, turn your palm down and wave your fingers or hand. To silently indicate a "no," shake a finger slowly to and fro.

Eating & Drinking

Lunch is the main meal of the day and usually the best time to talk business, though the serious discussion doesn't tend to start until after the coffee. Dinners are generally lighter and more formal; and when planning a rendezvous, it's essential to reserve a first-rate restaurant with a good menu and cellar. Bear in mind that dinner is usually served late—9 or 10pm. Spaniards often fill the gap between lunch and dinner by snacking on tapas (appetizers) at cafes and taverns.

If you're inviting Spanish friends to a meal and intending to include a spouse, it's best to extend the invitation to your visitor's spouse as well. If his spouse agrees to the invite, then it's okay to include yours too. As in most countries, it's expected for the person who makes the invitation to settle the check.

Business Etiquette

Things usually start off with casual commonplace observations and pleasantries. Once the negotiations actually get moving, it may take longer to get to the nitty-gritty than in other more northerly European countries. As companies tend to be rank-focused, concentrate on those within your rank or higher. At the same time, the opinion of everyone in the company is important. You are an outsider and must ingratiate yourself. Thus, expect many questions about your business, background, and family. Intuition as much as objective fact is important in the Spaniards' impression of you, so remain warm and friendly in your demeanor. Anticipate that many of the people important to a decision may not be present in any given meeting.

You may find it useful to have a local intermediary who can help you establish appointments. Schedule meetings well in advance. As a visitor, you should be punctual but anticipate that your hosts may be less prompt. There's still a lot of truth to the joke that in Spain, the only things that start on time are bullfights and theater performances. You can generally expect a 15- to 30-minute delay for social and certain business appointments.

Gifts

Business gifts are typically given at the conclusion of successful negotiations. Gifts should be opened and appreciated immediately. If you want to give something bearing a company name in business, then a pen or desk accessory is a good choice, as are books or CDs. Too expensive a gift might just be misinterpreted as a bribe, though.

If you're invited to dine with Spanish people, it's not customary to bring a bottle of wine as you might at home. A nicely wrapped gift, preferably showing a quality brand-name item, is more appreciated. So are chocolates, pastries, or flowers—though dahlias *(dalias)* and chrysanthemums *(crisantemos)* usually signify bereavement and are best avoided in normal circumstances, and 13 flowers is considered unlucky. For children, university or sports team shorts are a good choice.

LOOKING BACK AT MADRID

Moorish Mayrit

Madrid missed out on the Phoenicians, Greeks, Carthaginians, and Romans who arrived and influenced so many other corners of early Spain. Nor was it ravaged by the subsequent destructive Visigoths and Vandals, for the simple reason that the place barely existed, periodic primitive settlements apart, until 854. That was the year the conquering Moors—having set up their capital in southerly Córdoba—arrived in the center of Spain and built a wooden *qasr,* or ***alcazar*** (fortress), in a place they called **Mayrit,** or Magerit (both of which mean "many springs" in Arabic and refer to the abundance of underground streams in the area). Poised on a rocky ridge where today's **Palacio Real** now stands, this was just one of a line of defensive watchtowers aimed at protecting Islam territory from northern invaders. Mayrit grew from these simple beginnings into a township of over 7,000, holding firm against increasing Christian attacks before Ramiro II briefly occupied the place, and Alfonso VI of Castile definitively conquered it and Toledo in 1086.

Christian Colony

The rough and ready township, filled mainly with agricultural laborers whose activities are still reflected today in such names as **Plaza de la Paja** (Square of Straw), was renamed Madrid, and though it suffered occasional Arab sieges, it held out as a Christian outpost that encouraged religious colonists to come and build churches and monasteries. One of the earliest of these—dating from 1217—was the Friary of Saint Francis of Assisi, constructed on the site where the big domed church of **San Francisco el Grande** stands today. Some Moors—known as *Mudéjares*—stayed on and helped build the **San Nicolas de los Servitas** and **San Pedro el Viejo** towers, whose architectural styles bore their name. These little churches are the oldest in Madrid and provide a charmingly evocative visit today, as does the nearby narrow-laned villagelike zone of **Morería**—just across the road from Vistillas Park—where a tiny, but productive, Jewish community also lived.

The growing burg became a strategic crossroads, linking the center of Spain with the south and west, and was officially given the status of a town in 1202. Madrid played a more important role in affairs of state after the perambulating *cortes,* or parliament, which followed the kings from one township to another, met here for the first time in 1339. By the 15th century, Madrid was a key trading center with its own modest marketplace erected on the very site later taken over by the Plaza Mayor. A new stronger wall was built, whose main entrance was the **Puerta del Sol**—today at the very heart of modern Madrid.

Catholic Capital

In 1469, Ferdinand of Aragón and Isabella of Castile married, uniting the country's ever-squabbling and fragmented Christian provinces into a single country for the first

madrid THEN & NOW: FROM AUTOS DE FE TO PORTRAIT PAINTINGS

Madrid's most magnificent square is unquestionably the **Plaza Mayor** (p. 190), right at the center of lovely old Austrias district. Its classical rectangular shape—surrounding colonnaded walkways—and striking steel gray Castilian rooftop spires have made it one of the most photographed sights in Spain. A few centuries back, the ruthless Inquisition used this splendid location to put nonbelievers (real or imagined) to death by burning them at the stake; tournaments and *corridas* (bullfights) held here around the same period were also a bit violent. Today, in contrast, all is peace and light. The Reyes (Three Kings) processions start from here every January 6, and a range of concerts and exhibitions entertain the public sporadically year round. The innumerable cafes and restaurants around its edges are perennially busy; and on weekends, aficionados can buy stamps and coins from an array of stalls located under the colonnades.

time. Together they created the Spanish Inquisition to enforce primacy of Catholicism and to persecute or drive non-Catholics, Jews, and Moors out of the country. Twenty-three years later, two key events in Spanish history occurred: The last Arab stronghold was defeated in Granada, and Columbus's first voyage to the Americas laid the foundations for a far-flung empire that would bring wealth and power to Spain during the following centuries.

Madrid (pop. 20,000) then was still only of interest as a royal hunting area (especially in the **El Pardo** parkland north of the city, which today contains a host of protected wildlife), but its life was transformed in 1561 when the obsessively bureaucratic Philip II made the town his capital for the simple reason that it was the geographical center of the country. The number of inhabitants expanded fourfold, to over 80,000, in barely 40 years, and some of the city's finest sights still standing today, including the **Plaza Mayor, Monasterio de las Descalzas Reales,** and beginnings of the **Retiro Park**—next to the now disappeared Palacio del Buen Retiro—were built. Philip also commissioned a vast, chilling architectural masterpiece, **El Escorial,** 50km (31 miles) north of the capital as his organizational power base. From here, he tried to quell the Protestant revolt in the Netherlands, return England to Catholicism by marrying Mary I ("Bloody Mary") and wooing her half-sister Elizabeth I (who rebuffed him), and authorized the disastrous 1588 Armada invasion, which began the downturn of Spain's role as an international power.

Fluctuating Fortunes

Just over a hundred years later, the French-raised Philip V became king and was challenged for the throne by the archduke, Charles of Austria. The resultant **War of the Spanish Succession** caused Spain to lose Flanders, its Italian possessions, and Gibraltar (still held by the British today). The "enlightened" Charles III (1759–88) next countered these overseas disasters by dealing effectively with Madrid's social and economic problems, cleaning up the "dark, foul-smelling" capital by building sewers, introducing street lights, constructing monuments, and creating the **Palacio Real,** wide tree-lined **Paseo del Prado,** and the incomparable **Botanical Gardens.**

Thanks to his weaker successor Charles IV, however, Napoleon was allowed to place his brother Joseph Bonaparte on the throne in 1808, triggering the horrific **Peninsula War.** Madrileños put up a spirited but hopeless resistance against these superior odds—notably in Malasaña district's tiny **Plaza del Dos de Mayo,** where a brave but thwarted uprising took place (immortalized by Goya in his *El Tres de Mayo de 1808 en Madrid* masterpiece, which graphically portrayed the executions that took place the following day)—but it took another 4 years for allied forces, under the duke of Wellington, to drive out the French and restore Madrid, and Spain, to the Spaniards.

Spain's subsequent constitutional monarchy slowly collapsed in the midst of ecclesiastic conflicts, a financially crippling war in Morocco, and the rebellion of Spanish colonists, which led the United States to step in and relieve Spain of the last of its colonies—the Philippines, Puerto Rico, and Cuba—in 1898.

In reaction, Madrid saw the birth of a temporarily brilliant intellectual and artistic movement, known as the **Generation of '98,** in which such great writers as Miguel de Unamuno, Antonio Machado, Ortega y Gasset, and Valle-Inclan attended *tertulias* in grand old Madrid cafes, of which only **Café Gijon** (p. 141) and **Café Comercial** (p. 216) still stand. Visit them today to sip a coffee and imagine these Hispanic counterparts of Balzac and Baudelaire discussing art at corner tables savoring *café* or anis.

Rise of the Right

After the *cortes,* or parliament, was dissolved in 1923, General Miguel Primo de Rivera formed a military directorate. King Alfonso XIII and his family fled when Primo de Rivera resigned and the subsequently formed republic ran the country, slowly disintegrating from liberalism into anarchy, and finally leading to the growth of the ultraconservative **Falange** party (*Falange española,* or Spanish Phalanx)—modeled after Italy and Germany's fascist parties. The country was split down the middle,

madrid THEN & NOW: REBELLING & REVOLTING

The main impression you have of the tiny **Plaza Dos de Mayo** (p. 216) in Malasaña—an old Castizo (traditional) district of narrow crisscrossed streets sandwiched between the bustling Gran Vía and elegant Chamberí—is that it, too, is totally devoted to hedonism. Few squares so small can be so crammed with people knocking back *cervezas* and *copas de jerez* with such abandon. But on May 2, 1802, this square was the setting for an altogether more serious event. That was the day the citizens of Madrid rose up, bravely but futilely, against the occupying Napoleonic forces. They had no chance against such well-armed, disciplined troops and were quickly repressed. The next day, many executions took place in the square: Events were graphically recorded by Goya in his famous *El Tres de Mayo de 1808 en Madrid* painting, in which a lone central figure surrounded by his doomed companions howls his last act of defiance against the French rifle squad. The only acts of revolt today are the occasional late-night *botellón,* in which boisterous youngsters bring bottles of wine and whiskey and mix them with Coca-Cola to form a dire beverage called *calimocho* and live it up till dawn—much to the consternation of local residents.

equally between left and right, and political violence was common. On July 18, 1936, the army, supported by Mussolini and Hitler, tried to seize power, igniting the **Spanish Civil War.** General Francisco Franco, arriving by plane from Morocco, emerged as leader of the Nationalist (rightist) forces; and Madrid, controlled by the popular front, endured a brutal siege that lasted 28 months. By 1937, the republican forces were cut in two, and Madrid was left to fend for itself, as the popular front had already moved to Valencia for greater safety. Though larger in numbers, the republicans were divided and poorly organized, no match for the well-oiled, single-purposed fascist machine. On March 28, 1939, 200,000 nationalist troops marched into Madrid, meeting no resistance. The war was over the next day, when the rest of republican Spain surrendered. The war lasted 2 years and 254 days, costing some one million lives.

The war appalled the world with its ruthlessness. Churches were burned and mass executions and sundry atrocities were commonplace. Most shocking of all was the Fascist bombing of the Basque town of **Guernica,** which became the subject of one of Picasso's most fabled works, viewed daily today by thousands in Madrid's **Reina Sofía** (p. 174) art museum. For other invocations of this national tragedy, visitors can also travel to the awesome granite-built **El Valle de los Caídos** (the Valley of the Fallen; p. 266) outside San Lorenzo de El Escorial, whose cross is visible from miles away. To see where General Franco (whose rightwing sympathies led him to, at least spiritually, support Hitler and Mussolini in World War II), until his death in 1975, subsequently ruled the country with an iron fist for 36 stable, but oppressive, years, you can visit the grandiose corridor-filled **El Pardo Palace** beside the small town and protected wooded park immediately north of Madrid (p. 188). Here at a desk in a surprisingly small room, like his predecessor Philip II in El Escorial, the dapper and puritanical dictator ran his own considerably smaller empire with similar cool and ruthless efficiency.

Dawn of Democracy

After the democratic 1977 elections, a new constitution was approved by the electorate and the king; it guaranteed human and civil rights, as well as free enterprise, and canceled the status of the Roman Catholic Church as the church of Spain. It also granted limited autonomy to several regions, including Catalonia and the Basque provinces, both of which, however, are still clamoring for complete autonomy.

There was one alarming hiccup. In 1981 a group of right-wing military officers seized the *cortes* (parliament building) in Madrid and called upon Juan Carlos de Borbon—Franco's cultivated protégé and chosen successor or so it seemed—to establish a Francoist state. The king, however, surprised the country by refusing to accept the mold of Franco's protégé and saved the day by allowing the fledgling democracy to overcome its first test. Under Felipe Gonzalez's subsequent Socialist administration—the country's first leftist government since 1939—Spain entered the European Community (now Union) in 1986.

The '80s was a progressive decade for Madrid with a highly innovative and imaginative Socialist mayor Enrique Tierno Galván at the helm, still revered and honored with a park in his name. This was the effervescent and optimistic period of the ***movida*** when the creative arts, long repressed, exploded with an unprecedented inventive energy. It was alas subsequently dampened by his pallid and reactionary '90s Partido Popular successor Álvarez de Manzano who—unlamented—ceded his role in 2004 to the more dynamic and progressive Alberto Ruiz-Gallardón.

MEMORABLE quotes

Historical and Social:

"Me duele todo." (Everything hurts.) Philip II's last words in El Escorial where he lay dying from multiple illnesses and lamenting the decline of what had been the world's greatest empire.

"I am responsible only to God and history." General Franco explaining why he didn't need to explain his actions to any mere mortal.

"Uno, grande y libre" (One, great and free) Franco again describing his Utopian vision of Spain.

"Con Franco vivimos mejor." (With Franco we live better.) Right wing party slogan eulogizing their leader's successes in the 1960s and '70s.

"Con Franco vivíamos mejor." (With Franco we lived better.) 20th-century parody of the above by now deceased Catalan crime writer Manolo Vásquez Montalbán (creator of gourmet private eye Pepe Carvalho), who was here indirectly commenting on Spain's loss of the communal sense it demonstrated when it had a fascist regime to oppose.

"Spain is Different" Tourist slogan of the 1960s aimed at enticing more visitors to the country.

In praise of Madrid:

"De Madrid al Cielo y desde allí un agujero para verlo" (From Madrid to heaven and from there a hole in the sky to look down on it) Anonymous paean to the capital, combining an admiration for both the city's vital lifestyle and its perennial profusion of clear luminous skies.

"Madrid me Mata." (Madrid slays me.) More praise, hip style, honoring the city's exhausting choice of day and night entertainment amenities. (There's even a website: www.madridmemata.es.)

"Madrid Limpio y Verde" (Madrid clean and green) The new ecological slogan praising Madrid's dedication to keeping the place trash free, unpolluted, and verdant.

"Madrid se Mueve, muévete con Madrid." (Madrid is on the move, so move with Madrid.) More ad work, this time announcing the city's relentless non-stop metro expansion progress.

"No quites el sayo hasta el cuarenta de Mayo." (Don't take your undervest off till the 40th of May.) More a general saying than a quote but highly relevant to Madrid, which has long cold winters, short hot summers, and virtually no spring. So sometimes it can be chilly well into June, especially in the mornings.

"España Va Bien." (Spain's doing all right.) Optimistic 1990s view of the country by former Partido Popular President José María Aznar during those (mainly) happier pre-economic-crisis times.

The Spanish economy now enjoyed an upswing, which created more new jobs than in any other country in the E.U. Old Spanish traditions disappeared, one by one. More families moved to the suburbs, and more women joined the workforce. A survey has revealed that only 25% of Spaniards still take the siesta. And—shock! horror!—Spain officially abandoned its time-honored peseta and, with an ease that confounded many, slipped seamlessly under the euro umbrella in March 2002.

All this positive progress received a sharp blow on March 11, 2004, when Al Qaeda–linked terrorists blew up three suburban trains in and near the main train station of Atocha, causing nearly 200 deaths. But the subsequent unity, resilience, and individuality of spirit of the Madrileños were demonstrated in a moving

3-million-strong demonstration the following day. "We were all on that train" became a popular slogan.

Three days later—after 8 years in the wilderness—the PSOE (Spanish Socialist Party), under the benign and pragmatic José Rodriquez Zapatero, was reelected to power. It was an overt rejection of former President Aznar's initial insistence—with no evidence—in blaming the train attacks on ETA, and his contribution to the Iraq incursion, which had been clearly rejected by up to 90% of the population.

After 4 decades of violence aimed indiscriminately at the military and civil population alike, the Basque terrorist organization ETA announced a "permanent" ceasefire in 2006. They broke this vow at the end of the year without warning, bombing the car park in the Barajas airport's gleaming new terminal 4, causing 2 deaths and 40 million euros of damage. Half a dozen assassinations of police and politicians since have shown their implacable, tunnel-vision strategy. In 2008, Zapatero was returned to power as president for a second term as the country's socialist leader, albeit with a slightly reduced majority. His popularity has waned further since then, mainly due to his inability to deal effectively with the twin problems of unemployment—which counts among the highest in Europe—and an economic crisis that has seen the majority of the population having to tighten its belt more severely than any time since the Civil War.

There are hints not only that the conservative PP (Partido Popular) is likely to be the next ruling government, but also that the extreme right, in particular the Falange group, are still hovering in the background. Witness the 2010 suspension by a host of leading "old guard" magistrates of crusading judge Balthazar Garzón when he tried to investigate the disappearance of hundreds of thousands of citizens during the early days of the Franco regime.

ART & ARCHITECTURE IN MADRID

Art through the Ages

While Arabic, Romanesque, and Gothic art were all prominent in many areas of Spain between the 10th and 15th centuries, Madrid and surrounding Castile didn't really feature any prominent styles until the 16th century when **Renaissance** art finally flowered. Its supreme artist was **El Greco** (1540–1614), the Toledo-based Cretan (real name: Domenikos Theotocopoulos) whose strangely lit scenes, broodingly dark colors, crowded compositions, eerily elongated figures, and overall mystical aura are unmistakable.

Next came 17th and 18th century **Baroque,** characterized by a theatrical and decorative style that combined intense realism with a further daring use of light and shade. Leading practitioners of this art form were Naples-based **José de Ribera,** noted for his earthily humanistic depictions, and Sevillan **Francisco de Zurbarán,** whose glowing candlelit figures create a uniquely intimate mood. Most famous of them all was court painter **Diego Velázquez,** who used an unrivalled naturalist technique to produce his palace family scene *Las Meninas* (1656), considered by many to be Spain's greatest painting.

The late 18th and early 19th centuries saw the pastel-hued **Bourbon Rococo** style, displayed to perfection in the **Palacio Real,** whose corridors and ceilings are frothily decorated with works by Bohemian **Anton Mengs** (1728–79) and Italian

Tiepolo (1696–1770). Top Madrid painter of this period was the inimitable **Francisco Goya** (1746–1828), whose gargantuan assembly of works began mildly with sunlit **Rococo** depictions of San Isidro fiestas and progressed via ornate **neoclassical** portrayals (as in his clothed or unclothed *Majas*) and increasingly darker and more vitriolic condemnations of the atrocities of war to personal "Black Paintings" that reflected his own tortured struggles with deafness and depression.

Cubism and **Surrealism**—with their often fractured and imploded look—are the most prominent themes of the 20th century. **Juan Gris** (1887–1927), with his extraordinarily colorful palette, virtually stands alone as the only true **cubist.** Málaga-born **Pablo Picasso** (1881–1973), a genius who ignored all barriers, moved from teenage realism into far more complex realms, linking cubism with surrealism along the way. His masterpiece *Guernica* (1937) was a shockingly bleak and confusing polemic of the Civil War's most barbaric act. In its early days the painting was so controversial it needed eight guards to watch over it. Now only one stands on duty. The Catalan **surrealists Salvador Dalí** (1904–89) and **Joan Miró** (1893–1983) meanwhile both plumbed their ids for imagery. Dalí vividly explored the unreal worlds of nightmares and paranoia, while Miró's more whimsical images and sculptures suggest an inner exploration of childhood. Since the Civil War, abstract surrealist **Antoni Tàpies** (b. 1923), who uses material like wood, metal, and cloth to create his works, has emerged as Spain's leading artist.

Madrid's Architecture

Though between the 8th and 15th centuries much **Arabic architecture** was built in provinces like Andalusia, **Madrid**'s old **alcazaba fortress** has long disappeared and the city only retains a few wall fragments known as the **Muralla Arabe** on the Cuesta de la Vega slopes just below the Almudena Cathedral. More complete are the pair of *Mudéjar* (Moorish) towers built by 12th and 14th century *moriscos* atop Madrid's oldest churches: **San Pedro el Viejo** and **San Nicolas de las Servitas.**

There's even less evidence of the 9th to 13th century **Romanesque** that abounds from Galicia to Catalunya, and though formidable 14th to 16th century **Gothic** cathedrals, with their conglomeration of stained glass windows, pointed arches, cross vaults, and flying buttresses, can be found in Castilian cities like Toledo, Burgos, and Leon, all we have in Madrid is the modest but charming **Casa de los Lujanes** just off the Calle Mayor.

We have to look again to the 16th century **Renaissance** period whose style was marked by intricate Moorish-looking facades called **Plateresque** due to their resemblance to the work of silversmiths *(plateros)* to find anything impressive. Philip II's austere, straight-lined **El Escorial monastery,** designed by Juan de Herrera (1530–97), is the prime example. The gray slate roofs and distinctive pointed spires of this monumental icon appear again in the capital's ubiquitous array of 17th and 18th century **Baroque** buildings, from Herrera's supreme **Plaza Mayor** and Juan Gomez de Mora's **Casa de la Villa** to the more lavish **Real Academia de Bellas Artes** designed by the Churriguera family in a proliferation of statues, carvings, and twisty columns stacked into pyramids.

As a backlash against the latter's excesses, mid-18th-century Bourbon architects conjured up a blend of mathematical simplicity and classical grandeur to inaugurate the Italian-inspired **neoclassical** style. For them big was beautiful and its prime example was the **El Prado** museum and its magnificent adjoining tree-filled Paseo which has the beauty and sophistication of a Parisian boulevard.

Nineteenth century Industrial Revolution–era buildings, with their combination of cast-iron and glass, are spearheaded by the Retiro's **Palacio de Cristal** (Crystal Palace) and (albeit renovated) **Atocha** railway station. In total contrast, Madrid's very own 20th-century **Neo-Mudéjar** style nostalgically re-created early Arabic structures by using fine red brick, arches, balconies, and tiles combined with modern iron. The finest examples of this are the **Ventas** bullring at the eastern edge of the Salamanca district and **Antiguas Escuelas Aguirre,** with its imposing minaret tower and high gallery rising above the junction of O'Donnell and Alcalá. (Since 2009, the latter has been transformed into an immaculate and well-equipped Arabic Cultural Center).

In the early 20th century, the **Neo-Plateresque** style imitated the Spanish Renaissance Plateresque style which had evolved 400 years earlier. Its style is elaborate and fussily intricate with an ornate predominance of curves, arches, and turrets.

Francoist utilitarianism, meanwhile, is personified by the bland and self-contained **Edificio España,** built by the Otamendi brothers in 1953, and the 32-story **Torre de Madrid,** which appeared 4 years later. Both of them overlook the Plaza España, in contrast to the romantic statues of Cervantes, Don Quixote, and Sancho Panza below.

Upper Castellana Avenue meanwhile contains the best examples of the city's futuristic Tokyo-cum-New York style architecture: the 1988 **Torre Picasso** designed by Minoru Yamasaki in the **AZCA** business development—the highest building in Madrid—and the slanting twin **Torres KIO,** also known as the Puerta de Europa, which were built in Plaza Castilla by a Kuwaiti consortium. These were eclipsed in 2009, however, when the four nearby steely gray **CTBA (Cuatro Torres Business Area)** towers (p. 189) reached completion, elevating Madrid's architectural ego to even greater heights.

The newest project in progress is the portentously named, 75,000-square-meter **Ciudad de Justicia** (City of Justice), designed by Iraqi-Brit Zaha Hadid, the world's leading female architect (her credits include the prestigious Pritkzer award). A vast flying saucer-lookalike, it is nestled in the expanding **Valdebebas** development between the IFEMA Feria and Barajas airport's Terminal 4. Its huge, steely circular shape can already clearly be seen from neighboring Juan Carlos Park. When completed in 2011, the building will house over 100 law courts, while the still-burgeoning area around it will contain a host of highly sought-after new apartments and duplexes. It will be surrounded by a brand new 470 hectare (1,160 acre) park with trees, gardens, and lakes, which will be three times the size of Juan Carlos.

MADRID IN BOOKS, FILM, TV & MUSIC

History, Fiction & Biography

If you want to know more about the Arabs' contribution artistically and culturally to Spain as a whole, read Titus Burckhardt's *Moorish Culture in Spain* (McGraw-Hill).

Spain's most famous artist was Pablo Picasso. The most controversial book about the late painter is *Picasso: Creator and Destroyer* by Arianna Huffington (Simon & Schuster). Spain's other headline-grabbing artist was Salvador Dalí. In *Salvador Dalí: A Biography* (Dutton), author Meryle Secrest asks: Was he a mad genius or a cunning manipulator?

Andrés Segovia: An Autobiography of the Years 1893–1920 (Macmillan), with a translation by W. F. O'Brien, is worth seeking out.

Denounced by some as superficial, James A. Michener's *Iberia* (Random House) remains the classic travelogue on Spain. The *Houston Post* claimed that this book "will make you fall in love with Spain."

The latest biography on one of the 20th century's most durable dictators is *Franco: A Concise Biography* (Thomas Dunne Books). Gabrielle Ashford Hodges documents with great flair the Orwellian repression and widespread corruption that marked the notorious regime of this "deeply flawed" politician.

The most famous Spanish novel is *Don Quixote* by Miguel de Cervantes. Readily available everywhere, it deals with the conflict between the ideal and the real in human nature. Despite the unparalleled fame of Miguel de Cervantes within Spanish literature, very little is known about his life. One of the most searching biographies of the literary master is Jean Canavaggio's *Cervantes,* translated from the Spanish by J. R. Jones (Norton).

Although the work of Cervantes has attained an almost mystical significance in the minds of many Spaniards, in the words of Somerset Maugham, "It would be hard to find a work so great that has so many defects." Nicholas Wollaston's *Tilting at Don Quixote* (André Deutsch Publishers) punctures any illusions that the half-crazed Don is only a matter of good and rollicking fun.

Ernest Hemingway completed many works on Spain, none more notable than his novels of 1926 and 1940, respectively: *The Sun Also Rises* (Scribner) and *For Whom the Bell Tolls* (Scribner), the latter based on his experiences in the Spanish Civil War. Don Ernesto's *Death in the Afternoon* (various editions) remains the English-language classic on bullfighting.

For an interesting selection of anecdotes and pieces written over the years on the capital, read *Madrid: A Travellers Companion* (Constable) by Hugh Thomas, author of the classic in depth *Spanish Civil War.* A more personal view of the city is provided in Elizabeth Nash's highly individual *Madrid: A Cultural and Literary Companion,* in Signal Books' "Cities of the Imagination" series.

If you want the full lowdown on the monuments and historical background of Castile, check out hispanophile Alistair Boyd's *Companion Guide to Madrid and Central Spain* (Collins). A succinct and offbeat introduction to the capital's surrounding towns and villages is further provided in (author of this guide) Peter Stone's *Madrid Escapes* (Santana Books).

If you're interested in checking out the country's 20th-century political and historical background, check out Madrid-based journalist Giles Tremlett's *Ghosts of Spain* (Walker & Company), U.K. scholar Paul Preston's Franco (Basic Books), and famed researcher Hugh Thomas's revised and enlarged classic *The Spanish Civil War* (Modern Library).

If you read Spanish, one important book of the moment is the rewarding 2010 biography of Spain's socialist president Jose Luis Rodriguez Zapatero: *El Maquiavelo de Leon* (Esfera). Written by a leading Spanish media figure, José García Abad, it should silence all those critics who think of Sr. Zapatero as Spain's buffoonish "Mr. Bean." (Though it has to be admitted there is a certain physical resemblance btw. the two at times.)

Films Set (Mainly) in Madrid

One of the city's most enthusiastic chroniclers on celluloid has been **Pedro Almodóvar** (Oscar winner in 2002 for the best foreign language movie ***All About My Mother*** and whose muse Penélope Cruz was nominated for a Best Actress award in his later film ***Volver***). Though his unique comic vision has not altogether been appreciated by many Madrileños—who regard his stylish films as perverse kitsch sagas of marginals and neurotics—atmospheric sub-classics such as ***Women on the Edge of a Nervous Breakdown*** and ***What Have I done to Deserve This?*** create their own hilarious Madrileño subworld in which the female plays a surprisingly dominant role.

More seriously complex and unsettling are the works of the similar sounding **Alejandro Almenábar**—Chilean born but settled in Spain—who kicked off in the mid-1990s with ***Tesis*** (about snuff movies), and followed up with a nightmarish Madrid-based duo: ***Abre Los Ojos*** (remade in the States as ***Vanilla Sky*** with Tom Cruise) and ***Los Otros*** (The Others), a supernatural period thriller—his first in English—which starred Nicole Kidman. His latest film to date—set for a change in Galicia—was the moving ***Mar Adentro*** (somewhat bizarrely translated in English-speaking countries as "The Sea Inside"), in which Javier Bardem plays a terminally ill paraplegic patient and the moral dilemma faced by those around him regarding the use or nonuse of euthanasia.

Equally sobering, though more conventionally dramatic, are the social commentary works of **Carlos Saura,** ranging from his early ***Los Golfos*** and ***De Prisa, De Prisa*** (both about young Madrileño criminals in the Franco era) to the '90s ***Taxi*** (on urban racism in the city). His realistic musical trilogy ***Carmen, Tango,*** and ***Flamenco*** shows another facet of this leading director's talents.

A leading light in the realms of inventive anarchy is **Alex de la Iglesia,** whose blackest of black comedies include ***Día de la Bestia*** in which a trio of would-be exorcists try to hunt down the Devil in his lair beneath the KIO towers; and ***La Comunidad,*** where the inhabitants of a crumbling block of apartments fight for possession of a hidden stash, finally settling their scores in a vertiginous Harold Lloyd–style battle on the city's statue-dotted rooftops.

Last but by no means least, the highly unprolific **Victor Erice** (with three films in 30 years) created an indelible image of an artist's struggle in the ***Quince Tree Sun,*** shot entirely on location in the garden of real life artist Antonio Lopez's own rambling Chamartín house. Strictly for cineastes, this one.

Spanish Classical Music

Three major **composers** stand out. **Isaac Albeñiz,** a child prodigy who played in piano concerts at the age of 4, with his *Iberia* suite; **Manuel de Falla,** an ascetic

DO YOU know . . .

Why Madrileños are known as "gatos" (cats)?

Most people believe this stems from the fact that Madrileños like to stay up late, especially on the weekend, when many of them barely sleep. Out on the tiles with a vengeance! (***Note:*** This expression literally means to stay up all night like cats, which are often out all night and on rooftops.) However, the official explanation is historical. During an Arabic siege at the time when the city went by the name of Magerit, a particularly adept soldier managed to climb the outer walls with the agility of a cat by inserting his dagger between gaps in the stones as footholds. The story passed into legend and the soldier and his family assumed the name of Gato. They eventually had a street—the Callejón del Gato—named after one of their descendants, a court poet at the time of Juan II named Juan Alvarez Gato.

Andaluz from Cádiz, for his *Three Cornered Hat* ballet; and **Enrique Granados,** with his lively *Goyescas.*

The most talented **musician** of modern times was cellist **Pablo (Pau) Casals,** while today's leading **opera singer** is **Plácido Domingo.** In the world of creative folk music the *cantautores* (singer-songwriters) **Joan Manuel Serrat** and **Joaquin Sabina** are generally rated the two best working today. And in the world of flamenco dance the charismatic **Sara Baras,** who has made several world tours, is the most genial and talented performer of the moment.

EATING & DRINKING IN MADRID

Traditional Madrid fare is hearty stuff, aimed mainly at combating the cold winters. Eating is a social activity, whether that means eating out late at night or having large family gatherings for lunch. If you're just having tapas (see below) you'll never be short of high-calorie, high-cholesterol items like *tortilla* (omelet), *callos* (tripe), and chorizo (spicy sausage), and if it's a main meal traditional favorites like *cocido* (a dry stew of lamb, chickpeas, and veal generously strewn with chunks of lard), *lechona* (roast suckling pig), which reaches its apex of fatty sublimity in nearby Segovia, *pierna de cordero* (leg of lamb), and *chuletones* (huge cutlets of beef from the nearby Castilian stronghold of Avila) still dominate. The portions are immense, but the prices, by North American standards, can be high.

The city is also nationally and internationally eclectic, with dishes available not only from every province in the country but also abroad, encompassing everything from Galician *percebes* (goose barnacles) and Greek *moussaka* to Japanese sushi and German bratwurst. Pioneering chefs have made fusion all the rage and though in some restaurants you need an overdraft to indulge in their exquisitely dinky "tasting menus," there are certain spots like Ferran Adrià's **Fast Good Madrid** (p. 165) where quality and affordability merge.

Vegetarian eating spots are on the rise and another budget-style newcomer—maybe less healthy—is the hybrid Asian local. A recent place to open near me in what was once a standard nonsense tapas bar is called the "Alhambra Turkish Indian Kebab café bar" and more of this ilk are appearing everywhere. And on the shining new light front, hygienic sandwich bars like the Rodilla chain, so sparkling and clinical it's hard to believe, provide small, neatly wrapped non-loaf-sized *bocadillos* containing inventive mixtures like pineapple and *cabrales* blue cheese or kiwi fruit with *jamón serrano.*

Meals

BREAKFAST The day starts with a continental breakfast of coffee, hot chocolate, or tea, with assorted rolls, butter, and jam. Spanish breakfast might also consist of *churros* (fried fingerlike doughnuts) or sometimes *porras* (basically larger *churros,* which Madrileños habitually down in threes—though you should be wary of eating more than a couple yourself as they're very filling). Either version can be accompanied by hot chocolate that is very sweet and thick, but most Spaniards simply have coffee, usually strong, served with hot milk: either a *café con leche* (half coffee, half milk) or *cortado* (a shot of espresso "cut" with a dash of milk). If you find it too strong and bitter for your taste, you might ask for a more diluted *café americano.*

LUNCH The most important meal of the day in Spain, lunch is comparable to the farm-style midday "dinner" in the United States. It usually includes three or four courses, beginning with a choice of soup or several dishes of hors d'oeuvres called *entremeses.* Often a fish or egg dish is served after this, then a meat course with vegetables. Wine is always part of the meal. Dessert is usually pastry, custard, or assorted fruit—followed by coffee. Lunch is served from 1 to 4pm, with "rush hour" at 2pm.

TAPAS After the early evening stroll, many Spaniards head for their favorite *tascas,* bars where they drink wine and sample assorted tapas, or snacks, such as bits of fish, eggs in mayonnaise, or olives.

Because many Spaniards eat dinner very late, they often have an extremely light breakfast, certainly coffee, and perhaps a pastry. However, by 11am they are often hungry and lunch might not be until 2pm or later, so many Spaniards have a late-morning snack, often at a cafeteria. Favorite items to order are an *empanada* (slice of meat or fish pie from Galicia) or the aforementioned *tortilla* (Spanish omelet with potatoes) accompanied by a *copa* of wine or a *caña* (small glass) of beer. (If you want a larger beer, ask for a *doble.*) Many request a large *tapa,* such as *calamares* (squid) or *callos* (tripe), also served with bread and wine (or beer).

DINNER Another extravaganza: A typical meal starts with a bowl of soup, followed by a second course, often a fish dish, and by another main course, usually veal, beef, or pork, accompanied by vegetables. Again, desserts tend to be fruit, custard, or pastries.

Naturally, if you had a heavy and late lunch and stopped off at a tapas bar or two before dinner, supper might be much lighter, perhaps some cold cuts, sausage, a bowl of soup, or even a Spanish omelet made with potatoes. Wine is always part of the meal. Afterward, you might have a demitasse and a fiery Spanish brandy, *orujo* (equivalent of the gritty French *marc* or Italian *grappa*), or anis (a more digestive anise-flavored liquor, a specialty of nearby Chinchón). The typical dining hour is 10 or 10:30pm.

The Cuisine

SOUPS & APPETIZERS Soups are usually served in big bowls. Cream soups, such as asparagus and potato, can be fine; sadly, however, they are too often made from powdered envelope soups such as Knorr and Liebig. Served year-round, chilled gazpacho, on the other hand, is tasty and particularly refreshing during the hot months.

In the *paradores* (government-run hostelries) and top restaurants, as many as 15 tempting hors d'oeuvres are served. In lesser-known places, avoid these *entremeses,* which often consist of last year's sardines and shards of sausage left over from the Moorish conquest.

EGGS These are served in countless ways. A Spanish omelet, a *tortilla española,* is made with potatoes and usually onions. A simple omelet is called a *tortilla francesa.* A *tortilla portuguesa* is similar to the American Spanish omelet.

FISH Spain's fish dishes tend to be outstanding and vary from province to province. One of the most common varieties is *merluza* (sweet white hake). *Langosta,* a variety of lobster, is seen everywhere—it's a treat but terribly expensive. Gourmets relish their seawater taste; others find them tasteless. *Rape* (pronounced "*rah*-peh") is the Spanish name for monkfish, a sweet, wide-boned ocean fish with a scalloplike texture. Also try a few dozen half-inch baby eels. They rely heavily on olive oil and garlic for their flavor, but they taste great. Squid cooked in its own ink is suggested only to those who want to go native. Charcoal-broiled sardines, however, are a culinary delight—a particular treat in the Basque provinces. Trout Navarre is one of the most popular fish dishes, usually stuffed with bacon or ham. Among the superb shellfish brought in daily from Spain's Atlantic coasts, *gambas* (prawns) and *mejillones* (mussels) are widely available. *Gambas al ajillo* (prawns cooked in garlic in a small earthenware dish) and *mejillones al vapor* (steamed mussels) are two popular variations.

PAELLA You can't go to Spain without trying its celebrated paella. Flavored with saffron, paella is an aromatic rice dish usually topped with shellfish, chicken, sausage, peppers, and local spices. Served authentically, it comes steaming hot from the kitchen in a metal pan called a *paellera.* (Incidentally, what is known in the U.S. as Spanish rice isn't Spanish at all. If you ask an English-speaking waiter for Spanish rice, you'll be served paella.)

MEATS Try the spit-roasted suckling pig, so sweet and tender it can often be cut with a fork. The veal is also good, and the Spanish *lomo de cerdo,* loin of pork, is unmatched anywhere. Tender chicken is most often served in the major cities and towns today, and the Spanish are adept at spit-roasting it until it turns a delectable golden brown. However, in more remote spots of Spain, "free-range" chicken is often stringy and tough.

VEGETABLES & SALADS Through more sophisticated agricultural methods, Spain now grows more of its own vegetables, which are available year-round, unlike days of yore, when canned vegetables were used all too frequently. Both potatoes and rice are staples of the Spanish diet, the latter a prime ingredient, of course, in the famous paella originating in Valencia. Salads are often made simply with just lettuce, onions, and tomatoes.

DESSERTS The Spanish do not emphasize dessert, often opting for fresh fruit. Flan, a home-cooked egg custard, appears on all menus—sometimes with a burnt-caramel sauce in a version known as Crema Catalana. Ice cream appears on nearly all menus as well. But the best bet is to ask for a basket of fruit, which you can wash at your table. Homemade pastries are usually moist and not too sweet. As a dining oddity—although it's not odd at all to Spaniards—many restaurants serve fresh orange juice for dessert.

OLIVE OIL & GARLIC Olive oil is used lavishly in Spain, the largest olive grower on the planet. You may not want it in all dishes. If you prefer your fish grilled in butter, the word is *mantequilla.* In some instances, you'll be charged extra for the butter. Garlic is also an integral part of the Spanish diet, and even if you love it, you may find Spaniards love it more than you do and use it in the oddest dishes.

What to Drink

DRINKS An excellent non-carbonated drink for the summer is called Tri-Naranjus, which comes in lemon and orange flavors. In summer you should also try an *horchata.* Not to be confused with the Mexican beverage of the same name, the Spanish *horchata* is a sweet, milklike beverage made of tubers called *chufas.* In hot weather *granizados* (crushed-ice drinks) of lemon, orange, or even coffee are very popular, but watch the price if you're having one in an outdoor cafe in the Castellana Avenue or Retiro Park.

COFFEE Even if you are a dedicated coffee drinker, you may find the *café con leche* (coffee with milk) a little too strong. I suggest *leche manchada,* a little bit of strong, freshly brewed coffee in a glass that's filled with lots of frothy hot milk. If you're really desperate for American style coffee, you can now opt for Starbucks, which has opened several Madrid branches in the past couple of years.

BEER Beer *(cerveza)* is now drunk everywhere and rapidly superseding wine as the most popular tipple. Domestic brands include San Miguel, Aguila, Cruz Blanca, Cruzcampo and, last but not least, Mahou (which is made in Madrid). Bottled or draft versions of the latter are widely available, usually in the form of a *caña,* which is a small glass drawn from the *barril* or cask.

Note: There is an old Madrid ruling that alcoholic drinks—beer, wine, *vermut*—must be accompanied by a nourishing tidbit in order to "lessen their noxious influence," so you usually get a small free *tapa* thrown in with your tipple, especially in the cheaper, more traditional bars.

WINE Sherry *(vino de Jerez)* has been called "the wine with a hundred souls." Drink it before dinner (try the topaz-colored *finos,* a dry and very pale sherry) or whenever you drop into some old inn or bodega for refreshment; many of them have rows of kegs with spigots. *Manzanilla,* a golden-colored medium-dry sherry, is extremely popular. The sweet cream sherries (Harvey's Bristol Cream, for example) are favorite after-dinner wines (called *olorosos*). While the French may be disdainful of Spanish table wines, they can be truly noble, especially two leading varieties, Rioja and Navarra. Wines from westerly Extremadura are also beginning to make an impact and several Extremeño wine bars have recently opened in the capital. If you're not too exacting in your tastes, you can always ask for the *vino de la casa* (house wine) wherever you dine. (This is likely to be a quaffable drop from Toledo or La Mancha.) The Priorat of Catalonia, meanwhile, is heavy, though its rival Penedés comes across as a more subtle vino. From Andalusia comes the fruity sherrylike Montilla. There are some good local sparkling wines *(cavas)* in Spain, such as Freixenet and Codorniú, especially the Non Plus Ultra variety. One brand, Benjamín, comes in individual-size bottles.

Thanks to irrigation, improved grape varieties, technological developments, and the expenditure of billions of euros, bodegas and vineyards are sprouting up throughout the country, opening their doors to visitors interested in how the stuff is grown, fermented, and bottled. These wines are now earning awards at wine competitions around the world for their quality and bouquet. Even Madrid province wines, ignored for years and still straining at the leash to prove themselves, have improved. The Jesús Díaz bodega from Colmenar de Oreja, south of the capital near Chinchón, has already won several prizes for its fragrant reds.

Interested in impressing a newfound Spanish friend over a wine list? Consider bypassing the usual array of Riojas, sherries, and sparkling Catalonian *cavas* in favor of, say, a Galician white Albariño from Rias Baixas, which some connoisseurs consider the perfect accompaniment for seafood. Among reds, make a beeline for vintages from the fastest-developing wine region of Europe, the arid, high-altitude district of Ribera del Duero, near Burgos, whose alkaline soil, cold nights, and sunny days have earned unexpected praise from winemakers (and encouraged massive investments) in the past 5 years.

SANGRIA The all-time favorite refreshing drink in Spain, sangria is a red-wine punch that combines wine with oranges, lemons, *gaseosa* (seltzer), and sugar. Be careful, however; many joints that do a big tourist trade produce a sickly sweet Kool-Aid version of sangria for unsuspecting visitors. Other places may also add an unwelcome amount of cheap *coñac* or anis to the drink.

SPIRITS Adventurous imbibers can try *orujo,* a fiery liquor or *aguardiente* (made from the stalks and skins of grapes) that tastes like a rough *grappa* and is sometimes offered free after a meal. Pacharán is a rose-purple anise-flavored sloe gin spirit from Navarra, a conventional after-dinner drink.

WHISKEY & BRANDY The Spanish reign supreme with brandies and cognacs (though Spanish *coñacs* tend to be sweeter and darker than their French counterparts). Try Fundador, made by the Pedro Domecq family in Jerez de la Frontera. If you find this a bit raw and want a slightly smoother *coñac,* ask for the "103" white label, while for something yet more mellow—and pricey—Magno or Carlos III are an appreciable step up. If money is no object, splash out on a Lepanto or Gran Duque de Alba, both of which are served from decanters and guaranteed to send you floating in a mellow haze up the Gran Vía.

PLANNING YOUR TRIP TO MADRID

3

In spite of the fact that the city has six million inhabitants, traffic congestion as bad as in any major European city, and 2 main summer months that are as hot as you know where, Madrid is a remarkably easy and, in many corners, even relaxing city to visit and get around in.

For a start, there are no messy customs requirements like visas to arrange before you go; and once you've arrived and settled in, there are plenty of well-informed **tourist offices** in both the city and its surrounding province to give you the lowdown on what to do and where to go. Transport by **metro** (subway) and **bus** is extremely efficient and frequent, with an increasing number of facilities for travelers with disabilities.

The currency is the **euro** (€), common now throughout practically the entire European continent—with a few stubborn exceptions, like Norway—and it's easy to combine visits to other countries, such as England and France, without having to worry about changing currency. For additional help in planning your trip and for more on-the-ground resources in Madrid, please turn to chapter 12.

VISITOR INFORMATION

Tourist Offices

You can begin your info search with Spain's tourist offices (www.okspain.org).

IN THE UNITED STATES For information before you go, contact the **Tourist Office of Spain,** 666 Fifth Ave., Fifth Floor, New York, NY 10103 (✆ **212/265-8822**). It can provide sightseeing information, events calendars, train and ferry schedules, and more. Branches of the Tourist Office of Spain are also located at: 8383 Wilshire Blvd., Ste. 956, Beverly Hills, CA 90211 (✆ **323/658-7188**); 845 N. Michigan Ave., Ste. 915E, Chicago, IL 60611 (✆ **312/642-1992**); and 1221 Brickell Ave., Ste. 1850, Miami, FL 33131 (✆ **305/358-1992**).

IN CANADA Contact the **Tourist Office of Spain,** 102 Bloor St. W., Ste. 3402, Toronto, Ontario M5S 1M9, Canada (✆ **416/961-3131**).

Spain

IN THE U.K. Write to the **Spanish National Tourist Office,** 22–23 Manchester Sq., London W1M 5AP (✆ **020/7486-8077**).

IN MADRID **The Patronato Municipal de Turismo,** Calle Mayor 69 (✆ **91-588-29-00;** Mon–Fri 9am–2pm) will provide you with up-to-date information on what to do and where to go in the Spanish capital.

Other tourist offices providing free maps and information can be found at Duque de Medinaceli 2, Barajas Airport, Puerta de Toledo, and the Atocha and Chamartín rail stations. Opening hours vary. The main **Madrid Office of Tourism** (Oficina Municipal de Información y Turismo) is at Plaza Mayor 3 (✆ **91-588-16-36**), and is open Monday to Friday 10am to 8pm, and Saturday 10am to 3pm.

Maps

The tourist offices can also supply you with free pocket-size **maps** of the city. Metro stations will in turn provide you with a free, up-to-date map of the ever-changing underground and suburban railway systems (the latter is known as the *cercanías* and divided into different price-colored zones). Be sure to also turn to the inside back cover of this book for a map of the Madrid metro.

You can buy larger and more detailed **city maps** in newspaper kiosks and in the bookshop section of stores like the **Corte Inglés** or **FNAC,** in the central Calle Preciados, near the Callao metro station, for around 5.50€.

ENTRY REQUIREMENTS

A valid **passport** is all that an American, Australian, British, Canadian, or New Zealand citizen needs to enter Spain. Visitors from these countries do not need a visa so long as their visit does not exceed 90 days.

Customs

WHAT YOU CAN BRING INTO SPAIN

You can bring most personal effects and the following items duty-free: two still cameras and 10 rolls of film per camera, tobacco for personal use, 1 liter each of liquor and wine (for travelers age 18 or over), a portable radio, a cassette or digital recorder, a laptop, a bicycle, sports equipment, and fishing gear.

WHAT YOU CAN TAKE HOME FROM SPAIN

U.S. Citizens: For specifics on what you can bring back and the corresponding fees, download the invaluable free pamphlet *Know Before You Go* online at www.cbp.gov. (Click on "Travel," and then click on "Know Before You Go! Online Brochure.") Or contact the U.S. Customs & Border Protection (CBP), 1300 Pennsylvania Ave. NW, Washington, DC 20229 (✆ **877/287-8667**) and request the pamphlet.

Canadian Citizens: For a clear summary of Canadian rules, write for the booklet *I Declare,* issued by the Canada Border Services Agency (✆ **800/461-9999** in Canada, or 204/983-3500; www.cbsa-asfc.gc.ca).

U.K. Citizens: For information, contact **HM Customs & Excise** at ✆ **0845/010-9000** (from outside the U.K., 020/8929-0152), or consult the website at **www.hmce.gov.uk**.

Australian Citizens: A helpful brochure available from Australian consulates or Customs offices is *Know Before You Go*. For more information, call the **Australian Customs Service** at ✆ **1300/363-263,** or log on to **www.customs.gov.au**.

New Zealand Citizens: Most questions are answered in a free pamphlet available at New Zealand consulates and Customs offices: *New Zealand Customs Guide for Travellers, Notice no. 4*. For more information, contact **New Zealand Customs,** The Customhouse, 17–21 Whitmore St., Box 2218, Wellington (✆ **04/473-6099** or 0800/428-786; **www.customs.govt.nz**).

WHEN TO GO

Climate

Spring and fall are ideal times to visit Madrid. **May** and **October** are the best months, in terms of weather and crowds. In my view, however, the balmy month of May (with an average temperature of 16°C/61°F) is the most glorious time for making your own discovery of the Spanish capital.

On Time in Spain

In Spain, a time change occurs the first weekend of spring. Check your watch. Many unsuspecting visitors have arrived at the airport too late and missed their planes.

August is the month when Madrid is traditionally at its most peaceful, as many of its inhabitants have escaped to the mountains or are sunning themselves on the Atlantic or Mediterranean coasts. About 75% of the city's restaurants and shops also decide that it's time for a vacation and close for the month, though visitors usually find enough for their needs. However, these days it's not quite the semi-ghost town it was in the past, as Madrileños have become increasingly attracted by the advantages of staggered holidays. Many now choose June, September, or October as their main vacation time, when those popular coastal areas are less hot, less crowded, and less expensive. Also with the new middle-class affluence, many Spaniards are not necessarily limited to their homeland for choice. Another factor is the increased number of resident immigrants, from South Americans to East Europeans, who by choice or for economic reasons tend to stay, live, and continue working throughout the summer.

The main problem with summers in Madrid is the ovenlike midsummer heat (mercifully dry), which, in July and August, can sometimes reach afternoon maximums of 40°C (104°F), though the abundance of air-conditioned locales and soothing lack of crowds produce a unique, daylong siesta atmosphere.

Weather Chart for Madrid

	JAN	FEB	MAR	APR	MAY	JUNE	JULY	AUG	SEPT	OCT	NOV	DEC
Temp (°C)	6	7	9	12	16	21	24	24	21	14	9	6
Temp (°F)	42	45	49	53	60	69	76	75	69	58	48	43
Rainfall (cm)	4	4.5	3	4.5	3.8	2.5	.8	1	2.8	3.8	5.8	4.3
Rainfall (in.)	1.60	1.80	1.20	1.80	1.50	1.00	.30	.40	1.10	1.50	2.30	1.70

Public Holidays (Fiestas)

Holidays include January 1 (New Year's Day), January 6 (Feast of the Epiphany), March 19 (Feast of St. Joseph), Good Friday, Easter Monday, May 1 (May Day), June 10 (Corpus Christi), June 29 (Feast of Sts. Peter and Paul), July 25 (Feast of St. James), August 15 (Feast of the Assumption), October 12 (Spain's National Day), November 1 (All Saints' Day), December 8 (Immaculate Conception), and December 25 (Christmas).

No matter how large or small, every city or town in Spain also celebrates its local saint's day. In Madrid, it's May 15 (St. Isidro). You'll rarely know what the local holidays are in your next destination in Spain. Try to keep money on hand, because you may arrive in town only to find banks and stores closed. In some cases, intercity bus services are suspended on holidays.

Calendar of Events

The Madrileño calendar is a colorful kaleidoscope of saint's days, fiestas, and bullfights. Art exhibitions are perennial features during the hot summers, and you can enjoy concerts in Parque del Retiro as well as other open areas. Check with the city tourism office for details (✆ **91-366-54-77;** www.esmadrid.com).

The dates given below may not be precise. Sometimes the exact days may not be announced until 6 weeks before the actual festival. Check with the National Tourist Office of Spain (see "Visitor Information," at the beginning of this chapter) if you're planning to attend a specific event.

For an exhaustive list of events beyond those listed here, check **http://events.frommers.com**, where you'll find a searchable, up-to-the-minute roster of what's happening in cities all over the world.

THE BIG THREE FIESTAS

Fiesta de San Isidro Held in honor of Madrid's patron saint, fiesta activities cover ceramic, crockery, and secondhand book fairs. Local couples, known as *chulos* and *chulapas,* parade in Castizo (traditional) dress and enjoy feasts, *romerías,* and music acts in key spots like the 16th-century Plaza Mayor and leafy Pradera de San Isidro (the setting for those idyllic celebratory images of yesteryear immortalized on canvas by Goya). During this 4-week period, the most consecutive daily bullfights are held. May 15.

Virgen de la Paloma This lively festival belies the midsummer image of Madrid as a temporarily lethargic ghost city, with practically everyone out of town basking on the Levante and Cantabrian coasts. On August 15, the La Latina quarter becomes a crowded riot of street bunting, drinking stalls, live music, and kiddies' events. A float decorated with bright carnations and bearing an 18th-century gold framed portrait of Madrid's patron saint (the Virgin of La Paloma) is carried through streets on August 15 by the city *bomberos* (firemen).

The Autumn Festival Held in October and November, the **Feria del Otoño** (✆ **91-580-25-75**) is the best music festival in Spain, with a lineup that attracts the crème de la crème of the European and South American musical communities. The usual roster of chamber music, symphonic pieces, and orchestral works is supplemented by a program of zarzuela (musical comedy), as well as Arabic and Sephardic pieces composed during the Middle Ages.

THE YEAR AT A GLANCE

JANUARY

Three Kings Day (Día de los Reyes). Parades are staged throughout the main arteries of the city in anticipation of the Feast of the Epiphany (Jan 6). Parades usually take place on January 5 or 6.

FEBRUARY

ARCO (Madrid's International Contemporary Art Fair). One of the biggest draws on Spain's cultural calendar, this exhibit showcases the best in contemporary art from Europe and America. At the Crystal Pavilion of the Casa de Campo, the exhibition draws galleries from throughout Europe, the Americas, Australia, and Asia, who bring with them the works of regional and internationally known artists. To buy tickets, you can contact El Corte Inglés (✆ **91-418-88-00**) or Madrid Rock (✆ **91-547-24-23**). The cost is between 22€ and 30€. You can get schedules from the tourist office closer to the event. Dates vary, but usually mid-February.

Madrid Carnaval. The carnival kicks off with a big parade along the Paseo de la Castellana, culminating in a masked ball at the Círculo de Bellas Artes on the following night. Fancy-dress competitions last until February 28, when the festivities end with a tear-jerking "burial of a sardine" at the Fuente de los Pajaritos in the Casa de Campo, followed that evening by a concert in the Plaza Mayor. Call ✆ **91-429-31-77** for more information. Dates vary; 5 days before Ash Wednesday.

MARCH

Semana Santa (Holy Week). Although many of the country's smaller towns stage similar celebrations (especially notable in Zamora, Valladolid, and Seville), the festivities in Madrid are among the most elaborate. From Palm Sunday until Easter Sunday, a series of processions with hooded penitents moves to the piercing wail of the *saeta,* a love song to the Virgin or Christ. *Pasos* (heavy floats) bear images of the Virgin or Christ. Make hotel reservations way in advance. Call the Madrid Office of Tourism (Oficina Municipal de Información y Turismo) for details (✆ **91-588-16-36**). Usually last week of March.

APRIL

Bullfights. Holy week traditionally kicks off the season in Madrid. This national pastime affords the visitor an unparalleled insight into the Spanish temperament. (See also "Animal-rights Issues" section later in this chapter.)

MAY

Dos de Mayo. May 2 sees the commemoration of the valiant, but unsuccessful, uprising against occupying French forces during the Peninsula War in 1808, which was brutally repressed and stirringly immortalized in Goya's famous *El Tres de Mayo de 1808 en Madrid* painting of firing-squad victims. Rock concerts and flamenco shows take place in the Dos de Mayo square in Malasaña, where the rebellion began, as well as in other parts of the city.

Fiesta de San Isidro. Madrileños run wild with a 10-day celebration honoring their city's patron saint. Food fairs, Castilian folkloric events, street parades, parties, music, dances, bullfights, and other festivities mark the occasion. Make hotel reservations early. Expect crowds and traffic (and beware of pickpockets). For information, write to Oficina Municipal de Información y Turismo, Plaza Mayor 3, 28014, or call ✆ **91-588-16-36.** www.munimadrid.es. See also "The Big Three Fiestas," p. 34. Second week of May.

Feria del Libro. This annual book fair is located in Parque del Retiro. Leading international novelists and historians come to promote their latest works and the number of stands increases annually. The *feria* covers 2 weeks from late May to early June.

JUNE

Corpus Christi. A major holiday on the Spanish calendar, this event is marked by big processions in Madrid, as well as in nearby cathedral cities such as Toledo. Dates vary in June.

JULY

Veranos de la Villa. Called "the summer binge" of Madrid, this program presents folkloric dancing, pop music, classical music, zarzuelas, and flamenco at various venues throughout the city. Open-air cinema is a feature in the Parque del Retiro. Ask at the various tourist offices for complete details (the program changes every summer). Sometimes admission is charged, but often these events are free. Mid-July until the end of August.

AUGUST

Fiestas of Lavapiés and La Paloma. These two fiestas begin with the Lavapiés on August 1 and continue through the hectic La Paloma celebration on August 15, the day of the Virgen de la Paloma. Thousands of people race through the narrow streets. Apartment dwellers hurl buckets of cold water onto the crowds below to cool them off. Children's games, floats, music, flamenco, and zarzuelas, along with street fairs, mark the occasion. For more information, call ✆ **91-429-31-77.** See also "The Big Three Fiestas," p. 34.

OCTOBER

Autumn Festival. Spanish and international artists alike participate in this cultural program, with a series of operatic, ballet, dance, music, and theatrical performances. From Strasbourg to Tokyo, this event is a premier attraction, yet ticket prices are reasonable. Make hotel reservations early, and for tickets write to **Feria del Otoño,** Plaza de España 8, 28008 Madrid (✆ **91-580-25-75**). See also "The Big Three Fiestas," p. 34. Late October to late November.

DECEMBER

Día de los Santos Inocentes. Another countrywide holiday. On this day, the Spanish play many practical jokes and, in general, do *loco* things to one another—it's the Spanish equivalent of April Fools' Day. December 28.

3 GETTING THERE & GETTING AROUND

Getting There

BY PLANE

All flights from the U.S. and other overseas countries arrive at Madrid's international airport, **Barajas,** which lies 15km (9 miles) east of the center. It's usually best to allow half an hour to get from the center to the airport. For flight information, ring ✆ **90-235-35-70.**

MAIN FLIGHT OPERATORS FROM NORTH AMERICA The national carrier of Spain, **Iberia Airlines** (✆ **800/772-4642;** www.iberia.com), offers more routes to and within Spain than any other airline, with nonstop service to Madrid from both New York and Miami. From Miami, Iberia takes off for at least eight destinations in Mexico and Central America, and in cooperation with its air partner, Ladeco (an airline based in Chile), to dozens of destinations throughout South America as well. Iberia also flies from Los Angeles to Madrid, with a brief stop in Miami, and offers services to Madrid through Montréal two and three times a week, depending on the season. Also available are attractive rates on fly/drive programs within Iberia and Europe.

Iberia's fares are lowest if you reserve an APEX (advance-purchase excursion) ticket at least 21 days in advance, schedule your return 7 to 30 days after your departure, and leave and return between Monday and Thursday. Fares, which are subject to change, are lower during off season. Most transatlantic flights are on carefully maintained 747s and DC-10s, and in-flight services reflect Spanish traditions, values, and cuisine.

American Airlines (✆ **800/433-7300;** www.aa.com) offers daily nonstop service to Madrid from its massive hub in Miami, with excellent connections from there to the rest of the airline's impressive North and South American network.

Delta (✆ **800/241-4141;** www.delta.com) maintains daily nonstop service from Atlanta (centerpiece of its worldwide network) to Madrid. Delta's Dream Vacation department maintains access to fly/drive programs, land packages, and escorted bus tours through the Iberian Peninsula.

Since 1991, **United Airlines** (✆ **800/241-6522;** www.ual.com) has flown passengers nonstop every day to Madrid from Washington. United also offers fly/drive programs and escorted motor coach tours. At the time of writing, **Continental Airlines** (✆ **800/231-0856;** www.continental.com) had just finalized a merger with United. They currently offer six or seven nonstop flights per week, depending on the season, to Madrid from Newark, New Jersey, an airport many New York residents prefer.

Europass: A Cost-Cutting Technique

A noteworthy cost-cutting option is Iberia's Europass. Available only to passengers who simultaneously arrange for transatlantic passage on Iberia and a minimum of two additional flights, it allows passage on any flight within Iberia's European or Mediterranean dominion for $250 for the first two flights and $133 for each additional flight. This is especially attractive for passengers wishing to combine trips to Spain with, for example, visits to such far-flung destinations as Cairo, Tel Aviv, Istanbul, Moscow, and Munich. For details, ask Iberia's phone representative. Iberia's main Spain-based competitor is **Air Europa (✆ 888/238-7672; www.air-europa.es)**, which offers nonstop service from New York's JFK Airport to Madrid, with continuing service to major cities within Spain. Fares are competitive.

US Airways (✆ **800/428-4322;** www.usairways.com) offers daily nonstop service between Philadelphia and Madrid. US Airways offers connections to Philadelphia from more than 50 cities throughout the United States, Canada, and The Bahamas.

MAIN FLIGHT OPERATORS FROM THE UNITED KINGDOM The two major carriers that fly between the United Kingdom and Spain are **British Airways** (**BA;** ✆ **0845/773-3377,** or 020/8759-5511 in London; www.british-airways.com) and **Iberia** (✆ **020/7830-0011** in London). In spite of the frequency of their routes, however, I suspect most vacationing Brits fly charter (see "Tips for British Travelers," below).

More than a dozen daily flights, on either BA or Iberia, depart from London's Heathrow and Gatwick airports. The Midlands are served by flights from Manchester and Birmingham, two major airports that can also be used by Scots flying to Spain. Approximately seven flights a day go between London and Madrid (trip time: 2–2½ hr.). The best air deals on scheduled flights from the United Kingdom are those requiring a Saturday-night stopover.

Low-cost flights are now provided from a variety of British cities to Madrid by **easyJet.** No tickets are issued and no specific seats allocated (though families with children do have priority). All bookings are made online. Check **www.easyjet.com**.

Ryanair also operates bargain-priced flights from London Stansted to **Valladolid** (55 min. away by high-speed train, and 2½ hr. by bus, from Madrid). Check **www.ryanair.com**.

Tips for British Travelers

A regular fare from the United Kingdom to Spain is extremely high, so savvy Brits usually call a travel agent for a deal—either a charter flight or some special air-travel promotion. These so-called deals are almost always available, due to great interest in Spain as a tourist destination. Another way to keep costs down is an APEX (advance-purchase excursion) ticket. Alternatively, a PEX (public excursion fare) ticket offers a discount without the strict booking restrictions. You might also ask the airlines about a Eurobudget ticket, which has restrictions or length-of-stay requirements.

British periodicals are always full of classified advertisements touting "slashed" fares to Spain. Good sources include the London-based magazine *Time Out*, the daily travel section of London's *Evening Standard,* and the Sunday edition of almost any newspaper.

Most vacationing Brits looking for air-flight bargains go charter. Delays can be frequent (some as long as 2 days and nights), and departures are often at inconvenient hours. Booking conditions can also be severe, and one must read the fine print carefully and deal only with a reputable travel agent. Stays rarely last a month, and booking must sometimes be made at least a month in advance, although a 2-week period is sometimes possible.

Charter flights leave from some British regional airports for Madrid airports. Figure on saving approximately 10% to 15% off regularly scheduled flight tickets. Recommended companies include **Trailfinders** (✆ **020/7937-5400** in London; www.trailfinders.com) and **Avro Tours** (✆ **020/8715-0000** in London).

In London, many bucket shops around Victoria Station and Earls Court offer low fares. Make sure the company you deal with is a member of the IATA, ABTA, or ATOL. These umbrella organizations will help you out if anything goes wrong.

CEEFAX, a British television information service included on many home and hotel TVs, runs details of package holidays and flights to Europe and beyond. Just switch to your CEEFAX channel to find a menu of listings that includes travel information.

Also check out those **easyJet** and **Ryanair** flights mentioned on p. 37 in "Main Flight Operators from the United Kingdom."

Getting into Town from Barajas Airport

BY METRO (SUBWAY) The most convenient way to reach the center of Madrid from Barajas airport is by **metro** line 8 (pink on the metro map), which departs from terminals 2 and 4. A one-way ticket costs the usual single fare of 1€ plus an airport travel supplement of 1€. The line operates daily from 6am to 1:30am.

Trains connect with the Nuevos Ministerios business area of Madrid, north of the center and about 12 minutes from the airport. From here is access to two other metro lines, 10 bus routes, and a number of commuter train *(cercanías)* lines. Facilities at Nuevos Ministerios also include 34 check-in counters for departing flights, such as those on Iberia. It's possible to check your luggage and receive boarding passes up to 24 hours in advance, except for the popular Madrid/Barcelona air shuttle.

BY BUS The no. 200 **bus** service from terminals 1, 2, and 3, and number 204 from terminal 4, each connect the airport with the Avenida de America metro and bus terminal close to the city center, stopping en route at subway stations 4, 6, 7, and 9. The fare is 3.50€ one-way, and buses depart every 10 to 15 minutes 'round the clock (apart from a 2-hr. gap btw. 2–4am) to or from the airport. An alternative route from all terminals to the Avenida de America station is by red no. 101 bus, which stops en route at the Canillejas metro station (line 5), east of the center.

BY TAXI The ride to and from Barajas Airport carries a 6€ surcharge, and there is a 3€ supplement from railway stations. In addition, there is a 2€ supplement on Sunday and holidays, plus a 2€ supplement at night (after 11pm). Other extra charges can include a fee for each suitcase the driver handles. It's customary to tip at least 10% of the fare. Expect to pay 25€ to 30€ and up, plus surcharges.

BY SHUTTLE Instead of a regular taxi, you can take an **AeroCITY** shuttle service (✆ **91-571-50-47**), transporting you in an air-conditioned minivan to your doorstep in Madrid. This service is sometimes less expensive than a regular taxi, depending on the number of people traveling in the vehicle at one time. Service is 24 hours daily.

BY CAR To get into the center of the city from Barajas, head south along the Autovia M-13, which runs past the airport as far as the A-2 highway. Turn right (west) and continue along the A-2 as far as the Avenida de America junction. Continue along this same road, which crosses the northern edge of the Salamanca district, as far as Calle Príncipe de Vergara. Turn left and continue till you reach Calle Alcalá at the point where it runs alongside Parque del Retiro. Turn right here and Calle Alcalá leads you straight to Puerta del Sol, in the heart of Madrid in a matter of minutes.

BY TRAIN

If you're already in Europe, you may want to go to Spain by train, especially if you have a Eurail Pass. Even if you don't, the cost is moderate. Rail passengers who visit from Britain or France should make *couchette* (bunk beds in a sleeper car) and sleeper reservations as far in advance as possible, especially during the peak summer season.

Since Spain's rail tracks are of a wider gauge than those used for French trains (except for the TALGO and Trans-Europe-Express trains), you'll probably have to change trains at the border unless you're on an express train (see below). For long journeys on Spanish rails, seat and sleeper reservations are mandatory.

The most comfortable and the fastest trains in Spain are the AVE, ALTARIA, TER, TALGO, and Electrotren. However, you pay a supplement to ride on these fast trains. Both first- and second-class fares are sold on Spanish trains. Tickets can be purchased in either the United States or Canada at the nearest office of French Rail or from any reputable travel agent. Confirmation of your reservation will take about a week.

If you want your car carried, you must travel Auto-Expreso in Spain. This type of auto transport can be booked only through travel agents or rail offices once you arrive in Europe.

To go from London to Spain by rail, you'll need to change not only the train but also the rail terminus in Paris. In Paris, it's worth the extra bucks to purchase a TALGO express or a "Puerta del Sol" express—that way, you can avoid having to change trains once again at the Spanish border. Trip time from London to Paris is about 6 hours; from Paris to Madrid, about 15 hours or so, which includes 2 hours spent in Paris changing trains and stations. One-way fares fluctuate between £150 and £550 depending on the time of day and year. Check with **www.eurostar.com** or **www.raileurope.com** for exact timetables and fares.

Madrid has two major railway stations. Trains from London and Paris sometimes arrive at the interconnecting northerly station of Chamartín (see below), but usually at the largest **Atocha** station, Av. Ciudad de Barcelona, next to the Glorieta del Emperador Carlos V. Trains to and from here connect mainly with southern and eastern Spanish destinations. New fast rail services, introduced between 2007 and 2008, include the Barcelona to Madrid Talgo, which now takes 3½ hours (though slower trains still take up to 5 hr.); the Valencia ALTARIA, which takes 3½ hours; and a Málaga Talgo, which covers the journey to the capital in 2½ hours. (The Córdoba–Madrid part of the trip only lasts an hour!). The pioneer quickie service—launched back in 1992—was the Seville AVE, which takes 2½ hours. You check in for all these trains in a comfortable airport-style lounge, with airport-style luggage security checks—stricter since the Al Qaeda Madrid railway bombings of March 11, 2004.

The other main station, **Chamartín,** just above Plaza Castilla at Augustín de Foxá expanded in 2007 into an immaculately spacious combined metro, train, and bus

> **Like the Wind**
>
> The Spanish railway system is getting faster and more efficient by the year. The quickest way to get to Toledo is now by train (30 min.). The high-speed AVE service, opened in 2007, between Madrid and Burgos, includes 30km (19 miles) of tunnels through the Guadarrama Mountains and now does the 200km (124-mile) trip to Valladolid in 55 minutes (reaching Segovia en route in a mere 22 min.!). A further AVE connection with Barcelona (also started in 2007) takes 3 hours, stopping en route at Zaragoza and Lleida—a big reduction from the (still-operating) standard Talgo service of 5 hours—and if you want to head for the sunny shores of Andalusia, another Talgo now covers the 500km (310-mile) trip to Málaga in 2½ hours. Fastest of all will be the ALTARIA service to Valencia, which is scheduled to cover the 300km (186 miles) by 2011 in just 90 minutes!

intercambiador, or junction. It also has *cercanías* (suburban train line) links with Atocha and Nuevos Ministerios (which in turn has a further metro connection with Barajas airport; see "Getting There by Plane"). Long-distance trains from here run to northerly cities such as Santander, Burgos, Bilbao, San Sebastian, and Barcelona (a slower service than from Atocha) and to many European capitals.

For information about connections from any of these stations, call **RENFE** (Spanish Railways), at ✆ **90-224-02-02,** daily from 7am to 11pm. For a Eurail Pass to travel from Madrid to other European countries, including neighboring Portugal, visit **www.eurail.com**.

For tickets, go to the principal office of **RENFE,** Alcalá 44 (✆ **91-506-63-29;** Metro: Banco de España). The office is open Monday through Friday from 9:30am to 8pm.

BY BUS

Long-distance buses run regularly from major capitals of Western Europe to Madrid, but the service is not popular, as it's quite slow. (And, at certain bargain times in spring and autumn, it's actually cheaper to fly.) The busiest routes are from London and are run by **Eurolines Limited,** 52 Grosvenor Gardens, London SW1W 0AU (✆ **0990/143-219** or 020/7730-8235; www.eurolines.co.uk). The journey from London's Victoria Station to Madrid is provided by two services. The faster one is the Express Service 180, which departs from London daily at 9pm, and arrives at Madrid's **Estación Sur** the following day at 9:30pm. (This station is also known as Mendez Álvaro—see more on this station and others below if you want to explore either the immediate area or Spain in general from there.) The slower one is Service 181, which leaves London at 9pm on the first day and arrives at Estación Sur at 12:30am on the third day.

BY CAR

If you're touring the rest of Europe in a rented car, for an added cost, you might be allowed to drop off your vehicle in Madrid.

Highway approaches to Spain are across France on expressways. The most popular border crossing is near Biarritz, but there are 17 other border stations between Spain and France. If you plan to visit the north or west of Spain (Galicia), the Hendaye-Irún border is the most convenient frontier crossing. If you're going to Barcelona or Catalonia and along the Levante coast (Valencia), take the expressway in France to Toulouse, then the A-61 to Narbonne, and then the A-9 toward the border crossing at La Junquera. You can also take the RN-20, with a border station at Puigcerdà.

If you're driving from Britain, make sure you have a cross-Channel reservation, as traffic tends to be very heavy, especially in summer.

The major ferry crossings connect Dover and Folkestone with Dunkirk. Newhaven is connected with Dieppe, and the British city of Portsmouth with Roscoff. Taking a car on the ferry from Dover to Calais on **P & O Ferries** (✆ **800/677-8585** in North America, or 08705/20-20-20; www.poferries.com) costs £40 one-way and takes 1¼ hours. This cost includes the car and two passengers.

Another ferry option is the **Norfolkline** (✆ **0844/499-0824;** www.norfolkline.com), which operates a 1¾ hour ferry service from Dover to Dunkirk for £20 to £40 one-way for a car and two passengers. The drive from Calais, Boulogne, or Dunkirk to the Spanish border will take about 15 hours.

You can take the Chunnel—the underwater Channel Tunnel linking Britain (Folkestone) and France (Calais) by road and rail. **Eurostar** tickets, for train service between London and Paris or Brussels, are available through Rail Europe (✆ **800/EUROSTAR;** www.eurostar.com). In London, make reservations for Eurostar at ✆ **0870/530-00-03.** The tunnel also accommodates passenger cars, charter buses, taxis, and motorcycles, transporting them under the English Channel from Folkestone, England, to Calais, France. It operates 24 hours a day, 365 days a year, running every 15 minutes during peak travel times, and at least once an hour at night. Tickets may be purchased at the tollbooth at the tunnel's entrance. With "Le Shuttle," gone are the days of weather-related delays, seasickness, and advance reservations.

Once you land, you'll have about a 15-hour drive to Spain.

If you plan to transport a rental car between England and France, check in advance with the rental company about license and insurance requirements and additional drop-off charges. And be aware that many car-rental companies, for insurance reasons, forbid transport of one of their vehicles over the water between England and France.

Getting Around By Metro (Subway)

The Madrid **Metro** celebrated its 90th anniversary in 2009. It opened its service with a single line that ran from the Puerta del Sol to Cuatro Caminos and the first rickety trains were wooden, snail paced, and very smoky. Since then the whole system has grown at a steady pace. This accelerated into a huge expansion and modernization program at the start of the new millennium and tracks now extend east to Barajas airport, south to Arganda del Rey (29km/18 miles from the center), and to the chic suburbs of the north and west. Out of a total of 12 lines, all easily identified by their different colors on the underground map, no fewer than seven (nos. 1 to 5, 7, and 11) were extended and completed between 2007 and 2008, in addition to a new *Metronorte* line (complementing the 7-year-old *Metrosur* line linking the southern satellite towns of Mostoles, Fuenlabrada, and Leganes), which extends the service to Alcobendas and San Sebastian de los Reyes on the northeasterly outskirts of the city. In 2007, a ***metro ligero*** (literally, "light subway" or jet-age tram similar to the service currently operating in Bilbao and eastern Barcelona) opened on separate lines to the affluent westerly residential towns of Pozuelo de Alarcón and Boadilla del Monte and northerly suburbs of Sanchinarro and Las Tablas. Other outlying new towns are easily reached by the excellent *cercanías* (suburban lines).

The metro system is perfectly straightforward to learn and use, and it's by far the quickest, simplest, and cheapest way to travel about the city. The central converging point is Sol station (Puerta del Sol), which was renovated and impressively expanded in 2010, and trains run every 3 to 5 minutes during the day and every 10 to 15 minutes at night. Service begins at 6am (7am on Sun) and finishes around 1:30am. Avoid rush hours 8 to 10am, 1 to 2pm, and 4 to 6pm. Fares are determined by zones traveled. The fare is 1€ for a one-way trip on zone A stops (central) and 1.50€ for zone A and B stops (includes trips to outer Madrid stations such as Arganda del Rey on line 9 and Mostoles on Metrosur). A combined metro and *metro ligero* (see above) ticket costs 2€ one-way. You can save money on public transportation by purchasing a combined 10-in-one *metrobus* ticket (which also includes bus travel) costing 9.50€ from any metro ticket office counter or vending machine as well as at most *estancos* (tobacco and stamp shops) and in many newspaper kiosks. It covers zone A stops plus trips on red metropolitan buses. For information, call © **91-429-31-77.**

Shiny comfortable modern trains are now standard in the city's underground system, with yesteryear's vintage vehicles gone and long forgotten. The days when people smoked on the platforms have long gone, too.

See the inside back cover of this book for a comprehensive map of the Madrid metro, or go to **www.metromadrid.es** and click on the link at the top-right corner to change to the English page.

BY BUS

A 150-line network of red buses also services the city and suburbs, with routes clearly shown at each stop on a schematic diagram. The buses, which have the first and last stop on their routes clearly marked, are fast and efficient because they travel along special lanes. Varied schedules operate generally between 6am and 11:30pm, and the time between buses varies from 5 to 20 minutes, depending on the service. Night service operates half-hourly from midnight to 3am and hourly from 3 to 6am, with departure points at Cibeles and Sol and is consolidated by the quarter-hourly ***buhometro*** (literally "night-owl metro") weekend and fiesta day bus service, which follows *all* the routes usually covered by the metro when it closes down between 1:30 and 6 or 7am. As with the metro, these bus services charge 1€ per zone A (central) ride and 9.50€ for a 10-trip *metrobus* ticket (including trips on the metro). In addition to being available at the above-mentioned metro counters, vending machines, *estancos* (tobacconists), and newspaper kiosks, tickets are also sold at **Empresa Municipal de Transportes,** Alcántara 24 (© **91-406-88-00**), where you can buy a guide to the bus routes. The office is open daily from 8am to 2pm.

If you want to go **farther afield** from Madrid, there are two major bus terminals (Estaciones de Autobuses) and three smaller terminals that provide long and shorter distance bus services to and from Madrid. Though their journeys are more leisurely than those of the faster trains, the long-distance ones are comfortable and economical and use excellent highway systems.

The biggest station, covering mainly southern and southeastern destinations, such as Granada, Sevilla, Málaga, and Valencia, with the operator Avanza (www.avanzabus.com

for timetables and routes), is **Estacion Sur,** Calle Méndez Álvaro (✆ **91-468-42-00;** 6:30am–midnight; Metro: Mendez Álvaro). Already mentioned in the section "Getting There by Bus," it's also the focal point for a huge variety of international destinations ranging from Morocco to Romania.

Second biggest is the central underground **Avenida de America** bus and metro station (✆ **91-745-63-00**). The **Continental Auto** company (✆ **91-533-04-00**) runs the most buses out of here, providing regular long-distance national services to northern and northeastern cities, including Oviedo, Santander, Bilbao, San Sebastian, Pamplona, and Barcelona.

If you prefer exploring **nearby areas** in the Comunidad de Madrid or Province of Madrid, as well as nearby provincial cities like Segovia, there are three other stations to know about:

The semi-urban **Moncloa** (✆ **91-896-90-28**) bus and metro station—adjoining the Parque del Oeste close to University City—operates services to destinations inside Madrid province such as El Escorial, Aranjuez, and Alcalá de Henares.

The **Estación La Sepulvedana** (✆ **91-530-48-00**) is located underground next to the **Príncipe Pío** railway station (see below). From here, buses run to Segovia and other destinations near Madrid.

And the **Plaza Castilla** terminus in the north of the city near Chamartín railway station (see above) operates services to towns and villages in the northern part of Madrid province—including some up to 100km/62 miles away—from an underground station, as well as farther services to nearby city destinations from the surface station.

BY CERCANÍAS (SUBURBAN LINE) TRAIN

This excellent provincial train service has 10 lines (C-1 to C-10) operating economically and punctually to a variety of key towns radiating outward from the capital, from Aranjuez up to San Lorenzo de El Escorial. **Atocha** station, Glorieta del Emperador Carlos V (Metro: Atocha RENFE), is the best departure point for southerly destinations, and **Chamartín** station, Calle Agustín de Foxá (Metro: Chamartín), for northerly ones. Trains run between the two stations and either station, in practice, can be used for all destinations. Tickets (one-way or round-trip) are obtainable from station ticket offices or from machines on which the destinations are clearly marked.

Estación Príncipe Pío or Norte, Paseo del Rey 30 (Metro: Príncipe Pío), is nestled below the Palacio Real, close to the Manzanares River—and known in Franco's time as the Estación Norte or Estacion de Francia when it served as the main exit and arrival point for northerly European destinations—and now provides a mainly commuter connection with Alcalá de Henares, and nearby "dormitory" towns, as well as with neighboring provincial capitals such as Avila and Guadalajara. Adjoining the station is a vast commercial center of shops and eating spots, plus a multiplex.

For a map of the *cercanías* routes, turn to the inside front cover of this book.

BY TAXI

Madrid city cabs are easy to identify as they are black or white and have a red band and small insignia of a bear and madroño tree—symbols of Madrid—on the side. You can hail them in the street or pick them up at taxi stands all over the city. A green light on the roof indicates that they're free *(libre)*. When you flag down a taxi, the meter should register 1.75€; for every kilometer thereafter, the fare increases by 1.25€. A supplement is charged for trips to the railway station or the bullring, as well as on Sunday and holidays.

Warning: Make sure the meter is turned on when you get into a taxi. Otherwise, some drivers assess the cost of the ride, and their assessment, you can be sure, will involve higher mathematics.

Also, there are unmetered taxis that hire out for the day or the afternoon. They are legitimate, but some drivers operate as gypsy cabs. Since they're not metered, they can charge high rates. They are easy to avoid—always take a black taxi with horizontal red bands or a white one with diagonal red bands.

If you take a taxi outside the city limits, the driver is entitled to charge you twice the rate shown on the meter.

To call a city taxi, dial ✆ **91-447-51-80.**

BY CAR

Driving in congested Madrid is a nightmare and potentially dangerous. It always feels like rush hour, although theoretically, these are from 8 to 10am, 1 to 2pm, and 4 to 6pm Monday through Saturday. Parking is next to impossible except in expensive garages. About the only time you can drive around Madrid with a minimum of hassle is in August, when thousands of Madrileños have taken their cars and headed for Spain's vacation oases on the Mediterranean or Atlantic coasts or up in the mountains. Save your car rentals for excursions from the capital. If you drive into Madrid from another city, ask at your hotel for the nearest garage or parking possibility and leave your vehicle there until you're ready to leave.

On the other hand, a car can be useful if you want to really get off the beaten track and explore Madrid Province—although bus and train transport to all the main places of interest (such as Chinchón, Alcalá de Henares, Aranjuez, and El Escorial) is extremely efficient and economical (see chapter 11, "Side Trips from Madrid").

CAR RENTALS If you decide you want to rent a car while in Madrid to explore its environs or even to move on, you have several choices.

Although several Spanish car-rental companies exist, I've received lots of letters from readers of previous editions telling me they've had hard times resolving billing irregularities and insurance claims, so you might want to stick with the U.S.–based rental firms.

Note that tax on car rentals is a whopping 15%, so don't forget to factor that into your travel budget. Usually, prepaid rates do not include taxes, which will be collected at the rental kiosk. Be sure to ask explicitly what's included when you're quoted a rate.

Avis (✆ **800/331-1212;** www.avis.com) maintains about 100 branches throughout Spain, including about a dozen in Madrid. If you reserve and pay for your rental by telephone at least 2 weeks before your departure from North America, you'll qualify for the company's best rate, with unlimited kilometers included. In addition to its office at Barajas Airport (✆ **91-393-72-22**), Avis has a main office in the city center at Gran Vía 60 (✆ **91-547-20-48**). You can also get competitive rates from **Hertz** (✆ **800/654-3131;** www.hertz.com), which has an office at Barajas Airport (✆ **91-393-72-28**) and another in the heart of Madrid in the Edificio España, Gran Vía 88 (✆ **91-542-58-03**).

Two other agencies of note include **Kemwel Holiday Auto** (✆ **877/820-0668;** www.kemwel.com.) and **Auto Europe** (✆ **800/223-5555;** www.autoeurope.com).

The companies above require that drivers be at least 21 years of age and, in some cases, not older than 72. To be able to rent a car, you must have a passport and a valid driver's license; you must also have a valid credit card or a prepaid voucher. An international driver's license is not essential, but you might want to present it if you have one; it's available from any North American office of the American Automobile Association (AAA). Most cars hired in Spain are stick shift, not automatic, and are air-conditioned.

PETROL/GAS Most cars run on unleaded gas (current cost 1.30€ per liter, or 4.90€ per gallon) and there's no shortage of gas stations.

DRIVING RULES Spaniards drive on the right side of the road. Drivers should pass on the left; local drivers sound their horns when passing another car and flash their lights at you if you're driving slowly (slowly for high-speed Spain) in the left lane. Autos coming from the right have the right-of-way.

Spain's express highways are known as *autopistas,* which charge a toll, and *autovías,* which don't. To exit in Spain, follow the SALIDA (exit) sign, except in Catalonia, where the exit sign says SORTIDA. On most express highways, the speed limit is 120kmph (75 mph). On other roads, speed limits range from 90kmph (56 mph) to 100kmph (62 mph). You will see many drivers far exceeding these limits.

The greatest number of accidents in Spain is recorded along the notorious Costa del Sol highway, Carretera de Cádiz.

If you must drive through Madrid—or any other Spanish city—try to avoid morning and evening rush hours. Never park your car facing oncoming traffic, as that is against the law. If you are fined by the highway patrol *(Guardia Civil de Tráfico),* you must pay on the spot. Penalties for drinking and driving are very stiff (breathalyzers are now being far more strictly used than in the past). The limit amounts to two standard glasses of beer or wine, so take care when washing down those tapas. A new penalty points system used against local drivers for speeding, overtaking on double lines, and other infractions has reduced accidents to a small extent, thus in theory making it fractionally safer on the roads, though the volatile Latin temperament is still loudly and frequently expressed by incontinent horn blowing.

MAPS For one of the best overviews of the Iberian Peninsula (Spain and Portugal), get Michelin map no. 990 (folded version) or map no. 460 (spiral-bound version). For more detailed looks at Spain, Michelin has a series of six maps (nos. 441–446) showing specific regions, complete with many minor roads.

For extensive touring, purchase *Mapas de Carreteras—España y Portugal,* published by Almax Editores and available at most leading bookstores in Spain. This cartographic compendium of Spain provides an overview of the country and includes road and street maps of some of its major cities.

The **American Automobile Association** (www.aaa.com) publishes a regional map of Spain that's available free to members at most AAA offices in the United States. Incidentally, the AAA is associated with the **Real Automóvil Club de España** (**RACE; ✆ 90-240-45-45;** www.race.es). This organization can supply helpful information about road conditions in Spain, including tourist and travel advice. It will also provide limited road service, in an emergency, if your car breaks down.

BREAKDOWNS These can be a serious problem. If you're driving a Spanish-made vehicle that needs parts, you'll probably be able to find them. But if you are driving a foreign-made vehicle, you may be stranded. Have the car checked before setting out on a long trek through Spain. On a major motorway, you'll find strategically placed emergency phone boxes. On secondary roads, call for help by asking the operator to locate the nearest Guardia Civil, which will put you in touch with a garage that can tow you to a repair shop.

As noted above, the Spanish affiliate of AAA can provide limited assistance in the event of a breakdown.

Highways to Madrid

All highways within Spain radiate outward from Madrid, connecting on both inward and outward journeys with the M-30 and M-40 highways that encircle the city. The following are the major highways into Madrid, with information on driving distances to the city.

ROUTE	FROM	DISTANCE TO MADRID
N-I	Irún	507km (315 miles)
N-II	Barcelona	626km (389 miles)
N-III	Valencia	349km (217 miles)
N-IV	Cádiz	625km (388 miles)
N-V	Badajoz	409km (254 miles)
N-VI	Galicia	602km (374 miles)

BY BICYCLE

While it's hardly recommendable to try and ride a bike in the city center due to the twin dangers of inhaling polluted air and getting knocked off your bike by hordes of impatient car drivers, there are, surprisingly, parts of the capital where you can enjoy a spin, such as the wooded parklands of the Casa de Campo and Dehesa de la Villa, which are full of easily navigable trails. Also, some city streets are closed to traffic on Sunday from 11am to 2pm (Calle Fuencarral, for example, btw. the Bilbao and Quevedo roundabouts), giving you a brief, hassle-free opportunity to explore more urban areas on two wheels. The ever-expanding network of urban and outer city bicycle trails has now expanded to 100km (62 miles). You can also hire bikes to explore the spacious green Juan Carlos Park on the eastern edge of the city (p. 192).

The following two city companies rent bicycles at reasonable prices:

You can hire a bike from **Karacol Sport,** Calle Tortosa 8 (✆ **91-539-96-33;** www.karacol.com; daily 10:30am–3pm and 5–8pm [Thurs till 9:30pm]; Metro: Atocha) for 20€ per day. A cash deposit of 50€ and photocopy of your passport are required. Their offices are conveniently located near Atocha railway station so it's easy to put the bike on the train and journey in relaxed style as far as amenable places such as Aranjuez, where the terrain is flat and you can explore parks and riverside trails.

At **Bicimania,** Calle Palencia 20 (✆ **91-533-11-89;** www.bicimania.com; Mon–Sat 10:30am–2pm and 5–8:30pm; Metro: Alvarado), in the westerly Tetuan district, you can rent a bike for all-day and weeklong excursions. It costs 16€-20€ for a single weekday, 40€ for an entire weekend, or 100€ for the week; a cash deposit of 150€ is required (500€ for bikes with back suspension). You'll also need to bring a copy of your passport.

For general information on cycling around Madrid province, go online to the Spanish only website www.amigosdelciclismo.com/rutas/madrid.

MONEY & COSTS

If there is one thing old Spaniards wax nostalgic over, it's not the police state they experienced under the dictatorship of Franco, but the prices paid back then. How they miss the days when you could go into a restaurant and order a meal with wine for 50 pesetas.

Regrettably, Spain is no longer a budget destination. In Madrid, you can often find hotels charging the same prices as in London or Paris.

Taken as a whole, though, Madrid remains slightly below the cost-of-living index of other major European capitals. Unless the current monetary situation is drastically altered, there is a reasonably favorable exchange rate in Spain when you pay in U.S. dollars.

Prices in Madrid are generally high, but you get good value for your money. Hotels are usually clean and comfortable, and restaurants generally offer good cuisine and ample portions made with quality ingredients. Trains are fast and on time, and most service personnel treat you with respect.

In Madrid, many prices for children—generally defined as ages 6 to 17—are lower than for adults. Fees for children under 6 are generally waived.

The Euro

In January 2002, the largest money-changing operation in history led to the deliberate obsolescence of many of Europe's individual national currencies, including the Spanish peseta. In its place was substituted the euro (abbreviation EUR), a currency that, at this writing, was based on the fiscal participation of a dozen nations of Europe. Exchange rates of participating countries are locked into a common currency fluctuating against the dollar. For more details on the euro, check out **http://ec.europa.eu/euro.index_en.html**.

FOR NORTH AMERICAN READERS At the euro's inception, the U.S. dollar and the euro traded on par (that is, $1 approx. equaled 1€). But since then, the euro has gained strength against the dollar. The current conversion rate is 1€ equals $1.27 For up-to-the minute exchange rates between the euro and the dollar, check the currency converter website **www.xe.com/ucc**.

FOR BRITISH READERS At the time of writing, £1 equals approximately US$1.52, and trades at 1.19€.

As above, for up-to-date rates at any time, check the Universal Currency Converter website **www.xe.com/ucc**.

Exchange rates are more favorable at the point of arrival. Nevertheless, it's often helpful to exchange at least some money before going abroad to take care of incidentals on your way to your hotel, such as your metro, bus, or taxi fare. Currency and traveler's checks (for which you'll receive a better rate than cash) can be changed at all principal airports, though standing in line at the ***cambio*** (exchange bureau) in Madrid's Barajas airport could make you miss the next bus leaving for downtown.

Before leaving, therefore, check with any of your local American Express or Thomas Cook offices or major banks. Or, order euros in advance from the following: **American Express** (✆ **800/221-7282;** www.americanexpress.com), **Thomas Cook** (✆ **800/223-7373;** www.thomascook.com), or **Capital for Foreign Exchange** (✆ **888/842-0880**).

THE EURO, THE U.S. DOLLAR & THE BRITISH POUND

Euro €	U.S. $	U.K. £	Euro €	U.S. $	U.K. £
1.00	1.27	.84	75.00	95.25	63.00
2.00	2.54	1.68	100.00	127.00	84.00
3.00	3.80	2.52	125.00	158.00	105.00
4.00	5.08	3.36	150.00	190.00	126.00
5.00	6.35	4.20	175.00	222.25	147.00
6.00	7.60	5.04	200.00	254.00	168.00
7.00	8.89	5.88	225.00	285.00	189.00
8.00	10.16	6.72	250.00	316.00	210.00
9.00	11.43	7.56	275.00	349.00	231.00
10.00	12.70	8.40	300.00	381.00	252.00
15.00	19.05	12.60	350.00	444.50	294.00
20.00	25.40	16.80	400.00	508.00	336.00
25.00	31.75	21.00	500.00	635.00	420.00
50.00	63.50	42.00	1,000.00	1,270.00	840.00

On arrival in Madrid, it's best to exchange currency or traveler's checks at a bank, not a *cambio,* hotel, or shop. Note the rates and ask about commission fees; it can sometimes pay to shop around and ask the right questions.

Many Madrid hotels don't accept dollar- or pound-denominated checks; those that do will almost certainly charge for the conversion. In some cases, they'll accept countersigned traveler's checks or a credit card, but if you're prepaying a deposit on hotel reservations, it's cheaper and easier to pay with a check drawn on a Spanish bank.

This can be arranged by a large commercial bank or by a specialist such as **Ruesch International,** 700 11th St. NW, 4th Floor, Washington, DC 20001-4507 (© **800/424-2923;** www.ruesch.com), which performs a wide variety of conversion-related tasks, usually for only $5 to $15 per transaction.

If you need a check payable in euros, call Ruesch's toll-free number, describe what you need, and note the transaction number given to you. Mail your dollar-denominated personal check (payable to Ruesch International) to the address above. Upon receiving this, the company will mail a check denominated in euros for the financial equivalent, minus the $2 charge. The company can also help you with many different kinds of wire transfers and conversions of VAT (value-added tax, known as IVA in Spain), refund checks, and also will mail brochures and information packets on request. Brits can contact **Ruesch International Ltd.,** Marble Arch Tower, 14 Floor, 55 Bryanston St., London W14 7AA, England (© **0207/563-3300**).

The currency exchange at Chamartín railway station (Metro: Chamartín) is open 24 hours and gives the best rates in the capital.

Many banks in Spain still charge a 1% to 3% commission, with a minimum charge of 3€. However, branches of **Banco Central Hispano** charge no commission. Branches of **El Corte Inglés,** the department store chain, offer currency exchange facilities at various rates. You get the worst rates at street kiosks such as Chequepoint,

Exact Change, and Cambios-Uno. Although they're handy and charge no commission, their rates are very low. Naturally, **American Express** offices offer the best rates on their own checks. ATMs are plentiful in Madrid.

ATMs

The easiest and best way to get cash away from home is from an ATM, sometimes referred to as a "cash machine," or a "cashpoint." In Spain, only four-digit PINs are valid, so be sure to change any five- or six-digit PIN you may have to a four-digit number before you go.

The **Cirrus** (✆ **800/424-7787;** www.mastercard.com) and **PLUS** (✆ **800/843-7587;** www.visa.com) networks span the globe; look at the back of your bank card to see which network you're on, then call or check online for ATM locations at your destination. Be sure you know your personal identification number (PIN) and daily withdrawal limit before you depart. ***Note:*** Many banks impose a fee every time you use a card at another bank's ATM, and that fee can be higher for international transactions (up to $5 or more) than for domestic ones (where they're rarely more than $2). In addition, the bank from which you withdraw cash may charge its own fee. For international withdrawal fees, ask your bank.

Credit Cards

Credit cards are another safe way to carry money. They also provide a convenient record of all your expenses, and they generally offer relatively good exchange rates. You can withdraw cash advances from your credit cards at banks or ATMs, provided you know your PIN. Keep in mind that you'll pay interest from the moment of your withdrawal, even if you pay your monthly bills on time. Also, note that many banks now assess a 1% to 3% transaction fee on all charges you incur abroad (whether you're using the local currency or your native currency).

American Express, Visa, MasterCard, and Diners Club credit cards are all widely accepted in Spain. Discover Card is not widely accepted in Spain.

Traveler's Checks

Traveler's checks are accepted in Spain at banks, travel agencies, hotels, and some shops, and you can buy them at most banks before you leave home. They are offered in denominations of $20, $50, $100, $500, and sometimes $1,000. Generally, you'll pay a service charge ranging from 1% to 4%.

Emergency Cash—The Fastest Way

If you need emergency cash over the weekend when all banks and American Express offices are closed, you can have money wired to you from **Western Union** (✆ **800/325-6000;** www.westernunion.com). You must present valid ID to pick up the cash at the Western Union office. However, in most countries, you can pick up a money transfer even if you don't have valid identification, as long as you can answer a test question provided by the sender. Be sure to let the sender know in advance that you don't have ID. If you need to use a test question instead of ID, the sender must take cash to his or her local Western Union office, rather than transferring the money over the phone or online.

The most popular traveler's checks are offered by **American Express** (© **800/807-6233,** or 800/221-7282 for cardholders—this number accepts collect calls, offers service in several foreign languages, and exempts Amex gold- and platinum-cardholders from the 1% fee); **Visa** (© **800/732-1322**)—AAA members can obtain Visa checks at most AAA offices or by calling © **866/339-3378;** and **MasterCard** (© **800/223-9920**).

American Express, Thomas Cook, Visa, and **MasterCard** offer **foreign currency traveler's checks,** which are useful if you're traveling to one country, or to the Euro zone; they're accepted at locations where dollar checks may not be.

If you carry traveler's checks, keep a record of their serial numbers separate from your checks in the event that they are stolen or lost. You'll get a refund faster if you know the numbers.

HEALTH

Spain should not pose any major health hazards. The rich cuisine—garlic, olive oil, and wine—may give some travelers mild diarrhea, so take along some antidiarrhea medicine, moderate your eating habits, and even though the water is generally safe, drink mineral water only. Fish and shellfish from the polluted Mediterranean should only be eaten cooked, though in Madrid most seafood comes from the cleaner Atlantic-washed Northern provinces, and you might risk the odd raw *percebe* (goose barnacle) if you can afford it.

The water is safe to drink through Spain; however, do not drink the water in mountain streams, regardless of how clear and pure it looks.

General Availability of Health Care

No shots of any sort are required before traveling to Spain. Once there, medicines for common ailments, from colds to diarrhea, can be obtained over the counter at local chemists or *farmacias.* Generic equivalents of common prescription drugs are also usually available in Spain. (However, it does no harm to bring over-the-counter medicines with you to be on the safe side.)

Contact the **International Association for Medical Assistance to Travelers** (IAMAT; © **716/754-4883** in the U.S., 416/652-0137 in Canada; www.iamat.org) for specific tips on travel and health concerns in Spain and for lists of local, English-speaking doctors. The United States **Centers for Disease Control and Prevention** (© **800/311-3435;** www.cdc.gov) provides up-to-date information on health hazards by region or country and offers tips on food safety. The website **www.tripprep.com**, sponsored by a consortium of travel medicine practitioners, may also offer helpful advice on traveling abroad. You can find listings of reliable clinics overseas at the **International Society of Travel Medicine** (www.istm.org).

Change of Diet

No need to go on a tempting cholesterol binge if you really don't want to. Vegetarians can follow their usual diet pattern in Madrid, as there is an increasing number of vegetarian eating spots available (see also "Going Green in Madrid," p. 127) as well as a multitude of *herbolarios,* or health-food shops.

Sun Exposure

Madrid has a dry, sunny climate (over 300 cloudless days a year), and it's best to take protective measures against sunburn and heatstroke. This is particularly valid in May and June, when the days are long and the sun's rays are deceptively intense. The temperatures then are not as oppressive as those of July and August when you feel more inclination to stay in the shade or seek solace in an air-conditioned locale. Limit your exposure to the sun, especially during the first few days of your trip if you're traveling to the south, and, thereafter, from 11am to 2pm. Use a sunscreen with a high protection factor, and apply it liberally. Remember that children need more protection than adults.

Visitors with eyesight problems should also take care to avoid the sun's strong glare, using prescription sunglasses.

What To Do If You Get Sick Away From Home

Spanish medical facilities are among the best in the world. If a medical emergency arises, your hotel staff can usually put you in touch with a reliable doctor. If not, contact your embassy or consulate (p. 286); each one maintains a list of English-speaking doctors. Medical and hospital services aren't free, so be sure that you have appropriate insurance coverage before you travel (p. 286).

If you suffer from a chronic illness, consult your doctor before your departure. Pack **prescription medications** in your carry-on luggage, and carry them in their original containers, with pharmacy labels; otherwise they won't make it through airport security. Carry the generic name of prescription medicines, in case a local pharmacist is unfamiliar with the brand name.

I list **additional emergency numbers** and **hospitals** in chapter 12.

SAFETY

Terrorism

Since the Al Qaeda bomb attacks on three suburban trains in and around Atocha station on March 11, 2004, which resulted in the deaths of 200 people, both political and public attention in Spain has been strongly focused on the global nature of terrorism now threatening Western society.

A direct or indirect consequence of the massacre was that after a massive protest demonstration of two million people in the streets of the city, voters unexpectedly returned the Socialist party to power in the March 14 general elections. The policy of the new president, Rodríguez Zapatero, had always been to oppose the war in Iraq, and one of his first acts was to authorize the full withdrawal of Spanish troops from that country just over 3 months later.

Life in Madrid continued more or less unchanged after this event, though the memory of it remains indelible. To date, there is nothing to suggest that Islamic terrorism constitutes a more serious threat in Madrid than in any other major world city. U.S. tourists traveling to Spain should exercise caution and refer to the guidance offered in the Worldwide Caution Public Announcements issued in the wake of the September 11, 2001, terrorist attacks, also bearing in mind the abovementioned March 11, 2004, tragedy.

After 4 decades of deadly bomb attacks on police and public (even including tourists), the ETA, the Basque separatist movement, announced a "permanent" ceasefire in 2006, which was quickly broken (see p. 18 for more on the ETA's history). The group killed a French policeman during an attempted car robbery near Paris in late 2009 and since then is apparently racked by internal dissensions, and members are now hunted as criminals in two countries. Of late they have become notably silent.

Whether this heralds the beginning of the end for them as a purported "political force" still remains to be seen.

"Conventional" Crime

While most of Spain has a moderate rate of "conventional" crime, and most tourists have trouble-free visits to Spain, the principal tourist areas have been experiencing an increase in violent crime. Madrid has reported growing incidents of muggings and violent attacks, and older tourists and Asian-Americans seem to be particularly at risk. Criminals frequent tourist areas and major attractions such as museums, monuments, restaurants, hotels, beach resorts, trains, train stations, airports, subways, and ATMs.

Reported incidents have occurred in key tourist areas, including the zones around the Prado Museum and Atocha train station, and parts of old Madrid such as Puerta del Sol, El Rastro flea market, and Plaza Mayor. Travelers should exercise caution, carry limited cash and credit cards, and leave extra cash, credit cards, passports, and personal documents in a safe location. Crimes have occurred at all times of day and night, though visitors and residents alike are more vulnerable in the early hours of the morning.

Thieves often work in teams or pairs. In most cases, one person distracts a victim while the accomplice performs the robbery. For example, a stranger might wave a map in your face and ask for directions or "inadvertently" spill something on you. While your attention is diverted, an accomplice makes off with the valuables. Attacks can also be initiated from behind, with the victim being grabbed around the neck and choked by one assailant while others rifle through the belongings. A group of assailants may surround the victim, maybe in a crowded popular tourist area or on public transportation, and only after the group has departed does the person discover he or she has been robbed. Some attacks have been so violent that victims have needed to seek medical attention afterward.

Theft from parked cars is also common. Small items such as luggage, cameras, or briefcases are often stolen from them. Travelers are advised not to leave valuables in cars when they park them and to keep doors locked, windows rolled up, and valuables out of sight when driving. "Good Samaritan" scams are unfortunately common. A passing car will attempt to divert the driver's attention by indicating there is a mechanical problem. If the driver stops to check the vehicle, accomplices steal from the car while the driver is looking elsewhere. Drivers should be cautious about accepting help from anyone other than a uniformed Spanish police officer or Civil Guard.

Dealing with discrimination

As Madrid's population slowly becomes more international, overt racial prejudice—never a dominant issue here anyway—appears to be diminishing, though as John Vorwald points out below ("A Note on Discrimination") there will always be a hard core of people—such as the fascist fringe supporters of certain Spanish football clubs—whose attitude is affected simply by the color of a person's skin.

In the aftermath of the March 11 rail bombings of 2004, there was a hardening of attitudes toward Arabic nationalities by certain members of the community, though there is less evidence of that now. Feelings toward the increasing numbers of Latin American immigrants were similarly soured by the appearance (in relatively small numbers) of young L.A.–style South American criminal bands such as the "Latin

A NOTE ON DISCRIMINATION

A fierce sense of national pride might lead many Spaniards to bristle at the suggestion that racism is a problem in their country, but events during the past decade and a new report by Amnesty International have brought to the fore concerns over racism and racial profiling in Spain. In January 2002, Rodney Mack, an African American and the principal trumpet player with the Barcelona Symphony Orchestra, was attacked and beaten in Madrid by four police officers who later said they mistook the musician for a car thief. The thief had been described as a black man of roughly Mr. Mack's height, and a police official later admitted that Mack was singled out because of "the color of his skin and his height." In April 2002, Amnesty International cited the Mack case in an exhaustive report accusing Spain of "frequent and widespread" mistreatment of foreigners and ethnic minorities. The report investigated more than 320 cases of abuse from 1995 to 2002, including deaths and rapes while in police custody, as well as beatings, verbal abuse, and the use of racial profiling by police. The report claims that an increase in racist attacks in Spain has coincided with a dramatic growth in the country's immigrant population over the last 20 years. Spanish officials, however, rejected the report, and Congressman Ignacio Gil-Lázaro of Spain's ruling Popular Party said, "The police and Civil Guard confront immigration in a deeply humanitarian way."

While Amnesty's report may rightfully dispel the notion that Spain is exempt from the problems of racism, it does not suggest that the country is Europe's only offender. In recent years, Amnesty has pointed up race-based abuses in numerous European nations, including Austria, Greece, and Italy, as well as the United States. Travelers of color may have a perfectly enjoyable trip in Spain, but visitors to the area should travel with the knowledge that racism and xenophobia may well be as serious a problem in Spain as anywhere in Europe or the United States. If you encounter discrimination or mistreatment while traveling in Spain, please report it to your embassy immediately.

—John Vorwald

Kings" and "Dominicans Don't Play" in the outer areas of the city. After a flurry of arrests and subsequent releases in 2009, things have calmed down and attempts by social groups to integrate these delinquent minorities more effectively into the community have proved reasonably successful.

On the sexual front, the city is as liberal as any with gay lifestyles. See "Gay & Lesbian Travelers," p. 54.

Sole female travelers and residents can also live a reasonably hassle-free existence. See "Women Travelers" and "Multicultural Travelers," p. 55.

SPECIALIZED TRAVEL RESOURCES

Travelers with Disabilities

Most disabilities shouldn't stop anyone from traveling. There are more options and resources out there than ever before. Because of Madrid center's narrow roads and endless flights of stairs, though, visitors with disabilities may have difficulty getting around the city. But conditions are slowly improving: Newer hotels are more sensitive to the needs of persons with disabilities, and the more expensive restaurants are generally wheelchair-accessible. Newer stations on the metro have increasing facilities, including more escalators or sliding stairs and lifts covering all levels. However, since most places of interest have very limited, if any, facilities for people with disabilities, consider taking an organized tour specifically designed to accommodate such travelers.

If you're flying around Spain, the airline and ground staff will help you on and off planes and reserve seats for you with sufficient legroom, but it is essential to arrange for this assistance *in advance* by contacting your airline.

Avis has an "Avis Access" program, which offers such services as a dedicated 24-hour toll-free number (✆ **888/879-4273**) for customers with special travel needs; special car features such as swivel seats, spinner knobs, and hand controls; and accessible bus service.

The community website **iCan** (www.ican-network.com) has destination guides and several regular columns on accessible travel. Also check out the quarterly magazine ***Emerging Horizons*** (www.emerginghorizons.com) and ***Open World*** magazine, published by SATH (see below).

For the blind or visually impaired, the best source is the **American Foundation for the Blind (AFB),** 15 W. 16th St., New York, NY 10011 (✆ **800/232-5463** to order information kits and supplies, or 212/502-7600; www.afb.org). It offers information on travel and various requirements for the transport and border formalities for Seeing Eye dogs. It also issues identification cards to those who are legally blind.

Other organizations that offer assistance to travelers with disabilities include **MossRehab** (www.mossresourcenet.org) and **SATH** (**Society for Accessible Travel & Hospitality; ✆ 212/447-7284;** www.sath.org.). **AirAmbulanceCard.com** is now partnered with SATH and allows you to preselect top-notch hospitals in case of an emergency.

FOR BRITISH TRAVELERS WITH DISABILITIES The annual vacation guide *Holidays and Travel Abroad* costs £5 from **Royal Association for Disability and Rehabilitation (RADAR),** Unit 12, City Forum, 250 City Rd., London EC1V 8AF (✆ **020/7250-3222;** www.radar.org.uk). RADAR also provides a number of information packets on such subjects as sports and outdoor vacations, insurance, financial arrangements for persons with disabilities, and accommodations in nursing care units for groups or for the elderly. Each of these fact sheets is available for £2. Both the fact sheets and the holiday guides can be mailed outside the United Kingdom for a nominal postage fee.

Another good service is **Holiday Care,** 2nd Floor Imperial Buildings, Victoria Road, Horley, Surrey RH6 7PZ (✆ **01293/774-535;** fax 01293/784-647; www.holidaycare.org.uk), a national charity that advises on accessible accommodations for elderly people or those with disabilities. Annual membership costs £25 (U.K. residents) and £40 (abroad). Once you're a member, you can receive a newsletter and access to a free reservations network for hotels throughout Britain and, to a lesser degree, Europe and the rest of the world.

Gay & Lesbian Travelers

In 1978, Spain legalized homosexuality among consenting adults. In April 1995, the parliament of Spain banned discrimination based on sexual orientation. Madrid is one of the country's major gay centers and the action is mainly located in the Castizo quarter of **Chueca** between the Gran Vía and Calle Genova (p. 234). Clubs here range from the relatively sedate to the downright outrageous, and there are also a couple of gay-theme bookshops. The tiny Plaza de Chueca bustles with outdoor cafe life in summer and is a good spot for impromptu encounters.

Women Travelers

Spain is not Mexico or Colombia, and in capital Madrid in particular, women are as emancipated as in any other main European city. If a degree of machismo still exists, it is minimal today; and women are increasingly reaching high positions in all walks of life (though not as many as they would like). As for women exploring the city on their own, the degree of hassle experienced is scarcely different from Paris or London.

Multicultural Travelers

As Madrid becomes increasingly multicultural, especially in areas such as Lavapiés, visitors and residents of all nationalities are naturally accepted by what is in effect a fairly open-minded society. A person of a different race or skin color rarely draws more than a second glance, unlike a few decades back when a dark face was a rarity in a 99% Castizo city.

That said, instances of racial conflict are not unknown, though these tend to be with African, Arabic, and Latin American locals rather than multinational visitors. (See the "Safety" section and "A Note on Discrimination," above.)

Student Travel

Check out the **International Student Travel Confederation** (**ISTC;** www.istc.org) website for comprehensive travel services information and details on how to get an **International Student Identity Card (ISIC),** which qualifies students for substantial savings on rail passes, plane tickets, entrance fees, and more. It also provides students with basic health and life insurance and a 24-hour helpline. The card is valid for a maximum of 18 months. You can apply for the card online or in person at **STA Travel** (**© 800/781-4040** in North America; 134-782 in Australia; 0871/2300-040 in the U.K.; www.statravel.com), the biggest student travel agency in the world; check out the website to locate STA Travel offices worldwide. If you're no longer a student but are still under 26, you can get an **International Youth Travel Card (IYTC)** from the same organization, which entitles you to some discounts. **Travel CUTS** (**© 800/592-2887;** www.travelcuts.com) offers similar services for Canadians and U.S. residents alike. Irish students may prefer to turn to **USIT** (**© 01/602-1904;** www.usit.ie), an Ireland-based specialist in student, youth, and independent travel.

Student travelers in Madrid should check out the **Madhostel** and **Cats Hostel,** p. 92 and 91, respectively, for two of the best-value young-at-heart accommodations in the city.

SUSTAINABLE TOURISM

Sustainable tourism is conscientious travel. It means being careful with the environments you explore and respecting the communities you visit. Two overlapping components of sustainable travel are **ecotourism** and **ethical tourism.** The

International Ecotourism Society (TIES) defines ecotourism as responsible travel to natural areas that conserves the environment and improves the well-being of local people. TIES suggests that ecotourists follow these principles:

- Minimize environmental impact.
- Build environmental and cultural awareness and respect.
- Provide positive experiences for visitors and hosts alike.
- Provide direct financial benefits for conservation and for local people.
- Raise sensitivity to host countries' political, environmental, and social climates.
- Support international human rights and labor agreements.

You can find some eco-friendly travel tips and statistics, as well as touring companies and associations—listed by destination under "Travel Choice"—at the **TIES** website, **www.ecotourism.org**. Also check out **Ecotravel.com**, which lets you search for sustainable touring companies in several categories (water-based, land-based, spiritually oriented, and so on).

While much of the focus of ecotourism is about reducing impact on the natural environment, ethical tourism concentrates on ways to preserve and enhance local economies and communities, regardless of location. You can embrace ethical tourism by staying at a locally owned hotel or shopping at a store that employs local workers and sells locally produced goods.

Responsible Travel (www.responsibletravel.com) is a great source of sustainable travel ideas; the site is run by a spokesperson for ethical tourism in the travel industry. **Sustainable Travel International** (www.sustainabletravelinternational.org) promotes ethical tourism practices, and manages an extensive directory of sustainable properties and tour operators around the world.

In the U.K., **Tourism Concern** (www.tourismconcern.org.uk) works to reduce social and environmental problems connected to tourism. The **Association of Independent Tour Operators** (**AITO;** www.aito.co.uk) is a group of specialist operators leading the field in making holidays sustainable.

Animal-rights Issues

Spain is not a country that has been particularly noted for its kindness to animals in the past. Fiestas, which include torturing of bulls by attacking them with lances in the Castilian town of Tordesillas, still prevail (though the notorious throwing-a-donkey-off-a-tower shebang that took place annually in an Extremaduran village has happily disappeared).

The main bone of contention is, of course, the **bullfight,** which is still immensely popular in Madrid (home of the world's biggest bullring, Las Ventas), though not in other parts of Spain such as Catalunya and the Canary Islands. Far from fading, this violent and colorful activity (a highly stylized "ballet of death" rather than a sport)—which attracts and appalls visitors in equal numbers—is positively booming in the Spanish capital. In Spring 2010, attempts by animal rights groups to have it banned were thwarted by spirited President of the Community, Esperanza Aguirre, who had it officially declared an event "Of Touristic Interest," thus ensuring an indefinite stay of execution for the spectacle (if not for the bulls).

Perhaps she has a point. (Let's harden our hearts here, show some Hemingway-esque grit, and eschew our animal-loving instincts.) After all, this is a national event unique in Europe (in Portugal and Southern France they have bullfights but don't kill

IT'S EASY BEING green

Here are a few simple ways you can help conserve fuel and energy when you travel:

- Each time you take a flight or drive a car, greenhouse gases release into the atmosphere. You can help neutralize this danger to the planet through "carbon offsetting"—paying someone to invest your money in programs that reduce your greenhouse gas emissions by the same amount you've added. Before buying carbon offset credits, just make sure that you're using a reputable company, one with a proven program that invests in renewable energy. Reliable carbon offset companies include **Carbonfund** (www.carbonfund.org), **TerraPass** (www.terrapass.org), and **Carbon Neutral** (www.carbonneutral.org).
- Whenever possible, choose nonstop flights; they generally require less fuel than indirect flights that stop and take off again. Try to fly during the day—some scientists estimate that nighttime flights are twice as harmful to the environment. And pack light—each 15 pounds of luggage on a 5,000-mile flight adds up to 50 pounds of carbon dioxide emitted.
- Where you stay during your travels can have a major environmental impact. To determine the "green" credentials of a property, ask about trash disposal and recycling, water conservation, and energy use; also question if sustainable materials were used in the construction of the property. The website **www.greenhotels.com** recommends green-rated member hotels around the world that fulfill the company's stringent environmental requirements. Also consult **www.environmentallyfriendlyhotels.com** for more green accommodations ratings.
- At hotels, request that your sheets and towels not be changed daily. (Many hotels already have programs like this in place.) Turn off the lights and air conditioner (or heater) when you leave your room.
- Use public transport where possible—trains, buses, and even taxis are more energy-efficient forms of transport than driving. Even better is to walk or cycle; you'll produce zero emissions and stay fit and healthy on your travels.
- If renting a car is necessary, ask the rental agent for a hybrid, or rent the most fuel-efficient car available. You'll use less gas and save money at the tank.
- Eat at locally owned and operated restaurants that use produce grown in the area. This contributes to the local economy and cuts down on greenhouse gas emissions by supporting restaurants where the food is not flown or trucked in across long distances.

the bull) and, hey, a big, big moneymaker. For purely economic reasons alone, it wasn't likely to be dropped anyway by the country's financial—as well as hard-line traditionalist—hub (especially in view of the current—2010—crisis, with unemployment rampant and the country teetering on the brink of inflation).

However, a gentler attitude toward animals in general is emerging among Spaniards. Pet shops are on the increase, and more Madrileños are proud owners of preened, pampered, and protected *perros* (dogs) than ever before (apparently distancing themselves from the traditional rural trend of keeping the poor creatures tied up most of the day and then using them only for hunting). And people who ill treat any animal—be it hamster, hound, or horse—are punished by the law, if only with comparatively small fines.

Except *el toro* (the bull). He looks like he's destined to suffer for some time yet, though Spain's socialist government—which is more attentive to humane issues than any ruling party before—uniquely turned its attention to other animals' welfare a few years back, when it declared its support for the Great Ape Project, proposing to grant life, liberty, and protection to chimpanzees, gorillas, and their kin, and ensuring their protection from ill treatment in circuses, scientific experiments, and even advertising campaigns. That's one small step for animalkind. Maybe there's still hope for the bull.

For information on animal-friendly issues throughout the world, visit **Tread Lightly** (www.treadlightly.org).

Ecotourism

A surprising amount of beautiful and unspoiled backwaters are within an hour or so of Madrid. If you don't want to hire a car, you can easily make your way to them by local train (*cercanías*) or bus. Get maps and reference books from **La Tienda Verde,** in Calle Maudes (p. 224). Check out **Cercedilla** and **Patones de Arriba,** in the "Side Trips from Madrid" chapter. Or take a 45-minute bus ride from the **Conde Casal** stop near the Claridge Hotel (a short stroll from the southeast corner of the Retiro Park) down to **Perales de Tajuña** and seek out the **Via Verde** route along the banks of the tiny River Tajuña. Here you can walk or cycle for over 35 km/22 miles along converted former rail routes past peaceful cornfields, vineyards, and orchards in a valley bordered by limestone hills, a world apart from the big city bustle.

PACKAGES FOR THE INDEPENDENT TRAVELER

Package tours are not the same thing as escorted tours. With a package tour, you travel independently but pay a group rate. Packages usually include airfare, a choice of hotels, and car rentals; and packagers often offer several options at different prices. In many cases, a package that includes airfare, hotel, and transportation to and from the airport will cost you less than just the hotel alone had you booked it yourself. That's because packages are sold in bulk to tour operators, who resell them to the public at a cost that drastically undercuts standard rates.

Recommended Package Tour Operators

One good source of package deals is the airlines. Most airlines offer packages that may include car rentals and accommodations in addition to your airfare.

Among the airline packagers, **Iberia Airlines** (✆ **800/772-4642** or 90-240-05-00 in Spain; www.iberia.com) leads the way. Other packages for travel in Spain are offered by **United Airlines** (✆ **800/241-6522;** www.united.com), **American Airlines Vacations** (✆ **800/321-2121;** www.aavacations.com), and **Delta Vacations** (✆ **800/872-7786;** www.deltavacations.com). Also worth a look is **Continental Airlines Vacations** (✆ **800/301-3800;** www.covacations.com). Several big **online travel agencies**—Expedia, Travelocity, Orbitz, and Lastminute.com—also do a brisk business in packages.

Another good place to start your search is the travel section of your local Sunday newspaper. Also check the ads in the back of national travel magazines like *Arthur Frommer's Budget Travel Magazine, Travel + Leisure, National Geographic Traveler,* and *Condé Nast Traveler.* One of the biggest packages in the Northeast U.S., **Liberty Travel** (✆ **888/271-1584;** www.libertytravel.com), usually boasts a full-page ad in Sunday papers. **American Express Travel** (✆ **800/941-2639;** www.travel impressions.com) is another option.

Solar Tours (✆ **800/388-7652;** www.solartours.com) is a wholesaler that offers a number of package tours to Madrid.

Club ABC (✆ **800/456-5050;** www.clubabc.com) is known for searching for low-cost airfare deals to Spain. The tour agent also features air and land packages to Madrid.

ESCORTED GENERAL-INTEREST TOURS

Escorted tours are structured group tours, with a group leader. The price usually includes everything from airfare to hotels, meals, tours, admission costs, and local transportation.

Despite the fact that escorted tours require big deposits and predetermine hotels, restaurants, and itineraries, many people derive security and peace of mind from the structure they offer. Escorted tours—whether they're navigated by bus, motor coach, train, or boat—let travelers sit back and enjoy the trip without having to drive or worry about details. They take you to the maximum number of sights in the minimum amount of time with the least amount of hassle. They're particularly convenient for people with limited mobility, and they can be a great way to make new friends.

Spanish Language Classes

Madrid is the ideal city to study Spanish. One of the best schools is **International House,** Zurbano 8 (✆ **91-310-13-14**; www.ihmadrid.com; Mon–Fri 9am–8:30pm; Metro: Alonso Martínez). In addition to teaching English to Spanish students, International House also has regular Spanish classes for foreign visitors given by local Spanish teachers. All levels are offered. Most suitable for short-stay visitors are weeklong intensive courses, generally with small groups of five or six students, that last 20 hours and cost 197€. Immersion, one-to-one courses, at 36€ per hour, are also available to fit the student's schedule.

On the downside, you'll have little opportunity for serendipitous interactions with locals. The tours can be jampacked with activities, leaving little room for individual sightseeing, whim, or adventure; and they often focus on the heavily touristed sites, so you may miss out on many a lesser-known gem.

Recommended Escorted Tour Operators

There are many escorted-tour companies to choose from, each offering transportation to and within Spain, prearranged hotel space, and such extras as bilingual tour guides and lectures. Many of these tours to Spain include excursions to Morocco or Portugal.

Some of the most expensive and luxurious tours are run by **Abercrombie & Kent International** (✆ **800/323-7308** or 630/954-2944; www.abercrombiekent.com), including deluxe 13- or 19-day tours of the Iberian Peninsula by train. Guests stay in fine hotels, ranging from a late medieval palace to the exquisite modern Hesperia on Avenida Castellana.

Trafalgar Tours (✆ **800/854-0103** or 212/689-8977; www.trafalgartours.com) offers a number of tours of Spain. One of the most popular offerings is an 18-day trip called "The Best of Spain" (this land-only package is from around $1,900; with land and air, it's from $2,799).

Insight Vacations' "Highlights of Spain" is an 11-day tour that begins in Madrid, sweeps along the southern and eastern coasts, and concludes in Madrid. The company offers the tour for $1,370 to $1,830 including airfare, accommodations, and some meals. For information, contact your travel agent or Insight International (✆ **800/582-8380;** www.insightvacations.com).

Petrabax Tours (✆ **800/634-1188;** www.petrabax.com) attracts those who prefer to see Spain by bus, although fly/drive packages are also offered. Tours feature stays in *paradores* (high-standard, state-run hotels—some modern, some in historic buildings). A number of city packages are available, plus a 10-day trip that tries to capture Spain in a nutshell, with stops in places ranging from Madrid to Granada.

STAYING CONNECTED

Telephones

If you don't speak Spanish, you'll find it easier to telephone from your hotel, but remember that this is often very expensive because hotels impose a surcharge on every operator-assisted call. In some cases, it can be as high as 40% or more. On the street, phone booths (known as *cabinas*) have dialing instructions in English; you can make local calls by inserting a .25€ coin for 3 minutes.

To call Madrid: If you're calling Madrid from abroad:

1. Dial the international access code: 011 from the U.S. and Canada; 00 from the U.K., Ireland, or New Zealand; or 0011 from Australia.
2. Dial the country code for Spain: **34.**
3. Dial **91** for Madrid and then the number. So, the entire number you'd dial (from the U.S.) would be 011-34-91-000-0000.

In 1998, all telephone numbers in Spain changed to a nine-digit system instead of the six- or seven-digit method used previously. Each number is now preceded by its provincial code for local, national, and international calls. For example, when calling Madrid from Madrid or another province within Spain, telephone customers must dial 91-000-00-00. Similarly, when calling Valladolid from within or outside the province, dial 979-000-00-00.

To make international calls from Madrid: Dial 00 and then the country code (U.S. or Canada 1; U.K. 44; Ireland 353; Australia 61; New Zealand 64).

Dial the area code and number. For example, if you wanted to call the British Embassy in Washington, D.C., you would dial 00-1-202-588-7800.

For directory assistance: Dial © **11818** if you're looking for a number inside Spain, and dial © **11825** for numbers to all other countries.

For operator assistance: If you need operator assistance in making an international call, dial © **1008** (for Europe, Morocco, Tunisia, Libya, and Turkey) or **1005** (for the U.S. and all other countries), and © **1009** if you want to call a number in Spain.

Toll-free numbers: Numbers beginning with **900** in Spain are toll-free, but calling a 1-800 number in your home country from Spain is not toll-free. In fact, it costs the same as an overseas call.

In Madrid some smaller establishments, especially bars, discos, and a few informal restaurants, don't have phones. Further, many summer-only bars and discos secure a phone for the season only, and then get a new number the next season. Many attractions, such as small churches or even minor museums, have no staff to receive inquiries from the public.

When in Spain, the access number for an **AT&T** calling card is © **800/CALL-ATT** (2255-288). The access number for **Sprint** is © **800/888-0013.**

Cellphones

The three letters that define much of the world's wireless capabilities are GSM (Global System for Mobiles), a big, seamless network that makes for easy cross-border cellphone use throughout Europe and dozens of other countries worldwide. In the U.S., T-Mobile, AT&T Wireless, and Cingular use this quasi-universal system; in Canada, Microcell and some Rogers customers are GSM; and all Europeans and most Australians use GSM. If your cellphone is on a GSM system, and you have a world-capable multiband phone, such as many Sony Ericsson, Motorola, or Samsung models, you can make and receive calls across civilized areas around much of the globe. Just call your wireless operator and ask for "international roaming" to be activated on your account.

For many, **renting** a phone is a good idea. (Even World Phone owners will have to rent new phones if they're traveling to non-GSM regions, such as Japan or Korea.) While you can rent a phone from any number of overseas sites, including kiosks at airports and at car-rental agencies, I suggest renting the phone before you leave home. North Americans can rent one before leaving home from **InTouch USA** (✆ **800/872-7626;** www.intouchglobal.com) or **RoadPost** (✆ **888/290-1606** or 905/272-5665; www.roadpost.com). InTouch will also, for free, advise you on whether your existing phone will work overseas; simply call ✆ **703/222-7161** between 9am and 4pm EST, or go to **http://intouchglobal.com/travel.htm**.

The **Spanish Cell Phone Company** provides short- and long-term mobile phone rentals, with low rates for outgoing calls and free incoming calls. For details, phone ✆ **68-755-85-29,** or check **www.puertademadrid.es/rentacellphone**. **On Spanish Time Cellphone Rental** (✆ **91-547-85-75** or 65-626-68-44; www.onspanishtime.com) will deliver a phone to your hotel.

Buying a phone can be economically attractive, especially if you are on an extended vacation. Once you arrive, stop by a local cellphone shop and get the cheapest package. Local calls may be as low as 10¢ per minute, and in many countries, incoming calls are free.

The major Spanish cellphone companies are **Movistar**—owned by Spain's largest telephone company Telefónica—**Orange,** and **Vodaphone.** All three have dozens of offices all over Madrid where you can rent or buy a mobile phone and SIM card. Information on their websites is in Spanish. **Movistar** (www.movistar.es) provides the best coverage in Spain and is linked with international providers, allowing you easy access to voice mail as you're traveling. **Orange** (http://tiendamovil.orange.es) is the most economical of the three, with some rates as low as 3¢ a minute, though, in general, their system has less reliable coverage than Movistar. **Vodaphone** (www.grupolidertel.com) is from the U.K. and offers mobile service throughout Europe. Vodaphone is ideal if you're thinking of visiting other European countries after Madrid.

Voice-over Internet Protocol (VoIP)

If you have Web access while traveling, consider a broadband-based telephone service (in technical terms, **Voice-over Internet Protocol,** or **VoIP**) such as Skype (www.skype.com) or Vonage (www.vonage.com), which allow you to make free international calls from your laptop or in a cybercafe. Neither service requires the people you're calling to also have that service (though there are fees if they do not). Check the websites for details.

Internet & E-mail

WITH YOUR OWN COMPUTER

Wi-Fi (wireless fidelity) is the buzzword in computer access, and more and more hotels, cafes, and retailers are signing on as wireless "hotspots," where you can get high-speed connection without cable wires, networking hardware, or a phone line (see below). The two hotel chains in Madrid that have taken most advantage of this innovative move in communications are **Room Mate** and **High Tech/Petit Palace**—who have, between them, over 28 hotels in the city (chapter 6). New Wi-Fi bring-your-own-computer cafes, too, are appearing, such as **Antipodes** (cafe and sushi bar) at Calle San Agustin 18 (✆ **91-429-21-57**), in the Huertas district;

and the Argüelles branch of **VIPs,** at Calle Princesa 5 (© **91-542-15-78**), just west of the Plaza España. (These are not to be confused with the profusion of cybercafes, which provide the computers but don't let you bring your own. See the next section.) The 50-odd **Starbucks** that have sprung up since 2005 in Madrid unfortunately **do not** have this capability at the time of writing.

Boingo (www.boingo.com) and **Wayport** (www.wayport.com) have set up networks in airports and high-class hotel lobbies. iPass providers (see below) also give you access to a few hundred wireless hotel lobby setups. You sign up for wireless access service much as you do cellphone service, through a plan offered by one of several commercial companies that have made wireless service available in airports, hotel lobbies, and coffee shops, primarily in the U.S. (followed by the U.K. and Japan). Best of all, you don't need to be staying at, say, the Four Seasons to use the hotel's network; just set yourself up on a nice couch in the lobby. The companies' pricing policies can be byzantine, with a variety of monthly, per-connection, and per-minute plans, but in general you pay around $35 a month for limited access—and as more and more companies jump on the wireless bandwagon, prices are likely to get even more competitive.

You can get Wi-Fi connection one of several ways. Many laptops have built-in Wi-Fi capability (an 802.11b wireless Ethernet connection). Mac owners have their own networking technology, Apple AirPort.

For those with older computers, an 802.11b/**Wi-Fi card** (around $60) can be plugged into your laptop. **Vincci,** another hotel chain (chapter 6), provides this service, charging around 40€ for a card, which you buy in reception and can use with your laptop—till your time runs out—in the lounge (*not* the bedroom, though you can, in fact, also connect free of charge there if you have an Ethernet connection).

For dial-up access, most business-class hotels throughout the world offer dataports for laptop modems, and a few thousand hotels in the U.S. and Europe now offer free high-speed Internet access. In addition, major Internet service providers (ISPs) have **local access numbers,** allowing you to go online by placing a local call. The **iPass** network also has dial-up numbers around the world. You'll have to sign up with an iPass provider, who will then tell you how to set up your computer for your destination(s). For a list of iPass providers, go to **www.ipass.com** and click on "Individuals Buy Now." One solid provider is **i2roam** (© **866/811-6209** or 920/235-0475; www.i2roam.com).

Wherever you go, bring a **connection kit** of the right power and phone adapters, a spare phone cord, and a spare Ethernet network cable—or find out whether your hotel supplies them to guests.

WITHOUT YOUR OWN COMPUTER

As access to portable connection sources such as Blackberry becomes more commonly used among today's media-wise travelers and more and more hotels—and not just the High Tech and Petit Palace Chains—automatically feature Wi-Fi connections, the number of cybercafes where you can use on-the-spot computers has actually decreased in central Madrid in the past few years. Their boom years were fruitful but short.

Probably the best of those still operating is **Work Center,** which has a variety of Internet branches spread throughout the city. The most central branch is at Plaza Canalejas, Calle Principe 1 (© **91-360-13-95;** www.workcenter.es), open 8am to 10pm Monday to Friday and 10am to 2:30pm and 5 to 8:30pm Saturday and Sunday.

ONLINE TRAVELER'S toolbox

Veteran travelers usually carry some essential items to make their trips easier. Following is a selection of handy online tools to bookmark and use.

- **www.madridman.com** provides chatty background information on where to stay and what to do once in Madrid, as told by American resident Scott Martin.
- **www.spain.info** (Tourism Board of Spain) has a good section on Madrid attractions, especially eating spots.
- **www.elmundo.es** (Spanish only), the Metropolí section of *El Mundo* newspaper, on Fridays, has the most comprehensive summary of everything going on in the capital.
- **www.madaboutmadrid.com** gives you a further rundown on city events, in English.
- **www.timeout.com**, **www.softguides.com**, and **www.webmadrid.com** each provide extensive cultural, entertainment, and dining listings, written by savvy locals.
- **www.turismomadrid.es** is the site of the Madrid Tourist Board.

To find more cybercafes, check **www.cybercaptive.com** and **www.cybercafe.com**.

To retrieve your e-mail, ask your **Internet service provider (ISP)** if it has a Web-based interface tied to your existing e-mail account. If your ISP doesn't have such an interface, you can use the free **mail2web** service (www.mail2web.com) to view and reply to your home e-mail. For more flexibility, you may want to open a free, Web-based e-mail account with **Yahoo! Mail** (http://mail.yahoo.com). Your home ISP may be able to forward your e-mail to the Web-based account automatically.

If you need to access files on your office computer, look into a service called **GoToMyPC** (www.gotomypc.com). The service provides a Web-based interface for you to access and manipulate a distant PC from anywhere—even a cybercafe—provided your "target" PC is on and has an always-on connection to the Internet (such as with Road Runner cable). The service offers top-quality security; but if you're worried about hackers, use your own laptop rather than a cybercafe computer to access the GoToMyPC system.

SUGGESTED MADRID ITINERARIES

4

Central Madrid is clearly the best and most rewarding part of the city to explore. You can cover quite a few of the capital's main monuments and architectural highlights in just a day. But the more time you have available, the more justice you can do to the daunting cornucopia of sights on display here. Here are some recommendations on how and where to spend your time.

GETTING TO KNOW MADRID

The center of the Spanish capital is a huddle of medieval alleyways and squares, with an elegant reminder of the old Habsburg capital between the Royal Palace and Plaza Mayor. Dissecting the center is the Manhattan-style Gran Vía. Across the wide modern Castellana Avenue, leading north to the Plaza Castilla, lies the spacious Parque del Retiro, surrounded by 19th-century residential areas. The lower part of Castellana Avenue is the most beautiful, stretching from the lush tree-shaded Paseo del Prado and running alongside the world-famous museum to cosmopolitan Recoletos, with the city's most elegant cafe terraces. Fanning out around Madrid, expanding new suburbs and fashionable American-style satellite towns are gradually absorbing much of the capital's booming five-million-plus population.

Equip yourself with a good city map before exploring the town. One of the best and most detailed is the Michelin version, which sells at around 6€ in the travel sections of large stores like the Corte Inglés, FNAC, or Casa del Libro (the latter's located near the Gran Vía metro stop). The free maps given away by tourist offices and hotels are generally less detailed, giving a mere outline of the fascinating maze of little streets that form the labyrinthine center.

Neighborhoods in Brief

Madrid can be divided into two main zones of real interest to visitors: the old traditional **Center,** with the Puerta del Sol and Gran Vía at its heart and surrounding 17th-century Austrias, and Castizo (traditional) **Argüelles, Chueca,**

Malasaña, Chamberí, and **Lavapiés** districts; and the newer **Ensanche** (extension) refers to all parts of Madrid built outside of the old city walls from the 18th century onward. This area includes the wide cosmopolitan **Castellana Avenue,** with its business offices and classy hotels; the grid-planned, once mansion-filled **Salamanca** barrio, home of some of Madrid's best shops and restaurants; and northern **Chamartín** district, with its easier-going residential atmosphere.

THE CENTER

The Austrias & Plaza Mayor The **Austrias** quarter, with its alleys and tiny plazas, is named after the 17th-century kings of Spain, and contains the city's most evocative churches. In 1617, the colonnaded **Plaza Mayor** became the area's hub; today, with its mix of Habsburg, French, and Georgian architecture, it is one of the key nighttime centers of tourist activity. It's filled with cafes, bars, and shops selling everything from turn-of-the-20th-century souvenir hats to stamps and rare coins over the weekend. Concerts, shows, and exhibitions are often held here; and at *Navidad,* it's a child's delight with a proliferation of Christmas trees and stalls selling gifts. The lavish *Reyes* (or Three Kings) processions originate from here on January 6 amid much excitement.

The square is bounded by Calle Mayor, Cava de San Miguel, and Calle de la Cruz. Westward from the Plaza, the narrow Arco de Cuchilleros is filled with long-established eating spots and *tabernas;* cavelike locales, called *mesones*—hewn into the base of Cava de San Miguel's old five-story buildings at the northern end of the plaza—provide wine, tapas, and musical entertainment. Touristy, but great fun. In a narrow atmospheric street called the **Cava Baja,** just before you reach the Plaza de la Cebada, you'll find the largest concentration of trendy wine bars, homey *tabernas,* and *posada-* (inn) style restaurants in all Madrid.

The nearby **Plaza de la Paja,** close to the city's two oldest churches, was actually the heart of the city and its main marketplace during the medieval period. On the western edge of this area is the diminutive Muslim Madrid zone, which is centered on Las Vistillas, just below the Almudena cathedral and Royal Palace—the zone enjoys views toward the distant Guadarramas. Below it to the west is the Campo del Moro park; the Manzanares River, with its bordering walkways; and the great green expanse of the Casa de Campo.

Puerta del Sol Just east of the Plaza Mayor, the semicircular "Gateway to the Sun" is the starting point for all road distances within Spain. Its attractions are more peripheral, ranging from the shops and department stores of northerly traffic-free Preciados to the countless arrays of bars and nightspots lining the southerly, narrow alleyed district of Huertas.

Dominated by the 18th-century Casa de Correos (seat of the regional government), whose New Year's clock chimes are traditionally witnessed by exhilarated crowds, all eating their 12 grapes in time with the chimes, the crescent-shaped square is perennially lively, and its symbolic statue of the Bear and the Madroño Tree is a favorite rendezvous spot. It's also a prime hunting ground for pickpockets and purse snatchers, so take care.

Gran Vía/Plaza de España Gran Vía is the city's main street, lined with cafes, restaurants, cinemas, department stores, and the headquarters of banks and corporations. As you walk along, note the changing styles of buildings on either side: You're actually time-traveling through the 4 decades it took to construct the avenue between the early and mid-1900s. Gran Vía cuts a bow-shaped east-west swathe across the center, between the neoclassical **Metrópolis** building near the Banco de España and the **Plaza de España,** where statues of Don Quixote and his faithful squire, Sancho Panza, are set in a park surrounded by olive trees and beside a fountain overlooked by the stark 1950s Torre España and Edificio Europa buildings.

Madrid Neighborhoods

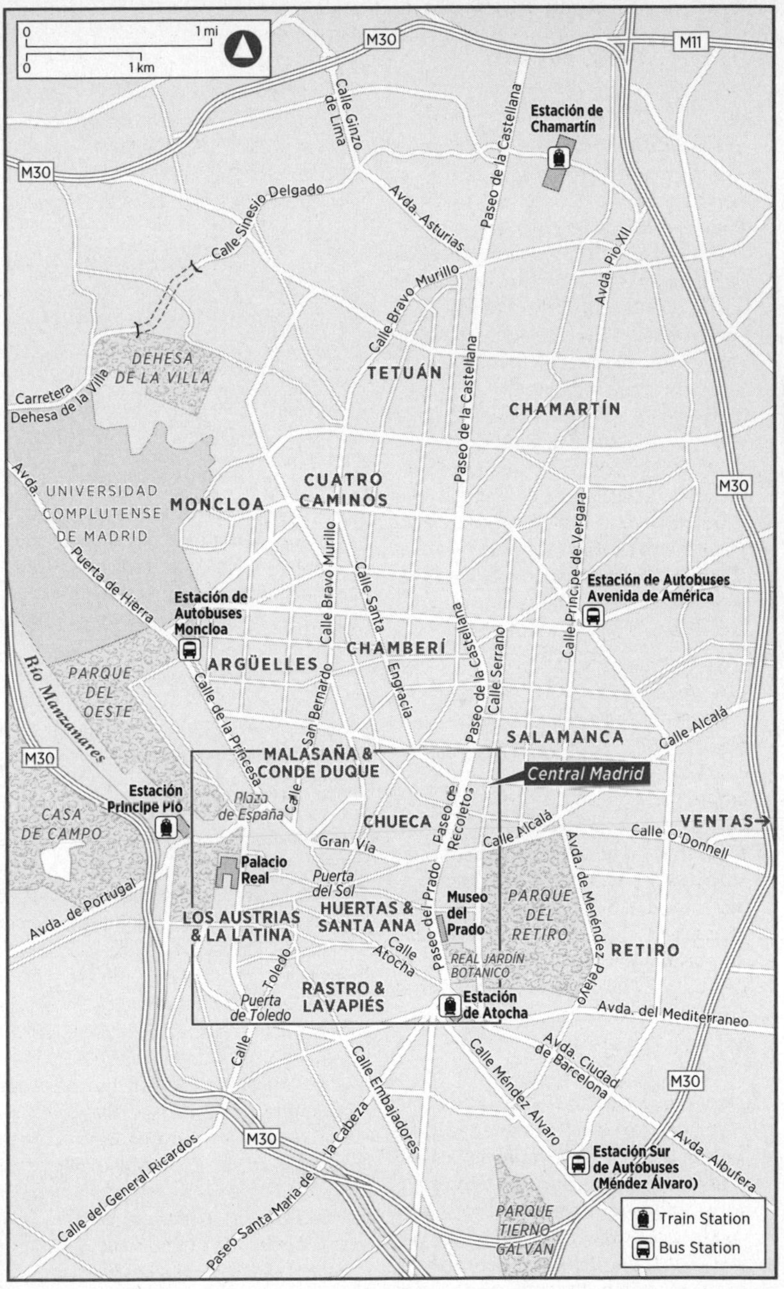

4–5° IZDA.: A miniguide TO DECIPHERING THE MYSTERY OF MADRID ADDRESSES

The numbers and abbreviations in Spanish addresses can seem complicated when the hotel, pension, gallery, or private residence is located *above* the ground floor. (***Remember:*** In Europe, the ground floor is the floor on the ground, and is the equivalent to the first floor in the U.S. The first floor in Europe is the one above the ground floor, which is equivalent to the second floor in the U.S.) Once you understand what all the symbols and abbreviations mean, however, you'll find that addresses in Spain are actually quite detailed and specific, explaining where the establishment is located with the utmost precision. Also note that in Spain, as in many other European countries, the building number comes after the street name. Here is a brief explanation of how addresses work:

The first number represents the number of the address on a particular **street** (for example, Hotel Adler is at Calle Velázquez 33). Sometimes the address may cover two street numbers, separated by a dash or the word *y,* which means "and" (for example, Hotel Occidental is at Miguel Angel 29–31, while Hotel Tryp Ambassador is at Cuesta Santo Domingo 5 y 7).

The second number, or the number after the street number(s), is followed by a **°** (degree symbol). This represents the ***piso* (floor)** that the establishment is on. For instance, Hotel Riesco is at Calle Correo 2–3°, which means the hotel is on the third floor at number 2 on Calle Correo; Hotel Astoria is at Carrera de San Jerónimo 30–32–5°, which means the hotel is on the fifth floor at nos. 30–32 on Carrera de San Jerónimo.

After the number with a degree symbol, you may see a third item. This will really only apply to a private residence or a small gallery. If there are only two units on a particular floor, you might see **izda.** or **dcha.** These abbreviations for the *izquierda* (left) or *derecha* (right), respectively, signal the location of the establishment within the building. For example, the Guillermo de Osma Art Gallery is at Claudio Coello 4–1° izda., which means the gallery is on the left side of the first floor of no. 4 on Claudio Coello. Alternatively, if the establishment is on a floor containing more than two apartments or galleries (generally, there may be up to six), you might see something with a superscript *a* or *o,* representing the unit number, such as 1° or 1ª *(primero/a)* for the first unit, 3° or 3ª *(tercero/a)* for the third unit, and so on. For example, Calle de Ferraz 32–34–2°–5° designates the fifth unit on the second floor at nos. 32–34 on Calle de Ferraz, and Calle del Amparo 21–3°–6ª is the sixth unit on the third floor of no. 21 on Calle del Amparo.

And just to complicate matters even more, finding an address within Madrid's grand boulevards and cramped meandering streets can sometimes be a problem, primarily because of the way buildings are numbered. On most streets, the numbering begins on one side and runs consecutively until the end, resuming on the other side and going in the opposite direction. Thus, no. 50 could be opposite no. 250. But there are many exceptions to this system. That's why it's important to know the cross street as well as the number of the address you're looking for. In fact, some addresses don't have a number at all. What they have is the designation *s/n,* which means *sin número* (without number). For example, the address of the Panteón de Goya (Goya's Tomb) is Glorieta de San Antonio de la Florida s/n.

In April 2010, the avenue celebrated the first centenary since its initial surfacing began. Purple carpets covered most of its surface, cars and buses were diverted, and inhabitants and visitors alike enjoyed the rare luxury of strolling along its temporarily peaceful and traffic-free length.

Argüelles/Moncloa Just to the northeast of Plaza España is **Argüelles,** a compact barrio of narrow crisscrossing lanes, sandwiched between promenade-like **Pintor Rosales** (which runs along the edge of Parque del Oeste) and the shop-filled Calle Princesa leading up to **Moncloa.** The latter is home to the kitsch '50s Ministerio del Aire building and, slightly to the north, a huge university campus area bounded by the green recreational zones of Puerta de Hierro to the north and Cea Bermúdez and Bravo Murillo avenues to the east. Students haunt its cafes, *tascas,* and more recent wine bars.

CASTIZO (TRADITIONAL) MADRID

Chueca This atmospheric area north of the Gran Vía includes the narrow streets of Hortaleza, Infantas, Barquillo, and San Lucas. Though appealing to all tastes and persuasions with a concentration of richly varied bars and restaurants of all price ranges and nationalities, it's also famed as the center of Madrid's gay scene. At night the entire area is very lively, especially in the tiny main square which is packed with cafe tables and chairs in summer.

Malasaña Centered on the famed Plaza Dos de Mayo, this traditional barrio is named after a teenage seamstress—Manuela Malasaña—who became an unwitting martyr for the Spanish cause during the Peninsula War, when the scissors she was carrying for her work were interpreted as a lethal weapon by the occupying French forces and she was summarily tried and executed. The neighborhood's grid system of crisscross narrow lanes is still bordered by traditional but now largely renovated 19th-century buildings and, at night, its many music bars are patronized by hard-rock and grunge fans.

Chamberí Though built in the late 19th century outside the old city walls, this originally working-class zone is more low-key and upmarket than its southerly counterparts Malasaña and Chueca. The focal point of Chamberí is the circular Plaza Olavide. Classy, elegant, and traditional, Chamberí is set among wide avenues with historic mansions—many of which now house foreign embassies. The barrio offers an attractive selection of restaurants, bookshops, art galleries, and museums, such as the charming Sorolla (where the famed Valenciano painter lived and worked for many decades; p. 186).

Lavapiés In decay until a few decades back, this former medieval working-class quarter south of the Plaza Mayor has seen many of its lanes turned into pedestrian zones with houses tastefully converted into studio flats. The area is filled with a new polyglot ambience, thanks to the recent immigrant influx from North Africa and the Middle East. The overall blend of the international and earthy bohemian has transformed the area into one of the most evocative and stimulating in Madrid.

THE ENSANCHE

Castellana Madrid's longest and most elegant avenue runs south from the **Plaza Castilla** to **Colon (Columbus) Square,** and its central pedestrian lanes are summertime open-air terraces filled with animated crowds. En route, it passes the high-rise AZCA business center, huge Santiago Bernabeu *fútbol* (soccer) stadium, and a choice of top hotels, expensive shops, apartment buildings, luxury hotels, and foreign embassies.

Next comes the shorter and more intimate **Recoletos,** linking **Colon** with the emblematic Cibeles fountain whose ever-busy roundabout is overlooked by the main post office (known as "the cathedral of post offices") and the 19th-century French- and Viennese-styled Banco de España. Its central median is often reserved for antique-book fairs, and its most famous buildings include the National Library and **Gran Café de Gijón** (p. 141).

The elegant final stretch is the **Paseo del Prado,** which leads down from Cibeles to Atocha railway station. Tree-shaded and maturely beautiful, it's home to such incomparable city gems as the Neptune statue, Bolsa (Stock Exchange), Ritz hotel, **Museo Nacional del Prado,** and **Botanical Gardens.** To the east of the garden lies **Parque del Retiro,** a magnificent park once reserved for royalty, with rose gardens, wide walkways, terrace cafes, fountains, statues (including the only one in the world dedicated to the devil), musicians and entertainers, a rowing lake (the Estanque), and Madrid's finest homage to the Industrial Revolution: the iron-, tile-, and glass-built **Casa de Cristal (Crystal Palace),** inspired by its 19th-century London namesake.

Salamanca Ever since the city walls came tumbling down in the 1860s, this elegant, stylish, and expensive neighborhood east of the center has been one of the most fashionable areas to live in Madrid. Some of the city's most traditional covered markets are tucked away here. Calle Serrano marks the western border of this neighborhood and is lined with international shops, stores, and boutiques. The U.S. Embassy is located halfway up the avenue, close to the Lazaro Galdiano Museum.

Chamartín The home of Madrid's main northerly railway station is also one of the city's most trendy but easy-going corners, with wide avenues, elegant boutique markets, and some charming hotels hidden behind flower-filled gardens. One of the city's largest contingents of long-term expatriates lives in this area, and it has a particularly attractive selection of international eating spots.

THE BEST OF MADRID IN 1 DAY

This is going to be a very busy day if you want to do the city's key sights full justice so conserve all your energy and have an early night beforehand. Start with the not-to-be-missed **Prado**—for many, the highlight of a Madrid visit.

Note: Seasonal opening hours of some attractions may require modification of the itinerary below: for example, from November to February. Start: Metro: Atocha or Banco de España. Bus: 9, 10, 34.

1 Prado Museum ★★★

As your minutes are precious here, pick out a few choice masterpieces (such as Velázquez's *Las Meninas*) and concentrate on your favorites. It will be difficult not to be sidetracked with such a wealth of beauty around you, but try to confine your time to a mere hour instead of the half-day you really need to do this museum justice. If you're making this visit on a Sunday morning it's free, so don't be put off by the longer-than-usual lines of eagerly waiting tourists. The bright and spacious new wing houses a hundred additional works by 19th-century artists, from Sorolla and Fortuny to the indispensable Goya. Temporary exhibitions here may include works by more modern artists such as Francis Bacon. See p. 174.

2 Botanical Gardens ★★★

Adjoining the museum, this compact backwater of calm and greenery was founded by Charles III. It had over 650 species when it opened in 1755; now you can count the wide variety of flowers, shrubs, and ancient trees into the thousands. As you wander its sylvan pathways, it's hard to believe you're in the heart of a big city. See p. 192.

3 Paseo del Prado ★★

Also the work of Charles III, this tree-lined gem, where you can walk shaded by a huge, mellow archway of green, is the most beautiful *paseo* in the capital, if not all of Spain. Flanked by the Ritz Hotel, Thyssen Museum (p. 175), and the Prado, it conjures up a picture of an elegant Bourbon Madrid of the 19th century (if we can forget the traffic for a moment).

4 Congreso de Diputados ★

Reach here after turning left at the **Neptuno** fountain and at the Plaza del Congreso. Admire the neoclassical facade, granite pillars, and bronze lion statues outside the mid-19th-century parliamentary building, designed by Pascual y Colomer. A botched coup was attempted in 1981 (bullet holes in the ceiling of the Sessions Chamber date from that inauspicious occasion). Bring your passport if you want to pay a Saturday morning visit. See chapter 8, "Walking Tour 3." You can also do a "virtual visit" via the website www.congreso.es.

5 Ateneo de Madrid ★

This 19th-century bastion of culture exudes a time warp atmosphere. Wander in, ask politely to see the well-worn lounges with their wooden walls and high chandeliers, and imagine yourself back in the time of Unamuno, Ortega y Gasset, and other literary giants of the "Generation of '98." (That's 1898.) Though the impressive upstairs library (members only, but you can peer through the glass door) now has Internet facilities, the mellow historic surroundings remain incongruously the same. See chapter 8, "Walking Tour 3."

6 Casa Museo de Lope de Vega ★

Probably the smallest museum in town, this well-preserved medieval house was the home of Spain's most famed and prolific 16th-century playwright and has a secret hidden gem of a garden at the rear. It's ironically located in a street named after his great novelist rival Cervantes. Best to book beforehand as it has severe limitations on the size of visiting groups. See p. 181 and chapter 8, "Walking Tour 3."

7 La Mallorquina Pastelería ☕

Rest your weary legs in the rather secretive upstairs cafe of La Mallorquina Pastelería, Puerta del Sol 8 (✆ 91-521-12-01), where the laid-back atmosphere contrasts pleasantly with the frenzy of the congested bar-cum-shop below. Great coffee plus a variety of cholesterol-filled pastries, including the Balearic Islands' favorite *ensaimada,* may tempt you into spoiling your lunch.

8 Puerta del Sol ★★★

Named after the sun-emblazoned gate of a medieval fort that stood here, this compact and ever-crowded urban hub—Madrid's answer to Times Square or Piccadilly Circus—is the only plaza in the city still to bear the name *puerta* (gate). Highlights are its 18th-century clock, whose chimes have marked the jubilant beginning of many a New Year, and an emblematic little statue of *El Oso*

The Best of Madrid in 1, 2 & 3 Days

The Best in 1 Day

1 Prado Museum
2 Botanical Gardens
3 Paseo del Prado
4 Congreso de Diputados
5 Ateneo de Madrid
6 Casa Museo de Lope de Vega
7 La Mallorquina Pastelería
8 Puerta del Sol
9 Plaza Mayor
10 Cava Baja's Casa Lucio
11 Austrias District
12 Plaza Oriente
13 Café Oriente

The Best in 2 Days

1 Retiro Park
2 Museo Thyssen-Bornemisza
3 Cibeles
4 Círculo de Bellas Artes
5 The Círculo de Bellas Artes Cafe
6 Real Academia de Bellas Artes de San Fernando
7 Convento de las Descalzas Reales
8 Casa Ciriaco
9 Palacio Real
10 Almudena Catedral
11 Parque de las Vistillas
12 Campo del Moro
13 Ermita de San Antonio de la Florida
14 Casa Mingo

The Best in 3 Days

1 Reina Sofia
2 Plaza del Cascorro/Rastro
3 Plaza de Lavapiés
4 Café Barbieri
5 Anton Martín Market
6 Filmoteca Cine Doré
7 Plaza Tirso de Molina
8 La Corrala
9 Casa Lastra Sidrería
10 Templo de Debod
11 Teleférico de Madrid
12 Casa de Campo
13 Lago

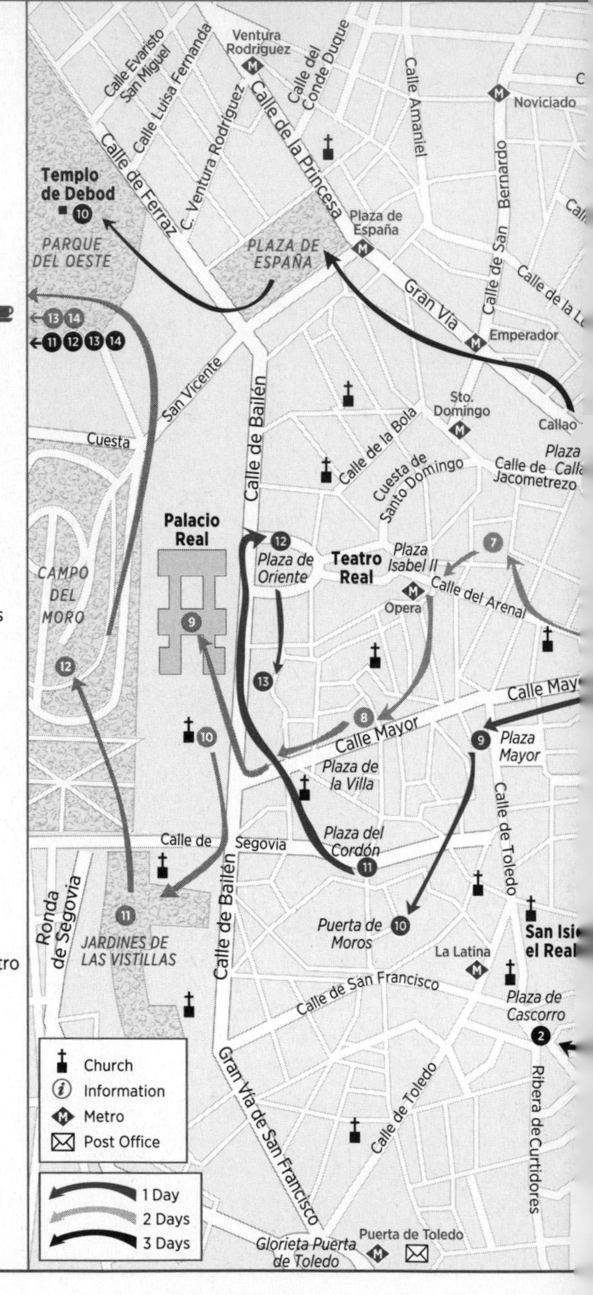

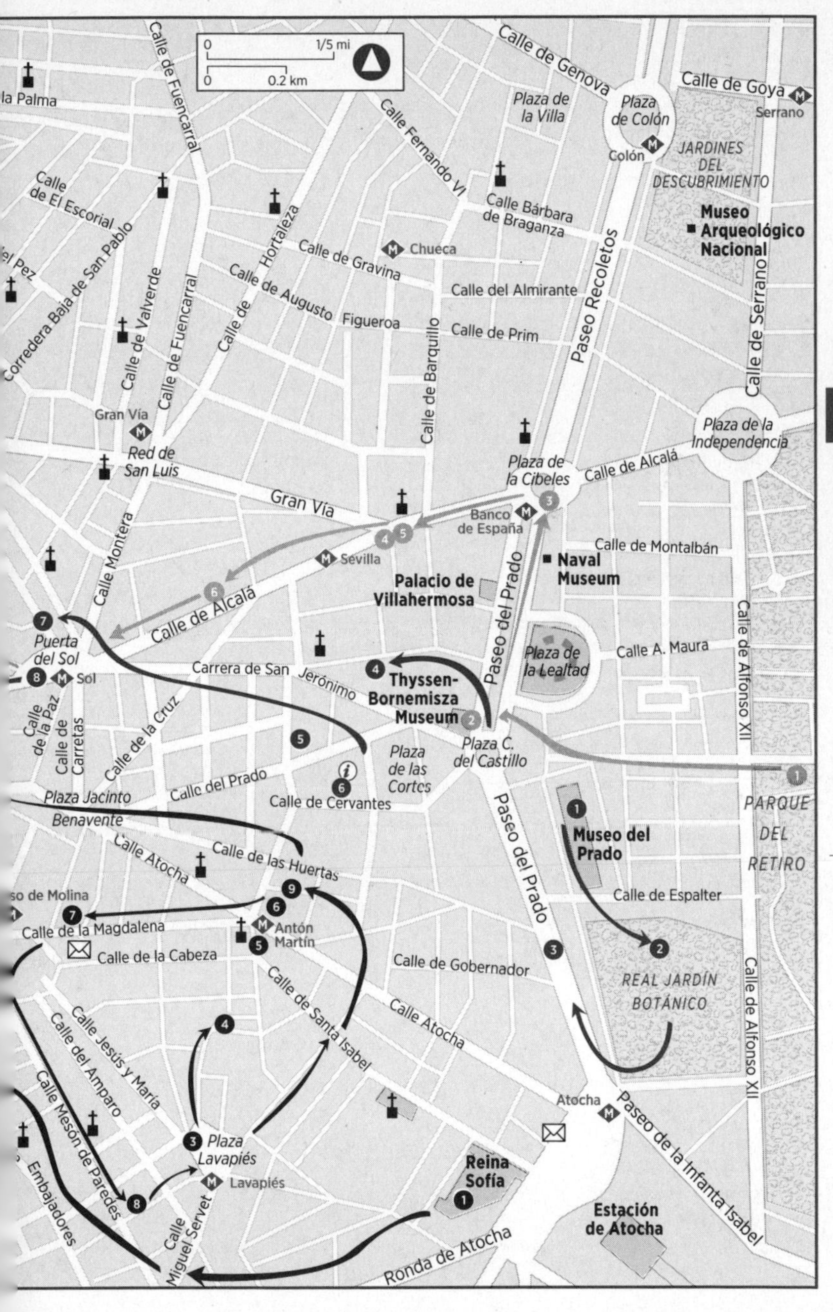
0 1/5 mi
0 0.2 km
la Palma
Calle de Fuencarral
Calle de Genova
Calle Fernando VI
Plaza de la Villa
Plaza de Colón
Colón
Calle de Goya
Serrano
JARDINES DEL DESCUBRIMIENTO
Museo Arqueológico Nacional
Calle Bárbara de Braganza
Calle de El Escorial
Calle de Hortaleza
Calle de Gravina
Chueca
Corredera Baja de San Pablo
Calle de Augusto Figueroa
Calle del Almirante
Calle de Prim
Paseo Recoletos
Calle de Serrano
Calle de Valverde
Calle de Fuencarral
Calle de Barquillo
Gran Vía
Red de San Luis
Plaza de la Independencia
Plaza de la Cibeles
Calle de Alcalá
Gran Vía
Banco de España
Calle de Montalbán
Sevilla
Naval Museum
Palacio de Villahermosa
Calle Montera
Calle de Alcalá
Paseo del Prado
Puerta del Sol
Sol
Carrera de San Jerónimo
Thyssen-Bornemisza Museum
Plaza de la Lealtad
Calle A. Maura
Calle de Alfonso XII
Calle de la Paz
Calle de Carretas
Calle de la Cruz
Plaza C. del Castillo
Plaza de las Cortes
Calle del Prado
Plaza Jacinto Benavente
Calle de Cervantes
Paseo del Prado
PARQUE DEL RETIRO
Museo del Prado
Calle Atocha
Calle de las Huertas
Calle de Espalter
Calle de la Magdalena
Antón Martín
Calle de la Cabeza
Calle de Gobernador
REAL JARDÍN BOTÁNICO
Calle de Santa Isabel
Calle Atocha
Calle Jesús y María
Calle del Amparo
Calle Mesón de Paredes
Calle de Alfonso XII
Atocha
Paseo de la Infanta Isabel
Plaza Lavapiés
Lavapiés
Reina Sofía
Embajadores
Calle Miguel Servet
Estación de Atocha
Ronda de Atocha

y el Madroño (The Bear and the Strawberry Tree), which was recently moved back to its original spot on the eastern side of the plaza at the city center end of Calle Alcalá. Sol is said to be the geographical center of the country, though the nearby town of Parla also claims this privilege. The whole square was refurbished in a neat but rather stark concrete-dominated style, complete with futuristic arched glass and steel entrances to the expanded metro station, in 2009. See p. 66 and chapter 8, "Walking Tour 3."

9 Plaza Mayor ★★★

Spain's most famous square has seen various, and sometimes violent, changes since its first appearance in the 15th century, but in these more peaceful days enjoys concerts, exhibitions, and one-off freebie treats such as the annual December serving of traditional *cocido* to the public by soldiers—one of many unofficial Christmastime traditions. Have your tongue-in-cheek portrait painted in 5 minutes by one of the various artists who set up their stalls beside the colonnades, and look out for the controversially bright and breezy murals portraying goddess Cibeles and offspring Proserpine on the Casa de la Panadería side (considered by some to resemble a comic strip). If you come on a Sunday, browse around the weekly stamp and coin market. See p. 190 and chapter 8, "Walking Tour 1."

10 Casa Lucio

Lunch in Casa Lucio, Cava Baja 35 (✆ 91-365-32-52; www.casalucio.es), a favorite of King Juan Carlos and visiting stars, dignitaries, and heads of state, including George W. The prize dish is the outwardly simple *huevos estrellados* (a fry-up of eggs and wafer-thin potatoes), here raised to a fine art. On a grander scale, the oven-baked beef steaks are out of this world. Try to get a first-floor table for the best atmosphere. See p. 127.

11 Austrias District ★★★

The narrow streets of Cuchilleros and Cavas Baja and Alta, and charming plazas de la Cebada and de la Paja, are at the heart of 16th-century Madrid, dating from the period when the Habsburgs ruled Spain. Here you'll find the city's oldest, and smallest, churches, **San Nicolas de las Servitas** and **San Pedro el Viejo,** twin reminders of a time when Madrid was a modest town of some 10,000 inhabitants. The tiny Morería section on its western fringe was once the Jewish quarter. See p. 180 and chapter 8, "Walking Tour 1."

12 Plaza Oriente ★★

Built over the remains of the old wooden Habsburg palace that burnt down in the 17th century, this attractive French-style semicircular plaza has lines of statues of the kings of Spain clustered round a central equestrian statue of Philip IV. A favorite with photographers, it's one of my favorite spots for relaxing over a drink.

13 Café Oriente

The great attraction of the Café Oriente ★★, Plaza de Oriente 2 (✆ 91-541-39-74; www.cafedeoriente.es), is not so much its plush mock baroque interior as its outside terrace area, which overlooks the square and magnificent facade of the Palacio Real (which you'll visit on your second day). Here you can sip your campari and soda in an atmosphere of historic splendor. See p. 132.

THE BEST OF MADRID IN 2 DAYS

Now you've got the essential lay of the land, having spent your first day in Madrid as outlined above. Use your second day as an opportunity to combine some leisurely wanderings among Madrid's top green areas—from the illustrious Retiro to the huge Casa de Campo—with a peek at farther cultural spots large and small, from the great Royal Palace that once housed kings to the tiny chapel where Goya is buried. And you'll get the chance to discover what radical changes—in the form of new walkways and gardens—the capital has carried out along the banks of its once tiny and ignored Manzanares River. **Start:** Metro: Retiro. Bus: 15, 146.

---

1 Parque del Retiro ★★★

Start with an early breakfast and a stroll among the joggers and tai chi exercisers as far as the Estanque (lake) in **Parque del Retiro.** Once the prerogative of royals alone, this rectangular oasis of greenery has become a popular rendezvous for residents ever since it was opened up to the public in 1868. See p. 192.

2 Museo Thyssen-Bornemisza

More exquisite art if you're game. This superb, multifaceted gallery, founded by the now defunct Baron Hans Heinrich and his wife, Carmen "Tita" Rivera, also has an impressive extension for temporary exhibitions. To get a rough idea of the museum's vast range, peep first at the Old Dutch masters and then at modernist masterpieces by Klee, Braque, and Picasso. See p. 175.

3 Cibeles

Madrid's most famous fountain lies at the meeting point of Alcalá and the Paseo del Prado, opposite the Banco España and main post office (Palacio de Comunicaciones). Sporting successes are traditionally celebrated with great enthusiasm in this square. When Spain defeated Holland to win the World Soccer Championship in Johannesburg in July 2010, the huge city fiesta that culminated here was the most extravagant and noisy even this lively city has seen, way superceding the shindig two years earlier when the national team beat Germany to win the UEFA Champion's League European Cup.

4 Círculo de Bellas Artes

This Art Deco gem has exhibitions in various salons as well as an adjoining excellent value cinema and an iconic ground floor cafe (see "Círculo de Bellas Arte," below, and p. 239). You can also pop up to the top floor and look at the library, even if you're not a member.

5 Círculo de Bellas Arte ☕

The Círculo de Bellas Arte's spacious and well-worn cafe, Calle Marqués de Casa Riera 2 (✆ 91-360-54-00), evokes a turn-of-the-20th-century aura, with its chandeliers, recumbent statue of a naked lady, and high wide windows overlooking the junction of Alcalá and the Gran Vía. TV morning interviews with established and up-and-coming politicians alike are often held against this backdrop, so you might get a glimpse of some future Spanish president. See p. 142.

6 Real Academia de Bellas Artes de San Fernando

Time for a quick peep at another unmissable temple of art, located just up Alcalá on the way to Puerta del Sol. This one's the oldest in Madrid and remarkable for its wealth of Spanish and Dutch masters. See the roomful of Goyas if nothing else. See p. 177 and chapter 8, "Walking Tour 3."

7 Convento de las Descalzas Reales

An oasis of calm in the midst of the urban mayhem, this 16th-century convent seems hundreds of kilometers from Madrid instead of just a stone's throw from the Gran Vía—though there is admittedly a slight sense of rush as you "do" the array of corridors and paintings in around 20 minutes. Some of these guided visits only have commentary in Spanish, so bring along an architectural guide book, if you've got one, to be on the safe side. See p. 183 and chapter 8, "Walking Tour 3."

8 Casa Ciriaco

After this surfeit of culture, tuck into a satisfying lunch at one of Madrid's remaining genuinely traditional eating spots, Casa Ciriaco, Calle Mayor 84 (© 91-548-06-20). Photos of eminent historic figures line the walls; pre-'30s radical thinkers used to meet here to put the world to right. Before the building became a restaurant, antiroyalists once threw a bomb at Alfonso XIII from one of the balconies. (He was unharmed, though many others were less fortunate.) These days, the mood is neither anarchic nor intellectual, but the hearty Castilian food is great nonetheless. See p 133.

9 Palacio Real

A Bourbon monument of granite and white stone, this vast Italian-designed 18th-century palace is one of Madrid's greatest architectural assets. Though it's not used much by today's royal family, official ceremonies are often held here, so best to check before your visit to make sure it's open. Fifty of its near 3,000 sumptuous salons are accessible to the public. If you come at midday on the first Wednesday of the month (excluding July and Aug), you'll catch the colorful changing of the guard. See p. 178 and chapter 8, "Walking Tour 1."

10 Almudena Catedral

Built over an unbelievably protracted period of 110 years—during which time its originally projected Gothic style eventually gave way to one of neoclassicism—this bright, but rather vacuous, 20th-century creation pales in comparison with the 11th-century mosque that long preceded it. It's worth a look for its 16th-century image of the Virgin of the Almudena in the crypt, the polychrome funeral casket of San Isidro, and the controversial abstract stained-glass windows, which provide some welcome color. See p. 176.

11 Parque de las Vistillas

Located at the southern end of the Puente de Segovia viaduct, close to the secretive Capilla del Cristo de los Dolores, this tiny area of parkland offers some of the best views in the city. Below you lies the green expanse of the Casa de Campo, while over to the northeast, you can see the distant purple-grey range of the Guadarrama Mountains, snow-capped in winter. During the San Isidro and Virgen de la Paloma fiestas, lively *verbenas* (fairs) held here fill the night air with music.

12 Campo del Moro

Though the name has 11th-century Moorish connotations (when the city was under siege), the charming Campo del Moro is in fact laid out like a rather lush English park. Designed in 1844 and first opened in 1931, it was closed during the Franco Era and finally reopened to the public in 1983. Today you can stroll at leisure among the flower beds, lawns, and fountains and enjoy the marvelous view of the Palacio Real towering above. See p. 191

13 Ermita de San Antonio de la Florida (Panteón de Goya)

Halfway along the Paseo de la Florida, which runs parallel to the Manzanares River, you'll find this delightful domed hermitage—the right-hand one of an identical couple. Some of Goya's most evocative frescoes (beautifully restored in 1996) depict the Miracles of Saint Anthony on the interior of the cupola. The artist himself is buried in front of the altar. See p. 187.

14 Casa Mingo

A great place for sampling cider—still or fizzy—and stuff cooked in it like delicious, calorie-loaded chorizo, Casa Mingo ★★, Paseo de la Florida 34 (© 91-547-79-18; www.casamingo.es), is a mere stone's throw from the Ermita de San Antonio de la Florida. This used to be a popular student hangout, and though it's not so cheap these days and sees a lot more tourists than students, it's still great fun—either inside under the rafters and beside the barrels or outside on the roof on hot summer evenings. See p. 166.

THE BEST OF MADRID IN 3 DAYS

One of the best and most surprising things about Madrid is how quickly one can move from narrow alleys and the medieval urban core to green wooded parklands. After spending your first 2 days as outlined above, use your third day to explore the dichotomies of Madrid: from the ultramodern Reina Sofía, to medieval Lavapiés. **Start:** Metro: Atocha. Bus: 9, 10.

---

1 Reina Sofía

Completing Madrid's top trio of art museums is this veritable mecca of modernity. Whether or not you go for the hyperfunctional look of the place outside—an uncompromising blend of concrete, glass, and steel—there's no doubt the Dalís and Tàpies inside are worth anyone's time. If you only see one thing, though, it has to be Picasso's groundbreaking *Guernica*, once considered so inflammatory a work it needed half a dozen guards close by to ensure no one tried to vandalize it. Now there's one guard around at the most. See p. 174.

2 Plaza del Cascorro/Rastro

This small square is at the top of Ribera de Curtidores, where the Sunday **Rastro,** or flea market, is held. (If your visit is actually on a Sun, you might want to switch the Reina Sofía for a bargain-hunting visit here; see p. 227.) The small but stirring monument at its center is in honor of Eloy Gonzalo, a young soldier who died on a suicide mission to Cuba while defending Spain's last Latin American possession in 1898. Saying *hola* to Eloy as you enter the square is said to bring you good luck.

3 Plaza de Lavapiés ★★

Steep narrow lanes—many of them pedestrian only—converge on this dusty triangular plaza, once the heart of a medieval Jewish stronghold. In just the past decade, its traditional Castizo atmosphere has been replaced by a bohemian multiethnic scene, with Senegalese, Chinese, Moroccans, Turks, and Indians bumping into you as you explore the district's eclectic array of shops, cafes, and eating spots.

Be sure to check out the new Valle-Inclan theater. Borderline seedy, the square positively bustles with life. See chapter 8, "Walking Tour 2."

4 Café Barbieri

The run-down, high-ceilinged Café Barbieri, Calle Ave María 45 (© 91-527-36-58), just off the square, has an intriguing bohemian ambience that goes with the territory. A cavernous, moodily lit spot where you can enjoy a reflective coffee or something stronger in the stimulating midst of the Lavapiés melting pot, it also offers a nice range of teas.

5 Antón Martín Market

A short puff uphill from Calle Ave María brings you to Plaza Antón Martín, where you can browse around one of Madrid's most typical old two-story markets. Stalls here sell a colorful selection of food from all over Spain as well as from tropical regions. Throbbing with life and color, it's the antithesis of the bland supermarket. Be sure to check out the good herbs and olive oil section. There's also a friendly little alcove cafe where you can hear youngsters banging out their steps on the floor of the flamenco dance school overhead as you sip your coffee. See p. 229.

6 Filmoteca Cine Doré

Situated next to the market, Madrid's most enchanting cinema has an Art Deco exterior and traditional interior. The place itself looks like it's from a scene in an Almodóvar flick and shows the most eclectic range of films in town. It also has a cafe and small bookshop stacked with esoteric books on the world of movies and, in summer, runs open-air shows on the roof. Up to five different films a day are shown in two separate salons in their original language, and the entrance fee of 2.50€ is a bargain. See p. 239

7 Plaza Tirso de Molina

Built on the site of a former convent and originally known as the Plaza del Progreso, this square at the northern end of Lavapiés was renamed after the great Golden Age playwright in 1941. Formerly an attractive if slightly seedy

19th-century plaza, it's now an extended semipedestrian zone with children's play areas and intermittent flower beds set amid the original trees. Tirso (or Fray [Friar] Gabriel Téllez, to give him his real name) will be pleased to note that the Zola-esque denizens who used to hang around his statue have been largely replaced by young students and pram pushing families.

8 La Corrala ★★

During the 19th century, many of Madrid's working-class population lived in tenements like these. With their characteristic patios and open balconies, they symbolized a basic communal lifestyle that made few concessions to individual privacy. In today's (comparatively) less-sociable world, most of them have disappeared and the few that still remain have subsequently achieved near-museum status. This one in Calle Meson de Paredes is the best preserved, though you can only view it from outside. See chapter 8, "Walking Tour 2."

9 Casa Lastra Sidrería

For good Asturian fare, go to Casa Lastra Sidrería, Calle Olivar 3 (✆ 91-369-08-37; www.casalastra.com). The tab can be expensive, so the fixed-menu lunch is the best value, especially if it includes *merluza* (hake). Go easy on the heady house cider if you want to do the rest of the day justice. **See p. 139.**

Take the metro to Argüelles:

10 Templo de Debod

Of all Madrid's fascinating sights, none is more incongruous than the Egyptian Temple of Debod, poised high on the edge of Parque del Oeste on the site of the former Montaña barracks and enjoying great views. The temple and two of its original three gateways were transported from their Nile-side habitat in 1968 in thanks for Spain's help with the Aswan Dam. Inside the temple are depictions of a Theban god with a ram's head symbolizing fertility. This is one of the city's major freebie attractions. See p. 184.

11 Teleférico de Madrid

For the best aerial view of the southern side of Madrid, take this 2.5km (1½-mile) cable car ride across the Manzanares River and Parque del Oeste into the Casa de Campo. An upbeat, rather dated, commentary in Spanish extols the beauties of the Palacio Real and Ermita de San Antonio de la Florida (or Panteon de Goya) as they float below. The departure point is in the middle of the splendid Paseo de Pintor Rosales, whose fortunate apartment owners not only enjoy the unrivaled vistas but also relax in the best array of terrace cafes you'll find in the city. See p. 195.

12 Casa de Campo

Thanks to this immense area of pines and shrubs (nearly 1,820 hectares/4,500 acres in all), Madrid claims to have more green zones than any other European capital. In olden days, kings hunted wild boar here. Today new predators, in the form of prostitutes, parade on the westerly fringe roads, but the green expanse's central trails and footpaths are quite free from such salacious influences and ideal for family picnics and strolls. See p. 191.

13 Lago

Surprisingly little-known, this circular lake with its high gushing central fountain in the southeast corner of the Casa de Campo is the ideal spot for a relaxing rowboat outing, while around the edge, an enticing choice of alfresco eating spots beckons, looking like *tavernas* on some Greek island. Here you can enjoy superb views of the city skyline, dominated by the classic outline of the Palacio Real. See p. 191.

14 Choose a *Taverna*

Enjoy an evening drink in one of the open-air spots beside the lake, such as the Restaurante Urogallo (✆ 91-526-23-69; www.elurogallo.net). In winter, return to Austrias.

WHERE TO STAY

Madrid's hotel capacity has mushroomed from virtually nothing to around 80,000 in little more than a century. The boom started modestly at the very end of the 1800s with the building of three hostelries: the Paris in Puerta del Sol, the Embajadores in Calle Victoria, and the Madrid in the Calle Mayor. (Before then—amazingly for a European capital—visitors could choose only from a motley selection of very basic rooms in coaching inns and boarding houses.)

But 1906, when King Alfonso XIII married Victoria Eugenia de Battenberg, marked the real turning point. The wedding kicked off a renaissance of top hostelries, starting with the building of the city's first world-class hotel, the Hotel Ritz Madrid in 1910. A gradual revision and expansion of the capital's lesser hostelries followed.

5

Today, Madrid's hotels, thanks to increasingly strict laws and well-planned renovations, include some of the finest in the world, ranging from *grand luxe* bedchambers fit for a prince to bunker-style beds in the hundreds of neighborhood *hostales* and *pensiones* (low-cost boardinghouses). In inexpensive hotels, by the way, be warned that you'll have to carry your bags to and from your room. Don't expect bellboys or doormen to be around to do it for you.

A large number of my recommendations are modern (at least inside), with an increased emphasis on innovative and creative character rather than the bland mass corporate style of many late-20th-century creations.

Best of the new arrivals (both first opened their doors in 2009) are the gleaming steel and glass **Eurostars Madrid Tower** (p. 111)—now the capital's tallest hotel—and the ultrachic **Selenza** (p. 105), which nestles in an art-gallery-filled street in the elegant confines of the Salamanca district.

Smoking footnote: All hotels may soon be required to have at least 70% non-smoking rooms. A parliamentary decision on private and public area smoking—proposing that Spain adheres to the tougher laws of most other European countries—is due in January 2011. The signs are that it will go ahead—in spite of inevitable protests by the hard-line 33% of the population who smoke full-time—and even the hoteliers themselves who fear losing money (see the "Smoking" section in the Fast Fasts section of chapter 12).

CHOOSING A HOTEL

The largest concentrations of hotels can be found around **Atocha Railway Station** and the **Gran Vía,** and though bargain seekers will find great pickings there, I downplay these two popular, but noisy, districts in my search for the most outstanding places to stay. The central areas near **Puerta del Sol** and **Plaza Mayor,** which provide a comprehensive cross-section of accommodations, also tend to be on the boisterous side, as you would expect in such busy central locations. However, you can't get more central and you won't find a wider variety of day and night amenities right on your doorstep. It's also not far to stumble home to after raiding the department stores or painting the town red!

The smart **Plaza de las Cortes,** just above the **Paseo del Prado,** offers select and slightly quieter hotels, as does the **Argüelles** area just west of the **Plaza España.** A number of newer hotels sit away from the center, especially on the streets just off the **Paseo de la Castellana**—a particularly popular choice for business travelers, thanks to the proximity of the AZCA center's international offices and easy metro access to Barajas airport (15 min.) from expanded and modernized **Nuevos Ministerios** station.

The cosmopolitan **Chamberí** and **Salamanca** districts, above the Malasaña district and Parque del Retiro, respectively, offer some of the most exclusive hotels in the city, while the residential zone of **Chamartín,** home of Madrid's other main railway station and great hub of Plaza Castilla, features a variety of leisure- and business-oriented hotels, within a 15-minute metro ride of Puerta del Sol.

Madrid also has a small number of apartotels. These combine the best of hotel and apartment facilities, designed for more self-sufficient visitors looking for the freedom to cook. Units come equipped with basic kitchen facilities and maid service is usually provided. The hotels typically have a restaurant on-site. The minimum stay is a week, though if time is no object, monthly or even longer stays are available. **Puerta del Sol, Chamberí,** and **Argüelles** (in Plaza España) all offer apartotel accommodations.

Booking a Room

TRAVELERS WITH DISABILITIES In recent years, newer hotels have taken more care to cater to travelers with disabilities by incorporating ramps, installing wider elevators, and even adapting certain rooms (mainly in higher category hotels). Check with the hotel in advance about specific needs and facilities available. The **FAMMA Association,** Calle Galileo 69 (✆ **91-593-35-50;** www.famma.org; Spanish only) provides a useful guide to wheelchair accessibility in Madrid.

AMENITIES & EXTRAS *Note:* In the hotel amenity details, mention of private bathrooms is made *only* if all the rooms in the hotel in question do *not* come with a bathroom. In some hotel bathrooms in Madrid, you may encounter a European phenomenon known as a **hip bath.** This bathtub is about half the length of a standard tub, large enough to sit in but not long enough to lie in. Think of it as a half-size or sit-down tub. In the reviews that follow, I note those hotels containing bathrooms with hip baths. **Breakfast** is not included in the quoted rates unless specified. A 7% government **room tax** is added to all rates. If you require a **nonsmoking room,** be sure to ask when you make your reservation. Not all hotels have them.

IF YOU HAVE AN EARLY flight

Unless it's absolutely necessary for you to stay at the bland outer suburb of Barajas where the airport is located, it's worth making the journey into Madrid. But if you find that, for business or other reasons, you have to stay there, one of the best options is **Meliá Barajas,** Av. de Logroño 35, 28042 (© **91-747-77-00;** www.solmelia.com), a government-rated four-star hotel standing in spacious grounds. With a classic modern decor, it is comfortable and inviting, offering midsize to spacious units, costing 140€ for a double or 360€ for a suite. The 270-unit, three-floor hotel also has a restaurant, bar, pool, room service, and babysitting. Each air-conditioned room comes with TV, hair dryer, minibar, and safe.

Another member of the Tryp chain, the 80-unit **Tryp Alameda Aeropuerto,** Av. de Logroño 100, 28042 (© **91-747-48-00;** fax 91-747-89-28; www.solmelia.com; AE, DC, MC, V; Metro: Barajas; bus: 115), is a case of two peas in a pod. When one hotel overflows, the other fills in the gap. Rooms are fairly bland, but comfortable, each with a tub/shower combo. The only difference is that this hotel has a small gym. On-site are a restaurant and bar, and amenities include pool, sauna, room service, babysitting, and laundry. In the room are air-conditioning, TV, hair dryer, minibar, and safe. Rates range from 165€ to 250€ for a double, and 350€ for a suite. Both chain members have free 24-hour shuttle service to the airport.

A final possibility is **Hotel Best Western Villa de Barajas,** Av. de Logroño 331, 28042 (© **91-329-28-18;** www.hotelvilladebarajas.com), a government-rated three-star member of the Best Western chain. Simpler than the two choices above, it charges only 120€ for a double room. Each midsize unit comes with a TV and phone as well as air-conditioning, and on-site are a restaurant and bar. It also offers free shuttle service to the airport.

GOVERNMENT RATINGS Spain officially rates its hotels by one to five stars. Five stars is the highest rating in Spain, signaling a deluxe establishment complete with all the amenities and the high tariffs associated with such accommodations. Top of the range come *gran lujo* (deluxe) hotels such as the **Ritz** and **Hesperia,** while standard five-star residences are beaten by the likes of **Westin Palace** and **Orfila.** Most of the establishments recommended in this guide tend to be three- and four-star hotels, as epitomized by solid midrange recommendations like the **Claridge.** Hotels granted one and two stars—like the **Santander** and **Persal**—are less comfortable, with limited plumbing and other physical facilities, although they may be perfectly clean and decent places. Similarly endowed *pensiones* (guesthouses), like the **Armesto** and **Riesco,** land at the bottom of the range aimed at dedicated budget travelers.

FROMMER'S STAR RATING SYSTEM These ratings reflect my personal evaluation of a hotel, based on a variety of overall factors ranging from atmosphere and character to facilities and standard of service. Those in the Very Expensive and Expensive categories are on a scale of one (highly recommended) to three stars (exceptional). Those in the Moderate and Inexpensive categories rate from zero (recommended) to two stars (very highly recommended). If, after a stay in one of the hotels listed in this guide, you have any views on the level of recommendation—or lack of it—please let me know.

RESERVATIONS Most hotels require at least a day's deposit before they will reserve a room for you. Preferably, this can be accomplished with an international money order or, if agreed to in advance, with a personal check or credit card number. You can usually cancel a room reservation 1 week ahead of time and get a full refund. A few hotel keepers will return your money up to 3 days before the reservation date, but some will take your deposit and never return it, even if you cancel far in advance. Many budget hotel owners operate on such a narrow margin of profit that they find just buying stamps for airmail replies too expensive by their standards. Therefore, it's important that you enclose a prepaid International Reply Coupon with your payment, especially if you're writing to a budget hotel. Better yet, call and speak directly to the hotel of your choice or send a fax.

If you arrive without a reservation, begin your search for a room as early in the day as possible. If you arrive late at night, you have to take what you can get, often for a much higher price than you'd like to pay.

BOOKING AGENCIES Check out **Madrid & Beyond** (✆ **91-758-00-63;** www.madridandbeyond.com), an Anglo-American travel company based in Madrid. Staffed by an enthusiastic, English-speaking team of U.K. and U.S. expats, they provide an in-depth knowledge of Spain, plus recommend and reserve quality hotels in Madrid and throughout the country (useful if you're thinking of doing some wider traveling). Their aim is to match each customer's taste and budget with a particular property, and arrange a variety of activities, including walking and cycling tours.

Travel agency **Viajes Aira** (✆ **91-305-42-24;** fax 91-305-84-19) takes hotel bookings at their Terminal 1 and 2 desks at Barajas airport's arrival area. They don't charge a booking fee and focus mainly on hotels in the moderate or midrange category (around 120€–180€ for a double). They're open 7am to midnight.

The privately run **Brújula** agency has booking desks at each of Madrid's two main railway stations (Atocha: ✆ **91-539-11-73;** Chamartín: ✆ **91-315-78-94**). They charge a booking fee of 3.50€ and cover every category of hotel, from inexpensive to five-star. They're open 7:15am to 9:30pm.

PARKING This is a serious problem. Few hotels have garages because many buildings turned into hotels were constructed before the invention of the automobile. Street parking is rarely available, and even if it is, you run the risk of having your car broken into. If you're driving into Madrid, most hotels (and most police) will allow you to park in front of the hotel long enough to unload your luggage. Someone on the staff can usually pinpoint the location of the nearest garage in the neighborhood, often giving you a map showing the way—be prepared to walk 2 or 3 blocks to your

House-Swapping

House-swapping is becoming a more popular and viable means of travel; you stay in their place, they stay in yours, and you both get an authentic and personal view of the area, the opposite of the escapist retreat that many hotels offer. Try **HomeLink International Home Exchange** (Homelink.org), the largest and oldest home-swapping organization, founded in 1952, with over 11,000 listings worldwide ($80 for a yearly membership). It has a number of apartments available for exchange in Madrid. You can also check the corresponding Spanish website **www.spainlink.net.**

car. Parking is noted in the hotel listings where it is available and with the corresponding neighborhood garage fees; where no parking information is listed, no parking is available.

best MADRID HOTEL BETS

- **Best Historic Hotel:** Inaugurated by Alfonso XIII in 1910, **Hotel Ritz Madrid** (© **800/225-5843** in the U.S., or 91-701-67-67), the gathering place of Madrid society, is still the capital's leading luxury choice. This Edwardian hotel is mellower than ever before, the old haughtiness of former management gone with the wind—it long ago rescinded its policy of not allowing movie stars as guests. ***Note:*** In summer, a tie is no longer obligatory and dress tends to be more informal (though the hotel still draws the line at shorts). The rich and famous continue to parade through its portals; today in the lobby you're likely to encounter nearly anyone, from the secretary-general of NATO to Paloma Picasso. See p. 104.
- **Best for Business Travelers:** The concierge at the **Park Hyatt Villa Magna** (© **800/223-1234** in the U.S., or 91-587-12-34) is one of the most skillful in Madrid, well versed in procuring virtually anything a traveler could conceivably need during a trip to the Spanish capital. One floor below lobby level, this five-star hotel's business center is well stocked, with access to translators, computers, scanners, fax machines, photocopiers, and even a well-informed technology concierge. There's a branch of Hertz car rental on the premises and enough stylish conference rooms (staffed with butlers and stocked with caviar, if the nature of your business meeting calls for it) to provide a place for any sales or executive meeting. See p. 105.
- **Best for a Romantic Getaway:** The **AC Santo Mauro** (© **91-319-69-00**) opened in 1991 in a villa designed by a French architect and built in 1894 for the duke of Santo Mauro. As a sign of the times, more recent visitors have included Julia Roberts and Richard Gere. The lavish property has an ageless grace, although it has been brought up to state-of-the-art condition. In good weather, guests retreat to a beautiful garden pavilion and enjoy many facilities such as a gym and indoor pool. It's resortlike in nature, although situated in Madrid. If you can afford it, go for one of the suites with a fireplace. See p. 109.
- **Best Hotel Lobby for Pretending You're Rich:** The **Westin Palace Hotel** (© **800/325-3535** in the U.S., 800/325-3589 in Canada, or 91-360-80-00), between the Paseo del Prado and Plaza de las Cortes, is a Victorian wedding cake of a place. To sit and people-watch in this lobby—the grandest Belle Epoque lobby in Madrid—is to be at the epicenter of Spanish political life. Head for the dazzling stained-glass cupola of the main rotunda lounge, and take in the fanciful ceiling frescoes and the custom-made carpets along the way. See p. 87.
- **Most Relaxing Hotel:** Located in a leafy residential backwater in the north of the city, **Residencia El Viso** (© **91-564-03-70**) is a distinctly rural hostelry, peaceful enough to be 100km (62 miles) out of town yet only 15 minutes from the lively center. See p. 113.
- **Best Service:** Madrid has grander hotels, but it's hard to find a staff as highly motivated, professional, and efficient as the one at the **InterContinental Madrid** (© **800/327-0200** in the U.S., or 91-310-02-00). Room service is offered around the clock, and the staff is adept at solving your Madrid-related problems. Nothing

seems to make them lose their cool, even when there's a long line at the desk. See p. 109.

- **Best Location: ME Madrid** (✆ **91-531-45-00**) is for those who want to be in the heart of Old Madrid, within easy walking distance of all those midtown Hemingway haunts. Dozens of the finest tapas bars are literally at your doorstep, and you can walk among the flower vendors, cigarette peddlers, and lottery-ticket hawkers, enjoying an atmosphere that's missing from the newer and more modern section of Madrid. See p. 87.
- **Best for Families:** The family-friendly, chain-run **Novotel Madrid Puente de la Paz** (✆ **800/221-4542** in the U.S., or 91-724-76-00), on the outskirts of town, is a good place for the entire clan. Rates are reasonable, and the bedrooms can easily be arranged to sleep children. There's also a pool, and the breakfast buffet is one of the most generous in Madrid. Children 15 and under stay free in their parent's rooms. See p. 114.
- **Best Budget Hotel:** In the very heart of Old Madrid, off the Plaza Mayor, **Hostal la Macarena** (✆ **91-365-92-21**), has been housing Frommer's readers comfortably and well—all for an affordable price—for decades. Surrounded by ancient buildings, the little inn is modest itself, but its welcome is warm, its staff is accommodating, and its price is right. See p. 101.
- **Best Views:** Located in Chamartín just above the gravity defying KIO buildings at the northern end of the wide Castellana, the 2009 built **Eurostars Madrid Tower** is the highest hotel in Madrid. Its rooms enjoy stunning vistas of not only the city, but also of the distant Guadarrama mountains. See p. 111.

NEAR THE PLAZA DE LAS CORTES

Very Expensive

Hotel Urban ★★★ Just a short walk up Carrera de San Jerónimo from the Spanish Parliament, the Urban is the imaginatively ambitious creation of Catalan businessman Jordí Clos. The reception and lobby areas are lined with statues from Papua New Guinea, while a several-story-high atrium with glass-walled elevators rises imposingly above one of the lounges. Other communal attractions include a small open-air swimming pool (June to mid-Sept) with an adjoining romantic rooftop "moonlit" dining room, **El Cielo** (p. 135), which combines with the elegant ground-floor Europa Deco restaurant to form as fashionable a duo of eating spots as you'll find in the entire city. Accommodation is of a similar sumptuously high standard, and the modern soundproofed rooms all feature rich leather and dark wood furnishings and have exquisite marble-layered bathrooms.

Carrera de San Jerónimo, 28014. ✆ **91-787-77-70.** Fax 91-787-77-99. www.derbyhotels.es. 96 units. 225€–350€ double; 330€–385€ junior suite; 585€ suite. AE, DC, MC, V. Parking 22€. Metro: Sevilla. **Amenities:** 2 restaurants; bar; outdoor pool; room service; laundry service; dry cleaning; nonsmoking rooms; rooms for those w/limited mobility. *In room:* A/C, TV, minibar, Wi-Fi.

Hotel Villa Real ★★★ Like the Urban, a member of the prestigious Derby hotel chain, this stylishly converted 19th-century mansion set beside a diminutive three-sided park directly faces the Spanish parliament *(Congreso de los Diputados)* between Puerta del Sol and Paseo del Prado. Its magnificent facade blends neoclassical and

Aztec motifs, while the mellow interior is dominated by a wealth of modern paintings and Roman mosaics—the latter being among the largest private collections in Spain. Each of the standard soundproofed accommodations offers a sunken salon with leather-upholstered furniture, and built-in furniture accented with burl-wood inlays. Although the rooms are immaculate but rather unimaginative in style, they're mostly large, with separate sitting areas and big, bright well-equipped bathrooms with tub/shower combos.

Plaza de las Cortes 10, 28014. © **91-420-37-67.** Fax 91-420-25-47. www.derbyhotels.es. 115 units. 200€-395€ double; 325€-475€ suite. AE, DC, MC, V. Parking 22€. Metro: Sevilla or Banco de España. **Amenities:** Restaurant; bar; babysitting; health club; room service. *In room:* A/C, TV, hair dryer, minibar.

Palacio del Retiro ★★★ This deluxe haven seriously challenges the city's other truly elegant hotels, including the sublime Ritz, for comfort, sophistication, and a touch of that old class. Tastefully converted and transformed from a grand 100-year-old Belle Epoque mansion (which resembles, as the name implies, a small palace), it stands just across the road from the verdant expanse of the Retiro, and most of its supremely comfortable and airy bedrooms enjoy splendid views of the classic park. Once the home of noble gentry, the hotel still exudes an aura of stylish grandeur, aided by a lavish decor that includes the original marble colonnades, Spanish ceramics, and Gallic stained-glass windows. (Its original aristocratic owners were known for their extravagant whims, as well as impeccable taste, and even are said to have used a private elevator to transport their private team of horses up to exercise on the roof, rather than in the busy park.)

Calle Alfonso XII, 28014. © **91-523-74-60.** Fax 91-523-74-61. www.slh.com. 50 units. 260€-405€ double; from 375€ suite. AE, DC, MC, V. Metro: Atocha or Banco de España. **Amenities:** Restaurant; bar; concierge; exercise room; room service; spa. *In room:* A/C, TV/DVD, CD player, minibar, Wi-Fi.

Westin Palace Hotel ★★★ Opened by no less a figure than King Alfonso XIII in 1912, the Palace is one of the largest, most ornate Victorian-style hotels in the city, with politicians, artists, and celebrities among its distinguished clientele. Widely regarded as the *gran dueña* (grande dame) of Spanish hotels and only slightly less prestigious than the nearby Ritz, its ground floor public area is dominated by a stunning atrium. The spaciously traditional rooms, most of which have been renovated, are all equipped with immaculate large bathrooms with tub/shower combos. Best and quietest accommodations are on the fourth, fifth, and sixth floors, but some side rooms tend to be noisy and lack views. The hotel faces the Paseo del Prado and Neptune Fountain and lies within easy walking distance of Plaza Santa Ana's lively blend of terrace cafes and some of Madrid's best antiques shops.

Plaza de las Cortes 7, 28014. © **800/325-3535** in the U.S., 800/325-3589 in Canada, or 91-360-80-00. Fax 91-360-81-00. www.westinpalacemadrid.com. 465 units. 425€ double; from 520€ suite. AE, DC, MC, V. Parking 22€. Metro: Banco de España. **Amenities:** 2 restaurants; bar; lounge; babysitting; gym; room service; sauna. *In room:* A/C, TV, hair dryer, minibar.

HUERTAS

Expensive

ME Madrid Reina Victoria ★ Built in 1923, this hotel has a government-protected ornate stone facade, though the hotel itself has changed hands several times—metamorphosing from visiting bullfighters' favorite, the Palacio de los Condes de

Where to Stay in Central Madrid

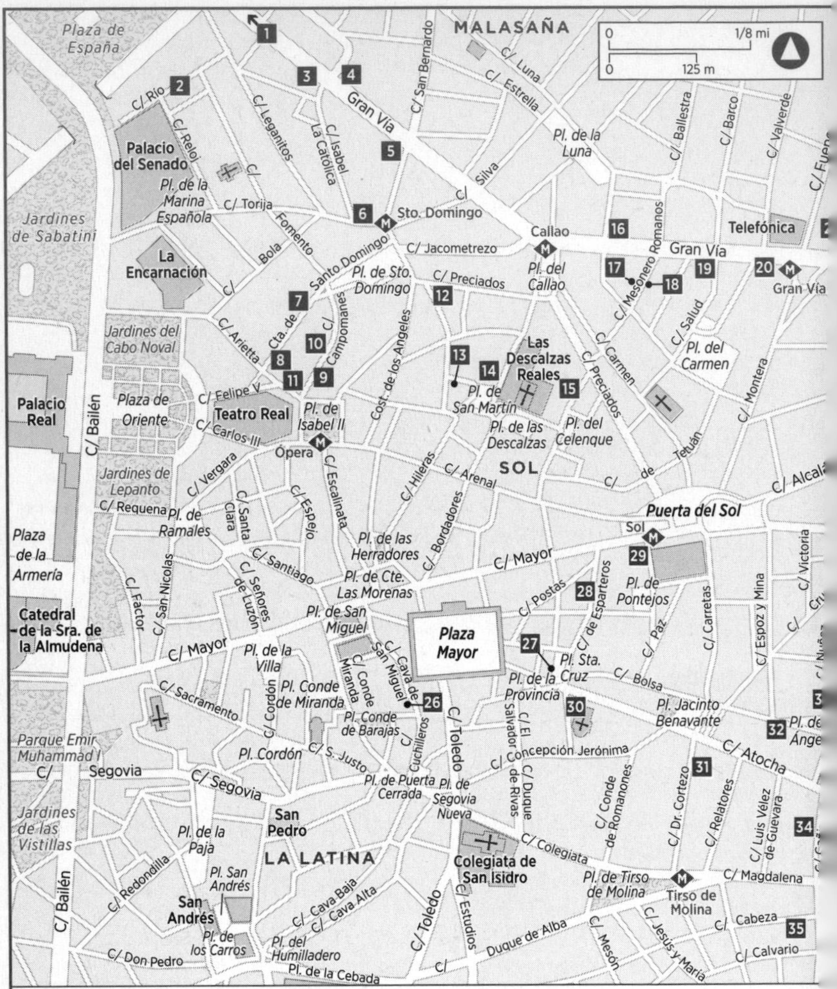

Adler Hotel **56**
Apartmentos Turistico Príncipe 11 **40**
Best Western Hotel Atlántico **16**
Best Western Hotel Carlos V **15**
Casa de Madrid **11**
Casón del Tormes **2**
Cat's Hostel **34**
Eurostars Madrid Tower **53**
Gran Hotel Velázquez **56**
High Tech Avenida **18**
Hostal Alcazar Regis **3**
Hostal Armesto **49**
Hostal Astoria **39**
Hostal Cervantes **51**
Hostal Lisboa **46**
Hostal La Macarena **26**
Hostal La Perla Asturiana **27**
Hostal Madrid **28**
Hostal Oporto **47**
Hostal Persal **32**
Hostal Residencia Don Diego **56**
Hostal Riesco **29**
Hotel Arosa **19**
Hotel Best Western Premier Santo Domingo **6**
Hotel Catalonia Las Cortes **44**
Hotel Emperador **5**
Hotel A. Gaudí **25**
Hotel Hospes **57**
Hotel Inglés **41**
Hotel Intur Palacio San Martín **14**
Hotel de las Letras **24**
Hotel Mediodía **63**
Hotel Meninas **10**
Hotel Mora **60**
Hotel Opera **8**

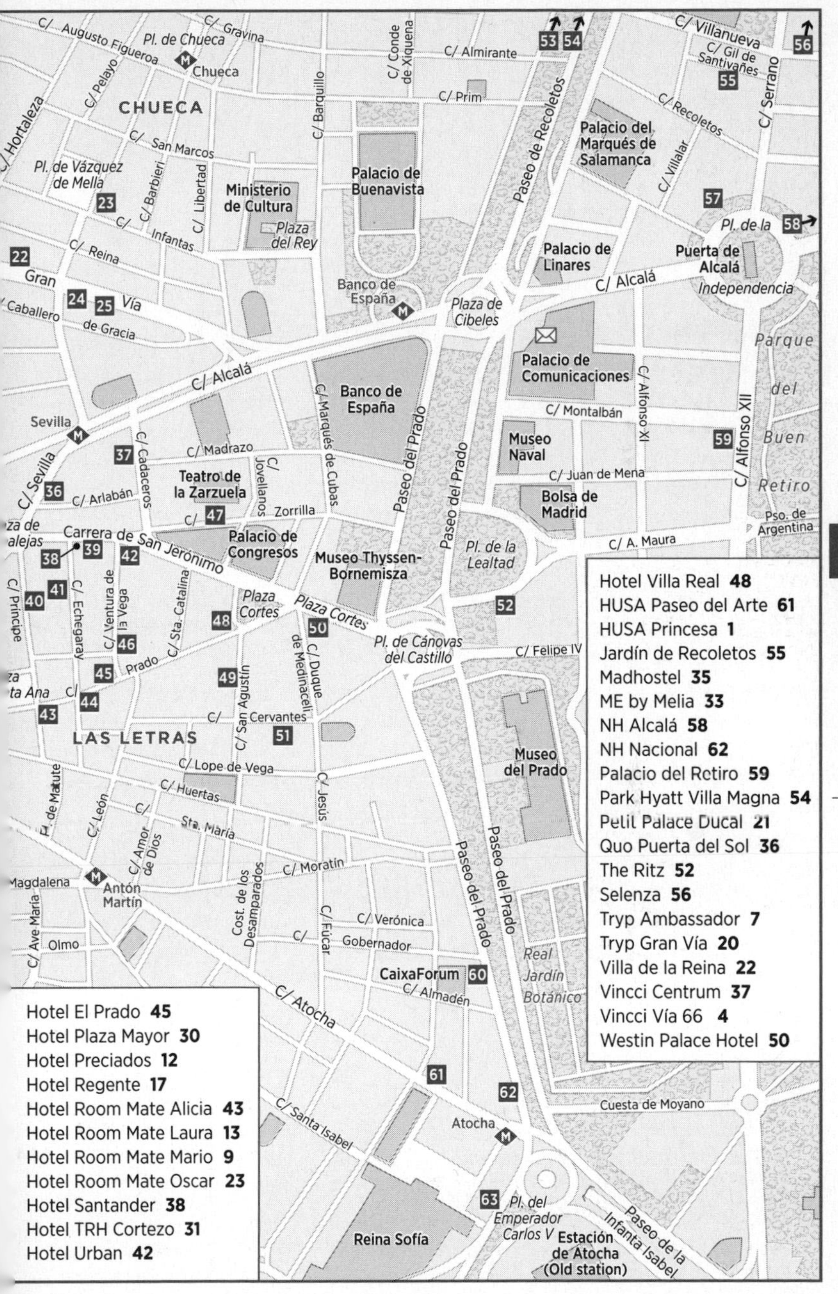

C/ Augusto Figueroa
Pl. de Chueca
C/ Gravina
Chueca
C/ Pelayo
CHUECA
C/ Hortaleza
C/ San Marcos
Pl. de Vázquez de Mella
23
C/ Barbieri
C/ Libertad
Ministerio de Cultura
Plaza del Rey
C/ Infantas
C/ Reina
22
Gran Vía
24
25
C/ Caballero de Gracia
C/ Barquillo
C/ Conde de Xiquena
C/ Almirante
C/ Prim
Palacio de Buenavista
Banco de España
Plaza de Cibeles
Paseo de Recoletos
53
54
C/ Villanueva
C/ Gil de Santivañes
55
56
C/ Serrano
C/ Recoletos
Palacio del Marqués de Salamanca
C/ Villalar
57
Pl. de la Independencia
58
Puerta de Alcalá
Palacio de Linares
C/ Alcalá
Parque del Buen Retiro
Palacio de Comunicaciones
C/ Alfonso XI
C/ Alfonso XII
C/ Montalbán
59
Museo Naval
C/ Juan de Mena
Bolsa de Madrid
Pso. de Argentina
C/ A. Maura
Banco de España
C/ Marqués de Cubas
Paseo del Prado
Sevilla
C/ Madrazo
37
C/ Cadaceros
C/ Sevilla
36
C/ Arlabán
Teatro de la Zarzuela
C/ Jovellanos
C/ Zorrilla
47
Palacio de Congresos
Museo Thyssen-Bornemisza
Pl. de la Lealtad
Carrera de San Jerónimo
38
39
42
41
40
C/ Príncipe
C/ Echegaray
C/ Ventura de la Vega
C/ Sta. Catalina
Plaza Cortes
48
50
52
C/ de Medinaceli
C/ Duque
Pl. de Cánovas del Castillo
C/ Felipe IV
46
45
C/ Prado
44
43
49
C/ San Agustín
C/ Cervantes
51
LAS LETRAS
C/ Lope de Vega
C/ Huertas
C/ Jesús
Museo del Prado
Pl. de Matute
C/ León
C/ Sta. María
C/ Amor de Dios
C/ Moratín
Magdalena
Antón Martín
Cost. de los Desamparados
C/ Verónica
C/ Gobernador
C/ Fúcar
C/ Ave María
Olmo
CaixaForum
60
C/ Almadén
Real Jardín Botánico
C/ Atocha
61
62
Cuesta de Moyano
C/ Santa Isabel
Atocha
63
Pl. del Emperador Carlos V
Reina Sofía
Estación de Atocha (Old station)
Paseo de la Infanta Isabel
Hotel El Prado 45
Hotel Plaza Mayor 30
Hotel Preciados 12
Hotel Regente 17
Hotel Room Mate Alicia 43
Hotel Room Mate Laura 13
Hotel Room Mate Mario 9
Hotel Room Mate Oscar 23
Hotel Santander 38
Hotel TRH Cortezo 31
Hotel Urban 42
Hotel Villa Real 48
HUSA Paseo del Arte 61
HUSA Princesa 1
Jardín de Recoletos 55
Madhostel 35
ME by Melia 33
NH Alcalá 58
NH Nacional 62
Palacio del Retiro 59
Park Hyatt Villa Magna 54
Petit Palace Ducal 21
Quo Puerta del Sol 36
The Ritz 52
Selenza 56
Tryp Ambassador 7
Tryp Gran Vía 20
Villa de la Reina 22
Vincci Centrum 37
Vincci Vía 66 4
Westin Palace Hotel 50

Teba, and the rather staid Tryp Reina Victoria, into today's state-of-the-art high-tech ME (Meliá España). The prestigious Meliá hotel company has equipped the hotel with all the latest communications facilities, from high-speed Internet to video conference rooms, while the luxuriously modern accommodations encompass standard doubles, self-contained studios, and top-quality suites. Some individual units are interconnected, allowing the hotel to combine two units into one, and the pristine en suite bathrooms all have hydromassage showers. The hotel stands beside one of the liveliest cafe-filled squares in Madrid, so you don't have to go too far to enjoy yourself at night.

Plaza Santa Ana 14, 28012. ✆ **91-701-60-00.** Fax 91-522-03-07. www.solmelia.com. 191 units. 260€ double; 395€ studio; 460€–750€ suite. AE, DC, MC, V. Metro: Tirso de Molina or Sol. **Amenities:** Restaurant; bar; babysitting; health club; room service. *In room:* A/C, TV/DVD, hair dryer, minibar, MP3 docking station, free Wi-Fi.

Moderate

Hostal Persal ★ This upmarket 1870s *hostal* was first built as a town house on the edge of the Old City before being totally refurbished at the beginning of the millennium to cater to jet-age clientele. Situated in an attractive square between Plaza Santa Ana and Plaza Mayor, the *hostal* is just a short stroll from central shops, bars, and restaurants. Cultural highlights, such as the Prado Museum, are a 10-minute walk away. The bargain-priced accommodations range from standard, compact, brightly but simply furnished doubles to larger family-size rooms accommodating up to four. The spare downstairs cafeteria is noted for its generous breakfast portions.

Plaza del Angel 12, 28012. ✆ **91-369-46-43.** Fax 91-369-19-52. www.hostalpersal.com. 80 units. 95€ double; 130€ triple; 150€ quad. AE, DC, MC, V. Metro: Sol or Tirso de Molina. **Amenities:** Cafe; concierge. *In room:* AC, satellite TV.

Hotel Catalonia Las Cortes ★ This Madrid member of the prestigious Hoteles Catalonia chain occupies a renovated 18th-century house halfway between Plaza de las Cortes and lively Plaza Santa Ana in a former bohemian zone known as the Barrio de las Letras. All rooms combine modern accessories, such as plasma TVs, with tastefully classical furnishings and decor—two rooms still feature colorful ceiling frescoes preserved from the original building—and immaculate en suite marble-topped bathrooms. The small restaurant provides a generous buffet breakfast. The staff is particularly friendly and helpful and will gladly point you in the direction of nearby top museums, including El Prado, as well as a host of local dinner spots.

Calle de Prado 6, 28014. ✆ **91-389-60-51.** Fax 91-389-60-52. www.hoteles-catalonia.com. 65 units. 140€ double. AE, DC, MC, V. Metro: Sol or Tirso de Molina. **Amenities:** Restaurant (breakfast only). *In room:* A/C, satellite TV.

Hotel Plaza Mayor ★ Located in the very heart of Madrid's historic Austrias district, close to the city's most famous square, this charming little hotel was converted from a historic church, the Iglesia de la Santa Cruz, which had fallen for many decades into decay and abandon. The surprisingly spacious bedrooms are well maintained and furnished in a contemporary style, with a marble-clad bathroom furnished with a shower or tub/shower combo. For the quality of comfort offered, the rates here are among the most affordable in Old Town. Best choice of all here, if your budget permits, is the luxurious Suite del Palomar.

Calle Atocha 2, 28012. ✆ **91-360-06-06.** Fax 91-360-06-10. www.h-plazamayor.com. 31 units. 85€–120€ double; 140€ triple. AE, DC, MC, V. Parking 18€. Metro: La Latina. **Amenities:** Coffee shop; reading and TV lounge; Internet access. *In room:* A/C, TV, hair dryer.

Hotel TRH Cortezo Tucked away in a short street between Calle de Atocha and Tirso de Molina square, with its many cafes and eating spots, the Cortezo is just a 5-minute walk from Plaza Mayor and Puerta del Sol. Rooms here all have comfortable beds and contemporary furnishings, and larger units boast an additional small lounge area with chairs and a desk. All have en suite bathrooms with tub/shower combos. The bright communal facilities include a cocktail bar and well-appointed restaurant, and just across the road is one of the best multiplexes (the Ideal Yelmo) in Madrid.

Dr. Cortezo 3, 28012. ✆ **91-369-01-01.** Fax 91-369-37-74. www.trhhotelcortezo.com. 85 units. 80€–135€ double; 185€–190€ suite. AE, DC, MC, V. Parking 22€. Metro: Tirso de Molina. **Amenities:** Restaurant; bar; babysitting; room service. *In room:* A/C, TV, hair dryer, minibar.

Room Mate Alicia ★ The compact, friendly, and very modern Alicia is the work of prestigious interior designer López Otero, who—with imagination and flair—has converted a formerly dour 20th-century industrial building into one of colorful Huertas's most stylish little hotels. An early Madrid member of the chic Room Mate chain, this location boasts sunlit rooms with cool minimalist decor and furnishings, plus fine views of the adjoining, ever-lively Plaza Santa Ana through large high windows. Accommodations range from doubles and suites to duplexes with their own small private pool. The hotel closes in August.

Calle de Prado 2, 28014. ✆ **91-389-60-95.** Fax 91-369-47-95. www.room-matehoteles.com. 34 units. From 120€ double; from 175€ suite; from 225€ duplex. AE, DC, MC, V. Metro: Sol or Tirso de Molina. **Amenities:** Lounge. *In room:* A/C, flatscreen TV, free Wi-Fi.

Inexpensive

Cat's Hostel This irrepressibly extraverted youth hostel, set in a converted 18th-century mansion, is extremely spacious, and the richly colored tiles and attractive archways of the ground floor lounge and adjoining patio—complete with gushing fountain—are evocatively Moorish in style. Most of the predominantly young visitors, however, are generally less interested in the decor than in taking advantage of the endless round-the-clock bars and nightspots within a stone's throw (including the famous Casa Patas flamenco hall on the same street; p. 240), not to mention the impromptu celebrations regularly held in the lounge. Reception is always open, perhaps in homage to the hostel's feline pedigree—cats don't sleep at night, so why should the desk staff? Rooms range from functional private doubles to basic, but adequate, dormitories accommodating up to 14. The cozy basement cave/bar is great for a chat over low-cost drinks.

Calle Cañizares 6, 28012. ✆ **91-369-28-07.** Fax: 91-429-94-79. www.catshostel.com. Units for 2 22€ per person; dorms for up to 14 persons 20€ per person, all with shared bathrooms. Rates include breakfast. Metro: Antón Martín. **Amenities:** Cave/bar; visiting DJs; satellite TV; free Internet; kitchen for guests' use; free left-luggage facilities; special surprise fiestas.

Chic & Basic Colors ★ Located on the second floor of a renovated old building (no elevator) in the very heart of Huertas and just a short walk from lively Plaza Santa Ana, this tiny chic hotel is an excellent budget value. All of its compact single and double bedrooms have different designs and are decorated in individual bright hues covering the spectrum of the rainbow. They also have comfortable modern furnishings and a small adjoining bathroom with shower. Communal areas include a lounge and cafe where you can informally meet other guests, use the (free) Internet connection, and relax over a *café con leche* or beer. Self-service breakfasts are included in the rates. The friendly staff makes both gay and hetero visitors equally welcome.

Calle Huertas 14-2°-izda., 28012. © **91-429-69-35.** Fax 91-429-69-35. www.chicandbasic.com. 10 units. 75€ single; 80€–100€ double. Rates include breakfast. MC, V. Metro: Tirso de Molina. **Amenities:** Cafeteria. *In room:* A/C, TV.

Hostal Armesto Tucked away in a side road a short walk from the Paseo del Prado on the edge of bar-filled Huertas, this unpretentious little *hostal,* run by a friendly and helpful couple, occupies the first floor of an atmospheric old building. The excellent-value rooms are neat and clean and each has its own private shower. Ask for a rear-view room that looks over the charming private garden of the adjoining San Agustín Palace for a tranquil insight into a secluded Madrid of yesteryear.

Calle San Agustín 6-1°, 28014. © **91-429-90-31.** 6 units. 60€ double. MC, V. Metro: Antón Martín. **Amenities:** Room service. *In room:* Fan, TV.

Hostal Astoria ★ Situated on the fifth floor of a 19th-century building, this unpretentious and highly affordable *hostal* is famed for its welcoming atmosphere and friendly staff. Situated between the El Prado and Thyssen museums and the countless bars and eating spots of lively Huertas, the Astoria is an excellent base for enjoying a wide choice of central attractions. The modestly comfortable rooms are bright and simply furnished, and complete with air-conditioning and adjoining bathrooms. Rooms facing the busy Carrera San Jerónimo tend to get noisy, so ask for one at the back if you want to enjoy some peace and quiet.

Carrera de San Jerónimo 30-32-5°, 28014. © **91-429-11-88.** Fax 91-429-20-23. www.hostal-astoria.com. 26 units. 75€–90€ double. MC, V. Metro: Sevilla. *In room:* TV, hair dryer, radio.

Hostal Cervantes One of Madrid's most genial family-run hotels, the Cervantes has long been a favorite with Frommer's readers and holidaymakers. Located on the immaculately maintained second floor of a stone-and-brick building, the *hostal* is accessible by stairway or a compact birdcage-style elevator. All rooms are equipped with comfortable bed, spartan furniture, and a tiny bathroom with a tub/shower combo. Though no breakfast is served, plenty of bars and cafes are virtually on your doorstep. You're also in easy walking distance of lively Plaza Santa Ana and the Prado Museum.

Cervantes 34, 28014. © **91-429-83-65.** Fax 91-429-27-45. 14 units. 60€ double. MC, V. Metro: Antón Martín. **Amenities:** Lounge. *In room:* TV.

Hostal Oporto ★ Tucked away in a narrow road behind the Thyssen Museum, this clean, immaculately kept *hostal,* with its rather bare and simple decor, is a real find for the budget traveler. You not only get a decent, comfortable bedroom with a private bathroom with shower, but also a warm welcome from the highly accommodating staff. Wintertime central heating is included, and there's a ceiling fan to keep the heat at bay during the short but torrid summers. Some larger rooms can accommodate three extra people, making them an ideal choice for families or groups of young people.

Calle Zorrilla 9, 28014. ©/fax **91-429-78-56.** www.hostaloporto.com. 12 units. 55€ double; 75€ triple. MC, V. Metro: Sevilla. *In room:* TV.

LAVAPIÉS

Inexpensive

Madhostel The "mad" here really does mean "like crazy" and is not just an abbreviation of Madrid. It's a 21st-century version of the standard youth hostel format, enjoying a permanent party atmosphere and an ideal choice for younger travelers looking for a fun stay in the city. Located in a spacious 19th-century Lavapiés *corrala*—a traditional building with communal terraces overlooking a central patio, complete with unexpected Mary Poppins–style rooftop views of old Madrid—Madhostel provides basic, but sociable, rooms—accommodating up to six persons—with or without a private bathroom, and of mixed or single genders. The chummy insomniac staff makes sure you feel at home whatever the hour.

Calle Cabeza 24, 28012. ✆ **91-506-48-40.** Fax: 91-506-48-41. www.madhostel.com. 35 shared units. Rooms for 4–6. Room with private bathroom 24€ per person; shared bathroom 22€ per person. Rates include breakfast. Metro: Antón Martín. **Amenities:** Bar; communal lounge and kitchen; reception; free Internet and Wi-Fi; flamenco stage for Spanish or pop shows. *In room:* A/C.

NEAR THE PLAZA ESPAÑA

Expensive

Gran Hotel Conde Duque ★ Attractively located in a quieter corner of central Madrid, this relaxing hotel, nestled beside a tree-lined plaza, is just a short stroll from Plaza España. Efficiently run by a Basque family, its ambience and clientele are predominantly Spanish. The warmly decorated bedrooms combine modern and traditional furnishings, with duvets and polished wooden floors. En suite bathrooms are large, immaculate, and well-equipped. An international touch—doubtless English-inspired—is its 5:30 to 7pm tea service in the lounge, where you can choose from up to 70 different teas. Museums and central attractions are in easy reach, and visitors can make use of neighboring health spa facilities, including a sauna.

Plaza Conde del Valle Suchil 5, 28015. ✆ **91-447-70-00.** Fax 91-448-35-69. www.hotelcondeduque.es. 143 units. 230€–285€ double. AE, DC, MC, V. Parking 22€. Metro: San Bernardo. **Amenities:** Restaurant; bar; airport transfer; babysitting; health club; room service. *In room:* A/C, TV, dataport (10€), hair dryer, minibar, radio.

Hotel Husa Princesa ★ This highly prestigious 10-story hotel is located in the Argüelles district beside the long leafy avenue that runs north from the Plaza España toward Moncloa. Renowned for its adroitness in combining top quality with relaxed comfort, the hotel is especially popular with airline staff, and the top two floors offer special "club class" or "steward services," including waiter-served coffee in the mornings and tapas in the afternoon. The elegant rooms have classic reproductions by the likes of Goya and Velázquez, and the attractive Malvasia dining room specializes in Mediterranean-style cuisine. If you're a fitness enthusiast, the hotel's very own gym and sports facilities are another bonus.

Calle Princesa 40, 28008. ✆ **91-542-21-00.** Fax 91-542-73-28. www.hotelhusaprincesa.com. 275 units. 325€ double; 500€–850€ suite. AE, DC, MC, V. Parking 25€. Metro: Ventura Rodríguez. **Amenities:** Restaurant; bar; health club; indoor pool; sauna; room service. *In room:* A/C.

Moderate

Apartohotel Rosales ★ The modern, well-appointed Rosales offers hotel and studio apartment accommodations. Attractively situated in the Argüelles district, just to the west of the Plaza España, Rosales is in easy walking distance of the terrace cafes on Pintor Rosales's promenade (Madrid's most stylish outdoor aperitif zone) and the *teleférico*. The generously sized units have en suite marble-covered bathrooms, and the studios also have small kitchenettes. Excellent value meals are available in the hotel's cafe and restaurant.

Calle Marqués de Urquijo 23, 28008. ✆ **91-542-03-51.** Fax 91-559-78-70. www.apartohotel-rosales.com. 40 units. 90€–180€ double; 160€–245€ apt; penthouse (Atico) 190€–300€. AE, DC, V. Parking 18€. Metro: Argüelles. **Amenities:** Restaurant; health club; room service; smoke-free rooms. *In room:* A/C, TV.

Hotel Casón del Tormes A well run four-story hotel with a smart red-brick facade and stone-trimmed windows, the Casón del Tormes stands on a quiet one-way street 1 block from Plaza de España. Rooms are generally spacious and comfortable, with color-coordinated fabrics and dark wood, including mahogany headboards. Bathrooms are very small, with tub/shower combinations. A long, narrow lobby with a marble floor opens into a separate room. There's a public parking lot near the hotel should you feel the urge to drive in this particularly busy part of town.

Calle del Río 7, 28013. ✆ **91-541-97-46.** Fax 91-541-18-52. www.hotelcasondeltormes.com. 63 units. 100€ double; 150€ triple. AE, DC, MC, V. Parking nearby 20€. Metro: Plaza de España. **Amenities:** Restaurant; bar; babysitting; room service. *In room:* A/C, TV, hair dryer.

ON OR NEAR THE GRAN VÍA

Expensive

Best Western Hotel Arosa ★ A favorite with international and business visitors alike, this friendly modern hotel is situated between the Gran Vía and Puerta del Sol. The refurbished rooms are all fully soundproofed, spotless, and equipped with comfortable wooden furnishings and pristine marble showers and bathrooms. Some pricier units have balconies where you can sit and sip a sherry as you watch the ever-changing scene of traffic and crowds in Madrid's most exhilarating thoroughfare. The over-the-top public-area decor (including an imitation leopard skin reception counter!) recalls the kitsch style of early Pedro Almodóvar movies and the freewheeling 1980s *movida* renaissance that followed 40 years of dictatorial repression.

Calle Salud 21, 28013. ✆ **91-532-16-00.** Fax 91-531-31-27. 180-200€ double. www.bestwesternarosa.com. AE, DC, MC, V. Metro: Gran Vía. Pets allowed. **Amenities:** Restaurant; bar; concierge; room service. *In room:* A/C, TV w/satellite programs and pay movies, dataport, hair dryer, minibar, radio.

Best Western Premier Hotel Santo Domingo ★ This stylishly atmospheric hotel, tucked away in a small square just below the center of the Gran Vía, has a marble-lined entrance that opens into an elegant interior filled with 18th-century ceramics, copies of Golden Age paintings, and romantic prints. Rooms are soundproofed, guarding against noise from the street and from its neighbors, and individually decorated in pastel-derived shades—some contain gold damask wall coverings, faux tortoiseshell desks, and striped satin bedspreads. Bathrooms are generally spacious and outfitted with ceramics, marble slabs, and tub/shower combos. Best units are the fifth-floor doubles, some of which have furnished balconies with great views over Old Madrid's tiled rooftops. The hotel restaurant offers a good choice of vegetarian dishes.

Plaza Santo Domingo 13, 28013. ✆ **91-547-98-00.** Fax 91-547-59-95. www.hotelsantodomingo.com. 120 units. Mon–Thurs 180€–240€ double; Fri–Sun 160€–200€ double. Rates include breakfast Sat–Mon mornings; otherwise 12€ extra. AE, DC, MC, V. Parking nearby 18€. Metro: Santo Domingo. **Amenities:** Restaurant; bar; babysitting; room service. *In room:* A/C, TV, hair dryer, minibar.

Hotel de las Letras ★ One of the newer members of the eminently stylish Epoque Hotels, this renovated early-20th-century gem stands in the heart of the

Gran Vía, enjoying sensational city views from its rooftop terrace. Wall inscriptions by notable Spanish writers fill the public areas amid the original tiles and stone carvings, while the luminous guest rooms boast original high ceilings and windows alongside an array of ultramodern amenities, ranging from plasma TVs to individual temperature controls. Some of the rooms also have a solarium terrace with a private Jacuzzi. The restaurant serves a terrific blend of Mediterranean and Oriental cuisine.

Gran Vía 11, 28013. ✆ **91-523-79-80.** Fax 91-523-79-81. www.hoteldelasletras.com. 103 units. 160€–250€ double; 250€–325€ suite. AE, DC, MC, V. Metro: Sevilla or Gran Vía. **Amenities:** Restaurant; bar; night club; health club; room service; spa; smoke-free rooms; rooms for those w/limited mobility. *In room:* A/C, plasma TV, fax-modem connections, minibar, Wi-Fi, temperature controls, pillow service.

Hotel Emperador ★★ One of Madrid's most sought-after watering holes, this extremely well run hotel is situated right on the Gran Vía; its Club Emperador (unofficially for members only) has long been a favorite hangout for residents and visitors alike. The spacious, traditionally furnished rooms enjoy a tranquil atmosphere in spite of the noisy neighboring thoroughfare; service is discreetly attentive. The icing on the cake here is its rooftop pool that enjoys exceptional city views, open in summer from 11am to 9pm—to the delight of guests seeking a cool refreshing dip in that ultrahot season. Book well ahead.

Gran Vía 53, 28013. ✆ **91-547-28-00.** Fax 91-547-28-17. www.emperadorhotel.com. 241 units. 220€–240€ double; 520€–540€ suite. AE, DC, MC, V. Metro: Gran Vía. **Amenities:** Bar; babysitting; concierge; health club; outdoor pool; room service; rooms for those w/limited mobility. *In room:* A/C, TV, hair dryer, minibar.

Hotel Gaudí ★ So called because it was built in 1898 by Emilio Salas y Cortés, one of the teachers of the great Barcelona architect Gaudí, this remarkable hotel is in a beautifully restored landmark modernist building complete with its original early-20th-century Neo-Plateresque facade (see p. 22). The stylish bedrooms come in a number of sizes, each one comfortably furnished and containing beautifully maintained bathrooms with tub/shower combos. The Gaudí effect continues in the stylish Pedrera restaurant (named after one of the legendary architect's key buildings in Barcelona), where you can enjoy genuine hearty Catalan cuisine right in the heart of Castilian Madrid.

Gran Vía 7–9, 28013. ✆ **91-531-22-22.** Fax 91-531-54-69. www.hoteles-catalonia.es. 184 units. 180€–220€ double; 300€–325€ suite. AE, DC, MC, V. Metro: Gran Vía. **Amenities:** Restaurant; bar; Jacuzzi; room service; sauna. *In room:* A/C, TV, hair dryer, minibar.

Tryp Gran Vía ★ A joint member of the famed international Tryp and Sol Meliá chains, this hotel is ideally located right on the bustling Gran Vía, surrounded by bars, cafes, and eating spots. Service is efficient and attentive, and public areas are comfortably and tastefully furnished. All rooms are neat, airy, and well equipped, and some have special provisions for travelers with disabilities. ***Note:*** If you fancy staying here during the bludgeoning heat of summer, bargain rates with discounts of up to 40% are available.

Gran Vía 25, 28013. ✆ **91-522-11-21.** Fax 91-521-24-24. www.solmelia.com. 175 units. 140€–155€ double. AE, DC, MC, V. Parking nearby 20€. Metro: Gran Vía. **Amenities:** Restaurant; bar/cafeteria; lounge; rooms for those w/limited mobility. *In room:* A/C, TV, hair dryer, minibar, radio.

Vincci Vía 66 This recent addition to the ultracool Vincci chain, in a renovated heritage building, stands halfway between Callao and the Plaza España on Gran Vía. Behind its towering white facade, the attractive wealth of original features includes a winding marble stairway and a forged elevator with stained-glass windows that takes you to the rooftop terrace with its panoramic city views. The decor throughout is a rich blend of grays, reds, and creams, from its carpeted and leather upholstered lounge to its spacious and comfortable rooms. New facilities include a well-equipped health spa and a variety of small business salons. Matching them for quality and originality is the bright minimalist dining room, with its creative range of international dishes.

Gran Vía 66, 28013. ✆ **91-550-42-99.** Fax 91-183-55-40. www.vinccihoteles.com. 116 units. 125€–185€ double; 270€–325€ executive double. AE, DC, MC, V. Metro: Gran Vía. **Amenities:** Restaurant; reception; spa w/sauna and massage treatment; roof terrace. *In room:* A/C, cable/satellite TV, Wi-Fi, pillow service.

Moderate

Best Western Hotel Atlántico This stylish Best Western affiliate hotel occupies five floors of a grand turn-of-the-19th-century building right on the Gran Vía. Rooms are neat, with tasteful downbeat furnishings, and insulated against noise. All are equipped with safes and Wi-Fi. The pristine en suite bathrooms with tub/shower combinations are agreeably spacious. A highlight is the top-floor lounge bar with its small outside rooftop terrace area, serving drinks and snacks and providing tantalizing vistas of the distant mountains from between the buildings.

Gran Vía 38, 28013. ✆ **800/528-1234** in the U.S. and Canada, or 91-522-64-80. Fax 91-531-02-10. www.hotel-atlantico.com. 80 units. 150€–175€ double; 190€–200€ triple. Rates include breakfast. AE, DC, MC, V. Parking nearby 20€. Metro: Gran Vía. **Amenities:** Restaurant; bar. *In room:* A/C, TV, hair dryer, minibar, Wi-Fi.

Hotel El Prado A member of the highly contemporary Hoteles Culturales Tematicos (HCT) chain, the cool red-brick Hotel El Prado (formerly the Green Hotel Prado) claims to be the first culturally themed hotel in Spain. The individual decor on each of its seven refurbished floors refers to a different wine region of Spain, from Andalusia at ground level to Madrid at the top. Rooms, named after specific wines such as Rioja, are sleekly outfitted with contemporary-looking, full-grained walls and free Wi-Fi, and each unit comes with its own small, but immaculate, tiled bathroom with shower. A full buffet breakfast, the only meal available here, is served in the smart downstairs cafe. The hotel stands in a narrow street leading up from the tranquil Plaza de las Cortes to the cafe-filled Plaza Santa Ana, and—keeping true to its name—is also a short walk away from Madrid's most famous museum.

Calle Prado 11, 28014. ✆ **91-369-02-34.** Fax 91-429-28-29. www.pradohotel.com. 48 units. 130€–150€ double; 160€ triple. AE, MC, V. Parking 20€. Metro: Antón Martín. **Amenities:** Cafeteria; bar; babysitting; meeting rooms; room service; wine-themed library. *In room:* A/C, satellite TV, hair dryer, minibar, free Wi-Fi.

Petit Palace Ducal Chueca Located in a renovated 19th-century mansion, with many original features still intact, this chic member of the High Tech chain is located on the southern fringe of Chueca close to the Gran Vía. Singles, couples, and families alike are well catered to by the welcoming young staff. Overall, the atmosphere is stylishly innovative, with red and black decor and up-to-date technological amenities such as free high-speed Internet access on PCs in all rooms. Top-floor rooms have a tiny terrace, and those at the front have good street views with double-glazed windows to keep the noise—and summer heat—at bay. Rooms are also available for nonsmokers and visitors with limited mobility, and all have en suite bathrooms with hydromassage showers.

Calle Hortaleza 3 (esquina Gran Vía 26), 28004. ✆ **91-521-10-43.** Fax 91-521-50-64. www.hthoteles.com. 58 units. 125€ single; 175€ double; 180€ family room. AE, DC, MC, V. Metro: Gran Vía. **Amenities:** Bar; generous breakfast buffet 11€; smoke-free rooms; rooms for those w/limited mobility. *In room:* A/C, TV, high-speed Internet access.

Room Mate Oscar ★★ Like its sister hotel Mario, this welcome addition to the Room Mate family was designed by the talented designer Tomás Alía. Its decor is an imaginative blend of frivolous and minimalist chic, and he boldly incorporates curves, colors, and even graffiti to update the original staid interior of the traditional building the hotel occupies. Rooms range from standard to executive doubles, some with balconies, and there are a few junior or regular suites. There are the usual Room Mate inclusions such as free Wi-Fi and a well stocked minibar. Situated in the colorful Plaza Vázquez de Mella, it's a stone's throw from the bustling Gran Vía and more intimately compact charms of the Chueca district.

Plaza Vázquez de Mella 12, 28004. ✆ **91-701-11-73.** Fax 91-521-87-18. www.room-matehotels.com. 75 units. 100€–210€ double; 160€–280€ junior suite. AE, DC, MC, V. Metro: Gran Vía. Parking 28€. **Amenities:** Babysitting; concierge. *In room:* A/C, TV, hair dryer, minibar, Wi-Fi (free).

Inexpensive

High Tech Avenida Gran Vía This slick, streamlined member of the High Tech chain of hotels occupies five totally renovated floors of a 1930s building on a street close to the popular flamenco club Torres Bermejas (p. 242). The neat, stylishly minimalist rooms range from doubles to family-sized rooms accommodating four. The more spacious, high-tech superior rooms have extras such as saunas, hydromassage showers, and Gran Vía views. All rooms are soundproofed, have Wi-Fi, and en suite bathrooms; some rooms cater to guests with limited mobility and nonsmokers.

Calle de Mesonero Romanos 14, 28013. ✆ **91-532-71-07.** www.hthoteles.com. 64 units. 95€–165€ double; 275€ family room. AE, DC, MC, V. Private parking nearby 25€. Metro: Callao or Gran Vía. **Amenities:** Cafeteria; lounge; babysitting; smoke-free rooms; rooms for those w/limited mobility. *In room:* A/C, TV, hair dryer, free Wi-Fi.

Hostal Alcázar Regis A charming, excellent value *hostal,* noted for its circular Greek-style "crown" and simple 19th-century decor, the Alcázar Regis is located on the fifth floor of a Gran Vía building, close to the Plaza España. Its public areas are pleasant, with wood paneling, lead-glass windows, parquet floors, and crystal chandeliers; and its immaculately refurbished high-ceilinged guest rooms have en suite bathrooms with tub/shower combinations. Its larger rooms accommodate up to four, making it an ideal budget family choice.

Gran Vía 61, 28013. ✆ **91-547-93-17.** www.hostal-alcazar.com. 10 units. 50€ single; 60€ double; 70€ triple; 90€ family size. No credit cards. Metro: Plaza de España or Santo Domingo. **Amenities:** Lounge. *In room:* A/C, TV.

Hotel H10 Villa de la Reina ★ Tastefully restored from an original 20th-century neoclassical building, the Villa de la Reina has also been updated with a variety of modern amenities. The attractively furnished rooms are handsomely decorated, enhanced by high ceilings and large windows that flood the room with light; the en suite bathrooms contain such extras as scales, bathrobes, and a vast selection of toiletries. Don't miss out on the first-rate breakfast buffet, which can include up to 60 home-baked products along with the standard fare of cereals, croissants, and fried eggs. And if you're feeling peckish in the early hours, the 24-hour Club H10 provides affordable meals plus free nonalcoholic drinks.

Gran Vía 22, 28013. ✆ **91-523-91-01.** Fax 91-521-75-22. www.h10hotels.com. 74 units. 150€–225€ double; 220€–375€ suite. AE, DC, MC, V. Parking 16€. Metro: Gran Vía. **Amenities:** Restaurant; bar; room service; smoke-free rooms. *In room:* A/C, TV, dataport, hair dryer, minibar.

Hotel Regente Located in the same street as the High Tech Avenida Callao, this very traditional hotel is close to a variety of central eating spots, bars, and shopping and is only a few steps way from Madrid's great central artery, the Gran Vía. Some of the Regente's facilities are new, but the no-frills decor and furnishings are from another era, pristinely renovated in a strangely evocative style that's best described as "period minimalist." It's an excellent centrally located value choice, with something for the young and young-at-heart to enjoy. Be warned: It can get noisy at times.

Calle de Mesonero Romanos 9, 28013. ✆ **91-521-29-41.** Fax 91-532-30-14. www.hotelregente.com. 154 units. 125€–140€ double. AE, DC, MC, V. Parking 28€ a day. Metro: Callao or Gran Vía. **Amenities:** Restaurant; cafeteria; bar; smoke-free rooms. *In room:* A/C, satellite TV, hair dryer, Wi-Fi, radio.

NEAR THE PUERTA DEL SOL

Expensive

Casa de Madrid ★★★ A mere stone's throw from the Royal Opera, on the second floor of an 18th-century mansion, is the city's most elegant B&B, a genuine aristocratic backwater from another era. Here in the heart of old Habsburg Madrid, owner Doña Maria Medina has furnished and decorated each of her individually themed bedrooms with valuable objets d'art and antiques, including Persian rugs. The rooms range from the modest single Zen room to a variety of internationally named and themed chambers, including the Indian, Greek, and Blue Rooms. If you want to splash out, try to book the large Damascus Suite. Continental breakfasts, included in the rates, are served on—what else?—silver trays, for another stylish touch.

Calle Arrieta 2, 28013. ✆ **91-559-57-91.** Fax 91-540-11-00. www.casademadrid.com. 17 units. 220€–240€ single; 275€–320€ double; 410€ Damascus suite. Rates include continental breakfast. AE, DISC, MC, V. Metro: Opera. **Amenities:** Library. *In room:* A/C, TV, minibar.

Hotel Intur Palacio San Martín ★ After serving as a U.S. embassy for over 150 years, this tastefully converted 15th-century mansion and coaching inn reverted to a private residence in 1951 before being finally transformed into one of Madrid's most character-filled hotels 50 years later, when it was officially designated a "building of historic interest" by the Patrimonio Nacional. Outstanding period features include the original facade and inner courtyard as well as wood paneling and stucco ceilings in the rooms. Extremely bright and spacious rooms also feature stylish period furnishings, lush carpeting, and traditional high windows. Many rooms overlook the Plaza de las Descalzas Reales. Best bets are those on the fifth floor with balconies. Both the splendid rooftop restaurant and the highly coveted presidential suite (complete with its own Jacuzzi) provide fine views of the picturesque Austrias district.

Plaza San Martín 5, 28013. ✆ **91-701-50-00.** Fax 91-701-50-10. www.hotelpalaciosanmartin.com. 97 units. 180€ double; 275€ suite. AE, DC, MC, V. Parking nearby 20€. Metro: Sol. **Amenities:** Restaurant (rooftop); health club; room service; smoke-free rooms. *In room:* A/C, TV w/pay movies, dataport, minibar, radio.

Hotel Preciados ★ ☺ Converted from a prominent 1881 structure into an atmospheric hotel 120 years later, the five-story Preciados is located on a shop-filled pedestrian street close to the Puerta del Sol in the very heart of the city. The original facade, entryway, and grand staircase remain intact, but practically everything else has been reconstructed from scratch for modern comfort. Bedrooms are midsize to spacious, and the bathrooms have modern plumbing and fittings, including large sinks and tub/shower combinations. Children are especially welcome here: Extra beds can be added to the standard rooms, and the restaurant has a special kiddies' menu. The restaurant used to be the famous Café Varela, a favorite of Madrid's literati; today it serves savory Mediterranean cuisine.

Preciados 37, 28013. ✆ **91-454-44-00.** Fax 91-454-44-01. www.preciadoshotel.com. 73 units. 160€–250€. MC, V. Parking 18€. Metro: Sol, Santo Domingo, or Callao. **Amenities:** Restaurant; bar; dance club; babysitting; room service. *In room:* A/C, TV, hair dryer, minibar.

Hotel Quo Puerta del Sol ★ 🎁 The traditional gray facade of this 100-year-old hotel conceals the high-tech amenities of a sleek modern interior of predominant reds, creams, and blacks, and hardwood floors and stainless-steel fittings created by top Spanish designer Tomas Alia. The comfortable midsize bedrooms are furnished in a cool contemporary style, with plush maroon chairs and white walls; all have en suite bathrooms with tub and shower. The first-rate restaurant specializes in "healthy-dietetic" breakfasts (18€) and internationally oriented main meals.

Sevilla 4, 28014. ✆ **91-532-90-49.** Fax 91-531-28-34. www.quopuertadelsolhotel.com. 61 units. 180€–290€ double; 300€–325€ suite. AE, DC, MC, V. Parking 25€. Metro: Sol. **Amenities:** Restaurant; bar; room service; smoke-free rooms. *In room:* A/C, satellite TV, hair dryer, minibar, Wi-Fi.

Tryp Ambassador ★ The Ambassador doesn't feel like part of a hotel chain. It's far too individual and still largely resembles the elegant baronial palace it was when the Dukes of Granada lived here in the 19th century. Many of the original features—such as the romantic *invernadero* (greenhouse)—have been retained, and the result is a lavishly restored four-story historic hotel with grandiose interconnected public areas. The rooms are conservatively furnished—most are large and soundproofed and come with twin beds. Bathrooms contain marble tub/shower combos, robes, and deluxe toiletries. The nearby Opera House and Royal Palace add to the overall regal atmosphere of the place.

Cuesta Santo Domingo 5 y 7, 28013. ✆ **91-541-67-00.** Fax 91-559-10-40. http://trypambassador.madridhotels.it. 182 units. 275€ double; from 350€ suite. AE, DC, MC, V. Metro: Opera or Santo Domingo. **Amenities:** Restaurant; bar; babysitting; room service. *In room:* A/C, TV, hair dryer, minibar.

Moderate

Best Western Hotel Carlos V A member of the Best Western chain, this very friendly family-run hotel is ideally positioned on a pedestrian-only street just off the Puerta del Sol, close to all central amenities. The second-floor restaurant and lounge areas are bright and attractive, and the comfortable accommodations obligingly cater to a variety of party sizes, offering connecting rooms, top-floor rooms with sun terraces, and group or family units. All have en suite bathrooms and some are reserved for nonsmokers. Lower-floor rooms tend to be noisy; try to get one higher up.

Calle Maestro Victoria 5, 28013. ✆ **91-531-41-00.** Fax 91-531-37-61. www.hotelcarlosv.com. 67 units. 125€–135€ double. Rates include buffet breakfast. AE, DC, MC, V. Parking nearby 16€. Metro: Sol. **Amenities:** Restaurant; bar; airport transfer; concierge; room service; free Wi-Fi. *In room:* A/C, TV, dataport, hair dryer, minibar.

Hostal Madrid Though its attractive facade dates from the 18th century, this well-run hotel boasts modern, state-of-the-art facilities and offers basic but colorful standard rooms and compact, well-equipped apartments for families or groups. Run by a youthful and welcoming staff that offers discount passes for city clubs and entertainment locales, it has a special appeal for younger visitors. The atmosphere is free and easy, and you can come and go as you please with your own key (no need to check in at reception).

Calle Esparteros 6-2°, 28012. ✆ **91-522-00-60.** Fax 91-532-35-10. www.hostal-madrid.info. 15 units. 85€–90€ double; 120€ triple; 250€ quad. MC, V. Metro: Sol. *In room:* TV, Wi-Fi.

Hotel Meninas ★ Named after Velázquez's famous portrait of a very young 17th-century princess surrounded by her royal entourage, this hospitable little hotel stands in a charmingly restored 19th-century building in a narrow, often-traffic-filled street parallel to the Hotel Opera. Modern extras include soundproofed rooms, Wi-Fi, and modernized bathrooms with tub and shower. Buffet breakfasts are served in a vaulted dining room; you can relax over a drink in the adjoining bar/lounge before dining in the hotel restaurant, located in the former wine cellars. Among the key nearby sights are the Royal Opera House and Royal Palace.

Calle Campomanes 7, 28013. ✆ **91-541-28-05.** Fax 91-541-28-06. www.hotelmeninas.com. 37 units. 180€ single; 250€–275€ double; 280€–320€ triple; 300€–350€ quad. AE, MC, V. Parking nearby 30€. Metro: Opera or Santo Domingo. **Amenities:** Breakfast room; bar; smoke-free rooms; rooms for those w/limited mobility. *In room:* A/C, TV, hair dryer, minibar, Wi-Fi.

Hotel Opera ★★ True to its name, this friendly and individual boutique-style hotel, with its cool red-brick exterior, wood paneling, and tinted-glass-decorated interior, is located close to Madrid's elegant Royal Opera House. The comfortable guest rooms, adorned with fabric-covered walls and equestrian-oriented prints, range from medium to fairly spacious, and those higher up also enjoy views of Plaza Isabel II and the Teatro Real (directly opposite the Opera House). Their adjoining marble-clad bathrooms have tub/shower combos, and some boast hydromassage jets. The English-speaking staff is most helpful in pointing out the excellent choice of local cafes, eating spots, and historic monuments.

Cuesta de Santo Domingo 2, 28013. ✆ **91-541-28-00.** Fax 91-541-69-23. 79 units. www.hotelopera.com. 140€–210€ double; 220€ triple. AE, DC, MC, V. Parking nearby 15€. Metro: Opera. **Amenities:** Restaurant; bar. *In room:* A/C, TV, hair dryer, minibar.

Room Mate Laura ★ Renovated in 2006 from a traditional 19th-century house, but with chic avant-garde decor and all mod cons, the Laura is another welcome addition to the nifty Room Mate chain, whose bright, lean style and jet-age amenities reach standards that would find approval either side of the Atlantic. Rooms are located in lofts or designed as duplexes, and each has free Wi-Fi plus a minibar and kitchenette. You couldn't be more centrally located and if you want to step out, the emblematic Plaza Mayor and Puerta del Sol (official center of the country) are in easy strolling distance.

Travesia de Trujillos 3, 28013. ✆ **91-701-16-70.** Fax 91-521-76-55. www.room-matehotels.com. 34 units. 125€ standard double; 150€ duplex; 180€ suite. AE, DC, MC, V. Parking 20€. Metro: Sol. **Amenities:** Babysitting; concierge. *In room:* A/C, TV/DVD, hair dryer, kitchenette, minibar, Wi-Fi (free).

Room Mate Mario Another stylish hotel close to the Opera House is this highly affordable member of the Room Mate group, which has been tastefully converted from a former youth hostel. Cool black-and-white corridors and avant-garde wall decor distinguish the public areas, while its compact guest rooms, inventively created by leading designer Tomas Alia, all have well-maintained en suite bathrooms with shower units. Some rooms have wheelchair access. (If you like maximum space, see if you can book no. 201, as it is the largest.) The multilingual reception staff is very helpful, especially when recommending local dining spots and pointing out local sights. Generous buffet breakfasts are included in the cost.

Calle Campomanes 4, 28013. ✆ **91-548-85-48.** Fax 91-559-12-88. www.room-matehoteles.com. 54 units. 100€–140€ double; 125€–180€ suite. Rates include buffet breakfast. AE, DC, MC, V. Parking 16€. Metro: Opera. **Amenities:** Rooms for those w/limited mobility. *In room:* A/C, flatscreen satellite TV, hair dryer, minibar, free Wi-Fi.

Vincci Centrum ★ A member of the Vincci hotel group, whose ultramodern designs and amenities mark the trend of minimalist hotels that have been appearing in increasing numbers, the Centrum is one of the best equipped and most ideally located of them all—equidistant from the Gran Vía, central Puerta del Sol, and museum-filled Paseo del Prado. A sleek modern design prevails in the midsize guest rooms, with bathrooms with tub/shower combos and immaculately tiled walls, while superior rooms, with their own private balconies, enjoy fabulous rooftop views of the city. Better bargains can be had on the weekend, as during the week the hotel is very popular with business travelers.

Calle Cedaceros 4, 28014. ✆ **91-360-47-20.** Fax 91-522-45-15. www.vinccihoteles.com. 87 units. 220€–280€ double. AE, DC, MC, V. Metro: Sevilla. **Amenities:** Restaurant/cafe; bar; limited room service; smoke-free rooms. *In room:* A/C, satellite TV, hair dryer, high-speed Internet, minibar.

Inexpensive

Hostal La Macarena ★ While still retaining its marvelous 19th-century Belle Epoque facade and original character—the creaky old elevator is as slow as ever—this perennial Madrid favorite has been nicely renovated in most other aspects by its new owners, Hostales Sil & Serranos. The small- to medium-sized rooms all have neat new furnishings, comfortable beds, and pristine bathrooms with sliding-glass panels for the shower area. Inner rooms are quieter (this is a popular after-dark area), but those with windows facing the street have double panes to keep the noise to a minimum. The *hostal* is on a street just below the eastern side of the Plaza Mayor near an array of cavelike *mesones*.

Cava de San Miguel 8, 28005. ✆ **91-365-92-21.** Fax 91-364-27-57. www.silserranos.com. 25 units. 65€ single; 75€–80€ double; 90€–95€ triple; 120€ quad. MC, V. Metro: Sol or Opera. **Amenities:** Bar; lounge. *In room:* Fan, TV, hair dryer.

Hostal La Perla Asturiana Just a block back from the Plaza Mayor, this is one of central Madrid's traditional old standbys for budget accommodations seekers. Don't expect luxury, but at these prices, and in this prime location, the down-to-earth standards are more than adequate. Each of the small rooms comes with a comfortable bed plus a simple but clean bathroom with a shower unit. No meals are served, but an almost inexhaustible choice of restaurants and tapas bars is virtually on your doorstep (avoid the terrace cafes around the Plaza Mayor itself, though, unless you want to get ripped off). The reception never closes and the courteous staff here makes you feel welcome 'round the clock.

Plaza Santa Cruz 3, 28012. ✆ **91-366-46-00.** Fax 91-366-46-08. www.perlaasturiana.com. 33 units. 50€–65€ double; 80€ triple. MC, V. Metro: Sol. **Amenities:** Lounge. *In room:* TV.

Hostal Lisboa Occupying four floors of a former town house, the comfortable but modernized Lisboa stands in a narrow lane just a short walk away from cosmopolitan Plaza Santa Ana and the Puerta del Sol. The smartly compact rooms are equipped with mainly double or twin beds and all have en suite bathrooms with shower stalls. The Lisboa does not serve breakfast, but an eclectic variety of budget-priced *tascas,* classy wine bars, and international restaurants line the neighboring streets. The multilingual staff is both efficient and helpful.

Ventura de la Vega 17, 28014. ✆ **91-429-46-76.** www.hostallisboa.com. 26 units. 50€ single; 65€ double. AE, DC, MC, V. Parking nearby 15€. Metro: Sol. **Amenities:** Lounge; babysitting. *In room:* A/C, satellite TV, hair dryer.

Hostal Riesco Run by the same hospitable family for the past 3 decades, this third-floor hotel is nestled in a restored 19th-century building, originally known as the "Casa de los Corderos" (House of the Lambs), on the corner of a narrow street that rises into the Austrias district. The polished-wood entry stairs and slow-moving traditional elevator—which only goes to even-numbered floors—belong to another era, and the genial decor includes stucco ceilings and bright gold fittings. Though the rooms are small, they are cozy with comfortable beds and chintzy curtains. Some have small terraces with colorful flowers and plants, and many have views of Madrid's famous central square. It's an amazing value and understandably one of the most popular budget hotels in the city, so book early if you want to stay here. (Check out the website with its genially eccentric English.)

Calle Correo 2–3°, 28012. ✆ **91-522-26-92.** Fax 91-532-90-88. www.hostalriesco.es. 28 units. 60€–70€ double; 80€ triple. No credit cards. Metro: Sol. **Amenities:** Lounge.

Hotel Inglés ★ Located in a landmark building from 1886, this traditional red-brick hotel (where, among past literary and musical international visitors, Virginia Woolf used to stay) overlooks a narrow street lined with bars and *tascas.* The well-maintained rooms are contemporarily furnished and come in a variety of shapes—mostly small, some in the back are quite dark—with compact bathrooms with shower stalls. The lobby is air-conditioned, but guest rooms are not (though they benefit from the effective heating during cold winter months). In summer, however, guests who open their windows at night often get some noise from the narrow Echegaray Street and the enclosed courtyard, so light sleepers beware (bring earplugs just in case). The service, though a trifle impersonal, is informed and efficient.

Calle Echegaray 8, 28014. ✆ **91-429-65-51.** Fax 91-420-24-23. 58 units. www.hotelinglesmadrid.com. 75€ single; 105€ double; 130€ suite. AE, DC, MC, V. Parking 16€. Metro: Sevilla. **Amenities:** Cafeteria; bar; babysitting; conference facilities; health club; room service. *In room:* TV, hair dryer.

Hotel Santander ★ First opened in the 1920s, the cozy and character-filled Santander is a legendary hotel that offers extremely reasonable value for your money. It lies just up the street from the Hotel Inglés and enjoys the same fascinating on-the-spot array of polyglot bars and eating spots and the wealth of other lively hedonistic amenities in Plaza Santa Ana and Plaza del Angel. The high-ceilinged air-conditioned rooms are clean and comfortable, and some larger rooms enjoy the added bonus of a separate tiny alcove with a chair to relax in. It's a genuine original and the ambience is enhanced by the warm and friendly reception service.

Calle Echegaray 1, 28014. ✆ **91-429-95-51.** Fax 91-369-10-78. www.thehotelsantandermadrid.com. 35 units. 80€–120€ double. MC, V. Metro: Sevilla. *In room:* A/C, TV.

Self-Catering

Apartamentos Turísticos Príncipe 11 Located just off Plaza Santa Ana and a short stroll from the Plaza Mayor, these modern, self-contained 40-sq.-m (431-sq.-ft.) units are ideally placed for central Madrid. Accommodations mainly comprise studios and apartments, with double or twin bedrooms, but also include a small number of suites and large family flats. There are also two-person *buhardillas* (attics or penthouses) with spacious terraces. All flats have fully equipped open-plan kitchenettes and bathrooms with washing machines. You have a choice of exterior or interior units, and though the former have atmospheric street views, they can get noisy.

Calle Príncipe 11, 28012. ✆ **90-211-33-11.** Fax 91-429-42-49. www.atprincipe11.com. 36 units. 90€ 2-person studio; 120€ 4-person studio; 140€ -160€ 2-person penthouse; 180€-200€ 6-person apt. AE, DC, MC, V. Metro: Sol. **Amenities:** Concierge. *In room:* A/C, satellite TV, dataport, kitchenette, maid service.

NEAR ATOCHA STATION

Expensive

NH Nacional ★ Originally built in 1900, in a prominent Belle Epoque style, the Nacional has retained its imposing period facade while now savoring a totally remodeled interior taking full advantage of the building's tall ceilings and large spaces. An impressive marble entrance hall is complete with Gothic columns and an overhead glass copula. The good-size bedrooms have eschewed their former rather dowdy decor in favor of a seamless designer style that includes avant-garde art; the en suite bathrooms all contain immaculate tub/shower combos. Atocha train station—the original reason for the hotel's existence—is virtually on your doorstep and exterior rooms have great views of the leafy and tranquil Botanical Gardens.

Paseo del Prado 48, 28014. ✆ **91-429-66-29.** Fax 91-369-15-64. www.nh-hotels.com. 214 units. 220€-250€ double; 450€-500€ suite. AE, DC, MC, V. Metro: Atocha. **Amenities:** Restaurant; bar; babysitting; room service. *In room:* A/C, TV, hair dryer, minibar.

Moderate

Husa Paseo del Arte This elegant and tastefully renovated hotel (formerly the Mercator) stands just across the road from the modern Centro de Arte Reina Sofía. Its public areas include a naturally lit modular lounge, and 16 of its comfortably air-conditioned guest rooms and suites are fully equipped for guests with limited mobility. Business visitors have access to conference rooms with Internet facilities, and there's a gym for keeping in shape. Breakfasts and main meals are available in the Trazos restaurant. The Atocha railway station is the other side of the neighboring roundabout.

Calle Atocha 123, 28012. ✆ **91-298-48-00.** Fax 91-369-12-52. 260 units. www.hotelhusapaseodelarte.com. 130€-275€ double; 250€-400€ suite. AE, DC, MC, V. Parking 16€. Metro: Atocha or Antón Martín. **Amenities:** Restaurant; cafeteria; bar; 2 lounges; babysitting; gym; room service; solarium. *In room:* A/C, TV, hair dryer, minibar.

Inexpensive

Hotel Mediodía Initially constructed in an early-20th-century neoclassical Franco-Belgian style, the inviting and very reasonably priced Mediodía still retains its original high ceilings, statues, and hanging lamps in the main entrance while also featuring partially modernized bedrooms blending bright modern decor with tall period windows and traditional wooden floors. The staff provides friendly and attentive service. The hotel is conveniently just across the road from Atocha station and the famed open-air bookstalls of the pedestrian Cuesta de Moyano.

Plaza de Emperador Carlos V 8, 28012. © **91-527-30-60.** Fax 91-527-30-66. www.mediodiahotel.com. 165 units. 85€–90€ double. AE, MC, V. Metro: Atocha. **Amenities:** Lounge. *In room:* TV.

Hotel Mora This modest but comfortable five-story hotel, located right beside the tree-lined Paseo del Prado and directly opposite the Botanical Gardens, is a short stroll from the Atocha railway station and the Reina Sofía and Prado museums. Recently refurbished throughout, the public areas include a bright, comfortable lounge, with stylish cream pillars, and an adjoining bar/cafeteria with a variety of breakfasts, from continental to American. The rooms are colorful, neat, and well-appointed, and some will accommodate an extra bed. Staff is very friendly and helpful.

Paseo del Prado 32, 28014. © **91-420-15-69.** Fax 91-420-05-64. www.hotelmora.com. 61 units. 75€–90€ double; 110€ triple. AE, DC, MC, V. Metro: Atocha. **Amenities:** Lounge; bar/cafeteria. *In room:* A/C, TV.

NEAR RETIRO/SALAMANCA

Very Expensive

Hesperia Madrid ★★★ An accredited member of the "Leading Hotels of the World," the stylishly minimalist Hesperia is dominated by Asian overtones such as the lime trees and stylish atrium in the lobby and the tiny Japanese gardens that dot the entire building. Rooms are immaculately compact, with top-quality fixtures and fittings, fashionable bathroom toiletries, and even pillows selected from a luxurious pillow menu. Top choice is the deluxe presidential suite, which enjoys marvelous city views from the split-level terrace and—like the other suites—has its own butler. Dine in the **Santceloni** dining room, whose gourmet chef Santa Santamaría has already earned the restaurant a Michelin rating (p. 152). Staff is efficient, friendly, and exceptionally attractive (another part of the hotel's charismatic appeal).

Paseo de la Castellana 57, 28046. © **91-210-88-00.** Fax 91-210-88-99. www.hesperia-madrid.com. 171 units. 350€–450€ double; 800€ and up suite. AE, DC, MC, V. Parking 25€. Metro: Gregorio Marañón. **Amenities:** Restaurant; bar; babysitting; concierge; access to health club; room service; sauna; smoke-free rooms and floor. *In room:* A/C, TV, minibar, Wi-Fi.

Hotel Ritz Madrid ★★★ The Ritz is a living legend among Madrid hotels, and its incomparable facade—declared a national monument—and interior high ceilings and graceful columns evoke the early-20th-century Belle Epoque era. One of *Les Grands Hôtels Européens,* the Ritz was built in 1908 by King Alfonso XIII, with the aid of César Ritz, in a time when spaciousness and luxury were standards. Therefore, the spacious and luxurious rooms—all now tastefully modernized—boast large closets, antique furnishings, and hand-woven carpets. Old dress codes live on, and the hotel requests that male guests wear a jacket and tie after 11am in the public areas. Passersby may like to sample the justly famed—if pricey—brunch in the Goya restaurant or on the beautiful summer garden terrace. Or spoil themselves with a superb afternoon tea with cakes and sandwiches at a deluxe 32€ per head!

Plaza de la Lealtad 5, 28014. ✆ **800/225-5843** in the U.S. and Canada, or 91-701-67-67. Fax 91-701-67-76. www.ritz.es. 167 units. 690€-795€ double; 1,450€-1,600€ suite. AE, DC, MC, V. Parking 27€. Metro: Banco de España. **Amenities:** Restaurant; bar; health club; room service; sauna. *In room:* A/C, TV, hair dryer, minibar.

Hotel Selenza June 2009 saw the opening of this, Spain's second Selenza Hotel (the first was in Estepona on the Costa del Sol), in a street lined with art galleries on the western edge of the Salamanca district. Like its southerly twin, it includes among its many deluxe amenities a splendid thalasso and spa where you can rejuvenate those tired musles after a day's city sightseeing. Unlike its purpose-built southern counterpart, it's located in a magnificent 19th-century Belle Epoque mansion, which has been tastefully renovated and refurbished with additional 21st-century accoutrements. The decor throughout is bright minimalist with tiled check flooring and elegant modern furnishings. A bonus for gourmets is the hotel's extremely stylish restaurant, already one of the city's best-rated, run by Michelin-star-awarded Catalan chef Ramón Freixa (p. 156).

Calle Claudio Coello 67, 28001. ✆ **91-781-01-73**. Fax 91-576-77-41. www.selenzahoteles.es. 44 units. 400€ double; 450€-600€ suite. AE, DC, MC, V. Metro: Serrano. **Amenities:** Ramón Freixa restaurant; bar; lounge; library; meeting room; small interior garden; room service; thalasso and spa; free international newspapers. *In room:* A/C, pay-to-view TV, DVD/CD player, minibar, free Wi-Fi, baby-care facilities, pillow service, access for those w/disabilities.

Park Hyatt Villa Magna ★★★ The glowing rose-colored granite facade of the Park Hyatt rises behind a small parkland of cedars, pines, and laurels halfway down Castellana Avenue. The elegant interior, in contrast, recaptures the period atmosphere of Carlos IV, with its paneled walls, marble floors, and bouquets of fresh flowers. Movie celebrities, pop stars, international sportsmen, heads of state, and senior politicians all feature high on the list of repeat visitors. Rooms in this luxury palace are plush but dignified and decorated in Louis XVI, English Regency, or Italian provincial style. Each comes with a neatly kept bathroom with a tub/shower combo. The staff is discreetly businesslike and helpful.

Paseo de la Castellana 22, 28046. ✆ **800/223-1234** in the U.S. and Canada, or 91-587-12-34. Fax 91-431-22-86. www.hotelvillamagna.com. 182 units. 450€-600€ double; 795€-850€ and up suite. AE, DC, MC, V. Parking 24€. Metro. Gregorio Marañón. **Amenities:** 2 restaurants; 2 bars; babysitting; health club; room service. *In room:* A/C, TV, hair dryer, minibar.

Expensive

Adler Hotel ★★ Located in the heart of elegant Salamanca, just a short walk from the Retiro, the Adler is another luxurious addition to the upmarket Madrid hotel scene. It occupies a converted 18th-century *palacete* complete with neoclassical decor, an interior designed by Pascual Ortega, and works by modernist artists such as Tapiès and Chillida. It blends a relaxed 1880s ambience with stylish 21st-century touches. Bedrooms have comfortable deluxe furnishings and totally modernized bathrooms equipped with tub/shower combinations. The charming *áticos* (penthouse rooms) comprise the much-sought-after fifth-floor accommodations. The on-site restaurant is noted, even in this upmarket section of town, for the quality of its cuisine.

Calle Velázquez 33, 28001. ✆ **91-426-32-30.** Fax 91-548-78-85. www.adlermadrid.com. 45 units. 350€-425€ double; 475€ suite. AE, DC, MC, V. Metro: Velázquez. **Amenities:** Restaurant; bar; babysitting; room service. *In room:* A/C, TV, hair dryer, minibar.

Hospes Madrid ★★ The charming and tasteful Hospes faces the white-stoned Plaza de la Independencia archway and main entrance to Parque del Retiro, and is discreetly integrated into a renovated town building in one of residential Madrid's most attractive corners. The interior is a blend of whites and grays, with creamy marble floors and walls merging with dark wood-toned doorways. Large-backed sofas and glass tables fill the naturally lit lounges. You can choose from a variety of gourmet dining, tapas, and snack-oriented eating spots right within the hotel. A highlight for health enthusiasts is the magnificent Bodyna spa and massage center, with its professional massage treatments and hot and dry saunas. The bright, spacious, high-windowed rooms are pure comfort, with polished bare wood floors covered with soft white carpets, original 19th-century pillars, and very generous size beds (for Spain) with stylish silver-hued period bedsteads.

Plaza de la Independencia 3, 28001. ✆ **91-432-29-11.** Fax 91-432-29-12. www.hospes.es. 41 units. 190€–26€ double; 775€–825€ suite. AE, DC, MC, V. Metro: Retiro. **Amenities:** Restaurant; lounge bar; tapas bar; gym; room service; sauna. *In room:* A/C, satellite TV, high-speed Internet and Wi-Fi, minibar, pillow service, terrace.

Hotel Catalonia Centro ★ Located in a superbly refurbished 19th-century building in the heart of the elegant Salamanca district, this is one of the Hoteles Catalonia group's most prestigious new Madrid hotels. Combining period character with fully modern amenities, it stands six stories high, with bay windows and decorative grills as key features of the traditional brick facade. The rooms all have parquet floors and warm wooden furnishings. Best of them all is the spacious junior suite, with its lounge, twin digital TVs, and magnificent city views.

Goya 49, 28001. ✆ **91-781-49-49.** Fax 91-781-49-48. www.hoteles-catalonia.com. 88 units. 150€–270€ double; 375€–400€ suite. AE, DC, MC, V. Metro: Goya. **Amenities:** Restaurant; Wi-Fi. *In room:* A/C, satellite TV, hair dryer.

Hotel Hesperia Emperatriz ★ Built in the 1970s and subsequently renovated in a combination of Laura Ashley and Spanish contemporary styles by Madrid's trendiest firm, Casa & Jardín, the Hesperia Emperatriz stands on a pleasant street just off the elegant Paseo de la Castellana. Rooms are comfortable and classically styled in cheery yellows and salmons, and come with neatly kept bathrooms containing tub/shower combos. Ask for a room on the seventh floor, where you get a private terrace at no extra charge. Best of all—and understandably in great demand—is the eighth-floor Emperatriz suite with its spacious balcony. Superior rooms catering especially to business travelers provide such extras as scanners, photocopiers, and printers. The hotel's Atrium restaurant is renowned for its cuisine and service.

López de Hoyos 4, 28006.. ✆ **91-563-80-88.** Fax 91-563-98-04. www.hesperiaemperatriz.es. 158 units. 180€–275€ double; 375€–460€ suite. AE, DC, MC, V. Metro: Gregorio Marañón. **Amenities:** Restaurant; bar; babysitting; room service; Wi-Fi. *In room:* A/C, satellite TV, hair dryer, minibar, office electronics (scanners, printers, and photocopiers) in Superior rooms.

NH Alcalá ★ This enduring hotel has a justifiably high reputation for service and atmosphere. Its long-established staff is renowned for its friendly and highly attentive service, while the warm period furnishings and decor include original wooden floors and traditional fittings. All rooms have been individually designed and refurbished, and central units overlook a charming garden patio. Each level has a special standout room planned by one of Spain's top modern designers, Agatha Ruiz de la Prada, who runs a boutique in the nearby fashionable Serrano Avenue. Parque del Retiro is just

family-friendly HOTELS

Meliá Castilla Children can spend hours and all their extra energy in the hotel's swimming pool and gymnasium. On the grounds is a showroom exhibiting the latest European automobiles. Hotel services include babysitting, providing fun for kids and parents too. Double rooms run 250€ to 295€. Capitán Haya 43; ✆ **91-567-50-00;** www.meliacastilla.com.

Hotel T3 Tirol This centrally located government-rated three-star hotel is a favorite of families seeking good comfort at a moderate price. It has a cafeteria. Doubles run 150€ to 195€. Marqués de Urquijo 4; ✆ **91-548-19-00;** www.t3tirol.com.

across the road, whenever you feel like a stroll among the greenery. For night owls, the hotel serves a *madrugada* (dawn) breakfast highlighted by the inevitable high-calorie *chocolate con churros.*

Calle Alcalá 66, 28009. ✆ **91-435-10-60.** Fax 91-435-11-05. www.nh-hotels.com. 146 units. 175€–275€ double. AE, DC, MC, V. Parking 20€. Metro: Príncipe de Vergara. **Amenities:** Restaurant; bar; concierge; room service; smoke-free rooms. *In room:* A/C, TV w/pay movies, hair dryer, minibar, radio, video games.

Vincci SoMa ★ Formerly known as Hotel Bauzá, this very latest addition (reopened in 2008) to the noted Vincci chain has retained the original's chic minimalist decor and aura of low-key comfort. Colors throughout the hotel are muted, as is the music, and the relaxed amenities include a tranquil library. The renovated dining room now features Mediterranean fusion dishes (plus chic additions such as an international list of mineral waters, known as the "H2O" menu). Except for occasional touches of red, the bedrooms are mostly monochromatic, and are especially noted for their sound systems, with CD players and PlayStations. Double-paned windows help block the outside traffic noise and the bathrooms have tubs and showers.

Calle Goya 79, 28001. ✆ **91-435-75-45.** Fax 91-431-09-43. www.vinccihoteles.com. 167 units. 150€–250€ double; 250€–300€ suite. AE, DC, MC, V. Parking 16€. Metro: Goya. **Amenities:** Restaurant; bar; gym; room service; sauna; smoke-free rooms; library. *In room:* A/C, TV, hair dryer, minibar.

VP Jardín de Recoletos ★ This contemporary apartment hotel, with its sedately attractive decor, stands on a narrow street near the lively hub of Plaza Colón. The inviting lobby has sleek marble floors and a stained-glass ceiling; the spacious rooms are traditionally furnished with small sitting and dining areas, wood trim, creamy white walls, and comfortable furniture in yellow and champagne. Well-equipped kitchenettes give you the inviting option of providing your own meals, though the hotel's superb buffet breakfast is a temptation not to be missed. All accommodations have well-equipped bathrooms, each with tub and shower, while "superior" rooms and suites offer hydromassage facilities as well as a big terrace.

Gil de Santivañes 6, 28001. ✆ **91-781-16-40.** Fax 91-781-16-41. www.vphoteles.com. 43 units. 180€–200€ double; 250€–275€ suite. Rates include buffet breakfast. AE, DC, MC, V. Parking 12€. Metro: Serrano. **Amenities:** Restaurant; cafe; limited room service. *In room:* A/C, TV, dataport, hair dryer, kitchenette, minibar.

Moderate

Ayre Gran Hotel Colón ★ The Ayre (formerly Fiesta) Gran Hotel Colón offers comfortable and reasonably priced accommodations in twin buildings separated by a small garden close to Parque del Retiro. Accommodations are divided into executive (in the Edificio Europa) and standard rooms (in the neighboring Edificio America), and all rooms have comfortable beds, smart modern decor, and compact bathrooms with stall showers. Some have private balconies. The hotel has an international restaurant, covered garage, and conference room with Wi-Fi for business visitors. One of the original Colón's founders was Manuel Ortega, an interior designer, which accounts for the beautiful stained-glass windows and murals in the public areas.

Pez Volador 1, 28007. ✆ **91-573-59-00.** Fax 91-573-08-09. http://ayre-grancolon-madrid.hotel-rez.com. 362 units. 125€–175€ double. AE, DC, MC, V. Parking 16€. Metro: Sainz de Baranda. **Amenities:** Restaurant; bar; nonsmoking lounge; babysitting; conference room w/Wi-Fi; health club; room service; sauna; solarium. *In room:* A/C, TV, hair dryer, minibar.

Gran Hotel Velázquez ★ This is one of the most attractive medium-size hotels in Madrid, with plenty of comfort and convenience. Opened in 1947 on an affluent residential street near the center of town, and unchanged in many ways since then, it has a 1930s-style Art Deco facade and a 1940s interior filled with well-upholstered furniture and richly grained paneling. Several public lounges lead off a central oval area, and recent additions include a business center with Wi-Fi. The comfortable rooms vary in size from standard doubles to suites large enough for entertaining, with a small separate sitting area; all have walk-in closets. Bathrooms are decorated in marble or tiles, with either stall showers or tubs.

Calle Velázquez 62, 28001. ✆ **91-575-28-00.** Fax 91-575-28-09. www.chh.es. 143 units. 250€–275€ double; from 350€ suite. AE, DC, MC, V. Parking nearby 20€. Metro: Velázquez. **Amenities:** 2 restaurants; bar; babysitting; room service. *In room:* A/C, TV, hair dryer, minibar.

Hotel Claridge This charming hotel lies southeast of Parque del Retiro in residential Conde Casal, about 5 minutes from all central attractions and sights by bus or metro. Soft carpets and triple glazing ensure the entrance and lounge are relaxing and quiet. Recent additions include small business salons, accommodating up to 15 people and equipped with Wi-Fi (which is also available on request in some guest rooms). The compact rooms and slightly larger suites are in turn pleasantly styled and include adjoining marble-surfaced bathrooms with tub/shower combos. Buffet breakfasts and main meals are served in the hotel's bright restaurant. If your booking dates are flexible, take advantage of the hotel's specially reduced weekend rates.

Plaza Conde de Casal 6, 28007. ✆ **91-551-94-00.** Fax 91-501-03-85. www.hotelclaridgemadrid.com. 150 units. Mon–Thurs 150€–195€ double, 195€ suite; Fri–Sun 95€–140€ double, 125€ suite. AE, DC, MC, V. Metro: Conde de Casal. **Amenities:** Restaurant; bar. *In room:* A/C, TV, hair dryer.

Inexpensive

Hostal Residencia Don Diego ★ Situated on the fifth floor of an elevator building on a bustling tree-lined avenue, in easy reach of many of the city monuments, the unpretentiously atmospheric Don Diego is one of Madrid's best value hotels. The vestibule contains an elegant winding staircase with iron griffin heads supporting its balustrade. Rooms are compact but comfortable for the price and the en suite bathrooms—similarly on the small side—are clean and adequate, with shower stalls. The English-speaking staff is friendly and service oriented, and keeps the place humming along efficiently.

Calle de Velázquez 45, 28001. ✆ **91-435-07-60.** Fax 91-431-42-63. www.hostaldondiego.com. 58 units. 90€-100€ double; 125€-140€ triple. MC, V. Metro: Velázquez. **Amenities:** Cafeteria. *In room:* A/C, TV.

CHAMBERÍ

Very Expensive

AC Santo Mauro ★★★ Set beside its own charming garden, this classic French-styled hotel is located inside a neoclassical villa built in 1894 for the duke of Santo Mauro. Many original features remain, though the former library is now a gourmet restaurant, **Belagua** (p. 159), the ballroom has been transformed into an imposing conference room, and a central vaulted ceiling overlooks an indoor pool. The interior is decorated with rich fabrics and Art Deco accents and furnishings. Accommodations are spacious throughout; choose from studios to duplex suites, all containing bathrooms with tub/shower combos. Each room has a sound system that comes with a wide choice of tapes and CDs, as well as many other lovely details, such as raw silk curtains, Persian carpets, antique prints, and parquet floors. Staff members outnumber rooms by two to one, ensuring impeccable service.

Calle Zurbano 36, 28010. ✆ **91-319-69-00.** Fax 91-308-54-77. www.ac-hotels.com. 54 units. 270€-425€ double; 450€-1,200€ suites. AE, DC, MC, V. Parking 18€. Metro: Rubén Darío or Alonso Martínez. **Amenities:** Restaurant; bar; babysitting; health club; indoor heated pool; room service; sauna. *In room:* A/C, TV, hair dryer, minibar.

Hotel Orfila ★★ 🎁 A classic example of elegant, tasteful decoration set in one of the city's most charming residential areas, this small 19th-century former palace once boasted its own theater and literary salon. Today it's a distinguished member of the highly luxurious Relais & Châteaux group, and its imposing central stairway and public areas betray its aristocratic Belle Epoque past. The lobby is located in a former courtyard, where horse-drawn carriages used to pull in for the night. The midsize-to-spacious bedrooms are decorated in a rich 19th-century style and have stylish bathrooms with tub/shower combinations. In the evening, dine in the Art Nouveau El Jardín de Orfila restaurant after savoring an aperitif in the secluded garden.

Orfila 6, 28010. ✆ **91-702-77-70.** Fax 91-702-77-72. www.hotelorfila.com. 32 units. 290€-395€ double; from 585€ suite. AE, DC, MC, V. Metro: Alonso Martínez. **Amenities:** Restaurant; bar; babysitting; room service. *In room:* A/C, TV, hair dryer, minibar.

InterContinental Madrid ★★ The dependable yet stylish InterContinental lies behind a barrier of trees in a neighborhood of apartment houses and luxury hotels. Its high-ceilinged public rooms are magnificent, with terrazzo floors and giant abstract mural mosaics of multicolored stones and tiles. Former infamous celebrities such as the late British hellraiser-actor Oliver Reed, who (not always welcomingly) livened the place up in the '70s, have given way today to a more staid business-oriented clientele. Most of the accommodations have private balconies, traditional furniture, and generous living space with very large beds, often king size. Tiled bathrooms are well equipped with robes, phones, and tub/shower combos. Generous extras include coffeemakers, working desk areas, Wi-Fi, and rental movies.

Paseo de la Castellana 49, 28046. ✆ **800/327-0200** in the U.S., or 91-310-02-00. Fax 91-319-58-53. www.ichotelsgroup.com. 310 units. 395€-460€ double; from 1,050€ suite. AE, DC, MC, V. Parking 25€. Metro: Gregorio Marañón. **Amenities:** 3 restaurants; bar; babysitting; health club; room service; sauna; solarium. *In room:* A/C, satellite TV, hair dryer, minibar.

Expensive

High Tech President Villamagna ★ As its name implies, this smartly renovated hotel, with its subdued decor and cool pearl and purple lighting, boasts state-of-the-art business facilities, including a well-equipped commercial center, laptops, and free high-speed Internet in all its rooms. Equally popular with laid-back holidaymakers, the attractive selection of standard doubles and spacious family rooms are all equipped with queen, twin, or bunk beds and stylishly furnished with faux-leather headboards, plus individual touches such as temperature controls. The en suite bathrooms are equipped with hydromassage showers and a sauna. The hotel is just off the Castellana, close to stylish cafes and in easy reach of central attractions. (***Note:*** Don't confuse it with the above-mentioned Park Hyatt Villa Magna, which is grander and pricier and located in the Castellana itself.)

Marqués de Villamagna 4, 28001. ✆ **91-577-19-51.** Fax 91-577-19-54. http://president.madridhotels.it. 104 units. 175€ double; 225€–250€ family room. AE, DC, MC, V. Metro: Rubén Darío. **Amenities:** Bar; sauna; smoke-free rooms; rooms for those w/limited mobility. *In room:* A/C, TV, hair dryer, minibar, Wi-Fi.

Hotel Occidental Miguel Angel ★ Ideally located just off Paseo de la Castellana, this sleek hotel's combination of contemporary styling, good furnishings, and efficient staff have established it as a Madrid favorite ever since its grand opening in 1975. Its attractive communal areas include an expansive sun terrace on several levels, with clusters of garden furniture surrounded by paintings of semitropical scenes, while its soundproofed rooms boast color-coordinated fabrics and carpets, and, in many cases, reproductions of classic Iberian furniture. The hotel's internationally famous Catalan-inspired **La Broche** restaurant (whose famed former chef Sergi Arola has now been replaced by the adept Angel Palacios) is among the foremost in the city's gourmet scene (p. 160). For health enthusiasts the "Lab Room" contains a climatized indoor pool and provides top-rate hydrotherapy treatment.

Miguel Angel 29–31, 28010. ✆ **91-442-00-22.** Fax 91-442-53-20. www.miguelangelhotel.com. 263 units. 260€–320€ double. AE, DC, MC, V. Parking 20€. Metro: Gregorio Marañón. **Amenities:** 2 restaurants; bar; babysitting; health club; room service; pool; sauna. *In room:* A/C, TV, hair dryer, minibar.

Self-Catering

Aparthotel Tribunal These smart well-appointed self-catering units, which range from small 25-sq.-m (269-sq.-ft.) studios to more spacious 50-sq.-m (539-sq.-ft.) apartments, are situated in the heart of Madrid between Chamberí and the Gran Vía, just a few steps from the Tribunal metro. Like the Prisma below, these units are not only fully equipped for do-it-yourself living, with one or two bedrooms, basic kitchenette, and en suite bathroom, but also enjoy hotel-style facilities such as maid service and a 24-hour reception desk. Unlike the Prisma, however, there's no restaurant on the premises, but whenever you don't feel like doing your own cooking, plenty of nearby cafes fit the bill. Ask for an exterior apartment, for views across the street of the Municipal museum with its baroque facade.

Calle San Vicente Ferrer 1, 28004. ✆ **91-522-14-55.** Fax 91-523-42-40. 106 units. www.hotel-tribunal.com. 90€–125€ double; 150€ 2-bedroom family unit. AE, DC, MC, V. Metro: Tribunal. **Amenities:** Reception desk; maid service. *In room:* A/C, satellite TV, hair dryer, kitchenette.

NH Suites Prisma ★ You have space enough to enjoy your Madrid stay in these 50-sq.-m (538-sq.-ft.) suites—which combine apartment and hotel amenities in the same building—so when you get tired of self-catering, you can eat in the hotel restaurant. In addition to the well-equipped lounge, kitchenette, and bathroom, the apartments also have a small office area—convenient if you're here on business. Located in the upper part of the Chamberí district, it's close to the Castellana and AZCA business center, with its banking and insurance offices, and a short trip by metro from the central Puerta del Sol and Plaza Mayor. If you're here in summer and enjoy swimming, one of the city's best outdoor pools, Canal de Isabel II (June–Sept only), is next to the nearby Calle Bravo Murillo (5 min. on foot).

Calle Santa Engracia 120, 28003. ✆ **91-441-93-77.** Fax 91-442-58-51. www.nh-hotels.com. 103 units. 90€–180€ double. AE, MC, V. Metro: Ríos Rosas. **Amenities:** Restaurant; cafe; bar; room service. *In room:* A/C, satellite TV w/pay movies, dataport, kitchen, Wi-Fi, maid service, video games.

CHAMARTÍN

Expensive

AC Cuzco ★ Popular with businesspeople and tour groups, the 15-story Cuzco stands beside Castellana Avenue in a commercial neighborhood of office buildings and government ministries, close to the main Congress Hall. Chamartín railway station is only a 10-minute walk, or two metro stops north. The hotel has been redecorated and modernized many times since it was completed in 1967, most recently in a chic gray cream minimalist style by its new owners, the noted AC (Antonio Catalan) chain. The rooms are spacious, with separate sitting areas and modern furnishings. Bathrooms come equipped with tub/shower combos.

Paseo de la Castellana 133, 28046. ✆ **91-556-06-00.** Fax 91-556-03-72. www.hotelaccuzco.com. 319 units. 170€–220€ double; 250€–550€ suite. AE, DC, MC, V. Parking 20€. Metro: Cuzco. **Amenities:** Restaurant; bar; babysitting; health club; room service; sauna. *In room:* A/C, TV, hair dryer, minibar.

Eurostars Madrid Tower ★★★ This ground-breaking new hotel extends over 31 floors of the gleaming steel-gray Sacyr Vallehermoso Tower—one of four in the 2009-completed 236m-high (774-ft.) Cuatro Torres Business Area just north of Plaza Castilla and a short stroll from the Chamartín railway. The imaginative interior, whose cool clinical public zones contrast strikingly with the intimate mellow warmth of the bedrooms, is the combined work of top Catalan architectural designers Josep Miret and Maria Vives. Highlights include the huge translucent 29th-floor Salon Gran Barcelona and splendid sauna and Jacuzzi rooms. No less than 22 well-equipped meeting rooms, boasting the latest in audio-visual technology, also make it an ideal choice for business visitors. The spacious bedrooms feature immaculate walnut wood furnishings and "intelligent" automatic sound, temperature, and light controls, all designed to ensure a permanent high degree of comfort for guests, while bathrooms are equipped with special hydromassage showers. Most rooms have incredible vistas (the higher up you are the better!).

Paseo de la Castellana 259B, 28046. ✆ **91-334 -27-00.** Fax 91-334-07-21. 24-hr. customer service from USA 93-295-99-08. www.eurostarsmadridtower.com. 500 units. 320€–400€ double; 450€–600€ suite. AE, DC, MC, V. Indoor parking. Metro: Begoña. **Amenities:** 30th-floor a la carte restaurant; 24-hr. lobby bar; babysitting; Jacuzzi; sauna; spa. *In room*: Automated intelligent control of sound, temperature and light, LCD panoramic TV, personalized phones, minibar, free Wi-Fi, en suite coffee and tea service, pillow service.

Hotel Don Pío This charmingly relaxed hotel stands in an attractive residential part of Chamartín east of the Castellana. Luxury standards plus extremely attentive service make this a firm favorite with business and holiday clientele alike. Traditional furnishings and dark wooden paneling welcome you in the lobby, and the large stylish rooms all have marble-finished bathrooms complete with hydromassage bathtubs. The hotel's restaurant is under a sunny plant-filled atrium. All central amenities are just a quarter of an hour away by metro, and if you enjoy swimming, a superb indoor Olympic size public pool is just up the road.

Av. Pío XII, 25, 28016. ✆ **91-353-07-80.** Fax 91-353-07-81. www.hoteldonpio.com. 41 units. 175€–195€ double. AE, DC, MC, V. Parking 16€. Metro: Pío XII. **Amenities:** Restaurant; cafe; concierge; room service. *In room:* A/C, TV, dataport, hair dryer, minibar.

Hotel Nuevo Madrid ★ This fairly recent member of Spain's famed Husa chain of hotels is located just across the M-30 highway, east of Chamartín station, in a peaceful residential corner of the city. It's an ideal choice for business and leisure visitors looking for relaxed accommodations away from the center yet within relatively easy reach of the central hot spots by bus or metro; the Ifema fairgrounds are about a 15-minute taxi drive away. The comfortably furnished rooms—some nonsmoking—have Wi-Fi and high-speed Internet access. You'll find the multilingual staff most friendly and informative.

Calle Bausá 27, 28033. ✆ **91-298-26-00.** Fax 91-298-26-01. www.hotelnuevomadrid.com. 431 units. 100€–125€ double; 150€ junior suites. AE, DC, MC, V. Metro: Pío XII or Duque de Pastrana. **Amenities:** Restaurant; bar; lounge. *In room:* A/C, satellite TV, hair dryer, minibar, Wi-Fi and high-speed Internet access.

NH Eurobuilding ★ The imposing Eurobuilding stands in a residential area just east of the Castellana surrounded by apartment houses, boutiques, nightclubs, and first-class restaurants. Eurobuilding actually consists of two buildings: The main one, Las Estancias de Eurobuilding, contains only suites, with sumptuously carved gold-and-white beds, large terraces for breakfast and cocktail entertaining, and all renovated in pastel shades; the other building houses comfortable double rooms, many with private balconies and views of the formal garden below. All accommodations have private bathrooms with tub/shower combos, and on-site fitness amenities include an outdoor and indoor swimming pool and "Spa Elyseum," with thermal cure programs.

Calle Padre Damián 23, 28036. ✆ **91-353-73-00.** Fax 91-345-45-76. www.nh-hotels.com. 490 units. 255€–295€ double; from 525€ suite. AE, DC, MC, V. Parking 22€. Metro: Cuzco. **Amenities:** Restaurant; bar; babysitting; health club; room service; outdoor pool; indoor pool; sauna. *In room:* A/C, TV, hair dryer, minibar.

Moderate

Hotel Aristos ★ This comfortable and relaxing hotel is situated in the same residential avenue as the Don Pío (see above). More like a friendly house than a hotel, the Aristos has been one of Chamartín's most popular retreats for over 3 decades, and its staff is renowned for their helpful and informal service. One of its main attractions is the garden where you can lounge and have a drink. Each of the tastefully renovated and comfortably furnished rooms has a small terrace and modern furniture, plus a private bathroom with a tub/shower combo. A gourmet highlight is the hotel's very own **El Chaflán** restaurant (p. 162).

Av. Pio XII 34, 28016. ✆ **91-345-04-50.** Fax 91-345-10-23. 23 units. www.hotelaristos.com. 160€-195€ double; 220€ triple. AE, DC, MC, V. Parking 16€. Metro: Pío XII. **Amenities:** Restaurant; lounge; room service. *In room:* A/C, TV, hair dryer, minibar, Wi-Fi (for a fee).

Husa Chamartín Owned by RENFE, Spain's government railway system, and a member of one of Spain's top hotel chains, Husa, this modern nine-story hotel adjoins the Chamartín railway station. The soundproofed and air-conditioned rooms are good sized and tastefully furnished, with marble-surfaced en suite bathrooms with stall showers. The hotel has a video screen that posts the arrival and departure of all of Chamartín station's trains. The airport and historic core of Madrid are just 15 minutes away by taxi or metro. The hotel boasts a number of well-equipped salons that can be used for conferences. Guests enjoy access at special rates to the nearby Chamartín Sports and Zen Clubs.

Agustín de Foxá s/n, 28036. ✆ **91-334-49-00.** Fax 91-733-02-14. www.hotelhusachamartin.com. 378 units. 185€ double; from 295€ suite. AE, DC, MC, V. Metro: Chamartín. **Amenities:** Restaurant; lounge; room service. *In room:* A/C, satellite TV, hair dryer, minibar, Wi-Fi.

Rafaelhoteles Orense ★ This smart silver-and-glass tower, which blends so well into the array of surrounding condominium complexes, is in fact the stylishly updated and renovated acquisition of the distinguished Rafael hotels group. The standard doubles and the more spacious junior suites are furnished with chic, bright, and semiminimalist decor of bare wood floors, gleaming white walls, and cozy chaise longues. Half of the rooms face Calle Pedro Teixera—a not too busy cul-de-sac leading off the busier Calle Orense; the other half face a quieter area in the back. The modern designer cafeteria is open 7am till midnight and serves everything from early buffet breakfasts to full meals. Business facilities include conference rooms with audiovisual accessories and Wi-Fi.

Pedro Teixeira 5, 28020. ✆ **91-597-15-68.** Fax 91-597-12-95. www.rafaelhoteles.com. 140 units. 150€-195€ double; 220€-275€ junior suites. AE, DC, MC, V. Metro: Santiago Bernabeu. **Amenities:** Cafeteria; conference room; room service. *In room:* A/C, satellite TV w/pay movies, hair dryer, minibar, Wi-Fi.

Residencia El Viso ★ 🎁 If your dream of Madrid is a peaceful and relaxing backwater in easy striking distance of the city center, then look no further than El Viso. Set in a converted 1930s Art Deco villa on a tree-lined residential barrio 15 minutes from bustling Puerta del Sol, it seems to be in another world. Its uniquely personal atmosphere and amenities are as charming as the setting. The intimately comfortable rooms all have en suite bathrooms. Though essentially renowned as a top-notch bed-and-breakfast, it also provides delicious lunches that are cooked by its owner, María; when the weather is warm, it's served on the shaded garden patio.

Calle Nervión 8, 28002. ✆ **91-564-03-70.** Fax 91-564-19-65. elviso@estanciases.es. 12 units. 160€-175€ double. AE, DC, MC, V. Parking nearby 20€. Metro: República Argentina. **Amenities:** Restaurant; health club; room service. *In room:* A/C, TV w/pay movies, minibar, radio.

AVENIDA AMERICA/BARRIO DE LA CONCEPCIÓN

Hotel Silken Puerta América ★ This unconventional hotel, part of the prestigious Silken group, is for design-addicts. The multicolored facade brightens up the predominantly gray cityscape around the Avenida de America bus and metro terminal.

Each of its 12 floors has been designed by a top international architect, from Norman Foster to Arata Isosaki. The individual rooms and suites have comfortable furnishings and highly imaginative decor, varying from an igloo-esque space with virtually no furnishings to a cool unit all in black and gray with sliding oak screens. The spacious public areas get just as much design attention—such as the elegant Lágrimas Negras dining room and minimalist Marmo cocktail lounge, with its gleaming Carrara marble bar top. You can work off any hedonistic indulgences in the hotel's well-equipped gym.

Av. de América 41, 28002. © **91-744-54-00.** Fax 91-744-54-01. www.hoteles-silken.com/HPAM. 342 units. 220€-390€ double; 700€-3,000€. AE, DC, MC, V. Free parking. Metro: Avenida de America. **Amenities:** Restaurant; bar; lounge; gym; covered swimming pool; room service; sauna; garden; rooms for those w/limited mobility. *In room:* A/C, satellite TV, hair dryer, minibar.

Novotel Madrid Puente de la Paz Originally intended to serve the accommodations needs of the cluster of multinational corporate headquarters that lie just across the M-30 highway, east of Avenida de America, this well-planned hotel provides smart and modern accommodations at prices so reasonable that it's now a great hit with regular tourists as well. Unusual for Madrid, it's also particularly easy and convenient for people who want to get around by car. The soundproofed rooms are laid out in a standardized but comfortable format, and—a special plus for families—the furnishings include sofas that can be transformed into comfortable beds.

Calle Albacete 1 (corner Av. Badajoz), 28027. © **800/221-4542** in the U.S. and Canada, or 91-724-76-00. Fax 91-724-76-10. www.accorhotels.com and www.novotel.com. 240 units. 185€-200€ double. Children 15 and under stay free in parent's room. AE, DC, MC, V. Parking 20€. Metro: Barrio de la Concepción. Drivers exit from M-30 at Barrio de la Concepción/Parque de las Avenidas, just before reaching the city limits of central Madrid, then look for the chain's trademark electric-blue signs. **Amenities:** Restaurant; bar; health club; pool; room service; sauna. *In room:* A/C, TV, hair dryer, minibar.

WHERE TO DINE

6

Madrid boasts the most richly varied cuisine in Spain. Its national eating spots cover everything from Andalusian gazpacho and Valencian paella (most famed of all Spain's rice and seafood dishes) to Galician pulpo (octopus), Asturian fabada (rich pork stew), and Basque bacalao (cod). And let's not forget Madrid's very own cocido (lamb and vegetable stew), callos (tripe) and, lesser known perhaps to visitors, oreja (ear: yes, you heard right). Plus neighboring Castile's outrageously delicious infanticide dishes: lechona (roast suckling pig) and corderito (baby lamb, best sampled in Segovia).

The region's dishes are both hearty and logical given the setting and winter climate, but the big surprise is that though Madrid is a landlocked city, surrounded by a vast arid plateau, it receives a daily supply of fish which is transported from the Atlantic north in large containers to supply top restaurants like La Trainera and Cabo Mayor with the country's best and freshest seafood.

Add to all that a new wave of sophisticated polyglot fusion cuisine, deft, brilliant, and light years away from the full-bodied traditionals mentioned above—and the scene takes on another dimension. Thanks to highly inventive and imaginative chefs like Sergi Arola, Santi Santamaria, and—latest newcomer to Madrid—Ramon Freixa (p. 156) the city's cuisine is now truly considered international. Ground-breaking Ferran Adriá in particular has gained such fame (the *New York Times* recently described him as the "dean of molecular gastronomy") that for a while he eclipsed even Gallic giants like Paul Bocuse. His much vaunted El Bulli restaurant in the northern Costa Brava will close for good in 2011, when he is scheduled to start a two-year tour of Asia in search of new culinary ideas. The restaurant will reopen at some later date as a school for chefs but never again to the public. In Madrid, however, Adriá's centrally located Terraza del Casino (p. 131) still continues to delight the public with its inventive dishes.

International restaurants are also growing in numbers, and you can take your pick from a range of European, Latin American, North African, Middle Eastern, and Asian eating spots. Among the latest of these to open are the charming Ethiopian **Mesob** (p. 146), which has introduced a whole new realm of exotic dishes to Madrileños and passing visitors alike, and ultrachic **Ingrid y Gaston,** which now provides the city's best Peruvian cuisine.

While browsing through this chapter, keep in mind that restaurants are categorized by the average cost of one entree, an appetizer, and a glass of wine. **Very Expensive** means a meal averages 40€ per person and up; **Expensive,** 25€–40€; **Moderate,** 15€–25€; **Inexpensive,** under 15€.

DINING OUT IN MADRID

Be sure to also read "Eating & Drinking in Madrid," p. 25, for an in-depth discussion of the food and drink of the Spanish capital.

Meal Times

Breakfast *(desayuno)* is taken in cafes or in your hotel between 7:30 and 10am, though if you want to make a very early start you'll find the occasional bar open around 5:30 or 6am.

It's the custom in Madrid to consume **lunch** *(almuerzo)* as the big meal of the day, from 2 to 4pm. After a recuperative siesta, Madrileños enjoy **tapas**—and indeed, no Madrid culinary experience would be complete without a tour of the city's many tapas bars (see "An Early-Evening *Tapeo,*" on p. 143, and "The Best of the *Tascas,*" on p. 166).

All this nibbling is followed by a lighter **dinner** *(cena)* in a restaurant, usually from 9:30pm to as late as midnight. Many restaurants, however, start serving dinner at 8pm to accommodate visitors from other countries who don't like to dine so late.

Most **restaurants** close 1 day a week, so be sure to check ahead. Hotel dining rooms are generally open 7 days. Generally, reservations are not necessary, except at popular, top-notch restaurants.

Types of Restaurants & Menus

Cafeterias usually are not self-service establishments but restaurants serving light, often American, cuisine. Go for breakfast instead of dining at your hotel, unless it's included in the room price. Some cafeterias offer no hot meals, but many feature combined plates of fried eggs, french fries, veal, and lettuce-and-tomato salad, which make adequate fare, or snacks like hot dogs and hamburgers.

Restaurants share one thing in common that cafeterias do not: By law, they must offer a fixed-price lunch menu that includes two main courses, a dessert, and (usually) wine. In simple, basic budget-priced ***economicas,*** these may cost as little as 10€ all-inclusive, while in top-quality **deluxe** eating spots with famous-name chefs—where more exotic and esoteric "tasting menus" are offered—they can be as high as 150€ to 200€ per head (often without wine). In between these two extremes—though distinctly nearer the *economicas* in price—comes a middle (15€–35€) range that includes historic ***tabernas,*** **all-purpose** eating spots serving an eclectically national and international choice of dishes, and **regional** restaurants that concentrate on the specific cuisines of different parts of Spain (Asturias and Galicia are most commonly represented here).

Order the *menú del día* (menu of the day) or *cubierto* (fixed price)—both fixed-price menus are based on what is fresh at the market that day. These are the dining bargains in Madrid, although often lacking the quality of more expensive a la carte dining. Usually each will include a first course, such as fish soup or hors d'oeuvres, followed by a main dish, plus bread, dessert, and the house wine. You won't have a

smoke-free DINING IN SIGHT?

At the time of writing this guide, after a lightly restrictive law passed, cafes, bars, and restaurants are still allowed to use their own discretion when deciding whether smoking on the premises should be allowed or not. Unwilling to lose customers, the vast majority opted for the former, much to the dismay of Spain's anti-smoking lobby. Though premises over 100 sq. m (1,100 sq. ft.) in area are required to have a small nonsmoking zone, entirely smoke-free locales remain in a distinct minority. Nicotine haters can nevertheless find solace in the occasional clear-aired oasis such as the inimitable and increasingly ubiquitous **Starbucks** and the vegetarian restaurant **Elqui** (p. 140).

A radical change is on the horizon, though. In June 2010, parliament voted by a huge majority to approve a new law enforcing stricter rules on smoking similar to those currently operating in France, Italy, Ireland, and Great Britain. The final decision—due in January 2011—could well see the end of smoking in a multitude of public areas not covered by the present law. These include restaurants, which would be totally smoke-free inside but allow smoking in open-air terrace areas. (For more details, see the "Smoking" section of Fast Facts, p. 289.)

large choice. The *menú turístico* is a similar fixed-price menu, but for many it's too large, especially at lunch. Only those with big appetites will find it the best bargain.

Tipping & Local Customs

Meals include **service and tax** (7%–12%, depending on the restaurant) but not drinks, which add to the tab considerably.

In most cases, service can seem perfunctory by North American standards. Waiters are matter-of-fact, do not fawn over you, or return to the table to ask how things are going. This can seem off-putting at first, but if you observe closely, you'll see that Spanish waiters typically handle more tables than their North American counterparts and they generally work quickly and more efficiently.

Follow the local custom and don't overtip. Theoretically, service is included in the price of the meal, but it's customary to leave an additional 10%.

Top restaurants, such as **Zalacaín** (p. 162), have a formal dress policy (jacket and tie for men). Call ahead if you're unsure.

best DINING BETS

- **Best for a Romantic Dinner: El Amparo** (**© 91-431-64-56**) sits in one of Madrid's most elegant enclaves, with cascading vines on its facade. You can dine grandly on nouveau Basque cuisine, enjoying not only the romantic ambience but also some of the finest food in the city. A sloping skylight bathes the interior with sunlight during the day, and at night lanterns cast soft, flattering glows, making you and your date look luscious. See p. 153.
- **Best for a Business Lunch:** For decades the influential leaders of Madrid have come to **Jockey** (**© 91-319-24-35**) to combine power lunches with one of the true gastronomic experiences in Madrid. In spite of increased competition, Jockey is still among the favorite rendezvous sites for heads of state, international

Where to Dine in Central Madrid

Al Natural **55**
Artemisa **47**
Asador Frontón **28**
Automático **33**
Bajamar **1**
Bali **1**
Bar Salamanca **25**
Café de Oriente **8**
Café del Círculo de Bellas Artes **51**
Caripén **2**
Casa Alberto **38**
Casa Ciriaco **13**
Casa Labra **10**
Casa Lastra Sidrería **29**
Casa Lucio **24**
Casa Paco **16**
Cervecería Alemana **40**
Comme Bio **12**
Cornucopia **5**
Delfos **4**
Do Salmon **42**
Donzoko **46**
Económico Soidemersol **34**
Edelweiss **54**
El Caldero **39**
El Cenador del Prado **41**
El Cielo del Urban **48**
El Cosaco **17**
El Estragón **18**
El Granero de Lavapiés **32**
El Mirador del Museo **57**
El Schotis **27**
El Viajero **23**
Elqui **35**
Errota-Zar **52**
Horcher **59**
Julian de Tolosa **20**
Kaiten Ginza Sushi Bar **56**
La Biotika **37**
La Bola **3**
La Botelleria de Maxi **26**
La Chata **21**
La Esquina del Real **9**

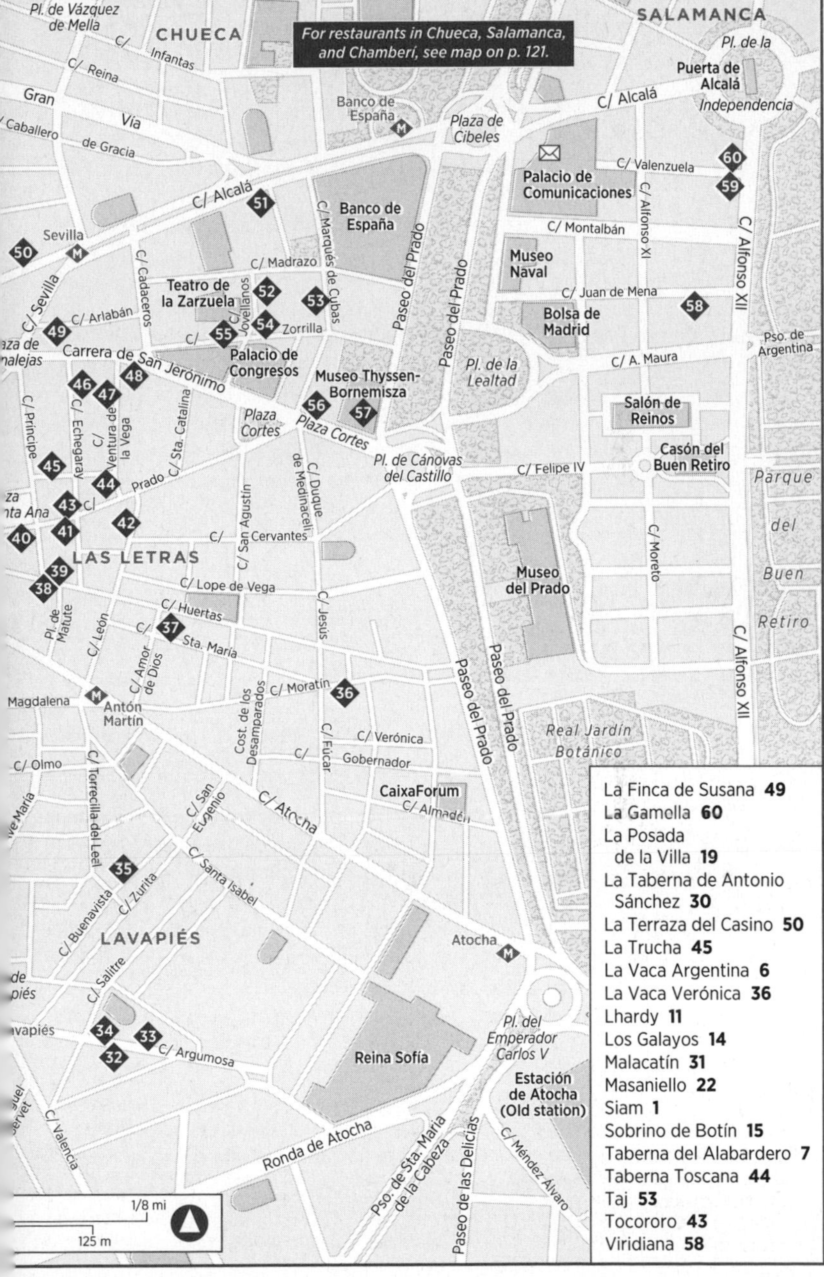
For restaurants in Chueca, Salamanca, and Chamberí, see map on p. 121.
CHUECA
SALAMANCA
LAS LETRAS
LAVAPIÉS
Pl. de Vázquez de Mella
C/ Infantas
C/ Reina
Gran Vía
C/ Caballero de Gracia
C/ Alcalá
Banco de España
Plaza de Cibeles
Puerta de Alcalá
Pl. de la Independencia
C/ Valenzuela
Palacio de Comunicaciones
C/ Alfonso XI
C/ Montalbán
Museo Naval
C/ Juan de Mena
Bolsa de Madrid
Pso. de Argentina
C/ A. Maura
Salón de Reinos
Casón del Buen Retiro
C/ Felipe IV
Parque del Buen Retiro
C/ Moreto
C/ Alfonso XII
Sevilla
C/ Sevilla
C/ Cedaceros
C/ Madrazo
C/ Marqués de Cubas
Paseo del Prado
Teatro de la Zarzuela
C/ Jovellanos
Zorrilla
C/ Arlabán
Carrera de San Jerónimo
Palacio de Congresos
Museo Thyssen-Bornemisza
Pl. de la Lealtad
Plaza Cortes
C/ Príncipe
C/ Echegaray
C/ Ventura de la Vega
C/ Sta. Catalina
Prado
C/ Duque de Medinaceli
Pl. de Cánovas del Castillo
C/ San Agustín
C/ Cervantes
Museo del Prado
C/ Lope de Vega
C/ Huertas
C/ Jesús
Pl. de Matute
C/ León
C/ Sta. María
C/ Amor de Dios
Magdalena
Antón Martín
C/ Moratín
Cost. de los Desamparados
C/ Verónica
C/ Fúcar
C/ Gobernador
Real Jardín Botánico
C/ Olmo
C/ Torrecilla del Leal
C/ San Eugenio
C/ Atocha
CaixaForum
C/ Almadén
C/ Santa Isabel
C/ Zurita
C/ Buenavista
Atocha
C/ Salitre
C/ Argumosa
Pl. del Emperador Carlos V
Reina Sofía
Estación de Atocha (Old station)
C/ Valencia
Ronda de Atocha
Pso. de Sta. María de la Cabeza
Paseo de las Delicias
C/ Méndez Álvaro
1/8 mi
125 m
La Finca de Susana 49
La Gamella 60
La Posada de la Villa 19
La Taberna de Antonio Sánchez 30
La Terraza del Casino 50
La Trucha 45
La Vaca Argentina 6
La Vaca Verónica 36
Lhardy 11
Los Galayos 14
Malacatín 31
Masaniello 22
Siam 1
Sobrino de Botín 15
Taberna del Alabardero 7
Taberna Toscana 44
Taj 53
Tocororo 43
Viridiana 58

celebrities, and diplomats. It's the perfect place to close that business deal with your Spanish partner—he or she will be impressed with your selection. See p. 159.

- **Best for a Celebration:** At night the whole area around Plaza Mayor becomes one giant Spanish fiesta, with singers, guitar players, and bands of roving students serenading for their sangria and tapas money. Since 1884 it has always been party night at **Los Galayos** (✆ **91-366-30-28**) too, with tables and chairs set out on the sidewalk for people-watching. The food's good as well—everything from suckling pig to roast lamb. What else would you expect from the best eating spot in the Plaza Mayor? See p. 128.
- **Best Views:** The cafe tables on the terrace of the **Café de Oriente** (✆ **91-541-39-74**) afford one of the most panoramic views of classical buildings and monuments in Madrid—a view that takes in everything from the Palacio Real (Royal Palace) to the Teatro Real. Diplomats, even royalty, have patronized this place, known for its good food and attractive Belle Epoque decor, which includes banquettes and regal paneling. See p. 132.
- **Best Decor: Las Cuatro Estaciones** (✆ **91-553-63-05**) has the most spectacular floral displays in Madrid. These flowers, naturally, change with the seasons, so you never know what you'll see when you arrive to dine. The entrance might be filled with hydrangeas, chrysanthemums, or poinsettias. The food is equally superb, a magnificent blend of classical and modern, but it's the stunningly modern and inviting decor that makes Las Cuatro Estaciones the perfect place for a lavish dinner on the town. See p. 160.
- **Best for Kids: Foster's Hollywood** (✆ **91-564-63-08**) wins almost hands-down. Since 1971 it has lured kids with Tex-Mex selections, one of the juiciest hamburgers in town, and what a *New York Times* reporter found to be "probably the best onion rings in the world." The atmosphere is fun too, evoking a movie studio with props. See p. 168.
- **Best Basque Cuisine:** Some food critics regard **Zalacaín** (✆ **91-561-48-40**) as the best restaurant in Madrid. Its name comes from Pío Baroja's 1909 novel, *Zalacaín El Aventurero,* but its cuisine comes straight from heaven. When the maitre d' suggests a main dish of cheeks of hake, you might turn away in horror—until you try it. Whatever is served here is sure to be among the finest food you'll taste in Spain—all the foie gras and truffles you desire, but many innovative dishes to tempt the palate as well. See p. 168.
- **Best American Cuisine:** Not everything on the menu at **La Gamella** (✆ **91-532-45-09**) is American, but what there is here is choice, inspired by California. Owner Dick Stephens, a former choreographer, now runs this prestigious restaurant in the house where the Spanish philosopher Ortega y Gasset was born. Even the king and queen of Spain have tasted the savory fare, which includes everything from an all-American cheesecake to a Caesar salad with strips of marinated anchovies. It's also known for serving what one food critic called "the only edible hamburger in Madrid," and that palate had tasted the hamburger at Foster's Hollywood (see above). Its wine list is comprehensive, covering a wide range of national and world vintages. See p. 154.
- **Best Continental Cuisine:** Although the chef at the small but enchanting **El Mentidero de la Villa** (✆ **91-308-12-85**) roams the world for culinary inspirations, much of the cookery is firmly rooted in French cuisine. Continental favorites

Where to Dine in Chueca, Salamanca & Chamberí

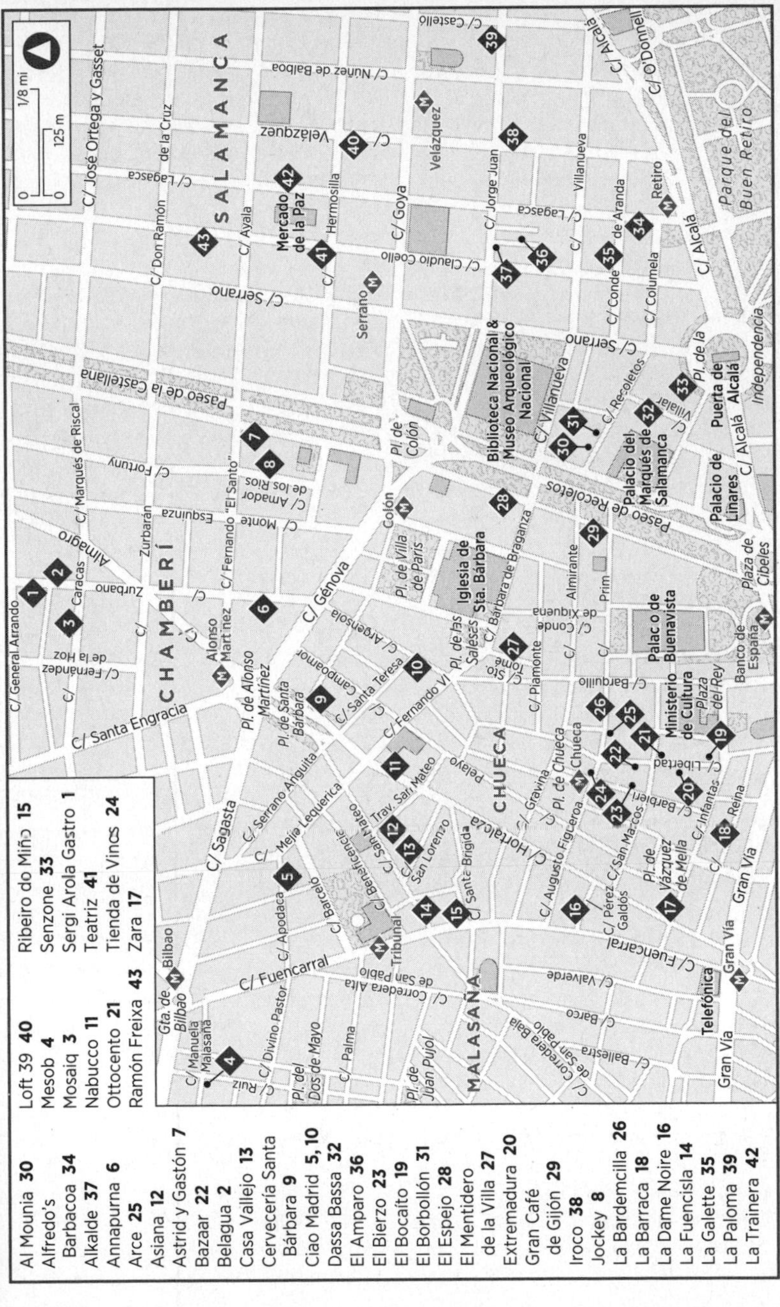

are updated here and given new twists and flavors, sometimes betraying a Japanese influence. From France come the most perfect noisettes of veal (flavored with fresh tarragon) that you're likely to be served in Spain. Even the Spanish dishes have been brought up-to-date and are lighter and subtler in flavor. See p. 147.

- **Best Seafood:** For the freshest of fresh Atlantic fish and nary a sign of a steak or leg of lamb, **La Trainera** (✆ **91-576-80-35**) on the elegant western edge of the Salamanca district close to shop-filled Serrano Avenue is without a par. Whatever you choose in this deceptively spacious marine-oriented haven, from luscious *bogavante* (lobster) to humble *almeja* (clam), will be of optimum quality.
- **Best Steakhouse:** Spanish steaks at their finest are offered at **Casa Paco** (✆ **91-366-31-66**). Señor Paco was the first in Madrid to sear steaks in boiling oil before serving, so that the almost-raw meat continues to cook on the plate, preserving the natural juices. This Old Town favorite also has plenty of atmosphere, and has long been a celebrity favorite as well. See p. 136.
- **Best Roast Suckling Pig:** Even hard-to-please Hemingway agreed: The roast suckling pig served at **Sobrino de Botín** (✆ **91-366-30-26**) since 1725 is the best and most aromatic dish in the Old Town. You'd have to travel to Segovia (home of the specialty) for better fare than this. Under time-aged beams, you can wash down your meal with Rioja wine. See p. 128.
- **Best Cocido: Malacatín** (✆ **91-365-52-41**). *Cocido madrileño* is the capital's favorite dish, a hearty combo of chickpeas, cabbage, salt pork, beef, and chicken designed to combat the winter cold. If you like it, come here: Having raised it to the peak of perfection, they've decided to serve nothing else. The restaurant is small, atmospheric, and excellent value—the fixed price also includes wine and dessert. Prior booking of both dish and table is essential. See p. 130.
- **Best Wine List:** Maybe the fact that it's half French has something to do with it, but **La Cava Real** (✆ **91-442-54-32**) in the heart of trendy Chamberí takes the palm when it comes for a really delectable cross section of wines, especially when you're given such expert advice on exactly which one to have. See p. 161.
- **Best Value Lunch:** For quality, good service, and simple but delicious dishes (like chargrilled vegetables and fresh pan-fried rice) at a highly competitive price, the bright modern **Finca de Susana** (✆ **91-369-35-57**) beats most of its rivals hands-down. You need to arrive earlier than usual in Spain for the bargain three-course lunch (say 1:30pm) in order to avoid the lines (no reservations). See p. 134. Similar good value is provided by its sister restaurant in Chueca: **Bazaar** (p. 150).
- **Best Vegetarian Fare: Al Natural** (✆ **91-369-47-09**). Obviously, politicians' gourmet tastes are changing—this totally "green" eating spot situated right behind the *Congreso de Diputados* enjoys the patronage of many a parliamentary member. Rice, vegetables, and veggie pizzas feature strongly, though some *platos* have chicken or fish included. It's packed by noon so try to get here early for lunch. See p. 142.

RESTAURANTS BY CUISINE

AMERICAN

Alfredo's Barbacoa (Chamartín & Salamanca, $, p. 164)

Foster's Hollywood ★ (near Plaza República Argentina, $, p. 168)

ARGENTINE

La Vaca Argentina (Near the Plaza España, $$, p. 145)

La Vaca Verónica (Plaza de las Cortes & Huertas, $, p. 138)

Ottocento (Chueca, $, p. 150)

ASTURIAN

Casa Lastra Sidrería (Lavapiés, $$$, p. 139)
Casa Mingo (Príncipe Pío, $, p. 166)

BASQUE

Alkalde ★ (Retiro/Salamanca, $$$, p. 152)
Arce ★ (on or near the Gran Vía, $$$, p. 147)
Asador Frontón ★ (Plaza Mayor & Austrias, $$$, p. 126)
Belagua (Chamberí, $$$, p. 159)
El Amparo ★★ (Retiro/Salamanca, $$$, p. 153)
El Bodegón (Retiro/Salamanca, $$$, p. 154)
El Borbollón (Paseo de Recoletos, $$$, p. 141)
Errota-Zar (Plaza de las Cortes & Huertas, $$, p. 137)
Goizeko Kabi ★ (Chamartín, $$, p. 163)
La Cava Real ★★ (Chamberí, $$, p. 161)
La Paloma ★ (Retiro/Salamanca, $$$, p. 155)
Pedro Larumbe ★ (Retiro/Salamanca, $$$, p. 156)
Príncipe de Viana ★ (Chamartín, $$$, p. 163)
Quintana 30 ★ (Argüelles/Moncloa, $$, p. 145)
San Mamés ★ (Cuatro Caminos, $$$, p. 169)
Taberna del Alabardero (Puerta del Sol, $$, p. 134)
Zalacaín ★★★ (Chamartín, $$$$, p. 162)

CALIFORNIAN

La Gamella ★★ (Retiro/Salamanca, $$$, p. 154)

CANTABRIAN

La Atalaya (Near Plaza República Argentina, $, p. 168)

CASTILIAN

Bar Salamanca (Plaza Mayor & Austrias, $, p. 129)
Café del Círculo de Bellas Artes ★ (Near Plaza de la Cibeles, $, p. 142)
Casa Alberto (Plaza de las Cortes & Huertas, $$, p. 166)
Casa Ciriaco (Puerta del Sol, $$, p. 133)
Casa Lucio ★ (Plaza Mayor & Austrias, $$, p. 127)
Casa Pedro (Fuencarral, $$$, p. 170)
El Bierzo (Chueca, $, p. 150)
El Molino de los Porches ★ (Near the Plaza España, $$$, p. 144)
Julian de Tolosa (Plaza Mayor & Austrias, $$$, p. 126)
La Gamella ★★ (Retiro/Salamanca, $$$, p. 154)

CATALAN

La Broche ★★★ (Chamberí, $$$, p. 160)

CONTINENTAL

El Mirador del Museo ★★ (Near Plaza de la Cibeles, $$, p. 141)
Horcher ★ (Retiro/Salamanca, $$$, p. 154)

CUBAN

Tocororo (Plaza de las Cortes & Huertas, $$, p. 138)
Zara (Chueca, $$, p. 149)

ETHIOPIAN

Mesob (Malasaña, $, p. 146)

EURO-AMERICAN

Cornucopia (Puerta del Sol, $$, p. 133)

EXTREMADURAN

Extremadura (Chueca, $$, p. 149)
Nicómedes ★ (Arturo Soria District, $$, p. 165)

FRENCH

Café de Oriente ★ (Puerta del Sol, $$, p. 132)
Caripén ★ (Puerta del Sol, $$$, p. 132)
El Borbollón (Paseo de Recoletos, $$$, p. 141)

KEY TO ABBREVIATIONS:
$$$$** = Very Expensive **$$$** = Expensive **$$** = Moderate **$ = Inexpensive

La Cava Real ★★ (Chamberí, $$, p. 161)
La Dame Noire (Chueca, $$, p. 149)
La Esquina del Real (Puerta del Sol, $$$, p. 132)
La Paloma ★ (Retiro/Salamanca, $$$, p. 155)
Pedro Larumbe ★ (Retiro/Salamanca, $$$, p. 156)
Zalacaín ★★★ (Chamartín, $$$$, p. 162)

FUSION

Asiana ★★★ (Chueca, $$$$, p. 146)
Fast Good Madrid ★ (Chamartín, $, p. 165)
Ramón Freixa ★★★ (Chamberí, $$$, p. 156)
Sergi Arola Gastro ★★★ (Chamberí, $$$$, p. 159)

GALICIAN

Do Salmon (Plaza de las Cortes & Huertas, $$, p. 136)
O'Pazo ★ (Cuatro Caminos, $$$, p. 169)
Ribeiro do Miño ★ (Chueca, $, p. 151)

GERMAN

Edelweiss (Near Plaza de la Cibeles, $$, p. 142)
Horcher ★ (Retiro/Salamanca, $$$, p. 154)

GREEK

Delfos (Puerta del Sol, $, p. 134)

GRILLED MEAT

La Posada de la Villa (Plaza Mayor & Austrias, $$, p. 128)

INDIAN

Annapurna (Chamberí, $$, p. 160)
Taj (Near Plaza de la Cibeles, $, p. 143)

INDONESIAN

Bali ★ (Near the Plaza España, $$, p. 144)

INTERNATIONAL

Dassa Bassa ★★ (Retiro/Salamanca, $$$, p. 153)
El Bodegón (Retiro/Salamanca, $$$, p. 154)
El Espejo ★ (Paseo de Recoletos, $$, p. 141)
El Viajero (Plaza Mayor & Austrias, $, p. 130)
Horcher ★ (Retiro/Salamanca, $$$, p. 154)
Iroco ★ (Retiro/Salamanca, $, p. 158)
Jockey ★★★ (Chamberí, $$$$, p. 159)
La Finca de Susana (Puerta del Sol, $, p. 134)
La Galette (Retiro/Salamanca, $$, p. 158)
La Terraza del Casino ★★★ (Puerta del Sol, $$$$, p. 131)
Lhardy ★★ (Puerta del Sol, $$$$, p. 131)
Loft 39 ★★ (Salamanca, $$$, p. 155)
Senzone Restaurant ★★ (Retiro/Salamanca, $$$, p. 156)
Sula ★ (Salamanca, $$, p. 157)
Viridiana ★★ (Retiro/Salamanca, $$$, p. 157)
Zalacaín ★★★ (Chamartín, $$$$, p. 162)

ITALIAN

Ciao Madrid (Chueca, $$, p. 148)
Masaniello (Plaza Mayor & Austrias, $, p. 131)
Nabucco (Chueca, $, p. 150)
Ottocento (Chueca, $$, p. 150)
Teatriz ★ (Retiro/Salamanca, $$, p. 158)

JAPANESE

Donzoko (Puerta del Sol, $$, p. 133)
Kaiten Ginza Sushi (Plaza de las Cortes & Huertas, $$, p. 137)
Nodo (Near Plaza República Argentina, $$, p. 168)

MADRILEÑO

La Bola (Near the Plaza España, $$, p. 144)
La Botillería de Maxi (Plaza Mayor & Austrias, $, p. 130)
Malacatín ★ (Plaza Mayor & Austrias, $, p. 130)
San Mamés ★ (Cuatro Caminos, $$$, p. 169)

Taberna de la Daniela ★ (Retiro/Salamanca, $$, p. 158)
Taberna del Alabardero (Puerta del Sol, $$, p. 134)

MEDITERRANEAN

Bazaar ★ (Chueca, $, p. 150)
Casa Benigna (Near Plaza República Argentina, $$, p. 165)
El Cenador del Prado ★ (Plaza de las Cortes & Huertas, $$, p. 136)
El Cielo del Urban ★★ (Plaza de las Cortes & Huertas, $$$$, p. 135)
El Mentidero de la Villa ★ (Chueca, $$$, p. 147)
El Olivo Restaurant ★★ (Chamartín, $$$, p. 163)
Las Cuatro Estaciones ★★★ (Chamberí, $$$, p. 160)
Santceloni ★★★ Retiro/Salamanca, $$$$, p. 152)
Sula ★ (Salamanca, $$, p. 157)

MOROCCAN

Al Mounia ★ (Paseo de Recoletos, $$$, p. 140)
Mosaiq ★ (Chamberí, $$, p. 161)

MURCIAN

El Caldero ★ (Plaza de las Cortes & Huertas, $$, p. 136)

PAELLA

Balear (Chamberí, $$, p. 161)
La Barraca (On or near the Gran Vía, $$$, p. 135)

PERUVIAN

Astrid y Gastón ★ (Retiro/Salamanca, $$$, p. 153)

RUSSIAN

El Cosaco (Plaza Mayor & Austrias, $, p. 129)

SCANDINAVIAN

Casa Benigna (Near Plaza República Argentina, $$, p. 165)

SEAFOOD

Bajamar (Near the Plaza España, $$$, p. 144)
Balear (Chamberí, $$, p. 161)
Cabo Mayor ★★ (Chamartín, $$$, p. 162)
El Pescador ★ (Retiro/Salamanca, $$$, p. 154)
La Barraca (On or near the Gran Vía, $$$, p. 135)
La Trainera ★ (Retiro/Salamanca, $$$, p. 155)

SPANISH

Café de Oriente ★ (Puerta del Sol, $$, p. 132)
Casa Mingo (Príncipe Pío, $, p. 166)
Casa Vallejo (Chueca, $$, p. 148)
Dassa Bassa ★★ (Retiro/Salamanca, $$$, p. 153)
Económico Soidemersol (Lavapiés, $, p. 140)
El Bocaíto ★ (Chueca, $$, p. 148)
El Bodegón (Retiro/Salamanca, $$$, p. 154)
El Buey (Retiro/Salamanca, $$, p. 157)
El Chaflán ★ (Chamartín, $$$$, p. 162)
El Schotis ★ (Plaza Mayor & Austrias, $$, p. 128)
Gran Café de Gijón ★★ (Paseo de Recoletos, $$, p. 141)
La Bardemcilla ★ (Chueca, $$, p. 149)
La Chata ★ (Plaza Mayor & Austrias, $, p. 130)
La Finca de Susana (Puerta del Sol, $, p. 134)
La Fuencisla ★ (Chueca, $$$, p. 147)
La Posada de la Villa (Plaza Mayor & Austrias, $$, p. 128)
La Terraza del Casino ★★★ (Puerta del Sol, $$$$, p. 131)
La Trucha (Plaza de las Cortes & Huertas, $$, p. 138)
Las Batuecas (Cuatro Caminos, $, p. 169)
Lhardy ★★ (Puerta del Sol, $$$$, p. 131)
Los Galayos ★★ (Plaza Mayor & Austrias, $$, p. 128)
Nodo (Near Plaza República Argentina, $$, p. 168)
San Mamés ★ (Cuatro Caminos, $$$, p. 169)

Sobrino de Botín ★★ (Plaza Mayor & Austrias, $$, p. 128)
Taberna del Alabardero (Puerta del Sol, $$, p. 134)
Tienda de Vinos ("El Comunista"; Chueca, $, p. 151)

STEAK

Casa Paco ★★ (Puerta del Sol, $$, p. 136)

TAPAS/TASCAS

Automático ★ (Lavapiés, $, p. 139)
Casa Alberto (Plaza de las Cortes & Huertas, $$, p. 166)
Casa Labra (Puerta del Sol, $$, p. 166)
Cervecería Alemana (Plaza de las Cortes & Huertas, $, p. 167)
Cervecería Santa Bárbara (Chueca, $, p. 167)
El Bocaíto ★ (Chueca, $$, p. 148)
La Bardemcilla ★ (Chueca, $$, p. 149)
La Taberna de Antonio Sánchez ★ (Lavapiés, $, p. 167)
Taberna Toscana (Plaza de las Cortes & Huertas, $, p. 139)

THAI

Siam (Near the Plaza España, $$, p. 146)
Thai Gardens ★★ (Chamartín, $$$, p. 153)

VALENCIAN

La Barraca (On or near the Gran Vía, $$$, p. 135)

VEGETARIAN

Al Natural ★ (Near Plaza de la Cibeles, $, p. 142)
Artemisa (Plaza de las Cortes & Huertas, $, p. 138)
Ceres (Cuatro Caminos, $, p. 169)
Comme-Bio (Puerta del Sol, $, p. 134)
El Estragón (Plaza Mayor & Austrias, $, p. 129)
Elqui (Lavapiés, $, p. 140)
Isla del Tesoro (Malasaña, $, p. 146)
La Biotika (Plaza de las Cortes & Huertas, $$, p. 137)
La Galette (Retiro/Salamanca, $$, p. 158)

PLAZA MAYOR & AUSTRIAS

Expensive

Asador Frontón ★ BASQUE Brainchild of former top pelota star Miguel Ansorena, this Basque bastion of hearty fare opened in 1980, on the first floor of a building overlooking Tirso de Molina square. As befits Spain's most macho province, the Asador specializes in grilled man-size meat dishes of the highest quality and its *chuletones de buey* (huge beef steak chops) are second to none. No need to be daunted by their size, as when served they are cut into strips for two to share. A popular starter is *pimientos del piquillo* (spicy peppers), and fish also features impressively in the form of *rape a la brasa* (grilled angler fish, also shared by two). Finish your meal with the house's own *cuajada* (junket) or *panchineta* (cream-filled puff pastry). Such has been the Frontón's success that it's expanded to two other branches in the northern part of the city, in the classy Salamanca district's Calle Velázquez and in Calle Pedro Muguruza, near Cuzco, where the menu is even broader.

Plaza Tirso de Molina 7 (entrance via Calle Jesús y María 1). ✆ **91-369-16-17.** www.asadorfronton.es. Main courses 25€–35€. AE, DC, MC, V. Oct–Apr daily; June–July and Sept Mon–Sat 1–3:30pm, 9–11pm. Closed Aug. Metro: Tirso de Molina.

Julian de Tolosa CASTILIAN Set in a 19th-century building in the center of Cava Baja, this popular eating spot is renowned for its generous-size quality steaks. The charming two-level dining area, with its red-brick walls, wooden beamed ceiling, and subtle halogen lighting, occupies the ground floor and basement areas. Maitre d'

GOING green IN MADRID

Being a "veggie" has long ceased to mean you need feel you're an outsider in the Spanish capital. Over the past decade and a half, the traditional dominance of carnivore-oriented establishments has been challenged by an ever-growing number of vegetarian restaurants. In this chapter, you find nine of the best (see "Restaurants by Cuisine," above).

You don't have to confine yourself to 100% green establishments to get the goods, though, as many standard Spanish eating spots offer a large choice of noncarnivorous platos.

Apart from the ubiquitous *tortilla* (made, *naturalmente,* with eggs Spanish-style and not from cornmeal Mexican-style), check out their menus for dishes like *pimientos fritos* (fried peppers), *berengenas al horno* (eggplant baked in the oven), *calabaza guisada* (stewed pumpkin), *setas al jerez* (mushrooms cooked in sherry), and *pisto* (Spain's answer to ratatouille with tomatoes, peppers, eggplant courgettes, and onions all cooked in oil and garlic: avoid the Manchego version, though, as this has bits of ham in it). *Jamón* (Mountain or cooked, Serrano or York) is scarcely regarded as "real" meat in Spain and can even appear in apparently innocuous dishes such as caldo (broth), so confirm with the waiter before you order.

Arabic, Indian, and Italian restaurants may also provide what you're looking for, with their inventive range of couscous, rice, and pasta-based dishes, and if fish is an acceptable option there are, of course, plenty of seafood restaurants to choose from, though these tend to be expensive. (Check the restaurant list for top-value spots like Ribeiro do Miño.)

Potato power: Anyone wanting a *racion*, or single dish, of something cheap and meat-free should try *patatas bravas* (potatoes sautéed brown and served in a picante sauce). Between Sol and Tirso de Molina, there's a trio of eating spots all called Las Bravas and all specializing in this simple but filling dish (still a modest 3.50€ dish). It's also widely available in tapas bars, sometimes at even cheaper prices.

Angela Halty will guide you through the contents of the succinct menu and its accompanying wine list of full-bodied reds. Supreme highlight is the legendary *chuletón de buey* (huge ox steak—rated as one of the best in Madrid) and supported by tasty basics such as *alubias rojas de Tolosa* (red Tolosa beans) and *pimientos del piquillo* (baked spicy peppers). Fresh *espárragos* (asparagus) and cogollos (lettuce hearts) are summer favorites. Also first-rate are the *merluza* (hake) and salty Idiazábal cheese. It's all good but not cheap. Don't forget to check the prices before you order!

Cava Baja 18. ✆ **91-365-82-10.** www.casajuliandetolosa.com. Main courses 20€–30€. AE, DC, MC, V. Mon–Sat 1:30–4pm and 9pm–midnight; Sun 1:30–4pm. Metro: La Latina.

Moderate

Casa Lucio ★ CASTILIAN Set on a narrow historic street whose edges once marked the perimeter of Old Madrid, this is a venerable *tasca* with all the requisite antique accessories. Dozens of cured hams hang from hand-hewn beams above the well-oiled bar. Among the clientele is a stable of sometimes surprisingly well-known public figures—perhaps even the king of Spain. The two dining rooms, each on a different floor, have whitewashed walls, tile floors, and exposed brick. A well-trained staff offers classic Castilian food, which might include Jabugo ham with broad beans, shrimp in garlic sauce, hake with green sauce, several types of roasted lamb, and a thick steak served sizzling hot on a heated platter, called *churrasco de la casa*. The gourmet showpiece, though, is a modest *campo* dish called *huevos estrellados,* literally "broken eggs" mixed with potatoes and here raised to a fine art.

Cava Baja 35. ✆ **91-365-32-52.** www.casalucio.es. Reservations recommended. Main courses 18€–32€. AE, DC, MC, V. Sun–Fri 1–4pm; daily 9pm–midnight. Closed Aug. Metro: La Latina.

El Schotis ★ SPANISH El Schotis was established in 1962 in the same bar-packed street as Casa Lucio, and its large and soberly old-fashioned dining rooms are the setting for an animated crowd of Madrileños and foreign visitors, who receive ample portions of conservative, well-prepared vegetables, salads, soups, fish, and above all, meat. Specialties of the house include roast baby lamb, grilled steaks and veal chops, shrimp with garlic, fried hake in green sauce, and traditional desserts. Although one reader found everything but the gazpacho ho-hum, this local favorite pleases thousands of diners annually. There's a bar near the entrance for tapas and before- or after-dinner drinks.

Cava Baja 11. ✆ **91-365-32-30.** Reservations recommended. Main courses 14€–28€; fixed-price menu 28€. AE, DC, MC, V. Mon–Sat 1–4pm and 8:30pm–midnight; Sun 1–4pm. Metro: La Latina.

La Posada de la Villa SPANISH/GRILLED MEAT Also in Cava Baja, this much loved 17th-century inn offers a modern, more sanitized version of the earthy grilled cuisine that fed the stonemasons who built the building's thick walls. Within a trio of dining rooms whose textured plaster and old stonework absolutely reek of Old Castile, you'll find a hardworking staff and a menu that focuses on a time-honored specialty—roasted baby lamb—that's ordered more often than anything else on the menu. Other excellent choices include different versions of hake, Madrid-style tripe, and the rich, savory stew *(cocido madrileño)* that many local residents remember fondly from the days of their childhood. Notice that many of the chairs have brass plaques bearing the names of famous patrons—I saw one labeled "Janet Jackson" last time!

Cava Baja 9. ✆ **91-366-18-60.** www.posadadelavilla.com. Reservations recommended. Main courses 14€–22€. DC, MC, V. Daily 1–4pm; Mon–Sat 8pm–midnight. Sun 1–4pm. Closed Aug. Metro: La Latina.

Los Galayos ★★ SPANISH This restaurant's location is among the most desirable in the city, on a narrow side street about three steps from the arcades of Plaza Mayor. Within two separate houses, the restaurant has flourished on this site since 1894. In summer, cascades of vines accent a series of tables and chairs on the cobblestones outside, perfect for tapas-sampling and people-watching. Some visitors consider an evening here among the highlights of their trip to Spain.

The ambience inside evokes Old Castile, with vaulted or beamed ceilings in several dining rooms. The Grande family, your multilingual hosts, prepares traditional versions of fish, shellfish, pork, veal, and beef in time-tested ways. Suckling pig, baby goat, and roasted lamb are almost always featured.

Calle Botoneras 5. ✆ **91-366-30-28.** www.losgalayos.net. Reservations recommended. Main courses 12€–28€. AE, DC, MC, V. Daily 9am–midnight. Metro: Sol.

Sobrino de Botín ★★ SPANISH Ernest Hemingway made this restaurant famous when, in the final two pages of his novel *The Sun Also Rises,* the main character Jake invited Lady Brett here for the Segovian specialty of roast suckling pig, washed down with abundant quantities of Rioja Alta (more affordable then). As you enter, you step back to 1725, the year the restaurant—which claims to be the oldest in the world—was founded. You'll see an open kitchen with a charcoal hearth, hanging copper pots, an 18th-century tile oven for roasting the suckling pig, and a big pot of soup whose aroma wafts across the tables. Painter Francisco Goya was once a dishwasher here. The two house specialties are roast suckling pig and roast Segovian lamb. From the a la carte menu, you might try the fish-based "quarter-of-an-hour" soup. Good main dishes include baked Cantabrian hake and filet mignon with potatoes. The dessert list features strawberries (in season) with whipped cream. You can accompany your meal with Rioja (Hemingway style) or Ribera del Duero wine.

Calle de Cuchilleros 17. ✆ **91-366-30-26** or 91-366-42-17. www.botin.es. Reservations required. Main courses 20€–120€; fixed-price menu 45€. AE, DC, MC, V. Daily 1–4pm and 8pm–midnight. Metro: Sol or Opera.

Inexpensive

Bar Salamanca 🎁 CASTILIAN It's well worth squeezing in to sample the hearty bargain value fare at this highly popular wine bar at the Austrias end of the Cava Baja. *Vino* is the main attraction here, but as in any Madrileño locale worth its salt, you can also enjoy a wide range of *raciones* at surprisingly reasonable prices for this area, from a full-bodied *cocido* to a variety of roasts, especially lamb. Other prime tapas and *raciones* to enjoy include *croquetas* (croquettes), *albóndigas* (meatballs), and *champiñones al cabrales* (mushrooms cooked with strong blue Asturian cheese). The comprehensive wine list covers Riojas, Ribera del Dueros, and Albariños by the glass (2.50€–5€) or bottle (10€–14€).

Cava Baja 31. ✆ **91-366-31-10.** Main courses 8€–16€. No credit cards. Tues–Thurs 1–4pm and 8:30pm–midnight; Fri–Sat 1–4pm and 8:30pm–1am; Sun 1–4:30pm. Metro: La Latina.

El Cosaco RUSSIAN One of the few Russian restaurants in Madrid sits adjacent to one of the most charming and evocative squares in town. Inside, you'll find a trio of dining rooms outfitted with paintings and artifacts from the former Soviet Union. Menu items seem to taste best when preceded with something from a long list of vodkas, many of them from small scale distilleries you might not immediately recognize. Items include rich and savory cold-weather dishes that go down better in the city's chilly winters than during the short sweltering summers, but which nevertheless provide satisfying alternatives from the all-Spanish restaurants in the same neighborhood. Examples include beef Stroganoff; quenelles of pike-perch with fresh dill; and thin-sliced smoked salmon or smoked sturgeon that's artfully arranged with capers, chopped onions, and chopped hard-boiled eggs. Red or white versions of borscht make a worthy starter, and blinis, stuffed with caviar or paprika-laced beef, are always excellent.

Plaza de la Paja 2. ✆ **91-365-35-48.** Reservations recommended. Main courses 10€–25€. AE, DC, MC, V. Mon 9pm–midnight; Tues–Sun 2–3:30pm and 9pm–midnight. Metro: La Latina.

El Estragón VEGETARIAN Set beside the Austrias' historic Plaza de la Paja (literally, Square of the Straw), this delightful veggie outpost (*estragón* means tarragon) offers a homey ambience with 20-odd tables set on three levels amid a decor of check tablecloths, russet terra-cotta tiles, and plaid curtains. The menu provides an eclectic choice of vegetarian dishes, from a vegetable-filled risotto verde to soy *albóndigas* (meatballs)—even a *cordon bleu* steak that contains no meat (only vegetables).

Popular appetizers are almond soup or pepper tart, and few can resist winding up with the delicious homemade chocolate tart with truffles. Unlike most green eating spots, it does in fact also have *pinchos* (kabobs) at the bar. The weekday fixed-lunch menu is good value but be warned: On weekends it doubles in price. A recent added bonus for website fanatics is the free Internet access.

Plaza de la Paja 10. © **91-365-89-82.** Main courses 12€–18€. Set lunch 15€; set dinner 25€. AE, DC, MC, V. Daily 1:30–5pm; 8:30pm–midnight. Metro: La Latina.

El Viajero INTERNATIONAL This bustling three-story restaurant is located right on Plaza de la Cebada close to the Rastro market and labyrinthine lanes of Lavapiés. Grilling is the big thing here, with an emphasis on Uruguayan *chorizo* (a sausage of red peppers and pork), *salchichas* (sausages), and beef, but the wide-ranging choices also cover salads, *pinchitos* (shish kabobs), and couscous. Prices are very reasonable and there's a first-rate prix-fixe menu. Lunchtime tends to be packed, and market visitors make it particularly busy on Sundays. On sunny summer days, you can eat on the terrace and enjoy the view.

Plaza de la Cebada 11. © **91-366-90-64.** Main courses 8€–20€; prix-fixe lunch 14€. AE, DC, MC, V. Tues–Sat 2–4:30pm and 9pm–12:30am; Sun 2–4:30pm. Closed last 2 weeks of Aug. Metro: La Latina.

La Botillería de Maxi MADRILEÑO A source of endless bad puns from "offally good" to the "offal truth," this genial old-style spit-and-sawdust establishment, located in the quieter lane parallel to Cava Baja, specializes in just that. Offal, or—to be more precise—dishes like *callos* (tripe in a rich sauce), or *entresijos* and *gallinejas* (both the latter are deep-fried lamb's gizzards, *gallinejas* generally being of a slightly higher quality). Acquired tastes or not, there are many who find these essentially *madrileño* dishes delicious from the word go, especially at Maxi's where you can be sure they're as good as it gets. If the thought of munching internal organs makes you squeamish—however well cooked and presented they may be—then there are the old standby *raciones* of aromatic *jamón Serrano, rabo de toro* (bull's tail), or pungent *cabrales* cheese to fall back on, plus the hearty *cocido madrileño* stew which is served on Thursdays and Saturdays. And whatever you have, you must accompany it with the hearty house red wine.

Cava Alta 4. © **91-365-12-49.** www.labotilleriademaxi.com. Main courses 10€–20€; set lunch Sat–Mon 14€, Tues–Fri 12€. No credit cards. Tues–Sat 1–4pm and 8:30pm–midnight; Sun 12:30–6pm. Metro: La Latina.

La Chata ★ 🎁 SPANISH The cuisine in one of Cava Baja's most perennially popular watering holes is Castilian, Galician, and northern Spanish. Set behind a heavily ornamented tile facade, the place has a stand-up tapas bar at the entrance, which is framed by hanging Serrano hams, cloves of garlic, and photographs of bullfighters. It is crowded from opening time onwards with visitors and locals alike who usually prefer to eat in the small atmospheric adjoining area where prices are more reasonable than in the main downstairs restaurant. Full meals might include roast suckling pig, roast lamb, *calamares en su tinta* (squid in its own ink), grilled filet of steak with peppercorns, or omelets flavored with strips of eel.

Cava Baja 24. © **91-366-14-58.** Reservations recommended. Main dishes (upstairs) 8€–16€; (downstairs) 12€–35€. AE, MC, V. Thurs–Mon 12:30–5pm; daily 8pm–1am. Metro: La Latina.

Malacatín ★ 🎁 MADRILEÑO Tucked away in a narrow street off the Plaza Cascorro, a stone's throw from the Rastro market, is this tiny century-old slice of old

Castizo Madrid. It's a tiny taberna where you sit on benches at basic wooden trestle tables and enjoy the place's one and only main dish: *cocido*. The very filling set menu includes wine (usually Valdepeñas) and dessert. If you feel like a tapa beforehand, you can sample *morcillas de León* (blood sausage from León) or *bacalao frito* (fried cod) at the bar—or a *caldo* (consommé) in cold weather—but don't forget to leave room for that prodigious main meal. As there are only two sittings—both at lunch-time—you'll need to be prepared for a siesta afterward anyway. Reservations at least one day beforehand are essential.

Calle Ruda 5. ✆ **91-365-52-41.** www.malacatin.com. Set *cocido* lunch 28€. Mon–Sat 2–4:30 (seatings at 2:30 and 3:30pm). No credit cards. Closed July–Aug. Metro: La Latina.

Masaniello ITALIAN This warmly hospitable rustic-style *trattoria* (named after a Naples revolutionary) is a lone unexpected outpost of Italian color in the midst of Cava Baja's proliferation of tabernas, wine bars, and former coaching houses transformed into atmospheric Castizo restaurants. Here *pasta* instead of *cocido* rules the day and you can enjoy real pizzas cooked in a genuine pizza oven by an Italian chef. The honest, down-to-earth Napoletana is a solid favorite, but under owner Luigi Fabriccini's guiding hand other more innovative specialities also fill the menu. Some standouts are *parmesana de berengena* (eggplant cooked in Parmesan cheese), *calzone, pappardelle,* and *spaghetti mare e monte*. Accompany your meal with a fine Chianti and finish off with the marvelous homemade *tiramisu,* if you have room (not forgetting a fiery *grappa* or *zambuca* with your espresso if you want the full treatment).

Cava Baja 28. ✆ **91-364-54-86.** Main courses 10€–20€. DC, MC, V. Sept–June Tues 9pm–midnight, Wed–Sun 2–4pm and 9pm–midnight; July Tues–Sun 9pm–midnight. Closed Aug. Metro: La Latina.

PUERTA DEL SOL

Very Expensive

La Terraza del Casino ★★★ SPANISH/INTERNATIONAL The mold-breaking Catalan chef Ferran Adrià created all the dishes on the menu here and flies in regularly to see that his cooks are following his orders. His deluxe eating spot lies on the top floor of Madrid's Casino, a former gents club whose history goes back the biggest part of a century, and his exquisite ever-changing culinary creations gravitate from one taste "explosion" to another. The panoramic city views from this culinary mecca are outstanding too—get to the top by elevator or via a grand 19th-century stairway. The decor is classically restrained with high ceilings and crystal chandeliers. Fresh seasonal ingredients are used to create his dishes, such as *raya* in oil and saffron with parsley purée and nuts on a bed of finely diced fries. More traditional dishes include the succulent *merluza a la gallega* (Galician hake), *crema de la fabada asturiana* (creamed Asturian bean soup), and the steeply priced *jamón Jabugo* (cured ham from acorn-fed pigs) served with a *menestra* (mixed vegetables) al dente. Only French champagne and Spanish wines are listed, some of the heartiest reds coming from the Ribera de Duero province of Castilla y Leon, near Valladolid.

Alcalá 15. ✆ **91-521-87-00.** www.casinodemadrid.es. Main courses 28€–45€; fixed-price menu 90€. AE, DC, MC, V. Mon–Fri 1:30–4pm and 9–11:45pm; Sat 9–11:45pm. Closed Aug. Metro: Sevilla.

Lhardy ★★ SPANISH/INTERNATIONAL Lhardy has been a Madrileño legend ever since it opened in 1839 as a gathering place for the city's literati and political leaders. At street level is what may be the most elegant snack bar in Spain. Within a dignified antique setting of marble and hardwood, cups of steaming consommé are dispensed from silver samovars into delicate porcelain cups, and rows of croquettes, tapas, and sandwiches are served to stand-up clients who pay for their food at a cashier's kiosk near the entrance. The ground-floor deli and takeout service is open daily from 9am to 3pm and 5 to 9:30pm.

The real culinary skill of the place, however, is on Lhardy's second floor, where you'll find a formal restaurant decorated in the ornate Belle Epoque style of Isabel Segunda. Specialties of the house include fish, pork, veal, tripe in a garlicky tomato and onion wine sauce, and *cocido,* the celebrated chickpea stew of Madrid. *Soufflé sorpresa* (baked Alaska) is the dessert specialty.

Carrera de San Jerónimo 8. ✆ **91-521-33-85.** www.lhardy.com. Reservations recommended in the upstairs dining room. Main dishes 15€–45€. AE, DC, MC, V. Mon–Sat 1–3:30pm and 8:30–11pm. Closed Aug. Metro: Sol.

Expensive

Caripén ★ FRENCH This restaurant stands in a historic district near the Royal Opera House and the Spanish Senate. It was once El Tablao, the flamenco club of Lola Flores, one of the most famous of all Spanish singer-dancers. Its Art Deco decor has been restored, and instead of flamenco, you get the inspired French bistro cookery of Daniel Boute. The restaurant is especially popular with the Madrid locals, or *gatos* (cats), because it serves until 2am when most other quality establishments are shuttered. (Local residents are called *gatos* because they like to roam about at night.) Go for the *mejillones de roca* (mussels in white wine and cream sauce), a perfectly prepared steak tartare, *foie* with *setas* (duck liver and mushrooms), or skate in black butter. You can finish off with such desserts as tiramisu, freshly made fruit tarts, or crepes.

Plaza de la Marina Española 4. ✆ **91-541-11-77.** Reservations recommended Fri–Sun. Main courses 15€–35€. MC, V. Mon–Sat 9pm–2am. Closed Aug. Metro: Opera/Santo Domingo.

La Esquina del Real FRENCH Next to the Teatro Real, you'll find this restaurant in an impressive 17th-century building with an ancient stone facade, thick granite walls, and the original wooden beams supporting old ceilings. This place has a sophisticated atmosphere, yet prices are very reasonable. One Madrid food critic recently called this place one of the city's "best-kept" culinary secrets. Jesus Oliva and Ismael Ballesteros, able successors to the former owner and chef, Marcel Magossian, continue his good work, extending a hearty welcome to patrons and feeding them well. Fresh ingredients are transformed into tasty concoctions, like large prawns with a delicate flavoring of raspberry vinaigrette or roast oxtail with mashed potatoes and fresh mushrooms. A rather common dish, veal fricassee in mushroom sauce, is transformed into something sublime here. To end your repast, you might opt for a combination platter of warm cheese, or try tart tatin, ice cream with a crunchy caramel sauce flambéed at your table.

Calle Unión 8, corner of Calle Amnistia 4. ✆ **91-559-43-09.** Reservations recommended Fri–Sun. Main courses 25€–45€. AE, MC, V. Mon–Fri 2–4pm and 9pm–midnight; Sat 9pm–midnight. Closed last 2 weeks of Aug. Metro: Opera.

Moderate

Café de Oriente ★ FRENCH/SPANISH The ever popular Oriente is one of the most beautifully located cafe-restaurants. From its terrace tables there's a spectacular view past statue-lined gardens of the Palacio Real (Royal Palace). The dining rooms—Castilian upstairs, French Basque downstairs—are regularly frequented by royalty and diplomats. Typical of the refined cuisine are vichyssoise, fresh vegetable flan, and many savory meat and fresh-fish offerings. Service is excellent. Most visitors try to get an outdoor table, though on cloudy winter days the interior, decorated in turn-of-the-20th-century style, with banquettes and regal paneling, is equally inviting. Pizza, tapas, and drinks (including Irish, Viennese, Russian, and Jamaican coffees) are served.

Plaza de Oriente 2. ✆ **91-547-15-64.** www.cafedeoriente.es. Reservations recommended in restaurant only. Cafe menu 22€; restaurant main courses 15€–35€; cafe, tapas 3.50€--5€.

Casa Ciriaco CASTILIAN In business for more than 90 years, this longtime favorite taberna-cum-restaurant is still run by the same family. Lying only 2 blocks from the Palacio Real, it has on occasion served dinners to members of the royal family along with a list of other impressive guests, including bullfighters, artists, and scholars. These distinguished guests are drawn to the unpretentious family atmosphere and the time-tested recipes. Nouvelle cuisine here means anything being served in 1900, including the classic Madrid *callos* (tripe), which is an acquired taste for many diners. One of the most enticing offerings is *perdiz* (partridge) served with fava beans. *Liebre* (hare), another good choice, is served with white beans. *Gambas a la plancha* (grilled prawns) is a good appetizer, or you might choose to start with one of the hearty soups of the day, including a specialty of Castile: sopa castellana. A few fish dishes appear, including *trucha* (mountain trout), and *cochinillo asado* (roast suckling pig) is a specialty. Accompany your feast with a glass (or two) of Rioja wine. There is another branch of Casa Ciriaco at Calle Marqués de Riscal 8 in the Chamberí district, near the Ruben Darío metro station.

Calle Mayor 84. ✆ **91-548-06-20.** Reservations recommended. Main courses 12€–28€. MC, V. Thurs–Tues 1–4pm and 8pm–midnight. Closed Aug. Metro: Sol.

Cornucopia EURO-AMERICAN Set on a narrow side street adjacent to the medieval Plaza de Descalzas Reales, this restaurant occupies the mezzanine level of what was originally a 19th-century private palace. Its glamour and allure derive from its ownership by three partners, one American and two Spanish. Within a pair of elegant and airy dining rooms whose gleaming parquet floors remain from the original decor, you can admire the frequently changing paintings, all available for sale. Menu items include mussels with fennel and a roasted red pepper sauce over black fettuccini; grilled baby hen with mushrooms and sherry sauce; and grilled pork tenderloin stuffed with brie and bacon, and served with a pomegranate-apple compote and a red wine reduction sauce. Desserts are sumptuous and might include a dollop of such original homemade ice creams as *mojito*. Named after a traditional Cuban cocktail, it's flavored with mint, lemon, and rum. All the food is well prepared, the ingredients are fresh, and the staff is among the most inviting in Madrid.

Calle Navas de Tolosa 9. ✆ **91-521-38-96.** www.restaurantecornucopia.com. Reservations recommended. Main courses 10€–25€; fixed-price lunch (Tues–Sat only) 12€; fixed weekday (except Fri) evening menu 16€. AE, DC, MC, V. Tues–Sat 1:30–4pm; Tues–Sun 9–1:30pm. Closed 1 week in Aug. Metro: Opera or Callao.

Donzoko JAPANESE Now in its third decade, the Donzoko is one of Madrid's longest established Japanese eating spots. Particularly popular with party-going groups of young clientele due to its location in lively Echegaray Street and the monumental menu, which covers every everything from sushi to sukiyaki (veal strips with wok-cooked vegetables for two; often viewed by Madrileños as a Nipponese version of their *cocido*). *Sashimi* and prawn *tempura* also grace the list, and of course *sake* (rice wine) is the appropriate drink for the occasion. Decor is functional to weird—you're greeted by a metal water fountain in the small entrance patio—and the service is attentively cool.

Calle Echegaray 3. ✆ **91-429-57-20.** Main courses 12€–25€. AE, DC, MC, V. Mon–Sat 1:30–3:30pm and 8:30–11:30pm. Metro: Sevilla.

Taberna del Alabardero BASQUE/MADRILEÑO/SPANISH In close proximity to the Royal Palace, this little Spanish classic is known for its selection of tasty tapas, ranging from squid cooked in wine to fried potatoes dipped in hot sauce. Photographs of famous former patrons, including Nelson Rockefeller and the race-car driver Jackie Stewart, line the walls. The restaurant in the rear is said to be one of the city's best-kept secrets. Decorated in typical tavern style, it serves a savory Spanish and Basque cuisine with market-fresh ingredients. The huge wine list covers the whole spectrum of what's best in Spanish vineyards.

Felipe V 6. ✆ **91-547-25-77.** www.alabardero.eu. Reservations required for restaurant only. Bar: tapas 3.50€–12€; glass of house wine 2.50€, glass of vintage dessert wine 5€–8€. Restaurant: main courses 15€–30€; tasting menu 55€. AE, DC, MC, V. Daily cafeteria: 10am–2am; restaurant: 1–4pm and 9pm–midnight. Metro: Opera.

Inexpensive

Comme-Bio VEGETARIAN This new concept in vegetarian eating opened in 2001 with two branches, one in the central Calle Mayor and the other in Chamberí. Each serves soups, *seitanes*, risottos, and pastries (as well as some tempting nonvegetarian "biological" meat dishes)—complete with additional special kiddie menu—in a bright open buffet dining area with large windows, a terrace, and a special air-conditioned section for smokers. The adjoining shop dispenses a comprehensive range of organic products—right down to ecologically approved pet food!

Mayor 30. ✆ **91-354-63-00.** Main courses 10€–25€; buffet lunch 12€. DC, MC, V. Daily 1:30–4pm and 8:30pm–midnight. Metro: Sol.

Delfos GREEK Located right in the heart of town, this is one of Madrid's smartest Greek eating spots, offering the full gamut of Hellenic fare and then some. The atmosphere is friendly and the taberna-style decor gets you in the right mood to enjoy the food. *Pikalia megali* is the ideal full-bodied appetizer, combining many familiar Greek tidbits on a single platter including taramasalata, tzatsiki, black olives, feta cheese, and dolmades (stuffed grape leaves). The Hellenes' favorite meat, lamb, scores highly here: Try the delicious Delfos version cooked with nuts and honey. Anise-flavored ouzo is the ideal aperitif to kick off with, and for those who've acquired the taste, the tangy resinated white wine, retsina, accompanies the meal to perfection. Though it is deceptively quaffable, beware: In sufficient quantities it packs quite a kick.

Cuesta de Santo Domingo 14. ✆ **91-548-37-64.** Main courses 9€–20€; set lunch 12€. AE, DC, MC, V. Tues–Sat 1:30–4:30pm and 8pm–midnight. Sun 1:30–4:30pm. Metro: Santo Domingo.

La Finca de Susana 🎁 SPANISH/INTERNATIONAL Set in a quiet street close to Alcalá and a short walk from the Puerta del Sol, this airy open-plan restaurant with its bright modern decor offers a winning combination of inventive quality cuisine and highly affordable prices. Vegetables in tempura batter and an exceptional choice of rice and fish dishes head the individual specialities and the desserts are simple and delicious. Service is smart and efficient and best value is its set weekday lunch. This is one place you should eat earlier than the usual Spanish hours as there's no booking and queues soon gather, especially at lunchtimes, due to its understandable popularity. (Try 1:30pm instead of an hour later.)

Calle Arlaban 4. ✆ **91-369-35-57.** www.lafincs-restaurant.com. Main courses 8€–16€. AE, DC, MC, V. Daily 1–4pm and 8:30–11:45pm. Metro: Sevilla.

ON OR NEAR THE GRAN VÍA

Expensive

La Barraca VALENCIAN This long established Valencian-style restaurant, designed and built like an old Levante country house, is renowned for its tasty seafood and rice-based dishes. There are four different dining rooms, three of which lie one flight above street level, all of them colorfully cluttered with ceramics, paintings, photographs, Spanish lanterns, flowers, and local artifacts. The house specialty, paella a la Barraca, is made with pork and chicken. Specialties in the appetizer category include *desgarrat* (a salad of cod and red peppers), mussels in a white-wine sauce, and shrimp sautéed with garlic. In addition to the recommended paella, you can select at least 16 rice dishes, including black rice and queen paella. Main-dish specialties include brochette of angler and prawns and rabbit with herbs. Lemon-and-vodka sorbet brings the meal to a fitting finish.

Reina 29. ✆ **91-532-71-54.** www.labarraca.es. Reservations recommended. Main courses 12€–30€; *menu del dia* 34€. AE, DC, MC, V. Daily 1–4pm and 8:30pm–midnight. Metro: Gran Vía or Sevilla.

PLAZA DE LAS CORTES & HUERTAS

Expensive

El Cielo del Urban ★★ MEDITERRANEAN Madrid's most exciting penthouse eating spot, patronized by a wide range of beautiful and "important" people (from top models and frivolous TV chat show performers to dead serious politicians) can be found on the top floor of the elegant avant-garde Hotel Urban (see chapter 5, "Where to Stay") beside the rooftop swimming pool and enjoying spectacular city views. The restaurant's decor is a blend of edgy and Baroque with bare floorboards, black metal chairs, tables with fine cotton tablecloths and large candelabras that are lit at night, and an overhead glass skylight crisscrossed by steel trellises. Among its eclectic delights are a fantastic *carpaccio de gambas rojas con vinagreta de soja y algas nori* (carpaccio of red prawns with soya sauce vinaigrette and seaweed), ultra-fresh *Ostras Napoleon* (huge oysters from the Galician Rías), and *tartare de solomillo de wagyu estilo Kobe* (Japanese style raw ox steak), as well as some outrageously mouth-watering *postres* (desserts). The superb (and pricey) menu del Cielo is served with Dom Perignon champagne.

In the Hotel Urban, Carrera de San Jerónimo 34. ✆ **91-787-77-80.** Reservations required. Main courses 30€–65€; menu del Urban 145€; gourmet menu del Cielo 220€. AE, DC, MC, V. Daily 1:30–4pm, 8:30–11:30pm. Metro: Sevilla.

Moderate

Casa Paco ★★ STEAK Madrileños defiantly name Casa Paco, just beside the Plaza Mayor, when someone dares to denigrate Spanish steaks. They know that here you can get the thickest, juiciest, tastiest steaks in Spain, priced according to weight. Señor Paco sears his steaks in boiling oil before serving them on plates so hot that the almost-raw meat continues to cook, preserving the natural juices. Located in the Old Town, this two-story restaurant has three dining rooms but reservations are imperative. If you face a long wait, sample the tapas at the bar in front. Around the walls are autographed photographs of notables.

Casa Paco isn't just a steakhouse; you can start with fish soup and proceed to grilled sole or baby lamb, or try *Casa Paco cocido,* the house version of Madrid's famous chickpea and pork soup. Finish with a luscious dessert, but don't expect coffee here as Paco no longer serves it. (When he did customers tended to linger, keeping tables occupied while potential patrons had to be turned away.)

Plaza Puerta Cerrada 11. ✆ **91-366-31-66.** www.casapaco1933.com. Reservations required. Main courses 12€–28€; fixed-price menu 30€. DC, MC, V. Mon–Sat 1–4pm and 8:30pm–midnight. Closed Aug. Metro: Sol, Opera, or La Latina.

Do Salmon GALICIAN As the name implies, this is predominantly a seafood restaurant offering good solid *gallego* specialities such as *pulpo a la feira* (octopus cooked in olive oil and with paprika sauce) as well as national favorites like *lenguado en salsa tartare* (grilled sole in rich tartar sauce). Hearty meat dishes also feature on the menu, and for carnivores I recommend the traditional *codillo con grelos* (ham knuckle with turnip tops). The service is quietly impersonal and the decor unspectacular—verging on mid-1950s drab—but it's the quality of the food that counts. Portions are generous (no measly nouvelle cuisine rationing here) and prices extremely reasonable, which is why the place has a staunch band of loyal regulars.

León 4. ✆ **91-429-39-52.** Main courses 8€–24€; set lunch (Tues–Fri only) 12€. Tues–Sun 1–4pm and 9pm–midnight. AE, MC, V. Closed mid-Aug to mid-Sept. Metro: Antón Martín.

El Caldero ★ MURCIAN Set in the narrow pedestrianized Huertas Street, this is probably the only restaurant in Madrid specializing in dishes from the still little-known Levante province of Murcia. Founded 30 years ago by Antonio Valero, it's now run by his son Alfredo, who provides the same high standard of marine cuisine. As with its more famous neighbor Valencia, Murcia's regional specialty is rice, served here in a variety of dishes headed by *paella* and *arroz al caldero* (rice cooked in seafood and shellfish stock). The fish in general is excellent, especially the *dorada a la sal* (gilt head bream cooked in salt), and fresh Levantine vegetables also feature prominently on the menu in dishes such as *verduras a la piedra.* Its prize dessert *tocino del cielo* (a light pudding made with egg yolk and syrup) is mouthwateringly delicious.

Huertas 15. ✆ **91-429-50-44.** www.elcaldero.com. Main courses 14€–29€. AE, DC, MC, V. Daily 1:30–4pm; Tues–Sat 9pm–midnight. Closed mid-Aug to mid-Sept. Metro: Antón Martín.

El Cenador del Prado ★ MEDITERRANEAN Founded by brothers Ramón and Tomás Herranz in the 1980s, this eccentric and beautiful eating spot is like no other in Madrid. In the anteroom, an attendant will check your coat into an elaborately carved armoire before the maitre d' ushers you into one of a trio of rooms. Two of the rooms have cove moldings, English furniture, and floor-to-ceiling gilded mirrors. A third room is ringed with lattices and flooded with sun from a skylight. Bright maroon and orange walls and glittering chandeliers create a modernist-cum-baroque mood and the main dining area basks in a glass-domed conservatory setting. Cuisine is a blend of Hispanic and Middle East Mediterranean with exquisite entrees like hummus with peppers and superb main fish courses such as *rodaballo con leche merengada* (turbot cooked in cinnamon-flavored milk). You might also enjoy such specialties as crepes with salmon and Iranian caviar; a casserole of snails and oysters with mushrooms; sea bass with candied lemons; or medallions of venison served with pepper-and-fig chutney. The fixed *menú de degustación* (tasting menu) is very good value.

Prado 4. © **91-429-15-61.** www.elcenadordelprado.com. Reservations recommended. Main courses 14€–25€; fixed-price menu 23€; vegetarian menu 25€; tasting menu 45€. AE, DC, MC, V. Mon–Fri 1:45–4pm; Mon–Sat 9pm–midnight. Closed Aug 12–19. Metro: Sevilla or Antón Martín.

Errota-Zar BASQUE Next to the House of Deputies and the Zarzuela Theater, Errota-Zar means "old mill," a nostalgic reference to the Basque country, home of the Olano family, owners of the restaurant. A small bar at the entrance displays a collection of fine cigars and wines, and the blue-painted walls are adorned with paintings of Basque landscapes. The restaurant has only about two dozen tables, which can easily fill up. The Basque country is long known as the gastronomic capital of Spain, and Errota-Zar provides a fine showcase for its cuisine. Try such appetizers as the rare Tolosa kidney bean or fried anchovies. Many Basques begin their meal with a *tortilla de bacalao* (salt cod omelet). For main dishes, sample the delights of *chuletón de buey* (oxtail) or *kokotxas de merluza en aceite* (the cheeks of the hake fish cooked in virgin olive oil). Hake cheeks may not sound appetizing, but Spaniards and many foreigners praise this dish. The best homemade desserts are *cuajada de la casa,* a thick yogurt made from sheep's milk, or *tarta de limón,* a lemon cake. You might also try rice ice cream in prune sauce.

Jovellanos 3, 1st floor. © **91-531-25-64.** www.errota-zar.com. Reservations recommended. Main courses 18€–35€; special *menú completo* 65€. AE, DC, MC, V. Mon–Sat 1–4pm and 9pm–midnight. Closed last half of Aug. Metro: Banco España or Sevilla.

Kaiten Ginza Sushi JAPANESE This outwardly unassuming but quietly excellent Oriental eating spot is located right opposite the Palace Hotel and just round the corner from the Thyssen museum. You can choose between a self-service bar where you pick your dishes from an inviting array that continually passes on a moving table if you're in a hurry and a sit-down restaurant if you want to take your time and relax. Starters include a delicious eggplant with cream of soya sauce, and vegetable dishes such as tempura are also highly recommended. Top speciality in both is—what else?—sushi prepared from the freshest of fresh market fish. The service, like the establishment, is low-key and attentive.

Plaza de las Cortes 3. © 91-429-76-19. Main courses 12€–30€. AE, DC, MC, V. Tues–Sat 1:30–4pm and 8pm–midnight. Sun 1:30–4pm. Metro: Banco de España.

La Biotika VEGETARIAN For well over a decade, vegetarian cuisine has been making notable progress on the Madrid scene. This intimate and charming spot just east of the landmark Plaza Santa Ana is an excellent example. It serves the capital's best macrobiotic vegetarian cuisine, and does so exceedingly well. I always begin with one of the homemade soups, which are made fresh daily, then have one of the large, fresh salads. The bread is also made fresh daily. One specialty is a "meatball without meat" (made with vegetables but shaped like a meatball). Tofu with zucchini and many other offerings appear daily.

Amor de Dios 3. ✆ **91-429-07-80.** www.labiotika.es. Main courses 8€–12€; *menú del día* 10€–12€. No credit cards. Daily 10am–midnight. Sun noon–4pm. Metro: Antón Martín.

La Trucha SPANISH With its Andalusian tavern ambience, La Trucha boasts a street-level bar and small dining room with arched ceiling and whitewashed walls. The decor is made festive with hanging braids of garlic, dried peppers, and onions. On the lower level, the walls of a second bustling area are covered with eye-catching antiques, bullfight notices, and other bric-a-brac. There's a complete a la carte menu including *trucha* (trout), *pescaíto frito* (fried fish, usually anchovies and whitebait), *verbenas de ahumados* (a selection of smoked delicacies), a glorious stew called *fabada* (made with beans, Galician ham, black sausage, and smoked bacon), and a *comida casera rabo de toro* (home-style oxtail). No one should miss nibbling on the tapas *variadas* in the bar.

If this branch turns out to be too crowded, there's another **Trucha** at Núñez de Arce 6 (✆ **91-532-08-82**).

Manuel Fernández y González 3. ✆ **91-429-58-33.** Reservations recommended. Main courses 15€–28€. AE, MC, V. Mon–Sat 11am–midnight. Metro: Antón Martín or Sevilla.

Tocororo CUBAN Attractively located close to Plaza Santa Ana, this is Madrid's finest Cuban restaurant. The nostalgia is evident in the pictures of old Havana, and in the paintings of famous artists such as Lam y Mattos that adorn the walls. The waitstaff is as lively as the pop Cuban music playing on the stereo. The dishes are typical Caribbean dishes, such as ceviche (marinated fish), ropa vieja (shredded meat served with black beans and rice), or lobster enchilada. If you prefer a simpler repast, try a selection of *empanadas y tamales* (fried potato pastries and plantain dough filled with onions and ground meat). Special cocktails of the house include mojitos and daiquiris. There are live shows on Friday and Saturday evenings.

Prado 3 (at the corner of Echegaray). ✆ **91-369-40-00.** www.el-tocororo.com. Reservations required Thurs–Sat. Main courses 12€–24€; fixed-price menu 15€. AE, DC, MC, V. Tues–Sun 1–4pm and 8pm–midnight. Closed last 2 weeks of Feb and last week of Sept. Metro: Sevilla.

Inexpensive

Artemisa VEGETARIAN There are two branches of this very popular and established vegetarian establishment. The most popular is probably this modern and simply decorated eating spot in the heart of bohemian Huertas parallel to Calle Echegaray. For starters try the inventive *crema de ortiga* (nettle cream), *sopa de menta y calabacín* (mint and pumpkin soup), or *quiche de puerros* (leek quiche). Main courses include an excellent vegetarian *paella,* and you can sip an "ecological" wine with your meal. Choose from over 20 different versions of herbal teas to accompany your dessert (give the *pastel persa,* Persian pastry, a try). A second branch is located at Tres Cruces 4 (✆ **91-521-87-21;** Metro: Callao). Good news for nicotine haters: Both establishments are strictly nonsmoking.

Ventura de la Vega 4. ✆ **91-429-50-92.** www.restaurantartemisa.com. Main courses 10€–15 €; set menu 14€; special combined tasting dish for 2: 25€. AE, DC, MC, V. Daily 1:30–4pm and 9pm–midnight. Metro: Sevilla.

La Vaca Verónica ARGENTINE "Veronica the Cow" is the charmingly eccentric name for this culinary haven located in the heart of the Huertas district. Healthy pasta and salad dishes predominate, and *carabineros* (large grilled shrimp) and generous sized *filetes* are among its eclectic seafood and meat choices. Specialities include *dorada en sal* (sea bream baked in salt) and *bandeja de carne roja* (a selection of grilled meats). The set menus are exceptionally good value and if you have a sweet tooth—and aren't counting the calories—the *tarta de chocolate* is a must. The colorful decor reflects its Argentine origins, and at dinnertime the tables are intimately candlelit.

Moratín 38. ✆ **91-429-78-27.** www.lavacaveronica.es. Main courses 10€–20€; set midday menu 16€. AE, DC, MC, V. Sat–Fri 1–4:30pm and 9pm–midnight; Sun 1–4:30pm. Metro: Antón Martín.

Taberna Toscana TAPAS Many Madrileños begin their nightly *tasca* crawl here. The ambience is that of a village inn that's far removed from 21st century Madrid. You sit on crude country stools, under sausages, peppers, and sheaves of golden wheat that hang from the age-darkened beams. The long, tiled bar is loaded with tasty tidbits, including the house specialties: *croquetas* (croquettes of fish or chicken purée), *morcilla* (rich black sausage), *lacón y cecina* (boiled ham), *habas* (broad beans) with Spanish ham, and *chorizo* (hard pork sausage)—almost meals in themselves. Especially delectable are the kidneys in sherry sauce and the snails in hot sauce.

Manuel Fernández y Gonzales 10. ✆ **91-429-60-31.** www.tabernatoscana.es. Beer (caña) 1.80€; glass of wine from 1.80€; tapas 4€–12€. MC, V. Tues–Sat noon–4pm and 8pm–midnight. Metro: Sol or Sevilla.

LAVAPIÉS

Expensive

Casa Lastra ASTURIAN Inspired by the cuisine of Spain's green northerly province of Asturias, the menu at this 1926-built tavern has attracted a devoted following, both among homesick Asturians and newer international converts. The decoration is in a regional style, with cowbells, dried sausages, "pigtails" of garlic, and wood clogs. This restaurant and cider house—the national drink of the province—is known for serving very big portions, which means you might skip the starters. However, if you do indulge, I recommend *fabes con almejas* (white beans with clams) and *chorizo a la sidra* (spicy Spanish sausage cooked in cider). As a main course, *merluza* (hake) is also cooked in cider. If you're here in winter, order a fabulously hearty *fabada,* the meat, sausage, and bean casserole of the province. Milk-fed lamb is also roasted to perfection, and goat meat is yet another specialty, as is the strong *cabrales* cheese made from a blend of milk from goats, sheep, and cows. For dessert, locals order *carbayón,* which is made from sweetened egg yolks and almonds, although this may be too sweet for most tastes. Everything is washed down with natural (unfizzy) cider, which might be more potent than you think.

Olivar 3. ✆ **91-369-08-37.** www.casalastra.com. Main courses 15€–30€; fixed-price menu Mon–Thurs 16€. AE, DC, MC, V. Thurs–Tues 1–4pm; Thurs–Sat and Mon–Tues 8pm–midnight. Closed July. Metro: Antón Martín.

Inexpensive

Automático ★ 🎁 TAPAS This classic tapas hangout is among the most popular in Lavapiés and in summer its terrace—one of many in lively Argumosa street—draws animated crowds of habitués and visitors. On Sundays it's packed to the gills due to the proximity to the Rastro market. Atmosphere apart, the inventive and bargain priced range of tidbits you get with your *caña* of beer or *chato* of wine are something else. *Bacalao* (salt cod), *mojama* (salted tuna), *cecina* (jerked beef), *migas* (fried bread crumbs), *morcilla patatera* (traditional blood sausage), and homemade pâtés line its comprehensive repertoire. On winter evenings, recorded blues and jazz classics enliven the indoor lounge/bar.

Argumosa 17. ✆ 91-530-99-21. Tapas/raciones 3€–11€. Tues–Sun 7pm–12:30am; Fri–Sat 12:30pm–12:30am. Metro: Lavapiés.

Económico Soidemersol SPANISH As the name implies, this is a place you can eat at without straining the budget. Formerly known simply as the Económico, it's a legendary eating spot that has preserved its traditional food and friendly neighborhood atmosphere while undergoing renovations and opening a sunny outside terrace. Go for standards like *gazpacho, lentejas* (lentils), *tortilla,* and *callos* (tripe). If you're feeling ultra-adventurous, try the chewy *oreja* (pig's ears). (Incidentally, the restaurant's name is *los remedios* spelled backward and *remedios* means cures or remedies. Enough said.)

Argumosa 9. ✆ **91-539-73-71.** Main courses 8€–12€; set lunch 12€. MC, V. Daily 1–5pm and 8pm–midnight. Closed mid-Aug to mid-Sept. Metro: Lavapiés.

Elqui VEGETARIAN The city's number-one self-service vegetarian eating spot sprang up around a decade ago in the burgeoning international melting pot of Lavapiés. Chef Carlos Urrutia's inventive combinations of cereals cooked with fresh vegetables soon earned it a large following, and today its bargain all-you-can-eat lunchtime buffet of *ensaladas* (salads), main hot dishes, and *postres* is a sellout so best to get there early. Mediterranean dishes such as hummus, couscous, and nut and ricotta crepes feature strongly on its very reasonable a la carte evening menu, and the *plato de baile* of brown rice, mushrooms, asparagus, and tofu is a must. There's a short list of organic wines and a wider range of herbal teas. In this toxin-free establishment, caffeine and nicotine are definitely out, so no lighting up after the meal please! The Elqui also arranges 8-hour-long vegetarian cooking courses.

José Antonio de Armona 22. ✆ **91-468-04-62.** Main courses 8€–12€; set buffet lunch 12€. No credit cards. Tues–Thurs and Sun 1:30–4pm; Fri–Sat 1:30–4pm and 9–11pm. Closed last 3 weeks of Aug. Metro: Antón Martín or Lavapiés.

PASEO DE RECOLETOS

Expensive

Al Mounia ★ MOROCCAN Widely acknowledged as the top Moroccan spot in Madrid, the Al Mounia first opened in 1968 under the auspices of owner-host Sahri and his daughter, stunning a then more traditional and provincial scene with its exotic cumin- and pistachio-flavored cuisine, atmospheric mosaics, embossed tiled decor, and high standards of service. Today it's particularly popular with couples or party groups. The imaginative maghrebi menu extends far beyond the conventional couscous, and gourmet standouts are its delicious ginger and saffron flavored vegetable broth, *pastilla* (pigeon pie), and *metaui* (Berber roast lamb). After the meal there's a great choice of outrageously delicious oriental pastries and dried fruits to choose from the dessert trolley, accompanied ideally by fresh mint tea. The restaurant's cellar includes a selection of excellent Moroccan wines.

Calle Recoletos 5. ✆ **91-435-08-28.** www.almounia.es. Main courses 18€–35€; set inclusive menus 40€–50€. AE, DC, MC, V. Tues–Sat 1:30–3:30pm and 9pm–midnight. Closed Semana Santa holy week in April and in Aug. Metro: Banco de España.

El Borbollón BASQUE/FRENCH For over four decades, the welcoming Castro family has presided over this little charmer lying between Calle Serrano and Paseo de Recoletos, near both Plaza Cibeles and Plaza Colón. For two decades, they have welcomed some of the more discerning palates in Madrid. Eduardo Castro, the chef, is a local personality and a whiz in the kitchen. His duck pâté is a masterpiece and among his highly regarded main dishes are whiskey-marinated chateaubriand, garlic flavored Segovian lamb cutlets, and steaks cooked with savory green peppers. Seafood is also top-notch, with grilled *rape* (monkfish), *rodaballo* (turbot), and *merluza* (hake) appearing regularly on the menu, and rich game dishes such as partridge are featured in the autumn.

Paseo de Recoletos 7. ✆ **91-431-41-34.** www.elborbollon.es. Main courses 16€–34€. AE, DC, MC, V. Daily Mon–Sat 1–4pm and 9pm–midnight. Metro: Retiro or Colón.

Moderate

El Espejo ★ INTERNATIONAL Located right beside the elegant Recoletos Paseo, this stylish cafeteria boasts one of the most attractive Art Nouveau decors in Madrid. If the weather is good, you can sit at one of the outdoor tables and be served by uniformed waiters who carry food across the busy street to a green area flanked with trees. On cloudier days, you can enjoy the views of the tile maidens with vines and flowers entwined in their hair that cover the walls inside. There's also an adjoining spacious dining room where you can savor quality dishes like grouper ragout with clams, steak tartare, guinea fowl with Armagnac, and duck with pineapple. Try profiteroles with cream and chocolate sauce for dessert.

Paseo de Recoletos 31. ✆ **91-308-23-47.** www.restauranteelespejo.com. Reservations required. Main courses 15€–28€; lunchtime menu del día 25€; special set menus 40€–80€. AE, DC, MC, V. Daily: Cafeteria service11am–2am (3am Sat–Sun); restaurant 1–4pm, 9pm–midnight. Metro: Colon.

Gran Café de Gijón ★★ SPANISH If you want food and atmosphere like it was in Franco's heyday, drop in here. Each of the old European capitals has a coffeehouse that traditionally attracts the literati—in Madrid it's the Gijón, which opened in 1888 in the heyday of the Belle Epoque. Artists and writers still patronize this venerated old cafe, spending hours over a coffee as did famous literary characters in the past like Ortega y Gasset and Miguel de Unamuno—who came to have their *tertulias* (artistically oriented chats) here. Open windows look out onto the wide paseo, and a large terrace is perfect for sun worshippers and bird-watchers. Along one side of the cafe is a stand-up bar; on the lower level is a restaurant. In summer, sit in the garden to enjoy a *blanco y negro* (black coffee with ice cream) or a mixed drink.

Paseo de Recoletos 21. ✆ **91-521-54-25.** www.cafegijon.com. Reservations required for restaurant. Main courses 15€–28€; fixed-price menu 14€–30€. AE, DC, MC, V. Daily 7am–3am. Metro: Colón.

NEAR PLAZA DE LA CIBELES

Expensive

El Mirador del Museo ★★ CONTINENTAL One of the most agreeable new summer dining spots in Madrid is the rooftop terrace restaurant of the Museo Thyssen-Bornemisza, which enjoys fabulous vistas of the neighboring tree-filled Paseo del Prado. A member of the gourmet-oriented Paradis group, it provides an excellent value menu, which imaginatively blends old and new dishes, including culinary treats like *vichysoisse con couscous o gazpacho, arroz con sepia* (rice with cuttlefish), and *pechuga de pato con salsa con cebolla en mostaza dulce* (duck breast with onion in sweet mustard). Fish dishes like *bacalao pil pil* and meaty favorites such as *cordero asado* also feature, and there's a host of mouth-watering desserts.

Paseo del Prado 8. ✆ **91-420-39-44.** Reservations required. Main courses 23€-40€. AE, DC, MC, V. May-Oct Wed-Mon 8pm-1am. Metro: Banco de España.

Moderate

Edelweiss GERMAN This soberly styled German standby has provided good-quality food and service at moderate prices since World War II. It's close to the Cortes so you'll often see politicians lunching here, enjoying the hearty portions of food, mugs of draft beer, and fluffy pastries. The ideal combination would be to start with Bismarck herring, then dive into goulash with spaetzle or *Eisbein* (pigs' knuckles or *codillo de cerdo*) with sauerkraut and mashed potatoes (minimum two persons), the most popular dish at the restaurant. Finish with the homemade apple tart or Black Forest gâteau.

Jovellanos 7. ✆ **91-532-33-83.** Reservations recommended. Main courses 14€-25€; fixed-price lunch 24€. AE, DC, MC, V. Daily 1-4pm and Mon-Sat 8pm-midnight. Metro: Banco de España.

Inexpensive

Al Natural VEGETARIAN The charming Al Natural, situated on a central but usually quiet road just behind the Cortes building, is as exotic a vegetarian's mecca as you could wish to find and a soothing escape for both the weary city explorer and occasional stressed political celebrity. Its atmospheric decor and healthily inventive dishes make a winning combination. The painted backdrop of fruit and greenery is subtly illuminated by amber lighting, luxuriant plants hang from the ceiling, and the background music is sensual and relaxing. The dining area is surrounded by warm wood paneling, and among the many veggie treats on offer I recommend the *pita napolitana* (Neapolitan style pita bread), *escalope de seitán y roquefort* (escalope of seitan and Roquefort cheese), and *champiñones Stroganoff* (mushrooms Stroganoff). Round off the meal with a healthy yogurt and aromatic *tila* (lime flower) tea.

Zorilla 11. ✆ **91-369-47-09.** www.alnatural.biz. Main courses 12€-22€; set menu 14€. AE, DC, MC, V. Mon-Sat 1-4pm and 8:30pm-11:30pm; Sun 1-4pm. Metro: Banco de España.

Café del Círculo de Bellas Artes (La Pecera) ★ 🎁 CASTILIAN You can easily get into this former members-only club if you pay a modest 1€ entry fee (which also allows you to see whatever exhibitions are on in its galleries). The high-ceilinged cafe-restaurant up the steps from the wide hall boasts 1920s-style ceilings, chandeliers, artistic statues, and soaring pillars. From its huge windows, you get a clear view of the ever-changing scene in Alcalá Street outside, though passersby can equally easily see what's going on inside, which is how it's earned itself the nickname *la pecera,* or aquarium. At lunchtime you can join politicians and bankers from the nearby parliament or the Banco de España to enjoy a variety of pork, beef, fresh fish, and chicken dishes. The reasonably priced set menu is changed every day, and once a week the chef prepares a sturdy traditional *cocido* (the Madrileños' favorite meat and vegetable stew). At night no dinners are served, but people flock here to devour tapas of *gambas* (shrimps) or *boquerones* (fried anchovies) with their glasses of Rueda blanco or Ribera del Duero tinto wine.

AN EARLY-EVENING *tapeo*

What's more fun than a pub-crawl in London or Dublin? In Madrid, it's a *tapeo,* and you can drink just as much or more than in those far northern climes. One of the unique pleasures of Madrid, a *tapeo* is the act of strolling from one bar to another to keep yourself amused and fed before the fashionable Madrileño dining hour of 10pm.

Most of the world knows that tapas are Spain's delectable appetizers, and restaurants around the world now serve them. In Madrid they're served almost everywhere, in *tabernas, tascas,* bars, and cafes.

Although Madrid took to tapas with a passion, they may have originated in Andalusia, especially around Jerez de la Frontera, where they were traditionally served to accompany the sherry produced there. The first tapa (which means a cover or lid) was probably *chorizo* (a spicy sausage) or a slice of cured ham perched over the mouth of a glass to keep the flies out. Later, the government mandated bars to serve a "little something" in the way of food with each drink to dissipate the effects of the alcohol. This was important when drinking a fortified wine like sherry, as its alcohol content is more than 15% higher than that of normal table wines. Eating a selection of tapas as you drink will help preserve your sobriety.

Tapas can be relatively simple: toasted almonds; slices of ham, cheese, or sausage; potato omelets; or the ubiquitous olives. They can be more elaborate too: a succulent veal roll; herb-flavored snails; *gambas* (shrimp); a saucer of peppery *pulpo* (octopus); stuffed peppers; *anguila* (eel); *cangrejo* (crabmeat salad); *merluza* (hake) salad; and even bull testicles.

Each bar in Madrid gains a reputation for its rendition of certain favorite foods. One bar, for example, specializes in very garlicky grilled mushrooms, usually accompanied by pitchers of sangria. Another will specialize in *gambas.* Most chefs are men in Madrid, but at tapas bars or *tascas,* the cooks are most often women—often the owner's wife.

For a selection of my favorite bars, see "The Best of the *Tascas*" on p. 166. There are literally hundreds of others, many of which you'll discover on your own during your strolls around Madrid.

Alcalá 42. ✆ **91-360-54-00.** www.circulobellasartes.com. Set lunch menu 12€–15€; evening tapas 3.50€–12€. MC, V. Sun–Thurs 9:30am–1am; Fri–Sat 9:30am–3am. Metro: Banco de España.

Taj INDIAN If curry is your thing then don't be put off by the sounds and appearance of this somewhat unchic eating spot—complete with artificial flowers and banal background Muzak. Attractively situated in a peaceful lane between the Cortes and Cibeles, it offers the real McCoy: genuinely hot lamb and tandoori chicken curries as well as a comprehensive *degustación* choice of entrees such as samosas, pakora, nan, and Bombay duck. The special vegetarian menu includes dessert and Indian tea. Friendly and attentive staff make the visit all the more enjoyable.

Marqués de Cubas 6. ✆ **91-531-50-59.** www.restaurantetaj.com. Main courses 10€–20€; set lunch 15€; vegetarian menu 17€; tasting menu 19€. AE, DC, MC, V. Mon–Thurs 1–4pm and 8:30–11:30pm; Fri–Sun 1–4pm and 8:30pm–midnight. Metro: Banco de España.

NEAR THE PLAZA ESPAÑA

Expensive

Bajamar SEAFOOD Bajamar, one of the best fish houses in Spain, is centrally located at the northwestern end of the Gran Vía, close to Plaza España. Both fish and shellfish are flown in fresh daily, the prices depending on what the market charges. Lobster, king crab, prawns, and soft-shell crabs are all priced according to weight. There is a large array of reasonably priced dishes as well. The service is smooth and professional and the menu is in English. For a (justifiably pricey) appetizer order half-dozen giant *ostras* (oysters) or *cigalas* (seawater crayfish). The special seafood soup is a most satisfying meal in itself; the lobster bisque is also worth trying. Some of the noteworthy main courses include *rodaballo gallego* (Galician style turbot), *paella marinera* (seafood paella), and *calamaritos en su tinta* (baby squid cooked in its own ink). The simple desserts include the chef's *flan* (caramel custard).

Gran Vía 78. ✆ **91-548-48-18.** Reservations recommended. Main courses 25€–70€. AE, DC, MC, V. Daily 1–4pm and 8pm–midnight. Metro: Plaza de España.

El Molino de los Porches ★ CASTILIAN This authentic Castilian asador specializes in tasty roast meats. The *cordero* (lamb), *cabrito* (kid), and *cochinillo* (baby pig) are all good choices, as is the first-rate estafado de rabo de toro (bull's tail stew). This spot is a popular hangout for bullfighters and their entourage. It's also a popular place for weddings and receptions, with musical groups performing, so book in advance and don't be surprised if things get a bit noisy. The attraction here, as in many restaurants in this attractive Argüelles Avenue bordering the parklands of the Parque del Oeste, is the outdoor terrace area where you can relax in summer.

Paseo del Pintor Rosales 1. ✆ **91-548-13-36.** Main courses 25€–45€; set menu 40€. AE, DC, MC, V. Daily for lunch and dinner 1:45–4:30pm and 8:45pm–midnight. Free parking. Metro: Ventura Rodriguez.

Moderate

Bali ★ INDONESIAN The one and only Indonesian restaurant in town is located in a quieter corner of the center, just off the Plaza de España end of the Gran Vía. The Bali has long been a refuge for hedonists seeking an exotic alternative to hearty Castilian fare. Go for the rijsttafel, a delicious selection of Oriental tapas served up on a candle-heated grill. Or sample the excellent set menu. Individual recommended main dishes include *pollo satay* with peanut sauce and *terong* (eggplant with pungent tomato purée).

San Bernardino 6. ✆ **91-541-91-22.** Menu 32€. AE, DC, MC, V. Mon–Sat 1–4pm and 8pm–midnight; Sun 1–4pm. Metro: Plaza de Espana.

La Bola MADRILEÑO This is *the taberna* where you can still savor something of the atmosphere of 19th-century Madrid. Just north of the Teatro Real, it's one of the few remaining full-blooded restaurants in the city (apart from a couple of maroon-shuttered tapas-oriented tabernas like Casa Alberto) with a bright russet facade. Timeless attractions include the gently polite waiters, Venetian crystal, and aging velvet. Ava Gardner, with her entourage of bullfighters, used to patronize this establishment. *Lenguado* (sole) and *merluza vasca* (Basque style hake) are among the best fish choices, while the meaty highlight is still the traditional Madrileño *cocido* cooked in earthenware pots by wood fire (though connoisseurs consider it's become

vineyards & WINERIES

Spanish red wines are some of the best in the world and its famed *Riojas* and *Penedeses* are widely available and remarkably affordable. Better value still—and barely known even in the rest of Spain—are the honest traditional wines emerging from Madrid province's own underrated vineyards.

Three of the top wine-producing regions in the Madrid province are **Colmenar de Oreja, San Martín de Valdeiglesias,** and **Chinchón. Colmenar de Oreja**'s prize-winning red and white Jesús Díaz wines are made from the Malvar and Airén grapes, while **San Martín de Valdeiglesias**'s strong (13%–13.5% alcohol) Señoría de Valderrábano reds are made from the Garnacha variety. **Chinchón** (of anis fame) also produces a hearty and palatable red called Viña Galinda. Look for these and other Comunidad de Madrid wines from **Arganda del Rey** and **Villarejo del Salvanés** in the supermarkets (2.75€–4.50€ a bottle) and restaurants (7€–12€ a bottle). They're worth a try.

For wider information on Spanish wines in general, contact **Wines from Spain,** c/o the Commercial Office of Spain, 405 Lexington Ave., 44th Floor, New York, NY 10174-0331; ✆ **212/661-4959.**

rather lightweight in its efforts to cater for an increasingly international clientele). Refreshing dishes to begin your meal with include *gambas a la plancha* (grilled shrimp) and *ensalada de pimienta roja* (red-pepper salad).

La Bola 5. ✆ **91-547-69-30.** www.labola.es. Reservations required. Main courses 15€–35€. No credit cards. Daily 1–4pm and 8:30–11pm. Metro: Opera.

La Vaca Argentina ARGENTINE Located close to the Opera House and Isabel II square, this is one of several branches of the popular Argentine chain that caters wholeheartedly to serious carnivores. Decor, as in the other restaurants, is modern and functional though the genuine cowhide lined walls are a nod to its land of origin. Service tends to be distracted, even coolly distant (perhaps the waiters yearn for the far-off pampas). Steaks are suitably huge but well matched by the delicious salads and imaginative pasta dishes, and the tasty Argentine starters include *empanada* (small meat pie) in chile sauce.

Cañas del Peral 2. ✆ **91-541-33-18.** www.lavacaargentina.net. Main courses 14€–36€. Daily 1:30–4:30pm and 8:30pm–midnight. Metro: Opera.

Quintana 30 BASQUE A refreshing newcomer on the Argüelles/Moncloa culinary scene is this adventurous eating spot, opened in February 2010; it has already gained a solid reputation for its comfortable ambience and friendly service under the supervision of maitre d' Miguel Valdés. In the kitchen, meanwhile, Angel Muñano, a former head leading light in the prestigious Goizeko culinary group, specializes in Basque dishes made from fresh market produce. Tasty starters include *mousse al cabracho* (scorpion fish mousse) and *croquetas de espinacas y pasas* (raisin and spinach croquettes), and his main courses *bacalao al horno* (oven-baked cod) and *chipirones encebollados* (baby squid cooked with onions) are exceptional. (Half-*racion* versions are also available for those on either a diet or a budget.)

Calle Quintana 30, 28008. ✆ **91-542-65-20.** Main courses 15€–35€. AE, MC, DC, V. Mon–Sat 10am–4pm and 8:30pm–midnight. Metro: Argüelles.

Siam THAI A near Buddhist sense of calm and peace fills this intimate eating spot, located in a quiet zone close to other polyglot restaurants just a short stroll from the Plaza España. Specializing in delicacies from Thailand, where multilingual Texan owner David Haynes lived many years before moving to Madrid to create this genuine labor of love, it's one of the best Asian eating spots in town. Authentic imported ingredients are used in creating gourmet treats such as hot prawn soup, spicy green curry, and rehashed veal cooked with cashews and limes. Among the simple but delicious desserts are oranges in rose water, and as a change from coffee you can choose from a wide range of special teas. The fixed-price lunch menu is good value.

San Bernadino 6. ✆ **91-559-83-15.** Main courses 12€–24€; set lunch 15€; tasting menu 26€. Daily 1–4pm and 8:30pm–midnight. Metro: Plaza España or Noviciado.

MALASAÑA

Inexpensive

Isla del Tesoro VEGETARIAN A vegan's delight on Madrid's expanding green scene, "Treasure Island" has been a mainstay of bohemian Malasaña for quite a while. Universal vegetarian dishes are imaginatively prepared and the restaurant, surprisingly, does not frown on the increasing ostracized smoker client. The adventurous menu of the day regularly changes its choice from country to country and the Japanese tray of specialities is particularly inventive. Try the *buen rollito,* which consists of pasta stuffed with fruit, cheese, fresh spinach, and nuts or the ever-popular main salad buffet.

Manuela Malasaña 3. ✆ **91-593-14-40.** www.isladeltesoro.net. Main courses 10€–18€; set lunch 12€. Mon–Sat 1:30pm–4pm and 9pm–midnight. Metro: Bilbao.

Mesob 🎁 ETHIOPIAN Opened at the end of 2009, this atmospheric watering hole on the northern edge of Malasaña is that rarity in Madrid: a genuine Central African restaurant. The colorful and (for most visitors) unfamiliar dishes are remarkably good value. For a starter try *fatira,* which consists of scrambled eggs with thin strips of pasta and is far tastier than it sounds. A yummy main course is *oro wot* (chicken with ginger, marrow, egg, and cheese), while *yebeg altcha* is a mouth-watering baby lamb served in a hot spicy sauce. *Injera,* the country's very own sharp-flavored pancakey bread, is also provided—local tradition is to place your food on it. It's all very relaxing and the friendly waiters—mainly female—wear traditional Ethiopian clothing. Only minor reservations: The red-hot spicy sauces are tempered slightly for local tastes and the tables are on the small side.

Manuela Malasaña 17, 28004. ✆ 91-445-81-70. Main courses 10€–15€. Tues–Sun 1:30–4pm and 8:30pm–midnight. Metro: Bilbao.

CHUECA

Very Expensive

Asiana ★★★ 🎁 ORIENTAL FUSION This unique eating spot is one of the most secretively exclusive in all Madrid. Tucked away down a narrow lane in the earthy but chic bohemian zone of Chueca, it's a labor of love that's been created by gourmet chef Jaime Renedo in his mother's lavishly Oriental antiques shop. Consisting of just six—or sometimes seven—tables, the restaurant is located in a spacious alcove-filled basement amid huge Chinese vases and Buddhist figures. This is one place you simply cannot walk into unannounced. You must reserve your table beforehand by international credit card, and when you do arrive, ring the doorbell to be allowed to enter. All of which adds to the intriguingly private—almost conspiratorial—atmosphere of the place, a kind of club for appreciators of really fine cuisine. Only dinners are served and the eclectic and inventive tasting menu changes nightly. Past menus have featured delights such as melon gazpacho with lobster and ravioli with potato mousse, while sublime desserts have included marshmallow of yuzu with ginger. Prepare to be surprised by all manner of sublime mixtures when you dine here—it's an unforgettable experience.

Travesia de San Mateo 4. ✆ **91-310-09-65.** Reservations must be made to reserve a table. Tasting menu 100€-120€ excluding wine. AE, DC, MC, V. Tues-Sat 9:30pm-midnight. Closed first 3 weeks in Aug. Metro: Tribunal or Alonso Martínez.

Expensive

Arce ★ BASQUE Arce has brought some of the best modern interpretations of Basque cuisine to Madrid, thanks to the enthusiasm of owner/chef Iñaki Camba and his wife, Theresa. Within a comfortably decorated dining room, you can enjoy dishes made of the finest ingredients using flavors designed to dominate your taste buds. Examples include a salad of fresh scallops and an oven-baked casserole of fresh boletus mushrooms, seasoned lightly so the woodsy vegetable taste comes through. Look for unusual preparations of hake and seasonal variations of such game dishes as pheasant and woodcock.

Augusto Figueroa 32. ✆ **91-522-59-13.** www.restaurantearce.com. Reservations recommended. Main courses 18€-40€; tasting menu 75€. AE, DC, MC, V. Mon-Fri 1:30-4pm; Mon-Sat 9pm-midnight. Closed the week before Easter and Aug 15-31. Metro: Chueca.

El Mentidero de la Villa ★ MEDITERRANEAN The Mentidero ("Gossip Shop" in English) is a truly multicultural experience. The owner describes the cuisine as "modern Spanish with Japanese influence and a French cooking technique." That may sound confusing, but the result is an achievement; each ingredient manages to retain its distinct flavor. The kitchen plays with such adventuresome combinations as veal liver in sage sauce; a spring roll filled with fresh shrimp and leeks; noisettes of veal with tarragon; filet steak with a sauce of mustard and brown sugar; and medallions of venison with purée of chestnut and celery. One notable dessert is the sherry trifle. The postmodern decor includes trompe l'oeil ceilings, exposed wine racks, ornate columns with unusual lighting, and a handful of antique carved merry-go-round horses.

Santo Tomé 6. ✆ **91-308-12-85.** www.mentiderodelavilla.es. Reservations required. Main courses 25€-45€. AE, DC, MC, V. Mon-Fri 1:30-4:30pm; Mon-Sat 9pm-midnight. Closed Aug. Metro: Alonso Martínez or Colón.

La Fuencisla ★ SPANISH Near El Museo Romántico is this small but comfortable restaurant that for nearly half a century has been serving meals in the traditional Spanish style. A family business, La Fuencisla (named as an offering to the Virgin of Segovia) is run by Señor and Señora de Frutos. The man of the house greets the visitors in the front while his wife creates tasty homemade meals in the kitchen. The dishes—which are typical of the Segovian kitchen prepared with fresh ingredients according to time-tested recipes—feature such highly praised delights as *chuletas parrilladas de lechona de cordero* (grilled chops of milk-fed lamb). Begin with fresh asparagus in country butter and aromatic garlic or savory mussels in a marinara sauce. Filet of tuna freshly baked in the oven is another gastronomic pleasure. For desserts, the cooks always prepare homemade tarts, which are especially good when the fresh fruit comes in. Otherwise, you might opt for the rice pudding or *flan de coco* (coconut pudding).

San Mateo 4. ✆ **91-521-61-86.** www.fuencisla.restauranteok.com. Reservations recommended. Main courses 15€–28€; *menú completo* 50€. AE, DC, MC, V. Mon–Sat 2–4pm and 9pm–1am. Closed Aug. Metro: Tribunal.

Moderate

Casa Vallejo SPANISH This hardworking bistro with a not terribly subtle staff offers less exposure to international clients than some of its competitors. Despite that, you'll find a sense of culinary integrity that's based on a devotion to fresh ingredients and a rigid allegiance to time-tested Spanish recipes. Occupying a turn-of-the-20th-century building, it contains room for only 42 diners at a time. If you want to get the best out of eating here, try some of the simple-sounding but delicious home-cooked specialities like *revuelto de morcilla* (scrambled eggs with black pudding), *pimentos de piquillo rellenos de vieras* (small hot red peppers stuffed with scallops), and *albóndigas de la casa* (home-cooked meatballs). Creamy desserts not to be missed include the *flan de la casa* (caramel custard). Budget gourmands in Madrid praise the hearty flavors here, the robust cookery, and the prices.

San Lorenzo 9. ✆ **91-308-61-58.** Reservations recommended. Main courses 9€–20€; fixed-price menu Mon–Fri 14€–22€. MC, V. Mon–Sat 2–4pm; Tues–Sat 9:30pm–midnight. Metro: Tribunal or Alonso Martínez. (There is another branch in Calle Juan Ramón Jimenez 22. Same hours. ✆ 91-350-27-33. Metro: Cuzco).

Ciao Madrid ITALIAN These two highly successful Italian restaurants are run by members of the extended Laguna family. The Calle Apodaca branch opened in 1996, four years after the first Caio Madrid was launched in Calle Argensola (see below). Both maintain the same hours, prices, menu, and a decor inspired by the tenets of minimalist Milanese decor, with good-tasting food items that include risottos and pastas, such as carpaccio, ravioli, or tagliatelle with boletus (wild mushrooms). No one will mind if you order pasta as a main course (lots of clients here do, accompanying it with a green salad). If you're in the mood for a more substantial main course, consider osso buco, veal scaloppine, chicken, or veal parmigiana, and any of several kinds of fish. For dessert don't miss the excellent tiramisu.

Apodaca 20. ✆ **91-447-00-36.** Reservations recommended. Pastas 9€–14€; main courses 12€–24€. AE, DC, MC, V. Mon–Fri 1:30–3:45pm; Mon–Sat 9:30pm–midnight. Closed Sept. Metro: Tribunal. (There's another location at Calle Argensola 7; ✆ **91-308-25-19;** closed Aug; Metro: Alonso Martínez).

El Bocaíto ★ SPANISH/TAPAS Inside this 150-year-old house, four original columns of wood encircle the high ceiling, and bullfighting posters adorn the white-tile walls. Behind a bar shaped into two horseshoes, the staff cooks and prepares some of the most appreciated tapas in Madrid, much appreciated by showbiz celebs such as Pedro Almodóvar (who once proclaimed it his favorite tapas bar). The selection ranges from simple delights like *jamón Serrano* (cured Serrano ham), *boquerones* (fresh anchovies), *gambas fritas* (fried shrimp), and *esparragos verdes con huevos revueltos* (green asparagus in scrambled eggs) to more sophisticated delicacies such as *bacalao con caviar* (salt cod pâté with caviar), and *mejimecha* (marinated mussels with ham and onions in béchamel sauce) is sublime. If you're hungry, try the *plato* *combinado* (a combination platter of practically all the tapas) together with a glass of their very palatable Rioja house wine.

Libertad 4-6. ✆ **91-532-12-19.** www.bocaito.com. Reservations recommended. Tapas 4.50€–8€; plato combinado of tapas 14€; main courses 12€–25€; tasting menu 45€. MC, V. Mon–Fri 1–4pm and 8:30pm–midnight; Sat 8:30pm–midnight. Closed last 2 weeks in Aug. Metro: Chueca.

Extremadura EXTREMADURAN In case you're wondering, Extremadura is the most westerly province in central Spain, famed until recently mainly for the fact that Spain's two great New World explorers, Cortez and Pizarro, came from here. During the past decade, its cuisine has also started making waves, and this homely restaurant serves up hearty traditional regional dishes with a few stylish and eccentric touches of its own. The heartiness comes with the entrees, more than generous portions of cheeses, pâtés, and salads, while the main-course fish and meat dishes are accompanied by such specialist fare as *ortigas* (cooked nettles), *borrajas* (borage), and *criadillas de tierra* (truffles). Venison ragout, roast kid, fresh trout, and *migas* (fried bread crumbs with meat, tomatoes, and grapes) are among the top regional highlights, and the *menú de degustación* is just the job if you've a big appetite. Excellent value Extremadura wines dominate the cellar, and fiery homemade *orujos* (eau de vies complete with soused snakes or lizards in the bottle) are the ideal after dinner digestif.

Libertad 13. ✆ **91-531-82-22.** www.restauranteextremadura.com. Main courses 10€–24€; *Menú de degustación* 30€; set menus 40€–48€. DC, MC, V. Mon 1–4pm; Tues–Sat 1–4pm and 8pm–midnight. Metro: Chueca.

La Bardemcilla ★ SPANISH/TAPAS Formerly known as the Café Latino, this warm Chueca locale has been run for several years by the cinematic Bardem family (Oscar winner Javier, sister Mónica, brother Carlos, and mother Pilar). Family photos and scenes from movies bedeck the walls, and tapas and *raciones* bear names from Bardem films (mostly Javier's) such as *Croquetas Jamón-Jamón.* Mingle with the largely cool clientele at the comfortable bar near the entrance and sample a *caña* with some olives, or enjoy a more leisurely dinner in the noisy and comfortable restaurant at the back. *Solomillo a la luna* (sirloin steak) and *chuletas de cordero* (lamb chops) are recommended main dishes on the carnivore-oriented menu, and there's an interestingly varied wine list.

Augusto Figueroa 47. ✆ **91-521-42-56.** www.labardemcilla.com. Tapas 4€–12€; main courses 14€–25€. AE, MC, V. Mon–Fri noon–5:30pm and 8pm–2am; Sat 8pm–2am. Metro: Chueca.

La Dame Noire FRENCH This is one for lovers of the pseudo baroque, a tongue-in-cheek locale where maroon-orange walls with artificial protruding legs and leopard skins, overhead fans, candles, and gilt prevail. The leather-clad waiters look like epicene extras in a minor Almodóvar movie, and the food is all but eclipsed by the kitsch atmosphere. The set-price Gallic-style dinner incorporates a variety of tasty dishes, from *mejillones a la crema* (creamed mussels), goat's cheese salad, and Burgundian snails to pepper or tartare steak. Desserts include rich chocolate pastel and tarte Latin. Choose a reasonably priced Navarra wine to accompany the meal.

Pérez Galdós 3. ✆ **91-531-04-76.** Set dinner (wine not included) 25€. AE, DC, MC, V. Sun–Thurs 9pm–midnight; Fri–Sat 9pm–2am. Metro: Gran Vía or Tribunal.

Zara CUBAN Small, cozy, and lively. That's Zara, the joint creation of Pepe Martínez and Inés Llanos, who forsook their native Caribbean island 4 decades ago to set up this landmark of Cuban cuisine in central Madrid. Prices are reasonable, the service is first-rate, and it's well worth waiting in a queue to sit at one of the check-clothed tables if the place is busy (which is most of the time). Recommended are the standard *ropa vieja* (shredded meat with chickpeas and tomato sauce), *arroz con frijoles y cerdo* (rice with pork and beans), and *picadillo de ternera con arroz y plátano frito* (spicy veal with rice and fried banana), while top desserts include a delicious *pasta de guayaba con queso* (guava jelly with cheese). Its cocktails are legendary, especially the rum-based daiquiris, which are claimed by many to be the best in the capital.

Infantas 5. ✆ **91-532-20-74.** www.restaurantezara.com. Main courses 10€–20€; set menus 22€–28€. AE, DC, MC, V. Mon–Fri 1–5pm and 8–11:30pm. Closed Aug. Metro: Chueca or Gran Vía.

Inexpensive

Bazaar ★ MEDITERRANEAN Located right in the heart of throbbing, trendy Chueca is this excellent value eating spot, frequented in the main by an attractive set of Madrileño youth and run by the same company who own the equally successful Finca de Susana on the other side of the Gran Vía. The decor here is similarly light, stylish, and airy, and the chef's repertoire equally creative and vibrant. Typically inventive dishes include a starter of fresh tomato soup made with basil ice cream while (outwardly) more standard fare ranges from a savory kettle of stew beef to tantalizingly flavored chicken brochettes. For dessert, I recommend their renowned *chocolatísimo,* a medley of mouth-watering chocolate delights.

Libertad 21. ✆ **91-523-39-05.** www.restaurantbazaar.com. Reservations not required. Main courses 9€–20€. AE, MC, V. Mon–Sat 1:15–4pm and 8:30–11:45pm. Metro: Chueca.

El Bierzo CASTILIAN Good honest fare from the northerly Castilian region of El Bierzo is the order of the day at this long established down-to-earth eating spot. One of Chueca's most popular and established home-cooking establishments, it boasts excellent value set lunch and dinner menus and is usually vibrant and filled with local regulars. *Costillas* (beef ribs), *lentejas con arroz* (lentils with rice), and *setas al ajillo* (wild mushrooms cooked in garlic) are among the favorite dishes, and there's a particularly wide choice of low-priced *tortillas* (omelettes) plus a good range of tapas and *raciones* if you fancy something lighter.

Barbieri 16. ✆ **91-531-91-10.** Main courses 9€–20€; set menu (lunch and dinner) 12€. AE, DC, MC, V. Mon–Sat 1–4pm and 8–11:30pm. Metro: Chueca.

Nabucco ITALIAN In a neighborhood of Spanish restaurants, the Italian trattoria format here comes as a welcome change. The decor resembles a postmodern update of an Italian ruin, complete with trompe l'oeil walls painted like marble. Roman portrait busts and a prominent bar lend a dignified air. You might begin your meal with a selection of antipasti or sample spinach and ricotta, both of which feature high on the vegetarian side of the menu. Main choices include first-rate low-cost *pizza* (pizzas), plus *cannelloni, osso buco,* and a wide selection of *vitello* (veal) dishes.

Hortaleza 108. ✆ **91-310-06-11.** www.nabuccorestaurante.com. Reservations recommended. Pizza 6.50€–10€; main courses 8€–18€. AE, DC, MC, V. Daily 1:30–4pm; Sun–Thurs 8:45pm–midnight; Fri–Sat 8:45pm–1am. Metro: Alonso Martínez.

Ottocento 🎁 ITALIAN/ARGENTINIAN Launched in 2007 and another welcome addition to the affordable Chueca list, this new wave Italian-Argentinian eating spot has slipped gently into the same 1840 building where the traditional Carmencita (a former meeting place for poets and artists) flourished for so many years. Mercifully,

family-friendly RESTAURANTS

Children visiting Spain will delight in patronizing any of the restaurants at the Parque de Atracciones in the **Casa de Campo**. Another good idea is to go on a picnic (see "Picnic, Anyone?" later in this chapter).

For a taste of home, there are always the fast-food chains: Dunkin' Donuts, McDonald's, Burger King, and Kentucky Fried Chicken are everywhere. Remember, however, that the burgers and chicken will have a slightly different taste from those served back home.

A place with juicy hamburgers, plus lots of fare familiar to American kids, is **Foster's Hollywood** (p. 168). Or try taking the family to a local *tasca,* where children are bound to find something they like from the wide selection of tapas.

all the original features have been fully retained, including the lovely 19th-century tile work, though now, instead of *cocidos* and Castilian roasts, you get provolone cheese and smoked Panini starters and amazing homemade Tuscan and Lombardian dishes like spinach and ricotta ravioli and potato gnocchi with parmesan cheese as main courses. Adventurous rice-based risotto dishes include *nero di sepia* (shrimps in squid ink) and more robust meat dishes from the southern hemisphere include *Bife de Chorizo,* a huge Pampas-style steak cooked in chimichurri sauce. For dessert, the tiramisu with mascarpone mousse and amaretto and coffee syrup is already a great favorite. In addition to the usual good Spanish wines, there's also Venetian Valpolicella or a Trivento Balbec from Mendoza if you fancy a more international tipple.

Libertad 16. ✆ **91-522-38-48.** www.ottocento.es. Reservations recommended. Main courses 7€–22€. AE, DC, MC, V. Tues–Sun 1–4pm and 9pm–midnight. Metro: Chueca.

Ribeiro do Miño ★ 🎁 GALICIAN Set in a quiet Chueca street between the busier thoroughfares of Horteleza and Fuencarral, this spacious multiroomed restaurant is probably the liveliest seafood eating spot in Madrid. It's nearly always packed and, considering what you'd pay for similar fish dishes elsewhere, the prices tell you why. Service is an admirable combination of the easygoing and the professional. No bookings are taken so if you want to be sure of a table, get there early and avoid weekends. Otherwise be prepared to wait. Shellfish is exceptional and the mainstay of the piscatorial menu is the shared platter of *gambas* (shrimp), *cangrejo* (crab), and *almejas* (clams). *Pulpo gallego* (Galician-style octopus) is a regular feature, and *percebes* (goose barnacles) occasionally show up (though this will thwart any plans for a budget meal). Salads are generous and the low-priced Ribeiro de la Casa *vino blanco* washes down the meal to perfection. You also get a glass of yellow green *orujo* (strong digestive spirit) on the house after your dessert.

Santa Brigida 1. ✆ **91-521-98-54.** www.marisqueriaribeiradomino.aliste.info. Main courses 10€–30€; special shellfish platter (minimum 2) 32€; set menus with wine, coffee, and spirit included 40€–50€. No credit cards. Tues–Sun 1–4pm and 8–11:30pm. Closed Aug. Metro: Tribunal.

Tienda de Vinos SPANISH This splendidly unadorned traditional bodega-restaurant is a serving slice of old Madrid in the heart of Chueca: quite fashionable with—among others—actors and journalists looking for Spanish fare without frills. It's officially known as Tienda de Vinos (the Wine Store), though residents have called the place "El Comunista" (The Communist) ever since the 1930s due to the political affiliations of many of its patrons then, including its long-deceased owner (whose great-grandsons sometimes put in an appearance). There is a menu, but no one ever looks at it—just ask what's available. Nor do you get a bill; you're just told how much to pay. Guests sit at simple wooden tables with wooden chairs and benches; walls are decorated with old posters, calendars, pennants, and clocks. Start with gazpacho, garlic or vegetable soup, or *lentejas* (lentils), and follow that with perhaps *chuletas de cordero* (lamb chops), *callos* (tripe in a spicy sauce), *albondigas* (meatballs), or *riñones al jerez* (kidneys in sherry). It's not as cheap as it used to be, of course, but it's still remarkable value.

Augusto Figueroa 35. ✆ **91-521-70-12.** Main courses 7.50€–16€. No credit cards. Mon–Sat 1–4pm and 9pm–midnight. Metro: Chueca.

RETIRO/SALAMANCA

Very Expensive

Santceloni ★★★ MEDITERRANEAN Santi Santamaría is justly ranked among the top three chefs of Spain, along with his chief rivals, Juan Mark Arzak and Ferran Adrià. Many rate him as higher even than that illustrious duo. He made his fame in his restaurant outside Barcelona and this much-praised branch in landlocked Madrid has met with equal success; his enticing and imaginative cuisine is essentially Mediterranean and uses the freshest ingredients available that day in the marketplace. The wine list is eclectic and adventurous and dishes range from exquisite starters like terrine of tuna and foie gras, an unusual combination that is both appealing and sensually captivating, to supremely inventive main courses like caviar with pork jowl and creamy potatoes and frogs' legs with garlic paste and parsley emulsion. The seafood dishes are similarly impressive, including such captivating items as red prawns with sweet-tasting and lightly sautéed onions and the more conventional but no less delicious John Dory with fennel. One of the best examples of Santamaría's innovative wedding of unlikely ingredients is cream of pumpkin with crisp sweetbreads and black olives, a tasty "troika" that breaks all the rules yet comes off masterfully. Need I say more. So bring along your very best credit card and dig in.

In the Hotel Hesperia, Paseo de la Castellana 57. ✆ **91-210-88-40.** www.restaurantesantceloni.com. Reservations required. Main courses 28€–70€; gastronomic menu 160€; special "de Mercado" menu 190€. AE, DC, MC, V. Mon–Fri 2–4pm; Mon–Sat 9–11pm. Closed Aug. Metro: Gregorio Marañón.

Expensive

Alkalde ★ BASQUE Decorated like a Basque inn, with beamed ceilings with hams hanging from the rafters, the Alkalde has been serving top-quality Spanish food in this traditional setting for many years. Upstairs is a large *típico* tavern, while downstairs extends a maze of stone-sided cellars that are pleasantly cool in summer (although the whole place is air-conditioned). The restaurant's rich choice of dishes does full justice to what's regarded as Spain's most culinarily gifted province, with sumptuous starters that range from *pimientos de piquillo asados en sarmientos* (spicy stuffed peppers roasted with vine shoots) to *gambas a la plancha* (market fresh grilled shrimps) and main attractions that include *merluza con chipiron, tinta y arroz* (hake with baby squid in its ink and rice), *mollejas y hongos con foie* (sweetbreads and mushrooms with foie gras), and *zancarrón de ternera estofado* (stewed leg of veal). After such indulgences, my favorite dessert here is the house's simple but delicious *crema casera quemada* (gently browned custard cream).

Jorge Juan 10. ✆ **91-576-33-59.** www.alkalderestaurante.com. Reservations required. Main courses 27€–50€; fixed-price menu from 55€. AE, DC, MC, V. Daily 1:15pm–midnight. Closed Sat–Sun in July–Aug. Metro: Retiro or Serrano.

Astrid y Gastón ★ PERUVIAN Founded by the husband and wife team of Astrid and Gastón Ecurio, who already run top eating spots in Lima, Bogotá, and other Latin American capitals, this elegant gourmet haven right on the Castellana offers some of the very best in Peruvian cuisine. Gaston's *ceviche,* a traditional dish based on seafood and shellfish, comes in a variety of versions including coriander flavored hake and clams, and another favorite with Madrileño regulars is his tuna and avocado *causa limeña.* Exotic meat lovers should try his delicious *cabrito medio oriente* (curried kid). The setting is coolly relaxing and the service unfussily excellent.

13 Paseo de la Castellana. ✆ **91-702-62-62.** www.astridygastonmadrid.com. Reservations required. Main courses 25€–34€. MC, V. Mon–Sat 1:30–3:30pm and 8:30–11:30pm. Metro: Gregorio Marañón.

Dassa Bassa ★★ SPANISH/INTERNATIONAL Run by former TV celebrity chef Darío Barrio, who here runs a small family team with his wife Itziar as the maitre d', this bright new in spot draws media folk and beautiful people. The high prices are justified, and in fact it is rated by some restaurant reviewers as being among the city's new top 10 nosh spots. Discreet from the outside with no name sign and modest white shutters, it looks like just another stylish 19th-century Salamanca district house. Barrio was yet another protégée of the great Catalan chef Ferran Adrià, but individual dishes like his simple-sounding but marvelous *patatas con trufas* (mashed potatoes with truffles) are totally his own. He offers two menus, one the so-called *reducido* or "reduced" version, comprising 17 exquisitely delicate minidishes, and the other a full-on "gastronomic" menu of half a dozen larger *platos.* The most flamboyant offering is probably his *rabo de toro limpio al vino tinto-chocolate con garbanzos guisados* (boned chunk of bull's tail with wine, chocolate, and stewed chickpeas!), said to be a recipe from his clearly resourceful *abuela* (grandma). Deliciously original too is a red beet-ice-cream-mango blended dessert. Barrio's so-called "playful personal statements" (as he calls some of his more out-there dishes) may have a pretentious ring, but they certainly deliver the goods.

Villalar 7. ✆ **91-576-73-97.** www.dassabassa.com. Reservations required. *Reducido* menu 80€; gastronomic menu 120€. AE, MC, V. Tues–Sat 1–3:30pm and 9–11pm. Metro: Retiro.

El Amparo ★★ BASQUE One of Madrid's most elegant gastronomic enclaves, El Amparo is built around the courtyard of an old *corrala* whose facade is covered by cascading vines. Inside, three tiers of rough-hewn wooden beams surround tables set with pink linens and glistening silver, above which a sloping skylight floods the interior with sun by day, while at night, pinpoints of light from the high-tech hanging lanterns create intimate shadows. Polite, uniformed waiters serve well-prepared, highly inventive nouvelle cuisine dishes like *cigalas salteadas de con raviolis de queso* (crayfish seasoned with ravioli cheese, honey, and rosemary) and *lechona con manzana y membrillo* (roast suckling pig with apple and quince seasoning). The standout dessert (another exquisite mouthful) is the *brioche caramelizado con ciruelas al vino tinto y crema de café* (caramelized brioche with plums marinated in red wine and coffee cream).

Callejón de Puigcerdà 8 (at corner of Jorge Juan). ✆ **91-431-64-56.** Reservations required. Main courses 18€–40€. AE, MC, V. Mon–Fri 1:30–3:30pm; Mon–Sat 9–11:30pm. Closed week before Easter. Metro: Serrano.

El Bodegón INTERNATIONAL/BASQUE/SPANISH El Bodegón looks and feels like a gentleman's club for hunting enthusiasts. International globetrotters are drawn here like flies, especially in the evening, as the restaurant is near such deluxe hotels as the Castellana and the Miguel Angel, and even the monarchy (King Juan Carlos and Queen Sofía, no less) have dined here. Waiters provide a dignified service, and even bottled water is served champagne-style, chilled in a silver floor stand. There are two main dining rooms, both conservative and oak-beamed in the country-inn style, serving the very best in Basque dishes. I recommend starting with cream of crayfish bisque or velvety vichyssoise. Main-course selections include the vegetarian *alubias de Tolosa* (fresh Tolosan broad beans), or a very gamey *pichón con ciruelas* (pigeon in a plum purée).

Pinar 15. ✆ **91-562-31-37.** Reservations required. Main courses 20€–40€. AE, DC, MC, V. Mon–Fri 1:30–4pm; Mon–Sat 9pm–midnight. Closed holidays and Aug. Metro: Rubén Darío or Gregorio Marañón.

El Pescador ★ SEAFOOD El Pescador (the Fisherman) is, as its name implies, a popular spot for seafood lovers, with over 30 kinds of fish on the menu. Many of the larger *mariscos* or shellfish, variously named *langostinos, cigalas, santiaguinos,* and *carabineros* according to their size, are on display in water tanks. The fresh Atlantic fish that feature on the menu are directly air-freighted from Galicia on Spain's north-west Atlantic facing coast, and many of them are sold in the neighboring Pescadería Coruñeses shop, arguably the finest fish emporium in all Madrid. Two Pescador highlights well worth trying are the *lenguado evaristo,* a whole sole so large it can only be ordered for two people, and the magnificent *langosta a la americana con arroz* (American style lobster with rice). ***Warning:*** Many dishes are expensive and priced by weight, so check first with the waiter before you order. Sometimes a price per kilo may be listed, which can be confusing. White Ribeiro and Albarinho wines again from Galicia best accompany the fish.

José Ortega y Gasset 75. ✆ **91-402-12-90.** Reservations required. Main courses 18€–50€. MC, V. Mon–Sat 1–4pm and 8:30pm–midnight. Closed Aug. Metro: Lista or Diego de León.

Horcher ★ GERMAN/INTERNATIONAL/CONTINENTAL The original Horcher restaurant was launched in Berlin in 1904. Forty years later, prompted by a tip from a high-ranking German officer that his country was losing the war, Herr Horcher moved his restaurant to Madrid. For years it was known as the best dining room in the city, and though fierce competition may have since robbed it of that crown, it's still going strong. It continues its grand European traditions, including excellent service and formal wear among guests. As an entree, try the *Carpaccio de venado con granos de mostaza y higos picantes* (veal carpaccio with grain mustard and spicy figs) or *blinis de huevas de salmon y crème fraiche* (blinis with salmon eggs and fresh cream), and for a main course, *rodaballo en manta de pisto* (turbot with ratatouille) or *rable de liebre en hohaldre* (hare wrapped in puff pastry). For dessert, the house specialty is crepes Sir Holden, prepared at your table.

Alfonso XII 6. ✆ **91-532-35-96.** www.restaurantehorcher.com. Reservations required. Jackets and ties for men. Main courses 36€–90€. AE, DC, MC, V. Mon–Fri 1:30–4pm; Mon–Sat 8:30pm–midnight. Metro: Retiro.

La Gamella ★★ CALIFORNIAN/CASTILIAN La Gamella had already established its gastronomic reputation in the Madrid province town of Navagalamella before 1988, the year its Illinois-born owner Dick Stephens moved his restaurant into the 19th-century building where the Spanish philosopher Ortega y Gasset was born.

The prestigious Horcher, one of the capital's legendary restaurants (see above), is just across the street, but the food at La Gamella is nowadays rated better. Mr. Stephens has prepared his delicate and light-textured specialties for the king and queen of Spain, as well as for Madrid's most talked-about artists and merchants, many of whom he knows and greets personally between sessions in his kitchen. The russet-colored, high-ceilinged design invites customers to relax as they ponder over an eclectic menu whose items include ceviche of Mediterranean fish, sliced duck liver in truffle sauce, garlic chicken and goat cheese served over caramelized endive, and an array of well-prepared desserts that includes an all-American cheesecake. The highlight for some is what has been called "the only edible hamburger in Madrid," generous in size and quality and covered with a rich salad so that it's impossible to eat without a knife and fork (unthinkable anyway to use your hands in such a genteel establishment).

Alfonso XII 4. ✆ **91-532-45-09.** www.lagamella.com. Reservations required. Main courses 20€–50€; set lunch 22€; tasting menu 38€. AE, DC, MC, V. Daily 1:30–4pm and 9pm–midnight. Closed 4 days around Easter. Metro: Retiro.

La Paloma ★ BASQUE/FRENCH A showcase for the culinary talents of chef-owner Segundo Alonso, who first made his name at the nearby exclusive El Amparo, this small but comfortable restaurant is located in a restored house with high ceilings and wooden beams in the Salamanca district. Many loyal fans followed him here and have since become regulars. His robust French and Basque dishes are some of the finest of their kind in Madrid, and his especially celebrated meat dishes include *manitas de cerdo con salsa de trufa* (pigs' trotters with foie gras sauce), *mollejas de ternera glaseadas* (glazed veal sweetbreads), and *rabo de toro* (bull's tail) stewed in red-wine sauce. The top fish choice has to be his *rodaballo a la placha con pasta de tomate con tomillo o erizos de mar* (grilled turbot with tomato paste and thyme or sea urchin), and for dessert, you must try his superb fresh dates with Chantilly cream.

Jorge Juan 39. ✆ **91-576-86-92.** www.rtelapaloma.com. Reservations recommended. Main courses 18€–34€; *menú completo* 65€. AE, DC, MC, V. Mon–Sat 1:30–3:45pm and 9pm–11:45pm. Metro: Vergara or Velázquez.

La Trainera ★ SEAFOOD It may look small from outside, but this elegant restaurant occupies a quartet of dining rooms within a turn-of-the-20th-century building in the glamorous shopping neighborhood of Serrano. Look for Basque-inspired platters of very fresh seafood, which arrive grilled, baked, fried, or drizzled with subtle combinations of herbs, wines, and olive oils. No meat of any kind is served here, but the fish is super fresh, brought straight from the huge Mercamadrid market where the owner has his own stall. Delicious specialties range from *rodaballo a la plancha* (grilled turbot) to *bogavante a la Americana* (American-style lobster) and *changurro en concha* (Basque-style minced crab served in a conch shell). You might want to start off with a platter of fresh *mariscos* (shellfish) set atop a bed of artfully arranged seaweed, but check the price first as these goodies are market-priced by weight.

Lagasca 60. ✆ **91-576-80-35.** www.latrainera.com. Reservations recommended. Main courses 20€–80€. AE, DC, MC, V. Mon–Sat 1–4pm and 8pm–midnight. Metro: Serrano.

Loft 39 INTERNATIONAL You can dine out in affordable style in a sleek linear dining room at this, one of the Salamanca district's more recently established culinary outposts. The decor is an eye-catching blend of mellow ochre and cream, framed by blue shuttered windows, and the service is both friendly and discreetly attentive. You may want to start with *salmorejo con lascas de jamon* (garlicky tomato dip with mountain ham) or the scrumptiously salty *ensalada de veieras con algas* (scallops and seaweed salad). For the main course, sample the melt-in-the-mouth tartar steak Loft 39 or *bacalao frito estilo Madrileño con pochas de pimientos rojos y avellanas* (Madrid-style fried cod with red peppers and hazelnuts). Finish in taste bud–stunning style with their simple but exquisite chocolate soufflé.

Calle Velázquez 39. ✆ **91-432-43-86.** www.restauranteloft39.com. Reservations required. Main courses 16€–35€. AE, DC, MC, V. Daily 1:30–4pm and 9pm–midnight. Metro: Velázquez.

Pedro Larumbe ★ BASQUE/FRENCH This stylish dining spot is located beside the Castellana Avenue and near Plaza Colón in a century-old building that used to be the headquarters of the famous newspaper *ABC*. Run by National Gastronomic Award winner Pedro Larumbe, it has three elegant dining areas: the classic Salón Pompeyano, the Art Deco Salón Fundador, and the beautifully tiled Patio Andalús. This Navarrese chef likes to combine *fin-de-siècle* decor with turn-of-the-20th-century cookery, and his specialties are often from the tried-and-true recipes of yesterday, as evoked by his *solomillo a la mostaza,* or steak with mustard sauce. Other prime dishes are the Basque-influenced *merluza en salsa verde con mejillones* (hake in green sauce with mussels) and delightful *ensalada de bocavante con salsa de almendras* (lobster salad with almond dressing). The service is impeccable, the wine list well chosen, and the desserts something to write home about: Try the tiramisu with a sweet wine and caramel sauce.

Serrano 61. ✆ **91-575-11-12.** www.larumbe.com. Reservations required. Main course 20€–35€; *menú completo* 60€. AE, DC, MC, V. Mon–Fri 1:30–4pm and 9pm–midnight; Sat 9pm–midnight. Closed Aug 15–30 and Easter week. Metro: Rubén Darío or Núñez de Balboa.

Ramón Freixa ★★★ FUSION When the Salamanca district's Hotel Selenza (p. 105) opened in 2009, it also heralded the birth of one of Madrid's most elegant new eating spots, named after meticulous and innovative chef Ramón Freixa. Freixa was trained in the prestigious Escuela de Hostelería in San Pol de Mar and is also owner of one of Catalunya's finest restaurants, the Racó de Freixa, recently awarded a Michelin star. Among his more inventive specialties are *ostra a la plancha con corazones de lechuga aliñados* (grilled oyster with dressed lettuce hearts) and *guiso de trigo tierno con almendras y cucurbitáceas* (tender wheat stew with almonds and marrow), while his more traditional *bacalao con sanfaina* are triumphs of comparative simplicity.

Claudio Coello 67. ✆ **91-781-01-73.** www.ramonfreixamadrid.com. Main courses 18€–35€; tasting menus 70€–100€. AE, DC, MC, V. Tues–Sat 1:30–3:30pm and 9–11pm. Metro: Serrano.

Senzone Restaurant ★★ INTERNATIONAL This ultra-cool, minimalist gray and cream hued eating spot is located on the ground floor of the Hospes Madrid (p. 106) near the Plaza de la Independencia. Its cuisine is lovingly created by young culinary chef-about-town Francisco Morales, who places a strong emphasis on healthy and natural foods. Among his top dishes are *bacalao en costra de fécula de patata* (cod cooked in a delicate potato crust) and the exotically bizarre *nécora negra con guindillas* (tiny black crab served with hot chili peppers), all presented as virtual works of art. Morales's wife, Rut Cotroneo, is the restaurant's highly knowledgable sommelier. (The wine list is *very* comprehensive and well-balanced.) Before your meal, relax over a fino in the comfortable lounges and wander around the intimate wood-paneled library with its window vistas of the Plaza de la Independencia. There's also an adjoining tapas bar and a chill-out patio, which is candlelit at night.

Plaza de la Independencia 3. ✆ **91-432-29-11.** Reservations required. Main courses 12€–25€. AE, MC, V. Tues–Sat 1:30–4pm and 8:30–11pm. Metro: Retiro.

Sula ★ INTERNATIONAL/MEDITTERANEAN As well as offering some of the most enticing multinational cuisine you'll find in the mainly snootily staid Salamanca district, the chic minimalist Sula is also one of the area's best spots for seeing famous faces (at least those known on the Madrid celeb circuit). First, pop into the small basement bar for a tasty tapa of *croquetas* or *calamares* accompanied by a glass of Rioja wine or a delicious snack of *gran reserva jamón* (vintage mountain ham), washed down with a glass of Moët et Chandon champers for 10€. They'll enhance rather than spoil your appetite for the main restaurant's rather dainty sized *raciones,* which include *ensalada de bacalao marinado* (marinated codfish salad), Adrià -inspired fusion fantasies like *espuma de higado de pato* (duck liver foam), and traditional fare like *Rabo to Toro* (bull's tail).

Calle Jorge Juan 33. ✆ **91-781-61-97.** www.sula.es. Reservations required. Small dishes 3€–17€; weekday executive menu 23€; "San Isidro" menu 45€. Mon–Sat 1:30–3:30pm and 10:30–11:30pm; bar Mon–Sat noon–midnight. Metro: Velázquez.

Viridiana ★★ INTERNATIONAL Viridiana—named after the 1961 Luis Buñuel film classic—is widely regarded as one of the finest restaurants of Madrid, renowned for the creative imagination of its chef and part-owner, Abraham García, who has lined the walls with stills from Buñuel films. (He is also a film historian, not just a self-taught chef.) Menu specialties are contemporary adaptations of traditional recipes, and they change frequently according to availability. Examples of the individualistic cooking include a salad of exotic lettuces served with smoked salmon, a chicken pastilla laced with cinnamon, baby squid with curry served on a bed of lentils, roasted lamb served in puff pastry with fresh basil, and the choicest langostinos from Cádiz. An intriguing Spanish-Mexican offering is his (take a deep breath) *flores de calabaza con jamón iberico y queso de Oaxaca en tortillas al mole poblano* (pumpkin flowers with Iberian ham and Oaxaca cheese wrapped in Mexican tortillas and covered with traditional mole sauce). All the dishes are sublime, and the inviting ambience makes you relax as you sit back to enjoy dishes that dazzle the eye.

Juan de Mena 14. ✆ **91-531-52-22.** www.restauranteviridiana.com. Reservations recommended. Main courses 28€–65€. V. Mon–Sat 1:45–4pm and 8.30pm–midnight. Closed 1 week at Easter. Metro: Banco de España.

Moderate

El Buey SPANISH This *casera* (homey) eating spot, with its cozy ambience and colorful bullfight decor, lies in residential Salamanca close to Goya and Alcalá Street. Twin of a more boisterous branch near Opera, it's a meat-eater's haven, specializing in quality steaks and joints cooked to individual needs. After an initial *picoteo* (selection of tidbits such as olives, stuffed anchovies, or *jamón Serrano*), go for the main favorite, *lomo de buey* (ox loin or beef filet). Noncarnivorous specialities on the menu may alternatively include *pimientos rellenos de mariscos* (peppers stuffed with shellfish) and homemade desserts such as *crepes rellenos de chocolate* (chocolate-filled crepes) are good follow-ups.

General Pardiñas 10. ✆ **91-578-38-71.** www.elbuey.es. Main courses 14€–28€. AE, DC, MC, V. Mon–Sat 1–4pm and 9pm–midnight. Metro: Principe de Vergara.

La Galette VEGETARIAN/INTERNATIONAL La Galette was one of Madrid's first vegetarian restaurants, and it remains one of the best. Small and charming, it lies in a residential and shopping area in the exclusive Salamanca district, near Plaza de la Independencia and the northern edge of Retiro Park. There is a limited selection of meat dishes, but the true allure lies in this establishment's imaginative preparation of vegetables. Examples include baked stuffed peppers, omelets, eggplant croquettes, and even vegetarian hamburgers. Some of the dishes are macrobiotic. The place is also noted for its mouth-watering pastries. The same owners also operate La Galette II, in the same complex.

Conde de Aranda 11. ✆ **91-576-06-41.** www.lagalette2.com. Reservations recommended. Main courses 8.50€–24€; fixed-price lunch 12€. AE, DC, MC, V. Mon–Sat 2–4pm and 9pm–midnight. Metro: Retiro.

Taberna de la Daniela ★ 🎁 MADRILEÑO With its traditional zinc-top bar and wall tiles, this much-loved Castizo taberna is among the very best Madrileño eating spots for enjoying *cocido*. The chef even includes a junior version (*cocido pequeño*) on his *menú infantil*. The great seafood specialties here are *bacalao pil pil* (Basque cod in a spicy green sauce) and *besugo la madrileño besugo* (or sea bream), being the most highly esteemed fish in the capital due to its exquisite flavor. Other homemade dishes include *sopa de fideos* (noodle soup) and *huesos de tuétano* (marrow bone). The dining area, set back beside pillars from the tapas bar, is quiet and relaxing, and the service is friendly.

General Pardiñas 21. ✆ **91-575-23-29.** Reservations recommended. Main courses 12€–25€. MC, V. Daily noon–4pm and 9pm–12:30am (Sat–Sun till 1am). Metro: Goya.

Teatriz ★ ITALIAN Decorated by the famed French architect and designer Philippe Starck, this old theater is now transformed into a top-notch Italian restaurant. Theater seats have long given way to dining tables, but Starck kept many of the elements of the old thespian's locale. As you head for the restrooms, you encounter a stunning fountain of marble, silver, and gold, with everything bathed in a bluish light, giving you the impression that you're in a nightclub. The kitchen closes at midnight, but the bar remains open until 3am. The dishes are cleverly crafted. One of the best pastas is a tortellini filled with Parmesan-flavored ground meat. There are also Spanish favorites like the rib-sticking *estofado de rabo de buey* (bull's tail stew). Top desserts to finish off with are the fresh cheese mousse with mango ice cream and velvety smooth tiramisu.

Hermosilla 15. ✆ **91-577-53-79.** Reservations recommended. Main courses 12€–22 €; *menú completo* 254€. AE, DC, MC, V. Daily 1:30–4pm and 9pm–12:30am. Closed Aug. Metro: Velázquez or Serrano.

Inexpensive

Iroco ★ INTERNATIONAL This well-run and popular Salamanca restaurant, decorated in a slick New York-ish style, is known for its *nueva cocina* (nouvelle cuisine). It attracts a business crowd for its lunch and a trend-setting and younger crowd in the evening. The Asian fusion prawn rolls make a delightful starter as does the white fish salad soused in a delightful sherry vinaigrette. For main courses you can sample enticing dishes like marinated tuna steak (grilled to perfection) or eggplant lasagna served with fresh mushrooms and lots of creamy mozzarella. Seafood enthusiasts also appreciate the Atlantic coast *merluza* (hake) served in an asparagus sauce. Desserts are always tempting and the flans (caramel custards) made fresh daily.

Velázquez 18. ✆ **91-431-73-81.** Reservations required. Main courses 14€–25€. AE, DC, MC, V. Daily 1:30–4pm and 8:30pm–midnight. Metro: Goya.

CHAMBERÍ

Very Expensive

Jockey ★★★ INTERNATIONAL This is a deluxe culinary citadel. For decades, this was the premier restaurant of Spain. A favorite of international celebrities, diplomats, and heads of state, it was once known as the Jockey Club, although "Club" was eventually dropped because it suggested exclusivity. The restaurant, with tables on two levels, isn't large. Wood-paneled walls and colored linen provide a cozy ambience. Against the paneling are a dozen prints of jockeys mounted on horses—hence the name.

Since Jockey's establishment shortly after World War II, each chef who has come along has prided himself on coming up with new and creative dishes. You can still order Beluga caviar from Iran, but might settle happily for the gooseliver terrine or slices of Jabugo ham. Cold melon soup with shrimp is soothing on a hot day, especially when followed by grill-roasted young pigeon from Talavera or sole filets with figs in chardonnay. Stuffed small chicken Jockey style is a specialty, as is *tripa madrileña*, a local dish. The well-stocked cellar offers a choice of no less than 700 varieties of wines and spirits!

Amador de los Ríos 6. ✆ **91-319-24-35.** www.restaurantejockey.net. Reservations required. Main courses 25€–50€; special menu 80€. AE, DC, MC, V. Daily 1–4pm and 9pm–midnight. Closed Aug. Metro: Colón.

Sergi Arola Gastro ★★★ FUSION The Catalan masterchef who put La Broche (p. 160) on the culinary map moved house and opened this new top spot in the Chamberí district, creating yet another must on the Madrid gourmet circuit. Just about the most discreetly located major restaurant in the country, it nestles unobtrusively in a quiet Chamberí street just a two-minute stroll away from his former locale. Among his many highly inventive dishes, keep a special eye out for the *tosta de lenguado y láminas de boletus con crema de ajo* ("toast" of sole with razor-thin slices of boletus mushrooms cooked in garlic sauce) and *crema de calçots con huevo frito y vieiras* (cream of *calçots* with fried egg and scallops). To accompany your meal there's a mind-boggling choice of over 500 hand-picked wines, including some of the very best vintages from Spanish and international vineyards. The cozy lounge bar also provides stunning cocktails served by barman supreme Diego Cabrera and "gastro snacks" and accompanying *raciones* such as *almejas vinagretas* (clams in vinaigrette sauce).

Calle Zurbano 31. ✆ **91-310-21-69.** www.sergiarola.es. *Gastro tapas y raciones* 7€–40€; various menus 110€–160€; tasting menu 170€ (250€ with select wine included). Metro: Gregorio Marañón.

Expensive

Belagua BASQUE This glamorous restaurant was originally built in 1894 as a small palace in the French neoclassical style. In 1991, Catalan designer Josep Joanpere helped transform the building into a carefully detailed hotel (the Santo Mauro), which I recommend separately (p. 109). On the hotel premises is this highly appealing postmodern restaurant, today one of the capital's finest. Assisted by the well-mannered staff, you'll select from a menu whose inspiration and ingredients change with the seasons. Examples include watermelon-and-prawn salad, light cream of cold ginger soup, haddock baked in a crust of potatoes tinted with squid ink, filet of monkfish with prawn-and-zucchini sauce, and duck with honey and black cherries.

Depending on the selection that day, dessert might include miniature portions of flan with strawberry sauce plus an array of the day's pastries. The restaurant's name, incidentally, derives from a village in Navarre known for its natural beauty.

In the Santo Mauro Hotel, Zurbano 36. © **91-319-69-00.** Reservations recommended. Main courses 20€–40€. AE, DC, MC, V. Daily 1:30–3:30pm and 8:30–11:30pm. Closed Aug. Metro: Rubén Darío or Alonso Martínez.

La Broche ★★★ CATALAN Previously helmed by top chef Sergi Arola, La Broche is now in the equally able hands of his erstwhile disciple Angel Palacios, a recent winner of the prestigious Bocusse Trophy. Enter the elegant and spacious lobby of the Hotel Occidental Miguel Angel (p. 110) and, on your left, you'll find the select dining enclave that attracts discerning gourmets. Deluxe ingredients, personally selected by the chef and changed to take advantage of the best in any season, are fashioned into some of the capital's most flavor-filled dishes. Start with raw seafood and seawater gelée, and then proceed into the heavenly and continually changing main courses. Even the bread placed on your table is freshly made and the creative desserts such as *helado de yoghurt de rosas con mandarina y almendra amarga.* (yogurt ice cream made from roses, mandarin oranges, and bitter almond yogurt) are out of this world.

Miguel Angel 29–31. © **91-399-34-37.** www.labroche.com. Reservations required. Main courses 25€–45€; special tasting menu 120€. AE, DC, MC, V. Mon–Fri 2–3:30pm and 9–11:15pm. Closed Aug. Metro: Gregorio Marañón.

Las Cuatro Estaciones ★★★ MEDITERRANEAN Las Cuatro Estaciones is placed by gastronomes and horticulturists alike among their favorite Madrid dining spots, and it is neck-and-neck with the Jockey (see above) in the prestige stakes. In addition to superb food, the establishment prides itself on decorating its salons with masses of flowers that change with the season. Depending on the time of year, the mirrors surrounding the multilevel bar near the entrance reflect thousands of hydrangeas, chrysanthemums, or poinsettias. Each person involved in food preparation spends a prolonged apprenticeship at restaurants in France before returning home to try his or her talents on the taste buds of discerning Madrileños. Representative specialties include crab bisque; a petite marmite of fish and shellfish; and a nouvelle cuisine version of blanquette of monkfish so tender it melts in your mouth. The desserts include daily specials brought temptingly to your table.

Ibáñez Ibero 5. © **91-553-63-05.** Reservations required. Main courses 45€–65€; fixed-price dinner 60€. AE, DC, MC, V. Mon–Fri 1:30–4pm; Mon–Sat 9pm–midnight. Closed Easter and Aug. Metro: Guzmán el Bueno.

Moderate

Annapurna INDIAN Regarded by many as the best Indian restaurant in Madrid, this refined restaurant stands in a relaxing Chamberí backwater just west of the Castellana. Immaculate and helpful service and a stylish dining room with charming views of an interior garden enhance the superlative cuisine. You might start with a delicious meat and vegetable *samosa,* and then go on to a main course choice of Jeenga Annapurna (shrimp in tamarind sauce) or one of the Annapurna's incomparable Roghan Josh curries, aromatic Kahmiri Pulao basmati rice dishes, or oven tandoori roasts. Among the array of desserts is the Gajar Halva (a carrot-and almond-based tartlet), and pistachio, saffron, and cardamom ice cream are equally tempting. The service is discreetly impeccable.

Zurbano 5. ✆ **91-319-87-16.** www.annapurnarestaurante.com. Reservations recommended. Main courses 18€–40€; special lunch menus 35€–40€; *menús de degustación* 40€. AE, DC, MC, V. Mon–Fri 1:45–4pm and 9–11:45pm; Sat 1:45–4pm. Closed public holidays. Metro: Alonso Martínez.

Balear PAELLA/SEAFOOD True to its Mediterranean name, this genial eating spot is a very popular place for seafood. Journalists, writers, poets, and artists in particular have a special place in their hearts for Balear. Its warm and welcoming yellow-and-white dining room is filled with potted plants. The menu is positively ruled by paellas, which come in no less than 14 different permutations that include chicken, pork, cod, spider crabs, and shellfish (including lobster), as well as a *ciega* (blind) version in which all fish bones and shells have been removed and an all-black version tinted with squid ink for extra flavor. There's even a vegetarian paella in case (inexplicably) you don't like fish. Further choices cover Catalan fideuá alternatives that substitute noodles for rice and that supreme standout among fishy delights: the sumptuous, but pricey, *caldereta de langosta* (lobster stew).

Sagunto 18. ✆ **91-447-91-15.** www.restaurantebalaear.net. Reservations recommended. Main courses 10€–25€. AE, MC, V. Daily 1:30–4.30pm; Tues–Sat 8pm–midnight. Metro: Iglesia.

La Cava Real ★★ FRENCH/BASQUE If the wine is as important to you as the meal itself, this is the place for you. When the tavern opened in 1983, it was the first real wine bar Madrid had ever seen. Since then, many others have appeared, but La Cava Real (which is linked to Spain's largest oenophiles' club) remains one of the very best. Just don't mention the word *beer* here and you should do fine. There are more than 350 wines in the cellar, and you can order a staggering 50 of them by the glass, which allows you to sample more than one tipple at the same meal if you so desire. Turn to the skilled maitre d', Chema Gómez, for advice on which vintage to choose. The chef, Javier Collar, matches the wines with a smooth and well-executed blend of the finest French and Basque dishes. Witness his *pimientos rellenos de bacalao* (peppers stuffed with cod), *rape envuelto en calabacín* (angler fish wrapped in vegetable marrow), and grilled and sweet-tasting *merluza* (hake) from the Bay of Biscay. He also provides tasty seasonal game fare and in autumn, dishes such as *perdiz* (partridge) and *codorniz* (quail). For desserts the cheese selection deserves an award on its own.

Espronceda 34. ✆ **91-442-54-32.** Reservations required. Main courses 15€–30€; *menú de degustación* 55€–65€. AE, DC, MC, V. Mon–Sat 1:30–4pm and 9pm–midnight. Closed Aug. Metro: Río Rojas.

Mosaiq ★ MOROCCAN Vividly decorated in exotic turquoise, orange, and cream hued silks, Mosaiq is a visual treat even before you get started on the delicious food. One of Madrid's most stimulating non-Spanish eating spots, with the added bonus of discreetly attentive service, it specializes in North African and Middle Eastern dishes of the highest order. The three dining areas all have traditional low-level tables with cushions and hassocks. For the main course go for Kafta (very spicy lamb brochettes), Tajine de Pollo (chicken tagine), or a standard Mediterranean fish such as *dorada al horno* (baked sea bream). Main dishes are usually served with rice, raisins, and pine nuts, and accompanied with traditional pita bread. After your meal you can choose from an excellent selection of teas.

Caracas 21. ✆ **91-308-44-46.** www.mosaiqrestaurante.com. Main courses 12€–24€; tasting menu for 2: 35€ per person. AE, DC, MC, V. Mon–Sat 1:30–4:30pm and 9pm–midnight (till 2am Fri–Sat); Sun 1:30–4:30pm. Metro: Alonso Martínez.

CHAMARTÍN

Very Expensive

El Chaflán ★ SPANISH One of Madrid's hot chefs, Juan Pablo Felipe Pablado, is a master in the kitchen here. He can take almost any dish, including the classics, and give it a new flavor and texture. (You can watch the whole cooking process through a double-glazed window, as you eat in a warmly relaxing gray-green dining room that's illuminated by an overhead skylight.) For example, he virtually deconstructs the most famous soup of Spain, gazpacho, and reassembles it into *glaces* and mousses. There's a firm hand in control here, and the chef personally selects the best produce, fish, and local meats to concoct his dishes. The roast suckling pig would rival any in Segovia, where they say this dish is prepared better than anywhere else in the world. The interesting seafood menu includes lesser-known Spanish fish dishes like marinated *corvina* (sea bass) and *urta* (sea bream) with winkles, while his notable selection of cheeses has won a Gourmet Club award.

Av. Pío XII 34. ✆ **91-350-61-93.** www.elchaflan.com. Reservations required. Main courses 22€–36€; fixed-price menus 45€–100€; tasting menus 65€–145€. AE, DC, MC, V. Mon–Fri 1:30–4pm; Mon–Sat 9–11:30pm. Metro: Pío XII.

Zalacaín ★★★ INTERNATIONAL/BASQUE/FRENCH Named after the intrepid hero of Basque author Pío Baroja's 1909 novel, *Zalacaín El Aventurer,* Zalacaín is small, exclusive, and very classy, with an old-world formal etiquette that still requires men to wear jackets and ties. Royalty and media celebrities appear regularly among its clientele. Outstanding in both food and decor (it's received prestigious Michelin and Gournetour awards in the past), the restaurant has the atmosphere of an elegant old mansion. Housed at the garden end of a modern apartment complex, it's reached by an illuminated walk from Paseo de la Castellana close to such deluxe hotels as the Castellana and the Miguel Angel. It's specialized in "haute cuisine" based on seasonal products since opening its doors back in 1973, and today's menu still features the occasional nouvelle touch among its many Basque and French specialties. Gems include *manita de cerdo rellena de setas* (pigs' feet stuffed with wild mushrooms), *ostras con caviar y gelatina de jerez* (oysters with caviar and sherry jelly), and *ravioli relleno de foie gras y trufas* (ravioli stuffed with foie gras and truffles). For dessert, try the superlative strawberry purée with cheese ice cream.

Alvarez de Baena 4. ✆ **91-561-48-40.** www.restaurantezalacain.com. Reservations required. Main courses 30€–55€; special tasting menu 110€. AE, DC, MC, V. Mon–Fri 1:15–4pm; Mon–Sat 9pm–midnight. Closed week before Easter and Aug. Metro: Gregorio Marañón.

Expensive

Cabo Mayor ★★ SEAFOOD Near Chamartín train station, this is one of the most popular and stylish restaurants in Madrid, even attracting Spanish royalty on occasions. An open-air staircase leading to the entranceway descends from a manicured garden on a quiet side street where a battalion of uniformed doormen stands ready to greet arriving taxis. The restaurant's decor is nautically inspired, with hardwood panels, brass trim, pulleys and ropes, a tile floor custom-painted with sea-green and blue replicas of waves, and hand-carved models of fishing boats. Some dozen bronze statues honoring fishers and their craft are displayed in brass portholes in illuminated positions of honor. Favorite fishy entrees are the exquisite *ensalada de bogavante* (lobster salad) and Cantabrian fish soup, while main course highlights include the *dorada guisada con tomillo* (stewed sea bream with thyme) and *salmón con salsa de jerez* (salmon in sherry sauce). A meat classic is the melt-in-your-mouth *ternera en salsa de cassis* (veal in cassis sauce), and desserts are topped by a rice mousse with pine-nut sauce.

Juan Ramón Jiménez 37. ✆ **91-350-87-76.** Reservations recommended. Main courses 18€–48€. AE, DC, MC, V. Mon–Sat 1:30–4pm and 8:45–11:45pm. Closed 1 week at Easter. Metro: Cuzco.

El Olivo Restaurant ★★ MEDITERRANEAN Locals praise the success of a non-Spaniard (in this case, French-born Jean Pierre Vandelle) in recognizing the international appeal of two of Spain's most valuable culinary resources: olive oil and sherry. Designed in tones of green and amber, this is the only restaurant in Spain that wheels a cart stocked with 40 regional olive oils from table to table. As an aperitif you can pick from over 100 brands of *vino de Jerez*—from dry *manzanillas* to sweet *olorosos*—in the hotel's famed sherry bar.

Menu specialties prepared by Chef Gonzalo Omiste include grilled filet of *rape* (monkfish) marinated in herbs and olive oil, then served with black-olive sauce over compote of fresh tomatoes, and four preparations of *bacalao* (cod) arranged on a single platter and served with a *pil-pil* sauce (cod gelatin and herbs whipped into a mayonnaise-like consistency with olive oil). Among the other delicious olive-based dishes are *ensalada de bogavante a las finas hierbas* (lobster salad with fine herbs).

General Gallegos 1. ✆ **91-359-15-35.** Reservations recommended. Main courses 19€–38€; fixed-price menu 45€; tasting menu 55€. Sherries 2€–5€ a glass. AE, DC, MC, V. Tues–Sat 1–4pm and 9pm–midnight. Closed Aug 15–31 and 4 days around Easter. Metro: Plaza de Castilla.

Príncipe de Viana ★ BASQUE Another of the city's classic Basque favorites, the Principe de Viana offers a wide choice of inventive dishes that range from traditional *bacalao ajoarriera* (cod with red peppers and tomatoes) to more adventurous creations like *mollejas en vinagreta de soja* (sweet meats in a soy vinaigrette). Those with a sweet tooth will be more than satisfied with the dessert of cream cheese and mango sorbet. From the nicely varied wine list, you might choose the smooth white Albarino from Galicia, which goes especially well with fish, or you could try thc Basque country's very own sharp green white Xacolí, a definite appetite-enhancer.

Manuel de Falla 5. ✆ **91-457-15-49.** Reservations required. Main courses 15€–28€. AE, DC, MC, V. Mon–Fri 1–4pm and 9–11:30pm; Sat 9–11:30pm. Closed Aug. Metro: Lima or Cuzco.

Thai Gardens THAI Part of a high-class chain whose branches extend from Casablanca to Sao Paolo, this trendy Thai restaurant is a favorite with celebrities and visitors looking for something special. After 13 years in the Salamanca district, it relocated to northerly residential Chamartín in 2007, and most of its dedicated regulars have continued to patronize it there. The chef and cuisine remain unchanged, and traditional delights like Khum Phom Pha Prawns and Kai Satee kabobs (using MSG-free ingredients mainly flown in from Thailand) continue to appear on the menu. Here in a warmly recreated Oriental setting, the attentive and friendly staff, dressed in colorful Thai costumes, serve you.

Paseo de la Habana 6. ✆ 91-577-88-84. www.thaigardensgroup.com. Main courses 20€–35€; tasting menu 45€. AE, DC, MC, V. Daily 2–4pm and 9pm–midnight. Metro: Serrano.

Moderate

Goizeko Kabi ★ BASQUE This restaurant serves some of the best Basque dishes in Madrid in an intimate, understated interior. Particularly delicious as a starter is *txangurro y pisto de bacalao* (crab and cod purée served in a conch shell). *Bacalao* (cod), the Basque country's specialty par excellence, appears on the main menu in various versions. My favorite is *bacalao al pil-pil,* which is served in a particularly delicious pungent green sauce. Also marvelous are the *tacos de rape con almejas* (chunks of angler fish with clams) and *kokotxas de merluza* (tender and creamily cooked "cheeks" of hake). Desserts offer further delights, such as the *mousse de naranja con lágrimnas de chocolate* (orange mousse with a coating of bitter chocolate) and the scrumptious if more experimental *helado de pan de centeno* (black bread ice cream).

Comandante Zorita 37. © **91-533-01-85.** www.goizekogaztelupe.com. Reservations recommended. Main courses 18€–45€; tasting menu 80€. AE, DC, MC, V. Mon–Sat 1–4pm and 8:30pm–midnight. Metro: Alvarado or Nuevos Ministerios.

Inexpensive

Alfredo's Barbacoa AMERICAN Located in a residential corner of Chamartín just off the Castellana, Alfredo's is a restaurant popular with Americans longing for home-style food. Al himself arrives at his small intimate bar/restaurant wearing boots, blue jeans, and a 10-gallon hat (though he's originally from New York, it's clear his spiritual home is Texas), and his friendly welcome has made the place a center for both his friends and newcomers to Madrid. Start off helping yourself at the salad bar—you can get a lot on your plate in one trip. Then perhaps order a hamburger (Super Alfredo's with cheese and bacon is the most filling). As the restaurant's name implies, this will be of the barbecued variety, just like the spare ribs and chicken. Star dish is the top sirloin steak, which is as big and juicy as they get in Madrid. And as a side dish, it's a rare treat to be able to have *mazorca* (corn on the cob) in a restaurant in Spain (though they grow the stuff here in abundance, they unappreciatively tend to feed it to the pigs!).

The original **Alfredo's Barbacoa,** Lagasca 5 (© **91-576-62-71**), is still in business, and also under Al's auspices.

Juan Hurtado de Mendoza 11. © **91-345-16-39.** www.alfredos-barbacoa.es. Reservations recommended. Main courses 8€–20€. AE, DC, MC, V. Mon–Sat 1–4:30pm and 8:30pm–midnight (Fri–Sat until 1am). Metro: Cuzco.

Picnic, Anyone?

On a hot day, do as the Madrileños do: Secure the makings of a picnic lunch and head for Casa de Campo (metro: El Batón), those once-royal hunting grounds in the west of Madrid across the Manzanares River. Children delight in this adventure, as they can also visit a boating lake, the Parque de Atracciones, and the Madrid zoo.

Your best choice for picnic fare can be bought right in the center at Rodilla, Barquillo 8 (© 91-523-90-10; www.rodilla.es; metro: Chueca), where you can find neatly prepared, squeaky clean European-sized (smaller than the huge old Spanish half loaf size) sandwiches, pastries, and takeout tapas. The sandwiches, including vegetarian, meat, and fish, begin at 1.50€. It's open Monday and Tuesday from 8:30am to 10:30pm; Wednesday, Thursday, and Sunday from 9am to 11pm; Friday and Saturday from 9am to 11:30pm.

Fast Good Madrid ★ 🎁 FUSION As the name implies, you get your grub in double–quick time here. What you may not realize, though, is that this bright and cheery place, located in the NH Eurobuilding in the northerly zone of Cuzco just below Plaza Castilla, is the brainchild of no less a personage than Spain's master chef Ferran Adrià. So what you get—at a truly budget price—is inventive quality food. McDonald's or Burger King, this ain't. The nifty, squeaky clean menu includes yummy delights such as pasta con parmesan and Panini Brie, Bacon, and Spinach, all neatly prepared and quite scrumptious. You can help yourself at the salad bar, or get table service for hot dishes like *hamburguesa de ternera* (tarragon flavored veal hamburger), served with olive oil and fries. The colorful but chic comic strip–inspired decor fits the fun mood exactly, and the casually clad staff is young, chirpy, and relaxed. There's also a lower-priced, smaller-portioned but equally tasty children's menu.

Padre Damián 23. ✆ **91-343-06-55.** www.fast-good.com. Main courses 8€–12€. AE, MC, V. Daily noon-midnight. Métro: Cuzco.

IN THE ARTURO SORIA DISTRICT

Moderate

Nicómedes ★ 🎁 EXTREMADURAN This colonial-style building has been completely transformed by the charming and hospitable Suárez sisters, Concha and Elena, into a modern-looking château of five floors with beautiful, tall bay windows that allow natural light to flood into the dining areas. In fine weather, customers often dine out on the summer terrace. The inventive cuisine focuses strongly on the western Portugal-bordering province of Extremadura, and that region's traditional goat cheese with glazed onions is a favorite opener. Also popular are *bolsitas rellenas de gamba y queso fresco* (crispy pasta balls stuffed with shrimp and freshly made cheese), while main course highlights include the traditional *solomillo de buey* (fondue of ox steak) and (more Cantabrian than Extremaduran in origin) *lomitos de dorada con verduras a la plancha* (slices of sea bream with grilled vegetables). For dessert, try the homemade cake of the day or more exotic *flan de azafrán y cardamomo con helado de melocotón* (saffron and cardamom flavored caramel custard with peach ice cream). Among the huge choice of wines, you might sample the region's hearty red Monasterio de Tentudia.

Moscatelar 18. ✆ **91-388-78-28.** www.nicomedesrestaurante.es. Reservations recommended. Main courses 12€–24€. AE, DC, V. Tues–Sat 1:30–3:30pm and 9:30pm–midnight; Sun 1:30–3:30pm. Closed Aug. Metro: Esperanza or Arturo Soria.

NEAR PLAZA REPÚBLICA ARGENTINA

Moderate

Casa Benigna MEDITERRANEAN/SCANDINAVIAN This charming bistro—the only one in town to offer a choice of both cool Nordic and sunny southern cuisines—lies in residential northerly Chamartín. Decorated in typically inviting

THE BEST OF THE *tascas*

Don't starve waiting around for Madrid's fashionable 9:30 or 10pm dinner hour. Throughout the city you'll find *tascas,* bars that serve wine and platters of tempting hot and cold hors d'oeuvres known as tapas: mushrooms, salads, baby eels, shrimp, lobster, mussels, sausage, ham, and, in one establishment, bull testicles. Keep in mind that you can often save euros by ordering at the bar rather than occupying a table. Here are six of my favorites:

Casa Alberto CASTILIAN/TAPAS/TASCAS One of the oldest *tascas* in the neighborhood, Casa Alberto first opened its doors in 1827 and has thrived ever since. On the street level of a house where Miguel de Cervantes lived briefly in 1614, it contains an appealing mixture of bullfighting memorabilia, engravings, and reproductions of Old Master paintings. Many visitors opt only for the tapas, continually replenished from platters on the bar, but there's a sit-down dining area for more substantial meals. Specialties include fried squid, shellfish in vinaigrette sauce, chorizo in cider sauce, and several versions of baked or roasted lamb.

Huertas 18. ✆ **91-429-93-56.** www.casaalberto.es. Reservations recommended. Main courses 12€–24€. AE, DC, MC, V. Tues–Sat 1–4pm; Tues–Sun 8:30pm–midnight. Metro: Antón Martín.

Casa Labra TAPAS Founded in 1860 and run by the Molina family for the past 6 decades, the mellow brown-walled Casa Labra is located a mere stone's throw from the Puerta del Sol. Said to have started up as a favorite meeting spot of the 19th-century Socialist party, it's one of the center's oldest and most popular tapas bars, invariably crowded and full of atmosphere. Of the many tidbits on offer, don't miss the croquetas de bacalao (deep-fried cod croquettes)—so cheap and delicious that they often create lines of eagerly panting aficionados. Accompany them with an equally low-priced caña (small glass) of cold Mahou beer or the house's white Valdepeñas wine. The adjoining restaurant provides a relaxed and secluded eating experience and is priced accordingly.

Tetuan 12. ✆ **91-532-14-05.** www.casalabra.es. Tapas 2.50€–3€ or 1.30€ per croquette; caña of beer or glass of wine 1.40€; main courses in restaurant 12€–20€. No credit cards. Daily 9:30am–3:30pm and 6–11pm. Metro: Sol.

Casa Mingo ASTURIAN/SPANISH Casa Mingo has been known for decades for its cider, both still and bubbly. The perfect accompanying tidbit is a piece of the local Asturian *cabrales* (goat cheese), but the roast chicken is the specialty of the house, with a large number of helpings served daily. There's no formality here; customers share big tables under the vaulted ceiling in the dining room amid a virtually all-wood decor and a wall lined with huge wine barrels. In summer, the staff sets up tables and wooden chairs on the sidewalk, and they open a terrace on the roof for dining. This is not so much a restaurant as a *bodega/taverna* that serves food.

Paseo de la Florida 34. ✆ **91-547-79-18.** www.casamingo.es. Main courses 8€–14€. No credit cards. Daily 11am–midnight. Metro: Príncipe Pío, then 15-min. walk.

Cervecería Alemana TAPAS/TASCAS Just round the corner from Casa Alberto directly on one of the liveliest little plazas in Madrid, this place earned its name because of its long-ago German clients. (It was also a great Hemingway favorite.) Though the bar clings to its turn-of-the-20th-century traditions, young Madrileños are fond of stopping in for a mug of draft beer. You can relax in the atmospheric old lounge or—depending on the weather—sit at one of the outside tables leisurely sipping your chosen tipple, as the waiters make no attempt to hurry you along. If you're feeling peckish, try the fried sardines or a Spanish omelet. Many of the *tascas* on this popular square are crowded and noisy—often with blaring loud music—but this one is quiet and a good place to have a conversation.

Plaza de Santa Ana 6. ✆ **91-429-70-33.** Beer 2.75€-4.50€; tapas and raciones 2.75€-15€. No credit cards. Sun-Thurs 11am-12:30am; Fri-Sat 11am-2am. Metro: Tirso de Molina.

Cervecería Santa Bárbara TAPAS/TASCAS Unique in Madrid, Cervecería Santa Bárbara is an outlet for a beer factory, which has in fact been producing beer since the early 19th century. Today, to keep up with the times, the management has done a lot to make it modern and inviting. Hanging globe lights and spinning ceiling fans create an attractive ambience, as does the black-and-white checkerboard marble floor. You go here for beer, of course: *cerveza negra* (black beer) or *cerveza dorada* (golden beer). The local brew (Mahou) is best accompanied by homemade potato chips or fresh shrimp, lobster, crabmeat, or barnacles. You can stand at the counter or go directly to one of the wooden tables for waiter service. In summer, you can sit outside at terrace tables overlooking the small tree-lined Santa Bárbara square.

Plaza de Santa Bárbara 8. ✆ **91-319-04-49.** www.cerverceriasantabarbara.com. Beer 2.75€-5€; tapas and raciones 3.50€-20€. MC, V. Daily 11:30am-midnight. Metro: Alonso Martínez.

La Taberna de Antonio Sánchez ★ TAPAS/TASCAS Named in 1830 after the founder's son, who was killed in the bullring, this charismatic *tasca*—rated the oldest in central Madrid—is full of bullfighting memorabilia, including the stuffed head of the animal that gored young Sánchez. Also featured on the dark-paneled walls are three works by the Spanish artist Zuloaga, who had his last public exhibition in this restaurant near Plaza Tirso de Molina. A limited array of tapas, including garlic soup, is served with Valdepeñas wine drawn from a barrel, though many local guests ignore the edibles in favor of smoking cigarettes and arguing the merits of this or that bullfighter. It's also becoming increasingly known to international visitors, so it's not unusual to see groups of animated young German or Italian tourists sampling the goods, too. A restaurant in the back serves Spanish food with a vaguely French influence.

Mesón de Paredes 13. ✆ **91-539-78-26.** Tapas 2.75€-4€; main courses in restaurant 8€-16€; fixed-price lunch Mon-Fri 12€. MC, V. Daily 1-4pm; Mon-Sat 8pm-midnight. Metro: Tirso de Molina.

Mediterranean style with murals of rural landscapes and divided into four intimate salons, it's run by the family of Jorge García, whose close relatives in Norway are the inspiration for the Scandinavian recipes. The exquisitely prepared dishes, based on the finest ingredients, cover everything from Norwegian herring in marinades to Levante style *arroz abanda,* a variation of traditional paella using different varieties of seafood. One eclectic standout is the roast ribs of tender baby lamb, while for vegetarians there's a delicious *parrillada de verduras,* or grilled fresh vegetables. For dessert, opt for the Norwegian cookies with wild berries or freshly made crepes with apple sauce.

Benigno Soto 9. ✆ **91-413-33-56.** Reservations required. Main courses 25€–55€; set menu 20€; tasting menu 45€. AE, MC, V. Mon–Sat 1:30–4pm and 9–11:30pm; Sun 1:30–4pm. Metro: Concha Espina.

Nodo 🎁 SPANISH/JAPANESE Ironically named after the old Franco-era news agency (Noticias Documentales) which used to be housed across the road, this hip eating spot offers a pole-opposite image of cool minimalism and ultrachic decor which tends to attract a high number of celebrity customers. There's nothing commonplace about the food, either. The restaurant's owner, Alberto Chicote, has successfully fused East and West gourmet tastes with dishes like *tataki de atún con ajo blanco malagueño* (Asian tuna with Málaga white garlic sauce). Other individual delights include *chipirones en su tinta* (baby squid cooked in its own ink), sushi, guachalomo, and "parcels" of leaf-enclosed fish. Simple but exotically named desserts like white chocolate bombe and *napoleón de fresas* finish off the meal. Service is extremely attentive and prices are not as high as you might expect.

Velázquez 150. ✆ **91-564-40-44.** www.restaurantenodo.es. Main courses 14€–24€. AE, DC, MC, V. Mon–Thurs 1:30–4pm and 9pm–midnight; Fri–Sun 1:30–4pm and 9pm–1am. Metro: República Argentina.

Inexpensive

Foster's Hollywood ☺ AMERICAN When your addiction to Stateside food becomes overwhelming, head here. When Foster's opened its doors in 1971, it was not only the first American-style restaurant in Spain, but also one of the first in Europe. Since those early days, it has grown to 25 restaurants in Madrid plus several more in the capital's surrounding province. A popular hangout for both locals and visiting Yanks, it offers a choice of dining rooms, ranging from classical club to a faux film studio with props. The varied menu includes Tex-Mex selections, ribs, steaks, sandwiches, freshly made salads, and, as its signature product, hamburgers grilled over natural charcoal. The *New York Times* once claimed that it had "probably the best onion rings in the world."

Paseo de la Castellana 116–118. ✆ **91-564-63-08.** www.fostershollywood.es. Main courses 8€–22€; midday menu 12€. AE, DC, MC, V. Sun–Thurs 1pm–midnight; Fri–Sat 1pm–2am. Metro: Nuevos Ministerios.

La Atalaya CANTABRIAN The owner of this pleasant restaurant, Gena Sánchez, hails from Santander in northern Spain and, in the typical style of her hometown, has decorated the yellow walls of her establishment with a plethora of modern paintings. The food is also typical of Spain's green northern coast, with an emphasis on fresh fish. Every Thursday and Saturday, the chefs prepare the most typical dish of Santander, a hearty cabbage soup. Called *cocido montanés,* it is also made with sausage, green beans, and black pudding. *Sopa de pescado,* or fish soup, is one of the finest of its kind in Madrid. You might opt for a *torta de queso caliente,* a warm cheese soufflé. For dessert, traditional regional puddings are served.

Joaquín Costa 31. ✆ **91-562-87-45.** Reservations recommended. Main courses 12€–25€; set menu 25€; special tasting menu 40€. AE, DC, MC, V. Tues–Sat 1:30–4pm and 9pm–midnight. Closed Aug. Metro: República de Argentina.

CUATRO CAMINOS

Expensive

O'Pazo ★ GALICIAN This deluxe Galician restaurant is viewed by local cognoscenti as one of the top seafood places in the country. The fish is flown in daily from Galicia and mostly priced by weight at market rates. In front is a cocktail lounge and bar, all polished brass, with low sofas and paintings. Carpeted floors, cushioned Castilian furniture, soft lighting, and colored-glass windows complete the picture. The fish and shellfish soup is delectable, although some clients gravitate to the seaman's broth as a beginning course. Main dishes range from baby eels to sea snails, from Galician-style scallops to zarzuela (a seafood casserole).

Reina Mercedes 20. ✆ **91-553-23-33.** Reservations required. Main courses 15€–35€. MC, V. Mon–Sat 1–4pm and 8:30pm–midnight. Closed Aug. Metro: Nuevos Ministerios or Alvarado. Bus: 3 or 5.

San Mamés ★ BASQUE/SPANISH/MADRILEÑO Situated in the northwest of the city in a historic building, this restaurant has been in the hands of the García family more than half a century and is decorated with colorful ceramic tiles and photographs of the celebrities who have dined here over the years. Its two homelike rooms exude an atmosphere of secluded intimacy. Here you'll find very tasty and well-flavored Madrileño and Basque dishes, with ingredients carefully chosen from the market by the owners. The most typical local dish is *callos a la madrileña,* a tripe stew with meat and chickpeas, beloved by their habitués; the number-one Basque option is *bacalao ajoarriero* (salt cod prepared with green peppers, tomatoes, and onions).

Bravo Murillo 88. ✆ **91-534-50-65.** Reservations recommended. Main courses 18€–30€; fixed-price menus 30€–45€. AE, DC, MC, V. Mon–Fri 1:30–4pm and 8:30–11pm; Sat 1:30–4pm. Closed Aug. Metro: Cuatro Caminos.

Inexpensive

Ceres VEGETARIAN Located in the northwestern corner of the city, this is one of the longest running green restaurants in Madrid, with a dedicated and faithful band of regulars, so best to book a table before coming in. The eclectic range of dishes is based on fresh market ingredients, and there is a small on-the-spot shop selling local products. The vegetarian *croquetas* (croquettes) are superb, and for dessert you must try its *tartas integrals* (whole meal tarts). Smoking, surprisingly for a vegetarian restaurant, is not frowned on, so be warned.

Topete 32. ✆ **91-553-77-28.** Reservations recommended. Main courses 10€–20€; midday menu 12€. Mon–Sat 1–4pm; Fri–Sat 8:30–11pm. Metro: Alvarado.

Las Batuecas SPANISH Owned by José Pascual and his family for over half a century, this temple of good home cooking has long been a popular culinary escape point (the name "Batuecas" means "daydreaming") for students, businessmen, and folk of leisure. Built on two floors with three separate restaurants, the place is totally unpretentious with rustic decor. But folks come here not for the decor but for the *comida casera* (home-cooked) dishes like *tortilla de callos* (omelet with tripe), *calamares en su tinta* (squids cooked in their own ink), or *berenjenas rebosadas* (sliced eggplant batter-fried). One of the tastiest and heartiest main dishes is shoulder flank of lamb roast, perfectly done. Note that dinner is served only 2 nights a week (Thurs–Fri).

Av. Reina Victoria 17. ✆ **91-554-04-52.** www.restaurantelasbatuecas.com. Reservations required. Main courses 15€–28€; *menú completo* 20€. No credit cards. Mon–Sat 1–4pm; Thurs–Fri 9–11pm. Closed Aug. Metro: Guzmán El Bueno or Cuatro Caminos.

FUENCARRAL

Expensive

Casa Pedro CASTILIAN Largely unknown to outside visitors, this culinary oasis in the earthy northerly suburb of Fuencarral (a town in its own right two centuries ago) is the second-oldest restaurant in Madrid after Sobrino de Botin. Founded in 1825 as a modest eating house for passing travelers, it was first known as *La Casa de la Silvestra* and then *La Casa de la Pascuala,* in honor of the consecutive chunky Amazons who supervised its ever-busy kitchen. In the 1940s, it acquired a new patron who upped its menu and standard of fare, and today it's entering its fifth generation of family ownership. The restaurant is divided into several different sections (separate rooms of the original house), where from its array of Castilian *asados* (roasts) you can savor a mouth-watering *conejo* (rabbit) dish that's considered by many to be the best in Madrid. Before your meal, pop in for a sip of sherry or wine at the restaurant's vintage adjoining *bodega* (cellar).

Nuestra Señora de Valvarde 119, Fuencarral. ✆ **91-734-02-01.** www.casapedro.com. Main courses 12€–38€. AE, DC, MC, V. Mon–Sat 2–4:30pm and 9pm–midnight; Sun 2–4:30pm. Metro: Fuencarral.

EXPLORING MADRID

7

As visitors have been discovering for decades now, there's much more to Madrid than just the Prado Museum. In fact, you're spoiled for choice. Cultural amenities run the gamut from grandiose palaces and churches to information-crammed museums and art galleries.

Green belts continue to expand, with kilometers of new grassy and tree-filled areas annually added to the city's outskirts, river banks, and historic central parks and gardens (p. 191). Leisure and sports facilities also abound, whether you want to participate or simply sit on the side as a spectator.

Traffic, as in all European cities whose centers were originally designed for the horse and carriage, is a problem, especially at rush-hour times. Best therefore to avoid driving downtown yourself unless you absolutely need to. But don't let the traffic stop you from getting out and exploring. It's easy to get around with the inexpensive and well-run combination of bus, metro (subway), and *cercanías* (suburban line train) transport. Taxis too are still a good value. So dive in and enjoy the fun.

THE MAJOR MUSEUMS: THE "GOLDEN TRIANGLE" OF ART

Tip: A cheap way to see many of the Spanish capital's cultural attractions is the **Madrid Card,** which combines a transportation pass (including Madrid Vision bus tours) with free entry to various museums and art centers. The cost is 47€ for a day, 60€ for 2 days, and 74€ for 3 days. Buy it at the main Plaza Mayor tourist office, on Madrid Vision buses, at newspaper kiosks, or online at **www.madridcard.com**.

Museo Caixa Forum An imaginative, if smaller, new rival to the "big three" museums listed below, the Swiss designed Caixa Forum is the result of an ingenious transformation from a former industrial center (that supplied the city with its electricity) into a bright, avant-garde establishment specializing in exhibits by contemporary artists such as Miquel Barceló. Video displays and concerts are also part of the scene, and there's a small but well-stocked first-floor bookshop. If you feel like a drink or snack between viewings, you can visit their cozy, top-floor cafe. Offbeat exterior features include a striking orange-cum-rust-hued facade, a lushly

Exploring Central Madrid

Almudena Cathedral **12**
Banco de España **32**
Bolsa de Comercio de Madrid (Stock Exchange) **33**
Caixa Forum **22**
Campo del Moro **6**
Casa de Campo **13**
Casa Museo de Lope de Vega **26**
Centro Cultural Conde Duque **4**
Edificio Metrópolis **29**
El Rastro **17**
El Real Jardín Botánico (Royal Botanical Garden) **23**
Iglesia de San Isidro **16**
La Casa de las Siete Chimeneas (House of the Seven Chimneys) **34**
Monasterio de la Encarnación **5**
Monasterio de las Descalzas Reales **9**
Museo Arqueológico Nacional **37**
Museo Cerralbo **3**
Museo de Cera de Madrid (Wax Museum) **38**
Museo de Historia **40**
Museo de la Real Academia de Bellas Artes de San Fernando (Fine Arts Museum) **28**
Museo de San Isidro **14**
Museo del Ferrocarril (Railway Museum) **20**
Museo del Prado **25**
Museo Nacional Centro de Arte Reina Sofía **19**
Museo Nacional de Artes Decorativas **36**
Museo Naval **30**
Palacio de Comunicaciones **31**
Palacio Real (Royal Palace) **7**
Parque del Oeste **1**
Parque del Retiro **24**
Plaza Mayor **10**
Puerta de Alcalá **35**
Real Basílica de San Francisco el Grande **18**
Real Fábrica de Tapices (Royal Tapestry Factory) **21**
San Nicolás de los Servitas Church **11**
San Pedro el Leal **15**
Sociedad General de Autores de España **39**
Teatro Real **8**
Templo de Debod **2**
Thyssen-Bornemisza Museum **27**

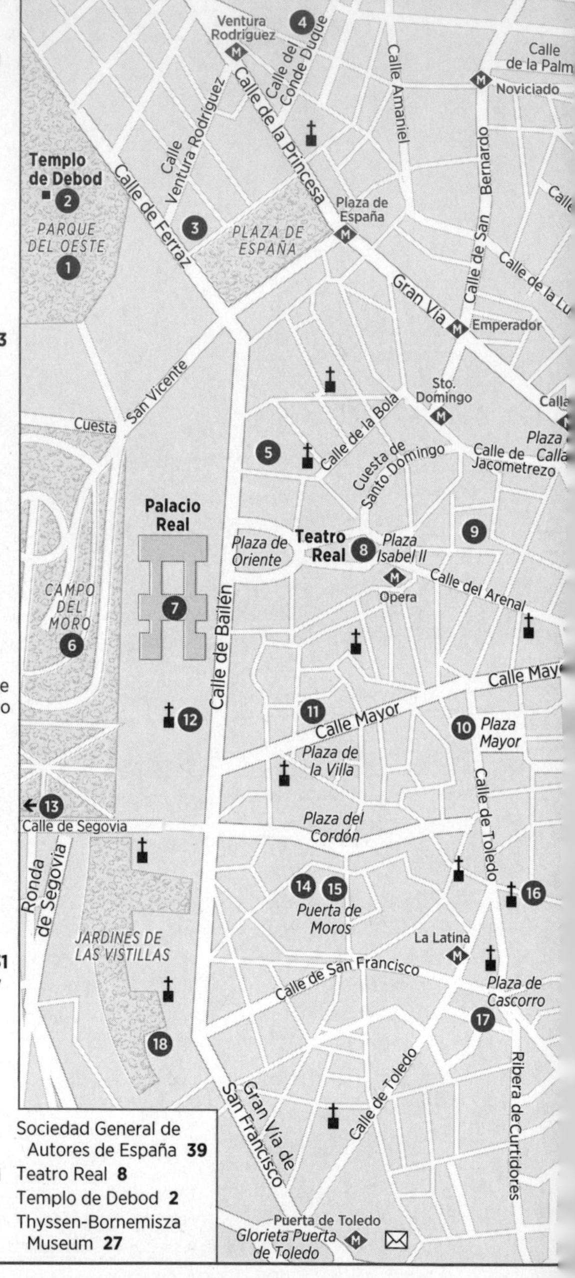

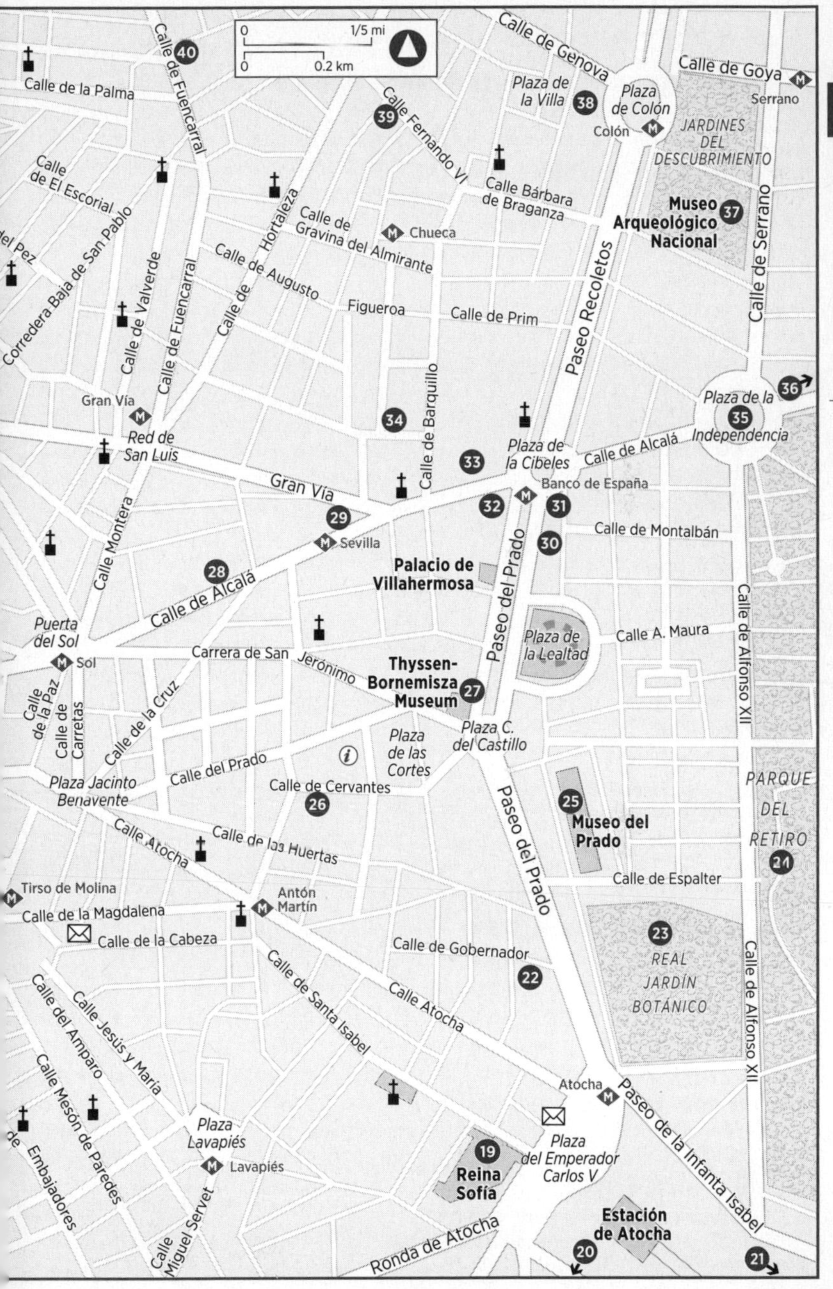
0 1/5 mi
0 0.2 km
Calle de Genova
Calle de Goya
Serrano
Plaza de la Villa
Plaza de Colón
Colón
JARDINES DEL DESCUBRIMIENTO
Calle de la Palma
Calle de Fuencarral
Calle Fernando VI
Calle Bárbara de Braganza
Museo Arqueológico Nacional
Calle de El Escorial
Calle de Gravina del Almirante
Chueca
Corredera Baja de San Pablo
Calle de Hortaleza
Calle de Augusto
Calle de Valverde
Calle de Serrano
Paseo Recoletos
Figueroa
Calle de Prim
Calle de Barquillo
Gran Vía
Red de San Luis
Plaza de la Cibeles
Calle de Alcalá
Plaza de la Independencia
Banco de España
Calle de Montalbán
Calle Montera
Sevilla
Palacio de Villahermosa
Paseo del Prado
Puerta del Sol
Sol
Carrera de San Jerónimo
Plaza de la Lealtad
Calle A. Maura
Thyssen-Bornemisza Museum
Calle de Alfonso XII
Calle de la Paz
Calle de Carretas
Calle de la Cruz
Plaza C. del Castillo
Plaza de las Cortes
Calle del Prado
Plaza Jacinto Benavente
Calle de Cervantes
PARQUE DEL RETIRO
Museo del Prado
Calle Atocha
Calle de las Huertas
Calle de Espalter
Tirso de Molina
Antón Martín
Calle de la Magdalena
Calle de la Cabeza
REAL JARDÍN BOTÁNICO
Calle de Gobernador
Calle de Santa Isabel
Calle del Amparo
Calle Jesús y María
Calle Mesón de Paredes
Atocha
Paseo de la Infanta Isabel
Plaza Lavapiés
Lavapiés
Plaza del Emperador Carlos V
Reina Sofía
Calle de Embajadores
Calle Miguel Servet
Ronda de Atocha
Estación de Atocha

verdant "vertical garden" which climbs the wall of a neighboring building, and a bizarre statue of an elephant balancing on its trunk located in a patio between the entrance and ever-busy Paseo del Prado.

Paseo del Prado 36. ✆ **91-330-73-00.** Free. Daily 10am–8pm. Metro: Atocha.

Museo Nacional Centro de Arte Reina Sofía ★★★ As the Prado has filled the role of repository for traditional art in Madrid, the Reina Sofía, nicknamed the "MoMA of Madrid," has provided for the world of modern art; it is the greatest repository of 20th-century art in Spain. Set within the echoing, futuristically renovated walls of the former General Hospital—originally built between 1776 and 1781—the museum is a sprawling, high-ceilinged showplace named after the Greek-born wife of Spain's present king. Once designated "the ugliest building in Spain" by Catalan architect Oriol Bohigas, the Reina Sofía has a design that hangs in limbo somewhere between the 18th and the 21st centuries. It incorporates a 50,000-volume art library and database, a cafe, a theater, a bookstore, Plexiglas-sided elevators, and systems that calibrate security, temperature, humidity, and the quality of light surrounding the exhibits.

Special emphasis is paid to the great artists of 20th-century Spain: Juan Gris, Salvador Dalí, Joan Miró, and Pablo Picasso (the museum has been able to acquire a handful of his works). What many critics feel is Picasso's masterpiece, *Guernica,* now rests at this museum after a long and troubled history of traveling. Banned in Spain during Franco's era (Picasso refused to have it displayed here anyway), it hung until 1980 at New York's Museum of Modern Art. The fiercely antiwar painting immortalizes the town's shameful blanket bombing by the German Luftwaffe, fighting for Franco during the Spanish Civil War. Guernica was the cradle of the Basque nation, and Picasso's canvas made it a household name around the world.

In 2008, the museum opened its roof terrace to the public from 10am to 9pm, allowing visitors hitherto unseen panoramic vistas of the city including the treetops of the Retiro Park. Dance performances and poetry reading evenings continue to be regular features here.

Santa Isabel 52. ✆ **91-467-50-62.** www.museoreinasofia.es. Admission 6€ adults, 3€ students, free for children 17 and under and seniors 65 and over. Free Sat 2:30–9pm and all day Sun. Mon and Wed–Sat 10am–9pm; Sun 10am–2:30pm. Free guided tours Mon and Wed at 5pm, Sat at 11am. Metro: Atocha. Bus: 6, 8, 10, 14, 19, 24, 26, 27, 32, 34, 36, 37, 41, 45, 47, 54, 55, 57, 59, 60, 78, 85, 86, 102, 116, 118, 119, 141, 148, or 247.

Museo Nacional del Prado ★★★ With more than 7,000 paintings, the Prado is one of the most important repositories of art in the world. It began as a royal collection and was enlarged by the Habsburgs, particularly Charles V, and later the Bourbons. In paintings of the Spanish school, the Prado has no equal; on your first visit, concentrate on the Spanish masters (Velázquez, Goya, El Greco, and Murillo). I say "on your first visit," because you will immediately see that you simply need more than 1 day to take in even just the highlights of this museum.

Major Italian works are exhibited on the ground floor. You'll see art by Italian masters—Raphael, Botticelli, Mantegna, Andrea del Sarto, Fra Angelico, and Correggio. The most celebrated Italian painting here is Titian's voluptuous Venus being watched by a musician who can't keep his eyes on his work.

The Prado is a trove of the work of El Greco (ca. 1541–1614), the Crete-born artist who lived much of his life in Toledo. You can see a parade of "The Greek's" saints, Madonnas, and Holy Families—even a ghostly John the Baptist.

You'll find a splendid array of works by the incomparable Diego Velázquez (1599–1660). The museum's most famous painting, in fact, is his *Las Meninas,* a triumph in the use of light effects. The faces of the queen and king are reflected in the mirror in the painting itself. The artist in the foreground is Velázquez, of course.

The Flemish painter Peter Paul Rubens (1577–1640), who met Velázquez while in Spain, is represented by the peacock-blue *Garden of Love* and by the *Three Graces.* Also noteworthy is the work of José Ribera (1591–1652), a Valencia-born artist and contemporary of Velázquez, whose best painting is the *Martyrdom of St. Philip.* The Seville-born Bartolomé Murillo (1617–82)—often referred to as the "painter of Madonnas"—has three *Immaculate Conceptions* on display.

The Prado has an outstanding collection of the work of Hieronymus Bosch (ca. 1450–1516), the Flemish genius. *The Garden of Earthly Delights,* the best-known work of "El Bosco," is here. You'll also see his *Seven Deadly Sins* and his triptych *The Hay Wagon. The Triumph of Death* is by another Flemish painter, Pieter Breughel the Elder (ca. 1525–69), who carried on Bosch's ghoulish vision.

Francisco de Goya (1746–1828) ranks along with Velázquez and El Greco in the trio of great Spanish artists. Hanging here are his unflattering portraits of his patron, Charles IV, and his family, as well as the *Clothed Maja* and the *Naked Maja.* You can also see the much-reproduced *El Tres de Mayo de 1808 en Madrid,* plus a series of Goya sketches (some of which, depicting the decay of 18th-c. Spain, brought the Inquisition down on the artist) and his expressionistic "black paintings."

The spacious, modern, two-story Jerónimos building at the rear of the main museum was added in 2007. Constructed around a stylish and naturally lit central cloister, it features temporary exhibitions of sculpture and painting by modern artists like Cy Twombly and Francis Bacon. Other communal facilities here include a cafe, auditorium, and souvenir shop (9am–7:15pm).

Paseo del Prado. ✆ **91-330-28-00.** www.museodelprado.es. Admission 8€ adults, free for children 17 and under and seniors 65 and over. Audio guides 4€. Tues–Sun 9am–8pm. Free Tues–Sat 6–8pm, and Sun and fiestas 5–8pm. Closed Jan 1, Good Friday, May 1, and Dec 25. Metro: Banco de España. Bus: 10, 14, 27, 34, 37, or 45.

Museo Thyssen-Bornemisza ★★★ Until around 1985, the contents of this museum virtually overflowed the premises of a legendary villa near Lugano, Switzerland. One of the most frequently visited sites in Switzerland, the collection had been laboriously amassed over a period of about 60 years by the Thyssen-Bornemisza family, scions of a century-old shipping, banking, mining, and chemical fortune with roots in Holland, Germany, and Hungary. Experts had proclaimed it as one of the world's most extensive and valuable privately owned collections of paintings, rivaled only by the legendary holdings of Queen Elizabeth II.

For tax and insurance reasons, and because the collection had outgrown the boundaries of the lakeside villa that contained it, the works were discreetly marketed in the early 1980s to the world's major museums. Amid endless intrigue, a litany of glamorous supplicants from eight different nations came calling. Among them were Margaret Thatcher and Prince Charles; trustees of the Getty Museum in Malibu, California; the president of West Germany; the duke of Badajoz, brother-in-law of King Carlos II; even emissaries from Walt Disney World in Orlando, Florida, all hoping to acquire the collection for their respective countries or entities.

Eventually, thanks partly to the lobbying by Baron Hans Heinrich Thyssen-Bornemisza's fourth wife, a Spanish-born beauty (and former Miss Spain) named

Carmen Tita Cervera, the collection was awarded to Spain for $350 million. Controversies over the public cost of the acquisition raged for months. Despite the brouhaha, various estimates have placed the value of this collection between $1 billion and $3 billion.

To house the collection, an 18th-century building adjacent to the Prado, the Villahermosa Palace, was retrofitted with the appropriate lighting and security devices, and renovated at a cost of $45 million. Rooms are arranged numerically so that, by following the order of the various rooms (nos. 1–48, spread out over three floors), a logical sequence of European painting can be traced from the 13th through the 20th centuries. The nucleus of the collection consists of 700 world-class paintings. They include works by, among others, El Greco, Velázquez, Dürer, Rembrandt, Watteau, Canaletto, Caravaggio, Hals, Memling, and Goya.

Unusual among the world's great art collections because of its eclecticism, the Thyssen group also contains goodly numbers of 19th- and 20th-century paintings by many of the notable French Impressionists, as well as works by Picasso, Sargent, Kirchner, Nolde, and Kandinsky—artists whose previous absence within Spanish museums had become increasingly obvious.

In addition to European paintings, major American works can also be viewed here, including paintings by Thomas Cole, Winslow Homer, Jackson Pollock, Mark Rothko, Edward Hopper, Robert Rauschenberg, Stuart Davis, and Roy Lichtenstein.

The museum's modern extension occupies the site of two mansions (one the former Palace of Goyeneche) on adjoining Marqués de Cubas Street. Known as the **Carmen Thyssen-Bornemisza Collection,** it occupies two floors, with Salas A to H on the second floor and Salas I to P on the first. The latter includes sculptures by Rodin, Fauvism, North American and German Impressionism, Post Impressionism, and Early Avant-Gardes of the 20th century. Among the standouts are works by Braque *(Marina a l'Estaque)* and Picasso *(Los Segadores)*. The second-floor display contains 17th- to 19th-century paintings by Italian, Dutch, and Flemish artists. Realism and Early Impressionism are the main themes. Salas E and F feature some magnificent North American landscapes.

Palacio de Villahermosa, Paseo del Prado 8. ✆ **91-369-01-51** or 91-420-39-44. www.museothyssen.org. Admission 8€ adults, 4€ students and seniors 65 and over, free for children 11 and under. Additional special exhibits: 8€ adults. Combination tickets for both exhibitions 13€. Tues–Sun 10am–7pm (July–Aug till 11pm). Metro: Banco de España. Bus: 1, 2, 5, 9, 10, 14, 15, 20, 27, 34, 37, 45, 51, 52, 53, 74, 146, or 150.

NEAR THE PLAZA MAYOR & PUERTA DEL SOL

Almudena Cathedral This highly controversial building—built on the site of Santa María de la Almudena, which in turn occupied the site of Madrid's first Muslim mosque—must be one of the longest-delayed projects in modern times: 110 years from inception to conception, in fact. Work began in 1883, following a neo-Gothic plan by the Marqués de Cubas. The first thing to be completed was the crypt, which today still retains the 16th-century image of Madrid's patroness, the Virgen de la Almudena. After that, progress was halted until 1944, when new architect Fernando Chueca took over, introducing a neoclassical style. It was eventually finished in 1993 and graced with a visit from the Pope. The bright interior reflects an uncertain blend of hybrid styles and its stained-glass windows are of the "pop art" variety, recently revealed to have been copied. (In defense, their creator claims they are "a vision from God.") The building hit the headlines back in 2004 with the sumptuous wedding of Prince Felipe and Doña Letizia (a former newscaster), the first such royal event in nearly a century, but since then (to date) no similarly eye-catching ceremonies have taken place. You can also pay a visit to the (more interesting) neo-Romanesque crypt to see its well-preserved 16th-century image of the Virgin.

Calle Bailen 8-10. ✆ **91-542-22-00.** Free admission to cathedral 10am-7:30pm. Entrance to crypt 4€ 10am-8pm. Daily 9am-8:30pm. Metro: Opera. Bus: 3, 39, or 148.

Iglesia de San Isidro This huge, twin-towered baroque church—also known as La Colegiata from its early days as part of a Jesuit college—acted as a substitute cathedral from 1885 until the completion of the Almudena. Designed by Pedro Sánchez in the style of the Gesu in Rome, and built by Francisco Bautista in the 17th century, it shelters the remains of Madrid's patron saint San Isidro and his wife, Santa María de la Cabeza. On the Thursday of Easter week, their two images are taken out and paraded around the streets of Madrid.

Calle Toledo 37. ✆ **91-369-20-37.** Free admission. Sept-July Mon-Sat 7:30am-1pm and 6:30-8:30pm; Aug Mon-Sat 7:30am-8:30pm and Sun 7:15am-8:30pm. Metro: La Latina or Tirso de Molina. Bus: 17, 18, 23, 35, or 60.

Museo de la Real Academia de Bellas Artes de San Fernando (Fine Arts Museum) ★★ An easy stroll from Puerta del Sol, the Fine Arts Museum is located in the restored and remodeled 17th-century baroque palace of Juan de Goyeneche. The collection—more than 1,500 paintings and 570 sculptures, ranging from the 16th century to the present—was started in 1752 during the reign of Fernando VI (1746–59). It emphasizes works by Spanish, Flemish, and Italian artists. You can see masterpieces by El Greco, Rubens, Velázquez, Zurbarán, Ribera, Cano, Coello, Murillo, Goya, and Sorolla.

The same building also accommodates the **Museo de Calcografia Nacional** (✆ **91-524-08-83;** Mon–Sat 10am–2pm, 5–8pm, and Sun 10am–2pm; free admission), which contains original plates used by Goya and other painters for engraving on copper or brass (an art known as chalcography). Limited edition prints are on sale here.

Alcalá 13. ✆ **91-524-08-64.** http://rabasf.insde.es. Tues-Sat 5€ adults, 2.50€ students, free children 17 and under and seniors 65 and over. Free Wed. Tues-Fri 9am-2pm and 4-7pm; Sat 9am-2:30pm and 4-7pm; Sun, Mon, and fiestas 9am-2:30pm. July-Aug Thurs till 8:30pm. Guided tours 11am (also 5pm Tues except July-Sept). Metro: Sevilla or Sol. Bus: 3, 15, 20, 51, 52, 53, or 150.

Museo de San Isidro Situated in San Andrés square in the heart of the Austrias, this more recent addition to Madrid's historical museums contains interesting perspectives on the city's progress through the ages, via Paleolithic, Roman, and Muslim eras to the present day, using plans, sketches, models, paintings, and archaeological finds transferred from the Municipal Museum. The museum stands on the site where San Isidro, Madrid's patron saint, is said to have rescued his son from a well, into which the latter had fallen, by making the water rise. The well, purportedly the original, is located in the middle of the building.

Plaza de San Andrés 2. ✆ **91-366-74-15.** Free admission. Mon-Fri 9:30am-8pm and Sat-Sun 10am-2pm; Aug Mon-Sat 9:30am-2:30pm. Metro: La Latina. Bus: 60.

HOP ON A bus

You can explore Madrid by public transport for next to nothing, traveling as far as you like on the urban **red line buses** for 1€ a trip. Even more economical is the 10-pack Metrobus ticket (9€), valid for both buses and the metro, which works out to only .90€ a trip. (A one-way combined bus and metro ticket will otherwise cost you 2€). You can buy tickets at any metro station or newspaper kiosk. To orient yourself, pick up a *Consorcio Transportes de Madrid* from one of the kiosks in the Puerta del Sol (1.50€). This city bus map marks all bus routes clearly. I've chosen a few of the best red line bus trips around the city. Hope you enjoy them.

33: Príncipe Pío to Casa de Campo This short run starts at the Príncipe Pío bus, metro, and train junction at the end of Paseo de la Florida, just northwest of the Royal Palace. First you follow the tree-lined avenue to the west of the Campo del Moro, and then you turn right across the Manzanares River at Puente de Toledo (Toledo Bridge) before passing through the built-up zone of Puerta del Angel. From here you cross the busy Paseo de Extremadura to enter the green parklands of the Casa de Campo, stopping at the Parque de Attracciones (a fun park for teenagers), Batán (where bulls are penned in a small farm building prior to participating in *corridas* at the Ventas bullring), and the zoo. It's a great trip for families with children. Service runs every 15 minutes from 10am to 10pm.

54: Atocha to Vallecas This route starts at Atocha and heads southeast along the Ciudad de Barcelona and Albufera avenues, via the lively junction of Puente Vallecas and across the M-40 highway to the Villa de Vallecas—a self-contained town which retains its earthy individuality (it still has its own *fútbol* team) in spite of now being part of the Madrid community. "Gentrification" in the form of duplex flats, pedestrian *paseos,* and tree-lined avenues has transformed the center, but it remains at heart a traditional character-filled place, whose huge, 18th-century church of San Pedro Ad Vincula is a cultural monument. On your way back to Madrid, jump off at the Calle Pío Felipe stop just above the Buenos Aires metro station and stroll on to the high grassy knolls of Cerro del Tío Pío park. From here you can enjoy panoramic views of Madrid, and on very clear days you can see the Gredos Mountains of Avila

Palacio Real de Madrid ★★ No longer occupied by royalty, but still used for state occasions, Madrid's Royal Palace stands on a ridge above the Manzanares River and Campo del Moro park. It was begun in 1738 on the site of the Madrid Alcázar, which burned to the ground in 1734. Some of its 2,000 rooms—which that "enlightened despot" Charles III called home—are open to the public; others are still used for state business. The palace was last used as a royal residence in 1931, before King Alfonso XIII and his wife, Victoria Eugénie, fled Spain.

Highlights of a visit include the Reception Room, the State Apartments, the Armory, and the Royal Pharmacy. To get an English-speaking guide, say *"inglés"* to the person who takes your ticket.

The Reception Room and State Apartments should get priority here if you're rushed. They include a rococo room with a diamond clock; a porcelain salon; the province 100km (60 miles) to the west. Service runs every 5 minutes from 6am to 10pm.

75: Callao to Colonia Manzanares This route takes you up the Gran Vía to Plaza España, where you turn left down the Cuesta de San Vicente to the Príncipe Pío junction, then west along Avenida de la Florida to turn again left opposite the Casa Mingo restaurant and the Ermita de San Antonio de la Florida (an ornate chapel that contains some important Goya frescoes). Crossing the bridge over the Manzanares River, you enter the uniquely laid-back world of Colonia de Manzanares, which is nestled between the river and Casa de Campo. Its center is a small conglomeration of shops and cafes bordered by avenues of mature residential villas with gardens; on its riverside promenade you may see people fishing. The unexpected aura of peace and relaxation of this charming backwater seems light years—rather than just a 20-minute bus ride—away from the bustling Gran Vía. Service runs every 10 to 15 minutes from 6:15am to 11:30pm.

146: Callao to Barrio de la Concepción Here is your chance to check out the changing architectural styles and moods as you progress along the length of Madrid's great east-west artery, Calle Alcalá. Starting at the center of the Gran Vía, you first pass the emblematic Cibeles fountain-statue and flamboyant turn-of-the-20th-century Palacio de Comunicaciones (Post Office) before continuing uphill to the neoclassical Puerta de Alcalá archway, opposite the main entrance to Retiro Park. From here the avenue extends farther east with the Retiro and Neo-Mudéjar Antiguas Escuelas Aguirre building on your right, plus the shop-filled Velázquez and Príncipe Vergara streets of the elegant 19th-century Salamanca district on your left. Passing through Goya and Manuel Becerra squares to the Ventas bullring, you finally cross the M-30 bridge and turn left into the newer (ca. 1940s), homelier district of Barrio de la Concepción, which runs parallel to Alcalá. Step off at the tiny Calero park and stroll among the flowers, trees, and playgrounds, where hordes of toddlers play on swings next to a pine-shrouded open-air summer cinema—one of only two in Madrid. Then relax at an outdoor terrace table in the adjoining promenade-like Calle Virgen de Nuria and enjoy a Mahou beer and tapas in the sun. Service runs every 5 to 10 minutes from 7am to 11:30pm.

Royal Chapel; the Banquet Room, where receptions for heads of state are still held; and the Throne Room. The empty thrones of King Juan Carlos and Queen Sofía are among the highlights of the tour.

The rooms are literally stuffed with art treasures and antiques—salon after salon of monumental grandeur, with no apologies for the damask, mosaics, stucco, Tiepolo ceilings, gilt and bronze, chandeliers, and paintings.

If your visit falls on the first Wednesday of the month, look for the changing of the guard ceremony, which occurs at noon and is free to the public.

In the Armory, you'll see the finest collection of weaponry in Spain. Many of the items—powder flasks, shields, lances, helmets, and saddles—are from the collection of Carlos V (Charles of Spain). From here, the comprehensive tour takes you into the Pharmacy.

Right in front of the Palacio Real is the **Plaza de Oriente,** a semicircular area of gardens and regal statues centered on an imposing re-creation of Felipe IV on horseback. Brainchild of Joseph Bonaparte and finished in the reign of Isabel II, it has an elegant European aura.

Plaza de Oriente, Calle de Bailén 2. ✆ **91-454-87-00.** Admission with guided tour 10€; self-guided 8€, add 1€ if painting gallery included; 3.50€ students, children 5–16, and seniors 65 and over, add .50€ if painting gallery included. Audio guides 2€. Mon–Sat 9am–6pm; Sun 9am–3pm. Metro: Opera or Plaza de España. Bus: 3, 39, or 148.

Real Basílica de San Francisco el Grande Prior to the inauguration of the Almudena, this imposing 18th-century church shared honors with San Isidro as the most important religious building in Madrid. Its dome is larger than that of St. Paul's in London, and its interior is filled with a number of ecclesiastical works, notably a Goya painting of St. Bernardinus of Siena. A guide will show you through.

Plaza de San Francisco el Grande, San Buenaventura 1. ✆ **91-365-38-00.** Admission 1€. Tues–Sat 11am–1pm and 4–6:30pm. Metro: La Latina or Puerta del Toledo. Bus: 3, 60, C, 148, or M4.

San Nicolás de los Servitas Church Officially confirmed as the oldest church in the city, San Nicolás still retains a slightly renovated 12th-century *Mudéjar* bell tower, built by Muslims under Christian rule though the rest of the church was reconstructed 3 centuries later. The tiny interior contains paintings by Pedro de Mena and sculptures by Nicolás Busi.

Plaza San Nicolás. ✆ **91-559-40-64.** Free admission. Mon 8:30am–1pm; Tues–Sat 9–9:30am and 6:30–8:30pm; Sun 10am–2pm and 6:30–8:30pm. Metro: Opera. Bus: 3.

San Pedro el Leal Also known as San Pedro el Viejo, and roughly the same size as San Nicolás, this is Madrid's second-oldest church and boasts the city's other remaining *Mudéjar* tower, said to still be in its exact original form. Built in the 14th century, the tower has a slight incline and has been jokingly called Madrid's answer to the Leaning Tower of Pisa. (For a more modern comparison with the famed Italian structure, see the listing for KIO Towers, later in this chapter.)

Costanilla de San Pedro. ✆ **91-365-12-84.** Free admission. Daily 6–8pm. Metro: La Latina. Bus: 50 or 55.

ALONG OR NEAR THE PASEO DEL PRADO

Bolsa de Madrid (Stock Exchange) For a fascinating look into the workings of the Spanish stock market, visit this impressive building designed by 19th-century architect Enrique María Rapulles. Located in the same small square as the Ritz hotel and just a short walk from the Prado, its neoclassical facade attracts almost as much attention as that of its illustrious neighbors. Visits are made at noon on weekdays, but you must make a prior call to arrange an appointment. You can view the stock exchange floor through a glass partition above and see a small exhibition on the history of the market.

Plaza de la Lealtad 1. ✆ **91-589-22-64.** www.bolsamadrid.es. Free admission. Individual visits Thurs at noon. Group visits Mon–Fri from 10am. Reservations essential. Metro: Banco de España. Bus: 10, 14, 27, 34, 37, or 45.

VIVA LA corrida!

There were moves to have the *corrida de toros* (bullfighting) banned throughout the whole country at the beginning of 2010, but feisty Madrid Community President Esperanza Aguirre thwarted them and had the event declared "Of Touristic Interest," thus preserving it for some time to come. Madrid is a traditional stronghold of the "fiesta brava," and many Madrileños would rather have red hot *banderillas* thrust in their eyes than give up one of the strongest and most colorful symbols of Spanish courage and good old-fashioned *machismo.* (In contrast, rival Barcelona—which has long looked toward the rest of Europe for its cultural influence and in recent decades ignored or even scorned *la corrida*—may well soon ban it.)

The capital itself has long drawn the finest matadors in Spain. If a matador hasn't proven his worth in the **Plaza de Toros Monumental de las Ventas,** Alcalá 237 (✆ **91-356-22-00;** www.las-ventas.com; Metro: Ventas), then he hasn't been recognized as a top-flight artist. The major season begins during the Fiestas de San Isidro, patron saint of Madrid, on May 15. This is the occasion for a series of fights, during which talent scouts are in the audience. Matadors who distinguish themselves in the ring are signed up for Majorca, Málaga, and other places. The bullfight season ends during the last 2 weekends in October (Feria del Otoño).

The best way to get tickets to the bullfights is to go to the stadium's box office (Fri–Sun 10am–2pm and 5–8pm). Concierges for virtually every upper-bracket hotel can also acquire tickets. Alternatively, you can contact one of Madrid's best ticket agents, **Localidades Galicia,** Plaza del Carmen 1 (✆ **91-531-27-32;** Metro: Sol), open Tuesday to Saturday from 9:30am to 1:30pm and 4:30 to 7pm, Sunday from 9:30am to 1:30pm. Tickets to bullfights are 18€ to 160€ depending on the event and the position of your seat. (See also www.bullfightticketsmadrid.com.) Front-row seats are *barreras. Delanteras*—third-row seats—are available in the *alta* (high) and the *baja* (low) sections. The cheapest seats, *filas,* have the worst view and are in the sun *(sol)* the entire time. The best and most expensive seats are in the shade *(sombra).* Bullfights are held on Sunday and holidays throughout most of the year, and every day during certain festivals, which tend to last around 3 weeks, usually in the late spring. Starting times are adjusted according to the anticipated hour of sundown on the day of a performance, usually 7pm from March to October, and 5pm during late autumn and early spring. Late-night fights by neophyte matadors are sometimes staged under spotlights on Saturday around 11pm. During the winter months of November to February, bullfights are replaced by a short circus season. See the "Especially for Kids" section.

Casa Museo de Lope de Vega Just uphill from the Paseo, this atmospheric town house, former home of Spain's foremost "Golden Age" playwright, who lived here for 25 years, is paradoxically situated in a street named after the country's greatest novelist. A 17th-century gem with delightful gardens at the back, it's well worth the visit.

Cervantes 11. ✆ **91-429-92-16.** Tues–Sun 10am–3pm. Free. Metro: Antón Martín. Bus: 34, 38, or 45.

Museo Nacional de Artes Decorativas In 62 rooms spread over several floors, this museum, near the Plaza de la Cibeles, displays a rich collection of furniture, ceramics, and decorative pieces. Emphasizing the 16th and 17th centuries, the eclectic collection includes Gothic carvings, alabaster figurines, festival crosses, elaborate dollhouses, elegant baroque four-poster beds, a chapel covered with leather tapestries, and even kitchens from the 18th century.

Calle de Montalbán 12. ✆ **91-532-64-99.** http://mnartesdecorativas.mcu.es. Admission 3€ adults; 1.50€ students, children, and seniors. Tues–Fri 9:30am–3pm; Sat–Sun 10am–2pm. Free Sun and fiestas. Metro: Banco de España. Bus: 14, 27, 34, 37, or 45.

Museo Naval de Madrid The history of nautical science and the Spanish navy, from the time of Isabella and Ferdinand until today, comes alive at the Museo Naval. The most fascinating exhibit on display is the map made by the first mate of the Santa María to show the Spanish monarchs the new discoveries. Also on display are souvenirs of the Battle of Trafalgar.

You can also visit the museum's library at nearby Calle Juan de Mena 2 (✆ **91-523-83-78;** Mon–Fri 9am–2pm).

Paseo del Prado 5. ✆ **91-379-52-99.** www.museonavalmadrid.com. Free admission. Tues–Sun 10am–2pm. Closed Aug. Metro: Banco de España. Bus: 2, 14, 27, 40, 51, 52, or M6.

NEAR MALASAÑA

Museo de Historia Famed for its outstanding Baroque facade, this renovated 18th-century building—formerly known as the Museo Municipal—houses a comprehensive collection of documents, models, paintings, drawings, and sketches covering the history of the Spanish capital. Formerly an orphanage, it's located on the eastern edge of the Malasaña district a short walk up from the Gran Vía. At present (2010), the museum is closed for refurbishing work: It's scheduled to re-open in 2011.

Calle Fuencarral 78. ✆ **91-588-86-72.** www.munimadrid.es/museodehistoria. Free admission. Tues–Sat 10am–9pm and Sun 11am–2:30pm. Investigation service available (advance reservation required; ✆ 91-701-18-63). Mon 10am–2pm. Metro: Tribunal. Bus: 3, 10, or 49.

NEAR THE PLAZA DE ESPAÑA

Centro Cultural Conde Duque A remarkable conversion from 18th-century barracks to one of Madrid's most evocative cultural centers, the Conde Duque is peacefully situated a short walk away from the Plaza España. Two galleries display permanent exhibitions of modern and abstract art and two vast patios are used for open-air sculpture exhibitions. This is also home of the refurbished Museo Municipal de Arte Contemporáneo, whose collection includes Bosch and Goya paintings donated by financial magnate José Lazaro Galdiano. Other attractions include a video library and concert venue. Popular and classical concerts are occasionally held here.

Conde Duque 11. ✆ **91-588-58-34.** www.munimadrid.es/condeduque. Free admission. Tues–Sat 10am–2pm and 6–9pm; Sun 10:30am–2pm. Metro: Noviciado or Ventura Rodríguez. Bus: 1, 2, 44, 74, 133, 202, 749, or C.

Monasterio de la Encarnación ★ Central Madrid's other royally endowed Habsburg monastery is quietly nestled in a charming little square between the Royal Palace and Plaza España. Though paling slightly in comparison with the incomparable Descalzas Reales, it still remains by any other standards a must-see. Founded by

Margaret of Austria and Philip III in 1611 and rebuilt by Ventura Rodriguez after a disastrous fire nearly destroyed it in 1767, it's inhabited by Augustine Recoletos nuns who remain out of sight in their cloisters during visiting hours. The facade is a fine example of post-Herreran style and inside hides an impressive selection of polychrome sculptures and paintings, highlighted by Ribera's superb portrait of John the Baptist. Most extraordinary of its many salons is the Reliquario, where the solidified blood of Saint Pantaleon, permanently kept in a glass orb, supposedly liquefies for 24 hours every year beginning at midnight on July 27 (the eve of his saint's day). According to legend, if it does not liquefy, disaster will follow. On display all around it are the bone fragments and bronze, copper, and gold reliquaries of other saints and martyrs. The main cloister and church are also well worth a look. Tours are conducted in Spanish.

Plaza de la Encarnación 1. ✆ **91-454-88-00.** Admission 3.60€ adults, 2€–2.90€ children 5–16 and seniors 65 and over. Combined with visit to Monasterio de las Descalzas (see below) 6€. All visits are guided. Tues–Thurs and Sat 10:30am–12:45pm and 4–5:45pm; Sun 10:30am–1:45pm. Metro: Opera or Santo Domingo. Bus: 25, 39, or 148.

Monasterio de las Descalzas Reales ★★ In the mid–16th century, aristocratic women—either disappointed in love or "wanting to be the bride of Christ"—stole away to this convent to take the veil. Each brought a dowry, making this Habsburg gem, which was founded by Joan of Austria in the 16th century, one of the richest convents in the land. By the mid–20th century, it sheltered mostly poor women. True, it still contained a priceless collection of art treasures, but the sisters were forbidden to auction anything; in fact, they were literally starving. The state intervened, and the pope granted special dispensation to open the convent as a museum in 1960. A quarter of a century later, the European Council rated it "Museum of the Year," and today the public can look behind the walls of what had been a mysterious presence on one of the most beautiful squares in Old Madrid.

In the Reliquary are the noblewomen's dowries, one of which is said to contain bits of wood from Christ's Cross; another, some of the bones of St. Sebastian. The most valuable painting is Titian's *Caesar's Money.* The Flemish Hall shelters other fine works, including paintings by Hans de Beken and Breughel the Elder. All of the tapestries were based on Rubens's cartoons, displaying his chubby matrons. Tours are in Spanish.

Plaza de las Descalzas Reales s/n. ✆ **91-454-88-00.** Admission 5€ adults, 2.50€ children 5–16 and seniors 65 and over. Combined with a visit to Monasterio de la Encarnacion (see above) 6€. All visits are guided. Tues–Thurs and Sat 10:30am–12:30pm and 3–5:45pm; Fri 10:30am–12:30pm; Sun 11am–1:15pm. Metro: Callao. Bus: 1, 2, 5, 20, 46, 52, 53, 74, M1, M2, M3, or M5. From Plaza del Callao, off the Gran Vía, walk down Postigo de San Martín to Plaza de las Descalzas Reales; the convent is on the left.

Museo Cerralbo This very personal museum close to the Debod temple was once owned by the 17th marquis of Cerralbo, Enrique de Aguilera y Gamboa. Housed in an Italian-style 19th-century mansion, it provides a unique visiting experience, as its contents are laid out in exactly the same order as when he was living there. The marquis was a great traveler as well as an erudite man of letters, and the museum is filled with collections (bequeathed to the state on his death in 1922) gathered during his colorful life. Forty years later, it was declared a national monument. Among its multitude of artistic treasures and eclectic knick-knacks (estimated at around 50,000) are paintings by Titian, Tintoretto, Zurbarán, and El Greco (including his classic *Ecstasy of St. Francis of Assisi*), sculptures, 18th-century English watches,

Venetian lamps, Saxon porcelain, and European and Japanese armor. The garden, planned in a classical-romantic style, has a small central pond and surrounding busts of Roman emperors. At the time of writing, the museum is closed for renovation, but it should be open to the public again by 2011.

Ventura Rodríguez 17. ✆ **91-547-36-46.** http://museocerralbo.mcu.es. Admission 2.40€ adults, 1.20€ students, Sept–June free for those 17 and under and seniors 65 and over. Free Wed and Sun. Sept–June Tues–Sat 9:30am–3pm, Sun 10am–3pm; July–Aug Tues–Sat 9:30am–2pm, Sun 10am–2pm. Metro: Ventura Rodríguez or Plaza España. Bus: 25, 39, 46, 74, or 138.

Templo de Debod This Egyptian temple near Plaza de España once stood in the Valley of the Nile, 31km (19 miles) from Aswan. When the new dam threatened the temple, the Egyptian government dismantled it and presented it to Spain. Taken down stone by stone in 1969 and 1970, it was shipped to Valencia and taken by rail to Madrid, where it was reconstructed and opened to the public in 1971. Photos upstairs depict the temple's long history. The museum is located in the open garden area adjoining Pintor Rosales Avenue close to the Parque del Oeste, with panoramic views west to the Casa de Campo and northwest to the Sierra de Guadarrama.

Paseo Pintor de Rosales 2. ✆ **91-366-74-15.** Free admission. Apr 1–Sept 30 Tues–Fri 9:45am–1:45pm and 6:15–8:15pm; Oct 1–Mar 31 Tues–Fri 9:45am–1:45pm and 4:15–6:15pm; Sat–Sun 9:45am–1:45pm year-round. No smoking or use of flash cameras allowed. Metro: Plaza de España or Ventura Rodríguez. Bus: 25, 39, 46, 74, or 138.

NEAR ATOCHA

Real Fábrica de Tapices (Royal Tapestry Factory) At this factory, founded nearly 300 years ago by Philip V and located a short walk southeast of Atocha railway station, the age-old process of making exquisite (and very expensive) tapestries is still carried on with consummate skill. Nearly every tapestry is based on a cartoon of Goya, who was the factory's most famous employee. Many of these patterns, such as *The Pottery Salesman,* are still in production today. (Goya's original drawings are in the Prado.) Some of the other designs are based on cartoons by Francisco Bayeu, Goya's brother-in-law.

Fuenterrabía 2. ✆ **91-434-05-50.** www.realfabricadetapices.com. Admission 4€ Mon–Fri, guided tours 10am–2pm. Closed Aug and fiestas. Metro: Menéndez Pelayo. Bus: 10, 14, 26, 32, 37, 54, 102, 141, C, or M9.

SALAMANCA

Museo Arqueológico Nacional This stately mansion is a storehouse of artifacts from the prehistoric to the baroque. One of the prime exhibits here is the Iberian statue *The Lady of Elche* ★★★, a piece of primitive carving (from the 4th c. B.C.), discovered on the southeastern coast of Spain. Finds from Ibiza, Paestum, and Rome are on display, including statues of Tiberius and his mother, Livia. The Islamic collection from Spain is outstanding. Other collections include Spanish Renaissance lusterware, Talavera pottery, Retiro porcelain, and some rare 16th- and 17th-century Andalusian glassware. Many of the exhibits are treasures that were removed from churches and monasteries. A much-photographed choir stall, from the palace of Palencia, dates from the 14th century. Also worth a look are the reproductions of the Altamira cave paintings (chiefly of bison, horses, and boars), discovered near Santander in northern Spain in 1868.

PRIVATE galleries

Madrid has about 150 private art galleries, where you can view and buy the work of modern artists of all styles. Some of the best galleries are located on Claudio Coello in the Salamanca district. These include **Guillermo de Osma,** Claudio Coello 4-1° izda. (✆ **91-435-59-36;** www.guillermodeosma.com; Mon–Fri 10am–2pm and 4:30–8:30pm, Sat noon–2pm; Metro: Retiro; bus: 2, 19, 20, 21, 28, 53, or 146); **Paz Feliz,** Claudio Coello 17 (✆ **91-575-86-86;** Mon–Fri 10am–2pm and 5–8pm, Sat 11am–2pm; Metro: Retiro or Serrano; bus: 1, 21, 53, or 74); and **Jorge Alcolea,** Claudio Coello 28 (✆ **91-431-65-92;** www.galeriajorgealcolea.com; 10:30am–2:30pm and 5:30–9:30pm; Metro: Retiro or Serrano; bus: 1, 21, 53, or 74). If you're keen on sculptures, visit **Capa Esculturas,** Claudio Coello 19 (✆ **91-431-05-93;** www.capaesculturas.com; Mon–Fri 10am–2pm and 5–8pm, Sat 11am–2pm; Metro: Retiro or Serrano; bus: 1, 21, 53, or 74).

A prominent gallery in Chueca district is **Oliva Arauna,** Barquillo 29 (✆ **91-435-18-08;** www.olivarauna.com; Mon–Fri 10am–2pm and 5–8pm, Sat 11am–2pm; Metro: Chueca; bus: 2, 19, 20, 21, 28, 53, or 146).

The museum is being renovated and will not be fully re-opened until 2012. In the meantime, a number of ground floor exhibits can be viewed free of charge.

Serrano 13. ✆ **91-577-79-12.** http://man.mcu.es. Free admission (till 2012). Tues–Sat 9:30am–8:00pm; Sun 9:30am–3pm. Metro: Serrano or Retiro. Bus: 1, 9, 19, 51, or 74.

Museo Arte Público As its name implies, this small "museum" is really an open-air public collection of mainly bronze abstract sculptures by the likes of Chillida and Miró—dating from the 1920s—situated next to the busy Castellana Avenue. At its center is a sparkling cascade designed by sculptor Eusebio Sempere, a tiny gem.

Paseo de la Castellana 41. ✆ **91-588-86-72.** www.munimadrid.es/museoairelibre. Free admission. Daily dawn–dusk. Metro: Ruben Darío. Bus: 5, 14, 27, 45, or 150.

Museo Lázaro Galdiano ★★ Imagine 37 rooms in a superbly renovated 19th-century mansion bulging with artworks, including many by the most famous old masters of Europe, and you have an idea of what this museum is like. Visitors usually take the elevator to the top floor and work down, lingering over such artifacts as 15th-century hand-woven vestments, swords and daggers, royal seals, 16th-century crystal from Limoges, Byzantine jewelry, Italian bronzes from ancient times to the Renaissance, and medieval armor.

Bosch evokes his own peculiar brand of horror on one of the gallery's most striking paintings, whose canvas is peopled with creepy fiends devouring human flesh. The Spanish masters are the best represented—among them El Greco, Velázquez, Zurbarán, Ribera, Murillo, and Valdés-Leal.

One section is devoted to works by the English portrait and landscape artists Reynolds, Gainsborough, and Constable. Italian artists exhibited include Tiepolo and Guardi. Salon 30—for many, the most interesting—is devoted to Goya and includes paintings from his "black period." Located slightly out of the way in the far southwest corner of Salamanca, close to the American Embassy, this gem of a museum is usually enjoyably underpopulated, a nice contrast to the overcrowded Prado, Thyssen, and Reina Sofía museums.

Serrano 122. ✆ **91-561-60-84.** www.flg.es. Admission 4€. Free Wed. Wed–Mon 10am–4:30pm. Mon and Wed–Fri, 3rd floor closes at 2pm. Closed fiestas. Metro: Rubén Darío or Gregorio Marañón. Bus: 9, 16, 19, 27, 45, 51, 61, 89, or 114.

CHAMBERÍ

Museo Sorolla From 1912, painter Joaquín Sorolla and his family occupied this elegant Madrileño town house off Paseo de la Castellana. His widow turned it over to the government, and it is now maintained as a memorial. Much of the house remains as Sorolla left it, right down to his stained paintbrushes and pipes. The museum wing displays a representative collection of his works.

Although Sorolla painted portraits of Spanish aristocrats, he was essentially interested in the common people, often depicting them in their native dress. On view are the artist's self-portrait and the paintings of his wife and their son. Sorolla was especially fond of painting beach scenes of the luminous Alicante coast.

General Martínez Campos 37. ✆ **91-310-15-84.** http://museosorolla.mcu.es. Admission 3€ adults, free for children 17 and under and seniors 65 and over. Free Sun. Tues–Sat 9:30am–8pm; Sun 10am–3pm. Metro: Iglesia or Rubén Darío. Bus: 5, 16, 61, 40, or M3.

MONCLOA

Museo de América (Museum of the Americas) This museum near the university campus houses an outstanding collection of pre-Columbian, Spanish-American, and Native American art and artifacts. Various exhibits chronicle the progress of the inhabitants of the New World, from the Paleolithic period to the present day. One exhibit, "Groups, Tribes, Chiefdoms, and States," focuses on the social structure of the various peoples of the Americas. Another display outlines the various religions and deities associated with them. Also included is an entire section dedicated to communication, highlighting written as well as nonverbal expressions of art.

Av. de los Reyes Católicos 6. ✆ **91-549-26-41.** http://museodeamerica.mcu.es. Admission 3€ adults, 1.50€ students, free for children 17 and under and seniors 65 and over. Free Sun. Tues–Sat 9:30am–3pm; Sun 10am–3pm. Metro: Moncloa.

Museo del Traje Located a 10-minute metro ride from the Gran Vía, in the heart of the University City just above Moncloa, this museum displays more than 500 costumes, even frocks from the 1700s, along with bullfighters' "suits of light." Spanish folk dress is highlighted as well, along with Chanel designs and a 1967 dress made of metal by designer Paco Rabanne. Movie scenes demonstrate the fashions, including Bogie's *Casablanca* and Audrey Hepburn in Givenchy as she appeared in *Funny Face*. Attracting the most attention is Marilyn Monroe in a subway-blown Travilla in *The Seven Year Itch*. Some of the exhibits are hands-on—for example, you can try on a corset or the frame of a hoop skirt, or even check out your derrière in a bustle. On-site is an excellent Basque restaurant, Bokado, whose more adventurous dishes include a gazpacho made with watermelon and lobster.

Avenida Juan de Herrera 2. ✆ **91-550-47-00.** http://museodeltraje.mcu.es. Admission 3€ adults, 1.50€ students. Free for children 17 and under and seniors 65 and over; free for all Sat from 2:30pm and all day Sun. Tues–Sat 9:30am–7pm, Sun 10am–3pm; July–Aug Thurs till 10:30pm. Metro: Moncloa or Ciudad Universitaria. Bus: 46, 82, 83, 84, 132, or 133.

PRÍNCIPE PÍO

Ermita San Antonio de la Florida and the Panteón de Goya (Goya's Tomb) ★ Nestled on an avenue close to the Manzanares River and just to the northwest of the Príncipe Pío bus and rail stations are two beautiful domed hermitages, built between 1792 and 1798. The one on the right contains Goya's tomb and one of his most unusual masterpieces—an elaborately beautiful fresco depicting the miracles of St. Anthony on the dome and cupola. This has been called Goya's Sistine Chapel (though admittedly this is on a smaller scale than Michelangelo's masterpiece). Already deaf when he began the painting, Goya labored dawn to dusk for 16 weeks, painting with sponges rather than brushes. By depicting common street life—stonemasons, prostitutes, and beggars—Goya raised the ire of the nobility who held judgment, until the patron, Carlos IV, viewed it. When the monarch approved, the formerly outrageous painting was deemed acceptable. Discreetly placed mirrors help you see the ceiling better.

Glorieta de San Antonio de la Florida s/n. ✆ **91-542-07-22.** www.munimadrid.es/ermita. Free admission. Tues–Fri 9:30am–8pm; Sat–Sun 10am–2pm (in summer daily 10am–2pm only). Metro: Príncipe Pío. Bus: 41, 46, 75, or C.

VENTAS

Museo Taurino (Bullfighting Museum) This museum might serve as a good introduction to bullfighting for those who want to see the real event. Here you'll see the death costume of Manolete, the *traje de luces* (suit of lights) that he wore when he was gored to death in 1947 at age 30 in Linares's bullring.

Other memorabilia evoke the heyday of Juan Belmonte, the Andalusian who revolutionized bullfighting in 1914 by performing close to the horns. The ubiquitous Goya is in evidence again here with his colorful painting of a matador, and displays of photographs and relics trace the history of bullfighting in Spain from its ancient origins to the present day.

Plaza de Toros Monumental de las Ventas, Alcalá 237. ✆ **91-725-18-57.** Free admission. Mar–Oct Tues–Fri and Sun 9:30am–2:30pm; Nov–Feb Mon–Fri 9:30am–2:30pm, Sun 10am–1pm. Metro: Ventas. Bus: 12, 21, 38, 53, 146, M1, or M8.

OUTSIDE THE CITY CENTER

Cerro de los Angeles (Hill of the Angels) Located 10km (6 miles) south of Madrid on the outskirts of Getafe, this 670m rise (2,200-ft.) surrounded by pines rivals the town of Pinto as official geographical center of Spain. It offers marvelous views of the fertile plains and less picturesque industrial estates of Southern Madrid. The hill's baroque **Ermita de Nuestra Señora de los Angeles** and **Convento de las Carmelitas Descalzas** date from the 17th century, and the towering white-stoned **Monumento de Sagrado Corazón,** with its 9m-high (30-ft.) statue of Jesus, was built from public subscriptions after the original monument—inaugurated by King Alfonso XIII in 1919—was dynamited by Republican forces in 1936 at the beginning of the Civil War. Amid the pines, you'll find picnic areas and kiddies' play zones, and there's a small cafeteria up near the statue. A colorful pilgrimage wends its way here from Getafe, south of Madrid, every May.

Carretera de Andalucía Km 13. Bus: 446 from Legazpi Sq. Easier access by car. From Atocha, drive down the Paseo de Delicias as far as Legazpi, and from there pass under the M-30 circular road and across the Manzanares River to join the A-4 Carretera de Andalucía. Follow this for some 8km (5 miles). Just after Getafe's Poligono Industrial (Industrial Estate) de Los Olivos, you'll see the turnoff to Cerro de los Angeles on your left.

Museo del Aire de Madrid/Museo Aeronáutica y Astronáutica Named **Cuatro Vientos** (Four Winds) after an airplane that crashed in the Mexican jungles of Campeche during a long-distance flight via Cuba in the 1930s, this time warp paradise for vintage plane observers is 8km (5 miles) west of Madrid, close to the satellite town of Alcorcón. There's a wide variety of military and civil airplanes dating from 1911 to the 1970s on display, both out in the open and in various large hangars. One of the most evocative is the English-piloted Dragon Rapide, in which General Franco flew to mainland Europe from Africa and the Canaries in 1936 to launch his coup attempt and initiate the Civil War, which ended democratic rule of the country for nearly 40 years. A small on-site cafeteria is open from 10am to 1:30pm.

Carretera Extremadura Km 10.5. ✆ **91-509-16-90.** www.aire.org/museo. Free admission. Tues–Sun 10am–2pm. Green line bus: 512, 513, 514, and 516 from Príncipe Pío.

Real Palacio de El Pardo Just 15km (10 miles) north of the city center in the tiny town of El Pardo, surrounded by a magnificent expanse of protected—and alas largely private—parklands filled with deer and birdlife, is the palace where General Franco lived and performed his duties as head of state for 35 years (till his death in Nov 1975). Originally a 15th-century hunting lodge, it was enlarged by Charles I (whose son Philip II added many important art works), badly damaged by a fire in 1604, and rebuilt by 18th-century architect Francesco Sabatini. The frescoes, paintings, and tapestries displayed in its salons today date from this and the following 2 centuries. An additional highlight is the elegant little theater built for Maria Luisa of Parma, Charles IV's Italian wife, where—it is said—Franco used to enjoy watching films that he himself had banned for moral or political reasons. The charming gardens are also a delight to wander around, and just a 5-minute stroll away you can visit the **Convento de los Capuchinos** (Carretera del Cristo; ✆ **91-376-08-00;** free admission; daily 9am–1pm, 4:30–9pm) and see a splendid Baroque wooden sculpture of Christ by Gregorio Fernández.

Calle Manuel Alonso. ✆ **91-376-15-00.** www.patrimonionacional.es. Admission 6€. Apr–Sept Mon–Sat 10:30am–5:45pm, Sun 9:30am–1:30pm; Oct–Mar Mon–Sat 10:30am–4:45pm. Bus: 601 from Moncloa.

ARCHITECTURAL STANDOUTS

Banco de España On the other side of Cibeles Square from the Correos building, Spain's most prestigious bank is housed in an equally impressive 19th-century French Second Empire–influenced landmark designed by Eduardo Adaro and Severiano Sanz de Lastra. Standouts inside include a Carrara marble stairway, glass-domed central patio, and a variety of stained-glass windows. Guided tours can be arranged, and the bank's collection of Goyas can be viewed by appointment.

Plaza de Cibeles or Paseo del Prado 2. ✆ **91-338-53-65.** www.bde.es. Guided tours by arrangement Mon and Wed–Thurs 9:30 and 11:30am. Write at least 1 week in advance to the Protocol Service, Banco de España, Alcalá 50, Madrid 28014. Metro: Banco de España. Bus: 1, 9, 74, 146, or 150.

Cuatro Torres Business Area (CTBA) ★ This quartet of business-oriented skyscrapers, completed in 2009, and visible from as far as 60km (40 miles) away, represents the new face of 21st-century Madrid. Their slender steel gray and gleaming glass outlines loom high at the northern end of the Castellana Avenue, beside the Chamartín railway station, dwarfing the nearby KIO Towers (see below). The big daddy is **Torre Caja Madrid,** a twin-columned edifice of reinforced concrete, designed by the ubiquitous Norman Foster; and, at 250m (820 ft.), it's the biggest building in the city. The **Torre de Cristal,** designed by Argentinian César Pelli, reaches only 1m (3 ft.) shorter, and the **Torre Sacyr Vallehermoso,** by Spanish designers Carlos Rubio Carvajal and Enrique Álvarez-Sala Walther, is 236m (774 ft.) high. The latter accommodates a five-star hotel, Eurostars Madrid Tower (p. 111), whose restaurant enjoys the best views in the capital. The "baby" of the group is the 223m (732-ft.) **Torre Espacio.**

Plaza Castilla. Metro: Plaza Castilla. Bus: 5, 27, 66, 70, 124, or 147.

Edificio Metrópolis Another familiar Madrid landmark standing out as prominently as a ship's bow, is this French-built 1911 structure designed by the brothers Jules and Raymond Février for the Union and Fenix Insurance Company. Topped by the bust of a phoenix symbolizing winged victory, its ornate dome of dark slate and gilt towers above the junction of Alcalá and the beginnings of the Gran Vía. Colonnaded floors have statues representing trade, agriculture, industry, and mining. Now owned by Metropolis Insurance, it remains largely unchanged in appearance since the beginning of the century (though the phoenix was replaced by a newer one in the 1970s). Unfortunately the building is not open to the public, so its charms can only be viewed from outside.

Calle de Alcalá 39. Metro: Sevilla. Bus: 1, 5, 9, 15, 20, 51, 52, 74, 146, or 150.

KIO Towers Madrid's very own ultramodern twin version of the Leaning Tower of Pisa, this pair of highly controversial gravity-defying *torres* was built at the beginning of the booming '80s to symbolize a new economic dawn. Financed by the Kuwaiti Investment Office (hence the name), their completion was delayed well over a decade due to a financial scandal. Evocative icons of smoked glass and concrete, they stand at the northern end of the Castellana Avenue on either side of Plaza Castilla like jet-age exit gates to the city, though their once uniquely dominant presence has now been eclipsed by the four huge CBTA towers farther up the avenue (see above).

Plaza Castilla. Metro: Plaza Castilla. Bus: 5, 27, 66, 70, 124, or 147.

La Casa de las Siete Chimeneas (House of the Seven Chimneys) Located in the historic Plaza del Rey on the western edge of Chueca, this remarkable little Habsburg building was the late-16th-century creation of El Escorial architect Juan de Herrera. Celebrated visitors over the years have included Charles I of England and the Marquis of Esquilache, who caused a minor mutiny when he tried to abolish the wearing of capes and broad-brimmed hats in the 18th century.

Plaza del Rey. Metro: Banco de España. Bus: 1, 9, 74, 146, or 150.

Palacio de Comunicaciones This is the grandiose name for Madrid's imposing Correos (Post Office) building, which was completed at the end of World War I by Antonio Palacios and Joaquín Otamendi. An extravagant wedding cake lookalike that gleams cream-ochre above the Plaza de la Cibeles, it's one of the most emblematic images of 20th-century Madrid. An ambitious blend of Spanish and Viennese Art Nouveau, the building is anything but functional in style, and contrasts strongly with the stark modernity of many buildings lining the nearby Castellana Avenue. Inside, it's just as dramatic, with high ceilings, soaring pillars, marble floors, and a palatial staircase. You won't find a more impressive place to buy stamps for your postcards.

Plaza de Cibeles. ✆ **91-521-65-00.** Mon–Fri 8:30am–9:30pm; Sat 9:30am–9:30pm; Sun 8:30am–2pm. Metro: Banco de España. Bus: 5, 14, 27, 37, 45, 53, or 146.

Palacio de Cristal (Crystal Palace) Modeled on London's Crystal Palace of the 1850s, Madrid's greatest wrought-iron and glass-domed Industrial Revolution structure was launched just 30 years later to stage an exhibition of Philippine tropical plants. It stands in the heart of the Retiro Park, reflecting charismatically in a small lake inhabited by ducks, grey lag geese, and black swans, and forms one of Madrid's most enduring bucolic images. Exhibitions of modern art, ranging from surrealistic metal sculptures to aviary shows, are regularly held inside the building.

Parque del Retiro. ✆ **91-574-66-14.** Free admission. Oct–May Mon and Wed–Sat 10am–6pm; June–Sept Mon and Wed–Sat 11am–8pm.

Plaza Mayor ★★ In the heart of Madrid, this famous square was known as the Plaza de Arrabal during medieval times, when it stood outside the city wall. The original architect of Plaza Mayor itself was Juan Gómez de Mora, who worked during the reign of Philip III. Under the Habsburgs, the square rose in importance as the site of public spectacles, including the abominable *autos de fé,* in which heretics were burned. Bullfights, knightly tournaments, and festivals were also staged here.

The buildings on the square burned three times—in 1631, 1672, and 1790—but each time the plaza bounced back. After the last big fire, it was completely redesigned by Juan de Villanueva.

Nowadays, a Christmas fair is held around the equestrian statue of Philip III (dating from 1616) in the center of the square. On summer nights, the Plaza Mayor becomes the virtual living room of Madrid, as tourists sip sangria at the numerous cafes and listen to scheduled and spontaneous music performances. The walls of the former **Casa de la Panadería,** on the square's northern side, feature murals that some have compared unflatteringly to comic strips.

Metro: Sol.

Puerta de Alcalá Designed by the prominent Italian architect Francesco Sabatini for Carlos III, this granite neoclassical gateway, comprising five arches topped by warrior angels and cupids, marked the eastern edge of the city up to the mid-1800s. Today it stands in the middle of the Plaza de Independencia roundabout, surrounded by a small flowery garden area, just opposite the entrance to the Retiro and next to the beginning of stylish Calle Serrano.

Plaza de la Independencia. Metro: Retiro. Bus: 1, 9, 19, 20, 28, 51, 52, or 146.

Sociedad General de Autores de España This extraordinary building, former home of banker Javier González Longoria (and also known as Palacio Longoria), is the only example of Catalan Art Nouveau architecture in Madrid. Gaudí and other exponents of this distinctive style never really got a look in, probably because of the fierce rivalry between the Spanish capital and Barcelona. Designed at the beginning of the century by José Grases Riera in a style that also shows French influence, the building bears more than a passing resemblance to an exotic fairy-tale sand castle. Today it's home of the Association of Spanish Writers and Artists; and though it's not open to the public, the unique exterior alone is well worth a look.

Calle Fernando VI 6. Metro: Alonso Martínez. Bus: 3, 40, or 149.

PARKS & GARDENS

Madrid is now officially one of the leafiest capital cities in the world, thanks to energetic programs for planting a multitude of trees, flowers, and grasslands organized in the last decade by the Comunidad de Madrid. Some parks—such as Casa de Campo and the Retiro—have been around for centuries, but new green zones are springing up annually. This overall change from just a few decades ago is remarkable.

Campo del Moro ★ These extremely beautiful gardens slope westward from the Royal Palace toward the River Manzanares. Named after a medieval Arab chieftain who attempted a vain siege of the fortress that occupied the spot where the palace now stands, the park boasts a well-tended profusion of lawns, trees, and flowers. The park also has two magnificent fountains: the 17th-century Triton, originally located in the Aranjuez Palace gardens, and the Las Conchas, built by Ventura Rodríguez a century later. (Incidentally, the still signposted Museo de Carruajes, or Carriage Museum, tucked away in a corner of the grounds, has been closed for many years.) You can only enter the park from the lower side beside the Paseo de la Virgen del Puerto (which involves a longish roundabout walk via Cuesta de la Vega, if you are visiting the Royal Palace first).

Paseo de la Virgen del Puerto. ✆ **91-454-88-00.** Free admission. Oct-Mar Mon-Sat 9am-6pm, Sun 9am-6pm; Apr-Sept 10am-8pm, Sun 9am-8pm. Metro: Príncipe Pío. Bus: 26, 33, 39, 41, 138, or 500.

Casa de Campo ★ Until 1931, this parkland, which lies south of the Royal Palace across the Manzanares River, was exclusively a hunting ground and leisure area for royalty. You can see the gate through which the kings rode out of the palace grounds, either on horseback or in carriages, on their way to the tree-lined park. A lake in the park is usually filled with rowers. You can have drinks and light refreshments around the water or go swimming in a municipally operated pool. Children will love the zoo and the Parque de Atracciones (p. 195). Neat gardens, walkways, and piazzas—part of the capital's ambitious 14km-long (9-mile) Río Madrid plan—line the widened and regenerated Manzanares River. A century-old pedestrian bridge, renovated and re-opened to the public in 2009, now relinks the park with the Príncipe Pío roundabout and smaller Campo del Moro Park (see above).

Casa de Campo is easy to reach by metro: Take the no. 10 (dark blue) line to **Lago,** which is just inside the southern section of the park, beside the circular lake; or take the no. 10 or no. 6 circular (gray) line to **Princípe Pío,** and enter the park by crossing the roundabout at the adjoining Paseo de la Florida, and then take the bridge over the Manzanares River. For a more scenic ride, take the *teleférico* (cable car; p. 195).

Paseo de la Florida and Avenida de Portugal. Free admission. Daily 8am-9pm. Metro: Lago or Batán.

El Capricho de Alameda de Osuna ★ Just below the southern end of Juan Carlos park, in complete contrast to it, is this fully mature, French-style park, designed by J. B. Mulot (Marie Antoinette's gardener) for the duchess of Osuna at the end of the 18th century. It's cool, green, and tranquil, with every conceivable kind of European tree, plus gazebos, lodges, an artificial lake with islands, and a labyrinthine hedge maze (alas, the latter is not open to the public). After years of abandonment and decay (it was used as a military barracks during the Civil War), it was initially restored to its full glory in the mid-1970s, with later work carried out in the 1990s.

Paseo de la Alameda de Osuna. ✆ **91-558-87-90.** www.parquedelcapricho.iespana.es. Free admission. Sat–Sun and fiestas only. Oct–Mar 9am–6:30pm; Apr–Sept 9am–9pm. Metro: El Capricho. Bus: 101 or 105.

El Real Jardín Botánico (Royal Botanical Garden) ★ A short walk west of the Retiro, adjacent to the Museo Nacional del Prado, the garden celebrated its 250th anniversary in 2005. However, the garden hasn't always been in this location. Founded in the 18th century by Fernando VI at the Huerto de Migas Calientes, it was subsequently moved to its present location by Carlos III. Today it contains more than 104 species of trees and 30,000 types of plants. Also on the premises are an exhibition hall and a library specializing in botany.

Plaza de Murillo 2. ✆ **91-420-30-17.** www.rjb.csic.es. Daily except Aug from 10am. Closing hours vary from 6 to 8pm according to the month. Adults 2.50€, students 1.25€, free for children 9 and under and seniors 65 and over. Metro: Atocha. Bus: 10, 14, 19, 32, or 45.

Parque del Oeste Beautifully laid out by landscape gardener Cecilio Rodríguez at the beginning of the 20th century, this peaceful and relaxing park slopes from the northwestern edge of Arguëlles down toward the River Manzanares and Casa de Campo. Meandering paths follow a well-marked "nature route" past birch, cedar, cypress, and pine trees; every May, a rose festival is held in the 17,000-sq.-m (182,986-sq.-ft.) Rosaleda, close to the *teleférico* and the terrace cafe–lined Pintor Rosales Promenade. The main entrance is at Moncloa, where Paseo de Moret meets the Avenida Arco de la Victoria.

Paseo de Moret and Avenida Arco de la Victoria. Daily dawn–dusk. Metro: Moncloa. Bus: 16, 44, 61, or 133.

Parque del Retiro ★ Originally a playground for the Spanish monarchs and their guests, this park extends over 140 hectares (350 acres). The huge palaces that once stood here were destroyed in the early 19th century; only the former dance hall, the Cáson del Buen Retiro (housing the modern works of the Prado), and the building formerly housing the Army Museum remain. The park boasts numerous fountains and statues, plus a large, pristine carp-filled lake where you can go rowing or take a 15-minute trip in a solar-powered pleasure boat. You can also view two exposition centers, the Velázquez and Crystal palaces (built to honor the Philippines in 1887—see "Architectural Standouts," above), and a lakeside monument, erected in 1922 in honor of King Alfonso XII. If you're here in early June, look out for the annual *Feria de Libros,* when book-filled stalls line the northern sector of the park and authors (famous or otherwise) sign copies of their latest works for eager collectors. In summer, the rose gardens are worth a visit, and you'll find several places for snacks and drinks.

Calle de Alfonso XII. Free admission. Daily 24 hr., but it is safest 7am–8:30pm. Metro: Retiro.

Parque Juan Carlos I This huge park, laid out in 1992 to celebrate Madrid's selection as European Cultural Capital, sprawls beside a golf course at the far western end of the city between Barajas airport and the Feria de Madrid buildings. A vast conglomeration of waterways, gardens, exercise areas, and cycling and walking paths, with views north to the distant Guadarrama Mountains, it's an airy alternative respite from the congestion and hassle of the city center. The abundant olive groves were here long before the park was conceived, but the pines, oaks, and eucalyptus will need a few more years of growth before the park can achieve a sense of completeness. Highlights are the "Jardin de Tres Culturas," with its twinkling fountains and Moorish arches, and the "Estufa Fria," a semi-glassed-in botanical garden area with trees and shrubs from various countries.

Av. de Logroño s/n. www.parquejuancarlos.net. June–Sept Sun–Thurs 7am–1am, Fri–Sat 7am–3am; Oct–May Sun–Thurs 7am–11pm, Fri–Sat 7am–midnight. Metro: Canillejas or El Capricho (south entrance) or Campo de las Naciones (north entrance). Bus: 122.

Parque Tierno Galván This is one of Madrid's newer parks, built in honor of the city's popular 1980s mayor Enrique Tierno Galván. Located in the southwest of the city, close to the Méndez Álvaro bus station (also known as Estación Sur), it's a sunny open park with lawns, cypresses, panoramic city views, and a Greek-style outdoor amphitheater where occasional concerts are held. It's also the site of three major family attractions: the IMAX cinema, the planetarium, and the Angel Nieto motorcycle museum (named after Spain's former world champion motorcyclist).

Calle Planetario s/n. ✆ **91-588-29-00.** Daily dawn–dusk. Metro: Méndez Álvaro. Bus: 102 or 148.

Quinta de la Fuente del Berro An oasis of unexpected peace beside the busy M-30 at the western end of the Salamanca district, this mature gem of a park dates from the 17th century and manages to support a wide selection of trees from all over the world within its small confines. Near the upper entrance is an information section with a cafe/restaurant, small art gallery, and a library. Around the park is the tiny district known as Quinta del Berro, where a number of stylish detached 1920s villas stand sedately in quiet tree-lined lanes.

Calle Alcalde Sainz de Baranda s/n. ✆ **91-455-01-29.** June–Sept 7am–midnight; Oct–May 7am–10pm. Metro: O'Donnell. Bus: 15 or 28.

ESPECIALLY FOR KIDS

El Planetario de Madrid Also in Tierno Galván park is Madrid's impressive Planetarium with regular 45-minute shows taking you on virtual-reality trips across the solar system without moving you from your seat. Though the narration is Spanish only, the movie is sensational enough to keep kiddies of all ages watching.

Parque Tierno Galván. ✆ **91-467-38-98.** www.planetmad.es. Admission 3.55€ adults, 1.55€ children 2–14 and seniors 65 and over, 2.75€ groups. Tues–Fri 11am–1:45pm and 5–7:45pm; Sat–Sun 11:45am–1:45pm and 5–8:45pm. Metro: Méndez Álvaro. Bus: 102 or 148.

Faro de Madrid Topped by what looks like a control tower and boasting a marvelous panorama of city and countryside alike, this thin 90m-high (300 ft.) tower (the "Lighthouse of Madrid") rises on the western outskirts of University City, just above Moncloa and right opposite the Museo de América. With the aid of telescopes, you can check out the Plaza Mayor's rooftops or (on a clear day) the rugged peaks of the Guadarramas 97km (60 miles) away. An elevator takes you up to the glassed-in viewing area, and diagrams point out the main city highlights. A major advantage is that relatively few people know about it, so you rarely have to wait in line (thankfully, since elevator space is limited). Currently the Faro is being refurbished but is due to reopen to the public again in 2011.

Av. de los Reyes Católicos. ✆ **91-544-81-04.** www.elfarodemoncloa.com. Admission 1€. June–Sept Tues–Sun 11am–1:45pm, 5:30–8:45pm; mid-Sept to May Tues–Sun 10am–2pm and 5–7pm, Sat–Sun 10:30am–5:30pm. Metro: Moncloa. Bus: 12, 44, or 133.

Faunia Initially set up in 2001 under the name *Parque Biológico de Madrid,* Faunia (as it is now called) aims at educating children (and adults) about the natural world by using state-of-the-art technology. A variety of ecosystems, from tropical rainforests to deserts and polar regions, have been ingeniously created within its 140,000-sq.-m (1.5-million-sq.-ft.) grounds. A wide variety of vegetation and hundreds of species of animals are on view. Facilities include dining areas, a nursery, an animal hospital, and a lake. Though it's out in the eastern suburbs of the city, it can be easily reached by metro or bus.

Av. de las Comunidades 28. ✆ **91-301-62-10.** www.faunia.es. Admission 25€ adults, 19€ children 3–9 and seniors 60 and over. Mon–Fri 10:30am–8pm; Sat–Sun 10:30am–9pm. Metro: Valdebernardo. Bus: 71.

IMAX Madrid Incredibly realistic 3-D and Omnimax presentations of science, travel, and wildlife movies make this very special movie house a must for the kids, even though the shows only last an hour and are in Spanish. It's located inside Tierno Galván Park, in southwest Madrid, just a short walk from the Mendez Álvaro bus station and metro.

Calle Meneses s/n, Parque Tierno Galván. ✆ **91-467-48-00.** www.imaxmadrid.com. Admission 7€ mornings (5.90€ Mon) and 10€ afternoons and evenings (9€ Mon). Mon–Thurs and Sun noon–1pm and 5–10pm; Fri–Sat noon–1pm and 5–11pm. Metro: Méndez Álvaro. Bus: 102 or 148.

Museo de Cera de Madrid (Wax Museum) The kids will enjoy seeing a lifelike wax Columbus calling on Ferdinand and Isabella, as well as Marlene Dietrich checking out Bill and Hillary Clinton. One of the latest inclusions is 2010 Wimbledon, French Open, and U.S. Open winner Rafael Nadal, who's a great hit with teenagers. The 450 wax figures also include heroes and villains of World War II. Two galleries display Romans and Arabs from the ancient days of the Iberian Peninsula; a show in multivision gives a 30-minute recap of Spanish history from the Phoenicians to the present.

Paseo de Recoletos 41. ✆ **91-319-26-49.** www.museoceramadrid.com. Admission 16€ adults, 12€ children 4–10 years and seniors 60 and over, free for children 3 and under. Daily 10am–2:30pm and 4:30–8:30pm; Sat, Sun, and fiestas 10am–8:30pm. Metro: Colón. Bus: 27, 45, or 53.

Museo del Ferrocarril (Railway Museum) Located just south of Atocha in the barrio of Delicias, this ironwork trainspotter's delight was built in 1880 by Gustave Eiffel. Once trains ran from here as far as Portugal, but all services stopped in 1968. Today—in a locomotive time warp—it's the only station in Madrid that still looks like it belongs to the 19th century. Climb aboard the trains (check out the 1950s Talgo that looks like the one Spencer Tracy took in the movie *Bad Day at Black Rock*), watch early locomotive movie footage, attend short "theater shows," and see the "clock room," whose array of timers includes the one that clocked up the very first train trip in Spain: from Barcelona to Mataró. Sometimes there's a buy-and-sell model-train market.

Paseo de las Delicias 61. ✆ **91-506-83-33** or 90-222-88-02. www.museodelferrocarril.org. Admission 4.50€ adults, 3€ children 4–12. Free Sat. Tues–Sun 10am–3pm. Theater shows Tues–Fri 10:30–11:45am. Closed Aug. Metro: Delicias.

Parque de Atracciones Now in its fourth decade, this lively park on the edge of the Casa de Campo boasts an enticing array of attractions aimed predominantly at youngsters. These include a toboggan slide, a carousel, pony rides, an adventure into outer space, a walk through a transparent maze, a visit to a jungle, a motor-propelled series of cars disguised as a tail-wagging dachshund puppy, and a gyrating whirligig clutched in the tentacles of an octopus named El Pulpo. The park also has diversions for young-at-heart adults, such as the exhilarating Montaña Rusa (roller coaster) and the American-designed Lanzadera (literally "launcher") which drops you 180 stomach-churning feet (55 meters) in a matter of seconds.

Casa de Campo. ✆ **91-463-29-00.** www.parquedeatracciones.es. Admission to all the amusements 29€ adults, 22€ children 3–6 years and seniors 65 and over, free for children 2 and under. Apr–May Tues–Fri noon–8pm, Sat–Sun noon–10pm; June–Aug Tues–Fri 11am–1am, Sat 11am–2am, Sun noon–1am; Sept Tues–Sun (variable hours; call to check before going); Oct–Mar Sat noon–8pm (sometimes 9pm), Sun 11am–8pm (sometimes 9pm). Take the *teleférico* cable car (p. 195); microbuses take you the rest of the way. Alternatively, take the suburban train from Plaza de España to Entrada de Batán.

Plaza de Toros Monumental de las Ventas ★ It's not all bulls and blood (p. 181) in this monumental Neo-Mudéjar–style (mock Arabic) 1920s Plaza de Toros—the largest in Spain—which, for at least 9 months of the year, attracts the finest *toreros* and greatest fighting bulls in the land. For periods of several weeks between November to March, when the air is distinctly cooler and the skies (for Madrid) are grayer, an entirely new mood takes over when the circus comes to town and, under a giant cover, elephants, clowns, and trapeze artists perform for kids of all ages in the bullfight arena. You can purchase tickets one of three ways: at the bullring; by calling ✆ **90-215-0025**; or by logging on to **www.taquillatoros.com**.

Calle Alcalá 237. ✆ **91-726-35-70.** www.las-ventas.com. Tickets 8€–60€ *sol* (sun), 15€–130€ *sombra* (shade). Metro: Ventas. Bus: 53 or 146.

Teleférico Strung high above several of Madrid's verdant parks, this cable car was originally built in 1969 as part of a public fairgrounds (Parque de Atracciones) modeled vaguely along the lines of Disneyland. Today, even for visitors not interested in visiting the park, the *teleférico* retains an allure of its own as a high-altitude method of admiring the cityscape of Madrid. The cable car departs from Paseo Pintor Rosales at the eastern edge of Parque del Oeste (at the corner of Calle Marqués de Urquijo) and carries you high above two parks, railway tracks, and over the Manzanares River to a spot near a picnic ground and restaurant in Casa de Campo. Weather permitting, there are good views of the Royal Palace along the way. The ride takes 11 minutes. At the Pintor Rosales entrance to the *teleférico* is the famed Bruin ice-cream parlor,

An Area You May Want to Avoid

The zone by the *teleférico* in the Casa de Campo has a very good self-service restaurant with a terrace section enjoying fine views of the park—an excellent place to enjoy a relaxing lunch before walking down a wood-fringed park to Lago. But some 500m (1,640 ft.) to the west, it's a different story. There, the road that runs just inside the park is a pickup zone for prostitutes and a drug zone, so you should avoid that particular section of the park entirely.

which has been around for decades and offers a wide choice of *helados* (ice creams) and *granizados* (iced drinks).

Paseo del Pintor Rosales s/n. ✆ **91-541-11-18.** www.teleferico.com. Adults 3.55€ one-way, 5.15€ round-trip, children 3–7 and seniors 65 and over 3.25€ one-way, 4.60€ round-trip. Apr–Sept daily noon to 8 or 9:30pm (depending on month); Oct–Mar Sat–Sun noon–7pm. Metro: Plaza de España or Argüelles. Bus: 21.

Zoo Aquarium de Madrid This modern, well-organized facility allows you to see about 3,000 animals from five continents. Most are in simulated natural habitats, with moats separating them from the public. There's a petting zoo for the kids and a show presented by the Chu-Lin band. The zoo/aquarium complex includes a 520,000-gallon tropical marine aquarium, a dolphinarium, and a parrot club. You can also take a camel, pony, or minitrain ride, and live your own *Jaws* experience at the walk-through shark tank.

Casa de Campo. ✆ **91-512-37-70.** www.zoomadrid.com. Admission 19€ adults, 15€ seniors and children 3–8, free for children 2 and under. Daily 10:30 or 11am to sunset. Metro: Batán. Bus: 33.

Out of Town

Aquasur In Aranjuez, this superb open-air pool with five giant slides is an ideal fun location for the kids if you're visiting Madrid in the full heat of summer. Catch the regular *cercanías* train from Atocha for the 40-minute trip. Free buses run from Aranjuez town center (Calle Príncipe) to the pool. It's a better value on weekdays.

Antigua Carretera Andalucía A4, Km 44, Aranjuez. ✆ **91-891-60-34.** Mon–Fri 6€ adults, 3€ children 3–9; Sat–Sun 10€–12€ adults, 6€ children 3–9. June–Sept 11am–8pm. Metro: Atocha RENFE, then *cercanías* train to Aranjuez; Bus: 423 or 423A from Mendez Nuñez Estación Sur.

Aquopolis-Villanueva de la Cañada One of two Aquopolis water parks in Madrid province (the other is in San Fernando de Henares), this well-equipped summer favorite is among the biggest pool leisure centers in all of Europe. Among its main attractions are its wave pools, huge water slides and—the coup de grace—a serpentine 65m-long (213-ft.) tube slide called the "Black Hole."

Av. de la Dehesa, Villanueva de la Cañada. ✆ **91-815-69-11.** www.aquopolis.es. Admission 23€ adults, 18€ children 3–9 and seniors 65 and over. Mid-June to mid-Sept noon–9pm. Metro: Moncloa. Bus: 627 from Moncloa bus station. Free bus service from Cuesta de San Vicente.

Museo de la Ciencia Cosmo Caixa Huge fun for kids of all ages is guaranteed at this interactive science museum on the outskirts of the northerly suburb of Alcobendas, just a short bus trip from Plaza Castilla. Activity rooms show how nature's laws work and how matter evolves from atomic structure to the most complex forms of life. There's also a Bubble Planetarium and two year-round exhibits worth a couple of hours of anyone's time. One exhibit is Toca Toca (Touch Touch), which has interactive touchable exhibits of small live animals like frogs and turtles in artificially created tropical settings; the other, more scientifically oriented exhibit is Clik de los Niños, in which children can play to their heart's content with various light and mechanism switches. In between visiting the different attractions, you can recharge with a snack and drink at the cafeteria.

Pintor Velázquez s/n, Alcobendas 16km (10 miles) from Madrid. ✆ **91-484-52-00.** Admission 3€ permanent exhibitions, 1.50€ per activity room, 2€ for children 8–16 and seniors 65 and over. Tues–Sun 10am–8pm. 10-min. cercanías train ride from Atocha station or 15-min. bus ride from Plaza Castilla.

Safari Madrid This animal-lover's paradise is located near the village of Aldea del Fresno just west of Navalcarnero, and is close to a lake and the beach-bordered Alberche River, where you can rent a paddleboat and swim in summer. A colorful range of nearly 500 animals, from tigers and monkeys to giraffes and elephants, roam wild in the extensive grounds—you can view them in safety from a car. An exciting highlight is the daily lion-taming show. Birds of prey are among the many species that fill the aviary, and for fans of slithery things, the reptile house boasts snakes galore.

Aldea del Fresno, Carretera de Extremadura N-V Km 32. ✆ **91-862-23-14.** www.safarimadrid.com. Admission 13€ adults, 9€ children 3–10. Daily 10:30am-6:30pm winter; 10:30am–9:30pm summer. Car essential. Take N-V to Navalcarnero, then M-507 to Aldea del Fresno.

Tren de la Fresa Known as the "Strawberry Train" because *fresas* (strawberries) are handed out by hostesses dressed in period costumes, this 50-minute trip from Atocha station to the town of Aranjuez is on an old steam train. This not only offers a relaxing and atmospheric way of travel, evoking an era of bygone days, but also gives you a full day out to visit Aranjuez palace and gardens and enjoy a lunch beside the Tagus River (p. 254). It is particularly popular in spring.

Estación de Atocha. ✆ **90-222-88-22.** 26€ adults, 18€ children 4–12. Departs 10:05am and returns from Aranjuez at 6:50pm. Closed mid-Oct to Mar and Aug to mid-Sept. Metro: Atocha RENFE.

Warner Brothers Movie World Spain's answer to Disney World lies a half-hour south of Madrid center. It's not cheap (and you're not allowed to take your own food and drink), but it's proved a smash for the family and could be worth stretching the budget for a day. Its five themed areas cover Old West Territory, Hollywood, DC Super Heroes, Cartoon Village, and Warner Bros. Studios.

San Martín de la Vega. ✆ **91-821-12-34.** www.parquewarner.com. Admission 38€ adults, 29€ children 5–11 years. Apr–June and July–Sept Mon–Thurs 11am–7 or 10pm, Fri–Sun 11am–midnight or 3am. Closed mid-Oct to Mar. By train C-3 from Atocha railway station. By car N-IV to Km 22, then M-506 to San Martín de la Vega (station at latter can also be reached by train from Atocha, changing at Pinto).

ORGANIZED TOURS

A large number of agencies in Madrid book organized tours and excursions to sights and attractions both within and outside the city limits. Although your mobility and freedom might be somewhat hampered, some visitors appreciate the ease and convenience of being able to visit so many sights in a single efficiently organized day.

In the City

BUS TOURS Many of the city's hotel concierges and all of the city's travel agents will book anyone who asks for a guided tour of Madrid or its environs with one of Spain's largest tour operators, **Pullmantours,** Plaza de Oriente 8 (✆ **91-541-18-07**). Regardless of their destination and duration, virtually every tour departs from the Pullmantours terminal, at the above address. Half-day tours of Madrid include an artistic tour priced at 39€ per person, which includes entrance to a selection of the city's museums, and a panoramic half-day tour for 22€.

The hop-on, hop-off **Madrid Vision Bus** lets you set your own pace and itinerary. A scheduled panoramic tour lasts a half-hour, provided that you don't get off the bus. Otherwise, you can opt for an unlimited number of stops, exploring at your leisure. The Madrid Vision makes four complete tours daily, two in the morning and two in the afternoon; on Sunday and Monday buses depart only in the morning. Check with **Trapsa Tours** (✆ **91-767-17-43**) for departure times, which vary. The full-day tour, with unlimited stops, costs 17€. Departures are from the company's main information and sales office on Calle Felipe IV, between the Museo Nacional del Prado and the Hotel Ritz. There are also several central stops throughout the center, including the Puerta del Sol and Plaza España, where you can pay for your tickets on the bus.

ORGANIZED WALKING TOURS If you're interested in organized walking tours of the city, the **Patronato Municipal de Turismo** (tourist office; p. 31) provides English-speaking guides and routes that cover the history, monuments, and leading figures of Madrid. Their office in the Plaza Mayor can give you details and sell you tickets. Local travel agencies also sell tickets for various sightseeing tours in and around Madrid.

For something a little more out of the ordinary, check out the program arranged by **Stephen Drake-Jones** (✆ **60-914-32-03;** www.wellsoc.org), an English former lecturer who's lived in the city for more than 30 years. His half-dozen erudite and slightly eccentric walks around old Madrid are pleasantly broken up by refreshments—liquid and otherwise—at local taverns.

Olé Spain Tours, Paseo Infanta Isabel 21 (✆ **91-551-52-94;** www.olespaintours.com; Mon–Fri 9am–2pm and 3:30–8pm; Metro: Atocha), can also pair you with a tour guide for walking tours around the city. They also organize tours by minibus or coach—depending on the size of the group—to nearby cities like Toledo and Segovia.

If you like eating and drinking as well as walking and would like some local experts to show you where and how to combine the two, then contact **Adventurous Appetites** (✆ **63-933-10-73;** www.adventurousappetites.com). The tapas bar tour is run by resident Englishman James Fraser; his trips depart from the statue of the bear and madroño tree in Puerta del Sol at 8pm, Monday to Saturday, and cost 50€ a head, including food and drinks in the first bar.

OUTSIDE THE CITY **Toledo** (p. 269) is the most popular full-day excursion outside the city limits. Pullmantours (see above) runs a tour from 55€ including lunch, that departs daily at 9:45am from the abovementioned departure point, and includes ample opportunities for wandering at will through the city's narrow streets. You can, if you wish, take an abbreviated morning tour of Toledo, without stopping for lunch, for 40€.

Another popular tour stops briefly in Toledo and continues on to visit the monastery at **El Escorial** and the **Valle de los Caídos** (Valley of the Fallen) before returning the same day to Madrid. With lunch included, this all-day excursion costs 75€.

The third major destination of bus tours from Madrid's center to the city's surrounding attractions is Pullmantours' full-day guided excursion to **Avila** and **Segovia** (p. 279), which takes in a heady dose of interesting medieval and ancient Roman monuments. With lunch included, the price per person is 60€–80€.

You can also take the **Tren de la Fresa** (p. 197) out to Aranjuez for the day.

SPORTS

Active

GOLF Golf is not so cheap in Madrid, where it still has the faint aura of being an elitist activity. (Weekends are particularly expensive, so avoid them if you can.) Among the few venues around the capital, the best is the **Club de Campo Villa de Madrid (Madrid Country Club),** Carretera de Castilla Km 2 (✆ **91-550-20-10;** www.clubvillademadrid.com; Mon–Fri club entry: Weekdays 16€, weekends 32€; weekday greens fees 50€; Sat–Sun greens fees 115€; hours depend on season; bus: 84 from Moncloa bus station), which has a challenging par-71 course. This is a full-fledged sports center with tennis, squash, horseback riding, pigeon shooting, and a swimming pool among its other facilities.

Another top-notch venue, located on the eastern outskirts of Madrid between the Juan Carlos Exhibition Halls and Barajas airport, is the **Golf Olivar de la Hinojosa,** Vía Dublin s/n, Campo de la Naciones (✆ **91-721-18-89;** www.golf olivar.com; greens fees 20€ for 9-hole course, 55€ for 18-hole course; hours depend on the season; Metro: Campo de las Naciones). You'll need a handicap card to play there.

HORSEBACK RIDING The closest place for taking to the saddle is the **Club de Campo Villa de Madrid** sports complex on the edge of the leafy Casa de Campo park (see "Golf," above, for details). At the nearby upmarket suburb of Pozuelo, you can also hire horses by the hour (15€) or day (45€–60€) at the **Club Hipico Mirasierra,** Carretera Fuencarral-El Pardo Km 3.5 (✆ **91-734-76-27**). Further countryside riding facilities are available at outlying towns such as **Cercedilla** and **Manzanares el Real** (p. 261).

SKIING The most popular resort near Madrid for this strictly midwinter activity (Nov–Feb) is **Puerto de Navacerrada** with its 15 ski slopes and chairlift up to the 2,100m (7,000-ft.) Bola del Mundo. **Valdesqui** near Cotos has 24 slopes and usually the best snow, while Valcotos has the most attractive setting. For up-to-date details on skiing accommodations, locations, and snow conditions around Madrid in general, contact **ATUDEM** (✆ **91-350-20-20**). As they only speak Spanish, you may want to get your hotel receptionist to help translate. Skiing conditions are generally limited and, for many, the main pleasure is seeing the beautiful surrounding countryside covered in a white blanket.

SWIMMING The best **indoor** public pool is the Olympic-size one at Chamartín (✆ **91-350-12-23**), which closes in August but is open the rest of the year. During the summer months from June to August the municipality has a wider variety of good-sized **open-air** pools. Among the best are those at **La Elipa** (closed for renovation work until summer 2011) and **Lago.** The **Comunidad de Madrid** also runs a popular summer pool at **Canal de Isabel II** (✆ **91-533-96-42**) in Chamberí. Entry for all these pools is around 4.50€.

TENNIS Reasonably priced courts are for hire (around 5€ per hr.) at large *polideportivos* (multifacility sports centers) run by the Madrid municipality. **Casa de Campo** (✆ **91-464-91-67**), **Barrio del Pilar, Barrio de la Concepción,** and **La Elipa** are among the main locales. Private courts with high membership and court fees are also available at the **Club de Tenis de Chamartín** (Calle Federico Salmon 2; ✆ **91-345-25-00;** www.ctchamartin.es).

THE "other" MADRID SOCCER TEAM

After decades of being eclipsed by the city's top team Real Madrid, rival **Atletico Madrid** finally broke loose by winning the European League cup in May 2010. Instead of celebrating in Cibeles, like Real M., it had its own nocturnal shindig beside Neptune's fountain, just down the Paseo del Prado. The team's 57,000 capacity Vicente Calderon stadium (at Paseo Virgen del Puerto 12; Metro: Piramides), set beside the impressively regenerated Manzanares River, will undoubtedly attract a wider public now. For online booking, call ✆ **90-226-04-03**, or visit www.clubatleticodemadrid.com.

WALKING The Guadarrama Mountains are nearer than you think. Just 1 hour and 20 minutes by suburban train from Chamartín takes you to the town of Cercedilla (see chapter 11), which has an information center and six graded trails into the hills. Another fine walking spot—reached by bus from Plaza de Castilla—is **Manzanares el Real,** with its beautiful and dramatic La Pedriza park, where many scenes from the Charleton Heston–helmed '60s epic *El Cid* were filmed (p. 261).

Spectator Sports

ATHLETICS Madrid's largest (20,000 capacity) athletic stadium, the **Estadio de la Comunidad de Madrid,** Av. de Arcantales s/n (✆ **91-720-24-00;** Metro: Las Musas; bus: 48), is in the process of expanding fourfold in the coming years (this in spite of the reduced incentive after the city's failure to win the bid to host the 2012 Olympics). Located on the ever-burgeoning eastern edge of the city, it features a variety of athletic events as well as periodic concerts.

BASKETBALL Basketball (*baloncesto* in Spanish) is almost as popular as *fútbol* all over Spain, and you can watch the sport in several locales throughout the city. The best is the 15,000-capacity **Palacio Vistalegre** stadium, Calle Utebo 1 (✆ **91-422-07-81;** www.palaciovistalegre.com; Metro: Vista Alegre; bus: 34, 35, 118, or 119), situated in the southwestern suburbs and rebuilt in 2000 over the old Plaza de Toros. It's still also a venue for bullfights as well as rock and opera concerts.

FÚTBOL If you're a fan of English-style football (soccer), then the place to go is **Santiago Bernabeu,** Paseo de la Castellana 144 (✆ **91-229-17-09;** www.realmadrid.es; ticket office Mon–Fri 6–9pm; tickets 16€–90€; Metro: Santiago Bernabeu; bus: 27, 40, 126, 147, or 150), Madrid's largest stadium. The total capacity is 75,000 spectators. This is the home of Spain's most successful team **Real Madrid,** regarded by diehard fanatics as even more important than the Prado or Palacio Real. The team's host of charismatic international stars includes star Cristiano Ronaldo, acquired by the highest sum ever paid for a player's transfer. When no games are in progress, you can visit the stadium as part of an informal tour (check at the ticket office) or simply wander in and have a drink at the cafe (which offers a great view of the pitch). Tickets to events can also be booked by phone (✆ **90-232-43-24**) using a credit card (MC, V) and picked up on the day of the match at Gate 14.

The supreme highlight for Spanish soccer came in July 2010 when, for the very first time, the national team won the **World Cup** in Johannesburg, beating Holland (after extra time) by one goal to none. The celebrations in Madrid lasted over 24 hours and, even by the city's OTT hedonistic standards, had to be seen—and heard—to be believed!

HORSERACING The **Hipódromo Madrid** race course, Av. Padre Huidobro, Carretera de La Coruña A6 Km 8 (✆ **91-740-05-40;** www.hipodromomadrid.com; 9€, 12€, or 30€ including parking; children 13 and under free; bus: 654, 655, or 658 from Moncloa bus station), also known as La Zarzuela, lies north of the city just past the elite sports complex of Puerta de Hierro. The racetrack is usually only open Sunday from 11am to 2pm, though in summer there are additional races at the same times, as well as occasional night races. The Hipódromo is closed in December. Check directly with the racetrack for relevant timetables during your visit.

STROLLING AROUND MADRID

8

Madrid is a very easy city to explore on foot as most of the key sights—palaces, churches, and museums—are closely grouped in and around the central narrow-alleyed Austrias district, and the city itself, though high up, is mostly flat. Plus, you don't have to go to the periphery of the city to find beautiful green areas and a bit of respite from the urban hustle. The Retiro and the Casa de Campo can both be reached in 15–30 minutes on foot from the Puerta del Sol.

WALKING TOUR 1: HABSBURG MADRID (THE AUSTRIAS)

START: **Southeastern corner of the Palacio Real.**

FINISH: **Calle del Arenal.**

TIME: **3 hours.**

BEST TIMES: **Sunday, when you can also visit the flea market of El Rastro.**

WORST TIMES: **Monday to Saturday from 7:30 to 9:30am and 5 to 7:30pm because of heavy traffic.**

This tour encompasses 16th- and 17th-century Madrid, including the grand plazas and traffic arteries that the Habsburg families built to transform a quiet town into a world-class capital.

1 Palacio Real (Royal Palace)

This imposing Bourbon-influenced palace is at the corner of Calle de Bailén and Calle Mayor. The latter street was built by Philip II in the 1560s to provide easy access from the palace to his preferred church, San Jerónimo el Real.

Walk east to:

2 Calle Mayor

Walk on the south side of the street. Within a block, you'll reach a black bronze statue of a kneeling angel, erected in 1906 to commemorate the aborted assassination of King Alfonso XIII (grandfather of the present king, Juan Carlos).

Walking Tour 1: Habsburg Madrid (The Austrias)

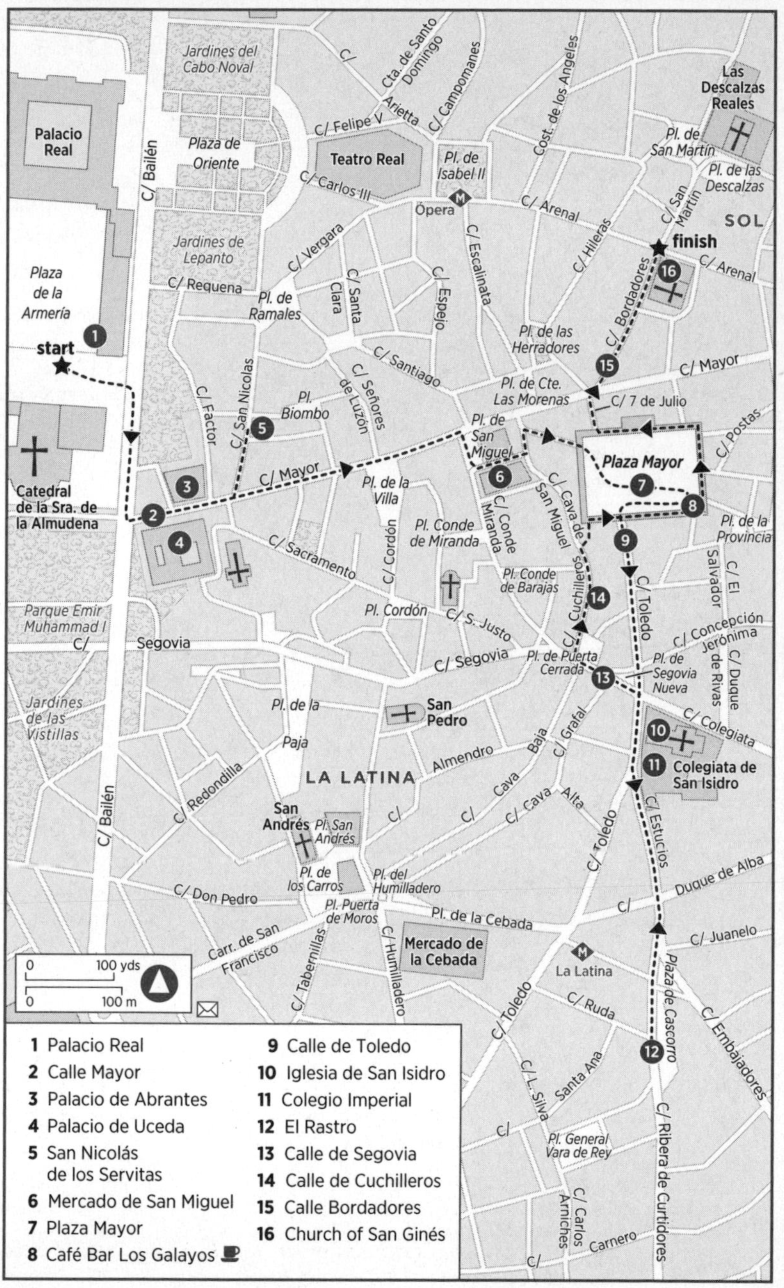

Across the street from the kneeling angel is the:

3 Palacio de Abrantes

Today, this charming small palace, at Calle Mayor 86, is occupied by the Italian Institute of Culture. You can browse through its ground-floor (all-Italian) bookshop and pop into its adjoining cafe.

On the same side of the street as the kneeling angel, to the statue's left, is the:

4 Palacio de Uceda

Almost opposite Palacio de Abrantes is this other small gem of a palace, at Calle Mayor 79, now the headquarters of the Spanish military (their version of the Pentagon). Both of these palaces are among the best examples of 17th-century civil architecture in Madrid.

Walk half a block east, crossing to the north side of Calle Mayor and detouring about 18m (60 ft.) to the left, down narrow Calle de San Nicolás. You'll come to the somber facade of the oldest church in Madrid, the 12th-century:

5 San Nicolás de los Servitas

Only a brick tower atop this tiny church remains from the original building at the Plaza de San Nicolás. It is one of the few examples of the *Mudéjar* style in the capital. The reredos at the high altar is the work of Juan de Herrera, architect of El Escorial.

Retrace your steps to Calle Mayor. Turn left and continue to walk east. You'll pass Plaza de la Villa on your right, and, 1 block later:

6 Mercado de San Miguel

This formerly traditional iron-canopied meat-and-vegetable market (Mon–Fri 9am–10pm, Sat 9am–2pm) in the Plaza de San Miguel was re-opened in 2009 after a meticulous two-year face-lift. Though all its *moderniste* 19th-century features have been lovingly retained, the original down-to-earth atmosphere has been replaced by an aura of cool glitzy chic. Today's revamped gourmet food stalls and ultratrendy cava and vermut bars are more popular with tourists than with locals, but the place does exert its own unique kind of nouveau riche allure (economic crisis or not).

Leave Plaza de San Miguel by Ciudad Rodrigo (there might not be a sign), which leads under a soaring granite archway and up a sloping street to the northwestern corner of:

7 Plaza Mayor

The capital's most beautiful and evocative square, a setting for occasional exhibitions and concerts, is a focal point of the city and the heart of vintage Austrias Madrid. At its center is an imposing equestrian statue of Felipe II (see this edition's cover photo).

8 Café Bar Los Galayos

Café Bar Los Galayos, Plaza Mayor 1 (✆ 91-366-30-28; www.losgalayos.net), has long been one of the best places for tapas along this square. If you're taking the walking tour during the day, you may want to return to this cafe/bar at night, when it is most lively. In summer, you can select one of the outdoor tables for your drinks and tapas. The cafe is open daily from noon to 1am.

Stroll through Plaza Mayor, crossing it diagonally and exiting at the closer of its two southern exits. A dingy, steep flight of stone stairs leads down to the beginning of the:

9 Calle de Toledo

This busy street, one of the oldest in the city, extends south toward La Latina on the edge of the Austrias district.

A short walk down at number 37, you'll come to the:

10 Iglesia de San Isidro

This quietly imposing church, topped by twin domes of yellow-stucco and granite and also known as the (deep breath) *Real Muy Ilustre y Primitiva Congregación de San Isidro de Naturales de Madrid,* is the legendary burial place of Madrid's patron saint and his wife, Santa María de la Cabeza. The church lost its status as a cathedral in 1992, when the honor went to the larger Church of La Almudena.

Adjacent to San Isidro is the baroque facade of the:

11 Colegio Imperial

Lope de Vega, Calderón, and many other famous men studied at this institute, which was also run by the Jesuits.

If your tour takes place on a Sunday morning, fork slightly left from here down Calle de los Estudios till you reach Plaza de Cascorro. There you'll find:

12 El Rastro

Madrid's world-famous flea market fills the long, narrow tree-lined Ribera de los Curtidores street that goes all the way down from the Plaza Cascorro, with its small statue honoring a hero of the war with Cuba, to the Ronda de Toledo. It starts every Sunday at 9am and is still buzzing around 3pm, when it officially finishes. Great bargains abound here but do watch your wallet.

If your tour takes place Monday to Saturday, skip the Rastro neighborhood. Instead, turn right onto:

13 Calle de Segovia

This street intersects Calle de Toledo just before it passes in front of the Iglesia de San Isidro.

Walk 1 block and turn right onto the first street:

14 Calle de Cuchilleros

Follow this street north past 16th- and 17th-century stone-fronted houses. Within a block, a flight of granite steps forks to the right. Climb the steps (a sign identifies the new street as Calle Arco de Cuchilleros) and you'll pass one of the most famous *mesones* (typical Castilian restaurants) of Madrid, the Cueva de Luis Candelas.

Once again you will have entered Plaza Mayor, this time on the southwestern corner. Walk beneath the southernmost arcade, and promenade counterclockwise beneath the arcades, continuing north underneath the square's eastern arcade. Then walk west beneath its northern arcade. At the northwest corner, exit through the archway onto Calle 7 de Julio. Fifteen meters (50 ft.) later, cross Calle Mayor and take the right-hand narrow street before you. This is:

15 Calle Bordadores

During the 17th century, this street housed Madrid's embroidery workshops, staffed exclusively by men. Today a handful of shops, more recently built, still sell charming traditional lace garments.

As you proceed, notice the 17th-century brick walls and towers of the:

16 Church of San Ginés

This church, at Arenal 15, is one of Madrid's oldest parishes and owes its present look to the architects who reconstructed it after a devastating fire in 1872.

At the end of this tour, you'll find yourself on traffic-congested Calle del Arenal, at the doorstep of many interesting old streets.

WALKING TOUR 2: THE CASTIZO QUARTER (LA LATINA & LAVAPIÉS)

START:	**Plaza General Vara del Rey.**
FINISH:	**Calle Mesón de Paredes.**
TIME:	**2 hours (at a slow pace).**
BEST TIMES:	**Any day.**
WORST TIMES:	**No particularly bad time, as rush-hour traffic doesn't affect much of this route.**

This short leisurely tour takes you across one of Madrid's oldest quarters: a warrenlike network of narrow lanes and medieval buildings that still represents the Castizo (traditional) heart of Madrid while attracting, in recent years, a genuine ethnic mix, with new resident nationalities ranging from Chinese and North African to Indian and Turkish.

---

1 Plaza Vara del Rey

We start our walk just west of El Rastro at this small intimate square named after a Spanish commander who died during the 1898 war with Cuba. The adjoining Museo de Artes Populares has examples of local arts and crafts.

Continue west to Calle Toledo and then south to the:

2 Puerta de Toledo

Originally planned to celebrate France's victory over Spain in 1808, this prominent archway at the end of Calle Toledo took 6 years to build and eventually served to commemorate the reverse: the expulsion of the French from Spain.

Turn east now through the Plaza Campillo Mundo Nuevo past the Ministerio de la Economía building and along the Ronda de Toledo to:

3 Glorieta de Embajadores

Together with Puerta de Toledo, this great roundabout forms the southern fringe of the Embajadores district, where many ambassadors moved in the 15th century when a plague was spreading through Madrid. Close by is the restored 18th-century *Fábrica de Tabaco* (Tobacco Factory).

Walking Tour 2: The Castizo Quarter (La Latina & Lavapiés)

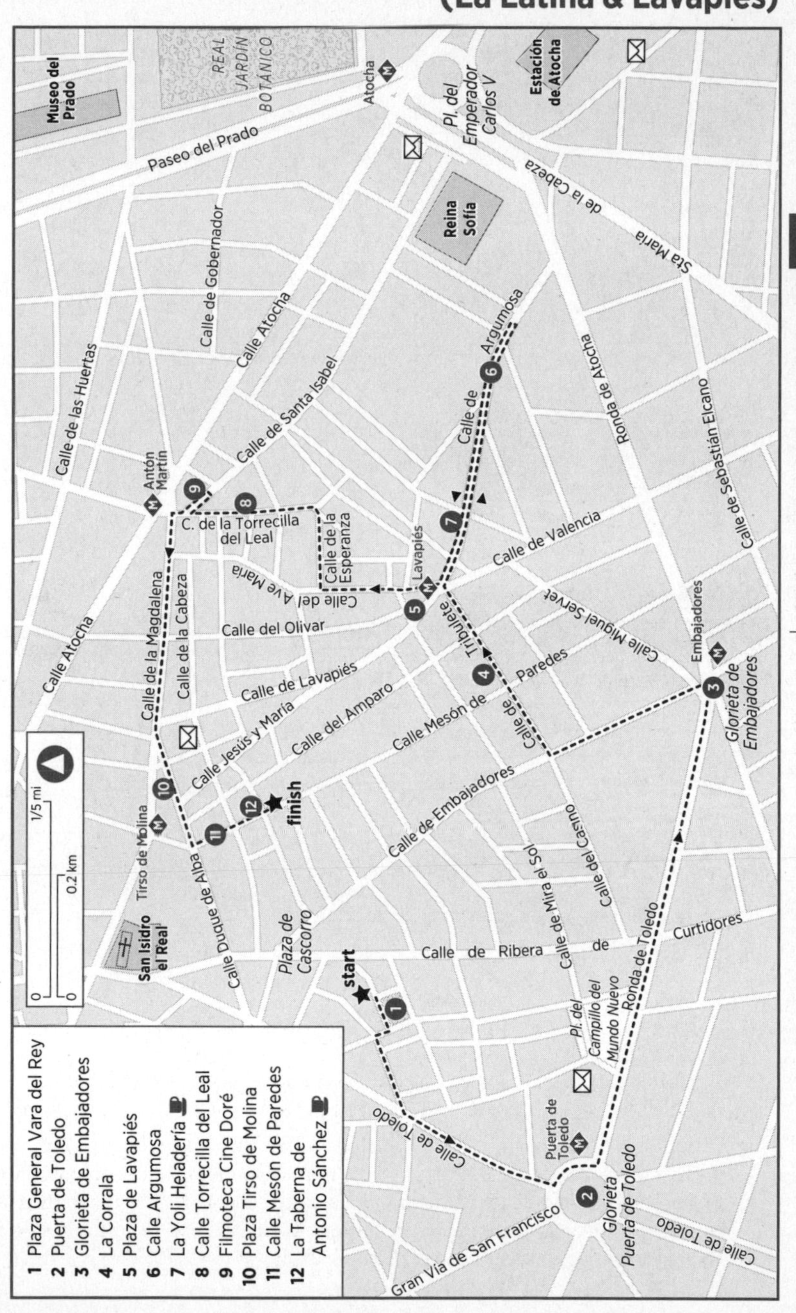

Continue west along Calle Embajadores, and then turn right into Calle de Tribulete arriving at:

4 La Corrala

Here, in a well-preserved example of the area's once widespread typical 16th-century architecture, is a building of windowless adjoining apartments, known as *corralas,* whose long continuous balconies overlook an open communal courtyard or well. This is one of the few such buildings that remain in Madrid. People still live in the apartments—some units as small as 26 sq. m (279 sq. ft.).

Westward along narrow Calle de Tribulete we come now to:

5 Plaza de Lavapiés

Named after a fountain that once adorned it, Lavapiés square is the focal point of this colorful barrio, medieval in character and multiethnic in atmosphere today. Arabic, Indian, Chinese, and Turkish shops and eating spots abound. Narrow lanes radiate upward and outward from it as they've done for centuries, but there's no trace of the fountain that gave it its name. (*Lavapiés* means, literally, "wash feet.")

From the square, take a southeasterly turn into:

6 Calle Argumosa

Known locally as the "promenade of Lavapiés," this wide, lively street leading east to the Ronda de Atocha is virtually one long row of cafes and bars with outdoor terraces in summer.

7 La Yoli Heladería

La Yoli Heladería, Argumosa 7 (✆ 91-528-80-09), is a small, modest-looking summer place, great not only for ice cream but also *granizado* (crushed ice drink of lemon or coffee) or *horchata* (a refreshing drink made of tiger nuts, water, and sugar). Sit on the tree-shaded pavement *terraza* and watch the world go by. The owners are very welcoming. Open April to October only; Monday to Thursday and Sunday 10am to midnight, Friday and Saturday 10am to 1am. No credit cards are accepted. Metro: Lavapiés.

Return to Lavapiés square and turn north into Calle Ave María, then right (east) at Calle Esperanza into:

8 Calle Torrecilla del Leal

Turn left and climb up this typically narrow and atmospheric street, which unobtrusively shelters two of the best wine and tapas bars in Madrid: Aloque (no. 20) and El Sur (no. 12). Both are ideal spots to pop into if you're taking an evening stroll (they don't open till 8pm).

Continue to the top and turn right at Plaza Antón Martín to reach the:

9 Filmoteca Cine Doré

Located next to Antón Martín square and its adjoining well-stocked two-story food market, this mecca for movie buffs offers, by far, the best value in Madrid (seats have remained constant at 2.50€ for the past three years; it's even cheaper if you're here long enough to buy a batch of 10 tickets for 20€). Despite threats a couple of decades back to raze it and build a block of modern offices in its place, this small ornate '50s monument to art managed to survive, thanks to the mass protest of artists, musicians, and writers. Programs cover the most adventurous and eclectic range of original language movies in Madrid. There are outdoor projections with a rooftop bar in summer and a small downstairs movie bookshop.

Return to Plaza Antón Martín and walk west along Calle de la Magdalena till you arrive at:

10 Plaza Tirso de Molina

Named after the prolific Golden Age playwright Tirso de Molina (the pseudonym of Fray [Friar] Gabriel Telléz, who died in 1648), this once historic but now blandly modernized square on the northern edge of Lavapiés is dominated by a statue in honor of him. Tirso was the first of many dramatists to write about the legendary romantic figure Don Juan.

On Sundays, the plaza is crowded with overflows from the Rastro market. On weekdays small children cavort in the square's play area, giving it a family feel. Close to the plaza are the Nuevo Apolo theater, with its eye-catching Art Deco–cum-Neo-Mudéjar facade and regular big musical productions, and the superb Asador Frontón (p. 126) restaurant, whose steaks are among the best in Madrid.

At the western end of the square turn left (south) into:

11 Calle Mesón de Paredes

This long narrow thoroughfare is one of the oldest streets in Lavapiés, leading right down to La Corrala and then continuing on to the Ronda de Valencia on the outskirts of the Old City. It's named after Simón Miguel Paredes, who ran one of the largest medieval *mesones* (hostelries) in Madrid. Though the *mesón* no longer exists, we have in its place one of the city's most distinctive *tabernas:* the cavernlike, bullfight-oriented Antonio Sanchéz (p. 167).

12 La Taberna de Antonio Sánchez

La Taberna de Antonio Sánchez, Mesón de Paredes 13 (✆ 91-539-78-26), is a snug 19th-century tavern, the oldest in central Madrid, whose atmospheric features include bullfight decor, dark-wood paneling, paintings by artist Ignacio Zuloaga, and a traditional zinc bar top. Here you can enjoy a glass or two of modestly priced wine together with a tasty tapa. Larger *raciones* are also available. Open daily from 1 to 4pm and Monday to Saturday from 8pm to midnight. MasterCard and Visa are accepted. Metro: Tirso de Molina.

WALKING TOUR 3: PUERTA DEL SOL, ALCALÁ & HUERTAS

START:	**Puerta del Sol.**
FINISH:	**Plaza Canalejas.**
TIME:	**2 hours (excluding a visit to the Monasterio de las Descalzas Reales).**
BEST TIMES:	**Any day.**
WORST TIMES:	**Avoid rush-hours on weekdays, 7:30 to 9:30am and 5 to 7:30pm, because of heavy traffic.**

This circular tour extends east from the Puerta de Sol to a fan-shaped area bordered by Calle Alcalá in the north and Calle Huertas in the south, taking in a wide range of historical, cultural, and fun sights along a compact route.

1 Puerta del Sol

This half-moon-shaped square is not only the acknowledged central point of the capital but also kilometer zero for the entire country (all distances in Spain are measured from outside the Casa de Correos on the south side of the square). Prior to assuming its present central position in the 19th century, this "Gateway of the Sun" marked the eastern entry point to the city. Traditionally symbolic of Madrid—and a favorite rendezvous point—is the bronze statue of the *Oso y el Madroño* (Bear and the Strawberry Tree), which was moved in 2009 from its long familiar position on the northern edge of the square at the entrance to the pedestrian Calle del Carmen over to the plaza's eastern edge, where the 8km-long (5-mile) Calle Alcalá ends. That same year saw the resurfacing of the entire square and final (if long delayed) completion of a newly expanded metro and suburban rail junction. This is now reached by an eye-catching, futuristic arched entrance of glass and steel.

From here, head west up Calle Arenal, and then take the second right turn into Calle San Martín to arrive at the:

2 Monasterio de las Descalzas Reales

Founded by Carlos V's daughter Juana of Austria in 1557, this haven of tranquillity, with its chapels, baroque art masterpieces, grandiose stairway, and (hidden) inner gardens, is still home to an enclosed order of nuns. Visitors are allowed in 20 at a time, which can make for large queues at times, so be prepared for a possible wait (p. 183).

Return to the Puerta del Sol, and then head east along Calle Alcalá past the impressive Ministerio de Economía y Hacienda building to the adjoining:

3 Real Academia de Bellas Artes de San Fernando

Started in 1744 by Felipe V and bought by Carlos III 30 years later, this art museum—located at Calle Alcalá 13—is the oldest in Madrid. It boasts a very rich collection of works by El Greco, Zurbarán, and Velázquez, as well as masterpieces by Van Dyck and Rubens. An entire room is devoted to Goya.

Cross the road and continue down the southern side of Alcalá, past the Sevilla metro station, until you reach Calle Marqués de Casa Riera. Turn right for the entrance to the:

4 Círculo de Bellas Artes

This multipurpose 1920s-style cultural center was refurbished in the 1990s and has four exhibition rooms. It boasts a superb cafe with high ceilings, where you can enjoy a drink and watch the city life outside swirl by. There is a top-floor library and adjoining bookshop, a theater, and a good value cinema showing international movies in their original language.

5 Casa Manolo

After the Círculo de Bellas Artes, turn right and then immediately left into Calle Jovellanos. There, opposite the Zarzuela (Comic Opera Theater), you'll find Casa Manolo at no. 7 (© 91-521-45-16), a marvelous old bar frequented by parliament office workers from just around the corner in Plaza de las Cortes. Unchanged over the decades, with a predominantly dark-wood decor and cozy alcoves, it serves great coffee and churros, plus inexpensive wines and what they claim are the best croquetas (croquettes of fish or chicken) in Madrid.

Walking Tour 3: Puerta del Sol, Alcalá & Huertas

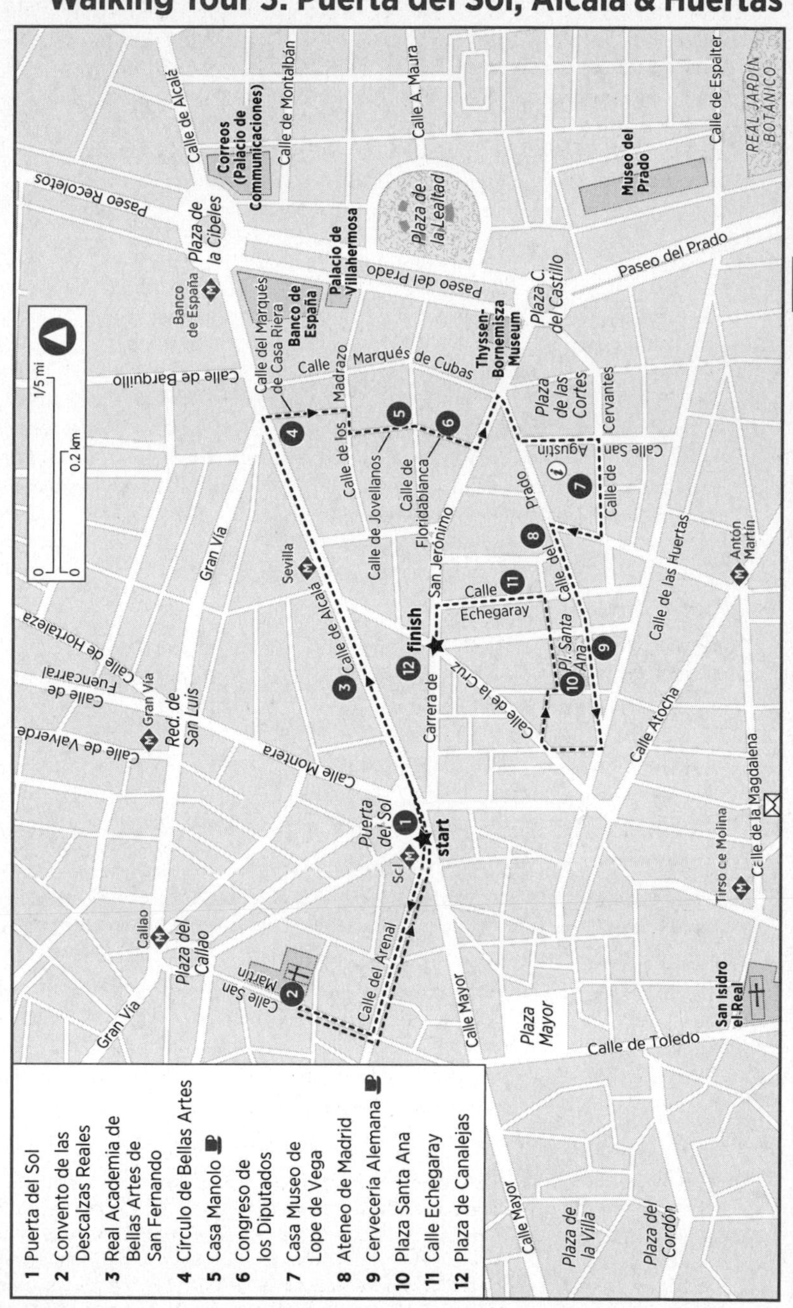

From here, turn left and immediately right down the small narrow Calle Floridablanca, which will bring you into Carrera de San Jerónimo. On your immediate right, you'll see the:

6 Congreso de los Diputados

This mid-19th-century building, also known as the Palacio de las Cortes, houses the lower house of Spanish parliament. Its classical portico and twin bronze lions facing the Plaza del Cortes create an impressive front entrance. Visitors can enjoy guided tours of the interior on Saturday mornings.

Cross the plaza, head south down Calle San Agustín and turn right (south) at Calle Cervantes to the:

7 Casa Museo de Lope de Vega

The prolific Golden Age playwright Lope de Vega Carpio wrote some of his 2,000-plus works in this small 16th-century house at no. 18, uniquely preserved and opened as a museum in 1935. Due to its size, only 10 people can visit it at one time (p. 181). Farther along is the Convento de las Trinitarias, where rival wordsmith Miguel de Cervantes's ashes were kept in an urn, which subsequently got mislaid. (The author of *Don Quixote,* incidentally, lived not on this street but on adjoining Calle León, though his abode was pulled down centuries ago. Only a commemorative plaque remains.)

Continue along Calle Cervantes to Calle León. Here turn right to Calle del Prado where almost opposite—at no. 21—you'll see the:

8 Ateneo de Madrid

Founded in 1820, this is one of the capital's great literary institutions and home of Spain's second-largest library. You have to pay a yearly subscription to be a member, but visitors are allowed to climb up the marble stairs; wander around; eye the array of portraits of key Spanish essayists, novelists, and poets; and soak up the untrammeled, slightly run-down 19th-century atmosphere. It also has a small unpretentious cafe, if you feel like a refreshing taste of something.

Turn left along Calle del Prado to arrive at:

9 Plaza Santa Ana

A legacy of the brief French rule under Joseph Bonaparte, this sunny square is one of the most popular in Madrid, filled with cafes that have open-air terraces in the center in summer and boasting a small statue to García Lorca. On its eastern side, in Calle Príncipe, is the stylish and very well preserved Teatro Español, which dates from the 18th century. A theater has existed on this spot since 1583, when the Corral del Príncipe would put on shows to a raucously demanding audience.

10 Cervecería Alemana

Try one of Hemingway's all-time favorites, the 80-year-old Cervecería Alemana, at Plaza Santa Ana 6 (✆ 91-429-70-33), for coffee or delicious cold beer. Sit at a table in the traditional wood-paneled interior in winter or outside in the square in summer.

Leave Plaza Santa Ana via Calle Príncipe to the north, and turn right into the tiny Manuel González y Fernández alley, passing—or pausing in—the Trucha tapas bar and tile-and-wood-decorated Viva Madrid cafe to arrive in:

11 Calle Echegaray

This long, narrow street, so quiet and unassuming by day, comes to life at night, when its multinational array of watering holes and eating spots makes progressing from one end to the other a very slow ramble. Among its highlights is La Venencia, a staunchly traditional and atmospheric cellar bar dating from the 1920s, which sells nothing but sherry by the glass (covering the full gamut from dry *manzanillas* to heavy *olorosos*) and small but delicious tapas of olives, cheese, and *jamón serrano* (mountain ham).

At the northern end of Calle Echegaray, turn left into Carrera de San Jerónimo and continue to the:

12 Plaza de Canalejas

Placed at the closely knit junction of four roads, this attractive but busy little square was once aptly named the Plaza de los Cuatro Calles. It owes its present name to the 19th-century politician José Canalejas, who was assassinated while peering in the window of a bookshop in the Puerta del Sol (just a couple of hundred meters away). Nearby, look out for the inimitable Lhardy's (p. 131) French restaurant, with its downstairs deluxe snack bar.

WALKING TOUR 4: GRAN VIA, MALASAÑA & CHUECA

START:	**Edificio Metropolis at junction of Gran Vía and Calle Alcalá.**
FINISH:	**Casa de las Siete Chimeneas in Chueca.**
TIME:	**2 to 3 hours.**
BEST TIMES:	**Weekends or midmornings.**
WORST TIMES:	**Rush-hour times 7:30 to 9:30am or 5 to 7:30pm (especially on the Gran Vía).**

This comprehensive walk takes you from east to west along the city's great central artery and returns via the intricate, narrow-laned districts of Malasaña and Chueca, with their traditional squares and architecture.

1 Edificio Metrópolis

The French-styled Metropolis building, built in 1911 for the Union and Fenix Español insurance company, stands at the beginning of the Gran Vía on the corner of the junction with Alcalá. An essential part of the central Madrid skyline, it looks back toward the equally symbolic Cibeles fountain and Correos building. On the pavement in front of it is a small statue in honor of La Violetera, or violet seller, representing all the young ladies who used to sell flowers, *Pygmalion*-style, to theatergoers. (International movie buffs may wish to note La Violetera was the heroine in an early flick, played by Sara Montiel, Spain's answer to Elizabeth Taylor.)

Start walking up the Gran Vía, and then make an immediate left deviation into Calle Caballero de Gracia to the:

2 Oratorio del Caballero de Gracia

One of the city's least-known ecclesiastical gems, this late-18th-century church is considered one of the finest examples of neoclassical work in Madrid. The Gran Vía was actually rerouted during its construction so that it could be preserved.

Return to the Gran Vía at the junction of Calle Montera and the San Luis roundabout. Passing the imposing 1924 Edificio Telefónica on your right, in its time Madrid's highest building, continue up the Gran Vía to the:

3 Plaza de Callao

Named after a naval battle fought between Spain and allied South American forces off Peru in 1866, this busy square stands just over halfway along the Gran Vía. Running off it toward the Puerta del Sol are the central pedestrian-only streets of Preciados and del Carmen, with their big shopping stores, and either side of it are some of Madrid's longest-established cinemas and theaters (Spanish-language showings only).

Continue on down to the end of the Gran Vía, where you reach the:

4 Plaza de España

Separating the Gran Vía from Calle Princesa, this large, perennially busy square is famed as much for its Don Quixote and Sancho Panza statue (on horseback in front of a taller one of Cervantes) as for the two concrete Francoist structures that tower beside it: Edificio España, built between 1947 and 1953 has 23 stories, while Torre Madrid (nicknamed "the Giraffe"), completed in 1953 with 10 more stories, was at its time the largest concrete building in the world. Both were designed by the prolific if stolid Otamendi brothers, Joaquin and Julian, and at the time of writing (Aug 2010) the Edificio España—formerly a hotel—remains empty after its purchase by the Banco Santander in 2005.

Cross the square at its northwesterly corner and walk up Calle Ferraz to Calle de Ventura Rodriguez. Turn right into it, and on your right is the:

5 Museo Cerralbo

This highly personal 19th-century mansion/museum provides an intimate contrast with the grandeur of the Paseo del Prado's "Big Three." It contains the lifetime personal collection of former owner Enrique de Aguilera y Gamboa, the 17th Marquis of Cerralbo, who died in 1922. All is as he left it, from his Japanese armor collection to his Goya and Zurbarán masterpieces. The museum is at present undergoing renovation work and due to re-open its doors to the public in 2011. See p. 183.

Leaving the museum, turn left along Ventura Rodriguez and cross Calle Ferraz to look at the:

6 Templo de Debod

Situated at the far end of the Parque del Oeste, on the western edge of the city (beside the tiny Ferraz gardens), this remarkable 4th-century temple, built by the Pharaoh Zakheramon, was transferred stone by stone from Egypt, in thanks for help given by Spain in building the Aswan Dam. There are spectacular views west from the edge of the park of the Casa de Campo and distant Guadarrama Mountains.

Walking Tour 4: Gran Vía, Malasaña & Chueca

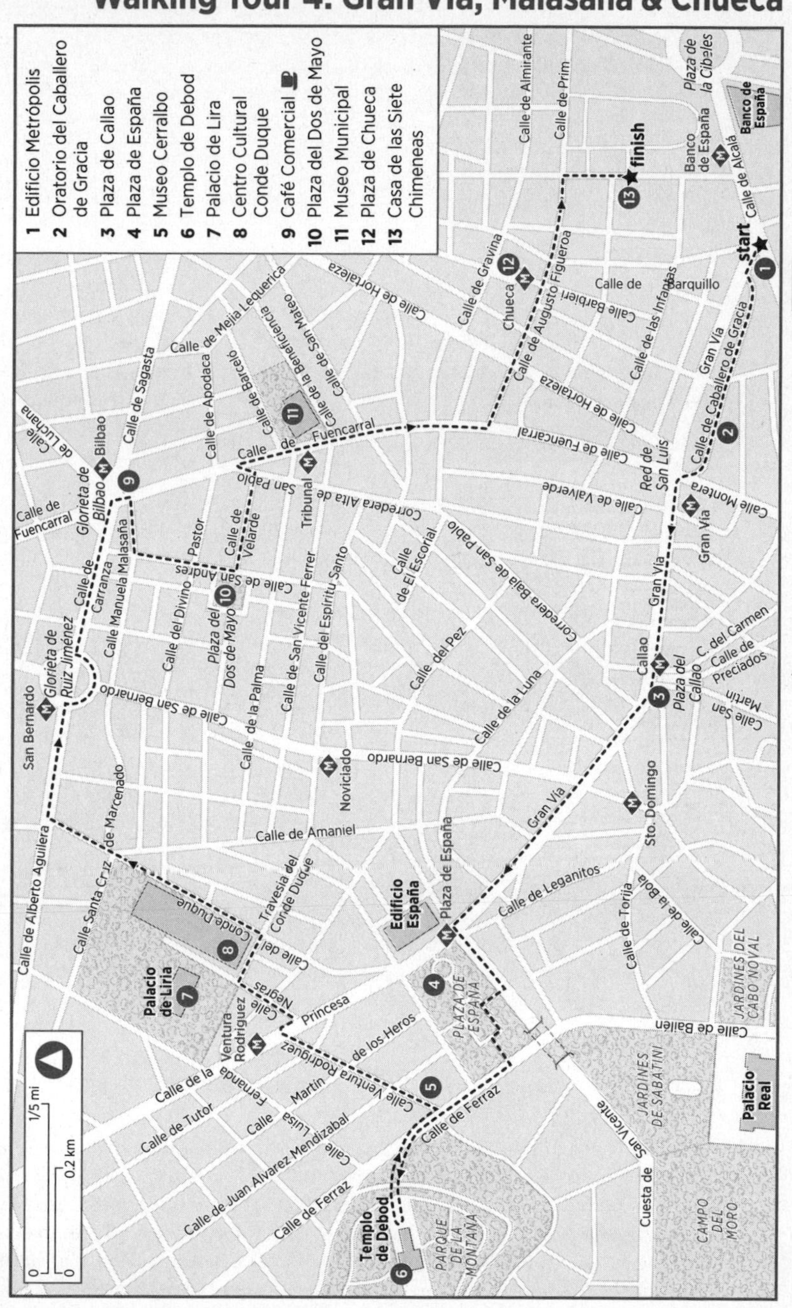

Return across Calle Ferraz and along Calle Ventura Rodriguez to reach Calle Princesa. Cross here to the:

7 Palacio de Liria

This marvelous neoclassical 18th-century palace can only be visited if you book in a group beforehand (write, call, or fax Princesa 20, Madrid; ✆ **91-547-53-02;** fax 91-541-03-77). The free tours take place each Friday at 10:45 and 11:30am, and 12:15pm. From outside, its gardens and imposing facade convey all the grandeur of an elegant bygone era. Formerly the private residence of the Duchess of Alba, its art collection includes paintings by Rembrandt, Rubens, and Goya.

Next take the lane to the right of the palace to join the Calle de Conde Duque, which leads to the:

8 Centro Cultural Conde Duque

Converted from a huge 18th-century barracks built for Felipe V's guards, complete with two spacious courtyards, this ambitious arts center provides around a dozen different exhibitions a year as well as concert performances and conferences. There's also a well-stocked video library.

Continue to the end of Calle Conde Duque and turn right (east) into Calle Alberto Aguilera, following the northern border of the Malasaña district. Cross the Glorieta de Ruíz Giménez roundabout and continue to the Glorieta de Bilbao.

9 The Café Comercial

Here's a chance to step back in time and sample what literary cafe life was like at the turn of the last century. The Café Comercial, Glorieta de Bilbao 7 (✆ 91-521-56-55), has dauntlessly clung to its age-old mood of unadorned—almost spartan—charm, where other establishments have yielded to crass developers. Its roomy interior, spare marble-topped tables, and painted iron pillars create a stimulatingly low-keyed aura. Coffee drinkers can spend hours uninterrupted here over their books, notepads, or thoughts, or exchange profound ideas on life with their companions. Along with the mellow—and, let's face it, snootier—Gijon in Recoletos, this place is a survivor from another age. (The only concession to modernity is the Internet cafe upstairs.)

Return into the Malasaña district by crossing Calle Fuencarral, which runs south, into the narrow Calle Mañuela Malasaña, named after the young woman who, so one story goes, was executed for carrying a dangerous weapon (namely scissors) by the occupying French forces during the Peninsula War. Turn left into Calle Andrés to reach another potent symbol of rebellion, the:

10 Plaza del Dos de Mayo

This small square, less impressive aesthetically than in its historical associations, celebrates the uprising of the populace against the French army on May 2, 1808. Formerly, it was the site of the Monteléon barracks, where captains Daoiz and Velarde launched their famed counterattack. Today a statue in their memory stands in the plaza, and the streets to the west and east of the square are named after them. An archway representing the main barracks gate stands next to the statue. The liveliest time here is during the San Isidro festivities in May, when concerts and outdoor parties are held. (Weekend *botellón* soirées, to which youngsters brought their own bottles of wine or spirits, mixed them with Coca-Cola, and lived it up till dawn, are still an occasional feature here, though officially banned.)

Head east from the square along Calle Velarde, and then turn right (south) into Calle Fuencarral. On your left after Calle Barceló is the:

11 Museo de Historia

Originally built as an 8th-century orphanage, this museum bears an ornate facade by Pedro de Ribera featuring San Fernando, patron saint of orphans. Inside is a vast array of maps, drawings, and photos of Madrid up to 1840. A major attraction is the superb large model of the entire city as laid out in 1833. The museum is currently closed for extensive refurbishment and scheduled to re-open in 2012. See p. 182.

Continue south down Calle Fuencarral and take the sixth street on your left, Calle Augusto Figueroa. Continue along this road across Calle Hortaleza. Two streets later you'll see Calle Barbieri on your right. Opposite this on your left is:

12 Plaza de Chueca

Dedicated to the zarzuela composer Federico Chueca, who died in 1908, this tiny square, with its surrounding 19th-century buildings, has evolved into the bustling epicenter of gay Madrid. In summer, the square is packed with as many cafe tables and raucous crowds as is humanly possible. Around the square, the Chueca district's intricate network of narrow lanes shelter what is probably the highest concentration of cafes, restaurants, bars, and clubs—some straight, most of them not—in the city. On weekends, the area barely sleeps. Not surprisingly, inhabitants of the apartments overlooking the square feel compelled to hang signs from their balconies pleading for a reduction in noise.

From here, return to Augusto Figueroa and turn left (east) till you reach Calle Barquillo. Turn right (south) and continue till you see on your right the:

13 Casa de las Siete Chimeneas

Built in 1585, The "House of the Seven Chimneys" achieved fame as the place where Charles I of England stayed in 1624 during a marriage-seeking visit to Madrid (in the end, his plan to wed the Infanta María was unsuccessful). Designed by Juan de Herrera, the Escorial architect, this superb Habsburg building is a surviving gem of Felipe II's regal Madrid, quietly set beside a charming plaza and topped by, of course, seven tall chimneys. Just a few minutes, yet a world away, from Plaza de Chueca.

SHOPPING IN MADRID

9

Seventeenth-century playwright Tirso de Molina called Madrid "a shop stocked with every kind of merchandise." That still holds true today, as an estimated 50,000 stores sell everything from high-fashion clothing to cheese and wine. The city hasn't totally sold out to colorless international franchises and still offers plenty of personal specialist shops—mainly around the Plaza Mayor and Puerta del Sol—selling a single product like fans, capes, espadrilles, or flamenco guitars. That said, chains like the Corte Inglés and FNAC have plenty in their favor, and if you're in a hurry, you could find just what you're looking for in one of their well-stocked central branches.

THE SHOPPING SCENE

Shopping Neighborhoods

THE CENTER The sheer diversity of shops in Madrid's center is staggering. Their densest concentration lies immediately north of the Puerta del Sol, radiating out from Calle del Carmen, Calle Montera, and Calle Preciados.

CALLE MAYOR & CALLE DEL ARENAL Unlike their more stylish neighbors to the north of Puerta del Sol, shops in this district to the west tend toward the small, slightly dusty enclaves of coin and stamp dealers, family-owned souvenir shops, clockmakers, military paraphernalia, and an abundance of stores selling musical scores.

GRAN VÍA Conceived, designed, and built in the 1910s and 1920s as a showcase for the city's best shops, hotels, and restaurants, the Gran Vía has since been eclipsed by other shopping districts. Its Art Nouveau/Art Deco glamour still survives in the hearts of most Madrileños, however. The bookstores here are among the best in the city, as are outlets for fashion, shoes, jewelry, furs, and handcrafted accessories from all regions of Spain.

EL RASTRO It's the biggest and most frenetic flea market in Spain, and its makeshift stalls draw collectors, dealers, buyers, and hopefuls from throughout Madrid and its suburbs every Sunday morning. For more information, refer to the "Flea Markets" section under "Shopping A to Z," below.

PLAZA MAYOR Under the arcades of the square itself are exhibitions of lithographs and oil paintings, and every weekend there's a loosely organized market for stamp and coin collectors. Within 3 or 4 blocks in every direction, you'll find more than the average number of souvenir shops.

On Calle Marqués Viudo de Pontejos, which runs east from Plaza Mayor, is one of the city's headquarters for the sale of cloth, thread, and buttons. Also running east, on Calle de Zaragoza, are silversmiths and jewelers. On Calle Postas, you'll find housewares, underwear, soap powders, and other household items.

NEAR THE CARRERA DE SAN JERÓNIMO Several blocks east of Puerta del Sol is Madrid's densest concentration of gift shops, crafts shops, and antiques dealers—a decorator's delight. Its most interesting streets include Calle del Prado, Calle de las Huertas, and Plaza de las Cortes. The neighborhood is pricey, so don't expect bargains here.

NORTHWEST MADRID A few blocks east of Parque del Oeste is this upscale neighborhood well stocked with luxury goods and household staples. Calle de la Princesa, its main thoroughfare, has shops selling shoes, handbags, fashion, gifts, and children's clothing. Thanks to the presence of the university nearby, there's also a dense concentration of bookstores, especially on Calle Isaac Peral and Calle Fernando el Católico, several blocks north and northwest, respectively, from the subway stop of Argüelles.

SALAMANCA DISTRICT This district is known throughout Spain as the quintessential upper-bourgeois neighborhood, with correspondingly exclusive shops. These include outlets run by interior decorators, furniture shops, fur and jewelry shops, several department stores, and design headquarters whose output ranges from the solidly conservative to the high tech. The main streets of this district are Calle de Serrano and Calle de Velázquez. The district lies northeast of the center of Madrid, a few blocks north of Parque del Retiro. Its most central metro stops are Serrano and Velázquez.

Hours

Major stores are open (in most cases) Monday to Saturday from 9:30am to 8pm. Many small stores take a siesta between 1:30 and 4:30pm. Of course, there is never any set formula, and hours can vary greatly from store to store, depending on the idiosyncrasies and schedules of the owner.

Shipping

Many art and antiques dealers will crate and ship bulky objects for an additional fee. Whereas it usually pays to have heavy objects shipped by sea, in some cases it's almost the same price to ship crated goods by airplane. Of course, it depends on the distance your crate will have to travel over land to the nearest international port, which, in many cases for the purposes of relatively small-scale shipments by individual clients, is Barcelona. Consequently, it might pay to call two branches of **UPS SCS** (UPS Supply Chain Solutions; www.ups-scs.com) from within Spain to explain your particular situation, and receive comparable rates. For information about sea transit for your valuables, call UPS SCS at their only Spanish branch, in Barcelona (© **93-478-81-86**). For information about **UPS Air Freight,** call the main Spanish office in Madrid (© **91-329-11-93**) for advice on any of the dozen air-freight pickup stations they maintain throughout Spain. These include, among many others, Barcelona, Alicante, Málaga, Bilbao, and Valencia. For more advice on this, and the formalities that you'll go through in clearing customs after the arrival of your shipment in your home country, contact the nearest local office via the online directory at **http://ups-scs.service.com/ups-scs/directory/index.htm**.

For most small- and medium-size shipments, air freight isn't much more expensive than ocean shipping. **Iberia**'s **Air Cargo Division** (✆ **800/221-6002** in the U.S.; www.iberia-cargo.com) offers air-freight service from Spain to New York, Chicago, Miami, or Los Angeles, as well as the United Kingdom and western Canada. What will you pay for this transport of your treasured art objects or freight? Here's a rule of thumb: For a shipment under 100 kilograms (220 lb.), from either Barcelona or Madrid to New York, the cost is approximately 4.40€ per pound. The per-pound price goes down as the weight of the shipment increases, declining to, for example, 1.50€ per pound for shipments of more than 1,000 kilograms (2,200 lb.). Regardless of what you ship, a minimum charge is enforced.

For an additional fee, Iberia or one of its representatives will also pick up your package. For truly precious cargo, ask the seller to build a crate for it. For information within Spain about air-cargo shipments, call Iberia's cargo division at Madrid's Barajas Airport (✆ **90-111-14-00**) or at Barcelona's airport (✆ **93-401-31-90**).

Remember that your air-cargo shipment will need to clear Customs after it's brought into your home country. This involves some additional paperwork, costly delays, and in some cases a trip to the airport where the shipment first entered the country. It's usually easier (and in some cases, much easier) to hire a commercial customs broker to do the work for you. **UPS SCS** can clear most shipments of goods for around $150, which you'll pay in addition to any applicable duty you owe your home government. For information, go online to **www.ups-scs.com/international/customs_broker.html**.

Tax & How to Recover It

If you are not a European Union resident and you make purchases in Spain worth more than 90€, you can get a tax refund. (The internal tax, known as VAT in most of Europe, is called IVA in Spain.) Depending on the goods, the rate usually ranges from 7% to 16% of the total worth of your merchandise. Luxury items are taxed at 33%.

To get this refund, you must complete three copies of a form that the store will give you, detailing the nature of your purchase and its value. Citizens of non-E.U. countries show the purchase and the form to the **Global Refund Office,** Terminal 1, Departure Gate A, Madrid-Barajas Airport (www.globalrefund.com).

The shop is supposed to refund the amount due you. Inquire at the time of purchase how they will do so and discuss in what currency your refund will arrive.

When the Weather & the Sales Are Hot!

The best sales are usually in summer. Called *rebajas,* they start in July and go through August. As a general rule, merchandise is marked down even more in August to make way for the new fall wares in most stores.

Bargaining

The days of bargaining are, for the most part, long gone. Most stores have what is called *precio de venta al público* (PVP), a firm retail price not subject to negotiation. With street vendors and flea markets, it's a different story because haggling *a la española* is expected. However, you'll have to be very skilled to get the price reduced a lot, as most of these street-smart vendors know exactly what their merchandise is worth and are old hands at getting that price.

SHOPPING A TO Z

Spain has always been known for its craftspeople, many still working in the time-honored and labor-intensive traditions of their grandparents. It's hard to go wrong if you stick to the beautiful handcrafted Spanish objects—hand-painted tiles, ceramics, and porcelain; hand-woven rugs; handmade sweaters; and intricate embroideries. And, of course, Spain produces some of the world's finest leather. Jewelry, especially gold set with Majorca pearls, represents good value and unquestioned luxury.

Some of Madrid's art galleries are known throughout Europe for discovering and encouraging new talent. Antiques are sold in highly sophisticated retail outlets. Better suited to the budgets of many travelers are the weekly flea markets.

Spain continues to make inroads into the fashion world. Its young designers are regularly featured in the fashion magazines of Europe. Excellent shoes are available, some highly fashionable. But American readers, be advised that prices for shoes and quality clothing are generally higher in Madrid than in the United States.

Antiques

The biggest concentration of antiques shops is Ribera de Curtidores, where the Sunday Rastro market is located (p. 227). You'll find a widespread choice in the prestigious Salamanca district, especially on Lagasca and Jorge Juan streets.

Centro de Anticuarios Lagasca You'll find about a dozen antiques shops here, clustered into one covered arcade. Though they operate as individual businesses, by browsing through each, you'll find an impressive assemblage of antique furniture, porcelain, and whatnots. Open Monday to Saturday from 10am to 1:30pm and 5 to 8pm. Lagasca 36. ✆ **91-577-37-52.** Metro: Serrano or Velázquez.

Galerías Piquer This huge arcade of new shops selling old things is set on the same street as the Rastro and has an equally varied choice of antiques and knick-knacks. It's all a bit neater and tidier, and, for some, lacks the full-blooded exhilaration of the gritty street market itself. Certainly worth a look, however, as the locales total up to 70 and you're bound to find something you like. The gallery opens Monday to Friday 10:30am to 2pm and 5 to 8pm, Saturday and Sunday 10:30am to 2pm. Times vary from shop to shop, so check the website. Ribera de Curtidores 29 (local 40). No phone. www.dai.es/piquer. Metro: Puerta de Toledo or La Latina. Bus: 17, 18, 23, 35, or 60.

Mercado Puerta de Toledo This deluxe selection of antique locales is located amid a conglomeration of 60-odd shops at the Puerta de Toledo, a short stroll from Ribera de Curtidores. Great places to look for quality vintage brass and ceramic goods. Open Tuesday to Saturday 10:30am to 9pm, Sunday 10:30am to 2:30pm. Ronda de Toledo 1. ✆ **91-366-72-00.** www.centropuertadetoledo.com. Metro: Puerta de Toledo.

Art Galleries

The widest selection of art galleries can be found in a trio of streets located in three separate and atmospherically different districts of Madrid: **Calle Claudio Coello,** in swanky Salamanca (which has the most galleries); **Calle Orfila,** in sedate Chamberí; and **Calle Almirante,** in bohemian Chueca. You'll also find a few near the Reina Sofía.

Estiarte This 30-odd-year-old gallery is the place to go for first-rate graphic art. Maz Ernst and Picasso are among past luminaries who've been represented here. Open Monday to Friday 10:30am to 2pm and 4:30 to 8:30pm, Saturday 10am to 2pm. Almagro 44. ✆ **91-308-15-69.** www.estiarte.com. Metro: Ruben Darío.

Galería Juana de Aizpuru This renowned Chueca gallery exhibits mainly vanguard and avant-garde art and sculptures by local and international artists such as Alex García Rodero and William Wegman. Open Monday 4:30 to 8:30pm, Tuesday to Saturday 10:30am to 2pm and 4:30 to 8:30pm. Closed in August. Barquillo 44. ✆ **91-310-55-61.** www.juanadeaizpuru.es. Metro: Chueca.

Galería Kreisler One successful entrepreneur on Madrid's art scene is Ohio-born Edward Kreisler, whose gallery, now run by his son Juan, specializes in figurative and contemporary paintings, sculptures, and graphics. The gallery prides itself on occasionally displaying and selling the works of artists who are critically acclaimed and displayed in museums in Spain. Open Monday to Saturday from 10:30am to 2pm. Closed in August. Hermosilla 8. ✆ **91-576-16-62.** Metro: Serrano. Bus: 27, 45, or 150.

Galería Marlborough Set on a stylish Chamberí street, this deceptively spacious gallery was designed by stateside architect Richard Gluckman. International artists from David Hockney to Luis Gordillo are regularly represented, and the gallery has branches in New York, London, and Monte Carlo. Open Monday to Saturday 11am to 2pm and 4:30 to 8:30pm. Orfila 5. ✆ **91-319-14-14.** www.galeriamarlborough.com. Metro: Alonso Martínez. Bus: 7, 40, or 147.

Galería Oliva Arauna The main focus of this gallery is sculpture, with a strong interest in photography and video. Samples of these three art forms are regularly represented in Arco and PhotoEspaña exhibitions. Open Monday to Saturday 10:30am to 2pm and 4:30 to 8:30pm. Closed afternoons in summer and the month of August. Barquillo 29. ✆ **91-435-18-08.** www.olivarauna.com. Metro: Chueca. Bus: 2, 19, 20, 21, 28, 53, or 146.

Galería Soledad Lorenzo This bright and spacious Chamberí gallery features works by top-notch contemporary Spanish painters such as Tàpies and Miguel Barceló. Open Monday 4:30 to 8:30pm, Tuesday to Saturday 11am to 2pm and 4:30 to 8:30pm (closed evenings mid-June to mid-Sept). Orfila 5. ✆ **91-308-28-87.** www.soledadlorenzo.com. Metro: Alonso Martinez.

Guillermo de Osma For lovers of early-20th-century avant-garde art created by artists ranging from Kandinsky to Klee, this discreet little gallery, tucked away on the first floor of an elegant Salamanca building, is a good place to look. At least three interesting shows are held each year. Open Monday to Friday 10am to 2pm and 4:30 to 8:30pm, Saturday from noon to 2pm. Claudio Coello 4–1° izda. ✆ **91-435-59-36.** www.guillermodeosma.com. Metro: Retiro. Bus: 2, 19, 20, 21, 28, 53, or 146.

Books

Booksellers This is a long-established bookshop with a very good choice of English-language books, from the latest U.K. and U.S. novels to travel, history, and teaching material. Plenty of children's literature and English-language DVDs and videos are available, plus a wide Spanish selection of fact and fiction. Open Monday to Friday 9:30am to 2pm and 5 to 8:30pm, Saturday 10:30am to 2:30pm. Fernandez de la Hoz 40. ✆ **91-442-79-59.** Metro: Gregorio Marañón.

Bookworld Stocked with an eclectic range of English-language books that amply covers fiction, history, travel, and biography, this is the newest member of Madrid's international bookshop scene. The shop is located in the heart of the Salamanca district, close to the Corte Inglés store, and is owned by a company that already has a long-established chain of bookshops in Málaga and Alicante coastal resorts. It has access to the very latest English-language publications, so if you don't see the book you want, they'll order it for you. Open in winter Monday to Saturday 10am to 8pm; summer Monday to Friday 10am to 2:30pm and 4:30 to 9pm, Saturday 11am to 7pm. Calle Goya 56, esq. Francisca Moreno. ✆ **91-578-23-16.** www.bookworldespana.com. Metro: Goya.

Casa del Libro By far the most comprehensive bookshop in Madrid, the three-story Casa del Libro is conveniently positioned right in the center of the Gran Vía. The basement offers a great selection of dictionaries and grammar books, while a ground-floor alcove has an up-to-date selection of English-language literature (alongside current French, German, Italian, and Portuguese tomes). The first floor houses a well-stocked international travel section with plenty of books on Madrid. Open Monday to Saturday from 9:30am to 9:30pm and Sunday from 11am to 9pm. Gran Vía 29. ✆ **90-202-64-02.** www.casadellibro.com. Metro: Gran Vía. Bus: 1, 2, 46, 74, 146, or 149.

Cuesta de Moyano A sort of smaller literary Rastro, this collection of wooden bookstalls and *kioskos* climbs a pedestrian street from the Atocha end of the Paseo del Prado—alongside the railings of the Botanical Gardens—right up to the southwestern corner of Parque del Retiro. A statue of 19th-century novelist Pío Baroja stands at the top. Practically all the books are secondhand and in Spanish, but whether you read Castilian or not, it's great fun to wander, browse, and simply absorb the scene, unchanged over many decades and one of the great traditional sights of outdoor Madrid. Most stalls are open daily from 10am to 7pm; Sunday mornings are the liveliest time. Claudio Moyano. No phone. Metro: Atocha. Bus: 6, 10, 14, 26, 27, 32, 34, 37, or 45.

Deviaje A top-notch travel book shop with a world-wide selection that includes many books in English. The informed and helpful staff will point you in the right direction, whatever far-off section of the world you want to read up on. Also has a good choice of maps. Serrano 41. ✆ **91-577-98-99.** www.deviaje.com. Metro: Ruben Darío or Serrano.

J & J Books and Coffee This friendly English-language *librería* is one of the best places to find secondhand book bargains. It's named after American husband-and-wife team Jamie and Javi, who wanted to create a meeting place for English-speaking residents and visitors as well as a comprehensive bookshop. A genial cafe sits on the ground floor, while the basement contains over 15,000 books ranging from horror stories to the classics. They also rent DVDs. Wednesdays and Thursdays are *intercambio* language evenings—when you get a chance to try out your Spanish with locals—and other social events include a Friday quiz night. Along with coffee, they serve cracking cocktails (their long "happy hour" is 4 to 7pm on weekdays, when you get two-for-one drinks). Open Monday to Thursday 11am to midnight, Friday and Saturday 11am to 2am, and Sunday 2 to 10pm. Espíritu Santo 47. ✆ **91-521-85-76.** www.jandjbooksandcoffee.com. Metro: Noviciado. Bus: 147.

La Tienda Verde This establishment consists of not one but two highly individual shops in the same Cuatro Caminos district street and offers a compact but comprehensive selection of travel, ecology, and nature books and maps, with a particular focus on Spain. An invaluable source of information for hikers, walkers, and mountaineers, its stock is almost entirely in Spanish. Open Monday to Friday 9:30am to 2pm and 5 to 8:30pm, Saturday till 8pm. Maudes 23 (books) and 38 (maps). ✆ **91-535-38-10.** www.tiendaverde.es. Metro: Cuatro Caminos. Bus: C (circular route).

Pasajes This first-rate Chamberí bookshop is on two levels and boasts an international stock that includes English-language fiction, nonfiction, children's books, and videos, as well as a wide variety of books in French, German, Italian, Portuguese, and Russian. Open Monday to Friday 10am to 2pm and 5 to 8pm, and Saturday 10am to 2pm. Génova 3. ✆ **91-310-12-45.** www.pasajeslibros.com. Metro: Alonso Martínez. Bus: 3, 7, 21, 40, or 147.

Petra's International Bookshop This small but cavernous shop extends back from a narrow street between Opera and the Gran Vía. It has a very comprehensive choice of both new and secondhand English-language books, as well as books in a variety of other languages. Here you can trade as well as buy. There's also a notice board and a regular coming and going of international visitors. Open Monday to Friday 11am to 2:30pm and 4:30 to 9pm, Saturday 11am to 2pm. Campomanes 13. ✆ **91-541-72-91.** Metro: Opera or Santo Domingo. Bus: 44, 133, or 147.

Capes

Capas Seseña Founded shortly after the turn of the 20th century, this shop manufactures and sells wool capes for women and men alike. The wool comes from the mountain town of Béjar, near Salamanca. Celebrities who have been spotted over the years donning Seseña capes include Picasso, Hemingway, and Hillary and Chelsea Clinton. Open Monday through Friday from 10am to 2pm and 4:30 to 8pm, Saturday from 10am to 2pm. Cruz 23. ✆ **91-531-68-40.** www.sesena.com. Metro: Sevilla or Sol. Bus: 5, 39, 51, or 52.

Carpets

Ispahan In this 19th-century building, behind bronze handmade doors, are three floors devoted to carpets from around the world, notably Afghanistan, India, Nepal, Iran, Turkey, and the Caucasus. One section features silk carpets. It's open Monday through Saturday from 10am to 2pm and 4:30 to 8pm. Serrano 5. ✆ **91-575-20-12.** Metro: Retiro. Bus: 1, 2, 9, 15, or 19.

Ceramics

Antigua Casa Talavera "The first house of Spanish ceramics" has wares that include a sampling of regional styles from every major area of Spain, including Talavera, Toledo, Manises, Valencia, Puente del Arzobispo, Alcora, Granada, and Seville. Sangria pitchers, dinnerware, tea sets, plates, and vases are all handmade. Inside one of the showrooms is an interesting selection of tiles, painted with reproductions of scenes from bullfights, dances, and folklore. A series of tiles also depicts famous paintings in the Prado. At its present location since 1904, the shop is only a short walk from Plaza de Santo Domingo. Open Monday to Friday from 10am to 1:30pm and 5 to 8pm, Saturday from 10am to 1:30pm. Isabel la Católica 2. ✆ **91-547-34-17.** Metro: Santo Domingo. Bus: 1, 2, 46, 70, 75, or 148.

Crafts

El Arco de los Cuchilleros Artesanía de Hoy Set within one of the 17th-century vaulted cellars of Plaza Mayor, this shop is entirely devoted to unusual craft items from throughout Spain. The merchandise is one of a kind and in most cases contemporary; it includes a changing array of pottery, leather, textiles, woodcarvings, glassware, wickerwork, papier-mâché, and silver jewelry. The hardworking owners deal directly with the artisans who produce each item, ensuring a wide inventory of handicrafts. The staff is familiar with the rituals of applying for tax-free status of purchases here, and speaks several different languages. Open January to September, Monday to Saturday from 11am to 8pm; October to December, Monday to Saturday from 11am to 9pm. Plaza Mayor 9 (basement level). ✆ **91-365-26-80.** www.elarcoartesania.com. Metro: Sol or Opera. Bus: 3 or 50.

Department Stores

El Corte Inglés This flagship of the largest department-store chain in Spain, which has several branches in all the major cities, sells hundreds of souvenirs and Spanish handicrafts, such as damascene steelwork from Toledo, flamenco dolls, and embroidered shawls. Some astute buyers report that it also sells glamorous fashion articles, such as Pierre Balmain designs, for about a third less than equivalent items in most European capitals. Services include interpreters, currency-exchange windows, and parcel delivery either to a local hotel or overseas. Open Monday to Saturday from 10am to 10pm. Some stores open Sunday noon to 8pm. Preciados 3. ✆ **91-379-80-00.** www.elcorteingles.es. Metro: Sol. Bus: 5, 15, 20, 39, 51, 52, or 53.

FNAC Located in the bustling pedestrian zone between Puerta del Sol and the Gran Vía, this multistory French store provides a wealth of media fare, from a multilingual book section with everything from current bestsellers to travel and history to a huge stock of DVDs and CDs (on the second floor there's a section where you can sit and listen before you buy). On the ground floor are a travel agency, cafeteria, and newsagents with a choice of international periodicals. Open Monday to Saturday from 10am to 9:30pm, Sunday noon to 9:30pm. Preciados 28. ✆ **91-595-61-00.** www.fnac.es. Metro: Callao. Bus: 44, 46, 75, 143, 146, 147, 148, or 149.

Embroidery

Casa Bonet The intricately detailed embroideries produced in Spain's Balearic Islands (especially Majorca) are avidly sought for bridal chests and elegant dinner settings. A few examples of the store's extensive inventory are displayed on the walls. Open Monday to Friday from 10:45am to 2pm and 5 to 8pm, Saturday from 10:15am to 2pm. Núñez de Balboa 76. ✆ **91-575-09-12.** Metro: Núñez de Balboa. Bus: 1 or 74.

Espadrilles

Casa Hernanz A short stroll south of Plaza Mayor, this store has been in business since the 1840s. In addition to rope-soled espadrilles (*alpargatas* in Spanish), they sell shoes in other styles, as well as hats. Open Monday to Friday from 9am to 1:30pm and 4:30 to 8pm, Saturday from 10am to 2pm. Toledo 18–20. ✆ **91-366-54-50.** Metro: La Latina. Bus: 17, 18, 23, 35, or 60.

Fans & Umbrellas

Casa de Diego Here you'll find a wide inventory of fans, ranging from plain to fancy, plastic to exotic hardwood, and cost-conscious to lavish. Some fans tend to be a bit overpriced; shopping around may increase your chances of finding a real bargain. Open year-round, Monday to Saturday from 9:45am to 8pm. Puerta del Sol 12. ✆ **91-522-66-43.** www.casadediego.net. Metro: Sol. Bus: 5, 15, 20, 51, 52, 53, or 150. Second location at Mesoneros Romanos 4. ✆ 91-531-02-23. Metro: Callao.

Fashions for Men

For the man on a budget who wants to dress reasonably well, the best outlet for off-the-rack men's clothing is one of the branches of the Corte Inglés department-store chain (see above). Most men's boutiques in Madrid are very expensive and may not be worth the investment. Note also that many of the stores in the "Fashions for Women" section below also feature a men's line.

Fashions for Women

Adolfo Domínguez This controversial Gallego designer from Orense has created a cool, laid-back style of clothing that caters to both sexes. Though too spare (verging on austere) for some tastes, its no-frills style and impressive cost-to-value ratio appeal greatly to others. Snazzier shoes and a sports range aimed at younger buyers are also

THE ZARAVOLUCIÓN

Many visitors to Spain are already familiar with the **Zara** clothing label. Now with over 1,000 (2,500, counting the Zara offshoot brands) outlets in 70 countries, including megastores in the fashion capitals of Milan, Paris, London, and New York, Zara is hard to ignore. But many are not aware and may be surprised to know that Zara is Spanish-owned.

Zara was started back in the early '70s by an industrious young Galician by the name of Amancio Ortega, now the richest man in Spain. He saw a necessity for stylish housecoats for the women in his rural village, and out of that an empire grew, starting with his very first shop in the Galician port-town of La Coruña in 1975. Today, Zara is one of the few fashion empires in the world that vertically controls the entire process, from textile manufacture to design to retail. Using a global network of buyers and trend-spotters, they interpret (many within the industry use the word "plagiarize") hot-off-the-catwalk pieces for men, women, and children at astoundingly affordable prices. They appeal to the full cross-generational demographic gamut, from urban tribes to executives. Zara's calendar doesn't just consist of four seasons; they produce and distribute clothing all year round in their behemoth headquarters in Ortega's native Galicia and Zaragoza. New, never-to-be-repeated models arrive every day, meaning converts return again and again and again.

A revolution needs a charismatic leader, and Ortega is no exception. Until he took the company public in 2001, the press possessed only one photo of a man estimated to be worth $10.3 billion. He imposes a strict "no-press" policy to his staff and never gives interviews. He never accepts any of the dozens of accolades awarded to him in person. What he has done is, in less than a generation, democratized fashion and made it possible to dress like a film star for a song.

available. Open Monday to Saturday 10:15am to 2pm and 5 to 8:30pm. There's another location at Serrano 18 (✆ **91-577-82-80;** www.adolfodominguezshop.com; Metro: Serrano). Ortega y Gasset 4. ✆ **91-576-00-84.** Metro: Núñez de Balboa. Bus: 1or 74.

Agatha Ruiz de la Prada A former leading light of the dynamic *movida* period of the late '80s, Agatha Ruiz de la Prada faded in popularity and then made a resurgence a decade ago in the ground floor of this Chamberí building built by her grandfather. Here you'll find the full gamut of her latest bright, accessible, easy-to-wear clothing. Children's and men's clothes are also made to order. Open Monday to Friday 10am to 2pm and 5 to 8pm. During the month of August, it also opens Saturdays from 10am to 2pm and 5 to 8pm. A second location (Serrano 27; Metro: Serrano) shares the same phone number. Marqués de Riscal 8. ✆ **91-319-05-01.** www.agatharuizdelaprada.com. Metro: Rubén Darío. Bus: 7, 40, or 147.

Sybilla The fashionistas of Madrid are buzzing with excitement over the clothes displayed in the tiny atelier here. Fashion critics have hailed Sybilla's clothing as "wearable, whimsical, and inevitably original." Everything is stylish. Habitués of the Goya ceremonies (Spain's answer to the Oscars) are often seen wearing top gear from here. The outlet also sells articles for the home, such as sheets, towels, and dishes. Open Monday through Friday from 10am to 2pm and 4 to 8:30pm, Saturday from 11am to 3pm and 5 to 8:30pm. Gran Vía 43. ✆ **91-547-12-39.** www.sybilla.es. Metro: Callao. Bus: 46, 74, 75, 133, 146, 147, or 150. Second branch at Callejón de Jorge Juan 14. ✆ 91-578-13-22. Metro: Retiro.

Zara One of Spain's top fashion shops, the Galician-run Zara offers stylish outfits at very reasonable prices. Apart from up-to-the-minute trendy clothes, Zara also provides quality suits and conventional office working gear. It's very popular, especially on Saturdays. Monday to Saturday open from 10am to 8:30pm. Princesa 45. ✆ **91-541-09-02.** www.zara.com. Metro: Argüelles. Bus: 1, 2, 44, 74, 133, or C (circular route).

Flea Markets

El Rastro Foremost among markets is the Sunday morning El Rastro (translated as either flea market or thieves' market), occupying a roughly triangular district of streets and plazas a few minutes' walk south of Plaza Mayor. Its center is Plaza Cascorro and Ribera de Curtidores. This market will delight anyone attracted to a mishmash of fascinating junk interspersed with bric-a-brac and paintings. ***Note:*** Thieves are rampant here (hustling more than just antiques), so secure your wallet carefully, be alert, and proceed with caution. Insofar as scheduling your visit to El Rastro, bear in mind that this is a flea market involving hundreds of merchants who basically pull up their display tables and depart whenever their goods are sold or they get fed up with the crowds. Sunday only. Opens at 9am (an hour earlier in summer), and winds down around 3pm. Metro: La Latina. Bus: 17, 18, 23, 35, or 60.

Food & Wine

Capperi Occupying the same premises as the former Al Dente, this pasta-oriented deli, also Italian run, offers a magnificent selection of gnocchi, lasagna, tagliatelle, spaghetti, fusilli, and the like. Some versions are deliciously stuffed with salmon, asparagus, or ricotta and spinach. Rich sauces and a fine selection of Italian olive oils, balsamic vinegars, and cheeses are also available, while the wines range from Valpolicellas to the lesser known Gattinaras and Ghemmes. You can also choose from a hearty range of grappas. Fernando VI 2. ✆ **91-308-17-74.** www.capperi.es. Metro: Alonso Martínez or Chueca. Bus: 3, 7, 21, 40, or 147.

González Quietly concealed in a character-filled Huertas street, this charming deli-cum-wine bar sells excellent cheeses and hams. Vintage wines by the glass or bottle are poured at the bar or in the cozily unpretentious inner salon, where discreet movie posters and stills bedeck the walls. Open Tuesday to Saturday 10:30am to 3pm, 7pm to midnight. León 12. ✆ **91-429-56-18.** Metro: Antón Martín. Bus: 6, 26, or 32.

Hespen & Suárez Kay Hespen and her husband, José Suárez, run this stylish deli, which may well remind you of New York, where Kay was a marketing expert and José was head chef at Plácido Domingo's restaurant. Products on its shelves range from Lebanese coffee and tandoori pasta to Japanese noodles. Their own products include bagels and take-away minestrone; and if you want to eat on the spot, you can sample their modest 10€ lunch menu, consisting of two courses plus a dessert (wine not included), or just enjoy a coffee and cake at the bar. Open Monday to Friday 8:30am to 10pm, weekends and fiestas 10am to 10pm. Barceló 15. ✆ **91-445-39-03.** Metro: Chueca. Bus 3, 40, or 149.

Isolée You can buy and take away worldwide fare ranging from sushi to mole from this chic deli/cafe-cum-fashion shop. You can also sample Isolée's very own innovative ChocolaTé (chocolate and tea!), sip a glass of Moët et Chandon in the Bubble Lounge, or enjoy a Parma ham ciapatta or healthy duck pâté with mango and spinach salad at the bar. The decor is a minimalist blend of pearl whites, pale grays, and blacks with bare wooden polished floorboards throughout; and in the small fashion section you can buy cool items such as Carlo Moretti glassware, Comme des Garçons perfumes, and Mihara Yasuhiro sneakers. Open Monday to Thursday 10:30am to 10pm, Friday and Saturday 10:30am to 8:30pm, and Sunday 4 to 10pm. Calle Infantas 19. ✆ **90-287-61-36.** www.isolee.com. Metro: Chueca. Bus 3, 40, or 149.

Lavinia If you can't find the wine you want here, you won't find it anywhere. Lavinia claims to be not only the largest wine shop in Madrid but also in the whole of Europe. Certainly it's big, and its two floors of racked *vinos* run the full range from to Tokai to Tío Pepe. Smart, bright, and ultramodern, it's light years away from the traditional concept of musty-barrel-lined bodegas, and the savvy multilingual staff complement it perfectly. Open Monday to Saturday 10am to 9pm. Ortega y Gasset 16. ✆ **91-426-06-04.** www.lavinia.es. Metro: Núñez de Balboa. Bus: 1 or 74.

Mallorca Madrid's best-established gourmet shop opened in 1931 as an outlet selling a pastry called *ensaimada,* and this is still one of the store's most famous products. Tempting arrays of cheeses, canapés, roasted and marinated meats, sausages, and about a dozen kinds of pâté accompany a spread of tiny pastries, tarts, and chocolates. Don't overlook the displays of Spanish wines and brandies. A stand-up tapas bar is always clogged with clients three-deep, sampling the wares before they buy larger portions to take home. Tapas cost from 2€ to 3.50€. Open daily from 9:30am to 9:30pm. Velázquez 59. ✆ **91-431-99-09.** www.pasteleria-mallorca.com. Metro: Velázquez. Bus: 1, 9, 19, 51, 74, or 89. There are nine other branches throughout the city center and surrounding suburbs.

Taste of America Set in the leafy residential northern part of the city at the end of Calle Serrano, Taste of America offers a wealth of stateside specialties including pretzels, fudge brownies, candy, and Newman's Own sauces. Additional Anglo-Saxon goodies on sale include marmite, Coleman's mustard, and cheddar cheese. Open Monday to Saturday 10am to 2pm and 4 to 8pm. Serrano 149. ✆ **91-411-46-42.**

www.tasteofamerica.es. Metro: República Argentina. Bus: 16, 19, or 51. There is a newer second branch in the northwesterly suburb of Pozuelo de Alarcón at Av. de Europa 23. ✆ **91-351-96-56**. Metro: Ligero Line 2: Avenida de Europa stop.

Food Markets

While on the booming outskirts of the city, and in nearby satellite towns such as Las Rozas and Madahonda, American-style malls and other modern commercial centers may be sprouting up at an alarming rate and superseding the traditional covered market, the latter still reigns supreme in the heart of Madrid. Vibrantly alive and brimming with atmosphere, with its goodies and kaleidoscope of colors it still survives as an indelible reminder of old Spain. As such, it's well worth taking a stroll around one whether you buy anything or not. Just to reassure yourself that some things never change, here are five prime examples.

Antón Martín This is one of the friendliest, and surprisingly least-known, of the traditional Madrileño markets, with two floors serving every conceivable kind of produce from Spain and farther afield. Adjoining street stalls sell a tantalizing variety of fish and smoked products. Calle Santa Isabel 5 (near Cine Doré). Metro: Antón Martín.

Chamartín A close rival to La Paz in the chic market stakes is residential Chamartín's traditional two-story food emporium. Noted for its small but immaculate fresh fish selection and marvelous range of olive oils and sauces, it also boasts an impressive range of quality meats, fruits, and vegetables. Bolivia 9. ✆ **91-457-53-50.** Metro: Colombia. Bus: 7, 16, 29, or 51.

La Cebada In spite of its ugly functional outward appearance, this La Latina landmark, right on the edge of the historic Plaza de la Cebada, is a bustling old-style market with an attractive variety of produce spread over two spacious levels. Plaza de la Cebada. ✆ **91-365-91-76.** Metro: La Latina. Bus: 60.

La Paz The neatest and most stylish market in Madrid, and possibly all of Spain, La Paz is located on the western edge of fashionable Salamanca. Pride of place goes to its charcuterie counters, but everything is top quality, hyperclean, and served with attentive professionalism. The classic cheese stall La Boulette boasts over 200 international cheeses. Ayala 28. ✆ **91-435-07-43.** Metro: Serrano. Bus: 1, 74, or 89.

Maravillas Situated between the northwesterly districts of Cuatro Caminos and Tetuan, this is the biggest of Madrid's old-style markets: noisier, grittier, more Rabelaisean than the previous two. Its choice of fish is the largest and most varied in the capital. Bargain-priced bar counters offer you as fine a coffee as you'll taste in the Ritz. Bravo Murillo 122. ✆ **91-533-40-30.** Metro: Alvarado. Bus: 3, 64, 66, 124, or 127.

San Miguel An exception to the above quintet, presumably representing a "market of the future," is the immaculately refurbished San Miguel, which re-opened in 2009. This Industrial Revolution wrought-iron-and-glass-facade building, set right in the heart of the Austrias district just below the Plaza Mayor, has been allowed to retain its charming original *moderniste* structure, but character-wise has metamorphosed into a highly sanitized "center of gastronomic recreation," where stalls sell fancy meat, fish, fruits, and vegetables alongside specialist goodies, while an equal number of new, pricey bars offer everything from traditional sherries and *vermuts* to imported French champagne and oysters. It's all very chic and with nary a grain of sawdust on the spotless floors. Plaza de San Miguel. ✆ **91-548-12-14.** Metro: Sol. Bus: 3.

Guitars

José Ramírez A true Spanish original, this long-established shop located just a stone's throw from the Puerta del Sol sells nothing but guitars. Not any old guitars, though. These handmade gems are purchased worldwide, and all shipping orders must be placed in the shop itself. Such is its fame that experts past and present, from Andrés Segovia to Dire Straits' Mark Knopfler, have had their guitars made here. You can also visit the workshop to see these instruments being made on weekdays. Open Monday to Friday 10am to 2pm and 4:30 to 8pm, Saturday 10:30am to 2pm. Calle de la Paz 8. ✆ **91-531-42-29.** www.guitarrasramirez.com. Metro: Sol.

Herbalists

Although vegetarian restaurants are a relatively recent phenomenon (p. 127), Spain has been a health-conscious country for some time, and herbalist shops (*herbolarios*) are traditional institutions. Here are two of the oldest.

Herbolario la Fuente 🎁 Founded in 1856, this family-run business began with a love of and fascination for plants and their curative powers. Making few concessions to modern fads or trends, all plants and herbs sold are freshly collected on a regular basis from the countryside and preserved either in large glass jars made at La Granja or in 19th-century drawers that slide into niches. Apart from relishing the guaranteed quality of their products, a visit here is a stimulating trip into the past. Open Monday to Friday 10am to 1:30pm and 5 to 8pm, Saturday 10am to 1:30pm. Pelayo 70. ✆ **91-308-13-98.** www.herbolariolafuente.com. Metro: Alonso Martínez. Bus: 3, 40, or 149.

Herbolario Morando In business since 1916, this veteran shop contains a large store of medicinal herbs, though in recent years market pressures have also drawn it into the spheres of garden produce, diet foods, spices, and natural cosmetics. Though it still retains the original drawers used for storing its products, today these are purely decorative. Open Monday to Friday 9:30am to 1:30pm and 4:45 to 8pm, Saturday 9:45am to 1:30pm, Sunday 10:30am to 2:30pm. Duque de Alba 15. ✆ **91-369-08-26.** Metro: La Latina. Bus: 17, 18, 23, 35, or 60.

Leather

Excrupulus Net Highly innovative shoe, jacket, and briefcase designs from Cataluña and Valencia—all of highest quality leather—are sold in this prestigious Chueca shop. You can also browse some sharp scarves and sunglasses, as well as the notable Muxart range of stylish windbreakers. Open Monday to Saturday 11am to 2pm and 5:30 to 8:30pm. Almirante 7. ✆ **91-521-72-44.** Metro: Chueca. Bus: 5, 14, 27, 37, 45, 53, or 150 (all to Recoletos).

Farrutx One of the most well-known names in the world of footwear, Farrutx originates from the Balearic island of Mallorca (its *zapaterías,* or shoe shops, are renowned for producing elegant quality goods). Belts and handbags feature highly among other leather products on sale here. Open Monday to Saturday 10am to 2pm and 5 to 8:30pm (from 5:30pm in July). Serrano 7. ✆ **91-577-09-24.** www.farrutx.com. Metro: Serrano. Bus: 1, 74, or 89.

Loewe ★ Since 1846, this has been the most elegant leather store in Spain. Its gold medal–winning designers have always kept abreast of changing tastes and styles, but the inventory still retains a timeless chic. The store sells luggage, handbags, and jackets for men and women (in leather or suede). Prices match the high quality of the goods. Open Monday to Saturday from 9:30am to 8:30pm. There's a second location located at Serrano 26 (✆ **91-577-60-56;** Metro: Serrano). Gran Vía 8. ✆ **91-522-68-15.** www.loewe.com. Metro: Banco de España or Gran Vía. Bus: 1, 2, 74, or 146.

Perfumes

Álvarez Gómez This is a marvelously old-fashioned *perfumería* that's been around so long it's newly fashionable again. The shop markets its own fragrances, many based on almost long-forgotten formulas. Even if you're not specifically looking for perfume, you'll find an array of unusual merchandise here, including tortoiseshell accessories, custom jewelry, and even women's handbags and belts. Open Monday through Friday 10am to 8:15pm, Saturday 10am to 2pm. Serrano 14. ✆ **91-431-16-56.** www.alvarezgomez.com. Metro: Serrano.

Perfumerías Oriental Located at the western edge of the Puerta del Sol, this shop carries one of the most complete stocks of national and international brands of perfume in Madrid. It also sells gifts, souvenirs, and costume jewelry. Open Monday through Saturday 10am to 8:30pm. Calle Mayor 1. ✆ **91-360-40-91.** Metro: Sol. Bus: 17, 31, or 51.

Porcelain

Lasarte This imposing outlet is devoted almost exclusively to Lladró porcelain; the staff can usually tell you about new designs and releases the Lladró company is planning for the near future. Open Monday to Friday 9:30am to 8pm, Saturday 10am to 8pm. Gran Vía 46. ✆ **91-521-49-22.** Metro: Callao. Bus: 46, 74, 75, 133, 146, or 150.

Shopping Malls

ABC Serrano Set within what used to be the working premises of a well-known Madrileño newspaper *(ABC)*, this is a complex of about 85 upscale boutiques that emphasize fashion, housewares, cosmetics, and art objects. Although each of the outfitters inside is independently owned and managed, most of them maintain hours of Monday to Saturday 10am to midnight. On the premises, you'll find cafes and restaurants to keep you fed between bouts of shopping, lots of potted and flowering shrubbery, and acres and acres of Spanish marble and tile. Serrano 61 or Castellana 34. ✆ **91-577-50-31.** www.abcserrano.com. Metro: Serrano. Bus: 1, 74, or 89 (Serrano); 7, 14, or 27 (Castellana).

Centro Comercial Plenilunio Set on the northeastern outskirts of the city, close to the Eisenhower junction section of the Barcelona highway, Plenilunio ("Full Moon") claims to be the largest commercial center in Spain, with over 200 shops ranging from top fashion shops, such as Bershka and Massimi Dutti, to innovative electronic equipment stores, such as Saturn (www.saturn.es). There are leisure and entertainment options, including multiscreen cinemas, bowling alleys, and a wellness center. Open Monday to Saturday 10am to 10pm and usually the first Sunday of every month. Av. Aragón s/n, Glorieta Eisenhower, Poligono de las Mercedes. ✆ **91-748-08-16.** www.pleniluniocc.com. Bus: 223, 224, 281, 282, or EMT 77.

Isla Azul Superseding even Plenilunio in size and amenities is this awesome minicity of banks, restaurants, food and fashion shops, and state-of-the-art movie houses (one of them boasting the largest screen in Spain!). Stylishly avant-garde in concept—it was the first Spanish building to be nominated as Europe's best commercial center in 2009—this exotic jet-age "Blue Island" has an innovative design that allows a maximum amount of natural light to illumine it. The center is located on the southern outskirts of town beside the regenerated suburb of Carabanchel. Open Monday to Saturday 10am to 10pm. Calle Calderilla 1. ✆ **91-511-46-80.** www.islazul.com. Metro: La Peseta (1km away).

La Vaguada This megamall has pretty much everything. Among its countless shops, cafes, and restaurants, you'll find an El Corte Inglés department store and a multiscreen cinema (Spanish-dubbed movies only). It's open Monday to Saturday and the first Sunday of every month 10am to 10pm (most shops, except for the department stores, close at 8:30pm; on Sun many shops open for shorter hours). Monforte de Lemos 36. ✆ **91-730-04-92.** www.enlavaguada.com. Metro Barrio del Pilar. Bus: 124 or 134.

MADRID AFTER DARK

Madrid abounds in dance halls, *tascas,* cafes, theaters, movie houses, music halls, and nightclubs. You'll have to proceed carefully through this maze, as many of these offerings are strictly for residents or for Spanish-speakers—especially the theaters.

Because dinner is served late in Spain, nightlife extends well into the early hours, in summer often ending at dawn. Madrileños are so fond of prowling around at night that they are known around Spain as *gatos* (cats). If you arrive at 9:30pm at a club, you'll have the place all to yourself, if it's even open. In most clubs, a one-drink minimum is the rule: Feel free to nurse one drink through the entire evening's entertainment.

10

In summer, free festivals abound as the city sponsors a series of plays, concerts, and films. Pick up a copy of the *Guía del Ocio* (available at most newsstands) for listings of these events. This guide also provides information about occasional discounts for commercial events, such as the concerts that are given in Madrid's parks. If you read Spanish, get Friday's *El Mundo* newspaper, as its accompanying "Metropoli" supplement gives you the complete lowdown on what's happening round the clock over the coming week.

Like flamenco clubs, discos tend to be expensive, but they often open for what is erroneously called afternoon sessions (7–10pm). Although discos charge entry fees, at an afternoon session, the cost might be as low as 5€; costs may rise to 20€ and beyond for a night session—that is, beginning at 11:30pm and lasting until the early morning hours. Therefore, you may choose to go early, dance until 10pm, and then proceed to dinner (at the fashionable hour).

Nightlife in Madrid can be roughly divided into the following "night zones":

PLAZA MAYOR/PUERTA DEL SOL The most popular areas can also be dangerous, so explore them with caution, especially late at night. They are filled with tapas bars and *cuevas* (drinking caves). It is customary to begin a *tasca* crawl here, going to tavern after tavern, sampling the wine in each, along with a selection of tapas. The major streets for such a crawl are Cava de San Miguel, Cava Alta, and Cava Baja.

GRAN VÍA This area contains mainly cinemas and theaters. Most of the after-dark action takes place on little streets branching off the Gran Vía.

PLAZA DE ISABEL II/PLAZA DE ORIENTE Another area frequented by tourists, many restaurants and cafes flourish here, including the famous Café de Oriente.

CHUECA Along such streets as Hortaleza, Infantas, Barquillo, and San Lucas, this is the gay nightlife district, with dozens of clubs. Cheap restaurants, along with a few female strip joints, are also found here. This area can also be dangerous in the early hours of the morning, though the customary presence of weekend revelers who throng the streets till around 3am often manages to deter potential pickpockets and muggers. The reasonably active police presence at night also helps.

ARGÜELLES/MONCLOA For university students, this part of town sees most of the action. Many dance clubs are found here, along with ale houses and fast-food joints. The area is bounded by Pintor Rosales, Cea Bermúdez, Bravo Murillo, San Bernardo, and Conde Duque.

THE PERFORMING ARTS

Madrid has a number of theaters, opera companies, and dance companies. To discover where and when specific cultural events are being performed, pick up a copy of *Guía del Ocio* at any city newsstand. The sheer volume of cultural offerings can be staggering. Below is a concise summary of the highlights.

Tickets to dramatic and musical events usually range in price from 7€ to 70€, with discounts of up to 50% granted on certain days of the week (usually Wed and matinees on Sun).

Concierges at most major hotels can usually get you tickets, if you are clear about your wishes and needs. They charge a considerable markup, part of which is passed along to whichever agency originally booked the tickets. You'll save money if you go directly to the box office. In the event your choice is sold out, you may be able to get tickets (with a reasonable markup) at **Localidades Galicia** at Plaza del Carmen 1 (© **91-531-27-32;** Metro: Sol). This agency also markets tickets to sporting events and bullfights (check out www.bullfightticketsmadrid.com). It is open Tuesday to Saturday from 9:30am to 1:30pm and 4:30 to 7:30pm, Sunday from 9:30am to 1:30pm. Otherwise, try **www.entradas.com** (© **90-248-84-88**), a 24-hour ticketing service (AE, MC, V are all accepted).

Major Performing-Arts Companies

Those who speak Spanish should check out the **Compañía Nacional de Nuevas Tendencias Escénicas,** an avant-garde troupe that performs new and often controversial works by undiscovered writers. On the other hand, the **Compañía Nacional de Teatro Clásico,** as its name suggests, is devoted to the Spanish classics, including works by the ever-popular Lope de Vega and Tirso de Molina.

Among dance companies, the national ballet of Spain—devoted exclusively to Spanish dance—is the **Ballet Nacional de España.** Their performances are always well attended. The national lyrical ballet company is the **Ballet Lírico Nacional.**

World-renowned flamenco sensation Antonio Canales and his troupe, **Ballet Flamenco Antonio Canales,** offer spirited high-energy performances. Productions are centered on Canales's impassioned *Torero,* his interpretation of a bullfighter and the physical and emotional struggles within the man. For tickets and information, you can call Madrid's most comprehensive ticket agency, the previously recommended

Localidades Galicia (see contact details above) for tickets to cultural events and virtually any other event in Castile. Other agencies with satellite offices located throughout Madrid include **Casa de Catalunya** (✆ **91-538-33-00**) and **Corte Inglés** (✆ **91-432-93-00;** www.elcorteingles.es/entradas).

Madrid's opera company is the **Teatro de la Opera,** and its symphony orchestra is the outstanding **Orquesta Sinfónica de Madrid.** The national orchestra of Spain—widely acclaimed on the continent—is the **Orquesta Nacional de España,** which pays particular homage to Spanish composers.

Classical Music Performance Halls

Check the program of *Fundación Juan March,* Calle Castello 77 (✆ **91-435-42-40;** www.march.es. Metro: Núñez de Balboa). Tapping into funds bequeathed by a generous financier (Sr. Juan March), it stages free concerts of Spanish and international classical music in a concert hall at its headquarters at Calle Castello 77. In most cases, these are 90-minute events, presented every Monday and Saturday at noon, and every Wednesday at 7:30pm.

Auditorio del Parque de Atracciones The schedule of this 3,500-seat facility might include everything from punk-rock music groups to the more highbrow warm-weather performances of visiting symphony orchestras. Check with Localidades Galicia (✆ **91-531-27-32** and **90-234-50-09;** www.parquedeatracciones.es) to see what's on at the time of your visit. Casa de Campo. Metro: Casa de Campo, Batán, or Lago.

Auditorio Nacional de Música Sheathed in slabs of Spanish granite, marble, and limestone and capped with Iberian tiles, this hall is the ultramodern home of the National Orchestra of Spain and the National Chorus of Spain. Standing just north of Madrid's Salamanca district, it ranks as a major addition to the competitive circles of classical music in Europe. Inaugurated in 1988, it is devoted exclusively to the performances of symphonic, choral, and chamber music. In addition to the Auditorio Principal (Hall A), whose capacity is almost 2,300, there's a hall for chamber music (Hall B), as well as a small auditorium (seating 250) for intimate concerts. Príncipe de Vergara 146. ✆ **91-337-01-39.** www.auditorionacional.mcu.es. Tickets 6€–60€. Metro: Cruz de Rayo.

Centro Cultural de la Villa Spanish-style ballet, along with zarzuelas (musical reviews), orchestral works, and theater pieces, are presented at this cultural center. Tickets go on sale 5 days before the event, and performances are usually presented at two evening shows (8 and 10:30pm). Plaza Colón. ✆ **91-480-03-00.** Tickets 12€–34€. Metro: Serrano or Colón.

Fundación Juan March This foundation sometimes holds free concerts at lunchtime. The advance schedule is difficult to predict, so call for information. Castello 77. ✆ **91-435-42-40.** www.march.es. Metro: Núñez de Balboa.

La Fidula Serving as a bastion of civility in a sea of rock 'n' roll and disco chaos, this club was converted from an 1800s grocer. Over the past 2 decades, it has been presenting chamber music concerts nightly at 11:30pm, with an additional show at 1am Friday to Sunday, in cooperation with the Royal Music Conservatory. The club offers the prospect of a tranquil, cultural evening on the town, at a moderate price. They take performances here seriously—late arrivals may not be seated for concerts. It is open Monday to Thursday and Sunday from 8pm to 3:30am, Friday and Saturday from 8pm to 4am. Calle Huertas 57. ✆ **91-429-29-47.** Cover 6€ for one show; 10€ for two shows. No live shows mid-June to Aug. Metro: Antón Martín.

Teatro de la Zarzuela Modeled on La Scala in Milan, this 150-year-old theater is the best place in Madrid to see the unfashionably nostalgic though still enjoyable Spanish operetta or zarzuela. A resident company gives spirited performances year-round, though the main season is October to July. Plays, ballet, and occasional opera and family shows also feature on the agenda, as does an annual program devoted to the 19th-century German Lied. Box office open noon to 8pm. Jovellanos 4. ✆ **91-524-54-00.** http://teatrodelazarzuela.mcu.es. Tickets 10€–80€. Shows usually start at 8pm. Metro: Banco de Espana.

Teatro Real This beautifully renovated theater is one of the world's finest stage and acoustic settings for opera. Its extensive state-of-the-art equipment affords elaborate stage designs and special effects. Today, the building is the home of the Compañía del Teatro Real, a company specializing in opera and occasional ballet, and often working with leading Spanish lyric talents, including Plácido Domingo. The theater is also a major venue for classical music. On November 19, 1850, under the reign of Queen Isabel II, the Royal Opera House opened its doors with Donizetti's *La Favorita*. Highlights of the 2010/2011 season range from Tchaikovsky's Eugene Onegin and Benjamin Britten's Turn of the Screw to the ever-popular Puccini's Tosca. Plaza Isabel II 7. ✆ **91-516-06-60.** www.teatro-real.es. Concerts 10€–125€; opera 20€–160€, or up to 280€ for opening night. Metro: Opera.

Mainstream Theater

Madrid offers many different theater performances, useful to you only if you are fluent in Spanish. If you aren't, check the *Guía del Ocio* for performances by English-speaking companies on tour from Britain, or select a concert or subtitled movie instead.

In addition to the major ones listed below, Madrid has at least 30 other theaters, including one devoted almost entirely to children's plays at the **Ciudad de los Niños,** which was moved from its former location in the Casa de Campo to the **Retiro Park** in 2009. Amateur groups stage dozens of other plays in such places as churches.

Nuevo Teatro Alcalá Specializing in Spanish versions of big Broadway hits such as Cats and Cabaret, this immaculately renovated theater lies just off Alcalá in the Salamanca district. Calle Jorge Juan 62. ✆ **91-426-47-79.** Advance bookings for tickets ✆ 90-288-87-88. Tickets 12€–75€. Metro: Príncipe de Vergara.

Teatro Bellas Artes In its early days, audiences at this long-established theater adjoining the Círculo de Bellas Artes cultural center enjoyed a prolific program organized by the colorful 19th-century novelist and playwright Ramón de Valle-Inclán. After a period of decline when relatively few plays were shown, the theater has bounced back and is now providing up to 10 stimulating works a year. Recent examples include Ingmar Bergman's *Autumn Sonata* and a modern version of Oedipus's *Phaedra*. The box office is open Tuesday to Sunday from 11:30am to 1:30pm, and 5pm till the beginning of the performance. Marqués de Casa Riera 2. ✆ **91-532-44-37.** Tickets 16€–30€. Metro: Banco de España.

Teatro de la Comedia This is the home of the Compañía Nacional de Teatro Clásico. Here, more than anywhere else in Madrid, you're likely to see performances from the classic repertoire of such great Spanish dramatists as Lope de Vega and Calderón de la Barca. There are no performances on Wednesday, and the theater is closed during July and August. The box office is open daily from 11:30am to 1:30pm and 5 to 6pm, and for about an hour before the performances. Renovation and expansion plans were drawn up in 2010 so the theater may be closed during 2011. Príncipe 14. ✆ **91-521-49-31.** Tickets 10€–25€; 50% discount Thurs. Metro: Sevilla. Bus: 15, 20, or 150.

Teatro Español This company is funded by Madrid's municipal government, its repertoire a time-tested assortment of great and/or favorite Spanish plays as well as international 20th-century works by the likes of Jean Genet and Ingmar Bergman. The box office is open daily from 11:30am to 1:30pm and 5 to 6pm. Príncipe 25. ✆ **91-429-62-97.** Tickets 5€–25€; 50% discount Wed. Metro: Sevilla.

Teatro Häagen-Dazs Calderón Disconcertingly renamed after its takeover by the internationally famous ice-cream company, this fine old theater (the largest in Madrid, with a seating capacity of 2,000) has switched from its traditional opera and flamenco programs to more modern entertainments such as 2010's *Jungle Book* and *Flashdance*. Shows begin most evenings at 8pm. Atocha 18. ✆ **91-429-58-90.** www.teatrohaagen-dazs.es. Tickets 25€–65€. Metro: Tirso de Molina.

Teatro Lara Reopened in the mid-1990s after years of disuse, the Teatro Lara stands on a steep narrow lane in Malasaña. It's a marvelous example of a 19th-century theater, and its evocatively traditional architecture has remained largely unchanged since refurbishment. Family plays and musicals such as *Annie* and *Blood Brothers* are generally shown here. The box office is open Tuesday to Sunday from 11:30am to 1pm and 5pm till the start of the show. Corredera Baja de San Pablo 15. ✆ **91-521-05-52.** www.teatrolara.com. Tickets 15€–25€. Metro: Callao.

Teatro Nuevo Apolo Nuevo Apolo is the permanent home of the renowned Antología de la Zarzuela company. It is on the restored site of the old Teatro Apolo, where these musical variety shows have been performed since the 1930s. A ballet-style *La Traviata* and flamenco version of Bizet's *Carmen* were among the favorites of 2010. Prices and times depend on the show. The box office is open daily from 11:30am to 1:30pm and 5 to 6pm. Plaza de Tirso de Molina 1. ✆ **91-369-06-37.** Tickets 20€–50€. Metro: Tirso de Molina.

Alternative Theater

Madrid offers a modest but fascinating choice of imaginative and original "alternative" shows—ranging from sharp satires to esoteric sketches. Unlike the more accessible mainstream theater, where you can usually get by without a full command of Spanish, knowledge of the language and thought processes is essential if you decide on a visit to one of these venues.

Alfil Though officially a mainstream theater, the Alfil's repertoire dips so frequently into the avant-garde—recent performances have included *Star Trip* (a surrealistic sendup of *Star Trek*)—that it's fair to include it in this section. A popular venue for stand-up comics—having in the past hosted the Internacional Teatro de Humor—it also provides a regular program of satirical and humorous plays. The box office opens 1 hour before each performance. Check with theater for exact shows and times. Calle Pez 10. ✆ **91-521-58-27** and 90-248-84-88. www.teatroalfil.com. Tickets 22€. Metro: Callao or Noviciado.

Cuarta Pared The "Fourth Wall" is another key fringe rendezvous. It boasts its own company as well as an enthusiastic training section and innovative contributors whose plays deal frankly and uncompromisingly with contemporary Spanish social themes. Another highly praised feature is its lively children's theater. The box office opens 1 hour before performances. Closed August. Ercilla 17. © **91-517-23-17.** www.cuarta pared.es. Tickets 12€–14€. Metro: Embajadores.

Sala Triángulo For alternative theater aficionados, this is the best of Madrid's offerings, presenting some of the most adventurously original satires and surrealistic sketches in town. Some programs may start at midnight. The box office opens 30 minutes before each show. Check with the theater for exact performance times. Open Thursday to Sunday. Calle Zurita 20. © **91-530-68-91.** www.teatrotriangulo.com. Tickets 10€–20€. Metro Antón Martín or Lavapiés.

English-Language Theater

The Madrid Players, with their combined troupe of American, English, and Spanish artists, put on spirited performances throughout the year in a range of venues. A standout is the Christmas Pantomime, for children of all ages, but they also do plays and musical shows, occasionally in alternative theaters such as the Sala Triángulo (listed above). Tickets range from 12€ to 16€. For details of performances and venues, call © **91-445-36-00** or 91-530-68-91. Also check www.madridplayers.org.

MOVIES

Mainstream

Cines Verdi The Chamberí-based, five-screen Verdi offers an enticing combination of mainstream and lesser-known international movies. There's also a small bar where you can enjoy a pre-movie coffee or glass of wine. Programs start at 4pm. Last performances start at 10:30pm. Bravo Murillo 28. © **91-447-39-30.** www.cines-verdi.com. Tues–Sun 7.50€; Mon and 1st show Tues–Fri 5€. Metro: Canal or Quevedo.

Golem The first of Madrid's four-screen cinemas—formerly the Alphaville—continues to show an adventurous blend of independent and lesser-known international movies. The comfortable basement restaurant was the original movie house. Programs start at 4:30pm. Late-night shows are on Friday and Saturday at 12:30am. Martín de los Heros 14. © **91-559-38-36.** www.golem.es. Tues–Sun 5€–7.50€; Mon (except holidays) 4.50€–6.50€. Metro: Ventura Rodríguez or Plaza España.

Princesa This larger, nine-screen multiplex is located in a small modern plaza adjoining Calle Princesa. It shows a wide selection of current international and national movies. Programs start at 4:05pm. Late-night shows on Friday and Saturday start at 12:30 or 12:45am. Princesa 3. © **91-541-41-00** or 90-222-91-22. www.cinesrenoir.com. Tickets 6.80€. Metro: Plaza de España or Ventura Rodríguez.

Renoir Four branches of these comfortable, well-run cinemas, all equipped with high-quality sound and picture, are scattered throughout the city. Each has compact-size *salas* showing an up-to-date blend of international movies. Programs start around 4pm. Late-night shows on Friday and Saturday start at 12:30am. **Renoir Cuatro Caminos,** Raimundo Fernández Villaverde 10 (© **91-541-41-00;** Metro: Cuatro Caminos), is close to northerly Cuatro Caminos's central roundabout and has a small bar. The 1896 **Renoir Plaza de España,** Martín de los Heros 14 (© **91-541-41-00;** Metro: Plaza de España or Ventura Rodríguez), is next to the Golem and shares the same street number. The **Renoir Princesa,** Princesa 5 (© **91-541-41-00;** Metro: Plaza de España or Ventura Rodríguez), is in the covered arcade running between Martín de los Heros and Calle Princesa—not to be confused with the larger nine-screen Princesa cinema listed above, which is up one level in the neighboring square and, confusingly, also part of the Renoir chain. And the **Renoir Retiro,** Narváez 42 (✆ **90-288-89-02;** Metro: Goya), is in stylish Salamanca, 2 blocks east of the Retiro park. www.cinesrenoir.com. Tickets 6.80€.

Yelmo Cineplex A favorite with locals and foreigners alike, this established eight-screen movie palace offers a good selection of the latest commercial productions. Programs start at 4pm. Late-night shows on Friday and Saturday start around midnight. Dr. Cortezo 6. ✆ **91-369-25-18** or 90-222-09-22. www.yelmocineplex.es. Tickets 5.80€-7.50€. Metro: Tirso de Molina.

Independent or Art House

In addition to the theaters listed below, French, German, Italian, and Brazilian **cultural centers** have regular V.O. *(versión original)* performances of their countries' movies, and the **Casa de América,** Paseo de Recoletos 2, often features offbeat Latin American films in Spanish or Portuguese.

Cine Doré (Filmoteca) Founded in 1953 and miraculously surviving philistine attempts in the '80s to turn it into a block of offices (thanks largely to a mass protest by journalists and artists), the Doré, or Filmoteca, is a movie buff's delight and a marvelous example of Art Deco architecture. Madrid's richest and most eclectic variety of original-version movies—from '20s classics to offbeat or commercial international productions—can be found here. It also offers bargain ticket prices, a cozy cafe, and a small but well-stocked movie bookshop. There are two indoor theaters plus an open-air one upstairs in summer. Situated right next to the Antón Martín covered food market on the northern edge of Lavapiés, it opens Tuesday to Sunday 4pm to midnight. Programs usually start at 5:30pm. Last performance 10pm. Santa Isabel 3. ✆ **91-369-11-25.** www.mcu.es/cine/index.html. Tickets 2.50€; block of 10 tickets (each useable for any show) 20€. Metro: Antón Martín.

Cine Estudio Círculo de Bellas Artes This stylishly renovated art cinema, just a few steps up the road from the Círculo de Bellas Artes cultural center, is noted for its varied alternative movie program. Pleasantly free of the crush that plagues some of the other movie houses, it's a relaxing backwater of comfort and taste. Programs start 5:30pm. Last performance 10pm. Marqués de Casa Riera 2. ✆ **91-522-50-92.** Tickets 4.50€. Metro: Banco de España.

La Enana Marrón As experimental a movie center as you'll find in Madrid, the tiny Enana Marrón (Brown Dwarf) nestles unobtrusively in a quiet lane between Chueca and Malasaña. A cineaste's cinema with a repertoire ranging from avant-garde retrospectives to new independent releases, it doesn't advertise so you'll need to ring, pass by, or check the website for current programs and timetables. There are also occasional seminars (in Spanish naturalmente) on film. Travesía de San Mateo 8. ✆ **91-308-14-97.** www.laenanamarron.org. Tickets 4€. Metro: Tribunal.

Pequeño Cine Estudio If you're a fan of '40s Hollywood film noir, British '50s comedies, or international classics in general, you're likely to find what you're looking for here in this modest shrine to celluloid nostalgia, tucked away in an offbeat corner of Chamberí. Three or four different films are shown every day from 4pm to midnight. Last program 10pm. Magallanes 1. ✆ **91-447-29 20.** Tickets 6.50€ Thurs-Tues, 5€ 1st session and Mon (except public holidays); 1€ seniors over 60 on Tues. Metro: Quevedo.

THE CLUB & LIVE MUSIC SCENE

Cabaret

Madrid's nightlife is no longer steeped in prudishness, as it was (at least officially) during the Franco era. You can now see glossy cabaret acts and shows with lots of nudity.

Café del Foro This old-time favorite in the Malasaña district suddenly became one of the most fashionable places in Madrid to hang out after dark in the 1990s. Patronizing the club are members of the literati along with a large student clientele. You never know exactly what the show for the evening will be, although live music of some sort generally starts at 11:30pm. Cabaret is often featured, along with live merengue, bolero, and salsa. There's a faux starry sky above the stage area, plus Roman colonnades that justify the name Café del Foro (Forum Café). Open daily from 7pm to 3am. Calle San Andrés 38. © **91-445-37-52.** Cover may be imposed for specialty act. Metro: Bilbao. Bus: 40, 147,149, or N-19.

Scala Meliá Castilla Madrid's most famous dinner show is a major Las Vegas–style spectacle, with music, water, light, and color. The program is varied, including international or Spanish ballet, magic acts, ice skaters, whatever. Most definitely a live orchestra will entertain you. It is open Tuesday to Saturday from 8:30pm to 3am. Dinner is served beginning at 9pm; the show is presented at 10:45pm. The show with dinner costs 80€, and if you partake you don't have to pay the cover charge, as it's included in the show/dinner price. Reservations are essential. Calle Capitán Haya 43 (entrance at Rosario Pino 7). © **91-571-44-11.** Cover 40€ including 1st drink. Metro: Cuzco.

Flamenco

Café de Chinitas One of the best flamenco clubs in town, Café de Chinitas is set one floor above street level in a 19th-century building midway between the Opera and the Gran Vía. It features an array of (usually) gypsy-born flamenco artists from Madrid, Barcelona, and Andalusia, with acts and performers changing about once a month. You can arrange for dinner before the show, although many Madrileños opt for dinner somewhere else and then arrive just for drinks and the flamenco. Open Monday to Saturday, with dinner served from 8 to 11pm and the show lasting from 10:30pm to 1am. Reservations are recommended. Torrija 7. © **91-559-51-35.** www.chinitas.com. Dinner and show 80€; show only (includes 1 drink) 40€. Metro: Santo Domingo. Bus: 1 or 2.

Candela Though this popular Lavapiés bar has no live music, the atmosphere is pure flamenco as gypsies and Andaluz performers regularly drop in and do their stuff. The "jam sessions" at the rear are deservedly famous, though it may be hard to get access. Open Monday to Thursday and Sunday 11pm to 5:30am, and Friday to Saturday 11pm to 6am. Olmo 2. © **91-467-33-82.** Metro: Tirso de Molina.

Casa Patas This club is now one of the best places to see "true" flamenco as opposed to the more tourist-oriented version presented at Corral de la Morería (see below). It is also a bar and restaurant, with space reserved in the rear for flamenco. Shows are presented midnight on Thursday, Friday, and Saturday and during Madrid's major fiesta month of May. The best flamenco in Madrid is presented here: As proof, flamenco singers and dancers often hang out here after hours. Tapas are available at the bar for 3€ to 16€. The club is open daily from 8pm to 2:30am. Cañizares 10. © **91-369-04-96.** www.casapatas.com. Admission 20€. Metro: Tirso de Molina.

THE SULTRY SOUND OF flamenco

The lights dim and the flamenco stars clatter rhythmically across the dance floor. Their lean bodies and hips shake and sway to the music. The word flamenco has various translations, meaning everything from "gypsified Andalusian" to "knife," and from "blowhard" to "tough guy."

Accompanied by stylized guitar music, castanets, and the fervent clapping of the crowd, dancers are filled with tension and emotion. Flamenco dancing, with its flash, color, and ritual, is evocative of Spanish culture, although its origins remain mysterious.

Experts disagree as to where it came from, but most claim Andalusia as its seat of origin. Although its influences were both Jewish and Islamic, it was the gypsy artist who perfected both the song and the dance. Gypsies took to flamenco like "rice to paella," in the words of the historian Fernando Quiñones.

The deep song of flamenco represents a fatalistic attitude toward life. Marxists used to say it was a deeply felt protest of the lower classes against their oppressors, but this seems unfounded. Protest or not, over the centuries, rich patrons, often brash young men, liked the sound of flamenco and booked artists to stage *juergas* or fiestas where dancer-prostitutes became the erotic extras. By the early 17th century, flamenco was linked with pimping, prostitution, and lots and lots of drinking, by audiences and artists alike.

By the mid-19th century, flamenco had gone legitimate and was heard in theaters and *café cantantes.* By the 1920s, even the pre-Franco Spanish dictator, Primo de Rivera, was singing the flamenco tunes of his native Cádiz. The poet Federico García Lorca and the composer Manuel de Falla preferred a purer form, attacking what they viewed as the degenerate and "ridiculous" burlesque of *flamenquismo,* the jazzed-up, audience-pleasing form of flamenco. The two artists launched a Flamenco Festival in Grenada in 1922. Of course, in the decades since, their voices have been drowned out, and flamenco is more *flamenquismo* than ever.

In his 1995 book *Flamenco Deep Song,* Thomas Mitchell draws a parallel to flamenco's "lowlife roots" and the "orgiastic origins" of jazz. He notes that early jazz, like flamenco, was "associated with despised ethnic groups, gangsters, brothels, free-spending bluebloods, and whoopee hedonism." By disguising their origins, Mitchell notes, both jazz and flamenco have entered the musical mainstream.

Corral de la Morería Right on the western edge of the Austrias quarter, the Morería (meaning, "where the Moors reside") sizzles with flamenco. Colorfully costumed strolling performers warm up the audience around 11pm; a flamenco show follows, with at least 10 dancers. It's much cheaper to eat somewhere else first, and then pay only the one-drink minimum. Open daily from 9pm to 3am. Morería 17. ✆ **91-365-84-46.** www.corraldelamoreria.com. Dinner and show 80€; show only (includes 1 drink) 35€. Metro: La Latina or Sol.

Corral de la Pacheca Located in the pricey Cuzco district, close to Castellana Avenue, this fashionable locale features flamenco performers who sing and dance. Open daily from 9pm to 3am. This show usually starts around 10pm. Juan Ramon Jimenez 26. ✆ **91-353-01-00.** www.corraldelapacheca.com. Dinner and show 75€–95€; show only (includes 1 drink) 35€. Metro: Cuzco.

Las Carboneras A fairly new competitor in the flamenco stakes, Las Carboneras is a stylish venue combining dinners and floor shows. Though decidedly commercial and priced accordingly, it offers top-value dance entertainment and regular invited quality acts. Open Monday to Saturday at 8:30pm and closes in the early hours. Shows are at 10:30pm Monday to Wednesday and 11pm Friday and Saturday. Plaza del Conde de Miranda 1. © **91-542-86-77.** www.tablaolascarboneras.com. 3-course meal with drinks 35€–60€; show only (includes 1 drink) 20€. Metro: La Latina or Opera.

Las Tablas ★ Fed up with faux flamenco on the tourist circuit and all those frilly costumes, two dancers, Antonia Moya and Marisol Navarro, opened their own little place. Some of the most authentic flamenco in Madrid is performed in their minimalist room. Sometimes the owners themselves star in a show. This place is for flamenco devotees. Shows are held nightly at 10:30pm, and reservations are needed Friday to Sunday. Plaza de España 9. © **91-542-05-20.** www.lastablasmadrid.com. Cover 24€ (includes 1 drink). Metro: Plaza de España.

Torres Bermejas Located in the very center of the city, on a narrow road leading off the Gran Vía, this colorful dinner and flamenco venue features regular live shows. Open nightly 8:30pm. Calle de Mesonero Romanos 11. © **91-532-33-22.** www.torresbermejas.com. Show and 1 drink 35€. Metro: Gran Vía.

Dance Clubs

In Madrid most clubs are open from around 6 to 9pm, later reopening around 11pm. They really start going at midnight or thereabouts.

Alquimia This stylishly individual disco has the unexpectedly relaxing atmosphere of an elegant old house. The eclectic, sometimes bizarre, repertoire of music is intended to accommodate all tastes. Open from 9pm. Villanueva 2. © **91-577-27-85.** Cover 12€ (includes 1 drink). Metro: Colón or Retiro.

Ananda Located close to the Atocha train station complex, this huge (2,000-sq.-m/22,000-sq.-ft.) nightclub boasts 10 bars and two dance floors, one inside and one outdoor. Things don't really liven up till around 2am, when a lavish dance show performed by drag queens begins. The Terrace is open nightly May to October from 11pm to sunrise. The Covered Zone is open October to May Thursday, Friday, and Saturday 11pm to sunrise. Calle Ciudad de Barcelona 2. © **91-781-95-40.** www.ananda.es. Cover 15€. Metro: Atocha.

Cool As its name suggests, this is one of the coolest clubs in the capital. Nowhere else in Madrid seems to blend a gay and straight (or else bi) crowd as successfully as this major production set on two levels. Sometimes the most stunning drag queens in Madrid appear here (often billed as "more beautiful than actual girls"). Video projections are always enticing, and the crowd of patrons in their 20s and early 30s is a medley of Madrileños and international folk, especially Brits and Yanks. One special feature of the club is the heavily attended Shangay Tea Dance, taking place on Sunday from 9am to 2am. If you're a "circuit queen" seeking out the hottest gay males in the Spanish capital, you're likely to encounter urban cowboys at this time. Open Friday and Saturday midnight to 6am, Sunday from 9pm to 2am. Isabel la Católica 6. © **91-548-20-22.** Cover 15€ (or up to 30€ when top DJs appear). Metro: Callao.

Joy Eslava Near the Puerta del Sol, this place has survived the passing fashions of Madrileño nightlife with more style than many of its (now-defunct) competitors. Virtually everyone in Madrid is likely to show up here, ranging from traveling sales reps in town from Düsseldorf to the youthful members of the Madrileño *movida*. Open nightly 11:30pm to 6:30am. Arenal 11. ✆ **91-366-37-33.** www.joy-eslava.com. Cover 16€ (includes 1 drink). Metro: Sol.

Kapital This is the most sprawling, labyrinthine, and multicultural disco in Madrid at the moment. Set within what was originally a theater, it has seven different levels, each sporting at least one bar and an ambience that's often radically different from the one you just left on a previous floor. Voyeurs of any age can take heart—there's a lot to see at the Kapital, with a mixed crowd that pursues whatever form of sexuality seems appropriate at the moment. Open Thursday to Sunday from 11:30pm to 5:30am. Drinks cost from 10€ each. Atocha 125. ✆ **91-420-29-06.** Cover 16€ (includes 1 drink). Metro: Atocha.

Kathmandu This is Madrid's club of the moment, where cutting-edge music echoes through the night—reggae, jungle, hip-hop, jazzy funk. At this alternative disco, be prepared for a dizzy psychedelic experience. Decidedly androgynous, it's an Oriental-inspired, ultramodern scoff at normalcy. The bar on the top floor is a curious retreat with Tibetan textiles draped from the ceiling. Nepalese art decorates part of the downstairs. At times the floor becomes so overcrowded, you think the club will sink, but it carries on with wild abandon. Open Thursday from 11am to 5am, Friday and Saturday from 10am until 6am. Señores de Luzón 3. No phone. Cover 10€–12€ (includes 1 drink). Metro: Sol.

Magik Room This small and friendly psychedelic-style disco is co-owned by Oscar winner Javier Bardem of Spanish-acting-family fame. Said to be the narrowest—and for many the coziest—place in town, it opens Tuesday to Thursday midnight to 5am, Friday and Saturday midnight to 5:30am; it doesn't really get going till the early hours. Colón 12. ✆ **91-531-34-91.** Metro: Tribunal.

Ohm/Bash Line This ultralively disco is known as **Bash Line** during the week and on Sundays. But on peak Friday and Saturday nights, it comes into its own as **Ohm,** a must with regular devotees to hedonism and newcomers in search of something alternative. Top DJs keep the action going, and organized theme parties are regular features. Open from Wednesday to Sunday midnight to 6am. Plaza de Callao 4. ✆ **91-531-01-32.** Cover 12€; Sat 14€. Metro: Callao.

Pachá Madrid The carefully contrived setting is pseudo-opulent, and the drinks sometimes hard to get because of the milling crowds. Despite that, Pachá thrives as one of the late-night staples in Madrid for the mid-20s to late-40s clientele (a crowd that often segregates itself by age into distinctly different areas). More than other nightclubs in Madrid, this has been the subject of complaints from neighbors about late-night noise. Open Tuesday to Sunday from 11pm to 5am. Barceló 11. ✆ **91-447-01-28.** www.pacha-madrid.com. Cover 12€–17€ (includes 1 drink). Metro: Tribunal.

Palacio de Gaviria Its construction in 1847 was heralded as the architectural triumph of one of the era's most flamboyant aristocrats, the Marqués de Gaviria. Famous as one of the paramours of Queen Isabella II, he outfitted his palace with the ornate jumble of neoclassical and baroque styles that later became known as *Isabelino*. In 1993, after extensive renovations, the building was opened to the public as a concert hall for the occasional presentation of classical music and as a late-night cocktail bar. No food is served, but the libations include a stylish list of cocktails and wines. The often-dull music doesn't match the elegance of the decor. Dance nights are usually Thursday through Saturday, everything from the tango to the waltz.

Cabaret is usually featured on most other nights. Monday to Friday from 9pm to 3am, Saturday and Sunday from 9pm to 5am. ***Note:*** Currently (2010) the Palacio de Gaviria is closed for refurbishment work, but it's scheduled to reopen in 2011, or 2012 at the latest. Arenal 9. ✆ **91-526-60-69.** www.palaciogaviria.com. Cover 8€–16€ (includes 1 drink). Metro: Sol or Opera.

Sala Wind This long-established club in the heart of the city delights its regulars with its eclectic nightly mood changes. A recent face-lift has made it even more popular, attracting a whole new crowd of early hours "aficionados," and whichever night you choose you're likely to find it packed to capacity. Open midnight to 6am Thursday to Saturday. Montera 25. No phone. Cover 14€ (includes 1 drink). Metro: Gran Vía.

Sala Stella (The Room) This weekend-only mecca, with its '70s decor and glistening mosaic ceiling, is one of the most stylish all-night spots around, featuring house techno music, a smooth DJ, and a tiny dance floor packed with seasoned revelers of the chic variety. Open Friday and Saturday 1 to 7am. Arlabán 7. ✆ **91-523-86-54.** Cover 14€ (includes 1 drink). Metro: Sevilla.

Sweet Don't get here too early. This place doesn't really swing into action till around 3am, by which time it's the hottest scene in Madrid. Steel doors open up to reveal a wildly campy scene that attracts a 90% gay clientele most nights. Look for suspended cages and a disco-ball dance floor packed with some of the prettiest girls and handsomest men in Madrid. Wear your most daring apparel. Open only Friday and Saturday from 11pm to daybreak. Dr. Cortezo 1. ✆ **91-869-40-38.** www.sweetfunkclub.com. Cover 15€ (includes 1 drink). Metro: Tirso de Molina.

Torero If you're not one of the *gente guapa* (beautiful people), head elsewhere. The seasoned bouncer at the door only admits those young men and women he judges to be beautiful; otherwise, it's away with you. If you can pass such a tough door policy, you'll find yourself in one of the city's most glamorous after-dark rendezvous spots. The club is on two levels, with the top floor being more attractive and Iberian, with leather chairs. The downstairs is more functional and less desirable. Some entertainment is provided on most nights, with drag shows a feature on Thursday. The latest Spanish recordings are played here, especially "pop Español." Hours are Friday and Saturday from 11pm to 6am, Sunday to Thursday from 11pm to 5am. Cruz 26. ✆ **91-523-11-29.** Cover 12€. Metro: Sol or Tirso de Molina.

Jazz

Café Central Off the Plaza de Santa Ana, beside the famed Gran Hotel Victoria, the Café Central has a vaguely turn-of-the-20th-century Art Deco interior, with an unusual series of stained-glass windows. Many of the customers read newspapers and talk at the marble-top tables during the day, but the ambience is far more animated during the nightly jazz sessions, which are ranked among the best in Spain and often draw top artists. Open Sunday to Thursday from 1:30pm to 2:30am, Friday and Saturday from 1:30pm to 3:30am; live jazz is offered daily from 10pm to midnight. Beer costs 5€. There's also a good lunchtime menu for just 12€. Plaza del Angel 10. ✆ **91-369-41-43.** www.cafecentralmadrid.com. Cover 10€–15€. Metro: Antón Martín.

Café Populart This club is known for its exciting jazz groups who encourage the audience to dance. It specializes in Brazilian, Afro-bass, reggae, and new-wave African music. When the music starts at 11:30pm, the drink prices nearly double: Beer costs 5€, whiskey with soda 10€. Open daily from 6pm to 2 or 3am. Huertas 22. ✆ **91-429-84-07.** www.populart.es. Metro: Antón Martín or Sevilla.

Clamores With dozens of small tables and a huge bar in its dark and smoky interior, Clamores, which means "noises" in Spanish, is the largest and one of the most popular jazz clubs in Madrid. Established in the early 1980s, it has thrived because of the diverse roster of American and Spanish jazz bands that have appeared here. The place is open daily from 7pm to around 4am, but jazz is presented only Tuesday to Saturday. Tuesday to Thursday, performances are at 11pm and again at 1am; Saturday, performances begin at 11:30pm, with an additional show at 1:30am. There are no live performances on Sunday or Monday nights, when the format is recorded disco music. Regardless of the night of the week, drinks begin at around 5€ each and can rise to 20€ depending on the act. Albuquerque 14. ✆ **91-445-79-38.** www.salaclamores.com. Metro: Bilbao.

Segundo Jazz It's over 3 decades since this spacious jazz haunt in Madrid's gritty Tetuan district opened, making Segundo Jazz officially the city's oldest jazz club. The eclectic range of artists performing varies from completely new faces to the most famous of Spanish jazz performers. *Cantautores* (singer-composers) and traditional bands both make regular appearances. Drinks range from 5€ to 12€, and the club is open daily from 7pm to 4am. Comandante Zorita 8. ✆ **91-554-94-37.** www.segundojazz.es. Metro: Nuevos Ministerios.

Pop & Rock

El Perro (de la Parte Atras del Coche) The bar's name ("the dog in the back of the car"—referring to the wobble-headed toy dog you still sometimes see in car rear windows) gives you a hint of the zany retro mood to expect here. Corny kitsch decor surrounds an eclectic mix of straight and bohemian clientele. You'll hear soul, funk, and rock-'n'-roll sounds, and live acts include heavy-metal groups. The club is open daily from 9pm to 3:30am. Calle de la Puebla 15. ✆ **91-521-03-25.** Cover 10€. Metro: Gran Vía.

Honky Tonk This lively spot in the Chamberí district combines live pop music and stylish dining with art and photography exhibitions. Open nightly 9pm to 5am. Entrance free until 3am. Covarrubias 24. ✆ **91-445-68-86.** www.clubhonky.com. Cover (after 3am) 10€. Metro: Alonso Martinez.

La Via Lactea Still a favorite with young, fun ravers, this pioneer bar dates from the late '70s, when the famed post-Franco *movida* began. The place specializes in rock and hip-hop, and its walls are lined with posters of pop stars of the past 2 or more decades, including the Beatles, the Who, and the Rolling Stones. Open nightly from 9pm. Velarde 18. ✆ **91-446-75-81.** www.lavialactea.net. Cover 8€. Metro: Tribunal.

Siroco This highly popular rock scene has live shows by Spanish and international pop groups till around 2am, followed by a lively blend of DJ-inspired soul and funk till the early hours. Open Thursday to Saturday from 9:30 or 10pm. San Dimas 3. ✆ **91-593-30-70.** www.siroco.es. Cover 8€–10€. Metro: San Bernardo.

Cuban Salsa/Brazilian

Café La Palma Live Cuban groups playing salsa dominate the agenda here. As in Paris, anything Cuban is chic in Madrid. This convivial club is one of the most happening in the capital. It's open daily from 4pm to 3am, but go after 10pm for the most action. A group mainly made up of people in their 20s and 30s come for the live music. La Palma 62. ✆ **91-522-50-31.** www.cafelapalma.com. Cover 6€–8€. Metro: Noviciado.

Galileo Galilei Under the same ownership as the popular Clamores (p. 245), this spacious venue hosts a wide selection of performers of all types and persuasions, from flamenco and jazz to eastern dance, though salsa is its specialty. The place used to be a cinema and still retains much of its original kitschy imitation-Greek decor. Open daily from 6pm to 3am. Galileo 100. ✆ **91-534-75-58.** www.salagalileogalilei.com. Cover 10€–20€ depending on artist appearing. Metro: Quevedo or Islas Filipinas.

La Negra Tomasa This Cuban music bar draws big crowds on weekends. A Caribbean setting is evoked by fishermen and palm fronds and pictures of Cuba on the walls. Cuban music and salsa attract a crowd in their 20s and 30s, and the place is very fashionable. The drinks served here—mojitos, daiquiris, and piña coladas—are familiar to barflies the world over. But have you ever had a Cubanito? It's tomato juice and lime with rum. Open daily from 1:30pm to 3am (till 5am Fri–Sun). Cádiz 9. ✆ **91-523-58-30.** www.lanegratomasa.es. Cover 8€–10€. Metro: Sol. Bus: 3, 15, 20, or 51.

Oba-Oba A little slice of Rio in Madrid, this established Brazilian club is now in its third decade of entertaining grateful customers with its sambas and serving up caipirinha cocktails. Regular live performances feature Brazilian artists. Opens daily from 11pm to 5:30am. Jacometrezo 4. No phone. Cover 10€. Metro: Callao.

THE BAR & PUB SCENE

Aloque Come to this cozy little bar with an even cozier little alcove at the back to sample their incomparable choice of wines, either by the glass or bottle. Latest "in" tipples are chalked on a blackboard, but there are over 300 national and international varieties to choose from—enough to satisfy the most demanding oenophile. Particularly interesting are the selections from burgeoning new Spanish areas such as Somontano near Huesca and Toro from the Zamora area of western Castilla. Excellent tapas ranging from *cecina de astorga* (smoked beef) to *carpaccio de buey con queso parmesano* (ox carpaccio with Parmesan cheese) match the quality of the vino. Open daily 7:30pm to 1am. Closed in August. Torrecilla del Leal 20. ✆ **91-528-36-62.** Metro: Antón Martín.

Balneario Clients enjoy potent drinks in a setting with fresh flowers, white marble, and a stone bathtub that might have been used by Josephine Bonaparte. Near Chamartín Station on the northern edge of Madrid, Balneario is one of the most stylish and upscale bars in the city. It is adjacent to and managed by one of Madrid's most elegant and prestigious restaurants, El Cabo Mayor, and often attracts that dining room's clients for aperitifs or after-dinner drinks. Tapas include endive with smoked salmon, asparagus mousse, and anchovies with avocado. Open Monday to Saturday from noon to 2:30am. Juan Ramón Jiménez 37. ✆ **91-359-56-96.** Drinks 5€–10€; tapas 3€–12€. Metro: Cuzco.

Bar Cock Built in the 1920s, this mellow, high-ceilinged bar attracts some of the most visible artists, actors, models, and filmmakers in Madrid. The name comes from the word *cocktail,* or so they say. The decor is elaborate and unique, and the martinis and gin fizzes are Madrid's best. Open daily from 7pm to 3am; closed December 24 to 31. Reina 16. ✆ **91-532-28-26.** www.barcock.com. Drinks from 5€ for beer; 8€–14€ for cocktails. Metro: Gran Vía.

Del Diego This hip spot is in competition with Chicote and the Cock as the most civilized place in town to enjoy a good cocktail. Try the superb daiquiris, or the excellent margaritas and dry martinis. Cool decor, low-key atmosphere, and smooth attentive service add to the charm of this discreet spot, tucked away in a quiet street just below the Gran Vía. Open daily Monday to Thursday 7pm to 3am and Friday and Saturday 7pm to 3:30am; closed the month of August. Reina 12. ✆ **91-523-31-06.** Cocktails start around 6€. Metro: Gran Vía.

The James Joyce Irish Pub This spacious and atmospheric bar, situated between Cibeles and the Puerta de Alcalá, is another Irish favorite with a more recently historic past and a penchant for name changes. Known until early 2006 as Kitty O'Shea's, it was called Café Lion in the 1940s when it was the key meeting spot for the literati. Today, local rugby club members gather for weekly get-togethers and fuel themselves on draft Guinness and no-nonsense pub food. The atmosphere is always good natured and easygoing, and in summer you can sit outside. In winter, the bar hosts regular live music shows. Open Monday to Thursday from 11am to 2am, Friday and Saturday from 11am to 4am. Alcalá 59. ✆ **91-575-49-01.** www.jamesjoycemadrid.com. Pint of beer 5€. Metro: Banco de España.

La Venencia On one of the traditional *tasca* streets in Old Madrid, this tavern has a distinct personality. It is dedicated to the art of serving Spain's finest sherry—and that's it. Don't come in here asking for an extra dry martini. My favorite remains Manzanilla, a delicate *fino* with just a little chill on it. To go with all that sherry, the genially informal waiters serve tapas of garlicky marinated olives, *jamón serrano* (mountain ham), *mojama* (cured tuna), or blue-cheese canapés. Ancient barrels form the decor, along with antique posters long turned tobacco-gold from cigarette smoke. Open daily from 7pm to 1:30am. Echegaray 7. ✆ **91-429-73-13.** Metro: Sevilla.

Moores If not the oldest Irish pub in Madrid, this is at least in the oldest building, as well as being the best and most centrally located of the city's three Moores establishments. It's in a medieval house with an atmospheric basement "interrogation room" where the dark inquisition ambience of yesteryear has been replaced by pool tables and Celine Dion sounds. The main salon is relaxing and comfortable with dark wood–paneled walls and cozy alcoves. Guinness is the tipple par excellence, and Wednesdays are curry evenings. Open daily noon to 1am. Felipe III 4. ✆ **91-365-58-02.** Pint of beer 5€. Metro: Sol.

Museo Chicote This is not a museum but simply Madrid's most famous cocktail bar. It's classic retro chic, with the same 1930s interior design it had when the foreign press came to sit out the Spanish Civil War. Long a favorite of artists and writers, the bar became a haven for prostitutes in the late Franco era. It's back in the limelight again, a sophisticated and much-frequented place for a rendezvous. Open daily from 8am to 3am. Drink prices can be high, but the waiters serve them with such grace you don't mind. Gran Vía 12. ✆ **91-532-67-37.** www.museo-chicote.com. Drinks begin at 7€. Metro: Gran Vía.

La Recoba Don't be put off by the narrow congested street and lines of cut-price Chinese retail shops outside. This Huertas locale, which stays open well into the early hours, is one of the most lively and popular in town. Outwardly a traditional taberna (dating in fact from 1930), it doubles as an Italian-Argentine restaurant and a cozy and animated *bar de copas*. Live shows including piano music and *cantautores* (singer-writers) take place from Thursdays to Sundays. Come here to enjoy a lively evening with youthful revellers. Magdalena 27, 28012. ✆ **91-369-39-88.** Metro: Anton Martín.

Teatriz Soft lighting and a decor by world-class designer Philippe Starck create one of the most stylish environments in Madrid. A meal in the restaurant (p. 158) averages around 20€ at lunch and 30€ in the evening, but if it's just a drink you're looking for, consider an extended session at any of the site's three bars. Here, the setting is not quite like a disco, but has a sound system almost as good. Hermosilla 15. ✆ **91-577-53-79.** Metro: Serrano.

Viva Madrid A congenial mix of students, artists, and foreign tourists cram into Viva Madrid. The interior is turn-of-the-20th-century, and antique tile murals and blatant Belle Epoque nostalgia contribute to an undeniable charm. In the good old days (the 1950s, that is), the fabled beautiful people showed up here, notably Ava Gardner and the bullfighter Manolete, when they couldn't take their hands off each other. But Orson Welles or even Louis Armstrong used to pop in as well. Crowded and noisy, it's a place where lots of beer is swilled and spilled. It's set within a neighborhood of antique houses and narrow streets near the Plaza de Santa Ana. Open Friday from noon to 1am, Saturday from noon to 2am. Manuel Fernández y González 7. ✆ **91-429-36-40.** Beer 4€; whiskey begins at 6€. Metro: Sol.

Cave Crawling

To capture a peculiar Madrid joie de vivre of the 18th century, visit some *mesones* and *cuevas,* many found in the *barrios bajos.* From Plaza Mayor, walk down the Arco de Cuchilleros until you find a gypsylike cave that fits your fancy. Young people love to meet in the taverns and caves of Old Madrid for communal drinking and songfests. The sangria flows freely, the atmosphere is charged, and the room is usually packed; the sounds of guitars waft into the night air. Sometimes you'll see a strolling band of singing students going from bar to bar, colorfully attired, with ribbons fluttering from their outfits.

Las Cuevas de Sesamo In a class of its own, this cavelike bar dating from the early 1950s draws a clientele of young painters and writers with its bohemian ambience. Hemingway was one of those early visitors (a plaque commemorates him). At first you'll think you're walking into a tiny snack bar—and you are. But proceed down the flight of steps to the cellar. Here, the walls are covered with contemporary paintings and quotations. At squatty stools and tables, an international assortment of young people listens to piano music and occasional guitar. Open daily from 7pm to 2am (till 3:30am Sat–Sun). Príncipe 7. ✆ **91-429-65-24.** Pitcher of sangria (for 4 people) is 12€ and beer 3.50€. Metro: Sevilla or Sol.

Mesón de la Guitarra My favorite *cueva* in the area, Mesón de la Guitarra is loud and exciting on any night of the week, and it's as warmly earthy as anything you'll find in Madrid. The decor combines terra-cotta floors, antique brick walls, hundreds of sangria pitchers clustered above the bar, murals of gluttons, old rifles, and faded bullfighting posters. Like most things in Madrid, the place doesn't get rolling until around 10:30pm, although you can stop in for a drink and tapas earlier. Don't be afraid to start singing a song in English if it has a fast rhythm—60 people will join in, even if they don't know the words. Open daily from 7pm to 1:30am. Cava de San Miguel 13. ✆ **91-559-95-31.** Beer and wine start at 2.50€; tapas 6€–15€. Metro: Sol.

Mesón del Champiñón In English, the name of this place is "house of mushroom," and you'll see the fungus depicted in various sizes along sections of the vaulted ceilings. The bartenders keep a brimming bucket of sangria behind the long stand-up bar as a thirst quencher for the crowd. A more appetizing way to experience the

SUMMER *terrazas*

At the first blush of spring weather, Madrileños rush outdoors to drink, talk, and sit at a string of open-air cafes, called *terrazas,* throughout the city. Some of the best (and most expensive) ones are along Paseo de la Castellana, between the Plaza de la Cibeles and the Plaza Emilio Castelar. You can wander up and down these boulevards, selecting one that appeals to you; then move on later to another one if you get bored. Sometimes these *terrazas* are called *chirinquitos.* You'll find them along other *paseos,* the Recoletos and the Prado, both fashionable areas but not as hip as the Castellana. For old traditional atmosphere, the terraces at the Plaza Mayor and in nearby Plaza Santa Ana are among the most atmospheric choices within the old city. Friday and Saturday are the most popular nights for drinking; many locals sit here all night. Most relaxing of all, though, are the *terrazas* along Paseo Rosales, beside the leafy Parque del Oeste in the westerly Argüelles district.

champiñón is to order a *racion* of grilled, stuffed, and salted mushrooms, served on toothpicks. Spanish families mingle with polyglot tourists in two tiny, slightly dark rooms in the back, where a jovial local plays organ music. Unless you want to be exiled to the very back, don't expect to get a seat; practically everybody prefers to stand. Open daily from 6pm to 2am. Cava de San Miguel 17. ✆ **91-559-67-90.** Dishes 7€–15€. Metro: Sol.

Gay & Lesbian Bars

Black & White This is the major gay bar of Madrid, in the center of the Chueca district. A guard will open the door to a large room—painted, as you might expect, black and white. A disco is in the basement, but the street-level bar is the premier gathering spot, featuring drag shows at 3am Thursday to Sunday, male striptease, and videos. Old movies are shown against one wall. Open Monday to Friday from 8pm to 5am, Saturday and Sunday from 8pm to 6am. Calle Libertad 34. ✆ **91-531-11-41.** www.discoblack-white.net. Beer 5€; whiskey 8€. Metro: Chueca.

Café Figueroa This turn-of-the-20th-century cafe attracts a diverse clientele, including a large number of gay men and lesbians. It's one of the city's most popular gathering spots for drinks and conversation. Open Sunday through Thursday from 4pm to midnight, Friday and Saturday from 4pm to 2:30am. Augusto Figueroa 17 (at corner of Hortaleza). ✆ **91-521-16-73.** Beer starts at 2.50€; whiskey from 6€. Metro: Chueca.

Cruising One of the predominant gay bars of Madrid, a center for gay consciousness-raising and gay cruising (though they say the name refers to automobile driving), this place has probably been visited at least once by every gay male in Castilla. There are practically no women inside, but always a hustler looking for a tourist john. It doesn't get crowded or lively until late at night. Open Monday to Friday from 8pm to 3:30am, Saturday and Sunday from 8pm to 4:30am. Pérez Galdos 5. ✆ **91-521-51-43.** Beer 3€–5€. Metro: Chueca.

Leather Club This is another of the premier bars for gay men in Madrid, but despite its supposed emphasis on leather and uniforms, only about 25% of the men who show up actually wear them. You'll find two bars on the establishment's street level and a disco in the basement. It's open Sunday through Thursday from 7pm to

3am, Friday and Saturday from 8pm to 3:30am. Pelayo 42. ✆ **91-308-14-62.** Cover 4€. Beer 5€. Metro: Chueca.

Rick's Rick's takes its name from "Everybody Comes to Rick's," the original title of the Bogie classic *Casablanca.* Many gay bars in the Chueca barrio are sleazy, but this is a classy joint—just like the Rick's in Morocco. It's decorated with Bogie paraphernalia, as well as marble floors and gilt columns. The only thing missing is a piano player singing "As Time Goes By"—and Bergman, of course. (Ingmar, more likely, in this case, as gay men patronize the place, with the occasional woman showing up, too.) Incongruously, it has a macho foosball table in the bar and cute lavender walls. Open daily from 11:30pm "until sometime in the early morning." Clavel 8. ✆ **91-531-91-86.** Cover 10€. Metro: Chueca.

A CASINO

Casino Gran Madrid Madrid's largest place for gambling, the Casino also appeals to nongamblers with a well-choreographed roster of dining and entertainment facilities, including two restaurants, four bars, and a nightclub. And if you happen to enjoy gambling, there are facilities for French and American roulette, blackjack, *punto y banco,* baccarat, and chemin de fer. Presentation of a passport at the door is essential—without it, you won't be admitted. Entrance costs 6€. A ticket is sometimes provided gratis by Madrid's larger hotels, so ask ahead. The casino and all of its facilities are open daily from 4pm to 5am.

An a la carte restaurant in the French Gaming Room offers international cuisine, with dinners costing from 40€ to 65€. A buffet in the American Gaming Room will cost around 30€. The restaurants are open 9:15pm to 2am.

The casino is 29km (18 miles) northwest of Madrid in the suburb of Torrelodones. If you don't feel like driving, the casino has buses that depart from Plaza de España 6 every afternoon and evening at 4:30, 6, 7:30, and 11pm and at 1am. Note that between October and June, men must wear jackets and ties; T-shirts and tennis shoes are forbidden in any season. Carretera La Coruña Km 29 (the A-6 hwy. running btw. Madrid and La Coruña), Torrelodones. ✆ **91-856-11-00** or 90-090-08-10. www.casinogranmadrid.es.

SIDE TRIPS FROM MADRID

11

Madrid makes an ideal base for excursions around central Spain and the scenic smaller towns and villages of Madrid province, a geographical kaleidoscope of plains, valleys, rivers, and mountains that belies the clichéd image of a beleaguered capital surrounded by arid badlands. Most of the day trips detailed in this chapter range from 30km to just over 90km (20–60 miles) outside the Spanish capital, allowing you to leave in the morning and be back by nightfall.

Public transport, either by train or bus, is particularly good in the region. It's both economical and efficient, usually getting you to your destination within an hour. And for a little extra outlay, the faster rail services to Segovia and Toledo will get you to either of those fascinating cities in half that time!

ALCALÁ DE HENARES

29km (18 miles) E of Madrid

Despite its outwardly modern appearance, Alcalá de Henares is a historic city with a glorious past. Its discreetly hidden medieval center still abounds with colleges, monasteries, and palaces, and its Calle Mayor (main street) is among the oldest in Madrid province. When a university was founded here in the 15th century, Alcalá became a cultural and intellectual center. Europe's first polyglot Bible (supposedly with footnotes in the original Greek and Hebrew) was published here in 1517, but the town declined during the 1800s when the university moved to Madrid. Today Alcalá is one of the main centers of North American academics in Spain, cooperating with the Fulbright Commission, Michigan State University, and Madrid's Washington Irving Center. Overall, the city has taken on new life. Commuters have turned it into a virtual suburb, dubbing it "the bedroom of Madrid." (Prominent among its noncommuting inhabitants is the perennial community of highly urbanized storks that nonchalantly squat in their roof- and spire-top nests or, wide-winged, wheel effortlessly overhead.)

Essentials

GETTING THERE **Trains** travel between Madrid's Atocha or Chamartín station and Alcalá de Henares every day and evening. Service is every 15 minutes (trip time: 23 min.) and round-trip fare from Madrid costs 5.50€ to 5.80€. The train station (© **90-224-02-02**) in Alcalá is at Paseo Estación.

Buses from Madrid depart from Av. América 18 (Metro: América) every 15 minutes. A fare is 1.95€ one-way, 3.30€ round-trip. Bus service is provided by Continental-Auto, and the Alcalá bus station is on Av. Guadalajara 36 (© **91-888-16-22**), 2 blocks past Calle Libreros.

Alcalá lies adjacent to the main national **highway** (N-11), connecting Madrid with eastern Spain. As you leave central Madrid, follow signs for Barajas Airport and Barcelona.

VISITOR INFORMATION The **tourist information office,** Callejón de Santa María 1 (© **91-889-26-94;** www.turismoalcala.com), provides a map showing all the local attractions. It is open daily from 10am to 2pm and 4 to 6:30pm (until 7:30pm July–Sept).

Exploring Alcala de Henares

Capilla de San Ildefonso Next door to the Colegio is the Capilla de San Ildefonso, the 15th-century chapel of the old university. It also houses the Italian marble tomb of Cardinal Cisneros, the founder of the original university. This chapel also has an *artesonado* (artisan's) ceiling and intricately stuccoed walls.

Plaza San Diego. © **91-882-13-54** or 91-885-40-00. Admission included in tour of Colegio (see below). Hours same as Colegio (see below).

Colegio Mayor de San Ildefonso Adjacent to the main square, Plaza de Cervantes, is the Colegio Mayor de San Ildefonso, where Lope de Vega and other famous Spaniards studied. You can see some of their names engraved on plaques in the examination room. The old university's plateresque **facade ★** dates from 1543. From here you can walk across the Patio of Saint Thomas (from 1662) and the Patio of the Philosophers to reach the Patio of the Three Languages (from 1557), where Greek, Latin, and Hebrew were once taught. Here is the Paraninfo (great hall or old examination room), now used for special events. The hall has a *Mudéjar* carved-panel ceiling. The Paraninfo is entered through a restaurant, Hostería del Estudiante (see "Where to Dine," below).

Plaza San Diego. © **91-885-41-22.** Admission 3€. Tours (mandatory) Mon–Fri 11:30am, 12:30, 1:30, 5, and 6pm; Sat–Sun 11 and 11:45am, 12:30, 1:15, 2, 4:30, 5:15, 6, 6:45, and 7:30pm.

Museo Casa Natal de Cervantes Visitors come to see the birthplace of Spain's literary giant Miguel de Cervantes, the creator of *Don Quixote,* who may have been born here in 1547. This 16th-century Castilian house was reconstructed in 1956 around a beautiful little courtyard, which has a wooden gallery supported by pillars with Renaissance-style capitals, plus an old well. The house contains many Cervantes manuscripts and, of course, copies of *Don Quixote,* one of the world's most widely published books (available here in many languages).

Calle Mayor 48. © **91-889-96-54.** www.museo-casa-natal-cervantes.org. Free admission. Tues–Sun 10:15am–1:30pm and 4:15–6:30pm.

Where to Dine

Hostería del Estudiante ★ CASTILIAN Located within the university complex, this remarkable building dating from 1510 is an attraction in its own right. It

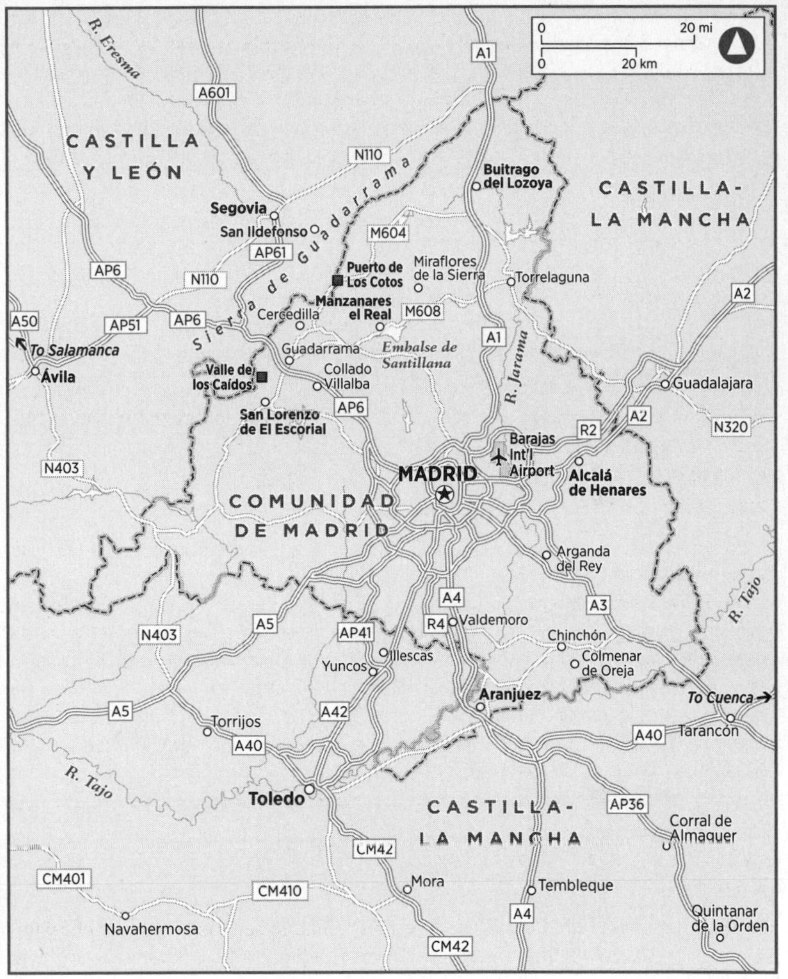

opened as a restaurant in 1929, and its traditional Castilian recipes haven't been altered since. In the cooler months, if you arrive early you can lounge in front of a 4.5m (15-ft.) open fireplace. Oil lamps hang from the ceiling, pigskins are filled with local wine, and rope-covered chairs and high-backed carved settees capture the spirit of the past. Run by the Spanish *parador* system, the restaurant offers a tasty (and huge) three-course set-price lunch or dinner, featuring such regional specialties as roast suckling lamb, *huevos comigos* (three eggs fried with mushrooms), and trout Navarre style. For dessert, try the cheese of La Mancha.

Calle Colegios 8. ✆ **91-888-03-30.** Reservations recommended. Main courses 22€–35€; fixed-price menus 28€. AE, DC, MC, V. Daily 1–4pm; Mon–Sat 9–11:30pm; Sun 9–10:30pm. Closed Aug.

ARANJUEZ

47km (29 miles) S of Madrid; 48km (30 miles) NE of Toledo

This Castilian town, at a confluence of the Tagus and Jarama rivers, was once home to Bourbon kings in the spring and fall. With the manicured shrubbery, stately elms, fountains, and statues of the **Palacio Real** and surrounding compounds, Aranjuez remains a regal garden oasis in what is otherwise an unimpressive agricultural flatland known primarily for its strawberries and asparagus.

Essentials

GETTING THERE **Trains** depart about every 20 minutes from Madrid's Atocha Railway Station to make the 40-minute trip to Aranjuez. It costs 3.15€ one-way and 5.70€ round-trip. Twice a day you can take an express train from Madrid to Toledo, which makes a brief stopover at Aranjuez. This trip takes only 30 minutes. Trains run less often along the east-west route to and from Toledo (a 40-min. ride). Spring highlight is the **Tren de la Fresa** (**Strawberry Express; ✆ 90-222-88-22**) trip, taking 50 minutes (the train is wooden and steam powered). Travel on this and you get to sample local strawberries handed out by hostesses in traditional costumes. See p. 197, in chapter 7, for more information. The Aranjuez station lies about 1.6km (1 mile) outside town. For information and schedules, call **✆ 90-224-02-02.** You can walk to the center in about 15 minutes, but taxis and buses line up on Calle Stuart (2 blocks from the city tourist office). The bus that makes the run from the center of Aranjuez to the railway station is marked "N-Z."

Buses for Aranjuez depart every 30 minutes, from 7:30am to 10pm, from Madrid's Estación Sur de Autobuses, Calle Méndez Álvaro. The hour-long journey costs 4.25€ one-way. In Madrid, call **✆ 91-530-46-05** for information. Buses arrive in Aranjuez at the city bus terminal, Calle Infantas 8 (**✆ 91-891-01-83**).

Driving is easy; it takes about 30 minutes once you reach the southern city limits of Madrid. To reach Aranjuez, follow the signs to Aranjuez and Granada, taking highway N-IV.

VISITOR INFORMATION The **tourist information office** is at Plaza de San Antonio 9 (**✆ 91-891-04-27**), open Monday to Friday from 10am to 2pm and 4 to 6pm.

Exploring Aranjuez

You can also visit **Aquasur** (p. 196), a giant open-air pool with slides, to beat the high heat of summer.

Casa del Labrador "The House of the Worker," modeled after the Petit Trianon at Versailles, was built in 1803 by Charles IV, who later abdicated in Aranjuez. The queen came here with her youthful lover, Godoy (whom she had elevated to the position of prime minister), and the feeble-minded Charles didn't seem to mind a bit. Surrounded by beautiful gardens, the "bedless" palace is lavishly furnished in the grand style of the 18th and 19th centuries. The marble floors represent some of the finest workmanship of that day; the brocaded walls emphasize the luxurious lifestyle; and the royal toilet is a sight to behold (in those days, royalty preferred an audience). The clock here is one of the treasures of the house. The *casita* lies .8km (a half-mile) east of the Royal Palace; those with a car can drive directly to it through the tranquil Jardín del Príncipe.

Calle Reina, Jardín del Príncipe. ✆ **91-891-03-05.** Admission 3.50€ adults, 2€ students and children. Apr–Sept Tues–Sun 10am–6:30pm; Oct–Mar Tues–Sun 10am–5:30pm.

Jardín de la Isla ★ After the tour of the Royal Palace, wander through the Garden of the Island. Spanish impressionist Santiago Rusiñol captured its evasive quality on canvas, and one Spanish writer said that you walk here "as if softly lulled by a sweet 18th-century sonata." A number of fountains are remarkable: the "Ne Plus Ultra" fountain, the black-jasper fountain of Bacchus, the fountain of Apollo, and the ones honoring Neptune (god of the sea) and Cybele (goddess of agriculture).

You may also stroll through the Jardín del Parterre, located in front of the palace. It's much better kept than the Garden of the Island, but not as romantic.

Directly northwest of the Palacio Real. No phone. Free admission. Daily Apr–Sept 8am–8:30pm; Oct–Mar 8am–6:30pm.

Palacio Real ★★ Since the beginning of a united Spain, the climate and natural beauty of Aranjuez have attracted Spanish monarchs: Ferdinand and Isabella; Philip II, when he managed to tear himself away from El Escorial; Philip V; and Charles III.

The structure you see today dates from 1778 (the previous buildings were destroyed by fire). The palace is lavishly and elegantly decorated: Salons show the opulence of a bygone era, with room after room of royal extravagance. Especially notable are the dancing salon, throne room, ceremonial dining hall, bedrooms of the king and queen, and a remarkable Salón de Porcelana (Porcelain Room). Paintings include works by Lucas Jordan and José Ribera. A guide conducts you through the huge complex (a tip is expected).

Plaza Palacio. ✆ **91-891-13-44.** Admission 5€ adults, 2.50€ students, 1.50€ children 5–16. Tues–Sun 10am–6:15pm. Bus: Routes from the rail station converge at the square and gardens at the westernmost edge of the palace.

Where to Stay

Hostal Castilla On one of the town's main streets north of the Royal Palace and gardens, the Castilla consists of the ground floor and part of the first floor of a well-preserved early-18th-century house. Most of the accommodations overlook a courtyard with a fountain and flowers. All units contain well-kept bathrooms with tub/shower combinations. Owner Martín Soria, who speaks English fluently, suggests that reservations be made at least a month in advance. Excellent restaurants are nearby, and the *hostal* has an arrangement with a neighboring bar to provide guests with an inexpensive lunch.

Carretera Andalucía 98, 28300 Aranjuez. ✆ **91-891-26-27.** 22 units. 60€ double. AE, DC, MC, V. Free street parking. Rates include breakfast. **Amenities:** Lounge. *In room:* A/C, TV.

Where to Dine

Casa José ★★ SPANISH/INTERNATIONAL Set near Town Hall and the Church of Antonio, this well-managed restaurant occupies a 300-year-old house in the heart of town; it's the premier restaurant of the entire area, and local gastronomes drive for miles around to dine here. The regionally based repertoire is prepared with an intelligent association of flavors. The menu focuses on fresh ingredients that the staff buys every morning at the town markets. The menu changes at least four times a year, with an emphasis on pork, veal, fish, chicken, and shellfish. Of special note are braised lamb chops in a fresh tomato and cilantro sauce; Jabugo ham with broad beans; shrimp in garlic sauce; hake with green sauce; and thick juicy steaks.

Calle Abastos 32. ✆ **91-891-14-88.** www.casajose.es. Reservations recommended. Main courses 18€–25€. AE, DC, MC, V. Tues–Sun 1–4pm and Tues–Sat 9pm–midnight.

Casa Pablo SPANISH An unpretentious and well-managed restaurant near the bus station in the town center, Casa Pablo was established in 1941. You can dine at tables set outside beneath a canopy while enjoying red and pink geraniums along the tree-lined street; in cooler weather you can eat upstairs or in the cozy rear dining room. The fixed-price menu includes four courses, a carafe of wine, bread, and gratuity. If it's hot out and you don't feel like having a heavy dinner, try a shrimp omelet or half a roast chicken; once I ordered just a plate of asparagus in season, accompanied by white wine. And if you've a yen for seafood, I recommend you try the *mero* (Mediterranean pollack of delicate flavor), grilled over an open fire.

Almibar 42. ✆ **91-891-14-51.** www.aranjuez.com/casapablo. Reservations recommended. Main courses 15€–30€. AE, MC, V. Daily 1–4:30pm and 8pm–midnight. Closed Aug.

El Rana Verde ★ SPANISH "The Green Frog," just east of the Royal Palace and next to a small bridge spanning the Tagus, is still the traditional choice for many. Opened in 1905 by Tomás Díaz Heredero, it is owned and run by a third-generation member of his family, who has decorated it in a 1920s style. The preferred tables are in the nooks overlooking the river. As in all the restaurants of Aranjuez, asparagus is a special feature. Game, particularly partridge, quail, and pigeon, can be recommended in season; fish, too, including fried hake and fried sole, makes a good choice. Strawberries are served with sugar, orange juice, or ice cream.

Reina 1. ✆ **91-891-32-38.** www.aranjuez.com/ranaverde. Reservations recommended. Main courses 12€–25€; fixed-price menu 18€–25€. MC, V. Daily 9pm–midnight.

BUITRAGO DEL LOZOYA

75km (47 miles) N of Madrid

The only township inside Madrid province to have retained its original Arabic walls, charming Buitrago is the last stop before the high Somosierra pass at the eastern end of the province's northerly mountain range. Poised like the prow of a ship on the curve of the Lozoya River, this small town of just over a thousand inhabitants boasts a picturesque medieval center and unique little Picasso museum. To the east lies the slate and shrub-dotted Sierra Negra (Black Mountains) replete with hidden streams, reservoirs, and villages, one of which, Montejo de la Sierra, shelters the most southerly beech tree forest in Europe.

Essentials

GETTING THERE **Continental Auto** buses (Línea Sierra Norte) depart from the Plaza Castilla Intercambiador station hourly, and the journey time is about 90 minutes. They operate between 6:15am and 11pm on weekdays and between 8am and 10:30pm on Saturday and Sunday. The last bus back to Madrid is at 8pm (✆ **91-314-57-55**).

Driving, take the northerly N-1 highway, which leads straight through Buitrago del Lozoya on its way to Burgos. Once clear of the city, you should get there easily in an hour.

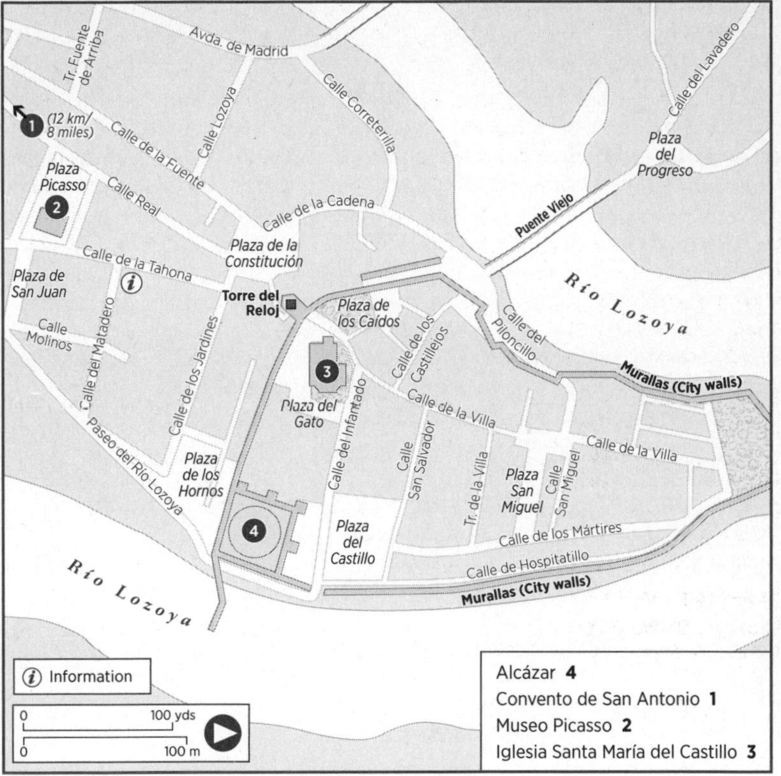

VISITOR INFORMATION The **town hall** in Buitrago (✆ **91-868-00-56**) gives useful local information.

Exploring Buitrago del Lozoya

IN TOWN

The ruined medieval castle **Alcázar** (no phone; free admission; daily 9am–1pm and 4–8pm) in the town center was declared a national monument in 1931. The well-preserved ramparts enclose the former courtyard where, amazingly, summer bullfights are now held. Early in the new year, notwithstanding the mountain cold, locals reenact biblical scenes in living tableaux, known here as the *Belén viviente.*

Within the castle grounds is the Gothic **Santa María del Castillo,** noted for its 17th-century sepulchers and *Mudéjar* tower. Unusually, the interior also features Bulgarian icons created by an artist living close by.

Las Murallas, the walls that surround the city, still intact from the times of the Arabic occupation, date from the 11th century. The tiny Paseo de la Concha (Shell Promenade) running alongside their eastern edge, beside the river, is a particularly peaceful and attractive spot.

Picasso Museum Located in the same building as the town hall, this unique little museum contains relics and souvenirs given to Picasso's barber, Buitrago native Eugenio Arias, when the two Spaniards shared a post–Civil War exile in southern France. Among the small but priceless exhibits are a wooden "Barber's Box" with pyrograph bullfight scenes and various ink sketches.

Plaza de Picasso s/n. ✆ **91-868-00-56.** Free admission. Tues–Fri 11am–1:45pm and 4–6pm, Sat–Sun 10am–2pm.

OUT OF TOWN

Convento de San Antonio 🎁 Founded in the 11th century, this little-known gem is the oldest convent in Madrid province. Noted for its exceptionally well-preserved tower, it nestles idyllically on the richly wooded slopes of La Cabrera Mountain, just 15km (9 miles) south of Buitrago and some 60km (37 miles) from the capital. The most practical way to get there is by hired car, though it's possible to catch the Buitrago bus from Madrid to the village of La Cabrera, at the base of the mountain, and take the steep 45-minute walk up. The trip's well worth the effort, whichever way you make it, as the views from the monastery are superb.

La Cabrera. ✆ **91-868-85-61.** Free admission. Tues, Thurs, Sat–Sun 11:30am–1pm and 5–6:30pm.

Where to Stay

Hostal Madrid-París A modest but comfortable converted stone house on the outskirts of town, just on your right as you arrive, the *hostal* offers excellent-value rooms and a neat traditional dining room.

Av. de Madrid 23. ✆ **91-868-11-26.** 25 units. 40€ double. V. **Amenities:** Restaurant. *In room:* A/C, TV.

Where to Dine

Mesón Serrano At this attractive old-fashioned hostelry specializing in Castilian roast dishes, try the outstanding lamb, which is cooked in a traditional oven.

Real 30 (facing the town hall). ✆ **91-868-01-13.** Main courses 15€–25€. V. Daily 1:30–5pm.

CERCEDILLA

57km (37 miles) NW of Madrid

By the time you reach this laid-back little town you're already in the foothills of the Guadarrama Mountains, and the hassle of the big city is far, far behind you. If you come by train, the center—with its cafes, small square, and alpine-style chalets and modern apartments—is hidden over to your right. The main attraction of Cercedilla, though, is that it's a walker's paradise with a variety of sylvan trails leading off from the pine-wooded Fuenfría Valley just ahead of you, blending into enticing ridges and peaks above the town.

Essentials

GETTING THERE By far the most convenient way to get to Cercedilla is by ***cercanías*** (suburban line C-8b) train from Chamartín. They run at least once an hour, and the journey time is an hour and 20 minutes. Once in town you can take an additional single-gauge train trip via Puerto de Navacerrada and spectacular pine forest scenery up to the 1,700m-high (5,576-ft.) Cotos—a ski center in winter and mountain walker's base in summer. This runs every 2 hours, and the trip lasts 40 minutes. The last train back to Madrid leaves Cercedilla at 10:35pm.

The **Larrea bus** company (✆ **91-530-48-00**) provides an hourly service (no. 684) from Moncloa bus station.

If you're **driving,** take the N-VI highway to Guadarrama town and then bear left on the M-995, which brings you to Cercedilla.

VISITOR INFORMATION **Tourist offices** (✆ **91-852-57-40**) are located at Av. Sierra de Guadarrama 30, and the **Town Hall** at Plaza Mayor 1 (✆ **91-852-57-40**) also provides local information. A kilometer (⅔-mile) inland from the railway station, you'll find the **Fuenfría Valley Information Center,** which gives details of six differently graded walks in the area along routes where tree trunks are marked in different colors according to each individual route, so you don't lose your way. It's open year-round from 9am to 6pm, except for Christmas and New Year fiesta days: December 25 and 31 and January 1 and 6.

Exploring Cercedilla

Though the surrounding scenery provides the key attraction, the town's main church, the **Iglesia Parroquial de San Sebastián**—originally medieval Romanesque and rebuilt after the Civil War—is well worth a look. It also enjoys spectacular views of the Guadarrama Valley.

In the Fuenfría Valley, a half-hour walk up the road that leads directly from the train station into the mountains brings you to the **Calzada Romana (Roman Road),** with original stones and remains of four Roman bridges along its route. It's a tiny section of a road that once connected the township of Titulcia, south of Madrid, with Segovia, on the other side of the mountains.

Where to Stay

Hostal El Aribel ★ This is the best and most atmospheric place to bed down. Vaguely Alpine in style, it was once a hostelry for miners. Today it's noted for its warm timber decor, neat well-appointed rooms, and friendly service. (A sister hotel, **Los Longinos,** with similar standards and amenities, adjoins it.)

Emilio Serrano 71. ✆ **91-852-15-11.** 50 units. 50€ double. V. **Amenities:** Bar; lounge. *In room:* TV.

Where to Dine

Casa Gómez This highly regarded traditional eating spot is on the first floor of a building opposite the railway station. Dishes like *sopa de hongos y castañas* (mushroom and chestnut soup) and *merluza con almejas y gambas* (hake with clams and prawns) are among the menu's main attractions.

Emilio Serrano 40. ✆ **91-852-01-46.** Dinner main courses 10€–16€; set lunch 12€. V. Fri–Sat 1–5pm and 9pm–midnight.

CHINCHON

52km (32 miles) SE of Madrid; 26km (16 miles) NE of Aranjuez

Many visitors to Chinchón are attracted by the ***cuevas*** **(caves),** where Anís de Chinchón, a strong digestive aniseed spirit, is manufactured. You can buy bottles of Chinchón *dulce, seco,* or *extra seco* at shops in the center of town. But it's the **Plaza Mayor ★★**, or main square, that's the real architectural highlight of Chinchón and the image that will linger on in your memory long after you've returned home. Dominated by its church, this photogenic arcaded plaza, which captivated artist Goya in the 18th century, is surrounded by three-story frame houses with wooden balconies. Its central lamppost is removed, cars that usually park there are told to park elsewhere, and—shazam—you have a colorful *plaza de toros,* where a half-dozen top bullfights take place between June and September.

Wander along the town's steep and narrow streets, past houses with large bays and spacious carriageways. Although closed to the public, the 15th-century **Chinchón Castle,** seat of the Condes of Chinchón, can be viewed from outside. The most interesting church, **Nuestra Señora de la Asunción,** dating from the 16th and 17th centuries, contains a painting by Goya.

GETTING THERE Regular L 337 **bus service** to Chinchón from Plaza Conde Casal (Metro: Conde Casal) is provided by **La Veloz** (✆ **91-409-76-02** for latest fares and timetables). Chinchón can also be reached from Aranjuez (earlier in this chapter), which is only a 15-minute ride away. **Buses** run twice a day from Aranjuez, but only Monday through Friday, leaving from Calle Almíbar next to the Plaza de Toros in Aranjuez. Schedules tend to be erratic, so call for information (✆ **91-891-01-83**). A one-way fare is around 1.80€.

You can find an alternative route to Chinchón if you're **driving** from Alcalá de Henares to Toledo. Halfway along the southwesterly C-300 bypass around the capital, turn off at the signs to CUEVAS DE CHINCHON. Another option is to take the E-901 southeast of Madrid toward Valencia, turning southwest at the turnoff for Chinchón.

Where to Stay

Hotel Nuevo Chinchón On the outskirts, this is the town's second-best address, rated just under the Parador (see below). Though it was actually built in 1994, the hotel's owners have invested lots of time and money in making it appear older and more nostalgic than it is. Low-slung and modern from the outside, it contains small bedrooms whose headboards are painted in old-fashioned folkloric patterns. All units have bathrooms equipped with showers. The overall effect is cozy, with a sense of low-key charm.

Urbanización Nuevo Chinchón, Carretera a Titulcia, Km 1.5, 28370 Chinchón. ✆ **91-894-05-44.** Fax 91-893-51-28. www.hotelnuevochinchon.com. 17 units. 80€–85€ double. AE, MC, V. Free parking. **Amenities:** Restaurant; bar; babysitting; outdoor pool (June–Sept only); room service. *In room:* A/C, TV, hair dryer.

Parador de Chinchón ★★★ Set near the town center, this hotel lies within the carefully restored 17th-century walls of what was originally an Augustinian convent. After a stint as a civic jail and as a courthouse, it was transformed in 1972 into a government-run *parador;* it is the best place to stay in town. A team of architects and designers converted it handsomely, with glass-walled hallways opening onto a stone-sided courtyard. The hotel has two bars and two dining halls. Severe but dignified rooms still manage to convey their ecclesiastical origins. Rooms range from small to medium, each with a quality mattress and fine linens along with well-maintained tiled bathrooms with showers.

Av. Generalísimo 1, 28370 Chinchón. ✆ **91-894-08-36.** Fax 91-894-09-08. www.paradores-spain.com/spain/pchinchon.html. 38 units. 150€–165€ double; 220€–240€ suite. AE, DC, MC, V. Parking 10€. **Amenities:** Restaurant; bar; babysitting; outdoor pool (June–Sept only); room service. *In room:* A/C, TV, hair dryer, minibar.

Where to Dine

Mesón Cuevas del Vino ★ SPANISH This establishment is known for its wine cellars. Hanging from the rafters are hams cured by the owners, along with flavorful homemade spiced sausages. Chunks of ham and sausage cooked in oil, plus olives and crunchy bread, are served. Your meal might begin with sliced chorizo (Spanish sausage); blood pudding; slices of La Mancha cheese; *sopa castellana* made with garlic, ham, and eggs; and thin-sliced cured ham. Main courses place heavy emphasis on roast suckling lamb and pig that emerge crackling from a wood-burning oven. Desserts include flan, biscuits coated in cinnamon and sugar, and liquefied and sweetened almonds presented in a soupy mixture in a bowl.

Benito Hortelano 13. ✆ **91-894-02-85.** www.cuevasdelvino.com. Reservations recommended on fiestas. Main courses 8€–25€. No credit cards. Wed–Mon 1:30–4pm and 8–11pm. Closed Aug 1–20.

MANZANARES EL REAL

48km (32 miles) N to NW of Madrid

Located near the source of the Manzanares River, this charming little town is well worth the trip for two very good reasons: first and foremost, to see its famous medieval castle, best-preserved in the entire province of Madrid; second, to explore the Cuenca Alta del Manzanares national park, whose astonishing Pedriza rock formations provide a fairy-tale backdrop to the town and the castle and are an ideal location for walking and picnicking.

Essentials

GETTING THERE **Hermanos de Colmenarejo SL** (✆ **91-314-64-08**) runs regularly from the Plaza Castilla Intercambiador station. The journey lasts about an hour (Rte. 724).

If you're **driving,** take the M-607 to Cerceda, and then swing right on to the M-608, which brings you straight to Manzanares.

VISITOR INFORMATION The **Town Hall,** Plaza del Pueblo 1 (✆ **91-853-00-09**), will give you full information on the town and its castle. There is also a small information kiosk at the entrance to the castle. Also see the website **www.manzanareselreal.org**.

Exploring Manzanares el Real

The **Castillo ★** (✆ **91-853-00-08**) stands beside the Santillana reservoir, its high turrets reflecting in the clear, still waters. Built in 1475 by the powerful Mendoza family, it was eventually converted into a palace. The original *Mudéjar* and Gothic walls remain, and the tastefully renovated interior hosts a library, observatory, exhibition room (named after the Marqués de Santillana), and tapestry-lined vestibule. From here climb to the parapets with their octagonal keep and trio of cylindrical towers, and enjoy the superb mountain and reservoir views. It's open Tuesday to Sunday June to September 10am to 1:15pm and 4 to 7:15pm, October to May 10am to 5:15pm. Admission is 2€. Concessionary charges 1€.

The **Iglesia Parroquial de Nuestra Señora de la Nieves** also dates from the 15th century and has a fine renaissance portal. It's home to a permanent colony of storks, who have made nests on its roof.

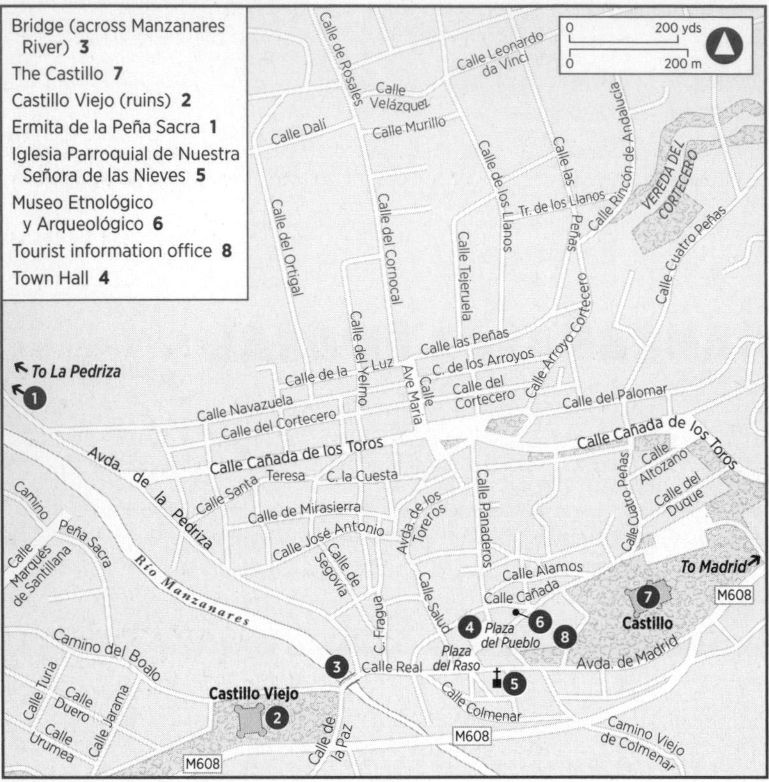

The tiny **Museo Etnológico y Arqueológico** is dedicated to ethnology and archaeology, with background prehistoric information on the surrounding area. It is within the Casa de Cultura, Calle de la Cañada 26 (✆ **91-853-03-40;** free admission; daily 5–9pm).

As spectacular a natural phenomenon as you'll find in the entire province, the surrealistically shaped granite formations of **La Pedriza ★** rise 2km (1¼ miles) north of the town, just off the road to Real de Cerceda. The surrounding paths and gullies of the Cuenca Alta de Manzanares national park are best avoided on weekends, especially in summer, when they tend to get packed with picnickers and hikers. Don't miss the marvelous views from the *mirador* at the Quebrantaherraduras Pass.

Near the entrance to the park, 3km (1¾ miles) above the town on Carretera de la Pedriza, you can visit the **Centro de Interpretación** (✆ **91-853-99-78**). This information center provides interesting facts on La Pedriza (such as geography, history, legends, and so on) and is open daily from 10am to 6pm. Short audiovisual shows about the park are given at 10 and 11:30am, and 1, 1:30, and 4:45pm. Admission is free.

The tiny 16th-century hermitage **Ermita de la Peña Sacra,** set high up in the national park's wild Peña Sacra (Holy Peak) area, also enjoys spectacular vistas. To get to it, follow Avenida de Pedriza up from the town. Unfortunately, the interior is now closed to the public (due to vandalism). You can, however, see the interior shrine through the window and take photographs of the simple but charming exterior. From its high vantage point, the Ermita enjoys spectacular views of the surrounding countryside.

Where to Stay

El Tranco This modest hostelry offers neat comfortable rooms and a comfortable atmosphere at very reasonable prices. It's popular and tends to get fully booked on weekends, so it's best to reserve in advance or go midweek.

Tranco 4. ✆ **91-853-00-63.** 9 units. 40€ double with shared bathroom, 50€ double with private bathroom. V. **Amenities:** Restaurant. *In room:* TV.

Where to Dine

Casa Goyo One of the town's favorite eating spots, the Goyo provides a wide variety of delicious but uncompromisingly traditional dishes ranging from *cabrito asado* (roast kid) to *chipirones en su tinta* (cuttlefish cooked in its own ink). It prides itself on using fresh market produce in all its dishes, which are priced accordingly.

Plaza del Sagrado Corazón 2. ✆ **91-853-94-84.** Main courses 15€–25€. V. Mon–Tues, Thurs–Sun 1:30–4pm and 9pm–midnight.

PATONES DE ARRIBA

60km (40 miles) NW of Madrid

A highly atmospheric village of black slate houses, Patones de Arriba (Upper Patones) clings to the rugged slopes of the Sierra Negra in the mountainous northwest corner of Madrid province, enjoying fine views of the Jarama Valley and the distant cliff-top township of Uceda, just inside the Guadalajara border. Its claims to fame are that it once had its own peasant king (who thought himself the equal of Felipe II) and it was one of the few spots unconquered by the French in the Peninsula War. After decades of abandon, it has reemerged in recent years as a favorite getaway for Madrileños, dotted with fine restaurants and tastefully converted houses, and surrounded by off-the-beaten-track walking trails. Its modern counterpart Patones de Abajo (Lower Patones), 2km (1¼ miles) below, is in contrast a functional town with a single main street bordered by modern low-level houses.

Essentials

GETTING THERE **Continental Auto SA** (✆ **91-533-04-00**) runs bus service (Rte. 197) several times a day from the Plaza Castilla Intercambiador through Torrelaguna to Patones de Abajo. From here you can catch a taxi or follow the steep path from the main road up a gorge to the village (half an hour's walk), depending on how energetic you're feeling.

Drive up the N-1 Burgos highway to Venturada, then take the N-320 to Torrelaguna, and finally the M-102, which brings you right to Patones de Arriba's tiny main square.

VISITOR INFORMATION Situated right on the square is the village's surprisingly well-equipped **Centro de Interpretación Rural de Patones** (✆ **91-843-20-26** weekdays, or 91-843-29-06 weekends; www.sierranorte.com/citeco) on Plaza de Llano, occupying a stone house with the grandiose name of Palacio de los Reyes de Patones. Here you can follow Patones's history from ancient times right up to the present via a series of plans, sketches, and scaled models. You can also watch a half-hour video. It's open Saturday, Sunday, and fiestas from noon to 6pm. Weekday visits can be arranged by appointment. The website **www.patones.es** also has useful information.

Exploring Patones de Arriba

The entire village is a scenic delight, where you can wander along higgledy-piggledy lanes, look at slate houses whose wild gardens overflow with luminous oleander bushes and outsize fig trees, and get enjoyably lost.

The larger town of **Torrelaguna** is just 7km (4⅓ miles) away and worth a visit on its own to see its monasteries, ancient walls, and magnificent 16th-century main square and church of Santa María Magdalena. Buses run to Torrelaguna and Patones de Abajo (below Patones de Arriba) directly from Madrid's Plaza Castilla station.

One of the walks to the north leads you to the dam **Presa de Atazar,** bordering a huge reservoir (largest in the province) fringed by pine woods. In summer, it's a great spot for picnicking or enjoying watersports. One minibus a day runs from Torrelaguna to Presa el Atazar and the neighboring village of El Atazar, departing at 11am, with return service to Torrelaguna at 5pm from El Atazar village.

Hidden away near the Atazar dam is the small but impressive **Cueva del Reguerillo,** whose stalactites and prehistoric sketches earned it a rating as an artistic-historic monument in 1931. A marked footpath from Patones de Abajo leads to the Reguerillo cave; it's approximately a 3-hour walk.

Where to Stay

El Tiempo Perdido ★★ Outwardly resembling just another village house, this is in fact one of the most original and prestigious little hotels in all of Madrid province. Its five individually furnished rooms have all been designed with superb taste by its French owner, with fine paintings, antiques, and quality linens. There's also a choice of classic videos, if you're a movie buff. Booking ahead is essential.

Travesía del Ayuntamiento 7. ✆ **91-843-21-52.** Reservations ✆ 65-038-17-30. 7 units. Double 190€–280€. MC, V. Fri–Sun and certain fiestas only. Closed Aug. **Amenities:** Lounge.

Where to Dine

El Poleo Regarded by many as Patones's top eating spot, this beautifully converted village house exudes atmosphere and style. The cuisine is mainly French Basque influenced, and specialties include *cordero en miel de Patones,* or roast lamb cooked in Patones honey. (Opposite is a twin eating spot, **El Jardín del Poleo,** with a large outdoor terrace ideal for summer dining.)

Travesía de Arroyo 1. ✆ **91-843-21-01.** Main courses 16€–30€. No credit cards. Fri–Sun 2–5pm and 9:30pm–midnight.

Rey de Patones Named after the village's former peasant king, this attractive and traditional restaurant is the oldest in Patones. It's definitely far from a vegetarian stronghold, as huge grilled steaks are the thing to have here. Because the owners live in the village, it's one of the few eating spots open during the week.

Asas 13. ✆ **91-843-20-27.** Main courses 15€–25€. No credit cards. Thurs–Tues 2–5pm and 9:30pm–midnight.

SAN LORENZO DE EL ESCORIAL ★

48km (30 miles) W of Madrid, 52km (32 miles) SE of Segovia

Without a doubt, one of the most unforgettable excursions from Madrid is to the austere royal monastery of San Lorenzo de El Escorial. Philip II ordered the construction of this granite-and-slate behemoth in 1563, 2 years after he moved his capital to Madrid. Once the haunt of aristocratic Spaniards, El Escorial is now a resort where hotels and restaurants flourish in summer, as hundreds come to escape the heat of the capital. Aside from the appeal of its climate, the town of San Lorenzo itself is not very noteworthy. But because of the monastery's size, you might decide to spend a night or two at San Lorenzo—or more if you have the time.

Essentials

GETTING THERE More than two dozen **trains** depart daily from Madrid's Atocha, Nuevos Ministerios, and Chamartín train stations. Trip time is little more than an hour. During the summer, extra coaches are added. For schedules and information, call ✆ **90-224-02-02.** A one-way fare costs 2.90€.

The railway station for San Lorenzo de El Escorial is located about 1.6km (1 mile) outside of town along Carretera Estación (✆ **91-890-07-14**). The Herranz bus company meets all arriving trains with a shuttle bus that ferries arriving passengers to and from the Plaza Virgen de Gracia, about a block east of the entrance to the monastery.

The Office of **Empresa Herranz,** Calle Reina Victoria 3, in El Escorial (✆ **91-890-41-22** or 91-890-41-25), runs some 40 buses per day (line 664) back and forth between Madrid's Moncloa station (Herranz Madrid; ✆ **91-896-90-28**) and El Escorial. On Sunday, service is curtailed to 10 buses. Trip time is an hour, and a round-trip fare costs 6.60€.

By **car,** follow the N-VI highway (marked on some maps as A-6) from the northwest perimeter of Madrid toward Lugo, La Coruña, and San Lorenzo de El Escorial. After about a half-hour, fork left onto the C-505 toward San Lorenzo de El Escorial. Driving time from Madrid is about an hour.

VISITOR INFORMATION The **tourist information office** is at Calle Grimaldi 2 (✆ **91-890-53-13**). It is open Monday to Thursday from 11am to 6pm, Friday to Sunday from 10am to 7pm.

Exploring San Lorenzo de El Escorial

Casa de Príncipe (Prince's Cottage) ★ This small but elaborately decorated 18th-century palace near the railway station was originally a hunting lodge built for

A Good Base for Exploring Castilla y Leon's Prize Cities

San Lorenzo (barely an hour from Madrid) makes a good base for visiting the Spanish capital and nearby Segovia, the royal palace at La Granja, and the Valley of the Fallen, or even—farther afield—Burgos, which is the site of one of Spain's very finest cathedrals.

Charles III by Juan de Villanueva. Most visitors stay in El Escorial for lunch, visiting the cottage in the afternoon.

Calle Reina s/n. ✆ **91-890-59-03.** Admission included in comprehensive ticket to El Escorial (p. 266). Sat-Sun and fiestas 10am-6:45pm.

El Valle de los Caídos (Valley of the Fallen) ★ This is Franco's El Escorial, an architectural marvel that took 2 decades to complete, dedicated to those who died in the Spanish Civil War. Its detractors say that it represents the worst of neofascist design; its admirers say they have found renewed inspiration by coming here.

A gargantuan cross nearly 150m high (492 ft.) dominates the Rock of Nava, a peak of the Guadarrama Mountains. Directly under the cross is a basilica with a vault in mosaic, completed in 1959. José Antonio Primo de Rivera, the founder of the Falange party, is buried here. When this Nationalist hero was buried at El Escorial, many people, especially influential monarchists, protested that he was not a royal. Infuriated, Franco decided to erect another monument. Originally it was slated to honor the dead on the Nationalist side only, but the intervention of several parties led to a decision to include all the *caídos* (fallen). In time, the mausoleum claimed Franco as well; his body was interred behind the high altar.

A funicular extends from near the entrance to the basilica to the base of the gigantic cross erected on the mountaintop above (where there's a superb view). When operating (it's closed indefinitely at the moment; see below), the funicular runs daily from 10:30am to 1:15pm and 4 to 6pm.

On the other side of the mountain, about a 10-minute walk from the mausoleum, is a Benedictine monastery that is sometimes referred to as "the Hilton of monasteries" because of its seeming luxury.

Note: At the time of writing, both the entire monument and the funicular service are **closed** to the public. There are no immediate plans to re-open. Consequently, the former afternoon bus service from San Lorenzo del Escorial no longer operates. You can only view the building from outside and if you want to do this, the best way to get there is by hired car via the following route. Drive to the entrance of the Cuelgamuros Valley, about 8km (5 miles) north of El Escorial in the heart of the Guadarrama Mountains. Once here, continue 6km (3½ miles) west along a wooded road to the underground basilica.

Real Monasterio de San Lorenzo de El Escorial ★★★ This huge granite fortress houses a wealth of paintings and tapestries and also serves as a burial place for Spanish kings. Foreboding inside and out, thanks to its sheer size and institutional look, El Escorial took 21 years to complete, a remarkably short time considering the bulk of the building and the primitive construction methods of the day. After his death, the original architect, Juan Bautista de Toledo, was replaced by Juan de Herrera, the greatest architect of Renaissance Spain, who completed the structure.

Philip II, who collected many of the paintings exhibited here in the New Museums, did not appreciate El Greco and favored Titian instead. But you'll still find El Greco's *The Martyrdom of St. Maurice,* rescued from storage, and his *St. Peter.* Other superb works include Titian's *Last Supper* and Velázquez's *The Tunic of Joseph.*

The **Royal Library** houses a priceless collection of 60,000 volumes—one of the most significant in the world. The displays range from the handwriting of St. Teresa to medieval instructions on playing chess. See, in particular, the Muslim codices and a Gothic *Cantigas* from the 13th-century reign of Alfonso X ("The Wise").

You can also visit the **Philip II Apartments;** these are strictly monastic, and Philip called them the "cell for my humble self" in this "palace for God." Philip became a religious fanatic and requested that his bedroom be erected overlooking the altar of the 90m-high (295-ft.) basilica, which has four organs and whose dome is based on Michelangelo's drawings for St. Peter's. The choir contains a crucifix by Cellini. By comparison, the Throne Room is simple. On the walls are many ancient maps. The Apartments of the Bourbon Kings are lavishly decorated, in contrast to Philip's preference for the ascetic.

Under the altar of the church, you'll find one of the most regal mausoleums in the world, the **Royal Pantheon,** where most of Spain's monarchs—from Charles I to Alfonso XII, including Philip II—are buried. In 1993, Don Juan de Borbón, the count of Barcelona and the father of King Juan Carlos (Franco passed over the count and never allowed him to ascend to the throne), was interred nearby. On a lower floor is the "Wedding Cake" tomb for children.

Allow at least 3 hours for a visit. The guided tour doesn't take you to all the sites, but you are free to explore on your own afterward.

Calle Juan de Borbón s/n. ✆ **91-890-59-03.** Comprehensive ticket 9€ adults, 5€ children, guided tour 10€. Free Wed. Apr–Sept Tues–Sun 10am–7pm; Oct–Mar Tues–Sun 10am–6pm.

Where to Stay

MODERATE

Hotel Botánico ★★ True to its name, the hotel stands in a lovely manicured garden. Although the building is traditionally Castilian, the decor seems vaguely alpine, with wood paneling and beams in the reception rooms. The clean, well-lit rooms are large and comfortable, with well-kept bathrooms containing tub/shower combinations. The hotel also has a restaurant.

Calle Timoteo Padros 16, 28200 San Lorenzo de El Escorial. ✆ **91-890-78-79.** Fax 91-890-81-58. 20 units. 125€–175€ double; 225€ suite. Breakfast included. AE, V. Free parking. **Amenities:** Restaurant; bar; babysitting; room service. *In room:* A/C, TV, hair dryer, minibar.

Hotel Victoria Palace ★ Tastefully renovated without losing its aura of style and comfort, the traditional Victoria Palace is simply the finest hotel in town. The rooms—some with private terraces, some with good views of El Escorial—are well furnished and all contain neatly kept bathrooms, mostly with tub/shower combinations. The rates are reasonable enough, and a bargain for a government-rated four-star hotel. The dining room serves some of the best food in town.

Calle Juan de Toledo 4, 28200 San Lorenzo de El Escorial. ✆ **91-896-98-90.** Fax 91-896-98-96. www.hotelvictoriapalace.com. 87 units. 140€–175€ double. AE, MC, V. Parking 12€. **Amenities:** Restaurant; bar; babysitting; outdoor pool (June–Sept); room service. *In room:* TV, hair dryer.

INEXPENSIVE

Hostal Cristina ★ An excellent budget choice, this hotel, which opened in the mid-1980s, is run by the Delgado family. Hostal Cristina doesn't pretend to compete with the comfort and amenities of the Victoria Palace (above) or even the Miranda & Suizo (below), but it has its devotees nonetheless. About 45m (150 ft.) from the monastery, it stands in the center of town, offering clean and comfortable, but simply furnished, rooms. Every room has a well-kept bathroom with a tub/shower combination. As the food served in the restaurant is good and plentiful, many Spanish visitors prefer to book here for a summer holiday.

Juan de Toledo 6, 28200 San Lorenzo de El Escorial. www.hostalcristina.es. ✆ **91-890-19-61.** Fax 91-890-12-04. 16 units. 50€–55€ double. MC, V. **Amenities:** Lounge. *In room:* TV.

Hotel Miranda & Suizo ★ On a tree-lined street in the heart of town, within easy walking distance of the monastery, this excellent middle-bracket establishment ranks as a leading government-rated two-star hotel. It's a Victorian-style building dating back to the late 19th century, with atmospheric lounges and comfortable guest rooms, some of which have terraces. The furnishings are comfortable, the beds often made of brass; sometimes you'll find fresh flowers on the tables. All units have bathrooms with tub/shower combinations. In summer, there is outside dining.

Calle Floridablanca 20, 28200 San Lorenzo de El Escorial. ✆ **91-890-47-11.** Fax 91-890-43-58. www.hotelmirandasuizo.com. 52 units. 85€–140€ suite. AE, DC, MC, V. Parking 8€. **Amenities:** Restaurant; bar. *In room:* A/C, TV, minibar.

Where to Dine

MODERATE

Charolés SPANISH/INTERNATIONAL The thick and solid walls of this establishment date, according to its managers, "from the monastic age"—and probably predate El Escorial. The restaurant was established around 1980, and has been known ever since as the best dining room in town. It has a flower-ringed outdoor terrace for use during clement weather. The cuisine doesn't quite rate a star, but chances are you'll be satisfied. The wide variety of choices are based entirely on fresh fish and meats and include such dishes as grilled hake with green or hollandaise sauce, shellfish soup, pepper steak, a *pastel* (pie) of fresh vegetables with crayfish, and herb-flavored baby lamb chops. Strawberry or kiwi tart is a good dessert choice.

Calle Floridablanca 24. ✆ **91-890-59-75.** Reservations required. Main courses 18€–32€. AE, DC, MC, V. Daily 1–4pm and 9pm–midnight.

La Cueva ★ CASTILIAN Founded in 1768, this restaurant captures the world of Old Castile, and it is only a short walk from the monastery. A *mesón típico* (typical Spanish bar) built around an enclosed courtyard, "the Cave" boasts such nostalgic accents as stained-glass windows, antique chests, a 19th-century bullfighting collage, faded engravings, paneled doors, and iron balconies. The cooking is on target, and the portions are generous. Regional specialties include Valencian paella and *fabada asturiana* (pork sausage and beans), but the fresh trout, broiled in butter, is the best of all. The menu's most expensive items are Segovian roast suckling pig and roast lamb (tender inside, crisp outside). Off the courtyard through a separate doorway is La Cueva's *tasca* (tapas bar), filled with Castilians quaffing their favorite before-dinner drinks.

San Antón 4. ✆ **91-890-15-16.** www.mesonlacueva.com. Reservations recommended. Main courses 12€–22€; *menú del día* 16€; *menú especial* (chef's special menu of the day) 25€. AE, MC, V. Tues–Sun 1–4pm and 8:30–11:30pm.

El Escorial After Dark

No longer the rather sober and restrained place it was during the long Franco era, the town comes alive at night, fueled mainly by the throngs of young people who pack into the bars and taverns, especially those along Calle Rey and Calle Floridablanca. One of my favorite bars, offering vats of wine or kegs of beer, is the **Regina Piano Bar,** Floridablanca (✆ **91-890-68-43;** www.reginapianobar.com).

TOLEDO ★★★

68km (42 miles) SW of Madrid; 137km (85 miles) SE of Avila

Don't miss a trip to Toledo—a place made special by its Arab, Jewish, Christian, and even Roman and Visigoth elements. A national landmark, the city that so inspired El Greco in the 16th century has remained relatively unchanged. You can still stroll through streets barely wide enough for a man and his donkey—much less for an automobile.

Surrounded on three sides by a bend in the Tagus River, Toledo stands atop a hill overlooking the arid plains of New Castile—a natural fortress in the center of the Iberian Peninsula. It was a logical choice for the capital of Spain, though it lost its political status to Madrid in the 1500s. Toledo has remained the country's religious center, as the seat of the Primate of Spain.

If you're driving, the much-painted skyline of Toledo will come into view about 6km (3½ miles) from the city. When you cross the Tagus River on the 14th-century Puente San Martín, the scene is reminiscent of El Greco's moody, storm-threatened *View of Toledo,* which hangs in New York's Metropolitan Museum of Art. The artist reputedly painted that view from a hillside that is now the site of **Parador Nacional de Conde Orgaz** (p. 275). If you arrive at the right time, you can enjoy an aperitif on the Parador's (p. 275) terrace and watch one of the famous violet sunsets of Toledo.

Essentials

GETTING THERE The high speed AVANT **train** service has 12 trains a day on weekdays and 7 a day at weekends—between 6:50am and 9:50pm—making the trip from Madrid's Atocha station in just 30 minutes. One-way fare is 9€. For more information, call ✆ **90-224-02-02;** in Toledo, call ✆ **92-522-30-99.**

Several **bus** companies run a regular bus service between Madrid and Toledo. Largest of these is **Continental-Auto.** Departures are from Madrid's Estación Sur de Autobuses (South Bus Station), Calle Méndez Álvaro (✆ **91-468-42-00** for information), every day between 6:30am and 10pm at 30-minute intervals. The fastest leave Monday to Friday on the hour. Those that depart weekdays on the half-hour, and those that run on weekends, take a bit longer. Travel time, depending on whether the bus stops at villages en route, is between 1 hour and 1 hour, 20 minutes. A one-way trip costs 4.50€.

A Great Scenic Drive

Another Toledan highlight is the Carretera de Circunvalación, the route that threads through the city and runs along the Tagus. Clinging to the hillsides are rustic dwellings, the *cigarrales* of the Imperial City, immortalized by 17th-century dramatist Tirso de Molina, who named his trilogy *Los Cigarrales de Toledo.*

Once you reach Toledo, you'll be deposited at the Estación de Autobuses, which lies beside the river, about 1.2km (¾-mile) from the historic center. Although many visitors opt to walk, be advised that the ascent is steep. Bus nos. 5 and 6 run from the station uphill to the center, charging 1€ for the brief ride. Pay the driver directly.

If you drive, exit Madrid via Cibeles (Paseo del Prado) and take the N-401 south.

VISITOR INFORMATION The **tourist information office** is at Puerta de Bisagra (✆ **92-522-08-43**). It's open Monday to Friday from 9am to 6pm, Saturday from 9am to 7pm, and Sunday from 9am to 3pm.

Exploring Toledo

Alcázar The Alcázar, located at the eastern edge of the old city, dominates the Toledo skyline. It became world famous at the beginning of the Spanish Civil War, when it underwent a 70-day siege that almost destroyed it. Today it has been rebuilt and turned into an army museum, housing such exhibits as a plastic model of what the fortress looked like after the Civil War, electronic equipment used during the siege, and photographs taken during the height of the battle. A walking tour gives a realistic simulation of the siege. Allow an hour for a visit. The long-closed Museo del Ejército (Army Museum) in Madrid reopened here in July 2010. Calle General Moscardó 4, near the Plaza de Zocodover. ✆ **92-522-16-73.** Admission 4€ adults, free for children 9 and under. Tues–Sun 9:30am–2pm. Bus: 5 or 6.

Casa y Museo de El Greco ★ Located in Toledo's *antiguo barrio judío* (the old Jewish quarter, a labyrinth of narrow streets on the old town's southwestern edge), the House of El Greco honors the great master painter, although he didn't actually live here. In 1585, the artist moved into one of the run-down palace apartments belonging to the Marquís of Villena. Although he was to live at other Toledan addresses, he returned to the Villena palace in 1604 and remained there until his death. Only a small part of the original residence was saved from decay. In time, this and a neighboring house became the El Greco Museum; today it's furnished with authentic period pieces.

You can visit El Greco's so-called studio, where one of his paintings hangs. The museum contains several more works, including a copy of *A View of Toledo* and three portraits, plus many pictures by various 16th- and 17th-century Spanish artists. The garden and especially the kitchen also merit attention, as does a sitting room decorated in the Moorish style.

Calle Samuel Leví 3. ✆ **92-522-40-46.** Admission 3€ adults, free for children 9 and under. Tues–Sat 10am–2pm and 4–6pm; Sun 10am–2pm. Bus: 5 or 6.

Catedral ★★★ Ranked among the greatest Gothic structures, the cathedral actually reflects several styles, since more than 2½ centuries elapsed during its construction (1226–1493). Many historic events transpired here, including the proclamation of Joanna the Mad and her husband, Philip the Handsome, as heirs to the throne of Spain.

Among its art treasures, the *transparente* stands out—a wall of marble and florid baroque alabaster sculpture overlooked for years because the cathedral was too poorly lit. Sculptor Narcisco Tomé cut a hole in the ceiling, much to the consternation of Toledans, and now light touches the high-rising angels, a *Last Supper* in alabaster, and a Virgin in ascension.

The 16th-century Capilla Mozárabe, containing works by Juan de Borgoña, is another curiosity of the cathedral. Mass is still held here using Mozarabic liturgy.

The Treasure Room has a 228kg (500-lb.) 15th-century gilded monstrance—allegedly made with gold brought back from the New World by Columbus—that is still carried through the streets of Toledo during the feast of Corpus Christi.

Other highlights of the cathedral include El Greco's *Twelve Apostles and Spoliation of Christ* and Goya's *Arrest of Christ on the Mount of Olives*. The cathedral shop,

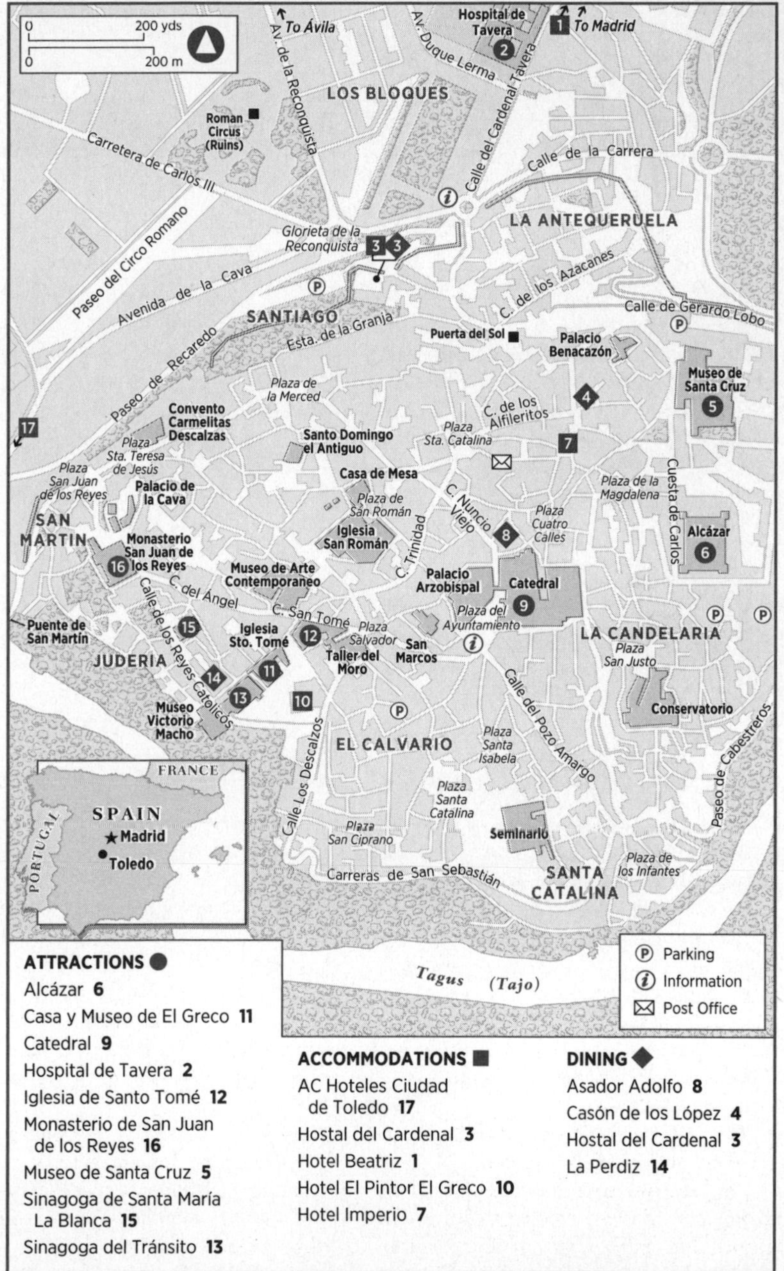
0 200 yds
0 200 m
To Ávila
Av. de la Reconquista
Av. Duque Lerma
Hospital de Tavera
To Madrid
Calle del Cardenal Tavera
LOS BLOQUES
Roman Circus (Ruins)
Carretera de Carlos III
Calle de la Carrera
LA ANTEQUERUELA
Paseo del Circo Romano
Glorieta de la Reconquista
Avenida de la Cava
C. de los Azacanes
SANTIAGO
Esta. de la Granja
Calle de Gerardo Lobo
Puerta del Sol
Palacio Benacazón
Paseo de Recaredo
Museo de Santa Cruz
Plaza de la Merced
C. de los Alfileritos
Convento Carmelitas Descalzas
Plaza Sta. Catalina
Santo Domingo el Antiguo
Plaza Sta. Teresa de Jesús
Plaza San Juan de los Reyes
Casa de Mesa
Plaza de la Magdalena
Palacio de la Cava
Plaza de San Román
C. Nuncio Viejo
Plaza Cuatro Calles
Cuesta de Carlos V
SAN MARTIN
Monasterio San Juan de los Reyes
Iglesia San Román
C. Trinidad
Alcázar
Museo de Arte Contemporaneo
Palacio Arzobispal
Catedral
C. del Ángel
Calle de los Reyes Católicos
C. San Tomé
Plaza del Ayuntamiento
Puente de San Martín
Iglesia Sto. Tomé
Plaza Salvador
San Marcos
LA CANDELARIA
Plaza San Justo
JUDERIA
Taller del Moro
Calle del Pozo Amargo
Conservatorio
Museo Victorio Macho
EL CALVARIO
Plaza Santa Isabela
Calle Los Descalzos
Plaza Santa Catalina
Paseo de Cabestreros
FRANCE
SPAIN
Madrid
Toledo
PORTUGAL
Plaza San Ciprano
Seminario
Carreras de San Sebastián
Plaza de los Infantes
SANTA CATALINA
Tagus (Tajo)
Parking
Information
Post Office
ATTRACTIONS
Alcázar 6
Casa y Museo de El Greco 11
Catedral 9
Hospital de Tavera 2
Iglesia de Santo Tomé 12
Monasterio de San Juan de los Reyes 16
Museo de Santa Cruz 5
Sinagoga de Santa María La Blanca 15
Sinagoga del Tránsito 13
ACCOMMODATIONS
AC Hoteles Ciudad de Toledo 17
Hostal del Cardenal 3
Hotel Beatriz 1
Hotel El Pintor El Greco 10
Hotel Imperio 7
DINING
Asador Adolfo 8
Casón de los López 4
Hostal del Cardenal 3
La Perdiz 14

where you buy tickets to enter, stocks a variety of quality souvenirs, including ceramics and damascene.

Cardenal Cisneros 1. ✆ **92-522-22-41.** Admission including Treasure Room 7€. Mon–Sat 10:30am–6pm; Sun 2–6:30pm.

Hospital de Tavera ★ This 16th-century Greco-Roman palace north of the medieval ramparts of Toledo was originally built by Cardinal Tavera; it now houses a private art collection. Titian's portrait of Charles V hangs in the banqueting hall. The museum owns five paintings by El Greco: *The Holy Family, The Baptism of Christ,* and portraits of St. Francis, St. Peter, and Cardinal Tavera. Ribera's *The Bearded Woman* also attracts many viewers. The collection of books in the library is priceless. In the nearby church is the mausoleum of Cardinal Tavera, designed by Alonso Berruguete.

Hospital de Tavera 2. ✆ **92-522-04-51.** Admission 4.50€. Daily 10:30am–1:30pm and 3:30–6pm.

Iglesia de Santo Tomé This modest little 14th-century chapel, situated on a narrow street in the old Jewish quarter, might have been overlooked had it not possessed El Greco's masterpiece *The Burial of the Count of Orgaz* ★★★, created in 1586. To avoid the hordes, go when the chapel first opens.

Plaza del Conde 4, Vía Santo Tomé. ✆ **92-525-60-98.** Admission 1.90€, 1.40€ students and seniors 65 and over. Daily 10am–6:45pm (closes at 5:45pm in winter). Closed Dec 25 and Jan 1.

Monasterio de San Juan de los Reyes ★ Founded by King Ferdinand and Queen Isabella to commemorate their triumph over the Portuguese at Toro in 1476, the church was started in 1477 according to the plans of architect Juan Guas. It was finished, together with the splendid cloisters, in 1504, dedicated to St. John the Evangelist, and used from the beginning by the Franciscan friars. An example of Gothic-Spanish-Flemish style, San Juan de los Reyes was restored after the damage caused during Napoleon's invasion and after its abandonment in 1835; since 1954, it has been entrusted again to the Franciscans. The church is located at the extreme western edge of the old town, midway between the Puente (bridge) of San Martín and the Puerta (gate) of Cambron.

Calle Reyes Católicos 17. ✆ **92-522-38-02.** Admission 1.90€ adults, 1.40€ seniors 65 and over, free for children 8 and under. Winter daily 10am–1:45pm and 3:30–6pm; summer daily 10am–1:45pm and 3:30–7pm. Bus: 2.

Museo de Santa Cruz ★★ Today a museum of art and sculpture, this was originally a 16th-century Spanish Renaissance hospice founded by Cardinal Mendoza—"the third king of Spain"—who helped Ferdinand and Isabella gain the throne. The facade is almost more spectacular than any of the exhibits inside. It's a stunning architectural achievement in the classical plateresque style (see p. 21). The major artistic treasure inside is El Greco's *The Assumption of the Virgin,* his last known work. Paintings by Goya and Ribera are also on display, along with gold items, opulent antique furnishings, Flemish tapestries, and even Visigoth artifacts. In the patio of the museum, you'll stumble across various fragments of carved stone and sarcophagi lids. One of the major exhibits is of a large astrolabe tapestry of the zodiac from the 1400s. In the basement, you can see artifacts, including elephant tusks, from various archaeological digs throughout the province.

Calle Miguel de Cervantes 3. ✆ **92-522-14-02.** Free admission. Mon–Sat 10am–6:30pm; Sun 10am–2pm. Bus: 5 or 6. Pass beneath the granite archway on the eastern edge of the Plaza de Zocodover and walk about 1 block.

Sinagoga de Santa María La Blanca ★ In the late 12th century, the Jews of Toledo erected an important synagogue in the *almohada* style, which employs graceful horseshoe arches and ornamental horizontal moldings. Although by the early 15th century it had been converted into a Christian church, much of the original remains, including the five naves and elaborate *Mudéjar* decorations, mosquelike in their effect. The synagogue lies on the western edge of the city, midway between the El Greco museum and San Juan de los Reyes.

Calle Reyes Católicos 2. ✆ **92-522-72-57.** Admission 1.90€, 1.40€ students and seniors 65 and over. Daily 10am–6pm. Bus: 2.

Sinagoga del Tránsito ★ One block west of the El Greco home and museum stands this once-important house of worship for Toledo's large Jewish population. A 14th-century building, it is noted for its superb stucco Hebrew inscriptions, including psalms inscribed along the top of the walls and a poetic description of the Temple on the east wall. The synagogue is the most important part of the **Museo Sefardí (Sephardic Museum),** which opened in 1971 and contains art objects as well as tombstones with Hebrew epigraphy, some of which are dated before 1492.

Calle Samuel Leví. ✆ **92-522-36-65.** Admission 2.40€. Tues–Sat 10am–2pm and 4–9pm; Sun 10am–2pm. Closed Jan 1, May 1, Dec 24–25, and Dec 31. Bus: 2.

Shopping

In swashbuckling days, the swordsmiths of Toledo were world-renowned. They're still here and still turning out swords today, though now they're souvenirs and not dueling weapons. Toledo is equally renowned for its *damasquinado,* or **damascene** work, the Moorish art of inlaying gold, even copper or silver threads, against a matte black steel backdrop. Today Toledo is filled with souvenir shops hawking damascene. The price depends on whether the item is handcrafted or machine made. Sometimes machine-made damascene is passed off as the more-expensive handcrafted item, so you have to shop carefully. Bargaining is perfectly acceptable in Toledo, but if you get the price down, you can't pay with a credit card—only cash.

The Pottery & Embroidery Towns of Old Castile

The best deals on pottery won't be found in Toledo. If you're interested in buying a number of items, consider a trip to **Talavera la Reina,** 76km (47 miles) west of Toledo, where most of the pottery is made. Since Talavera is the largest city in the province, it is hardly a picture-postcard little potter's village. Most of the shops lie along the main street of town, where you'll find store after store selling this distinctive pottery in multicolored designs.

Pottery hunters also flock to **Puente del Arzobispo,** another ceramic center, known for its green-hued pottery. From Talavera, drive west on the N-V to Oropesa, then south for 14km (9 miles) to a fortified bridge across the Tagus. In general, ceramics here are cheaper than those sold in Toledo.

Just past **Oropesa** at the turnoff to Lagartera is the village where the highly sought-after embroidery of La Mancha originates. Virtually every cottage displays samples of this free-form floral stitching, shaped into everything from skirts to tablecloths. Of course, shops in Toledo are also filled with samples of this unique embroidery.

Marzipan (called *mazapán* locally) is often prepared by nuns and is a local specialty. Many shops in town specialize in this treat made of sweet almond paste.

The province of Toledo is also renowned for its **pottery,** which is sold in so many shops at competitive prices that it's almost unnecessary to recommend specific branches hawking these wares. However, over the years I've found that the prices at the large roadside emporiums on the outskirts of town on the main road to Madrid often have better bargains than the shops within the city walls, where rents are higher.

Bermejo Established in 1910, this factory and store employs almost 50 artisans, whom you can observe at work as part of a visit. The outlet carries a wide array of damascene objects fashioned into Toledo's traditional *Mudéjar* designs. These include swords, platters, pitchers, and other gift items. Don't think, however, that everything this place manufactures follows the inspiration of the medieval Arabs. The outfit engraves many of the ornamental swords that are awarded to graduates of West Point in the United States, as well as the decorative, full-dress military accessories used by the armies of various countries of Europe, including France. Open Monday to Friday from 9am to 1pm and 3 to 6pm, Saturday from 8am to 1pm. Closing times are later in July and August, determined solely by business traffic. Calle Airosas 5. ✆ **92-528-53-67.** www.bermejoswords.com.

Casa Telesforo Many long-time residents of Toledo remember this place as the supplier of the marzipan consumed at their childhood birthday parties and celebrations. A specialist in the almond-and-sugar confection whose origins go back to the year 1806, it sells the best *mazapán* (marzipan) in town, cunningly made into such whimsical shapes as hearts, diamonds, flowers, and fish. Open daily from 9am to 10pm, later in summer, depending on the crowds. Plaza de Zocodover 13. ✆ **92-522-33-79.**

Felipe Suárez Established in the 1920s, this outfit has manufactured damascene work in various forms ranging from unpretentious souvenir items to art objects of rare museum-quality beauty that sell for as much as 12,000€. You'll find swords, straight-edged razors, pendants, fans, and an array of pearls. The shop maintains extended hours throughout the year, daily from 9:30am to 7pm. Paseo de los Canónigos 19. ✆ **92-522-56-15.**

Santiago Sánchez Martín This is one of the most painstaking and prestigious manufacturers of damascene work in Toledo. It specializes in the elaborately detailed arabesques, whose techniques are as old as the Arab conquest of Iberia. Look for everything from decorative tableware (platters, pitchers), to mirror frames, jewelry, letter openers, and ornamental swords. Open Monday to Friday from 9am to 2pm and 5 to 7pm. Río Llano 15. ✆ **92-522-77-57.**

Where to Stay

EXPENSIVE

AC Hoteles Ciudad de Toledo ★★ Just over a decade old, this hotel has emerged as a first-rate alternative to the Parador, for location and amenities alike. In fact, if El Greco were painting his *A View of Toledo* today, he might well have preferred this splendid site, whose panorama can hardly be bettered. On a beltway south of the city—follow the directions to the Parador—this deluxe property is a member of a chain that also includes the swanky Santo Mauro in Madrid. The epitome of luxury living and contemporary lines, you enter the hotel from the third floor and move down through the spiraling architectural design to reach the rest of the hotel. Bedrooms are spacious and luxuriously furnished, all in contemporary styling, each with tiled bathrooms containing tub/shower combinations. The suites have oversize bathtubs and hydromassage.

Carretera de Circunvalación 15, 41005 Toledo. ✆ **92-528-51-25.** Fax 92-528-47-00. www.ac-hotels.com. 49 units. 130€–150€ double; 190€–225€ suite. AE, MC, V. Free parking. Bus: 5. **Amenities:** Restaurant; bar; babysitting; room service. *In room:* A/C, TV, hair dryer, minibar.

Hotel Beatriz ★★ ☺ This was the first really luxe hotel constructed in the city. It's also the largest, although the staff still manages to give its guests personal attention. The building dates from the early 1990s but was completely refurbished post-millennium, making it your best bet for up-to-date technology.

Junior suites are blessed with a private Jacuzzi; the more expensive rooms have hydromassages. The furnishings are tasteful and comfortable, and the location is only a 5-minute drive from the Old Town. The activities here are the best of any hotel, including the bamboo-constructed Kiosk Bar with great cocktails. The piano bar features live music plus an on-site dance club. The hotel restaurant, Alacena (p. 277), is also Toledo's most luxurious.

Carretera de Avila Km 2.75, 45005 Toledo. ✆ **92-526-91-00.** Fax 92-521-58-65. www.hotelbeatriztoledo.com. 295 units. 90€–145€ double; 180€ junior suite; 295€ suite. AE, DC, MC, V. Parking 10€. **Amenities:** 2 restaurants; bar; babysitting; gym; outdoor pool; room service; sauna; rooms for those w/ limited mobility. *In room:* A/C, TV, hair dryer, minibar.

Parador de Toledo Conde de Orgaz ★★★ You'll have to make reservations well in advance to stay at this *parador,* which is built on the ridge of a rugged hill where El Greco is said to have painted his *A View of Toledo.* That view is still here, and it is without a doubt one of the grandest in the world. The main lounge has fine furniture—old chests, brown leather chairs, and heavy tables—and leads to a sunny terrace overlooking the city. On chilly nights, you can sit by the public fireplace. The guest rooms are the most luxurious in all of Toledo, far superior to those at Hotel María Cristina (see below). Spacious and beautifully furnished with reproductions of regional antique pieces, each has a private bathroom with a tub/shower combination.

Cerro del Emperador, 45002 Toledo. ✆ **92-522-18-50.** Fax 92-522-51-66. www.parador.es. 76 units. 150€ double; 195€ suite. AE, DC, MC, V. Free parking. Drive across Puente San Martín and head south for 4km (2½ miles). **Amenities:** Restaurant; bar; babysitting; outdoor pool (June–Sept only); room service. *In room:* A/C, TV, hair dryer, minibar.

MODERATE

Hostal del Cardenal ★★ Although long acclaimed as the best restaurant in Toledo (p. 278), the fact that this establishment has rooms available is still a well-kept secret. They're not as grand as those at the Parador, but they are choice nevertheless, sought by those wanting to capture an old Toledan atmosphere. The entrance to this unusual hotel is set into the stone fortifications of the ancient city walls, a few steps from the Bisagra Gate. To enter the hotel, you must climb a series of terraces to the top of the crenellated walls of the ancient fortress. Here, grandly symmetrical and very imposing, is the *hostal* (hostel), the former residence of the 18th-century cardinal of Toledo, Señor Lorenzana. Just beyond the entrance, still atop the city wall, you'll find flagstone walkways, Moorish fountains, rose gardens, and cascading vines. The establishment has tiled walls; long, narrow salons; dignified Spanish furniture; and a smattering of antiques. Each room has a private bathroom equipped with a tub/shower combination.

Paseo de Recaredo 24, 45003 Toledo. © **92-522-49-00.** Fax 92-522-29-91. www.hostaldelcardenal.com. 27 units. 95€–125€ double; 125€–160€ suite. AE, DC, MC, V. Free parking (limited places). Bus: 2 from rail station. **Amenities:** Restaurant; bar; babysitting. *In room:* A/C, TV, hair dryer.

Hotel María Cristina Adjacent to the historic Hospital de Tavera and near the northern perimeter of the old town, this stone-sided, awning-fronted hotel resembles a palatial country home. If you're willing to forgo the view from the Parador and the charm of Hostal del Cardenal, this hotel is generally cited as *número tercero* in Toledo. Originally built as a convent in 1560 and later used as a hospital, it was transformed into this comfortable hostelry in the late 1980s. Sprawling, historic, and generously proportioned, it contains clean, amply sized, attractively furnished guest rooms, each with a private bathroom, which are mostly equipped with tub/shower combinations. On-site is the very large and well-recommended restaurant, El Abside.

Marqués de Mendigorría 1, 45003 Toledo. © **92-521-32-02.** Fax 92-521-26-50. www.hotelesmayoral.com. 73 units. 115€ double; 185€ suite. AE, DC, MC, V. Parking 10€. **Amenities:** Restaurant; bar; room service. *In room:* A/C, TV, minibar.

Hotel Pintor El Greco ★ In the old Jewish quarter, one of the most traditional and historic districts of Toledo, this hotel was converted from a typical *casa toledana* (house in Toledo), which had once been used as a bakery. With careful restoration, especially of its ancient facade, it was transformed into one of Toledo's best and most atmospheric small hotels—the only one to match the antique charm of Hostal del Cardenal (see above), although, it too, seems relatively unknown. Decoration in both the public rooms and bedrooms is in a traditional Castilian style. Bedrooms come in a variety of shapes and sizes, as befits a building of this age, but all are equipped with small bathrooms with tub/shower combinations.

Alamillos del Tránsito 13, 45002 Toledo. © **92-528-51-91.** Fax 92-521-58-19. www.hotelpintorelgreco.com. 33 units. 110€–130€ double. AE, DC, MC, V. Parking 5€. **Amenities:** Lounge; babysitting. *In room:* A/C, TV, hair dryer, minibar.

Kris Doménico ★ ☺ A government-rated four-star hotel and one of the finest in Toledo, Doménico is located among Los Cigarrales, the typical country houses lying south of the city and offering panoramic views, though only a 5-minute drive to the historic core. The modern building is constructed in a classic and traditional style. Bedrooms are medium in size and comfortably furnished. Some of the rooms have windows in the roof for greater light. All units contain well-kept bathrooms with tub/shower combinations. The second- and third-floor rooms have terraces opening onto the swimming pool or views of the city. A terrace restaurant offers a fine national and international cuisine.

Cerro del Emperador, 45002 Toledo. © **92-528-01-01.** Fax 92-528-02-03. www.krishoteles.com. 50 units. 125€ double; 210€ suite. AE, MC, V. Free parking. Bus: 7. **Amenities:** Restaurant; bar; babysitting; outdoor pool (June–Sept only); room service. *In room:* A/C, TV, hair dryer, minibar.

INEXPENSIVE

Hotel Imperio Toledo Long a budget favorite, this modest hotel is a few yards from the Alcázar and Cathedral. Built in the '80s, the hotel was recently renovated (and just in time), adding more comfort to the small rooms. The furnishings are in a rather severe style, but the beds are comfortable and the bathrooms have tub/shower combinations. However, for the price, this is one of the city's best choices. Rooms on the second floor have balconies overlooking the street. A snack bar is on-site, but some fine restaurants lie just outside the door.

Cadena 5, 45001 Toledo. ✆ **92-522-76-50.** Fax 92-525-31-83. www.terra.es/personal/earroyop/inicio.htm. 21 units. 50€ double. AE, DC, MC, V. Parking nearby 14€. **Amenities:** Bar; lounge; babysitting. *In room:* A/C, TV.

Where to Dine

MODERATE

Alacena ★ TOLEDAN/SPANISH In the previously recommended Hotel Beatriz, this is the most elegant and comfortable restaurant in Toledo, although Hostal del Cardenal (see below) maintains a slight edge in cuisine. Using some of the area's best products and the finest produce shipped from the international markets in Madrid, Alacena's chefs are dedicated to flavor, taste, and texture. The chefs also celebrate the dying art of hunting, as evoked by such specialties as stewed partridge or sirloin of deer in a sauce of fresh mushrooms. Other specialties include filet of hare and Mediterranean rice dishes. Sometimes the chefs feature a specialty month, such as November, when they celebrate the cuisine of Galicia province in the northwest, shipping in turbot, hake, bullock, and goose barnacles caught off the coast of Spain.

In the Hotel Beatriz (p. 275), Carretera de Avila. ✆ **92-526-91-00.** Reservations recommended. Main courses 12€–25€. Fixed-price menu 36€–40€. AE, DC, MC, V. Mon–Sat 1:30–4pm; daily 8–11:30pm.

Asador Adolfo ★ SPANISH Less than a minute's walk north of the cathedral, Asador Adolfo is one of the finest restaurants in town (though I prefer the Hostal del Cardenal). Sections of the building were first constructed during the 1400s, although the thoroughly modern kitchen has recently been renovated. Massive beams support the dining room ceilings, and, here and there, the rooms contain faded frescoes dating from the original building.

Game dishes are a house specialty; such choices as partridge with white beans and venison consistently rate among the best anywhere. Other offerings include hake flavored with local saffron as well as a wide array of beef, veal, or lamb dishes. To start, try the *pimientos rellenos* (red peppers stuffed with pulverized shellfish). The house dessert is marzipan, prepared in a wood-fired oven and noted for its lightness.

Del a Granada 6. ✆ **92-522-73-21.** Reservations recommended. Main courses 18€–28€; fixed-price menu 35€; tasting menu 48€. AE, DC, MC, V. Daily 1–4pm; Mon–Sat 8pm–midnight. Bus: 5 or 6.

El Casón de Los López de Toledo ★★ CASTILIAN A short walk from the heartbeat Plaza de Zocodover, this charmer serves the lightest and most sophisticated cuisine in Toledo. Its setting alone would make it an enticing choice. In an antique building, it's a virtual museum, furnished with antiques, some from as far back as the 16th century. Castilian iron bars, *Mudéjar*-style wooden ceilings, Arab stucco decorations, a patio ringed with marble statues, a splashing fountain, and caged birds create a mellow atmosphere. And get this: Much of the furniture is for sale. Hopefully, some other diner won't buy the table out from under you when your main course arrives.

In this mellow ambience, sample the local countryside fare such as game, hare, rabbit, partridge, and pigeon. A recent specialty I enjoyed, loin of venison with fresh, garlic-flecked spinach in a velvety smooth mushroom cream sauce, was irresistibly juicy and a combination of blissful contrasts. Launch yourself with the garlic-ravioli soup, a first for many diners, and top the meal with an extravagant cheese and fresh plum mousse.

Sillería 3. ✆ **92-525-47-74** or 90-219-83-44. www.casontoledo.com. Reservations required. Main courses 15€–24€; set-price standard and "gran" menus 41€–71€. AE, DC, MC, V. Daily 1:30–4pm; Mon–Sat 9–11pm.

Hostal del Cardenal ★★ SPANISH Treat yourself to Toledo's best-known restaurant, located in the hotel of the same name (p. 275) and owned by the same people who run Madrid's Sobrino de Botín (p. 128). The chef prepares regional dishes with flair and originality. Choosing from a menu very similar to that of the fabled Madrid eatery, begin with "quarter of an hour" (fish) soup or white asparagus, then move on to curried prawns, baked hake, filet mignon, or smoked salmon. Roast suckling pig is a specialty, as is partridge in casserole. Arrive early to enjoy a sherry in the bar or in the courtyard.

Paseo de Recaredo 24. ✆ **92-522-08-62.** www.hostaldelcardenal.com. Reservations required. Main courses 12€–24€; fixed-price menu 24€. AE, DC, MC, V. Daily 1–4pm and 8:30–11:30pm. Bus: 2 from rail station.

INEXPENSIVE

Restaurante La Perdiz ★ CASTILIAN La Perdiz is named from the favorite dish of Toledans: partridge. That bird is best showcased here in a dish called *perdiz estofada a la toledana,* partridge stew with white wine, bay leaf, and onions. Another excellent choice is venison in a mushroom sauce. The menu also has some imaginative offerings such as a fresh fried cheese tossed in an orange dressing. On occasion a roast suckling pig is featured. The best dessert is that local favorite, marzipan, here served as a tart with almond biscuits. Locals cite the place, with good reason, for its quality cuisine at affordable prices. The same people who run La Perdiz also operate Asador Adolfo, Toledo's premier restaurant (see above). But prices at La Perdiz are far more reasonable.

Calle Reyes Católicos 7. ✆ **92-525-29-19.** www.grupoadolfo.com/restaurante-laperdiz.html. Reservations recommended. Main courses 12€–24€; set menu 24€. AE, MC, V. Tues–Sat noon–11pm; Sun noon–4pm.

Toledo After Dark

Begin your nighttime crawl through Toledo with a stop at **Bar Ludeña,** Plaza de la Magdalena 13, Corral de Don Diego 10 (✆ **92-522-33-84**), where a loyal clientele comes for delectable tapas. Fixed-price menus range from 10€ to 17€. Glasses of wine are sometimes passed through a small window to clients standing outside enjoying the view of the square. The bar is little more than a narrow corridor, serving *raciones* of tapas that are so generous they make little meals, especially when served with bread. The roasted red peppers in olive oil are quite tasty, along with the stuffed crabs and *calamares* (squid). Huge dishes of pickled cucumbers, onions, and olives are available. They also have a tiny dining room behind a curtain at the end of the bar serving inexpensive fare.

Despite the many tourists that throng its streets during the day, Toledo is quiet at night, with fewer dance clubs than you'd expect from a town of its size. If you want to hear some recorded music, head for **Bar La Abadía,** Plaza San Nicolás 3 (✆ **92-525-11-40**), where local residents, many of them involved in the tourism industry, crowd elbow to elbow for pints of beer, glasses of wine, and access to the music of New York, Los Angeles, or wherever. It's also fun to drop in to the **Cervecería Trébol,** Calle Santa Fe 1 (© **92-521-37-02**), to sample their wine, beer, excellent tapas, and *bombas* (stuffed potato bombs).

SEGOVIA ★★★

91km (54 miles) NW of Madrid; 68km (42 miles) NE of Avila

Gleaming Segovia, with its mellow stone built monuments, typifies the glory of Old Castile (now known as Castilla y Leon). It stands in the southwest of this castle-rich region, and Isabella herself was proclaimed queen here in 1474. Wherever you look, you'll see reminders of that golden era—whether it's the most spectacular **Alcázar Castle** on the Iberian Peninsula or, going farther back in time, the well-preserved, still-functioning **Roman aqueduct.** The city is located on the northwestern slope of the Guadarrama Mountains, where the Eresma and Clamores rivers converge, and its narrow, winding streets are best covered on foot if you want to fully view the Romanesque churches and 15th-century palaces along the way.

Essentials

GETTING THERE While the standard regional 15 **trains** a day that wind their scenic way over the mountains can take as long as 2 hours (one-way fare 5.90€), the super-fast Talgo to Valladolid and Burgos reaches Segovia—after passing though 33km (22 miles) of new tunnels that cut through the very heart of the Guadarramas—in a mere 22 minutes! (This rapid, mainly subterranean ride costs around 9€ one-way.) The Segovia station lies on the Paseo Obispo Quesada s/n (© **92-142-07-74**), a 20-minute walk southeast of the town center. Alternatively, you can board bus no. 3, which departs every quarter-hour for the Plaza Mayor.

Ten to 15 **buses** a day depart from Madrid's new Príncipe Pío underground bus station for Segovia. **La Sepulvedana** (© **91-538-48-00;** www.lasepulvedana.es) operates buses; a one-way ticket costs 6.65€. The scenic journey takes just over an hour.

By **car,** take the N-VI (on some maps it's known as the A-6) or the Autopista del Nordeste northwest from Madrid, toward Leon and Lugo. At the junction with Route 110 (signposted SEGOVIA), turn northeast.

VISITOR INFORMATION The **tourist information office** is at Plaza Mayor 10 (© **92-146-03-34**). It is open daily from 9am to 3pm and 5 to 7pm.

Exploring Segovia

Alcázar de Segovia ★★★ If you've ever dreamed of castles in the air, then all the fairy-tale romance of childhood will return when you view the Alcázar. Many have waxed poetic about it, comparing it to a giant boat sailing through the clouds. View the Alcázar first from below, at the junction of the Clamores and Eresma rivers. It's on the west side of Segovia, and you may not spot it when you first enter the city—but that's part of the surprise.

The castle dates from the 12th century, but a large segment, which contained its Moorish ceilings, was destroyed by fire in 1862. Restoration has continued over the years.

Royal romance is associated with the Alcázar. Isabella first met Ferdinand here, and today you can see a facsimile of her dank bedroom. Once married, she wasn't foolish enough to surrender her royal rights, as replicas of the thrones attest—both are equally proportioned. Philip II married his fourth wife, Anne of Austria, here as well.

Walk the battlements of this once-impregnable castle, from which its occupants hurled boiling oil onto the enemy below. Or ascend the hazardous stairs of the tower, originally built by Isabella's father as a prison, for a panoramic view of Segovia and the great plain north toward Leon.

Plaza de La Reina Victoria Eugenia. ✆ **92-146-07-59.** www.alcazardesegovia.com. Admission 4€ adults, 3€ children 8–14, free for children 7 and under. Free 3rd Tues of each month. Apr–Sept daily 10am–7pm; Oct–Mar daily 10am–6pm. Bus: 3. Take Calle Vallejo, Calle de Velarde, Calle de Daoiz, or Paseo de Ronda.

Cabildo Catedral de Segovia ★ Constructed between 1515 and 1558, this is the last Gothic cathedral built in Spain. Fronting the historic Plaza Mayor, it stands on the spot where Isabella I was proclaimed queen of Castile. Affectionately called *la dama de las catedrales,* it contains numerous treasures, such as the Blessed Sacrament Chapel (created by the flamboyant Churriguera), stained-glass windows, elaborately carved choir stalls, and 16th- and 17th-century paintings, including a reredos portraying the deposition of Christ from the cross by Juan de Juni. The cloisters are older than the cathedral, dating from an earlier church that was destroyed in the so-called War of the Comuneros. Inside the cathedral museum you'll find jewelry, paintings, and a collection of rare antique manuscripts.

Plaza Catedral, Marqués del Arco. ✆ **92-146-22-05.** Free admission to cathedral; cloisters, museum, and chapel room 2€ adults, free for children 11 and under. Spring and summer Mon–Sat 9am–7pm; off-season daily 9:30am–6pm. Sun 9am–2:30pm.

Iglesia de la Vera Cruz Built in either the 11th or the 12th century by the Knights Templar, this is the most fascinating Romanesque church in Segovia. It stands in isolation outside the walls of the old town, overlooking the Alcázar. It's believed that its unusual 12-sided design was copied from the Church of the Holy Sepulchre in Jerusalem. Inside you'll find an inner temple, rising two floors, where the knights conducted nightlong vigils as part of their initiation rites.

Carretera de Zamarramala. ✆ **92-143-14-75.** Admission 2€. Apr–Sept Tues–Sun 10:30am–1:30pm and 3:30–7pm; Oct–Mar Tues–Sun 10:30am–1:30pm and 3:30–6pm.

Monasterio del Parral ★ 🎁 The restored "Monastery of the Grape" was established for the Hieronymites by Henry IV (1425–74), a Castilian king known as "The Impotent." The monastery lies across the Eresma River about .8km (a half-mile) north of the city. The church is a medley of styles and decoration—mainly Gothic, Renaissance, and plateresque. The facade was never completed, and the monastery itself was abandoned when religious orders were suppressed in 1835. Today it's been restored and is once again the domain of the *jerónimos,* Hieronymus priests and brothers. Inside, a robed monk will show you the various treasures of the order, including a polychrome altarpiece and the alabaster tombs of the Marquis of Villena and his wife—all the work of Juan Rodríguez.

Subida del Parral 2 (across the Eresma River). ✆ **92-143-12-98.** Free admission. Mon–Sat 10am–2:30pm and 4–6:30pm; Sun 10–11:30am and 4–6:30pm. Take Ronda de Sant Lucía and cross the Eresma River.

Roman Aqueduct (Acueducto Romano) ★★★ This architectural marvel was built by the Romans nearly 2,000 years ago. Constructed of mortarless granite, it consists of 118 arches, and in one two-tiered section it soars 29m (95 ft.) to its highest point. The Spanish call it El Puente. It spans the Plaza del Azoguejo, the old market square, stretching nearly 720m (2,400 ft.). When the Moors took Segovia in 1072, they destroyed 36 arches, which were later rebuilt under Ferdinand and Isabella in 1484.

Plaza del Azoguejo.

Where to Stay

EXPENSIVE

Hostería Ayala Berganza ★★ Located next to the Romanesque church of San Millán, only a few minutes walk from the Aqueduct, this 15th-century building was once the abode of one of Spain's most famous painters, Ignacio Zuloaga (1870–1945). It has been turned into one of the most atmospheric little inns in Castile. Part of the hotel is the original Castilian palace, dating from the 15th century and declared a historic monument, plus a modern structure completed in 1998. Care and attention went into the design of the modernized bedrooms and two suites, each individually decorated and containing a private bathroom with tub and shower. In a stone-columned central patio, an excellent Castilian cuisine based on seasonal dishes and roasted meats from a wood-fired oven are served.

Calle Carretas 5, 40001 Segovia. ✆ **92-146-04-48.** Fax 92-146-23-77. www.innsofspain.com. 18 units. 120€–145€ double; 175€–220€ suite. Rates include breakfast. AE, MC, V. **Amenities:** Restaurant; coffee shop; bar; babysitting; garden. *In room:* A/C, TV, hair dryer, minibar.

Parador de Segovia ★★★ This 20th-century tile-roofed *parador* sits on a hill 3km (2 miles) northeast of Segovia (take the N-601) on an estate called El Terminillo, which used to be famous for its vines and almond trees, a few of which still survive. If you have a car and can get a reservation, don't hesitate: Make this your first choice. The guest rooms are deluxe, containing bathrooms with tub/shower combinations. Furnishings are tasteful (often in blond pieces), and large windows open onto panoramic views of the countryside. Some of the older rooms here are a bit dated, however, with a lackluster decor. The in house restaurant is one of the best places to enjoy a meal in Segovia.

Carretera Valladolid s/n (N-601), 40003 Segovia. ✆ **92-144-37-37.** Fax 92-143-73-62. www.parador.es. 113 units. 160€ double; from 230€ suite. AE, DC, MC, V. Covered parking 10€, free outside. **Amenities:** Restaurant; bar; babysitting; fitness center; outdoor pool (June–Sept); indoor heated pool (Oct–May); room service; sauna; 2 tennis courts (1 lit). *In room:* A/C, TV, hair dryer, minibar.

MODERATE

Hotel Infanta Isabel ★ Named after Queen Isabel, the great-grandmother of the present-day king, this hotel overlooks Segovia's charming central square and is within a stone's throw of the majestic cathedral. This is where Queen Isabel would stay when traveling to the nearby summer palace of La Granja. The present owners have modernized the interior considerably, but a good deal of the building's 19th-century grandeur, such as the staircase, remains. Each room is decorated in its own style, and each is furnished with an eye to comfort. Despite its style, the hotel has every convenience; bathrooms with tub/shower combinations strike a reassuring 20th-century note.

Plaza Mayor, 40001 Segovia. ✆ **92-146-13-00.** Fax 92-146-22-17. www.hotelinfantaisabel.com. 37 units. 80€–120€ double. AC, DC, MC, V. Parking 10€. **Amenities:** Bar; lounge; babysitting; room service. *In room:* A/C, TV, hair dryer, minibar.

Hotel Los Arcos This concrete-and-glass five-story structure opened in 1987 and is generally cited as the best in town. Well run and modern, it attracts the business traveler, although tourists frequent the place in droves as well. Rooms are generally spacious but furnished in a standard international bland way, except for the beautiful rug-dotted parquet floors. Built-in furnishings and tiny bathrooms with tub/shower combinations are part of the offering. Rooms are well kept, although some furnishings look worn.

Even if you don't stay here, consider dining at the hotel's La Cocina de Segovia, which is the only hotel dining room that competes successfully with Mesón de Cándido (p. 282). As at the nearby competitors, roast suckling pig and roast Segovia lamb—perfectly cooked in specially made ovens—are the specialties. There's also a tavernlike cafe and bar. In all, it's a smart, efficiently run, and pleasant choice, if not a terribly exciting one.

Paseo de Ezequiel González 26, 40002 Segovia. ✆ **92-143-74-62.** Fax 92-142-81-61. www.hotellosarcos.com. 59 units. 80€–115€ double. AE, DC, MC, V. Parking 10€. **Amenities:** Restaurant; bar; lounge; babysitting; health club; room service. *In room:* A/C, TV, hair dryer, minibar.

Las Sirenas Standing on the most charming old plaza in Segovia, opposite the Church of St. Martín, this hotel was built around 1950, and has been renovated several times. However, it has long since lost its Franco-era supremacy to Hotel Los Arcos (see above). It is modest and well maintained and decorated in a conservative style. Each bedroom is filled with functional, simple furniture and a well-kept bathroom with shower. Breakfast is the only meal served, but the staff at the reception desk can direct clients to cafes and *tascas* nearby.

Juan Bravo 30, 40001 Segovia. ✆ **92-146-26-63.** Fax 92-146-26-57. www.hotelsirenas.com. 39 units. 75€–100€ double. AE, DC, MC, V. **Amenities:** Breakfast salon. *In room:* A/C, TV.

Where to Dine

Casa Duque ★ CASTILIAN Set on the street that links Segovia's ancient Roman aqueduct with the city's medieval core, this restaurant was established in 1895, and has fed many successive generations of local residents ever since. The severely dignified interior looks almost unchanged since it was built. The decor includes heavy ceiling beams, exposed stone, rough-textured plaster, and battered 19th-century artifacts from long-ago farms. Come here for the kind of cuisine that was in vogue when the restaurant was built, with very few concessions to modern cuisine. Try the excellent version of cream of crabmeat soup; roasted suckling pig slow-cooked on a spit; savory roasted lamb with aromatic rosemary, thyme, and garlic; and different preparations of grilled chicken, veal, beef, and pork. An exceptional accompaniment for any of these might include kidney beans cooked with chunks of salted cod, fresh spinach, and mounds of mashed potatoes or rice.

Calle Cervantes 12. ✆ **92-146-24-87.** www.restauranteduque.es. Reservations recommended. Main courses 12€–24€; set menus 25€–60€. AE, DC, MC, V. Daily 12:30–5pm and 8–11:30pm.

Mesón de Cándido ★★ CASTILIAN For years this beautiful old Spanish inn, standing on the eastern edge of the old town, has maintained a monopoly on the tourist trade. Apart from the hotel restaurants—specifically La Cocina de Segovia at the Los Arcos—it is the town's finest dining choice. The Cándido family took it over in 1905, and fourth- and fifth-generation family members still run the place, having fed, over the years, everybody from Hemingway to Nixon. The oldest part of the restaurant dates from 1822, and the place has gradually been enlarged since then. The proprietor of the House of Cándido is known as *mesonero mayor de Castilla* (the major innkeeper of Castile). He's been decorated with more medals and honors than paella has grains of rice. The restaurant's popularity can be judged by the crowds of hungry polyglot diners who fill every seat in the six dining rooms. The a la carte menu includes two regional staples: *cordero asado* (roast baby lamb) and *cochinillo asado* (roast suckling pig). Some of the seating areas are cramped and confining. Opt for a table on the second floor, facing the aqueduct, or else one of the outdoor cafe tables in front.

Plaza del Azoguejo 5. ✆ **92-142-59-11.** www.mesondecandido.es. Reservations recommended. Main courses 14€–25€. AE, DC, MC, V. Daily 12:30–4:30pm and 8pm–midnight.

An Easy Excursion to La Granja

To reach La Granja, 11km (7 miles) southeast of Segovia, you can take a 20-minute bus ride from the center of the city. Six to ten La Sepulvedana buses a day leave from the Príncipe Pío bus station in Madrid. A one-way fare costs 7.40€. For information, call ✆ **92-538-48-00.**

Palacio Real de La Granja San Ildefonso de la Granja was the summer palace of the Bourbon kings of Spain, who replicated the grandeur of Versailles in the province of Segovia. Set against the snowcapped Sierra de Guadarrama, the slate-roofed palace dominates the village that grew up around it (which, these days, is a summer resort).

The founder of La Granja was Philip V, grandson of Louis XIV and the first Bourbon king of Spain (his body, along with that of his second queen, Isabel de Fernesio, is interred in a mausoleum in the Collegiate Church). Philip V was born at Versailles on December 19, 1683, which may explain why he wanted to re-create that atmosphere at Segovia.

Before the palace was built in the early 18th century, a farm stood here—hence the totally incongruous name *la granja,* meaning "the farm" in Spanish. Inside you'll find valuable antiques (many in the Empire style), paintings, and a remarkable collection of tapestries based on Goya cartoons from the Royal Factory in Madrid.

Most visitors, however, seem to find a stroll through the gardens, studded with chestnuts and elms, more pleasing, so allow adequate time for that. The fountain statuary is a riot of cavorting gods and nymphs, hiding indiscretions behind jets of water, providing for a spectacular display.

Plaza de España 17, San Ildefonso (Segovia). ✆ **92-147-00-19.** Admission 5€ adults, 2.50€ children 5–14, free for children 4 and under. Apr–Sept Tues–Sun 10am–6pm; Oct–Mar Tues–Sat 10am–1:30pm and 3–5pm; Sun 10am–2pm.

Segovia After Dark

Some of the most spontaneous good times can be created around the Plaza Mayor, Plaza Azoguejo, and the busy Calle del Carmen that runs into the Plaza Azoguejo. Each of those sites contains a scattering of simple bars and cafes that grow more crowded at night as the days grow hotter. If you want to go dancing, two of the most popular discos are **Mansión,** Calle de Juan Bravo (no phone), which is open nightly from 11pm till dawn for dancing, drinking, and flirting with the 20- to 30-year-old crowd; and its somewhat more stylish competitor, **Bar Ginasio,** Paseo del Salon (no phone), which is open nightly from 8pm till dawn; it's a bit more atmospheric and frequented by night-owls ages 25 to around 50.

FAST FACTS

FAST FACTS: MADRID

12

American Express For your mail or banking needs, you can go to the American Express office at the corner of Marqués de Cubas and Plaza de las Cortes 2, across the street from the Palace Hotel (✆ **91-322-55-00** or 91-322-54-45; Metro: Gran Vía). Open Monday through Friday from 9am to 7:30pm and Saturday from 9am to 2pm.

Area Code The Madrid area code is **91.**

Babysitters Most major hotels can arrange for babysitters, called *canguros* (literally, kangaroos) or *niñeras.* Usually the concierge keeps a list of reliable nursemaids and will contact them for you, provided you give adequate notice. Rates vary considerably. Although many babysitters in Madrid speak English, don't count on it.

Business Hours While many **shops,** especially the smaller ones, still retain the traditional opening times of 9 or 10am to 2pm and 5 to 8 or 9pm, many are now switching to a more flexible and extended *horario,* often staying open through lunchtime. Large stores such as the Corte Inglés and the Casa del Libro bookshop follow the latter schedule, for example, as do supermarkets like Al Campo and Carrefour. **Banks** are open Monday to Friday from 8:30am to 1:30pm, some with an extension till 5pm on Thursdays. Some are open on Saturday mornings.

Dentists For an English-speaking dentist, contact the **U.S. Embassy,** Serrano 75 (✆ **91-587-22-00**); it maintains a list of dentists who have offered their services to Americans. For dental services, also consult **Unidad Médica Anglo-Americana,** Conde de Arandá 1 (✆ **91-435-18-23;** Metro: Retiro). Office hours are Monday through Friday from 9am to 8pm and Saturday from 10am to 1pm, and there is a 24-hour answering service.

Doctors For an English-speaking doctor, contact the **U.S. Embassy,** Serrano 75 (✆ **91-587-22-00**).

Drinking Laws Alcoholic drinks are available in practically all the thousands of bars and hundreds of hotels and restaurants in the city, and, by law, cannot be served to minors under 18. Breathalyzers are now used more frequently than in the past, and drivers may be subjected to spot checks whether or not they've just had an accident or broken the law. The official permitted limit for drinking is the equivalent to 2 glasses of wine, or 2 *cañas* (small glasses) of beer or 2 glasses of spirits (given the size of Spanish measures, one glass here would suffice if you're thinking of driving yourself).

Drugstores For a late-night pharmacy *(farmacia),* look in the daily newspaper under *Farmacias de Guardia* to learn which drugstores are open after 8pm. Another way to find one is to go to any pharmacy, which, even if closed, always posts a list of nearby pharmacies that are open late that day. Madrid has hundreds of pharmacies, but one of the most central is **Farmacia Gayoso,** Arenal 2 (✆ **91-521-28-60;** Metro: Puerta del Sol). It is open Monday through Saturday from 9:30am to 9:30pm.

Electricity As in the rest of Europe, the electricity connection is 220 volts though on increasingly rare occasions it is 125 volts. Many hotels have 110-volt North American–style outlets for electric razors. For other appliances, you'll need a transformer, unless there is a voltage switch. You need a two-prong plug to connect into the mains.

Embassies & Consulates If you lose your passport, fall seriously ill, get into legal trouble, or have some other serious problem, your embassy or consulate can help. These are the Madrid addresses and hours: The **United States Embassy,** Calle Serrano 75 (✆ **91-587-22-00;** Metro: Núñez de Balboa), is open Monday through Friday from 9am to 6pm. The **Canadian Embassy,** Núñez de Balboa 35 (✆ **91-423-32-50;** Metro: Velázquez), is open Monday through Friday from 8:30am to 5:30pm. The **United Kingdom Embassy,** Calle Fernando el Santo 16 (✆ **91-319-02-00;** Metro: Colón), is open Monday through Friday from 9am to 1:30pm and 3 to 6pm. The **Republic of Ireland** has an embassy at Claudio Coello 73 (✆ **91-576-35-00;** Metro: Serrano); it's open Monday through Friday from 9am to 2pm. The **Australian Embassy,** Plaza Diego de Ordas 3, Edificio Santa Engracia 120 (✆ **91-441-93-00;** Metro: Ríos Rosas), is open Monday through Thursday from 8:30am to 5pm and Friday from 8:30am to 2:15pm. Citizens of **New Zealand** have an embassy at Plaza de la Lealtad 2 (✆ **91-523-02-26;** Metro: Banco de España); it's open Monday through Friday from 9am to 1:30pm and 2:30 to 5:30pm.

Emergencies The centralized number for fire, police, or ambulance is ✆ **112.**

Hospitals/Clinics **Unidad Médica Anglo-Americana,** Conde de Arandá 1 (✆ **91-435-18-23;** Metro: Retiro), is not a hospital but a private outpatient clinic offering the services of various specialists. This is not an emergency clinic, although someone on the staff is always available. The daily hours are from 9am to 8pm. For a real medical emergency, call ✆ **112** for an ambulance. See also the "Health" section in chapter 3, "Planning Your Trip to Madrid," p. 30.

Insurance **Medical Insurance** For travel overseas, most U.S. health plans (including Medicare and Medicaid) do not provide coverage, and the ones that do often require you to pay for services up front and reimburse you only after you return home.

As a safety net, you may want to buy travel medical insurance, particularly if you're traveling to a remote or high-risk area where emergency evacuation might be necessary. If you require additional medical insurance, try **MEDEX Assistance** (✆ **410/453-6300;** www.medexassist.com) or **Travel Assistance International** (✆ **800/821-2828;** www.travelassistance.com; for general information on services, call the company's **Worldwide Assistance Services, Inc.,** at ✆ **800/777-8710**).

Canadians should check with their provincial health plan offices or call **Health Canada** (✆ **866/225-0709;** www.hc-sc.gc.ca) to find out the extent of their coverage and what documentation and receipts they must take home in case they are treated overseas.

Travelers from the **U.K.** should carry their European Health Insurance Card (EHIC), which replaced the E111 form as proof of entitlement to free/reduced cost medical treatment abroad (✆ **0845/606-2030;** www.ehic.org.uk). Note, however, that the EHIC only covers "necessary medical treatment," and for repatriation costs, lost money, baggage, or cancellation, travel insurance from a reputable company should always be sought (www.travelinsuranceweb.com).

Travel Insurance: The cost of travel insurance varies widely, depending on the destination, the cost and length of your trip, your age and health, and the type of trip you're taking, but expect to pay between 5% and 8% of the vacation itself. You can get estimates from various providers through **InsureMyTrip.com**. Enter your trip cost and dates, your age, and other information, for prices from more than a dozen companies.

U.K. citizens and their families who make more than one trip abroad per year may find an annual travel insurance policy works out cheaper. Check **www.moneysupermarket.com**, which compares prices across a wide range of providers for single- and multi-trip policies.

Most big travel agencies offer their own insurance and will probably try to sell you their package when you book a holiday. Think before you sign. **Britain**'s **Consumers' Association** recommends that you insist on seeing the policy and reading the fine print before buying travel insurance. **The Association of British Insurers** (✆ **020/7600-3333;** www.abi.org.uk) gives advice by phone and publishes *Holiday Insurance*, a free guide to policy provisions and prices. You might also shop around for better deals: Try **Columbus Direct** (✆ 0870/033-9988**;** www.columbusdirect.net).

Trip-Cancellation Insurance: Trip-cancellation insurance will help retrieve your money if you have to back out of a trip or depart early, or if your travel supplier goes bankrupt. Trip-cancellation insurance traditionally covers such events as sickness, natural disasters, and Department of State advisories. The latest news in trip-cancellation insurance is the availability of **expanded hurricane coverage** and the **"any-reason"** cancellation coverage—which costs more but covers cancellations made for any reason. You won't get back 100% of your prepaid trip cost, but you'll be refunded a substantial portion. **TravelSafe** (✆ **888/885-7233;** www.travelsafe.com) offers both types of coverage. Expedia also offers any-reason cancellation coverage for its air-hotel packages. For details, contact one of the following recommended insurers: **Access America** (✆ **866/807-3982;** www.accessamerica.com); **Travel Guard International** (✆ **800/826-4919;** www.travelguard.com); **Travel Insured International** (✆ **800/243-3174;** www.travelinsured.com); and **Travelex Insurance Services** (✆ **888/457-4602;** www.travelex-insurance.com).

Language English is still not as widely spoken or understood in Madrid as in the popular Mediterranean coastal zones such as the Costa del Sol, Costa Brava, and Mallorca, though this situation is gradually improving. It's best to take a concise phrasebook to help you along. Frommer's very own *Spanish PhraseFinder & Dictionary* (Wiley 2006) fits the bill nicely here, covering a variety of subjects from socializing and shopping to health and safety. See Chapter 13 for a glossary.

Laundromats, Laundries & Dry Cleaning Try a self-service facility, **Lavandería Donoso Cortés,** Donoso Cortés 17 (✆ **91-446-96-90;** Metro: Quevedo); it's open Monday to Friday from 9am to 2pm and 3:30 to 8pm, Saturday from 9am to 2pm. A good dry-cleaning service is provided by **El Corte Inglés** department store at Raimundo Fernández Villaverde 79 (✆ **91-418-88-00;** Metro: Gregorio Marañón), where the staff speaks English.

Legal Aid Should you happen to break the law and get arrested, you will be assigned an *abogado de oficio,* or duty solicitor, free of charge. You'll also be allowed to phone your consulate, who will alternately put you in touch with an English-speaking lawyer.

Lost & Found Be sure to tell all of your credit card companies the minute you discover your wallet has been lost or stolen, and file a report at the nearest police precinct. Your credit card company or insurer may require a police report number or record of the loss. Most credit card companies have an emergency toll-free number to call if your card is lost or stolen; they may be able to wire you a cash advance immediately or deliver an emergency credit card in a day or two.

If you need emergency cash over the weekend when all banks and American Express offices are closed, you can have money wired to you via **Western Union**

(✆ **800/325-6000;** www.westernunion.com). Following are toll-free numbers for lost cards: Visa ✆ **900-99-11-24;** MasterCard ✆ **900-97-12-31;** and American Express ✆ **1-715-343-7977** (global hotline).

Luggage Storage & Lockers These can be found at both the Atocha and Chamartín railway terminals, as well as the major bus station at the Estación Sur de Autobuses, Calle Méndez Álvaro (✆ **91-468-42-00;** Metro: Méndez Álvaro).

Mail The local postage system is both reliable and efficient, though services such as FedEx are available if you prefer to use them.

Postage rates—in euros—for postcards and letters to North America from Spain are .64€ to 1.38€ up to 20g; to elsewhere in the European Union .78€ to 1.07€.

Post your letters in the post office itself or in yellow post boxes called *buzones.*

Buy stamps in an **Oficina de Correos** (Post Office) or—if you don't fancy queuing—in an *estanco* (a government licensed tobacconist easily recognized by its brown and yellow logo). For further information, check the Spanish postal service website **www.correos.es**.

If you don't want to receive your mail at your hotel or the American Express office, direct it to *Lista de Correos* at the central post office in Madrid. To pick up mail, go to the window marked *Lista,* where you'll be asked to show your passport. Madrid's central office is in **Palacio de Comunicaciones** at Plaza de la Cibeles (✆ **91-396-20-00**).

Newspapers & Magazines The Paris-based *International Herald Tribune,* which sometimes includes an English language version of *El País* (see below), is sold at most newsstands in the tourist districts, as are *USA Today,* the *Financial Times, Wall Street Journal*, and European editions of *Time* and *Newsweek.* Top Spanish newspapers are *El País, El Mundo, ABC,* and *La Razón.* The *Guía del Ocio,* a small magazine sold in newsstands, contains entertainment listings in Spanish, as does the *Metropolí,* which comes with *El Mundo* free on Fridays. *InMadrid* is an English Language freebie available at tourist offices, as well as some bookshops, bars, and cinemas. *The Broadsheet,* Calle del Correo 4, 2–4 Madrid (visits only by appointment; e-mail editorial@tbsmagazine.com; www.tbsmagazine.com), is an online magazine with general subjects on Spain in English. (It ceased publication as a printed periodical in 2008.)

Free Spanish newspapers that give you a briefer rundown on what's going on in the city and around the world are handed out at the entrances to metro stations. These publications include *Metro, Qué,* and *20 Minutos.*

Passports The websites listed provide downloadable passport applications as well as the current fees for processing applications. For an up-to-date, country-by-country listing of passport requirements around the world, go to the "International Travel" tab of the U.S. Department of State at **http://travel.state.gov**.

For Residents of Australia You can pick up an application from your local post office or any branch of Passports Australia, but you must schedule an interview at the passport office to present your application materials. Call the **Australian Passport Information Service** at ✆ **131-232,** or visit the government website at **www.passports.gov.au**.

For Residents of Canada Passport applications are available at travel agencies throughout Canada or from the central **Passport Office,** Department of Foreign Affairs and International Trade, Ottawa, ON K1A 0G3 (✆ **800/567-6868;** www.ppt.gc.ca). ***Note:*** Canadian children who travel must have their own passports. However, if you hold a valid Canadian passport issued before December 11, 2001, that bears the name of your child, the passport remains valid for you and your child until it expires.

For Residents of Ireland You can apply for a 10-year passport at the **Passport Office,** Setanta Centre, Molesworth Street, Dublin 2 (✆ **01/671-1633;** www.irlgov.ie/iveagh). Those under age 18 and over 65 must apply for a 3-year passport. You can also apply at 1A South Mall, Cork (✆ **21/494-4700**) or at most main post offices.

For Residents of New Zealand You can pick up a passport application at any New Zealand Passports Office or download it from their website. Contact the **Passports Office** at ✆ **0800/225-050** in New Zealand or 04/474-8100, or log on to **www.passports.govt.nz**.

For Residents of the United Kingdom To pick up an application for a standard 10-year passport (5-yr. passport for children under 16), visit your nearest passport office, major post office, or travel agency or contact the **United Kingdom Passport Service** at ✆ **0870/521-0410,** or search its website at **www.ukpa.gov.uk**.

For Residents of the United States: Whether you're applying in person or by mail, you can download passport applications from the U.S. Department of State website at **http://travel.state.gov**. To find your regional passport office, either check the U.S. Department of State website or call the **National Passport Information Center** toll-free number (✆ **877/487-2778**) for automated information.

Police In an emergency, dial ✆ **112.**

Restrooms Some public restrooms are available, including those in the Parque del Retiro and on Plaza de Oriente across from the Palacio Real. Otherwise, you can always go into a bar or *tasca,* but you should order something. The major department stores, such as Galerías Preciados and El Corte Inglés, have good, clean restrooms. For some amusing anecdotes on restroom experiences in Madrid, among many other world-wide spots, check out **www.thebathroomdiaries.com**.

Smoking Smoking restrictions currently apply to all working and most public places, though most bars and cafes still allow smoking except in certain categorized "nonsmoking zones."

However, things finally look set for a radical change. The first stage of a new bill proposing to ban smoking in all public places (especially restaurants and hotels) was approved by a vast majority in Madrid's Congreso de Diputados (Parliament) on June 23, 2010. The aim is for a law to be finally passed to this effect January 1, 2011, following the other European examples of Italy, Ireland, and—surprisingly—Turkey, formerly one of the world's most avid smoking countries. (If Turkey can do it, surely so can Spain!)

Restaurants are concerned that if this new bill becomes law they will lose customers, and **hoteliers** are even more worried. (See respective "Where to Dine" and "Where to Stay" chapters.) From having a few rooms set aside for nonsmokers—as is the case in some of the better hotels at present—**all** hotels will need to have a small number of rooms set aside for smokers, while most rooms will be for **nonsmokers**. Open-air terrace smoking in both will still be allowed.

Here are some relevant statistics to support the anti-smoking lobby: One-third of all Spaniards smoke on a regular basis. (You may think that's a gross underestimate when you see them puffing away in between sips of their morning coffees.) Since the 2006 law, the number of smokers has slightly *increased,* from 34% to 35%, though they smoke slightly less—around 12 a day instead of 14. (Top European smokers, incidentally, are the Greeks, who average 20 cigarettes a day.)

Taxes There are no special city taxes for tourists, except for the VAT (value-added tax; known as IVA in Spain) levied nationwide on all goods and services, ranging from 7% to 33%. For information on how to recover VAT, see p. 220.

Time Spain is 6 hours ahead of Eastern Standard Time in the United States. Daylight saving time is in effect from the last Sunday in March to the last Sunday in September.

Tipping Don't overtip. The government requires restaurants and hotels to include their service charges—usually 15% of the bill. However, that doesn't mean you should skip out of a place without dispensing an extra euro or two. The following are some guidelines:

Your hotel porter should get 1.50€ per bag. Maids should be given 1€ per day, more if you're generous. Tip doormen 1€ for assisting with baggage and 1€ for calling a cab. In top-ranking hotels, the concierge will often submit a separate bill, showing charges for newspapers and other services; if he or she has been particularly helpful, tip extra. For cab drivers, add about 10% to the fare as shown on the meter. At airports, such as Barajas in Madrid and major terminals, the porter who handles your luggage will present you with a fixed-charge bill.

In restaurants and nightclubs, a 15% service charge is added to the bill. To that, add another 3% to 5% tip, depending on the quality of the service. Waiters in deluxe restaurants and nightclubs are accustomed to the extra 5%, which means you'll end up tipping 20%. If that seems excessive, you must remember that the initial service charge reflected in the fixed price is distributed among all the help.

Barbers and hairdressers expect a 10% to 15% tip. Tour guides expect 2€, although a tip is not mandatory. Theater and bullfight ushers get from .50€ to 1€.

Water Reservoir supplies after the unusually wet winter of 2009/2010 filled reservoirs around Madrid to around 75% to 80% capacity, which is above average for the region. So at the time of writing, there were no restrictions on use or deterioration in the quality of the water. In general, it is perfectly okay to drink the tap water in Madrid, though there is a wide choice of bottled mineral water available in shops, bars, and restaurants if you'd rather play safe.

AIRLINE & HOTEL WEBSITES

MAJOR AIRLINES

Aeroméxico
www.aeromexico.com

Air France
www.airfrance.com

Alitalia
www.alitalia.com

American Airlines
www.aa.com

British Airways
www.british-airways.com

Continental Airlines
www.continental.com

Delta Air Lines
www.delta.com

EgyptAir
www.egyptair.com

El Al Airlines
www.elal.co.il

Finnair
www.finnair.com

Iberia Airlines
www.iberia.com

Japan Airlines
www.jal.co.jp

KLM
www.klm.com

Lufthansa
www.lufthansa.com

Northwest Airlines
www.nwa.com

Olympic Airlines
www.olympicairlines.com

Qantas Airways
www.qantas.com

Swiss International Air Lines
www.swiss.com

Thai Airways International
www.thaiair.com

Turkish Airlines
www.thy.com

United Airlines
www.united.com

US Airways
www.usairways.com

Virgin Atlantic Airways
www.virgin-atlantic.com

BUDGET AIRLINES

Aer Lingus
www.aerlingus.com

Air Berlin
www.airberlin.com

BMI Baby
www.bmibaby.com

easyJet
www.easyjet.com

Ryanair
www.ryanair.com

CAR-RENTAL AGENCIES

Auto Europe
www.autoeurope.com

Avis
www.avis.com

Budget
www.budget.com

Enterprise
www.enterprise.com

Hertz
www.hertz.com

National
www.nationalcar.com

Thrifty
www.thrifty.com

USEFUL TERMS & PHRASES

13

Most Spaniards are very patient with foreigners who try to speak their language. Although you might encounter several regional languages and dialects in Spain, Castilian (Castellano, or simply Español) is understood everywhere. In Catalonia, they speak Catalán (the most widely spoken non-national language in Europe with roots in French, Italian, and Latin), and you'll find variants of this tongue in Valencia, Alicante, and the Balearic Islands; in the Basque country, they speak Euskera (a complex "non–Indo European" language whose real origins remain a mystery); in Galicia, you'll hear Gallego (a Romance language closely linked to Portuguese); and in Asturias— with recently growing frequency— a tongue known as Babel (or Asturianu), which has Latin roots dating to the Roman occupation of the province. Still, a few words in Castilian will usually get your message across with no problem, wherever you are in Spain.

When traveling, it helps a lot to know a few basic phrases, so I include a list of certain simple phrases in Castilian Spanish for expressing basic needs. Two pronunciation points to note: In Spain, the "ll" sound is a combination of "l" and "y" rather than just "y," which is South American pronunciation, and the "rr" is pronounced with an exaggerated guttural Scottish or Germanic intonation.

BASIC VOCABULARY

English & Castilian Spanish Phrases

English	Spanish	Pronunciation
Good day	**Buenos días**	*bweh*-nohs *dee*-ahs
How are you?	**¿Cómo está?**	*koh*-moh es-*tah*
Very well	**Muy bien**	mwee byehn
Thank you	**Gracias**	*grah*-syahs
You're welcome	**De nada**	deh *nah*-dah
Goodbye	**Adiós**	ah-*dyohs*
Please	**Por favor**	pohr fah-*vohr*
Yes	**Sí**	see
No	**No**	noh
Excuse me	**Perdóneme**	pehr-*doh*-neh-meh
	Discúlpeme	dees-*kul*-peh-meh

English	Spanish	Pronunciation
Give me	**Déme**	*deh*-meh
Where is . . . ?	**¿Dónde está . . . ?**	*dohn*-deh es-*tah*
the station	**la estación**	lah es-tah-*syohn*
a hotel	**un hotel**	oon oh-*tel*
a gas station	**una gasolinera**	*oo*-nah gah-so-lee-*neh*-rah
a restaurant	**un restaurante**	oon res-tow-*rahn*-teh
the toilet	**el baño**	el *bah*-nyoh
a good doctor	**un buen médico**	oon bwehn *meh*-dee-coh
the road to	**el camino a/hacia . . .**	el cah-*mee*-noh ah/*ah*-syah
To the right	**A la derecha**	ah lah deh-*reh*-chah
To the left	**A la izquierda**	ah lah ees-*kyehr*-dah
Straight ahead	**Derecho**	deh-*reh*-choh
I would like	**Quisiera**	kee-*syeh*-rah
I want	**Quiero**	*kyeh*-roh
to eat	**comer**	ko-*mehr*
a room	**una habitación**	*oo*-nah ah-bee-tah-*syohn*
Do you have . . . ?	**¿Tiene usted . . . ?**	tyeh-neh oo-*sted*
a book	**un libro**	oon *lee*-broh
a dictionary	**un diccionario**	oon deek-syoh-*na*-ryo
How much is it?	**¿Cuánto cuesta?**	*kwahn*-toh *kwehs*-tah
When?	**¿Cuándo?**	*kwahn*-doh
What?	**¿Qué?**	keh
There is (Is there . . . ?)	**(¿)Hay (. . . ?)**	aye
What is there?	**¿Qué hay?**	keh aye
Yesterday	**Ayer**	ah-*yehr*
Today	**Hoy**	oy
Tomorrow	**Mañana**	mah-*nyah*-nah
Good	**Bueno**	*bweh*-noh
Bad	**Malo**	*mah*-loh
Better (Best)	**(Lo) Mejor**	(loh) meh-*hor*
More	**Más**	mahs
Less	**Menos**	*meh*-nohs
No smoking	**Se prohibe fumar**	seh proh-ee-beh foo-*mahr*
Postcard	**Tarjeta postal**	tar-*heh*-tah pohs-*tahl*
Insect repellent	**Repelente contra insectos**	reh-peh-*lehn*-teh *cohn*-trah een-*sehk*-tohs

MORE USEFUL PHRASES

English	Spanish	Pronunciation
Do you speak English?	**¿Habla usted inglés?**	*ah*-blah oo-*sted* een-*glehs*
Is there anyone here who speaks English?	**¿Hay alguien aquí que hable inglés?**	aye *ahl*-gyehn ah-*kee* keh *ah*-bleh een-*glehs*
I speak a little Spanish.	**Hablo un poco de español.**	*ah*-bloh oon *poh*-koh deh es-pah-*nyol*
I don't understand Spanish very well.	**No (lo) entiendo muy bien el español.**	noh (loh) ehn-*tyehn*-doh mwee byehn el es-pah-*nyol*
The meal is good.	**Me gusta la comida.**	meh *goo*-stah lah koh-*mee*-dah
What time is it?	**¿Qué hora es?**	keh *oh*-rah es
May I see your menu?	**¿Puedo ver el menú (la carta)?**	*pweh*-do vehr el meh-*noo* (lah *car*-tah)
The check, please.	**La cuenta por favor.**	lah *kwehn*-tah pohr fah-*vohr*
What do I owe you?	**¿Cuánto le debo?**	*kwahn*-toh leh *deh*-boh
What did you say?	**¿Mande?**	*mahn*-deh
More formal:	**¿Cómo?**	koh-moh
I want (to see) a room . . .	**Quiero (ver) un cuarto** or **una habitación . . .**	*kyeh*-roh (vehr) oon *kwahr*-toh, *oo*-nah ah-bee-tah-*syohn*
for two persons.	**para dos personas.**	*pah*-rah dohs pehhr-*soh*-nas
with (without) bathroom.	**con (sin) baño.**	kohn (seen) *bah*-nyoh
We are staying here only . . .	**Nos quedamos aquí solamente . . .**	nohs keh-*dah*-mohs ah-*kee* soh-lah-*mehn*-teh
1 night.	**una noche.**	oo-nah *noh*-cheh
1 week.	**una semana.**	oo-nah seh-*mah*-nah
We are leaving . . .	**Partimos (Salimos) . . .**	pahr-*tee*-mohs (sah-*lee*-mohs)
tomorrow.	**mañana.**	mah-*nya*-nah
Do you accept traveler's checks?	**¿Acepta usted cheques de viajero?**	ah-*sehp*-tah oo-*sted cheh*-kehs deh byah-*heh*-roh
Is there a laundromat near here?	**¿Hay una lavandería cerca de aquí?**	eye *oo*-nah lah-*vahn*-deh-*ree*-ah *sehr*-kah deh ah-*kee*
Please send these clothes to the laundry.	**Hágame el favor de mandar esta ropa a la lavandería.**	*ah*-gah-meh el fah-*vohr* deh mahn-*dahr ehs*-tah *roh*-pah a lah lah-*vahn*-deh-*ree*-ah

NUMBERS

English	Spanish	Pronunciation
one	uno	***oo*-noh**
two	dos	**dohs**
three	tres	**trehs**

English	Spanish	Pronunciation
four	cuatro	***kwah*-troh**
five	cinco	***seen*-koh**
six	seis	**says**
seven	siete	***syeh*-teh**
eight	ocho	***oh*-choh**
nine	nueve	***nweh*-beh**
ten	diez	**dyehs**
eleven	once	***ohn*-seh**
twelve	doce	***doh*-seh**
thirteen	trece	***treh*-seh**
fourteen	catorce	**kah-*tohr*-seh**
fifteen	quince	***keen*-seh**
sixteen	dieciséis	**dyeh-see-*says***
seventeen	diecisiete	**dyeh-see-*syeh*-teh**
eighteen	dieciocho	**dyeh-see-*oh*-choh**
nineteen	diecinueve	**dyeh-see-*nweh*-beh**
twenty	veinte	***bayn*-teh**
thirty	treinta	***trayn*-tah**
forty	cuarenta	**kwah-*rehn*-tah**
fifty	cincuenta	**seen-*kwehn*-tah**
sixty	sesenta	**seh-*sehn*-tah**
seventy	etenta	**seh-*tehn*-tah**
eighty	ochenta	**oh-*chehn*-tah**
ninety	noventa	**noh-*behn*-tah**
one hundred	cien	***syehn***
two hundred	doscientos	**doh-*syehn*-tohs**
five hundred	quinientos	**kee-*nyehn*-tos**
one thousand	mil	**meel**

TRANSPORTATION TERMS

English	Spanish	Pronunciation
Airport	**Aeropuerto**	ah-eh-roh-*pwehr*-toh
Flight	**Vuelo**	*bweh*-loh
Rental car agency	**Arrendadora de autos**	ah-rehn-da-*doh*-rah deh *ow*-tohs
Bus	**Autobús**	ow-toh-*boos*
Bus or truck	**Camión**	ka-*myohn*
Lane	**Carril**	kahr-*reel*
Nonstop	**Directo**	dee-*reck*-toh
Baggage (claim area)	**(Recibo de) Equipajes**	eh-key-*pah*-hehs
Intercity	**Foraneo**	foh-rah-*neh*-oh
Luggage storage area	**Guarda equipaje**	*gwahr*-dah eh-key-*pah*-heh

English	Spanish	Pronunciation
Arrival gates	**Llegadas**	lyeh-*gah*-dahs
Originates at this station	**Local**	loh-*kahl*
Originates elsewhere	**De paso**	deh *pah*-soh
Stops if seats available	**Para si hay lugares**	*pah*-rah see aye loo-*gah*-rehs
First class	**Primera**	pree-*meh*-rah
Second class	**Segunda**	seh-*goon*-dah
Waiting room	**Sala de espera**	*sah*-lah deh es-*peh*-rah
Toilets	**Sanitarios**	sah-nee-*tah*-ryos
	or **Servicios**	sair-vi-ssi-ohs
Ticket window	**Taquilla**	tah-*key*-lyah

EATING IN SPAIN

See "Eating & Drinking in Madrid" in chapter 2 for more vocabulary on restaurants, food, and drink.

The Basics

MEALS & COURSES

English	Spanish	Pronunciation
Breakfast	**Desayuno**	deh-sah-*yoo*-noh
Lunch	**Almuerzo**	al-*mwehr*-thoh
Dinner	**Cena**	*theh*-nah
Meal	**Comida**	ko-*mee*-thah
Appetizers	**Entremeses**	en-treh-*meh*-sehs
Main course	**Primer plato**	*pree*-mehr *plah*-toh
Dessert	**Postre**	*pohs*-treh

TABLE SETTING

English	Spanish	Pronunciation
Bottle	**Botella**	boh-*teh*-lyah
Cup	**Taza**	*tah*-thah
Fork	**Tenedor**	teh-neh-*dor*
Glass	**Vaso**	*bah*-soh
	or **Copa**	*koh*-pah
Knife	**Cuchillo**	koo-*chee*-lyoh
Napkin	**Servilleta**	sehr-vi-*lye*-tah
Spoon	**Cuchara**	koo-*chah*-rah

DECODING THE MENU

English	Spanish	Pronunciation
Baked	**Al horno**	ahl *ohr*-noh
Boiled	**Hervido**	ehr-*vee*-thoh
Charcoal grilled	**A la brasa**	ah lah *brah*-sah

English	Spanish	Pronunciation
Fried	**Frito**	*free*-toh
Grilled	**A la plancha**	ah lah *plan*-chah
Rare	**Poco hecho**	*poh*-koh *eh*-choh
Medium	**Medio hecho**	*meh*-dyo *eh*-choh
Well done	**Muy hecho**	mwee *eh*-choh
Roasted	**Asado**	ah-*sah*-thoh
Sauce	**Salsa**	*sahl*-sah
Spicy	**Picante**	pee-*kahn*-teh
Stew	**Estofado**	ess-toh-*fah*-doh

DINING OUT

English	Spanish	Pronunciation
Check/bill	**Cuenta**	*kwen*-tah
Waiter	**Camarero** *(masc.)* **Camarera** *(fem.)*	kah-mah-*reh*-roh kah-mah-*reh*-rah

Assorted Foods

BEVERAGES

English	Spanish	Pronunciation
Beer	**Cerveza**	thehr-*veh*-thah
Coffee	**Café**	kah-*feh*
Milk	**Leche**	*leh*-cheh
Pitcher	**Jarra**	*hah*-rah
Tea	**Té**	teh
Water	**Agua**	*ah*-gwah
Wine	**Vino**	*bee*-noh
Red	**Tinto**	*teen*-toh
Rosé	**Rosado**	roh-*sah*-thoh
White	**Blanco**	blahn-*koh*
Wine list	**Carta de vinos**	*kahr*-tah deh *bee*-nohs

MEAT, SAUSAGES & COLD CUTS

English	Spanish	Pronunciation
Beef	**Buey**	*bway*
Blood Sausage	**Morcilla**	mor-*thill*-ya
Duck	**Pato**	*pah*-toh
Chicken	**Pollo**	*po*-lyoh
Cold meat	**Fiambre**	*fyam*-breh
Cutlet	**Chuleta**	choo-*leh*-tah
Ham	**Jamón**	hah-*mohn*
Cooked ham	**Jamón York**	hah-*mohn* york
Cured ham	**Jamón Serrano**	hah-*mohn* seh-*rah*-noh

English	Spanish	Pronunciation
Kidneys	**Riñones**	ree-*nyoh*-nehs
Lamb	**Cordero**	kohr-*deh*-roh
Liver	**Hígado**	*ee*-gah-thoh
Meat	**Carne**	*kahr*-neh
Partridge	**Perdiz**	*pehr*-deeth
Pheasant	**Faisán**	fahy-*thahn*
Pork	**Cerdo**	*thehr*-doh
Rabbit	**Conejo**	koh-*neh*-hoh
Ribs	**Costilla**	kos-*tee*-lyah
Sausage	**Salchicha**	sahl-*chee*-chah
Spicy sausage	**Chorizo**	choh-*ree*-thoh
Steak	**Bistec**	*bee*-stehk
Sirloin	**Solomillo**	so-loh-*mee*-lyoh
Tripe	**Callos**	*kah*-lyohs
Turkey	**Pavo**	*pah*-voh
Veal	**Ternera**	tehr-*neh*-rah

SEAFOOD & SHELLFISH

English	Spanish	Pronunciation
Anchovy		
salt	**Anchoa**	ahn-*choh*-ah
fresh	**Boquerón**	boh-*keh*-rohn
Bass	**Lubina**	loo-*bee*-nah
Bream (porgy)	**Besugo**	beh-*soo*-goh
Clam	**Almeja**	al-*may*-hah
Cod	**Bacalao**	bah-kah-*lah*-oh
Crab	**Cangrejo**	kan-*greh*-hoh
Crayfish	**Cigala**	see-*gah*-lah
Cuttlefish	**Jibia, Sepia**	*hih*-byah, *seh*-pyah
Fish	**Pescado**	pess-*kah*-thoh
Flounder	**Platija**	plah-*tee*-hah
Grouper	**Mero**	*meh*-roh
Hake	**Merluza**	mehr-*loo*-thah
Lobster	**Langosta**	lahn-*goss*-tah
Mackerel	**Caballa**	cah-*ba*-lyah
Monkfish	**Rape**	*rah*-peh
Mussel	**Mejillón**	meh-hee-*lyohn*
Octopus	**Pulpo**	*pool*-poh
Oyster	**Ostra**	*ohs*-trah
Prawn	**Gamba**	*gahm*-bah
Red mullet	**Salmonete**	sal-moh-*neh*-teh
Salmon	**Salmón**	sal-*mohn*

English	Spanish	Pronunciation
Sardine	**Sardina**	sahr-*dee*-nah
Scallop	**Peregrina**	peh-reh-*gree*-nah
Shellfish	**Mariscos**	mah-*reess*-kohs
Shrimp	**Camarón**	ka-mah-*rohn*
Sole	**Lenguado**	len-*gwah*-doh
Squid	**Calamar**	kah-lah-*mahr*
Swordfish	**Pez espada**	*peth* ess-*pah*-thah
Trout	**Trucha**	*troo*-chah
Tuna	**Atún**	ah-*toon*
Turbot	**Rodaballo**	roh-dah-*ba*-lyoh

VEGETABLES & LEGUMES

English	Spanish	Pronunciation
Carrot	**Zanahoria**	thah-nah-*oh*-ryah
Cabbage	**Col**	kohl
Red cabbage	**Lombarda**	lom-*bahr*-dah
Celery	**Apio**	*ah*-pyoh
Chickpea	**Garbanzo**	gahr-*bahn*-thoh
Corn	**Maíz**	mah-*eeth*
Eggplant	**Berengena**	beh-rehn-*jeh*-nah
Fava (broad) beans	**Habas**	*ah*-bahs
Garlic	**Ajo**	*ah*-ho
Green beans	**Judías**	hoo-*dee*-yahs
Leek	**Puerro**	*pweh*-roh
Lentil	**Lenteja**	lehn-*teh*-hah
Lettuce	**Lechuga**	leh-*choo*-gah
Mushroom	**Seta**	*seh*-tah
Onion	**Cebolla**	theh-*bo*-lyah
Potato	**Patata**	pah-*tah*-tah
Salad	**Ensalada**	enn-sah-*lah*-dah
Spinach	**Espinaca**	ess-pee-*nah*-kah
Swiss Chard	**Acelgas**	ah-*thell*-gass
Tomato	**Tomate**	toh-*mah*-teh
Vegetables	**Verduras**	vehr-*doo*-rahs
Zucchini	**Calabacín**	kah-lah-bah-*theen*

MISCELLANEOUS

English	Spanish	Pronunciation
Banana	**Plátano**	*plah*-tah-noh
Bread	**Pan**	pahn
Bread roll	**Bollo**	*bo*-lyoh
Butter	**Mantequilla**	mahn-teh-*kee*-lyah

English	Spanish	Pronunciation
Caramel custard	**Flan**	flahn
Cheese	**Queso**	*keh*-soh
Egg	**Huevo**	*weh*-boh
Fruit	**Fruta**	*froo*-tah
Ice cream	**Helado**	eh-*lah*-doh
Omelet	**Tortilla**	tohr-*tee*-*l*ya
Pepper	**Pimienta**	pee-*myen*-tah
Rice	**Arroz**	*ah*-rohth
Salt	**Sal**	sahl
Sugar	**Azúcar**	ah-*thoo*-kahr

Index

See also Accommodations and Restaurant indexes, below.

General Index

A

B

O

P

Q

R

Accommodations

Restaurants

NOTES

NOTES